P9-CEC-932

Facebook® Marketing ALL-IN-ONE FOR DUMMIES®

2ND EDITION

by Amy Porterfield,
Phyllis Khare, and
Andrea Vahl

WILEY

John Wiley & Sons, Inc.

Facebook® Marketing All-in-One For Dummies®, 2nd Edition

Published by
John Wiley & Sons, Inc.
111 River Street
Hoboken, NJ 07030-5774
www.wiley.com

Published by John Wiley & Sons, Inc., Hoboken, New Jersey

Published simultaneously in Canada

For general information on our other products and services, please contact our Customer Care Department within the U.S. at 877-762-2974, outside the U.S. at 317-572-3993, or fax 317-572-4002.

For technical support, please visit www.wiley.com/techsupport.

Wiley publishes in a variety of print and electronic formats and by print-on-demand. Some material included with standard print versions of this book may not be included in e-books or in print-on-demand. If this book refers to media such as a CD or DVD that is not included in the version you purchased, you may download this material at http://booksupport.wiley.com. For more information about Wiley products, visit www.wiley.com.

Library of Congress Control Number: 2012952205

ISBN 978-1-118-46678-0 (pbk); ISBN 978-1-118-46679-7 (ebk); ISBN 978-1-118-46680-3 (ebk);
ISBN 978-1-118-46681-0 (ebk)

Manufactured in the United States of America

10 9 8 7 6 5 4 3 2 1

WILEY

About the Authors

Amy Porterfield has a foundation in traditional marketing and content development; she has worked with mega brands like Harley-Davidson Motorcycles, along with Peak Performance Coach Tony Robbins, where she oversaw his creative team and collaborated on multiple online marketing campaigns. She currently creates online programs to teach entrepreneurs and small businesses how to leverage social media to gain greater exposure, attract quality leads, and turn their fans and followers into loyal customers. Amy's most popular online programs, FBinfluence and FB Ads Insider, have helped thousands of entrepreneurs and small businesses find a voice online, strengthen their client relationships, and ultimately experience bigger profits.

Phyllis Khare is an in-demand speaker for all things social media (Twitter, Facebook, YouTube, LinkedIn, Pinterest, and Google+). She's the author of *Social Media Marketing eLearning Kit For Dummies* (a four-color book with a DVD and online learning environment) and co-author (along with the fabulous Amy Porterfield and Andrea Vahl) of the first edition of *Facebook Marketing All-in-One For Dummies*. Phyllis has been a featured guest and presenter for Social Media Examiner's Facebook Success Summit and its annual Small Biz Success Summit. She's also a presenter for MarketingProfs University and has a regular column "The Social Media Report" in iPhone Life magazine and contributes monthly posts to a variety of blogs including FiveStarSpeakers.com. With Andrea Vahl, Phyllis has recently launched Social Media Manager School, which helps train others to become social media managers and consultants, which is getting rave reviews from the participants.

Speaker, trainer, consultant, and in-demand writer of all things social media, Phyllis loves to teach and inspire everyone. Ever the cheerleader, she has been known to jump up and down in excitement about the marketing possibilities with social media.

Andrea Vahl is a social media consultant, strategist, and speaker who works with authors, retail businesses, technology companies, and B2B companies all over the world. She has spoken at events such as BlogWorld, Facebook Success Summit, Small Business Success Summit, as well as large corporate events. She is also the Community Manager for Social Media Examiner, consistently ranked by AdAge as one of the top Marketing blogs in the world. With Phyllis Khare, Andrea has recently launched Social Media Manager School, which helps train others to become social media managers and consultants. She uses her improv comedy skills to blog as Grandma Mary, Social Media Edutainer. Learning social media is way more fun with Grandma Mary. You can learn more about Andrea and Grandma at `www.andreavahl.com`.

Dedication

This book is dedicated to my husband, Hobie. You're just crazy enough to think I can do anything, and that makes me the luckiest girl ever.
–Amy Porterfield

To my first granddaughter, Prana Shakti Brown, and my first grandson, Archer. May your world be filled with an effortless integration of both the physical and online worlds. May your circle of friends be world-wide. You are why we continue to create. And to my Mom and Dad, who are always my biggest fans — even when they have no idea what I'm writing about!
–Phyllis Khare

To my parents, Marilyn and Carl Sodergren, who taught me everything I know about being social, and to my wonderful family Steve, Devin, and Henry, who so generously supported me through the second edition of this book.
–Andrea Vahl

Authors' Acknowledgments

From Amy Porterfield: I want to acknowledge my family (a.k.a. my cheerleaders). My husband, Hobie, my mom, Beverly, and my sister, Tracie — these three have given me the courage to go after everything I've ever wanted. And thank you to my dad, JB, for teaching me the work ethic needed to get the job done. I also want to thank my stepmom, Shay, for always making me feel like I am destined for greatness, no matter what!

I must also acknowledge my best friend Gina. Her commitment to seeing me succeed surprises me daily. We must have been business partners in another lifetime (or maybe that's in the works in just a few years?!). I also want to acknowledge my two amazing co-authors, Phyllis Khare and Andrea Vahl. As a real testament to networking, this book opportunity came to me because I sat next to Andrea at a networking dinner. Two years later, she recommended me to Wiley Publishing, and the rest is history. As for Phyllis, she was the voice of reason throughout this whole process, and her insight and knowledge were invaluable from day one. In addition, a big acknowledgment to Amy Fandrei, Susan Christophersen, and Nicole Sholly of Wiley Publishing. I know you ladies worked many late nights to see this book to completion, and not one minute of that hard work went unnoticed. And last, I want to thank Facebook for changing, updating, tweaking, and fully revamping your platform almost weekly — it made for a very interesting editing process, to say the least!

From Phyllis Khare: I'd like to acknowledge all the people at Wiley who worked on this project. There were so many people who contributed to the huge project. I don't know all their names, but please know that all of you are held in deep appreciation. This was truly a team project. I want to thank Amy Fandrei and Nicole Sholly, and of course I deeply want to acknowledge Amy Porterfield and Andrea Vahl. My two special writing companions. Bonded for life over Facebook! I'd also like to thank my family for supporting me as we wrote, and rewrote this book. Ron, Celestial, Wes, and Ron (the son) — you are the best. And to all the people who create and maintain social media platforms, thank you for creating such an amazing interface for people to use to open more doors to their lives and businesses.

From Andrea Vahl: I want to acknowledge my family and friends who supported me through this incredible journey, Steve, Devin, Henry, my parents and my sister and family, and the wonderful friends I've made online and off. I want to thank my incredible co-authors Phyllis and Amy; your friendship throughout this has meant the world to me. And especially Phyllis, who is my own social media success story connection — you never know where those connections will take you! Thank you to all my online friends, fans, links, followers, and community; I hope to meet you all someday and am happy to call you friends. Finally, I need to profusely thank Amy Fandrei and Nicole Sholly for their support and mentorship throughout this process. Thank you!

Publisher's Acknowledgments

We're proud of this book; please send us your comments at `http://dummies.custhelp.com`. For other comments, please contact our Customer Care Department within the U.S. at 877-762-2974, outside the U.S. at 317-572-3993, or fax 317-572-4002.

Some of the people who helped bring this book to market include the following:

Acquisitions, Editorial

Senior Project Editor: Nicole Sholly

Acquisitions Editor: Amy Fandrei

Copy Editor: Kathy Simpson

Technical Editor: Melanie Nelson

Editorial Manager: Kevin Kirschner

Editorial Assistant: Leslie Saxman

Sr. Editorial Assistant: Cherie Case

Cover Photos: © studiocasper / iStockphoto (computer/cart); © Dimitri Vervitsiotis / Getty Images (computer screen image)

Cartoons: Rich Tennant (`www.the5thwave.com`)

Composition Services

Project Coordinator: Sheree Montgomery

Layout and Graphics: Carl Byers, Joyce Haughey, Jennifer Mayberry

Proofreaders: Melissa D. Buddendeck, Lauren Mandelbaum

Indexer: BIM Indexing & Proofreading Services

Publishing and Editorial for Technology Dummies

Richard Swadley, Vice President and Executive Group Publisher

Andy Cummings, Vice President and Publisher

Mary Bednarek, Executive Acquisitions Director

Mary C. Corder, Editorial Director

Publishing for Consumer Dummies

Kathleen Nebenhaus, Vice President and Executive Publisher

Composition Services

Debbie Stailey, Director of Composition Services

Table of Contents

Introduction

One thing we know for sure from writing this book is that Facebook loves change. The folks at Facebook love to change things up — tweak the platform; upgrade programs; and above all, innovate each chance they get. This is great for everyone who's looking to use Facebook to grow a business but not so great for anyone who's writing a "how things work" book about Facebook marketing. On Facebook, how things work one day may not be how things work the next day! The good news is that we were able to stay on top of all the changes and pack this book with the latest and greatest Facebook marketing strategies.

That said, Facebook's unwavering dedication to innovation is exactly why it is the social networking powerhouse that it is today. With Facebook's constant growth and massive influence, it's obvious that Facebook isn't just a flash-in-the-pan phenomenon. These days, you can't surf the web, listen to the radio, watch TV, or even flip through a magazine without hearing or seeing something about Facebook.

Facebook represents a huge opportunity for your business. If you're in a business of any kind, you absolutely should consider Facebook to be a key player in your marketing strategy. With Facebook having close to 1 billion active users, your ideal audience is highly likely to be spending time there. You have a huge opportunity to capture the attention of, and build relationships with, the people who could potentially be your most loyal customers. When you fully leverage the power of Facebook, you can build an engaging Facebook presence, attract and engage quality customers, and quickly grow your business.

About This Book

Whether you're a complete newbie on Facebook or a veteran who's looking to take Facebook marketing to a new level, this book is for you. You can play many roles on Facebook, and this book gives you the tools to decide how Facebook fits into your overall marketing plan.

You may decide that you want to use Facebook as a mini hub — an extension of your own website where your fans first go to get to know, like, and trust you. After you've created a solid relationship with your fans, you can encourage them to visit your website to find out more about what you have to offer. Or you may want to use Facebook as a robust customer-service portal — a place where you answer client questions, help troubleshoot product challenges, and become the go-to source for all your clients' needs.

Your opportunities are endless, and this book helps you understand which opportunities are right for your business.

Foolish Assumptions

To get real results from the strategies and tips in this book, you don't need any special skills. As long as you have basic computer skills and can navigate around the internet with ease, you will be able to apply the strategies described throughout with little or no stress. This book is ideal for anyone who is looking to market a local business, an online business, or a brand on Facebook, but it can also be helpful for anyone who has a solid business idea and wants to learn how to launch a new business endeavor on Facebook.

Specifically, this book is for anyone who:

- Is fairly new to Facebook marketing and is looking for a way to grow their online exposure
- Doesn't have a Facebook Page but is interested in the right way to start one on Facebook
- Is already on Facebook and has a Page, but is looking to take that Page to the next level

The good news is that you don't have to be an online marketing pro to take advantage of all the strategies outlined in this book!

Conventions Used in This Book

We use a few specific conventions in this text for ease of comprehension. When we tell you to type something (in a box or a field, for example), we put it in **bold.** When we refer to text that you see onscreen, we put it in a typeface that `looks like this`. Terms in *italics* are defined as they relate to Facebook marketing. And when we provide a URL, it looks like this:

`www.dummies.com/go/facebookmarketingaiofd2eupdates`

What You Don't Have to Read

You don't have to read this book sequentially, and you don't even have to read all the sections in any particular chapter. You can skip sidebars and just read the material that helps you complete the task at hand.

How This Book Is Organized

Facebook Marketing All-in-One For Dummies, 2nd Edition, is divided into nine minibooks that take you from understanding why Facebook is important for your business marketing strategy all the way through studying advanced marketing tactics and measurement.

Each minibook is designed to be a complete, stand-alone guide to help you master the subject covered within. You can read this book cover to cover, or choose the areas that interest you and dive right in. The following sections describe all nine minibooks so that you can determine which ones will help you the most.

Book I: Joining the Facebook Marketing Revolution

You may wonder how Facebook can benefit your business. How do you get started — and, more important, why? This minibook helps you understand the potential that Facebook holds for any business and how to reap the rewards of a well-crafted Facebook marketing plan.

We lead you through the basics of searching for and finding your audience on Facebook, defining your goals, and putting in place the measurement tools you need to monitor your return on investment.

Book II: Claiming Your Presence on Facebook

Plant your flag and set up your Facebook Page in this minibook. Book II walks you through the setup process, including selecting a Page type and naming your Page, so that your business can start connecting with potential customers all over the world. You also get a complete tour so that you know how to navigate the Admin panel and editing dashboard.

Book III: Adding the Basics to Your Facebook Page

Find out all the different ways to post content to your Page, including videos, links, and photos. You also discover how to customize your tabs so that your Facebook Page is branded and stands out.

If you have a blog, you can automatically import the blog posts to save time. Connect your Page to your Twitter accounts to create a richer experience for your community members and also to save time.

Book IV: Building, Engaging, Retaining, and Selling to Your Community

Start by building visibility to your Page through your existing customers and then find creative ways to connect to new Facebook users. This minibook gives you plenty of ways to engage your customers and basic rules for participating in the conversation in a meaningful way. You also find out how to expand your e-commerce by bringing it to your Facebook Page with apps via an online Facebook store.

Book V: Understanding Facebook Applications

Explore the world of Facebook applications in this minibook; find out how applications can integrate with your Page to make it a better place for your community. Look at the best existing applications to add, and find out about custom iFrame applications that help you create any type of tab you can imagine.

Book VI: Making Facebook Come Alive with Events and Contests

In this minibook, you discover the ins and outs of creating and marketing your Event. If your Facebook Page needs a little fun, consider holding a contest to engage and grow your community. Book VI covers the different types of contests, how to follow Facebook's contest rules, and what applications can help you run your contest. Make sure that you're getting the most out of your contest efforts with promotional strategies and results analysis.

Book VII: Advanced Facebook Marketing Tactics

Get ready for Facebook 201 in this minibook, where you see how to create the ultimate "Facebook experience" for your audience. Topics include growing your Page, building social proof, and using the viral nature of Facebook to your advantage.

You find out how to use the Facebook social plug-ins to bring the Facebook experience to your own website and how to combine Facebook Offers with Promoted posts to connect with your community in a much bigger way. This minibook also covers how to tap into mobile marketing with Facebook Places and Facebook Deals.

Book VIII: Facebook Advertising

Are you looking to create a Facebook ad campaign? If so, this minibook is for you. Find out how to design your campaign, allocate a budget, and split-test your ads so that you get the most bang for your buck. Understand the differences among all the new Facebook ad types. See how to write a click-worthy ad that targets your specific client. Then dive into the report section to find out how well your ad performed.

Book IX: Measuring, Monitoring, and Analyzing

This minibook brings all the Facebook marketing strategies throughout this book together with analysis of your Page activity. Make sure that you're measuring your efforts and setting realistic targets for your Facebook Page. Explore and understand Facebook Insights, which tracks your progress, and compare third-party measurement tools to see which ones may be right for your business.

Icons Used in This Book

All through the book, special icons appear in the margin to draw your attention to particular bits and pieces of information. The following descriptions demystify these graphics:

This icon signifies a trick to use or another bit of helpful information that you may find especially useful.

When you see this icon, try to hang on to what we tell you; it's important to keep in mind.

You want to pay especially close attention on the rare occasions when you see this icon.

We use this icon sparingly; it indicates information that's safe to skip but that you might find interesting.

Where to Go from Here

This book can be read in any order you choose. Each chapter stands on its own and can help you tackle specific tasks. If you've just started thinking about marketing yourself on Facebook but don't know where to begin, head to Book I. If you already have a Facebook Page and a basic understanding of how Facebook works, you can begin optimizing your Page by starting with Book II. Your first stop may be the table of contents, where you can look up sections that you need any time.

Occasionally, we have updates to our technology books. If this book does have technical updates, they'll be posted at `www.dummies.com/go/facebookmarketingaiofd2eupdates`.

Book I

Joining the Facebook Marketing Revolution

"I know it's a short profile, but I thought 'King of the Jungle' sort of said it all."

Contents at a Glance

Chapter 1: Exploring Facebook Marketing

In This Chapter

- Discovering Facebook's marketing potential
- Looking at four key Facebook marketing strategies
- Mastering the art of Facebook engagement
- Examining Facebook's global market opportunities
- Understanding the basics of Facebook marketing
- Seeing the benefits of selling from the Facebook platform

Facebook is the most powerful social network on the planet. With around a billion active users, Facebook presents a unique opportunity to connect with and educate your ideal audience in a way that your website and your blog can't even come close to matching.

The reach of the Facebook platform has grown exponentially in the past few years and will only continue to get bigger. In fact, the number of marketers who say that Facebook is "critical" or "important" to their business has increased by 83 percent in just the past two years. Today, almost anyone or any company can find a following on Facebook, from big brands such as Starbucks to small, lesser-known mom-and-pop shops. Facebook's platform can turn a business into a living, breathing, one-to-one online marketing machine. Facebook is changing the game, and there's no better time than the present to jump on board.

In this chapter, we cover why Facebook should become a key marketing tool to help you grow your business. Specifically, we look at Facebook's massive marketing potential, its expansive capability to reach your ideal audience, and the core strategies you can implement today to seamlessly add Facebook to your marketing program.

Seeing the Business Potential of Facebook

We have good news and bad news for you when it comes to Facebook marketing. The bad news first: Facebook marketing isn't free. Sure, it doesn't cost actual dollars to get set up with a presence on Facebook, but it's sure to cost you both time and effort — two hot commodities that most business owners have very little of these days. You have to account for the time and energy it takes to plan your strategy, set it up, get yourself trained, execute your plan, build your relationships, and take care of your new customers after you start seeing your efforts pay off. And although you don't need to be tied to Facebook 24/7 to see solid results, dedicated time and effort is essential when creating a successful Facebook marketing plan, and your time and effort are anything but free. But here's the good news: This book can help you streamline your Facebook marketing efforts and eliminate the guesswork that often goes into figuring out anything that's new and somewhat complex.

Facebook marketing can help you create exposure and awareness for your business, increase sales, collect market data, enhance your customers' experience, and increase your position as an authority in your field. However, before you can start to see real results, you must determine why you're on Facebook.

If you take the time to ponder the following questions, you'll gradually begin to create a road map to Facebook marketing success:

- **Why do you want to use Facebook to market your business?** More specifically, what do you hope to gain from your use of Facebook, and how will it help your business?
- **Who is your ideal audience?** Get specific here. Who are you talking to? What are the demographics, needs, wants, and challenges of the person who will buy your products, programs, or services?
- **What do you want your ideal audience to do via your efforts on Facebook?** In other words, what feelings, actions, or behaviors do you want your audience to experience?

When you're clear about *why* you're on Facebook, you're better able to design a strategy that best fits your business needs. We explore many potential strategies through the course of this book. For now, though, in the name of helping you better understand how you can use Facebook to market your business, here's a list of just a few ideas you can implement when you embrace Facebook marketing:

You are not in the Facebook marketing business!

Remember this very important fact: You are *not* in the business of Facebook marketing. Your job is not to become an expert or master of Facebook. As you navigate this book, remember that your job is to be an expert at your business — and Facebook is a tool that you will use to do that. Take the pressure off yourself to master Facebook marketing. This will make all the difference as you master the strategies outlined throughout these pages.

- **Set up special promotions inside Facebook, and offer special deals exclusively to your Facebook community.** You could create a coupon that your visitors can print and bring into your store for a special discount, for example.
- **Offer Q&A sessions in real time.** Your visitors can post questions about your niche, product, or service; then you and your team can offer great advice and information to your Facebook community.
- **Highlight your Facebook fans by offering a Member of the Month award.** You could choose and highlight one fan who shows exemplary participation in your Facebook community. People love to be acknowledged, and Facebook is a fantastic platform for recognizing your best clients and prospects.
- **Highlight your own employees with an Employee of the Month feature on your Facebook Page.** Profile someone who's making a difference at the company. You can include photos and video to make it even more entertaining and interesting to your audience.
- **Sell your products and services directly inside Facebook.** Include a button that links your fans to an electronic shopping cart to enable them to buy in the moment. You have many opportunities to promote and sell your products and services on Facebook.

REMEMBER

The preceding list is just a glimpse of what you can do inside Facebook's powerful walls. Many more opportunities await you — but you'll have to read a few more of our minibooks to get acquainted with them.

Reaping the benefits for business-to-consumer companies

When it comes to business-to-consumer (B2C) companies, one of the greatest advantages of Facebook marketing is the ability to engage one-on-one with your ideal clients. By asking questions, encouraging conversations, and creating personal engagement with your customers and prospects, you can build relationships in a way that wasn't possible before social networking took the marketing world by storm.

REMEMBER

Although we all know that consumer brands with big marketing budgets can attract millions of followers on Facebook, there's still room for the little guys.

Here's a thought experiment: Rather than feel frustrated because your company can't compete with big-brand giants on Facebook, turn the success of those companies into an opportunity for you to model the best and learn from them. Here are four key strategies that the big B2C companies have adopted in their Facebook marketing strategies to help them stand out from the rest:

- **Acknowledge your fans.** The B2C giants on Facebook do a fantastic job of spotlighting their fans. When fans feel appreciated, they continue to engage with your Page.

  One great example of this strategy comes from Oreo, which knows a thing or two about standing out. In celebration of its 100th birthday, Oreo created a campaign to spotlight its fans' birthdays too. Every single day during the celebration, Oreo chose one fan who had a birthday that day and spotlighted that person in its Timeline cover photo, as shown in Figure 1-1. Oreo's Facebook Page has millions of fans, so those folks must be doing something right!

Figure 1-1: Oreo can wow its audience by creating unique experiences.

- **Know your audience.** When you're clear about who you're communicating with on Facebook, you can create experiences around your audience's interest and likes. An example of a B2C company that's in tune with its audience is Red Bull, as evidenced by that Page's custom apps and unique content.

  The team behind Red Bull's Facebook Page knows what its audience will respond to best and then delivers. A series of online games and apps for fans, for example, is geared toward sports and high-impact competitions, as shown in Figure 1-2.

- **Mix up your media.** Facebook strategies that infuse a variety of media, including photos and video, often draw a bigger crowd. One example is Old Spice's use of video in an (in)famous Facebook campaign.

  Old Spice was able to grab the attention of Facebook users with its Old Spice Guy videos, as shown in Figure 1-3. These videos showed a topless guy responding to fans' silly and often hilarious questions and quickly became viral sensations. When the two-day campaign ended, the Old Spice YouTube Channel had almost 8 million views and 616,000 fans on Facebook. That's impressive!

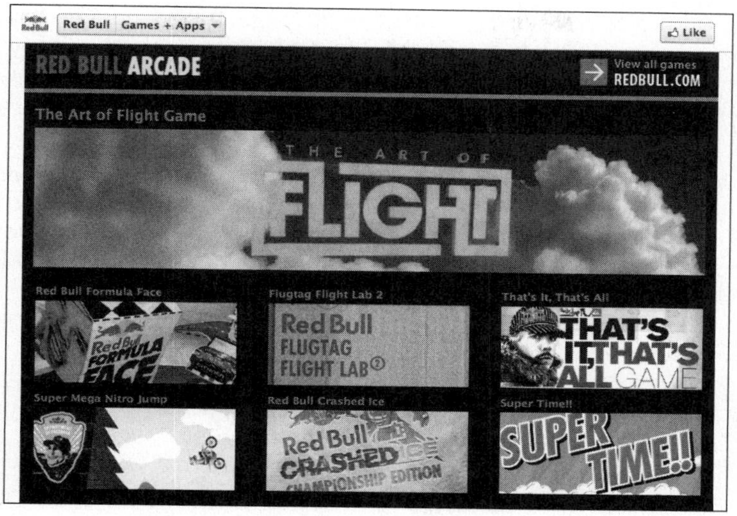

Figure 1-2: Red Bull keeps it fun with its Red Bull Arcade on Facebook.

Figure 1-3: Got a question for the Old Spice Guy?

Going viral

When a video, article, or other piece of content goes *viral,* it means that people are continually sharing that content through their online networks. Someone might post a funny video on YouTube, for example. People start to pass it along to their friends by e-mailing the link, posting it on their Facebook Pages, and tweeting about it. If a massive number of people begin to share the video, it will spread to others like wildfire, therefore becoming what many call a viral sensation.

✦ **Have fun.** Face it — most people log on to Facebook to have fun and connect with friends. Interacting with brands and businesses is not the No. 1 reason why people get on Facebook each day. That doesn't mean, however, that these users aren't a captive audience! The key is to infuse fun into your Facebook activity when appropriate.

Coca-Cola secured its spot at the top of many best-of-the-best Facebook Page lists with its fun, innovative promotions and playful, interactive features. Coke's Summer Snapshot contest, for example, encouraged fans to take photos of themselves holding their special Summer Coca-Cola cans. Figure 1-4 shows an example of a fan photo. Notice that others can vote on the photos — which, of course, allows everyone to get in on the fun.

Figure 1-4: A fan photo serves as part of Coca-Cola's summer campaign on Facebook.

TIP

Photos are viewed more than anything else on Facebook. They go viral quickly because when a fan posts a photo, that photo is sent to the News Feeds of all their friends. Hundreds of thousands of potential new fans will see these photos.

REMEMBER

When reviewing these four strategies illustrated by some well-known B2C companies, remember that you, too, can create these experiences for little or no cost. Again, model the best that's out there, and make the strategies work for your own business.

Reaping the benefits for business-to-business companies

We know that Facebook marketing works well for B2C businesses, but if you're a business-to-business (B2B) company, you may be wondering whether Facebook makes sense for your business. In short, the answer is yes! In fact, 41 percent of B2B companies have reported acquiring a customer through Facebook.

Not only can B2B companies incorporate the four key strategies mentioned in the preceding section, but B2B companies also have a unique advantage over B2C when it comes to Facebook marketing: Facebook's platform is designed to support *exactly what* B2B companies need to be successful in attracting clients and securing sales.

To better explain this idea, here are three factors that make B2B a perfect fit for Facebook marketing:

- **B2B has a smaller potential customer base.** This means that B2B companies don't have to constantly focus on growing their numbers of followers to hundreds of thousands; instead, they can put the majority of their focus on nurturing the relationships they already have. Facebook is a platform that thrives on one-to-one relationships.
- **Buying decisions in B2B rely heavily on word of mouth and reputation.** Businesses that are looking to make a huge buying decision often want to know what their peers are doing and how they feel about a product or service. Facebook's open network allows people to see who their peers are interacting with and what they're talking about at any given time, therefore making it easy to find out what others think about a product or service.
- **B2B generally has a higher average price point than B2C.** When the price of the product or service is considered to be high, the client is likely to seek out information and content to support buying decisions. On Facebook, content is king. The more high-value content a company can generate, the more likely it will be to attract the ideal client base and become a Facebook success story.

For B2B companies, connection, knowledge sharing, and reputation management are key ingredients of success. Facebook's unique platform can help optimize these key strategies.

Developing genuine relationships with customers and prospects

No matter whether your business is B2B or B2C, it really comes down to one person talking to another. No one wants to interact with a faceless brand, business, or logo. We all want to buy from a friend — someone we trust and feel comfortable engaging with regularly.

Facebook allows us to move beyond the obstacles of traditional marketing (very one-sided) and instead communicate with our clients and prospects on a one-on-one level by putting a face with a name, making the entire exchange more human.

Creating one-to-one customer engagement

Engagement is crucial in mastering Facebook marketing. If you build rapport and can get your Facebook community talking, your efforts will go a long way.

It's one thing to broadcast a special promotion on Facebook, but it's an entirely different experience to ask your fans a question related to your products and services and receive 50 responses from people telling you exactly how they feel about what you're selling. In many cases, this real-time engagement can be priceless! In Figure 1-5, the popular online shoe and clothing retailer Zappos.com asks its audience about winter fashion preferences.

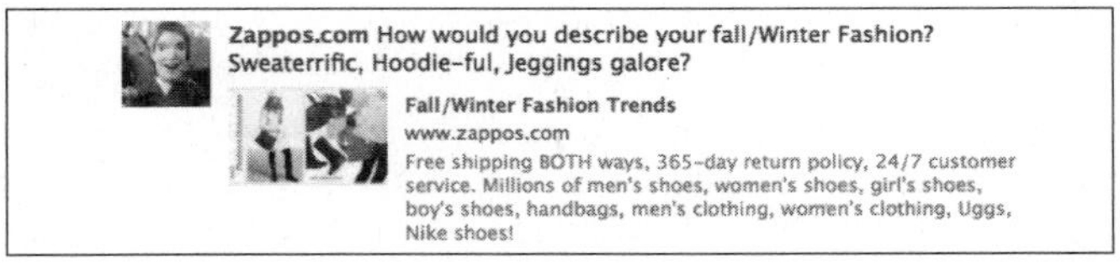

Zappos.com How would you describe your fall/Winter Fashion? Sweaterrific, Hoodie-ful, Jeggings galore?
Fall/Winter Fashion Trends
www.zappos.com
Free shipping BOTH ways, 365-day return policy, 24/7 customer service. Millions of men's shoes, women's shoes, girl's shoes, boy's shoes, handbags, men's clothing, women's clothing, Uggs, Nike shoes!

Figure 1-5: Ask (a question), and ye shall receive.

TIP: One very successful Facebook marketing strategy is to ask your followers interesting questions. It's human nature to enjoy talking about likes and interests; therefore, encourage sharing by asking your fans to express *their* thoughts about their likes and interests. It's a great way to increase fan engagement.

Providing prompt customer service

Before the days of social networking, phone calls, e-mails, and handwritten letters were just about your only options when it came to reaching out to your clients. Today, you can send a tweet or make a Facebook post to inform your customers of new features, benefits, or changes to your products or services. Social media allows you to get the word out quickly, making it easier for you to keep your customers informed and satisfied.

REMEMBER: If you optimize your Facebook marketing experience, you can provide your customers a superior customer experience — a much richer experience than you've ever been able to offer before. Not only can you create a social media experience in which you're keeping your customers informed, but you can also give them an opportunity to reach out to you.

Imagine this: You sell shoes. A client orders a pair of your shoes online and receives them in the mail. When the shoes arrive, they're the wrong pair. That client logs on to Facebook and posts this message:

> I just received my much anticipated pair of red stilettos in the mail today . . . too bad the company messed up and sent me sneakers instead! I'm frustrated!

At first glance, you may think that a post like that would hurt your business. On social sites like Facebook and Twitter, however, you can turn a potentially bad post into an opportunity to gain a customer for life.

Imagine that you respond within just five minutes with this post:

> Julie, we are so sorry that you received the wrong pair of shoes! We are shipping your red stilettos overnight, and make sure to look for the 50% off coupon we included in your box as well. Two pairs of shoes are always better than one!

Here's what's great: The opportunity for real-time problem solving is powerful. You not only just saved a sale and made Julie a happy customer, but also showed anyone watching on Facebook that you care about your clients and will go above and beyond the call of duty to make them happy. This type of experience wasn't possible before social media came on the scene.

TIP

You can find out more about online tools that will help you monitor who's talking about you online in Book IX, Chapter 3. These tools will help you stay in the know and in tune with your customers. They will also save you precious time and effort when managing your Facebook activity.

In addition to proactively monitoring Facebook for customer service issues, you can use many robust tools to create a virtual service desk directly inside Facebook. Livescribe, for example, has incorporated a support desk directly into its Facebook Page. As you can see in Figure 1-6, you can ask the folks at Livescribe a question, share an idea, report a problem, or even give praise directly from that Facebook Page.

Customers commonly use social media sites to post questions or complaints. If you provide a designated place for support, you're likely to keep your customers happy and turn them into repeat buyers!

What's even more important is that others can see these posts. Then fans and potential buyers can go to this custom app to get answers or see what others are saying about the products. It's another great way to educate fans about your products and services. In addition, this tool can cut down service calls when it's executed correctly, saving your company time and money.

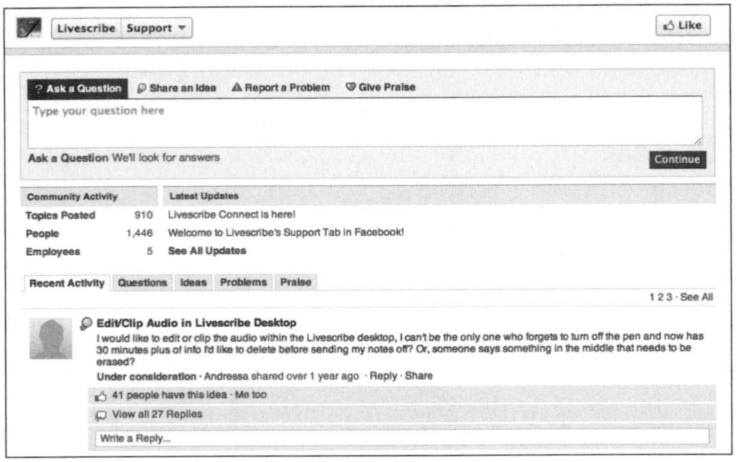

Figure 1-6: Check out the Livescribe Facebook support desk.

Creating a shopping portal

Facebook's expansion into the e-commerce sector might forever change the way we shop. In the past, creating an e-commerce website took a lot of money and even more time. Today, Facebook's platform — interwoven with third-party apps — has allowed millions of businesses to showcase their products and services and to sell them online. (To find out more about how third-party apps can be part of your Facebook marketing strategy, check out Book V.)

When it comes to the kinds of shopping interfaces you can create on Facebook, you have two options:

- **A storefront:** Here's where potential buyers come to browse products. When users want to buy, they click the Buy button and are then taken to a separate, e-commerce-equipped website to finalize the purchase. Currently, this type of shopping interface is the most popular, but we'll likely see the second interface option (see next bullet) catch up soon.
- **A fully functioning store:** Your second interface option involves creating a full-blown store where shoppers can browse and purchase without leaving the Facebook environment.

  You can find one example of such a fully functioning store on the Facebook Page for the Grandma Mary Show. Here, you'll find a buying experience within Facebook where you can buy an e-book directly from that Facebook Page, as shown in Figure 1-7.

REMEMBER

When Facebook users post about products they love, the users' friends naturally want to know more. This curiosity creates viral exposure for your products and services.

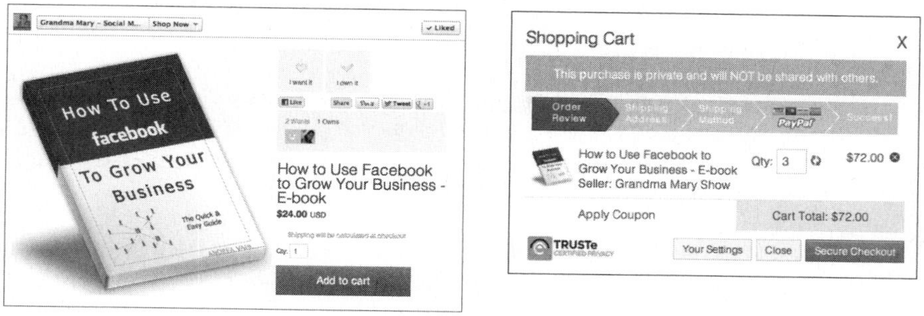

Figure 1-7: The Grandma Mary Show allows e-book purchases from directly inside the Facebook e-commerce platform.

Facebook offers an extremely valuable opportunity to showcase your products and services and to create a new portal where you can sell your goods.

Using Facebook with the Global Market

Few people would deny that the social media phenomenon, and Facebook specifically, is growing at a staggering pace. It's important to note that social media is exploding everywhere, not just the United States. Online users in Australia, Japan, and Italy all show even stronger adoption of social media than Americans do, and those in China, Denmark, and Sweden are said to be adopting social media at the same rates as Americans. To give you a glimpse of the magnitude of Facebook's global reach, here are some statistics provided by Facebook as of March 2012:

- Almost a billion active users are on Facebook.
- People spend more than 700 billion minutes per month on Facebook.
- Half of Facebook's active users log on to Facebook in any given day.
- People interact with more than 900 million objects (Pages, groups, Events, and community Pages).
- During March 2012, 398 million users were active on Facebook on at least six of the preceding seven days.
- More than 500 million active users access Facebook through their mobile devices monthly, and people who use Facebook on their mobile devices are twice as active on Facebook as nonmobile users.
- Young adults continue to be the heaviest Facebook users, but the most rapid growth is among those 50 years old and older. This group is the fastest-growing demographic on Facebook today.

- From 2008 to 2009, Facebook's international audience grew from 34 million to 95 million people. Today, more than 80 percent of users are outside the United States, and translations into more than 70 languages are available on the site.
- Although the United States is the largest country on Facebook, Indonesia is Facebook's second-largest market, with more than 45 million of its 200 million people online. The United Kingdom and Turkey are in the third and fourth spots.

With more than 80 percent of Facebook users being outside the United States, it's essential to understand Facebook's place in the global market. Facebook breaks down barriers and makes introducing your products and services to international audiences easier. Here are some opportunities you can explore to extend your brand's footprint in the global market:

- **Use Facebook advertising to reach international audiences.** You can target 25 countries with one Facebook Ad, or you can target one country at a time and drill down into specific cities within the country. You can also create multiple ads and target numerous cities in the countries you want to target with your ads. The more localized you make your ads, the better chance you have of reaching your ideal audience.
- **Translate your content.** With the rise of international markets on Facebook today, it's wise to consider translating your content on Facebook. In fact, English accounts for only 31 percent of language use online. Facebook has its own crowdsourced translation product: Facebook Internationalization. More than 300,000 users have helped translate the site through the translations application.

  In many countries, the majority of people do not have access to computers with Internet access. Mobile devices are making it possible for Facebook to reach more people, however. As we mention earlier in this chapter, more than 500 million Facebook users access the site via their mobile devices each month. Facebook Indonesia executive Chamath Palihapitiya reports that nearly every Indonesian Facebook user is accessing the platform via his or her mobile phone. That's a pretty astounding stat, to say the least!

Understanding Facebook Marketing Basics

Facebook can supercharge your existing marketing efforts by giving you a platform to grow your audience, create deeper connections, and create new experiences to foster loyal client relationships. Facebook's unique platforms that let you market and promote your brand online are your Profile and your Facebook Page.

The Profile (also called Profile Timeline) was initially designed to allow you to maintain your social relationships and communicate with your friends and family members online. Facebook made some significant changes to the Profile, however, and updated it with a Subscribe button. The Subscribe button, which is optional, allows Facebook users who aren't your Friends on Facebook to subscribe to your Profile updates, meaning that they can see your public posts in their News Feeds.

Subscribing to someone's personal account is a lot like following someone on Twitter. In other words, you don't have to be Friends with someone on Facebook to see their Public posts. If you're marketing a personal brand, the Profile with a Subscribe button may be perfect for your marketing outcomes. There are some strategic marketing reasons to have a personal account with the Subscribe button. We cover the complete marketing strategy for activating your Subscribe button in Book II, Chapter 1.

The second way to market on Facebook is via a Facebook Page. Pages are like digital storefronts, or places where your prospects can take a digital walk around your business to learn more about your brand and what you have to offer. Here you can highlight your best programs, products, and services to interact with an interested audience.

A large portion of this book is dedicated to creating and optimizing your Facebook Page. Before we get into the how-to's and strategies, though, we point out a few of the most important details you need to know to get off on the right foot.

Marketing on your Page and your Profile

Although you'll soon find out all you'll ever need to know about the differences between a Profile and a Page, for the purposes of starting things off, here's a quick rundown:

- **When you sign up for Facebook, you create a Facebook Profile.**

  A Profile is meant to be all about you. It has been referred to as a living scrapbook of your life. It highlights who you are and gives details about your life experiences over time. With the addition of the Subscribe button, you now have the option to make some of your posts public and other posts private. The opportunity to select who sees your posts gives you a unique advantage by allowing you to be selective and use your Profile to connect with family members and friends, as well as to post information about your business.

- **Promoting your business, brand, or any other entity other than a person for monetary gain via a Profile goes against Facebook's terms of service.**

It isn't against the rules, however, to mention your business and keep your relatives, friends, and those subscribed to your Profile informed about new happenings with your business.

- **A Facebook Page is designed specifically to highlight your business, and its purpose is to allow businesses to communicate with their customers and fans.**

  Those who follow your Facebook Page expect to see promotions and conversations about your programs and services, so it's perfectly acceptable to promote your business on a Facebook Page.

For a more comprehensive understanding of Profiles and Pages, check out Book II, Chapter 1.

Developing your Page to be a hub of activity

Your Facebook Page can serve as a meeting place for people who have similar interests and values. Involve your customers in your conversations by asking them questions and encouraging them to share their thoughts.

One way you can create a hub of activity is to encourage your fans to use your Facebook community as a platform where they can connect with other like-minded individuals.

You can become the go-to source in your industry, for example, making your Page the hub of your industry's latest news and happenings. By delivering valuable content via your Facebook Page, you're setting up your company as the authority — a trusted advisor.

One great example of a company using Facebook to position itself as the go-to source for an industry is 360i, a major player in the field of social media marketing (see Figure 1-8).

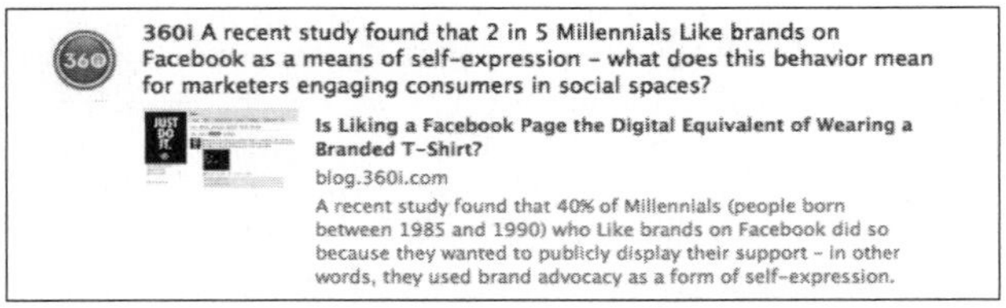

Figure 1-8: 360i Facebook engagement activity.

During the course of this book, you'll have the opportunity to familiarize yourself with many strategies that can help you create a unique hub of activity — including a whole slew of strategies in Book VII.

Understanding privacy options

After you set up your Facebook Profile, you have several privacy options to choose among to determine just how much or how little of your Facebook self you want to share. These options become even more important if you decide to activate the Subscribe button, making your Profile more accessible.

First, Facebook has what it calls an *inline audience selector,* which is a drop-down menu that lets you decide which group of people sees your post (see Figure 1-9).

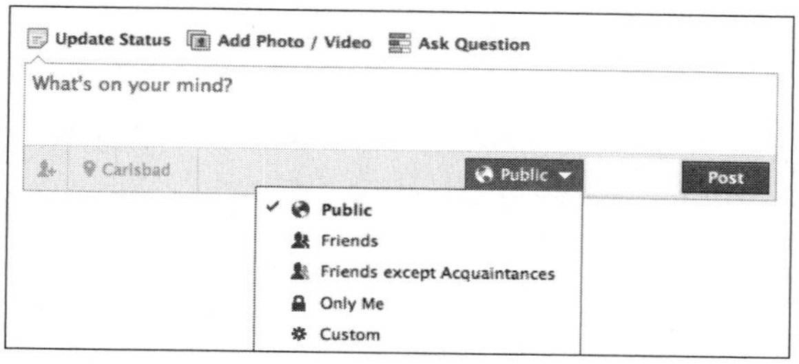

Figure 1-9: The inline audience selector's options.

With the inline audience selector, you can choose to display your post to five groups:

- ✦ **Public:** All your Facebook Friends and anyone who has subscribed to your Profile Timeline can see your post.
- ✦ **Friends:** All your Facebook Friends can see your post.
- ✦ **Friends Except Acquaintances:** All your Facebook Friends whom you manually selected as Close Friends can see your post.

  The group Friends Except Acquaintances is pulled from a custom list that you set up manually. We discuss the strategy behind custom lists in Book VII, Chapter 1.
- ✦ **Only Me:** You can post something that only you will see on Facebook, but we realize that this seems a bit silly to do!
- ✦ **Custom:** You can manually choose the individual Friends who see your post.

REMEMBER

You can not only select an audience when you post, but also change your selection at any time. To do this, hover on your posts' globe icon, as shown in Figure 1-10, and then choose your audience preference from the drop-down menu.

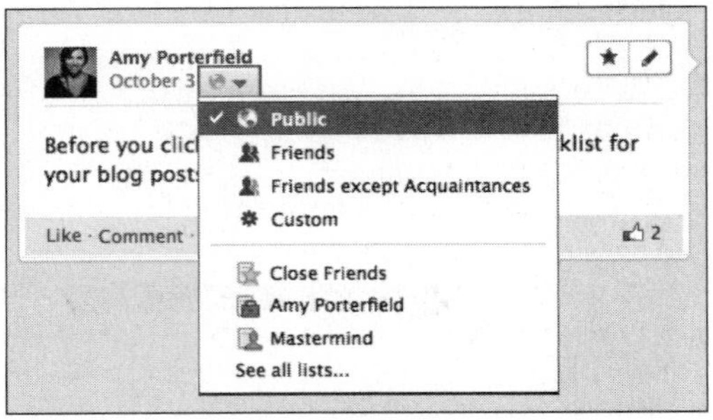

Figure 1-10: The audience selector allows you to change who sees your post.

Here's how to access your privacy settings:

1. **Point your browser to** `www.facebook.com`**, and log in to your account.**
2. **In the top-right corner of your screen, click the small arrow next to the Home link, and then choose Privacy Settings from the drop-down menu that appears.**

   On the Privacy Settings page, you can see all your options for setting your privacy controls on Facebook, as shown in Figure 1-11.

Facebook's privacy settings allow you to control exactly who sees what within your Facebook Profile. The challenge is that the privacy settings are extremely detailed, and Facebook changes or upgrades them often. But don't worry: When Facebook does make changes, it always notifies users, thereby keeping everyone informed.

Also included on the privacy options dashboard is the option to set your default privacy setting to Public, Friends, or Custom. You can also dive deeper into the settings and customize specific sections of your Profile Timeline, and we suggest that you do just that. To help you understand your level of privacy options better, here are the five main privacy areas:

- **How You Connect:** This area allows you to control how you connect with people on Facebook. Here, you can set the capabilities for people to send you Friend requests, post on your Timeline, and send you messages.
- **Timeline and Tagging:** *Tagging* is a way that people on Facebook can link to pictures, videos, and posts. We cover tagging in Book IV, Chapter 2, but for now, what you need to know is that this area allows you to control how people tag you on Facebook. Here, you have the option to control the privacy settings to ensure that you review these tags individually and approve them before they post on your Timeline

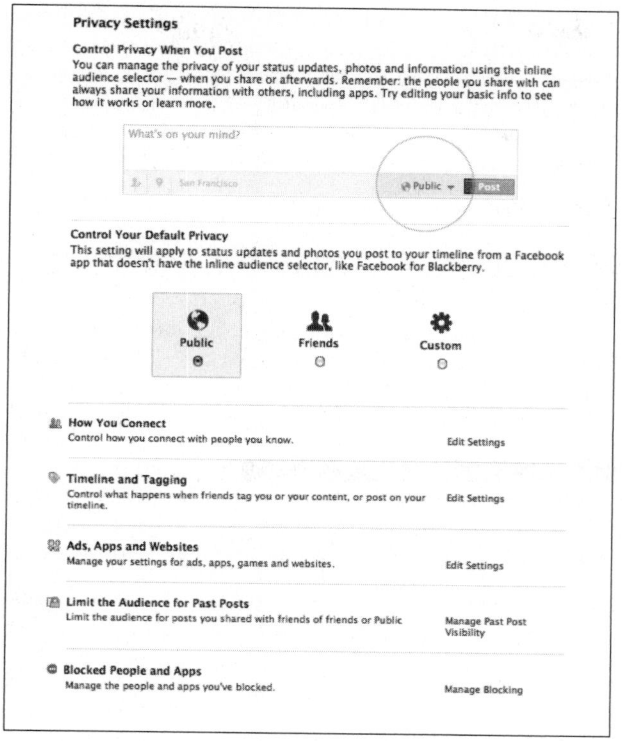
Privacy Settings
Control Privacy When You Post
You can manage the privacy of your status updates, photos and information using the inline audience selector — when you share or afterwards. Remember: the people you share with can always share your information with others, including apps. Try editing your basic info to see how it works or learn more.
What's on your mind?
San Francisco
Public
Post
Control Your Default Privacy
This setting will apply to status updates and photos you post to your timeline from a Facebook app that doesn't have the inline audience selector, like Facebook for Blackberry.
Public
Friends
Custom
How You Connect
Control how you connect with people you know.
Edit Settings
Timeline and Tagging
Control what happens when friends tag you or your content, or post on your timeline.
Edit Settings
Ads, Apps and Websites
Manage your settings for ads, apps, games and websites.
Edit Settings
Limit the Audience for Past Posts
Limit the audience for posts you shared with friends of friends or Public
Manage Past Post Visibility
Blocked People and Apps
Manage the people and apps you've blocked.
Manage Blocking

Figure 1-11: Privacy Settings page on Facebook.

- **Ads, Apps, and Websites:** This area allows you to control how your information is shared with ads, apps, games, and websites that are connected to Facebook.
- **Limit the Audience for Past Posts:** When Facebook changed to the new Profile Timeline layout (see Book II, Chapter 1), all your older posts became more readily visible. Because of this change, Facebook created this control to allow you to limit the visibility of your past posts.
- **Blocked People and Apps:** This area allows you to manage the people and the apps you've blocked.

To learn more about your privacy settings on Facebook, go to `www.facebook.com/about/privacy`.

TIP

You can change your privacy settings at any time. Experiment with the settings, and when you feel that you need to tighten or loosen the constraints, it's easy to log in to Facebook and make these changes.

Although it's true that you need to have a personal Profile in place before you can create a business Page, there's no way for others to see the connection between your new Page and your existing Profile — unless you tell them, of course. Only you know the connection, and you can keep it that way for eternity, if you like. People who choose to connect with you on your Page won't be able to access any information from your personal Facebook Profile.

Keeping things professional but personal

Facebook gives you the opportunity to give a face and personality to your company. Sure, many of us use Facebook in our day-to-day business (as we mention earlier in this chapter), but the vast majority of Facebookers are there to engage with their friends and have fun. And no matter how serious your product or service may be, you always have room for a little levity.

People want to know *you,* not your brand. Be careful about using jargon in your posts and coming across as too "corporate," because this is often seen as inauthentic on social networking sites. Talk to your Facebook community as though the people in it are your friends, not potential clients. The more real you are on Facebook, the more your fans will want to engage with you and your business.

Chapter 2: Creating Your Facebook Marketing Plan

In This Chapter

- Researching and targeting your ideal audience on Facebook
- Finding new connections using Facebook Search
- Understanding the core rules for a successful Facebook Page
- Creating a Facebook team that will help grow your community
- Measuring the success of your Facebook investment

Facebook has changed the game of marketing for everyone. In the past, people who were interested in your products or services would read a brochure, visit your bricks-and-mortar shop, or maybe watch a commercial to find out the information they needed before making a buying decision. Today, people go to Google or search popular social networks for answers to their questions instead. That's why you need an online presence, in real time, to answer their questions when they seek you out. After all, if you make customers wait, they can be knocking on a competitor's virtual door with a click of a button. With that in mind, it's essential that you create a solid, well-thought-out Facebook marketing plan that defines your goals and maps your online strategies.

By the end of this chapter, you'll be able to start putting your Facebook marketing plan to work. Begin by defining your target audience and finding that audience inside the virtual walls of Facebook.

Defining Your Ideal Audience on Facebook

Facebook has more than a billion active users as of this writing, so more likely than not, your brand will find an audience on Facebook. The key here is finding out where they are and what they do while they're inside this thriving social network.

The first step in creating a Facebook marketing plan involves identifying your *brand*. You want to determine who you are and who your customers are. Ask yourself what's unique about your product or service, and what about your product or service attracts buyers. Are you a life coach who teaches people how to find their true passion? Are you a yoga teacher who lives a green lifestyle and sells organic specialty soaps online? In a nutshell, who are you, and what do you do? After you get clear about your brand, you can identify your ideal audience.

Identifying the demographics of your ideal audience

Before you begin marketing on Facebook, you want to compile all the information you already have regarding the demographics of your ideal audience. Commonly used demographics include gender, race, age, location, income, and education. If you haven't done this research, one way to approach it is to survey your existing customers. Ask them questions to find out their specific demographics to help you understand who is buying your products or services.

To help survey your audience, you can use inexpensive (and often free) online tools to make the process easy and anonymous for your audience. Two great sites to explore are Polldaddy (`www.polldaddy.com`) and SurveyMonkey (`www.surveymonkey.com`).

With your audience demographic information in hand, using the tips and techniques we highlight in this chapter you can research similar Facebook users to find potential customers to target inside Facebook. The more information you collect before you start to market on Facebook, the more success you'll have finding new, potential clients. As you dig deeper into Facebook marketing in this chapter, we show you precisely how to use your existing information to find your ideal audience on Facebook.

Understanding the psychographics of your ideal audience

The more you understand your target audience, the better equipped you are to keep the attention of your existing audience and attract new clients as well.

In addition to identifying demographics, you'll want to identify your ideal audience's *psychographics*. Don't let the word scare you; it's easy to do, we promise.

Psychographics are attributes often related to personality, values, attitudes, or interests. Figuring out what a person likes or dislikes, or even favorite hobbies, can be priceless information as you market your products or services, because the more you know about your ideal audience, the better you can create marketing messages that will grab their attention and encourage them to take action.

One way to figure out the psychographics of your ideal audience is to simply ask them. Use your social media networks to post engaging, thought-provoking questions to learn more about your audience. Ask them about their interests, hobbies, and needs. People love to talk about themselves, and if they trust you, they'll often reveal even more than you initially asked.

As we mention earlier in this chapter, online surveys are another great way to learn more about your ideal audience. Offering prizes or giveaways in exchange for information is a great strategy to get people to participate in your surveys. Remember — the more you know, the smarter you can be in your overall marketing activity.

Figure out what your customers want to know from you. What information do you have that they want? If you cast too wide a net, you're likely to come up short in the end. Make sure to stay focused on the people who matter most to your business's success.

You'll also want to find out where your audience spends time while on Facebook. What Facebook Pages do they interact with often? Who do they follow? What do they post in their own personal Facebook Profiles? This information will tell you a lot about your Facebook audience. (In Book IX, we walk you through how to use the Facebook tracking tool, Insights, as well as third-party monitoring tools. Understanding these tools will help you monitor your ideal audience's activity and interactions on Facebook.)

After you know what your business is about, what you're selling, and who your audience is, you want to spend a little time on your tone. In other words, you want to talk to your Facebook audience in a manner that they're familiar with.

Always stay conversational, but try to use words and phrases that they use in their everyday conversations. If your audience is 14-year-old boys who love to skateboard, for example, you talk to them much differently than you would to an audience of new moms looking to connect with other moms. When you know your audience's lingo and style of communication, you can quickly become part of the community.

Finding Your Ideal Audience inside Facebook

One of the biggest benefits of marketing on Facebook is that you have access to the information that Facebook users add to their personal Profiles. Depending on users' Profile privacy settings, you may be able to see their date of birth, marital status, hometown, current location, political views, religious views, employment details, hobbies, interests, and bios. In the past, with traditional marketing, people would pay big bucks for this type of information, but now it's free to you — and at your fingertips.

A great tool you can use to locate your ideal audience on Facebook is Facebook Search. This tool allows you to enter keywords in a search field, and the people, groups, and Pages that are using your keyword(s) will show up in a list. Facebook Search is an ideal tool for anyone looking to connect with people who share interests or views.

When you do a search using Facebook Search, you can find information that users add to their About section and post in their status updates, as well as information about the groups and Pages users interact with. This tool is a very powerful one, to say the least.

Here's how to use Facebook Search:

1. **Log in to your Facebook account, and locate the search query field at the top of the page.**
2. **Enter the keyword or phrase you want to search for; then click Search.**

   In the search field, enter the keyword or phrase you want to search for inside Facebook. A drop-down list shows suggested people and Pages.
3. **Scroll down, and click See More Results For.**

   In the left column, the default filter for Search is All Results. Make sure that it's highlighted. To check out an example of a Facebook Search query, see Figure 2-1.

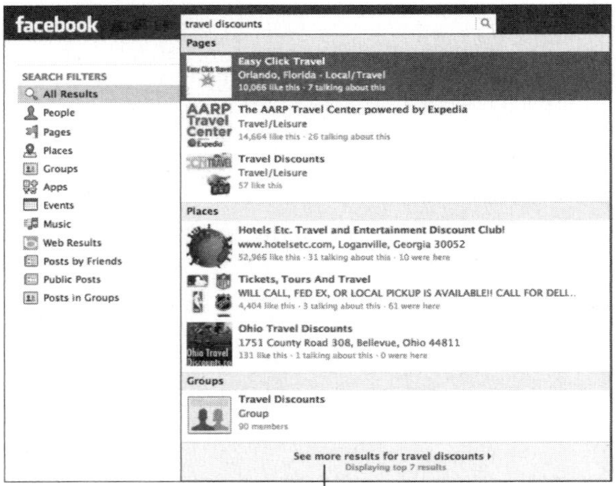

Figure 2-1: The Facebook Search page.

Click to see more search results.

The results for your keyword or keyword phrase will populate in different sections on Facebook. You can explore the following sections by clicking the links in the left column:

- People
- Pages
- Places
- Groups

- Apps
- Events
- Music
- Web Results
- Posts by Friends
- Public Posts
- Posts in Groups

For the purpose of finding your audience on Facebook, we suggest that you spend your time researching the People, Pages, Places, Groups, and Events links.

After you click a specific category, the search results for that keyword show up in one stream. Figure 2-2 shows an example search for the word *sushi* in the category Pages.

Choose a category

Figure 2-2: Click the category of your choice to see results for your keyword.

Filtering Facebook Search results

After you complete your search inquiry, you may be thinking, "Great! But now what do I do with all this info?" Here are a few strategies for putting that info to use in going after your ideal audience on Facebook:

- **Send a Friend request.** Identify the Facebook users you want to target, and Friend them on Facebook. If the Facebook user has enabled messaging, you may be able to send him a personal e-mail via Facebook. Sending a personal note is smart when sending a Friend request to make the connection more personal.

  To change your messaging settings, go into Privacy Settings, click "How to Connect," and choose which option works best for your preferences under the drop-down menu next to "Who can send you Facebook messages?" as shown in Figure 2-3.

Figure 2-3: Messaging options inside your Privacy Settings.

Be mindful when sending personal messages to people you do not yet personally know. Be careful to not come across as "spammy" or too pushy, but instead keep things friendly, casual, and to the point, as shown in Figure 2-4.

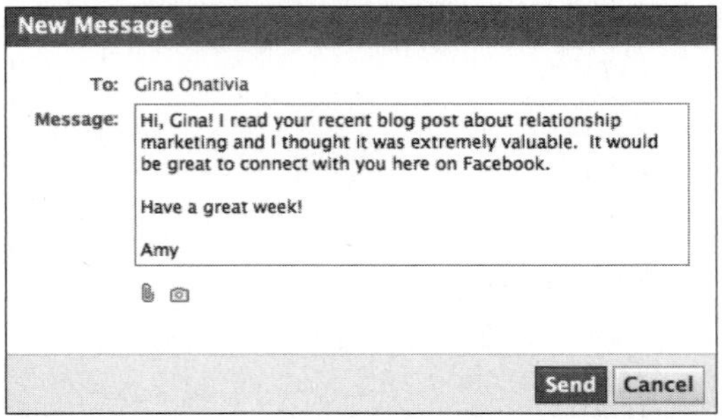

Figure 2-4: Attach a personal note to a Friend request.

- **Ask them to join your Page.** Invite your targeted users to like your Page by sending them an e-mail inside Facebook, including the link to your Facebook Page, and requesting that they check out your Page and click the Like button to join your community. In the e-mail, briefly tell them why it's a good idea to join your Page.

✦ **Join the groups that count the most.** The best strategy is to join active Facebook groups related to your brand or niche and become part of that community. After joining, consistently post helpful tips that will eventually connect people to your Facebook Page, as shown in Figure 2-5.

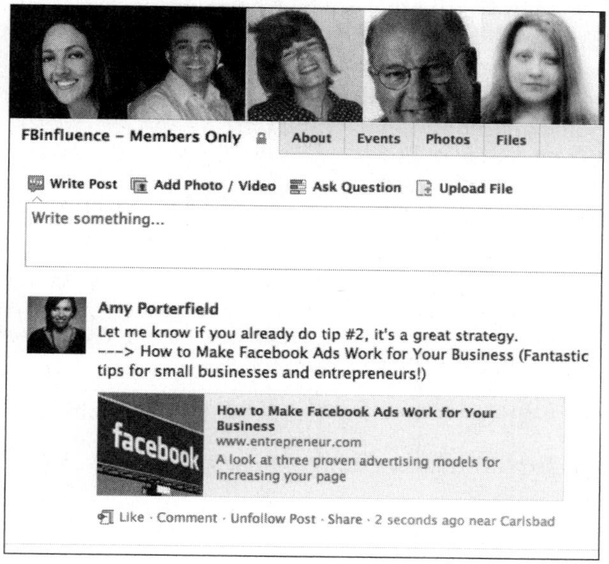

Figure 2-5: Post comments to a Facebook group devoted to your niche.

Using Facebook Ads to research your ideal audience

Even if you don't plan to use Facebook Ads as part of your overall Facebook marketing plan, you can still benefit from the Facebook Ads platform to find out to what degree your target audience is on Facebook.

Here's how you can access this valuable information:

1. **Log in to your Facebook account, and click the drop-down menu next to the word *Home* in the top-right corner of your page.**
2. **From the drop-down menu, choose Create an Ad.**
3. **When you're inside the Ads dashboard, choose your Page as the Facebook destination.**

   The What Do You Want to Promote? option appears. You have two choices: your Page itself or a specific post from your Page.
4. **Choose your Page name.**

   The People Will See option appears.

5. **Choose A New Ad About [Your Page Name].**

   The option to create an ad appears. You can ignore this option and instead scroll down to the next section, called Choose Your Audience, where you can dive in to learn more about your ideal audience inside Facebook (without paying a dime!).

6. **In the Location section, below Choose Your Audience, type a country name.**

   You can get more specific by choosing states, provinces, cities, and zip codes. You can enter multiple states, cities, and zip codes in the same location field; however, if you enter two or more countries in the country field, you will lose the option to list states, cities, and zip codes. You want to drill-down as much as possible to get a good representation of your ideal client on Facebook.

   TIP: To better understand the physical location of your fans, take a look at the demographics data in your Insights dashboard (the area where you will find metrics details for your Facebook Page). You can find out more about Insights in Book IX, Chapter 2.

7. **(Optional) Indicate a specific age or an age range, or specify gender.**

8. **In the Precise Interests section, enter a keyword that describes your audience.**

   (For this exercise, ignore Broad Categories.)

   After you type in a keyword, a drop-down menu appears, as shown in Figure 2-6. From that drop-down menu, you can choose the keywords that Facebook identifies as best choices based on your initial keyword. After you choose the keyword, press Return or Enter, and then you can be even more specific by selecting subcategories of your keyword.

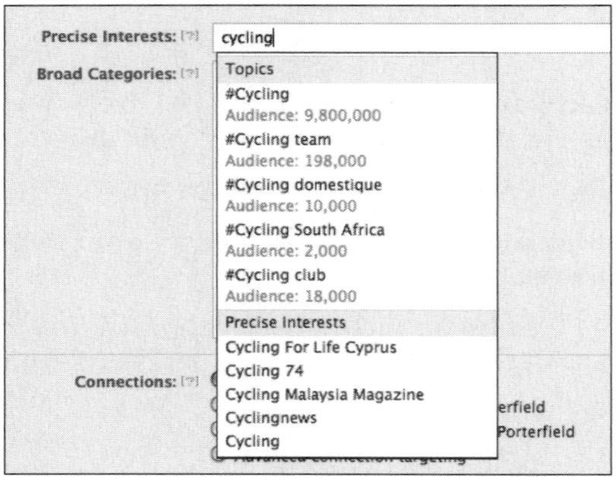

Figure 2-6: Search by Precise Interests.

Suppose that you choose *cycling* as your keyword because you know that your target audience consists of avid cyclists who will likely mention cycling in their personal Profiles. After you choose this keyword, you get to see options to drill-down even more. You can click any of the boxes that also relate to your target audience and thereby drill-down on your target audience even more, as shown in Figure 2-7.

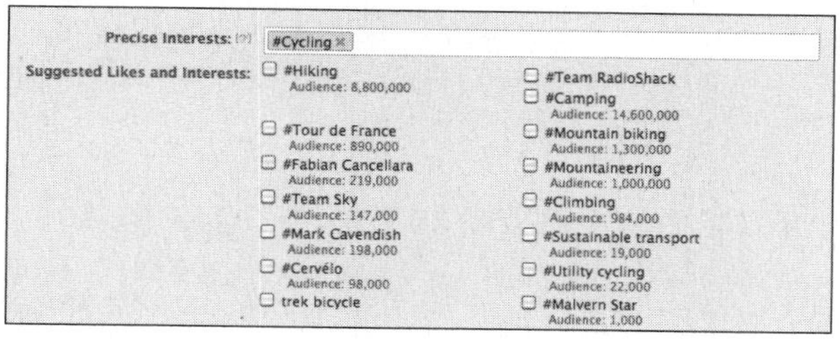

Figure 2-7: Deepen your search with subcategories.

After you enter the appropriate information for location, demographics, and interests, a number on the right side of the screen shows you how many people on Facebook match your ideal target audience criteria, as shown in Figure 2-8. If you have that nugget of information, you know whether your target audience is on Facebook.

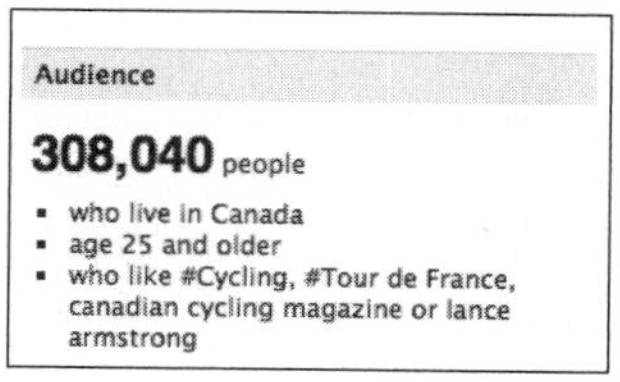

Figure 2-8: Check out how many people meet your ideal audience criteria.

Identifying the Core Goals of Your Facebook Marketing Plan

With Facebook growing by the minute, there's no question that it must be a part of your marketing mix. These days, however, it's not enough to sign up for a Facebook account, put up a Facebook Page, and hope that potential readers find you. Unfortunately, the *Field of Dreams* model ("Build it and they will come") doesn't apply.

Book II is dedicated to showing you everything you need to know about the importance of a Facebook Page and how to set one up strategically. To set up your Facebook marketing foundation, however, it's essential to create a Facebook marketing plan or strategy. Think of your strategy as a road map — the directions you need to create a thriving, active, loyal community on Facebook.

The strategy behind a Facebook marketing plan doesn't need to be complicated, but it does need to be carefully thought out. When it comes to growing a brand on Facebook, business owners and marketers commonly become stuck, often because they overcomplicate things. The goal of this section is to help you create a Facebook marketing plan without going absolutely crazy in the process.

Defining your Facebook marketing goals

As you think about crafting your Facebook marketing plan, understand what Facebook can do for your business. Consider these six Facebook marketing goals as you craft your new plan:

- Increasing overall exposure
- Building brand awareness
- Creating a loyal, engaged community
- Listening to your clients' needs, interests, and feedback
- Monitoring what people are saying about your brand
- Driving action (often in the form of sales of your products or services)

These six core goals will help you shape the specific outcomes you want to achieve from your Facebook marketing plan. We explore these core goals throughout the book to ensure you have the tools to create a successful Facebook marketing plan. One of the first steps when creating your marketing plan and determining your goals is to decide on a social media budget.

Deciding on a social media budget

You've likely heard that social media marketing is free. Well, we're sorry to break it to you here, but that's not exactly the case. It can be free, but in some areas, we encourage you to consider spending a little money to take your campaign to a professional level. Here are three areas where you should consider spending a little money:

- **Branding:** We suggest that you hire a designer to create a look and feel for all your social media profiles. All your profiles should be consistent across channels and match your branding as much as possible. With everything that you need easily accessible online these days, finding a designer for this task is affordable and quick. Sites like `www.freelance.com` and `www.tweetpages.com` are great resources to find designers to create your social media profiles. In Book III, Chapter 2, we show you how to use custom apps to brand your Facebook Page.

- **Social media consulting:** We often suggest that entrepreneurs and businesses that are new in the social media arena spend a little money educating themselves. Although we don't suggest that you run out and hire someone to take over your social media activity, we do suggest that you consult a social media expert for a review of your social media strategy to gain feedback on and insight into your new plan.
- **Facebook Ads:** The third area you may want to consider budgeting for is Facebook Ads — which leads us right into the next section.

Deciding whether a Facebook Ads campaign is right for you

Consider experimenting with Facebook Ads, even if you only plan to test them for a limited time with a small budget. You may be pleasantly surprised by the effectiveness of this advertising channel, because Facebook Ads allow you to promote your business, get more likes for your Facebook Page, and drive more leads to build up your sales funnel.

The reason why Facebook Ads are so popular is that the targeting is like that of no other advertising vehicle available today. You can target by gender, age, race, location, and interests — and even by who is or who isn't a liker of a specific Facebook Page. It's an impressive tool worth checking out, for sure.

TIP

We spend an entire minibook (Book VIII, to be exact) exploring Facebook Ads in greater depth. To get a quick taste of how Facebook advertising works, check out the Facebook description at `www.facebook.com/advertising`. And don't forget *Facebook Advertising For Dummies,* by Paul Dunay, Richard Krueger, and Joel Elad (John Wiley & Sons, Inc.).

After you establish your core goals for your Facebook marketing plan, you can focus on creating a successful Facebook Page.

Before you hire a social media consultant

If you decide to hire a social media consultant to review your social media marketing plan, treat the experience as though you're hiring a new employee. Ask for references, and do your due diligence to make sure that you're hiring a skilled, experienced consultant who has achieved real results for other clients. One way to start your search for a social media consultant is to search in Facebook by going to `www.facebook.com/search` and typing these keywords:

"social media consultant"

"social media marketing"

"social media marketer"

Rules for Successful Facebook Pages

One of the most important questions to ask as you create your Facebook marketing plan is, "What do I want to achieve with my Facebook Page and overall marketing on Facebook?"

To help you sort through the many layers of Facebook marketing, consider nine core rules as you create your Facebook Page:

- Be deliberate, and manage expectations.
- Focus on smart branding.
- Create fresh content.
- Give your Page a human touch.
- Cultivate engagement with two-way dialogue.
- Encourage fan-to-fan conversations.
- Make word-of-mouth advocacy easy.
- Create consistent calls to action.
- Monitor, measure, and track.

Dive into the following sections to explore the nine core rules for a successful Facebook Page.

Rule #1: Be deliberate, and manage expectations

Before you do anything else, you need to decide why you want to have a presence on Facebook. What is your overall vision for your Page? Often, your vision for Facebook will be aligned with your overall company vision.

If you own a high-end clothing store for women, for example, your company vision may be to offer the highest fashion and the best-quality clothing in your area to make women feel great about how they look. On Facebook, your vision for your store may be to create a community for women who love high fashion, giving them a place to talk about clothes and share ideas. Your Facebook Page can become a hub for fashion-minded women (and the best place for you to engage with your ideal audience on Facebook).

Having a clear vision does two things:

- It allows you and your team to clearly understand why you're on Facebook. When you understand the why, your actions are deliberate and have purpose.
- When you have a clear vision, you can communicate it to your Facebook fans, who then will know how to interact with your Page.

Your vision is only as strong as the person or team behind it. It's up to you to spread the word. The good news is that after you have a solid fan base, your fans will help spread your message and virally attract new followers. It's up to you to sell your vision to get others to pay attention.

Rule #2: Focus on smart branding

One way to understand the power of a Facebook Page is to look at it as a mini version of your own website. Some of the most successful Facebook Pages act as an extension of the brand and are essentially mini websites inside Facebook. Smart branding allows you to create a bridge from Facebook to your website. The key is to create a Page that sparks familiarity with your brand when your existing customers visit your Page.

Here are two examples of Facebook Pages (one of which is shown in Figure 2-9) that do a great job of mirroring their website branding. Check them out to see branding done right.

Social Media Examiner

Website: `www.socialmediaexaminer.com`

Facebook Page: `www.facebook.com/smexaminer`

Red Bull

Website: `www.redbull.com`

Facebook Page: `www.facebook.com/redbull`

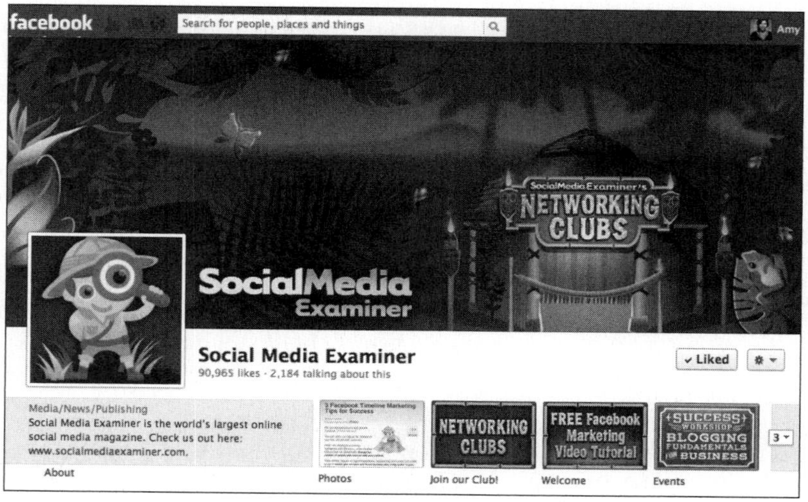

Figure 2-9: Smart branding via Social Media Examiner.

REMEMBER

You can't expect that consumers on Facebook will find you easily and automatically. Facebook users typically don't search actively for a brand's Facebook Page; instead, most users stumble upon a Page, either through a Friend's Page or from a hub such as your website. Branding your Page allows you to make your Page dynamic (stand out above the rest) and more viral in nature (increasing the number of people who will see it).

Rule #3: Create fresh content

To get the most reach for your content, make sure that your content educates, entertains, and empowers your fans. This will pique their interest and keep them coming back for more.

Also, publish everything you have in as many places as possible. You want to get your content online and seen by as many prospects as possible.

You can also monitor what others are publishing. If you see something that would be valuable to your audience — and isn't in direct competition with your business — publish that content (and make sure to give the content's publisher credit for it!). Third-party publishing is a great way to continue to add value for your fans without having to create all the content yourself.

To help create content consistently, we suggest that you create an editorial calendar. The task may sound daunting, but it's actually very simple. Here's how you do it:

1. **Create a six-month digital calendar.**

   You can do this in a word-processing program like Microsoft Word, or you can find digital calendars online. One of our favorite digital-calendar sites is `www.calendarsthatwork.com`.

2. **Decide how often you want to create content, and in what form.**

   Consider creating blog posts, video posts, articles, reports, podcasts, or any other form of media you know your audience will like. Mix it up, delivering your content in many formats to attract a wider reach of ideal clients.

3. **Brainstorm content ideas related to your brand or niche.**

   Again, think of what interests your clients most. (*Hint:* Check out your competition's content. This will help you decide what may be best for your audience.)

4. **Create a calendar of content.**

   Choose the specific dates on which you plan to post, and list the topic of the content and the type of delivery. You might add the following in the June 18 box, for example: *Blog post and Facebook update on "How to Create a Facebook Page."* It's as easy as that!

TIP

Stay diligent with your content calendar. After you create it, stick with it. The more disciplined you are in sticking to your content calendar, the more traction you will gain with your audience.

Rule #4: Give your Page a human touch

To give your Page a human touch, highlight the team behind it. Your fans don't want to connect with your brand or product; they want to connect with you. As you have likely heard numerous times, social media is about transparency and authenticity. People want to know that they're communicating with the real you; that's why first names and photos are the norm on Facebook.

Brands that allow their Page administrators to have real conversations with their fans are much more likely to have active, engaging Pages. Here are a few key strategies to give your Facebook Page a human touch:

- ✦ Address your fans by their first names, and craft your posts in the first-person singular voice.
- ✦ Use a conversational tone in your posts.
- ✦ Encourage your Page administrators to add their names at the end of their posts, as shown in Figure 2-10.

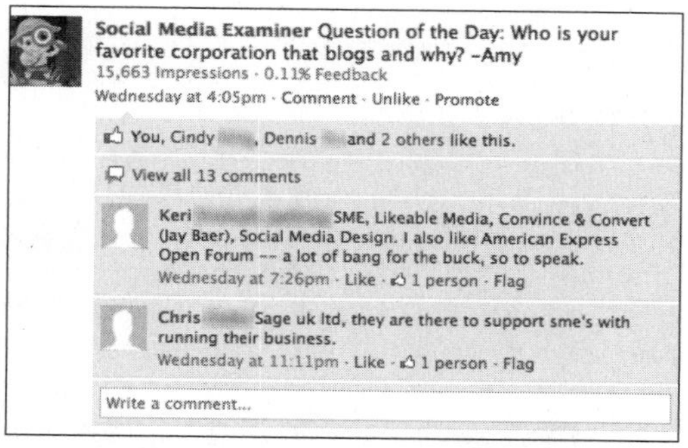

Figure 2-10: Have Page admins add their names to their posts.

- ✦ If you have multiple admins, add your Page administrators' photos and bios on a custom tab, as shown in Figure 2-11. This allows your fans to get to know the people that are representing your Page.

Don't make your Page another static website. Give it a human touch by encouraging your admin team members to be themselves, communicate with your fans as though they were talking to their friends, and give each post that spark of personality.

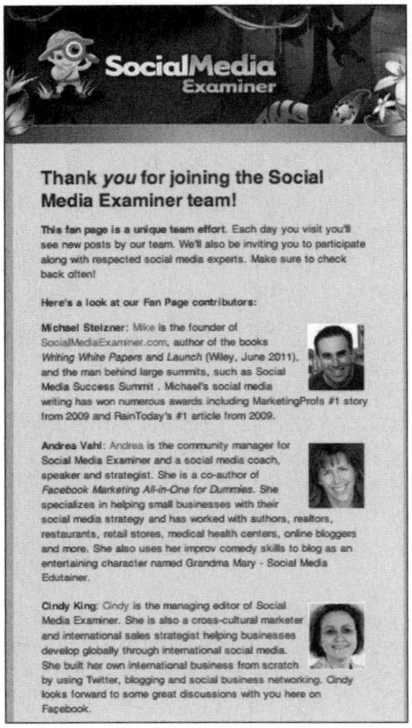

Figure 2-11: A Facebook Page tab that spotlights the Page administrators.

Rule #5: Cultivate engagement with two-way dialogue

In a nutshell, engagement is about getting your fans to take action, which means posting on your Page, commenting on your posts, clicking the Like button next to your posts, and sharing your content. A well-executed engagement strategy takes time and effort. More than anything, engagement is really about showing up daily and taking a genuine interest in the likes, interests, and opinions of your fans.

The rule for engagement is making it about your fans and not about you. Remember that people love to talk about themselves, so craft your posts and questions around them, and you're sure to see some great conversations begin to surface on your Page. Check out Figure 2-12 for an example of a question that's about the user — not about a brand.

REMEMBER

A massive fan base left disengaged is a recipe for disaster! Take action; start talking with your fans regularly.

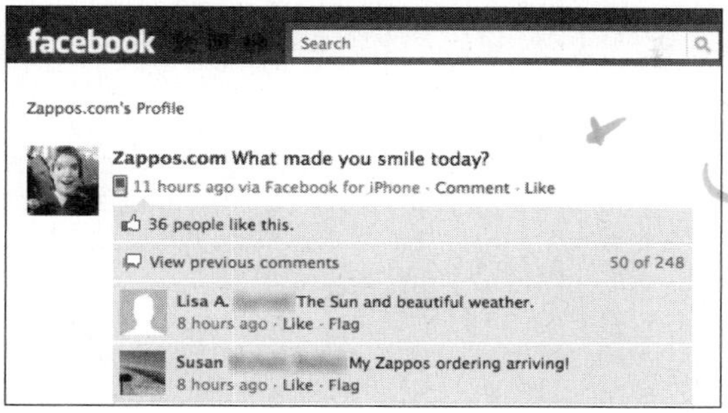

Figure 2-12: Make your posts less promotional and more inclined to engage people.

Rule #6: Encourage fan-to-fan conversations

The key here is to enhance your fans' experience by creating a community that encourages peer-to-peer communication. Here are a few key strategies you can use to get fans talking to one another:

✦ **Showcase fans.** Create a Member of the Month campaign or an opportunity to spotlight your fans directly on your Facebook Page, as shown in Figure 2-13. When fans are recognized, they tell their Friends — which encourages even more fan-to-fan interaction.

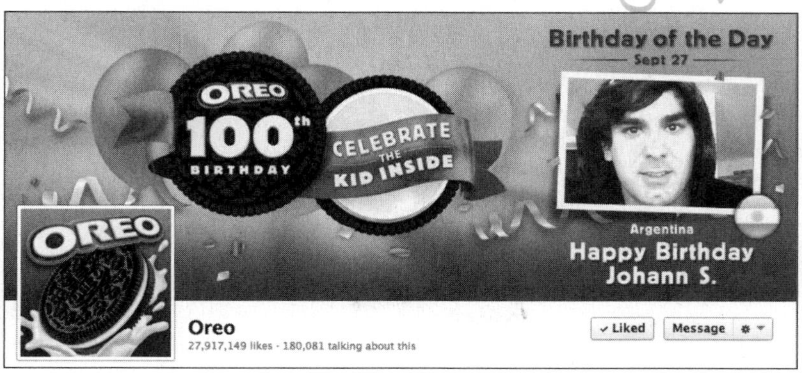

Figure 2-13: Oreo spotlights fan birthdays on their Timeline Cover photo.

✦ **Recognize top contributors.** When you have someone on your Page who likes to answer questions from fans, or who often offers tips or suggestions, take advantage of his or her enthusiasm. Ask the fan to be an ambassador for your Page, and encourage him to help out when appropriate. Give your biggest advocates specific guidelines and responsibilities, and reward them with perks. Their involvement will free up time for you to concentrate on other ways to grow your Page.

Rule #7: Make word-of-mouth advocacy easy

It's a fact that customers trust their friends and other customers more than they trust a brand. Think of it this way. If you were going to buy a new pair of running shoes, who would you listen to: your good friend who is an avid runner and who just purchased a pair, or the shoe manufacturer that's posting a promotion about those shoes on its Facebook Page? Gravitating toward the person you have a relationship with is human nature. That's precisely why word-of-mouth advocacy is essential.

To encourage word-of-mouth advocacy, you want to make it easy for your fans to talk about you. Here are a couple of suggestions:

- **Ask a fan to like a post or Share a post.** When you post a link to a new article on your Facebook Page, add a line at the end of the post that says, "If you like this article, please click the link to share it with your friends!" Keep the tone light and conversational, and your fans will be happy to oblige.
- **Do something that encourages self-expression.** People love to talk about themselves and share their thoughts, feelings, and feedback. Create an experience that makes them want to share your content with their friends. This is how the viral experience is created. To do this, you can create a poll on your Page or run a contest that gets your audience excited about engaging with you. We mention testing polls earlier in this chapter. (To find out more about contests on Facebook, check out Book VI, Chapter 2.)

Rule #8: Create consistent calls to action

To move your fans to action, you need to give them a reason to take action. Discounts or specials are great ways to reward your clients. You're saying, "Hey, I really appreciate your being a fan. Thanks for coming on over. I want to do something special for you now."

You can give out discount codes or even create a special custom app for your Page (see Book V, Chapter 2) and allow your fans to print the coupons.

REMEMBER

You want to keep your fans happy and get them to take action. Everybody loves a discount or a special, so think of ways you can incorporate these items into your Facebook marketing plan.

Another way you can encourage fans to take action is ask them to sign up for your online newsletter or sign up for a giveaway. This strategy is considered to be an *opt-in strategy,* and with custom apps, you can easily create an opt-in box (see Figure 2-14) to collect the names and e-mail addresses of your fans. Again, check out Book V, Chapter 2 for details about customized apps.

Figure 2-14: Add an opt-in box on a Facebook Page.

Rule #9: Monitor, measure, and track

Although it may not sound like a fun task, it's essential that you monitor, measure, and track your Facebook activity. In Book IX, we explore in depth the various ways for you to do this, but for the sake of your Facebook marketing plan, you want to make sure that you have surefire methods in place that enable you to consistently track your Facebook marketing progress.

The great thing about social media marketing is that it's not set in stone. In the past, you would have to print a marketing brochure for thousands (if not hundreds of thousands) of dollars and then cross your fingers, hoping that it worked — because if it flopped, you had to wait until that brochure ran out and then spend a handful of money to test something new.

On Facebook and other social sites, most of the time tweaking a marketing campaign is as easy as clicking a button. That's a huge advantage of marketing online.

The key here is being diligent about testing what's working and instantly tweaking what's not. When you get into this habit, you can see progress much faster than you ever did with traditional marketing endeavors.

Summing up the nine rules

REMEMBER

There's a lot of noise on the web about the do's and don'ts of social media marketing, and it tends to be overwhelming. These nine core rules are meant to simplify your process.

If you add a bunch of extra components to the rules, you're less likely to see the results you want — or, worse, you're likely to get overwhelmed and not take action. In short, ignore the chatter, and stick to the plan.

Creating a Facebook Page is fairly simple, but growing its momentum and getting it to thrive takes time, dedication, and some planning. Don't expect to create a Page and then see a massive following instantaneously. Create valuable content, encourage fans to share your Page with their friends, and tell people about it. With time and patience, you'll see your Page grow.

Setting Up the Resources and Manpower for Your Facebook Marketing Plan

After you nail down what goes into your Facebook marketing plan, you'll want to explore what resources and manpower you have at your disposal. If you're an entrepreneur or the owner of a small business, you probably don't have a large team. The good news is that you don't need a large team behind you to attract a captive audience on Facebook. By following the nine core rules of a Facebook Page that we describe in the preceding section — and by keeping your Facebook marketing plan simple — you can grow your Page to the level you need with only a few hands on deck. The following sections show you how to identify the people and resources you need to put your Facebook marketing plan to work.

Identifying your existing resources and manpower

First, do an internal assessment to identify your resources and manpower. For entrepreneurs and small-business owners, the essential players are at least two Page administrators (assign one admin the Page manager role, and the other person can be a content creator or moderator). We discuss all admin roles in more detail later in this chapter and in Book II, Chapter 3. Plus you will want to assign a designer and programmer to help with your branding. If you have the funds, we also suggest that you put some money toward a few sessions with a social media strategy consultant who will review your existing plan.

For larger businesses, if you have a marketing team, we suggest integrating your Facebook marketing plan into your existing marketing initiatives. Your Facebook marketing plan shouldn't be a stand-alone Facebook marketing tool; instead, it should be closely integrated into your overall marketing plan. Sit down with your existing marketing team, and go through the six Facebook marketing goals and nine core rules of a successful Facebook Page to see how they align with the programs and initiatives you already have in place.

Integrating your social media strategies

Along with your Facebook marketing plan, you'll likely want to consider other social media initiatives. Perhaps you'll want to include Twitter in your social media mix or create a YouTube channel as part of your social media outreach plan.

To get the most momentum for your social media marketing plan, don't separate your social media marketing efforts. One person, or one solid team, should oversee all social media efforts. It's important to have strong synergy among all social media sites; therefore, you want the person managing your Facebook Page to know firsthand what's taking place on your Twitter account, YouTube channel, and any other social site.

Deciding on in-house or outsourced marketing

After you decide to create a Facebook marketing plan, you have to decide who's going to run it. You have multiple options to consider for your social media management and support.

Option 1: Hire an agency (or consultant) to manage your Facebook Page

Like most things, this option has both pros and cons. We offer both sides for your consideration.

Pros:

- **You gain access to social media expertise and knowledge.** This is especially helpful if your knowledge is limited.
- **An agency or consultant can save you a tremendous amount of time.** If you're not consistently listening to your fans and interacting with them regularly, they will quickly lose interest in your Page. It might be a smart move for you to hire someone to take on this important task.
- **Social media experts tend to be in the know about the latest trends.** Because social media changes quickly, it's important to stay on the cutting edge and be the first to adopt new strategies or tools as they prove to be promising. An agency or consultant can advise you on the latest and greatest in social media marketing to keep you current and ahead of the pack.
- **You get expert advice on your social media content strategy.** One of the most important pieces of your Facebook marketing strategy is the

content you post on your social networks. An agency or consultant can help you create a content plan to align with your overall marketing plan.

- **An agency or expert has access to monitoring and tracking tools and technology that you may not have.** This is important, because an agency can quickly see what is working and what needs tweaking, allowing your campaign to be monitored in real time.

Cons:

- **An agency won't know your products or services as well as you do.** If you're not careful, an agency may end up representing you or your brand in ways that don't particularly inspire confidence. Potential customers often ask questions about a product or service via a company's Facebook Page. Ask yourself this question: If an agency or consultant were managing your Page, would that agency or consultant be able to give the prospects accurate information?

  Incorrect information could cost you a new client — or, worse, earn you backlash from your Facebook fans. One solution is to make sure that your agency or consultant has direct access to the appropriate people inside your company who can provide real-time support when needed.

- **An agency won't understand your brand as well as you do.** Successful brands have a specific voice, and it's critical that this voice be consistent throughout all your marketing initiatives. That said, it's paramount that your agency or consultant understand your brand voice and be clear on your brand personality and positioning. This clarity allows for a seamless transition between your company's communication style and the agency's communication on your behalf.

- **An agency won't know your company culture intimately and will be unaware of behind-the-scenes activities.** One of the most important aspects of Facebook marketing is the transparency factor. Your fans want to know your company and brand at an intimate level. That's what makes social media networking so attractive to consumers.

  Only you and those who work with you intimately know what your company stands for and what its values are. This is difficult to explain to someone from the outside who isn't experiencing it firsthand.

  REMEMBER

  Some of the most popular brands on Facebook allow their fans to get a glimpse of their company culture and what goes on behind the scenes. Zappos is a great example; see `www.facebook.com/zappos`.

  An agency or consultant isn't part of your culture and won't be able to communicate the special benefits of that culture to your fans unless you educate that agency or consultant in advance, which takes some dedication on your part.

- **If you (or someone on your team) don't manage your Facebook Page directly, you won't see what's happening on a day-to-day basis.** This situation means you lose a little control of what's taking place on your Page.

  One solution is to ask your agency or consultant to report to you on a regular basis, informing you about what's taking place on your Page, and letting you know about any challenges and what was done to take care of them.

If you do decide to hire an agency or consultant, make sure that you discuss what's expected; the procedures you want the agency or consultant to adhere to at all times; and the rules, guidelines, and any specific procedures to follow in case of a crisis on any of your social networking sites.

Option #2: Self-manage your Facebook marketing plan

Most small to midsize businesses manage their Facebook marketing plan in-house. Overall, this strategy has multiple benefits. If you're managing your strategy in-house, you essentially eliminate all the cons discussed in the preceding section.

Option #3: Use the hybrid model

If you're new in the social media arena (as most people are), consider hiring support to some degree. One solution that we suggest is the hybrid model. In essence, you hire an agency or consultant to help build your social media marketing strategy (including your Facebook marketing plan), and that agency or consultant can also support the launch of the strategy in the early stages. When things are off the ground and running smoothly (which may take about six months to get going), you and your team take over. You not only benefit from the agent's or consultant's expertise and experience, but also work in a certain amount of training so that you and your team are well equipped to take over after the agent's or consultant's contract ends.

Defining Your Admin Team

Among the most important roles on your Facebook Page are the administrator and administration team. You can have just one person manage your Page and oversee the management, monitoring, and content creation, but we suggest that you assign multiple admins to help support your Facebook Page activity. The great news is that you can assign different permissions to specific admin roles, meaning that you don't have to give full access of your Page to all your admins.

Having a few admins is a smart strategy because your admins can divide and conquer. With multiple admins, you can assign roles and responsibilities that are aligned with the admins' skills and strengths, and your Page will be more consistently managed when multiple people watch over day-to-day activity.

Make sure to assign each admin clear tasks to prevent overlap or confusion on your Page. Create a set of rules and guidelines to make sure that everyone is clear of the Page expectations for admins.

Filling the five admin roles

There are five admin roles:

- **Manager:** A manager has full access to your Page. A manager can manage admin roles (meaning that he or she can add and delete admins and assign admin roles), edit the Page, add apps, create posts, respond to and delete comments, send messages, create Ads, and view Insights.
- **Content creator:** A content creator can edit the Page, add apps, create posts, respond to and delete comments, send messages, create Ads, and view Insights.
- **Moderator:** A moderator can respond to and delete comments, send messages, create Ads, and view Insights.
- **Advertiser:** An advertiser can create Ads and view Insights.
- **Insights Analyst:** An insights analyst can view Insights.

Because you're able to assign different levels of access to your Page admins, take advantage of this feature by assigning some of your Facebook tasks to different people on your team.

Adding an admin

To add an admin to your Facebook Page, you have to be an admin manager of your Page. Only admin managers can add other admins. Here's how you do it:

1. **Log in to Facebook, and go to your Facebook Page.**
2. **From the Edit Page drop-down menu (located at the top of your Facebook Page in the Admin Panel), choose Admin Roles.**

   You're taken to your admin page.

   If you already have multiple admins, your current admins' images and names pop up. You also see a field where you can enter the name or e-mail address of a person you want to add as an admin, as shown in Figure 2-15.

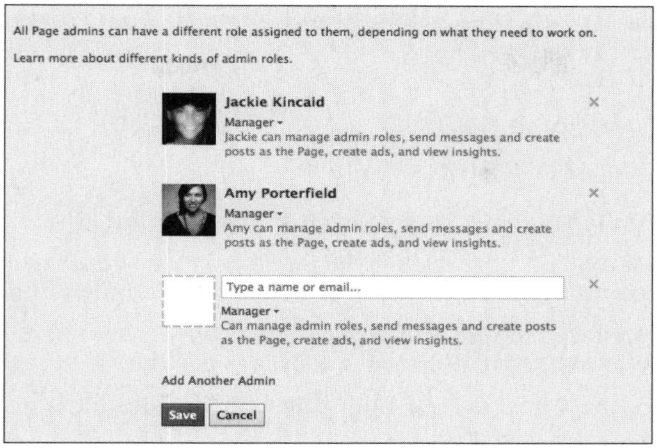

Figure 2-15: Add a new admin to your Page.

3. **Type the name or e-mail address of each person you want to add as an admin.**

   As you type the name, a drop-down menu appears, with possible choices of people you may be searching for.

4. **Click the correct name and his or her profile image in the drop-down menu, and the full name populates instantly.**

   If you want to add more admins to your Page, they must be Friends of your personal Profile, or they must have liked your Page. If you want to add someone who doesn't fit either description, you can add him as an admin by typing the e-mail address he uses to log in to Facebook. When you enter the e-mail address, that person receives an e-mail from Facebook, saying that he was made an admin of your Page.

5. **(Optional) Add more admins by clicking the Add Another Admin link, located above the Save button (refer to Figure 2-15).**

6. **If necessary, change the roles of your existing admins by clicking the drop-down menu below a name and choosing a new role from the menu, as shown in Figure 2-16.**

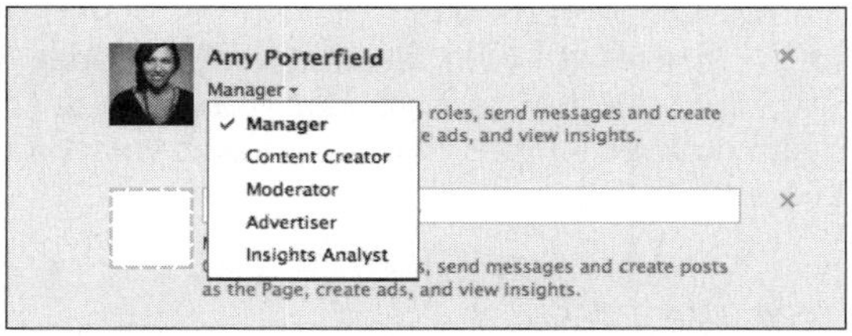

Figure 2-16: Choose a specific admin role for an admin.

7. **Click Save, and you will be prompted to add your Facebook password to secure the changes.**

Deleting an admin

To delete an admin, follow these simple instructions:

1. **Log in to Facebook, and go to your Facebook Page.**
2. **From the Edit Page drop-down menu (located at the top of your Facebook Page in the Admin Panel), choose Admin Roles.**

   You're taken to your admin page. If you already have multiple admins, your current admins' images and names pop up.
3. **Click the X next to the name of the admin you want to delete.**
4. **Click Save, and you will be prompted to add your Facebook password to secure the changes.**

   When you remove an admin, that person is automatically removed from your admin list. She won't receive notification that she's been removed as an admin.

Just as you're able to remove other admins of your Page, you can remove yourself as an admin. We don't recommend doing this, however. If you remove yourself as an admin of your Page, you lose all access to your Page, and you can no longer act as the owner of the Page. This means that you can't edit the Page, you can no longer post on behalf of the Page, and you can't access the Facebook Page dashboard. Therefore, always keep yourself as one of the admins of your Facebook Page.

Choosing the right Page manager

The *Page manager* is the admin of your Page who is ultimately responsible for managing the Page and making sure that it runs smoothly. In many ways, this admin manages the other admins who you've assigned to the Page. Additionally, the Page manager should be well aware of your Facebook marketing plan and should execute that plan on a daily basis.

A Page manager interacts with your fans daily, so it's paramount that you take the time to choose this person wisely. More often than not, the person you end up choosing is already on your internal team because he knows your brand and your clients better than someone from the outside does. If you do need to hire an outside source, make sure that you train that person well and monitor her activity closely.

Checking out personality traits

When looking for the right manager for your Page, you want to make sure that person's personality is a good fit for your audience. Here are six personality traits of a superstar Page manager:

- Natural communicator
- Problem solver
- Person who enjoys people
- Good listener
- Professional
- Positive and enthusiastic

REMEMBER

In addition to these traits, consider your ideal audience. Make sure that your Page manager will connect easily with your fans.

Searching for skills

Although personality traits are important for a Page manager, keep in mind that any successful Page manager must also possess these necessary skills:

- Solid understanding of social networking
- Social media savvy
- Strong commitment to helping people in social channels
- Ability to multitask and think quickly
- Knowledge and understanding of online marketing
- Ability to grasp how social media activity aligns with business goals

Making the final choice

To make the right decision, here are some important questions to ask before you decide who will ultimately manage your Facebook Page:

- Does this person show the ability to be social online?
- Does this person show a genuine interest in connecting with our clients?
- Can I trust this person to be professional and respectful at all times?
- Do people naturally gravitate toward this person?
- Will this person actively contribute to new ideas to grow the Page and make it better each day?

Considering a social media manager

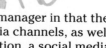

A *social media manager* differs from a Facebook Page manager in that the social media manager is responsible for all social media channels, as well as the overall social media marketing strategy. In addition, a social media manager must interact regularly with your internal marketing team (if you have one).

The size of your organization, your overall budget, and your access to resources are major factors in deciding whether a social media manager is right for your business.

A social media manager must possess personality traits and skill sets similar to those of Page manager. See "Choosing the right Page manager," earlier in this chapter, to review the necessary traits and skills.

In addition, the social media manager must know your company, brand, products, and services well, and must have a strong background in traditional marketing as well as a strong grasp of new media marketing trends. In a nutshell, social media manager is a higher-level position than Page manager and has many more responsibilities. Whereas you may be able to add the Page manager role to an existing employee's plate, the social media manager role is more robust and time-consuming, and requires more experience and a higher-level skill set than that of Page manager.

We suggest that you start small. First, identify and test a dedicated manager for your Facebook Page, and hire a social media consultant or agency for just a few months to get you up and running. Then review your activity, and decide whether a social media manager would add value and growth to your overall plan. Just as you would with a Page manager and admins of your Facebook Page, if you decide to hire a social media manager, make sure to create clear roles, responsibilities, and guidelines for this position.

Coordinating admin posts and strategies

It's important to assign clear guidelines and rules not only for your Page manager, but also for your multiple admins. To keep your admins on task without duplicating efforts, give them clear direction. That way, your Page will be updated regularly; your fans will be supported, and your admins won't be confused about their Page responsibilities. As previously mentioned in this chapter, an editorial calendar will come in handy when coordinating posts and marketing messages. To ensure all your admins are on the same page, it's a smart strategy to encourage each of them to use the same editorial calendar to track activity. Here are some guidelines to consider as you coordinate posts and strategies:

- **Decide how you want your admins to post on your Page.** Here are some questions you want to ask about your status updates and posts on your Timeline:
  - How often will you post updates to your Page?
  - What will you post about?
  - Will you include links in your posts to direct fans to content outside Facebook?

- Will you use third-party content, such as posts from your favorite blog sites and videos from YouTube, to add value?
- Will you mix up the media, using video, audio, and photos?

✦ **Determine a communication strategy.** There's a fine balance between controlling the conversations on your Page and allowing your fans to interact freely with each other without much policing on your part. Decide how your admins should manage this important balance. The goal is to monitor your Page so that it has no inappropriate behavior or content that could damage your reputation, but at the same time, not be too controlling (because you might stop conversations that otherwise would develop freely).

✦ **Assign and document roles.** One admin may be responsible for posting one third-party article a day, and another admin may be assigned the task of uploading company videos throughout the week. Other tasks could include posting questions, uploading company photos to a photo album, monitoring and responding to all fan posts, and posting on fan Pages to increase overall engagement. Whatever the tasks, make sure that your admins are clear on their duties so they're not confused.

✦ **Create internal guidelines.** Every Facebook Page should have a "do's and don'ts" list associated with it, and your internal team should use that list as a guide. Make very clear what you allow and what you won't tolerate on your Page. Include what can and can't be discussed, including company-related content and personal content. Decide how often you'll promote your programs and services, and explain what acceptable promotion looks like. Think about your company, your mission, and your goals, and carefully craft your guidelines around them. The time you spend on this task will spare you a lot of headaches in the future!

Measuring Your Return on Investment

Because we're still in the early days of social media marketing, measuring return on investment (ROI) is, in a word, tough. There's still much debate about what you can and can't measure because in many ways, social media is considered to be a soft marketing vehicle, meaning it's still debatable how we should measure hard metrics like dollars earned and customers acquired.

With that in mind, think about your marketing goals and what you plan to accomplish via your new Facebook marketing plan. If you start from there, you're sure to identify areas that you can measure to track your results.

Defining success

To define success, it's essential to have a solid Facebook marketing plan. You have to know what success looks like before you start. For you, success may include getting people to interact and leave comments on your Facebook Page, encouraging your Facebook fans to check out your website, and/or selling your products and services on your Facebook Page. It comes down to aligning your social media metrics with the metrics your company is already comfortable with. In Book IX, we drill into the specific areas you'll want to track and analyze to make sure that your Facebook marketing plan is working for you.

Measuring brand ROI

The best way to think about measuring brand ROI is to consider how recognizable your brand is to your target audience. It really comes down to identifying how often your fans are engaging with your Page. The number of likes you have is important, but the frequency at which your fans are responding to your questions or engaging with your posts is even more important. You want to track how many times your fans are clicking your links and responding to your posts with comments.

In addition, you want to consider how well your existing customers can identify with your brand on Facebook. Is your Facebook branding consistent with your website, products, and or services? You want to create a bridge from Facebook to your main hub, and you do this with consistent branding.

Measuring financial ROI

The best way to measure financial ROI for your Facebook marketing plan is to set benchmarks. You want to clearly document what you're working toward in terms of sales and how you can use Facebook as part of this strategy. You also want to decide whether your goal is to sell directly from your Page or to use your Page as a channel to funnel interested prospects to a sales page after you build their trust and offer them immense value. Measuring your financial ROI comes down to your sales strategy for your Page.

If your goal is to sell your products or services from your Facebook Page, you need to identify benchmarks for this process. Look at how many people you manage to attract to your Page daily; track which tabs they click and how long they stay on your Page overall. You can do all this by using Facebook Insights and third-party monitoring tools. In Book IX, we walk you through how to use Facebook Insights and third-party monitoring tools to help you better understand how to track your financial ROI for your Facebook marketing initiatives.

Book II

Claiming Your Presence on Facebook

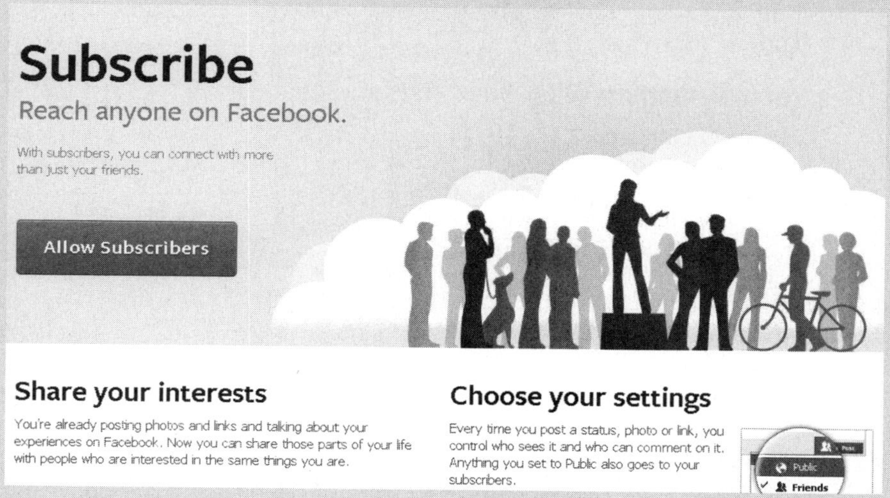

Subscribe
Reach anyone on Facebook.
With subscribers, you can connect with more than just your friends.
Allow Subscribers
Share your interests
You're already posting photos and links and talking about your experiences on Facebook. Now you can share those parts of your life with people who are interested in the same things you are.
Choose your settings
Every time you post a status, photo or link, you control who sees it and who can comment on it. Anything you set to Public also goes to your subscribers.
Public
Friends

Contents at a Glance

Chapter 1: Understanding Facebook Pages and Personal Accounts

In This Chapter

- Familiarizing yourself with Facebook's Page and account options
- Addressing privacy concerns
- Understanding why you need a personal Profile to have a business Page on Facebook
- Staying clear on when to use Facebook as your personal account or as your Page
- Taking the big view of how a Page works and where everything is located

Facebook offers many types of Pages to encourage community and networking. To create the biggest buzz around your product, service, or business, you need to be aware of Facebook's Page and account options and of the pros and cons of each. This chapter explains those options so that you can decide which type of Page best fits your needs.

We cover personal Profiles, business Pages, Places Pages, group Pages, Interest Pages (formerly known as Community Pages), and limited business accounts. Although each of these choices has merit, it's usually best to create a business Page for your product, service, or business (and we explain why in this chapter).

If you already have a personal Profile on Facebook (now called a Timeline), you know how easy it is to create an account. You may think it's a snap to set up your own business Page, too, and figure that you'll just skip this chapter. We have one word for you: Don't! You need to know some intricacies of the Profile/business Page that you might otherwise miss along the way.

REMEMBER

One of the most important things we discuss in this chapter is who can and cannot create a certain kind of Page. We go into detail as we discuss each type of Facebook Page, but the gist is this: You must be an authorized representative of an organization to create a business Page for it. If you aren't the authorized representative and want to create a space where fans of a certain topic or figure can share their thoughts and opinions, Facebook suggests that you create a group Page for them. We discuss group Pages in this chapter, too.

Reviewing Facebook Pages and Account Types

The two types of Pages most likely to interest you are personal Profiles and business Pages. That's because these are the two ways to establish a presence on Facebook. The personal Profile is now called the Timeline because of its chronological design, and it allows you to have subscribers (more on that in a moment), but it's still just a personal Profile. Business Pages also use the Timeline design. When we use the word *Timeline* in this chapter, we put either *personal* or *business* in front of it so you don't get confused. (That's a heroic goal on Facebook: not to get confused!)

The other Page types that you come across on Facebook can supplement your Facebook marketing efforts. The next few sections offer a brief review of these Page types and explain why you should avoid or embrace them. Everyone's needs are a little different, though, and you may find that one of the options listed here is a good fit for your particular endeavor on Facebook.

Facebook has a type of account called *business account,* which you need to open a business Page and run ads, and it's very limited; you can't like, share, or comment (important aspects of a social environment) anywhere on Facebook with this type of account. That said, at the end of this chapter, we include steps on how to open this type of account. All the authors of this book recommend that you start with a personal Profile and then open a business Page.

Navigating Your Personal Profile Timeline and the Subscribe Button

Close to 1 billion people use Facebook as a social space to keep up with friends, share photos and links, and share great stuff they find online. It's a space where people can connect after not being in touch for a long time or find people they would like to get to know better. It's a place for social interaction. It's where the social party is right now! It's time to join the party by creating a personal Profile and using Facebook as a social and commerce environment.

Facebook likes to keep the two uses — social and commerce — separate, but it recently created a Subscribe system as a way for public figures to market themselves in a personal Profile.

Subscribing to someone's personal Profile is a lot like following someone on Twitter. In other words, you don't have to be Friends with someone on Facebook to see that person's Public posts. We say *Public posts* because there are ways to post to smaller lists of people, like Close Friends and family members. A Public post is an open post; anyone can see it.

There's a very clear marketing strategy behind activating your Subscribe button on a personal Profile. We cover this strategy in just a moment, but here's the gist of it: If you're branding yourself, consider activating the Subscribe button on your personal Profile and possibly creating a business Page. If you're branding your business, open a business Page.

By creating a personal Profile and activating your Subscribe button, you can be Friends with your friends and relatives and ask your existing customers to subscribe to your personal Profile. If you also build your business Page on Facebook, you can go back to your subscribers and invite them to like your business Page, if appropriate. If you don't have this initial personal connection, the only way to invite people to your Page is through paid Facebook Ads, e-mail, or phone calls.

A personal Profile on Facebook is easy to open. One of the fastest-growing demographics of people joining are people over 35, so if that describes you, and you've never enjoyed a social space, it may feel a bit strange at first, but you'll catch on. Then you'll see how easy it is to engage and develop social connections for your business.

Creating a personal Profile

We feel that a Facebook personal Profile is a vital first step, especially if you're a public figure and plan to use the Subscribe option.

If you don't already have a personal Profile set up on Facebook, run (don't walk) to `www.facebook.com`, and set up an account. Facebook makes it super-easy. Right from the home page, enter your

- First and last name
- E-mail address (and then again as confirmation)
- Password
- Gender
- Birthday

Facebook requires all users to provide their real date of birth to encourage authenticity and provide only age-appropriate access to content. You will be able to hide this information from your personal connections (and people who like your business Page), if you want, and its use is governed by the Facebook Privacy Policy.

After entering the necessary personal information, click the Sign Up button. You now have a Facebook personal Profile. Figure 1-1 shows what your personal Timeline might look like after you've added Cover photos and made a few posts.

Figure 1-1: A personal Timeline.

On the Facebook home page, you may be tempted to click the link below the account creation fields that says *Create a Page for a Celebrity, Band, or Business.* Don't click it! This link creates what Facebook calls a business account. As we mention earlier in this chapter, a business account has limited functionality; it's for people who don't already have a Facebook personal Profile and who want to use Facebook only to administer a business Page and run ad campaigns.

When you create a business account, you won't be able to interact on Facebook in a normal way. It's very limiting. According to Facebook, you won't be able to share other posts, like Pages, or comment. You won't be able to view personal Profiles, and worst of all, business accounts can't be found in a search. There might be rare situations in which you need this type of account, though, and for such cases, you can find the instructions for opening a business account at the end of this chapter.

Some people worry that visitors will see the connection between their personal Profile and the business Page they create, so they make a bogus personal Profile before they open their business Page. We don't recommend doing this, either. Besides, Facebook frowns on creating fake accounts. By *frowns on,* we mean that Facebook might delete *all* your Facebook accounts if it discovers that you've been creating fake Profiles. Don't risk the wrath of Facebook by setting up a bogus account!

Be assured that people who choose to connect to your business Page won't be able to see that you're the Page owner or Admin (administrator), or have access to your personal Profile, unless you change your Page settings to list yourself publicly as an Admin of the Page.

It's all very clear from Facebook's side: You may create business Pages only to represent real organizations of which you are an authorized representative. There's no pretending to be someone you're not. In other words, even if you intended all along for the account you created to be just a great joke, Facebook lacks a sense of humor in that regard.

It's important to note that it's against Facebook policy to create a personal Profile that uses the name of the business — as in O'Grady's for the first name and Cleaners for the last name. If you do create a personal Profile for your business in this fashion, Facebook can (and will) delete all your accounts, and they won't be reinstated. In case you've made the mistake of creating a personal Profile with your business name, we explain how to change it in the next chapter.

Facebook will let you migrate your personal Profile to a business Profile Page, sometimes called a business Profile. We discuss the business account at the end of this chapter. In general, we don't recommend doing this particular type of migration.

If you already have a personal Profile with your real name, with many Friends who are actually business connections, you may want to explore the subscribe option and/or build a business Page and ask everyone to like it.

If your personal Profile has been functioning as a business, with a business name (like the O'Grady Cleaners example above), you may want to change the account name to your real name and then explore the Subscribe option and/or build a business Page and ask everyone to like it.

Activating the Subscribe button

We mention earlier in this chapter that there are some good marketing reasons to have a personal Profile with the Subscribe button activated. If you already have a large number of Facebook Friends who are more like potential customers or clients, and you haven't taken the time to create a business Page (and probably won't), this approach is for you! We go over all this more thoroughly in Book II, Chapter 4, and we cover it a bit more in Book IV, Chapter 5. In the meantime, if you're ready to open the Subscribe button on your personal Profile, read on.

Here's how to activate the Subscribe button on your personal Timeline Profile:

1. **With your personal Profile open, click the box on your Timeline called Subscribers.**

   If you have the new Timeline design, the Subscribe link is below the cover image. If you have the old design, look for the Subscribe link in your left menu.

   If you still don't see it, click to reveal all the rows of apps. And if you still don't see it, see the alternate method following these instructions.

2. **Click the Settings icon.**
3. **Turn on Subscriptions by choosing On from the Subscribers drop-down menu, as shown in Figure 1-2.**
4. **Adjust the settings to your liking.**
5. **Click Okay.**

Alternately, if you don't see the Subscription box on your Timeline, go to `www.facebook.com/about/subscribe`, and click the large green button to turn on your Subscribe button.

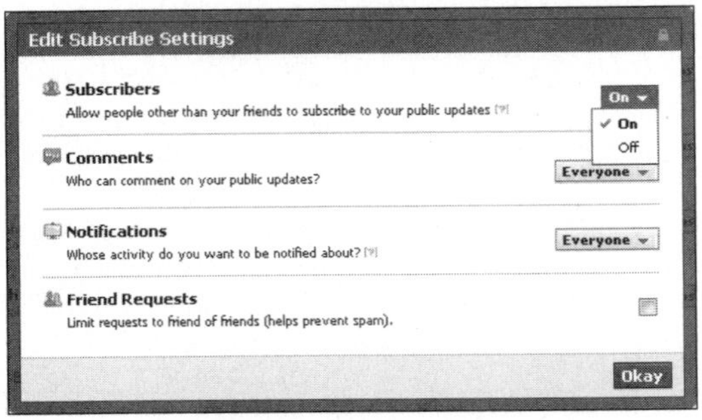

Figure 1-2: Here is where you adjust your settings for your Subscriptions.

The Subscribe button is optional. You can continue to enjoy a personal Profile and share with only Friends and family; you don't have to activate the Subscribe button.

Don't be confused when Facebook says, "Your Friends are already Subscribed." This just means that they'll see your updates, whether or not those updates are Public.

Here are some highlights of the personal Profile's subscribe system:

- After someone subscribes to you, that person sees your Public updates in his or her News Feed. People may also discover your Profile through the People to Subscribe To box on the right side of their News Feed or through their Friends' News Feed stories.
- Subscribers can Share your Public posts, which broadcasts your post and Profile to a larger audience.
- You can have an unlimited number of subscribers (no more 5,000 Friend limit).
- You can block people from being able to subscribe to you by adjusting your Privacy Settings Block List.
- You can connect with and promote to people on Facebook who prefer to subscribe to instead of like a business Page.

For a nice document that explains subscriptions, check out `https://developers.facebook.com/attachment/Subscriptions_PublicFigures_final.pdf`.

Talking about the Ticker

Before we move on to the Facebook Page, let's talk about the ticker. The *ticker* is a column of real-time notifications on the right side of your News Feed page. You see it when you're logged in to your personal Profile.

A nice thing about the ticker when you're using the personal Profile Subscription option is that your Public posts appear in the News Feeds of your subscribers. When someone comments on a post, the link and the comment appear in the ticker; therefore, more people have the opportunity to see it.

When you hover on any item in the ticker, a pop-up window displays the post and comments, and you can interact with it right there. You can also reply as your Page; more on that topic coming up in Book II, Chapter 3.

Another nice feature of the ticker is video viewing. If you post a video and someone sees it in his or her ticker, all that person needs to do is hover on the post to play the video right in the pop-up window.

Other business advantages of the ticker include

- Comments made on older posts (either as a Public post to your subscribers or as your business Page) are posted to the ticker, so you can continue to gain exposure even after a post is days, weeks, or months old by encouraging new comments and continuing to reply to new comments. Each engagement returns it to the ticker.
- When people like your business Page, that action appears in the ticker. Anyone seeing that notification can hover on it and like your Page, too, right from the pop-up window.
- Every time you add a picture to your personal or business Page, a notification appears in the ticker. When someone hovers on it, he or she can comment right there. Takeaway? Post a lot of pictures!

Now that you've set up a personal Profile Timeline, have started finding old and new friends on Facebook, and are trying out the Subscription system with your Public posts, you can explore a business Page.

Creating a Business Page

A business Page provides wonderful opportunities for marketing and promoting your business. It doesn't matter whether you're talking about a bricks-and-mortar business or a virtual consulting firm that you run out of your car. This Page can help your business grow, which we cover in Book I and throughout this entire book.

Facebook has deliberately tried to make business Pages as broad and useful as possible. You can create a business Page for all of the following:

- Local Business or Place
- Company, Organization, or Institution
- Brand or Product
- Artist, Band, or Public Figure
- Entertainment
- Cause or Topic

In Book II, Chapter 2, we explain each of these options in detail and discuss how to choose the one that's right for you. We also give you the steps for creating your business Page on Facebook.

As we note in the section on personal Profiles earlier in this chapter, you can opt to have only a personal Profile with the Subscribe button activated and post Public posts. You don't need to create a business Page at all. But creating a personal Profile and then creating a Facebook business Page makes sense for most people because of the many features of both. Figure 1-3 shows you a brief comparison of a personal Profile with Subscribe and a business Page.

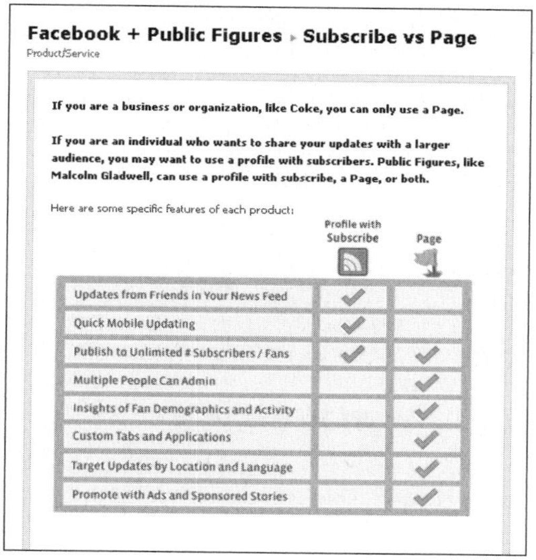
Facebook + Public Figures ▸ Subscribe vs Page
Product/Service
If you are a business or organization, like Coke, you can only use a Page.
If you are an individual who wants to share your updates with a larger audience, you may want to use a profile with subscribers. Public Figures, like Malcolm Gladwell, can use a profile with subscribe, a Page, or both.
Here are some specific features of each product:
Profile with Subscribe
Page
Updates from Friends in Your News Feed
Quick Mobile Updating
Publish to Unlimited # Subscribers / Fans
Multiple People Can Admin
Insights of Fan Demographics and Activity
Custom Tabs and Applications
Target Updates by Location and Language
Promote with Ads and Sponsored Stories

Figure 1-3: Subscriptions versus Pages.

These business Page features are integral parts of the reason why you should use a business Page as your product, service, or company hub on Facebook.

REMEMBER

If you're branding yourself and don't need any of the Page apps (you find out about them in Book V) or a detailed analytics system (Book IX), develop the personal Profile with the Subscribe button. If you're branding your business and need both ads and deep analytics, open a business Page.

Although you may want to keep your personal Profile private and connect only with certain people, you'll likely want as many people as possible to connect with your business on Facebook. The way to do that is via a Facebook business Page, which has no limits on the number of fans (that is, likes) you can have and lets you install applications as well.

Applications (commonly referred to as *apps)* are useful to business Pages. You can install apps for contact forms, newsletter signups, live video chats, and much more. Depending on which apps you install, you can use these apps to improve your fans' interaction with your page and to streamline your Facebook administrative duties. We tell you all about Facebook applications and give you our top suggestions for apps in Book V and throughout this book. We give you a little peek at what you can expect your business Page to resemble in Figure 1-4.

Figure 1-4: An example of a Facebook business Page.

Making a Places Page

A Places Page ties the computer Facebook experience to the mobile Facebook experience. Places is an effort by Facebook to create a community experience with your Facebook Friends while you're out and about. Places is Facebook's answer to other geolocation applications, like Foursquare and Gowalla. Places allows your fans to use their smartphones through `http://touch.facebook.com` to check in to your bricks-and-mortar store or restaurant when they visit. This check-in then shows up in their News Feeds so that their Friends will see it. The average Facebook user has 130 Friends, so that's a lot of extra promotion for you! Figure 1-5 shows what a Places Page on a mobile phone may look like when someone checks in.

Notice that this Page has set up a Check-In Deal with 10 percent off a consultation after four check-ins. Also notice the four tabs at the bottom: Activity, Wall, Info, and Photos. Currently you do not see any custom apps on the mobile interface.

Figure 1-5: A Facebook Places Check-In Page on a mobile interface has just a few elements.

Places Pages can be created by anyone at any time. When users check in via their smartphones by using `http://touch.facebook.com` or `http://m.facebook.com`, and the place the user is checking in to doesn't have a Places Page, he or she can create one. As a business owner, you can surely see why you'd want to retain control of your Places Page rather than leave that control to the masses. You have two options:

- ✦ If your business doesn't have a Places Page, you can create one and claim it as your official Places Page.
- ✦ If a Places Page is already created for your business, don't worry! You can still claim the Places Page as the official representative and obtain control of the page.

  After you've claimed your Places Page, you can offer Check-In Deals to people who check in.

We explain how to figure out whether your business already has a Places Page created, whether you need to create one, and how to create Deals in Book VII, Chapter 4.

After you've determined whether you have a Places Page, it's a good idea to *claim* your Facebook Places Page so that you have control of how that Page is administered. When you claim your Places Page (again, see Book VII,

Chapter 4), you're just confirming with Facebook that you're the owner of the company or an authorized representative acting on behalf of the company.

After you've claimed your Places Page, you have the opportunity to merge your Places Page with your business Page on Facebook. If you decide to merge your business Page and Places Page, a good process would be to create your business Page first and then claim or create your Places Page.

TIP

Merging a business Page and a Places Page retains everything from your business Page (photos, posts, events, video, ads), and the Page now contains a map, check-ins, and a place on the Timeline for recommendations.

REMEMBER

Including a physical street address when you create a business Page automatically adds your Places Page recommendation interface, too.

A merged Page looks a lot like Figure 1-6. Notice the number of people who have checked in. The Info link on a merged Page contains a map.

Figure 1-6: This is how a merged Places and business Page looks.

There's just a little more to add to this local Page process. If you create a local business-type Page, you still have to claim it. That's right. Even if there's no other Places Page anywhere on Facebook with your business name, and all you have is the Page you just created, you still have to claim it. Just go to your Admin panel and click Edit Page, and you should see a Claim This Page link. Click it, and go through the steps. You'll be able to verify your Page by e-mail or by regular mail.

Creating a Group Page

A group Page isn't officially a business-type Page. A group Page can supplement a business's Page, however. You have three options when it comes to creating a group Page:

- **Closed group Pages:** This type is the default. The members are *public* (meaning that they're visible to the Facebook community), but the content is private. You see the updates to this type of Page in your News Feed, with an icon. When you hover over it, the text says, "Shared with: Members of {group name}."
- **Open group Pages:** The members and content are public. Anything you post inside this group Page will show up on your Wall, as well as on your Friends' News Feeds.
- **Secret group Pages:** The members and content are private. The only ones who can see anything posted on a secret group Page are the members of this group.

Most group Pages look the same but simply have different privacy settings. Figure 1-7 shows what a group Page looks like to members. This particular group decided to use an image at the top of the Page, but you can also have the thumbnail images of the members across the top.

Figure 1-7: A Facebook group Page is a great way to collaborate on projects or discuss specific topics.

Although a group Page isn't considered to be an official business Page, it can offer some wonderful benefits to your business when it's used in conjunction with your business Page. To see what we mean, consider the following business uses for a group Page:

- **You can create a closed group Page for the members of a collaborative project.** The members of this type of group are public as a way to create a bit of mystery or buzz about an upcoming event for those who see the group listing in Facebook Search, but discussions between members are private.
- **You can create an open group Page for training.** A cool idea is to create an open group Page for coaching or training sessions. On the day and time of the event, everyone could go the group Page and ask questions in the group chat box, and the organizer could post answers in the post box. If you do this in an open group format, the group could be found in Facebook Group Search at `www.facebook.com/search.php?type=groups`, and in the Group Directory at `www.facebook.com/directory/groups`. What a wonderful and innovative way to advertise your expertise!
- **You can create a secret group Page for your staff.** With a secret group Page in place, your staff can post updates, links, videos, events, and documents that only those staff members in the group can see. They can have a group chat, and everyone can type text in the chat box at the same time. A Facebook group chat in the morning, before work starts, would be a fun way to start the day. Here's a great post on using Secret Groups for businesses:

  `www.socialmediaexaminer.com/how-to-use-secret-facebook-groups-to-enhance-your-business`

Setting Up an Interest Page

Interest Pages, formerly known as Community Pages, are Facebook Pages dedicated to a single cause or topic. Facebook automatically generates them from the fields that people fill out in their personal Profiles. These Pages should not be confused with the Cause or Community business Page options that individuals can create.

This section explains the generic Facebook-generated Interest Page, and we explain the Cause or Community option for a business Page in Book II, Chapter 2. We know that the terms are confusing, but these are two separate types of Pages. Figures 1-8 and 1-9 show how these pages differ.

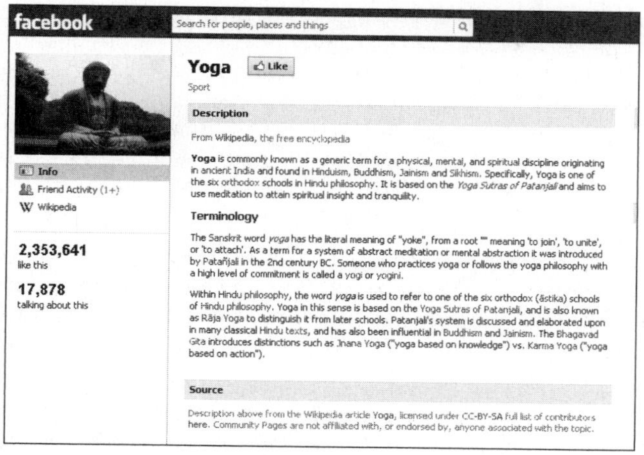

Figure 1-8: A generic, Facebook-generated Interest Page.

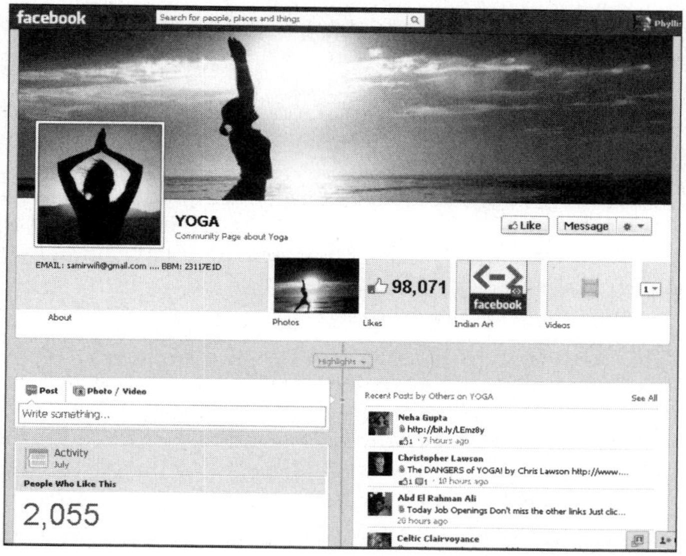

Figure 1-9: A Cause/ Community business Page has all the functions of a business Page.

Generic, Facebook-created Interest Pages are commonly disregarded because they lack the information and functionality of business Pages. They don't make good business hubs for several reasons:

- **No one owns an Interest Page.** You can't administer or impose your business culture on a generic community Page because it doesn't belong to you.

- **You can't post regularly to a generic Interest Page.** These pages pull in articles that you or your Friends post about a topic, but no one can contribute information directly to an Interest Page. The only way to have any post show up on an Interest Page is to use the keyword that is the Page's title. Use *yoga* in a post, for example, and it shows up on the Interest Page for yoga. In fact, as you can see in Figure 1-8, Interest Pages don't have a traditional Wall. Instead, you land on the Info tab, which is really just a landing page; you can't interact with the information.
- **You can't install applications on an Interest Page.** As we state earlier in this chapter, applications can be important parts of your marketing strategies because they add functionality and customization to your business Page.
- **Updates to Interest Pages don't appear in the News Feed.** Although an Interest Page has a Like button at the top (just as a business Page does), these pages don't generate News Feed stories, so you won't see anything from an Interest Page showing up in your personal News Feed (and neither will your customers and fans). If you click the Like button, though, that Page shows up in your personal Profile below Likes and Interests on your Info tab.

So how do you know whether you're looking at a generic, Facebook-generated Interest Page? There are several ways (refer to Figure 1-8):

- On an Interest Page, there's no large Cover photo, and the left navigation bar is limited to three options: Info, Friend Activity, and Wikipedia. If no Wikipedia information is available, that navigation option doesn't appear. There is no traditional Wall tab. On the other hand, a community business Page has a large Cover photo and up to four featured app boxes.
- Most Interest Pages display a related Wikipedia article if one is available. You may also see posts by your Friends or the global Facebook community that contain the keyword of the Interest Page. (If the Interest Page is for yoga, for example, any articles posted by your Friends that contain the word *yoga* show up here.)
- Many Interest Pages display a generic image as the Profile image, whereas others display an image related to the topic. Depending on the type of interest, you may see a gray square with a white silhouette of a specific image (such as a briefcase, a student in a mortarboard, or a molecule); a logo or image from a business, school, or topic; and so on. Sometimes, an image from the Wikipedia article is used in that space, as you see in Figure 1-8.

We encourage you to search your business name to see whether Facebook has created Interest Pages for it. When you find an Interest Page with your business name, you can start the process of claiming it. Look for the Know The Owner? button, and click it. Then enter your e-mail address and start the process to claim the Page (see Figure 1-10).

Click this button to claim the page.

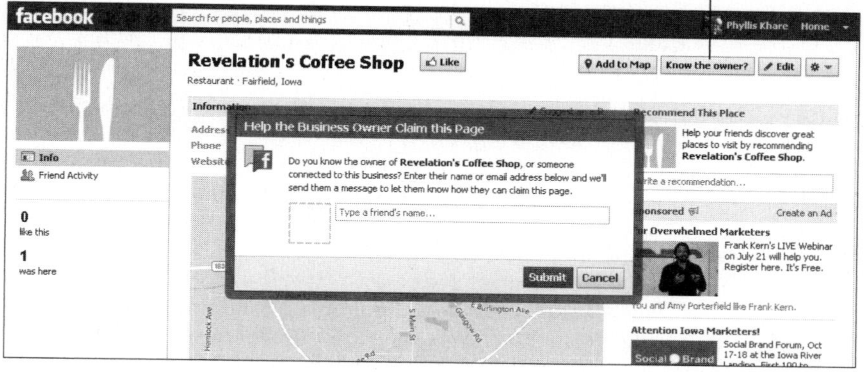

Figure 1-10: Find any Interest Pages with your business name, and start the process of claiming them.

Creating a Limited Business Account

If you prefer not to use Facebook as a regular social user with a personal Profile, you can create a business account. A business account has limited functionality; it's for people who don't already have a Facebook personal Profile and who want to use Facebook only to administer a business Page and run ad campaigns.

When you create a business account, you won't be able to interact on Facebook normally. The account is very limiting. You won't be able to share posts from others, like Pages, or comment. You won't be able to view personal Profiles. Worst of all, business accounts can't be found in a search. You will, however, be able to interact with people on your Page.

If you still feel that you want to create this type of account, follow these steps:

1. **Go to** `www.facebook.com`.
2. **At the bottom of the personal Profile form, click the link titled Create a Page for a Celebrity, Band, or Business.**
3. **Click to choose the type of business Page you'd like to create.**
4. **Complete the requested Page information.**

   You need to type the Page name, and depending on the Page type you choose, you may need to add the physical location.
5. **Select the check box next to I Agree to Facebook Pages Terms.**
6. **Type in the security words.**

7. **Click the Get Started button.**

   You will need to verify the e-mail address. Look for that e-mail and click the link to verify. Once clicked you're in the interface that lets you continue developing your new business-account Facebook Page.

   Business accounts are only for people who currently don't have a personal Profile. If you already have a personal Profile, you should log in to Facebook with that account and create your business Page. (To see how to create a business Page connected to your personal Profile, see Book II, Chapter 2.)

Your business account is live, and your browser opens your new business Page so that you can finish setting it up. Now, any time you log in to Facebook, you won't see a personal Profile News Feed, as most users do; instead, you'll see the Admin panel for your Page.

We don't recommend that you open this type of account in Facebook, but it's an option. If you use this type of account and try to interact on Facebook (by trying to comment on another post), you get an error-message dialog box asking you to open a personal account to complete the action.

Chapter 2: Creating Your Business Page

In This Chapter

- Choosing your Page name and type
- Modifying Page settings to match your needs
- Going through the steps to publish your new business Page
- Sharing your business Page with customers
- Managing missteps you might have taken

This chapter is all about creating your business presence on Facebook by opening a Facebook Page. We always think it's a good idea to read the instructions before building something new, and we suggest that here, too. Choosing your Page type and category might be very clear-cut for you, or maybe not. Reading and exploring how it works can be an interesting first step.

In this chapter, we take you through the steps to create your Facebook business Page. Then, we show you how to let people know that your Page is open for business. If you are reading this after you have created an account or business Page on Facebook and might have done it the wrong way, we address that, too, under managing missteps.

TIP: One way that we enjoy exploring how other people have done it is by going to `www.facebook.com/pages`. Notice the names of Pages; sort by the types at the top of the Page; hover your cursor over a linked Page name; and look at the little box that pops up with the type and category below the title. If you hover over the Starbucks name, for example, the box says Food/Beverages. You can learn a lot by seeing how other businesses have created their Pages.

Considering a Few Things Before You Start

Creating your Facebook business Page is an important process, and we want you to be as awake as possible while going through it. Some of the selections you make will determine many future functions, such as the information fields on your Info Page that you'll surely want to use in your marketing plan. In particular, you want to carefully consider what to name your Page and which type of business Page to create. You can change the Page type at any time, but you need to realize that this will change the types of informational fields you have available for use, too.

Choosing the right name for your business Page

The name you give to your business Page is extremely important because it becomes the title of your Page. When a customer, fan, or Friend searches for your business Page on Facebook, this name/title will enable her to find you. Because naming your Page is so important, we'd like you to mull over a few things. Here are a few naming do's and don'ts to consider before you create your business Page:

Page names must

- Use proper, grammatically correct capitalization
- Have logical, correct punctuation
- Include your name, if you're branding yourself
- Include your business keywords, if you're branding your niche or product

Page names can't use the following:

- Excessive capitalization or all capitals
- Symbols such as ! or ® or TM (but you can use a hyphen)
- Repeated and unnecessary punctuation
- Abusive terms
- The word *Facebook* or any variation of it

Facebook wants you to create concise Page names without long tag lines after the name. You have up to 75 character spaces for your Page name, and we encourage you to keep things short and sweet. All the businesses we know that created long Page names eventually wanted to shorten them. We created a Page with a very long tagline: iPhoneLife Magazine & iPhoneLife.com — *User created stories, tips & reviews.* Facebook approved it, and it was used that way for a year. Recently, Facebook gave Pages the capability to change their names, and this company jumped on that to modify the name to iPhone Life magazine. Normally you can't change a Page name after it has more than 200 likes, but this editing door opened for just a few days after a major Facebook update and the business jumped on it.

This option to change a Page name has come and gone two times since we started writing this chapter. We don't know if it will be around when you create your Page, so think the name through carefully in case you can't change it in the future. Facebook doesn't want you to use superfluous descriptions or unnecessary qualifiers, such as the word *official* in a Page name. Campaign names and regional or demographic qualifiers, though, are acceptable. Nike Football Spain is just fine, for example.

TIP

Stay clear of generic terms for your Page name, too. If you name a Page using a generic reference to the category, such as Jewelry instead of Sparkle's Jewelry Store, you may have your administrative rights removed, and the Page will become an uneditable, Facebook-generated Interest Page.

Choosing the right type of business Page

Facebook offers six types of Facebook Pages so that you can choose the one that best fits with your product, service, brand, or business. When you go to `www.facebook.com/pages/create.php`, you see the business Page options, as shown in Figure 2-1.

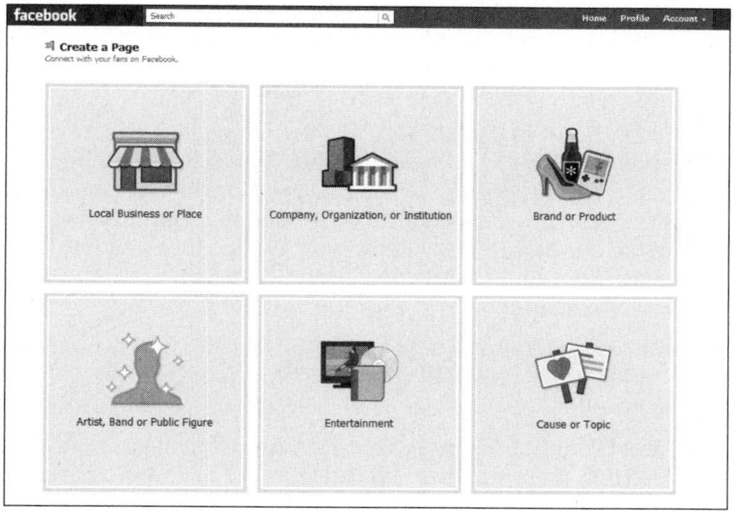

Figure 2-1: Choose one of these six options to create your business Page.

We know that you're probably wondering which type you should use for your own business Page. To help you, the following list gives you the skinny on what each Page type offers and when you should choose a particular Page type over another:

- **Local Business or Place:** This Page type is for bricks-and-mortar businesses. Choose this type only if you truly have a local, open-to-the-public type of business.

When you click the Local Business or Place option, you see a drop-down menu with 39 category choices. You can choose one of these categories to create a Page, or if none of the categories fits your business, you can choose the Local Business category and go from there. The Info Profile for this type of business Page is very detailed, with editing fields for hours of operation, parking options, and price ranges.

- **Company, Organization, or Institution:** This Page type is for a company that isn't necessarily open to the public the way a local business would be. Many of the categories in the drop-down menu are the same as those for the Local Business or Place type, but the resulting Info Page won't have the same detailed interface to fill in for prices, parking, and so on.

  If you have multiple stores in the same city, you need to sit down and decide on a company policy about Facebook Pages. Do you or your store managers want to manage one Page or a Page for each store? Starbucks runs one company Page, for example; Aveda has a custom link that helps you find a local store. Obviously, these are large corporations, but other companies give managers the option to open a Page as long as they adhere to company social media policies.

- **Brand or Product:** If you sell an actual physical product, this is the Page type to consider. Facebook offers many categories: cars, clothing, computers, pet supplies, and a generic product/service category.

- **Artist, Band or Public Figure:** Obviously, if you're a band or artist, this type is the one to choose, but this Page type also includes politicians, businesspeople, chefs, dancers, and actors. You may think that the actor category would be in Entertainment, but it isn't! It is under the Artist, Band or Public Figure type. Notice that you use this type for your band, but if you're only promoting your CD on Facebook, you can use the Entertainment type with the category Album.

  Just keep in mind that you must be the official, recognized, and authorized representative of whatever type and category of Page you create on Facebook.

- **Entertainment:** If you have a TV show or a magazine, or are creating a Page just for your music CD, select this Page type. There are close to 30 different categories listed here. We're still trying to figure out why Library is listed as a category under Entertainment. Is your library entertaining?

- **Cause or Community:** If you've been on Facebook for a while, don't confuse this type of Page with the Causes application. If you're new to Facebook and are creating a Page for a nonprofit or community organization, don't select this Page type! Select Company, Organization, or Institution, and select the category of Non-Profit.

Every Page type has an Info section. Also, many categories have specific fields in that Info section that are used when someone shares your Page with his or her Friends. Anyone can share your Page by using a Share link located after clicking the gear icon in the top-right corner of the Page. Most Page categories use the Company Overview text to populate the Share invitation. Clicking that Share link autopopulates a post that goes on your personal account Timeline and is visible in the News Feed. Because you're the Admin of the Page, you also have the option to use the Invite Your Friends function. This particular function is available only to Admins of the Page. Everyone else can only use the Share This Page option.

You can share to your own Timeline, someone else's Timeline, to a group, or in a private message. You can add personal text with a share post but not with an Invite Your Friends function. We go into detail on how to do all that in Book IV, Chapter 1.

One of the authors of this book recently changed her Page type from Brand or Product to Artist/Band/Public Figure, with a category of Business Person. It seemed to fit her a little better, even though she's also a teacher, author, and entertainer — other category choices for this Page type. This brings up the point that you can adjust the Page type and category setting later, if you need to. The interface is a bit different and can be accessed right from the top of your Page. The steps to change your Page type and category are at the end of this chapter and in Chapter 3 of this minibook.

Setting Up Your New Business Page

Goodness. Finally. Time to set up a new business Page on Facebook!

Are you ready? Before you attempt to create your business Page, first read through these steps and then follow along when you read them again:

1. **Log in to your personal Facebook account.**
2. **Go to** `http://facebook.com/pages/create.php`.

   Doing so brings up a screen showing six Page types. If you need to, take the time to click each Page type and then click the drop-down category list, as shown in Figure 2-2. Look for a category that matches your business.
3. **Select the type of Page to create.**

   New options become available for you to fill in.

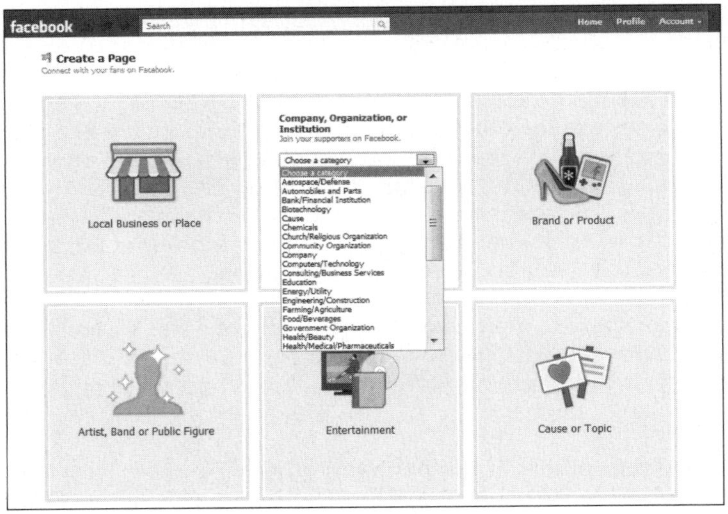

Figure 2-2: Find a category for your business.

4. **Select the category of Page you want.**

   The category you choose determines the types of Info fields that are available for your Page. All types, except Cause or Community, ask you to select a category for your Page. The reason to find the best category is that the category determines what details are shown on your business Page's Info link. The Book category, for example, displays an Info link with fields for the International Standard Book Number (ISBN); the Café category gives you fields for hours and types of credit cards you take.

5. **Type the requested information.**

   Depending on which business Page type you choose, you see different text fields to fill in. The Name field ends up being the title of the Page. Each of the six types calls the Name field something different: Local Business calls it Business or Place; Company calls it Company Name; Brand or Product calls it Brand or Product; Artist or Band calls it Name; Entertainment calls it Name; and Cause or Community calls it Cause or Community.

   Facebook likes (insists on) first letters being capitalized for Page names. You need to fill out all fields to be able to create your Page.

   TIP: Take the time to think through this whole naming business. Better yet, read the "Choosing the right name for your business Page" section, earlier in this chapter. You'll be able to change a Page name only up to the point at which you have 200 people who like your Page. After that point, you're stuck with it unless Facebook opens the link to change it again. So think it through.

6. **Select the I Agree to Facebook Pages Terms check box.**

   You must be the official representative of this person, business, band, or product to create this Page. If you're not, you're in violation of Facebook Terms and Services; Facebook can (and will) remove your Profile and not reinstate it.

7. **Click the Get Started button.**

   You've created a Facebook Page!

The first screen you see after clicking the Get Started button looks like Figure 2-3. Now Facebook takes you through a three-step process to fill in and open your Page to the public:

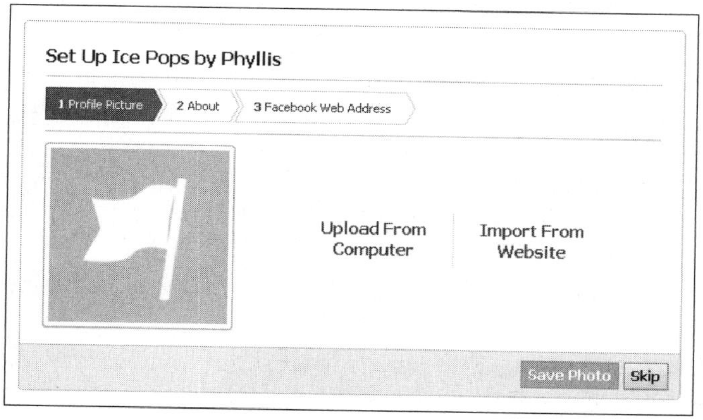

Figure 2-3: Facebook guides you as you customize your business Page.

1. **Upload a Profile picture.**

   A Profile picture isn't the large Cover photo you see on other Pages. This is the smaller, square image located in the bottom-left corner overlaying the Cover photo. The image can be any shape, but the viewable part is square (180 × 180 pixels). In just a moment, you can specify what part of this image becomes the thumbnail that will accompany your posts.

   After you've uploaded your Profile image, click Next.

2. **Fill in a basic description and any other site links, such as Twitter or a website.**

   In our testing, we found that you can add as many links as you want.

   When you have those links in place (always use the `http://` part of the URL so that the links will be hyperlinked), click Save Info.

3. **Set your vanity URL in the Web Address tab.**

   We have to state right here that this tab comes and goes. Sometimes we see this third tab, and sometimes we don't. If you see it, you're very lucky, as you can set your vanity URL right away, without having to develop 25 likes for the Page to get it.

A *vanity URL*, or username, is the part of a Facebook address for your Page. For example, `http://facebook.com/`**`TheMissPhyllisCollection`**. Before you get a username, the address might look like this: `https://www.facebook.com/pages/`**`The-Miss-Phyllis-Collection/139008436119989`**. If you see this step, think this through because in our experience, once you've set it you will only be able to change the URL for the Page once more.

Now Facebook takes you on a little guided tour, suggesting your next steps to take:

- ✦ **Like Your Own Page:** We suggest that you do this!
- ✦ **Invite Your Friends to Like the Page:** We don't like this because you haven't fixed your Page up yet! You haven't uploaded a large Cover photo or completed the Info Page yet. We take you through these tasks a bit later, and you'll be able to invite your Friends at any point, so we suggest that you click Next.
- ✦ **Invite Your E-mail Contacts:** Again, we don't suggest you do this step right now. You'll be able to return to this step later, so click Next.
- ✦ **Share Something:** This step is where you would create your first post as the Page. Unless you have something lined up to say, click Skip, and come back to this later too.

The guided tour ends, and Facebook rolls up to the top of your Admin panel. You can see how that looks in Figure 2-4.

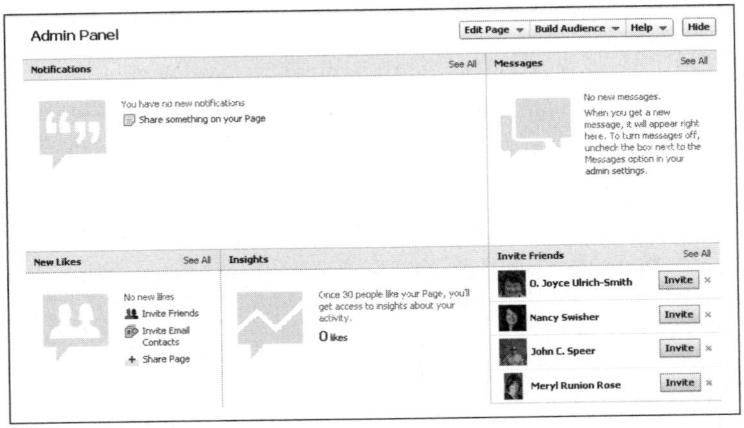

Figure 2-4: The Admin panel is your main interface for working with your new Page.

WARNING!

When you create a new Page, Facebook defaults it as published! Yikes! You may want to unpublish your Page to the public so that you can continue to work on it privately. Just look for the Edit Page button, and follow these steps:

1. **Click the Edit Page button.**

   This button is located at the top of your new Page.
2. **Choose Manage Permissions from the drop-down menu.**
3. **Select the top check box, Page Visibility (see Figure 2-5), so that only Admins can see this Page.**

   This option effectively unpublishes your new Page, hiding it from everyone except Page Admins.

Page Visibility check box

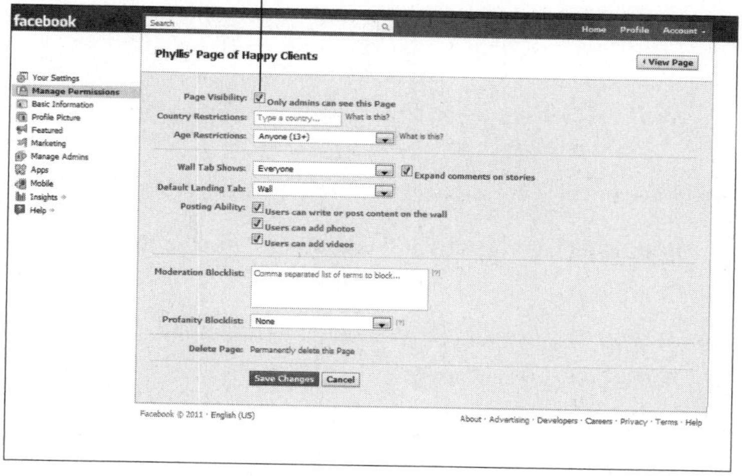

Figure 2-5: Click the Page Visibility check box to hide your Page from the public.

4. **Click Save Changes.**

   Your business Page is now visible only to you and any other Admins. After you've decked out your Page with a Cover image, detailed info, photos, and other fun things, you can publish the Page for all to see by coming back to this Page and clearing the Page Visibility check box.

Completing, Publishing, and Promoting Your Page

Now you need to complete your Page so that you can publish it and promote it. To see what a finished Local Business Page might look like for a food establishment, check out the Facebook business Page for Merante Brothers

Market, at www.facebook.com/meranteboys. Figure 2-6 shows the Cover photo, the custom apps, the Page category, the address, the phone number, and the hours. This is what you're going for when you go through this section and fill out more info.

Figure 2-6: This Local Business Page is full of vital information.

You have several steps to go through, as follows:

1. Adding a Cover photo and adjusting your Profile image thumbnail
2. Completing your Info Page
3. Adding Facebook-built apps and custom apps
4. Posting status updates
5. Publishing your Page
6. Adding milestones
7. Promoting this Page on your website
8. Setting up your mobile phone

In the following sections, we walk you through each of these steps. Try not to skip ahead, because these steps are important for forming your new Page!

Getting your Facebook images right

You know all about a picture saying a thousand words, right? Your Facebook Cover and Profile photos say a lot about you and your business, so you'll want to be sure to have images for both that convey a positive message. And now that Facebook creates a nice, little "hover card" when someone hovers over your Page name in the News Feed, you want to make sure it looks fantastic. This hover card will show the Cover photo, Profile photo, and the Page type.

Adding a Cover photo

You need to add a Cover photo to your Page — no ifs, ands, or buts about it.

If you're branding yourself, it's a good idea to feature your face in this Cover photo image, to help connect the human element to the rest of the Page that contains text and links. Adding this personal touch can make people feel more connected to you — and to what you're selling.

If you're branding your company, make sure that your logo or product image is on this image.

Whichever way you choose, the image fills the top position on your Page, as shown in Figure 2-7. If you're branding yourself, we highly recommend that you create and use a custom image that contains your logo and your photo.

The image size is 851 × 315 pixels. The space you get for a Cover photo is quite a bit larger than the space for a personal Profile picture and can really make a statement on your Page.

Figure 2-7: Use the Cover photo to make an impression and connect with your audience.

WARNING!

Facebook has some guidelines you need to follow for the Cover image, mainly that it *cannot* be any of the following:

- An ad
- A call to action
- A promotion
- A coupon
- Mostly text
- A copyright infringement

Facebook's stance (which you can find here: `www.facebook.com/help/?faq=276329115767498#How-should-I-choose-a-cover-photo-for-my-Page?`) may seem to be quite restrictive for businesses. Try to think of this image as what you're trying to brand as the "feeling" of your business. There are great strategies you can use with this image, which we outline in Books IV and IX. In general, think of changing this image with your other promotions so that they support one another.

To upload an image from your hard drive to your Facebook Page, follow these steps:

1. **If this is the first Cover photo you are adding, look for the Add a Cover button, where the Cover image will appear. If you are changing the Cover photo, you will need to hover over the Cover photo and click the Change Cover button.**

   A hidden link with a pencil icon comes up, as shown in Figure 2-8.

Figure 2-8: Start by uploading a great cover image.

2. **Click Add a Cover or the Change Cover button.**
3. **Click the Browse button in the Image dialog box that appears and then find the image on your computer that you want to upload.**

   As soon as you double-click the image file you want to upload, Facebook starts the upload process.

   The best size is 851 × 315 pixels. If you upload a larger image, you can drag it around to get the best placement. If the image is larger than 851 × 315, only a portion of it will appear as the Cover photo for your Page; when clicked, the image opens to the complete size of the photo. If the image is less than 300 pixels wide, Facebook displays an error message and tells you that the image is too small to use in this space.
4. **Adjust the image as necessary.**
5. **Click Save Changes.**

   After the file is uploaded, you go back to the Page.

6. **Click the image, and add a description that includes your best link (back to your website, for example).**

   Adding a description — with a link to your website — for every image needs to be second nature on Facebook. See Figure 2-9 for that interface.

Figure 2-9: Always add a photo description that includes a link to your website.

Cover photos are set to Public viewing. You can't change that viewing setting (and why would you?). You see the globe icon that Facebook uses to denote Public when you upload the image.

Adjusting your Profile thumbnail image

After you have your Cover image just right, you may want to check the thumbnail that Facebook generates for your Profile image. A *thumbnail* is a smaller version of your Profile image. In the world of Facebook, a thumbnail image shows up next to every status update or comment you make as your Page. As you can imagine, your thumbnail is a key component in branding your business Page.

And now that Facebook creates a nice, little "hover card" when someone hovers over your Page name in the News Feed, you want to make sure it looks fantastic. This hover card will show the Cover photo, Profile photo, and the Page type.

The Profile image is 180 × 180 pixels. If you upload an image larger than that, Facebook gives you a cropping interface to select a square part of the image.

After you have the Profile image uploaded, you may want to adjust the thumbnail image. Follow these steps to adjust the thumbnail image:

1. **Hover over your Profile image.**

   A hidden link with a pencil icon comes up.

2. **Click the Edit Profile picture link.**

   You see several links: Choose from Photos, Take Photo, Upload Photo, Edit Thumbnail, and Remove.

3. **Click the Edit Thumbnail link.**

   Doing so pulls up the Edit Thumbnail dialog box, as shown in Figure 2-10.

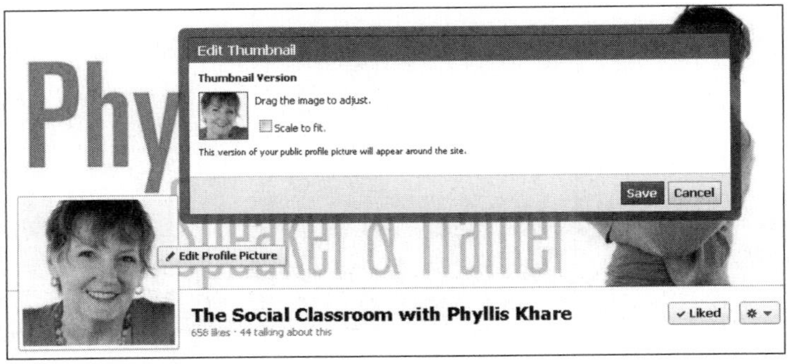

Figure 2-10: You can adjust your thumbnail to look just right.

4. **Drag the thumbnail image around until it looks good as a thumbnail, or choose Scale to Fit.**

5. **Click Save.**

REMEMBER: This is an image; therefore, it has a description area where you can add text and hyperlinks. Click the Photos app box; then click the Profile images album and the image itself. Add text and hyperlinks in the top-right corner where you see the words *Add a Description*.

Completing the Info Page

The next step is filling in the fields on the Info Page. Depending on the Page type and category, the fields will be different. The TV Show category has a field called Plot, for example, whereas the Book category has a field for the ISBN.

The following examples use the Company Page type and the Company category. Follow these steps:

1. **At the top of the Admin Panel, click the Edit Page button and then click Update Info.**

   This step opens the Page dashboard. Notice the Basic Information menu on the left side. If that menu isn't visible, click Basic Information.

2. **At the top of the Basic Information interface, change the Page type and category.**

   You can go back and change this at any time.

3. **In the Official Page field, don't enter any text.**

   Fill in this field only if you're creating a Page about a brand, celebrity, or organization that you don't officially represent. Don't add any text in this field if this is not the case, as Facebook will connect your Page to the Official Page and it is next to impossible to reverse. In most cases there is no need to type anything here.

   Leave it blank if this doesn't apply to you.

4. **Fill in the Username Selection field.**

   As noted in the "Setting Up Your New Business Page" section earlier in this chapter, if you see a Web Address tab where you can set a vanity URL, you're very lucky! If not, this is where you go after you have at least 25 people liking your Page so that you can select a vanity URL or username. You will either see a field where you can change what you've selected previously, or a notice that you still don't have 25 likes yet.

5. **Modify the Name and Start type section.**

   You can change the name of your Page in this space. After you have more than 200 likes, you have the option to change the name just one more time.

   The Start type and date are important to modify. If you use the current day, month, and year, you won't be able to add anything to the Page's Timeline from the past. If you think that you'll have milestones to add with a past date, make the Start date further back than that date. You can also decide whether you want this first date type to be Born, Founded, Started, Open, Created, or Launched. Milestones are explained in Book 3 of this minibook.

6. **In the Address section, add a physical address or not.**

   The Address section is important for local businesses.

   If you add a physical address in this section, your Page is now a Places Page. You have a new function on your Page where anyone can add a public Recommendation. Think this through. It's best to use this address space only if you have actual hours when your place of business is open. You will still have the subcategories you chose at the top of the Page, with a few added functions; people can check in to your business and use the Recommendation function. You will also need to then claim your Page, as we addressed in this Book II, Chapter 1.

7. **In the About field, enter your website URL and promotional or informational text.**

   The About field is vital. This bit of text is right below the Page's Profile image. People will be able to see about 170 characters. Make sure that you have an `http://` link as the very first thing so that you have a hyperlink to your website or products.

8. **Fill out the rest of the fields.**

   The next set of fields depends on your Page type. Fill out all the fields. One of them is the text that autopopulates the invitation that's generated when you (or anyone) shares the Page.

   Generally, the Company Overview or Description field is used for this sharing invite. You will check this sharing process in the next chapter, and this is where to revisit to edit the text.

9. **Click Save Changes.**

   The page will refresh with a note at the top saying Information Updated. To view your changes, click the View Page button.

   Now you see the About text below the Profile image and other information, depending on your Page type. You can see how that looks in Figure 2-11.

Figure 2-11: The About text is viewable on your Page.

Adding Facebook-built apps

Facebook has a set of apps built for Pages: Photos, Events, Notes, and Video. These apps are available as soon as you create a Page, but they may not show up in the featured app space. You need to add them first. Here's how to do that:

1. **Go to your Admin Panel, and click Edit Page.**

   A drop-down panel will appear.

2. **Click the Update Info link.**

   Your main Page dashboard appears, and you can see more choices in your left sidebar, including an Apps link.

3. **Click Apps.**

   This link shows you all the apps that are available to add to your Page. If this Page is brand new, you see only Photos, Events, Notes, and Video.

4. **If you want to add any of these apps, click the Edit Settings link next to it.**

   In the Edit Notes Settings dialog box that appears, you see two tabs: Profile and Additional Permissions, as shown in Figure 2-12.

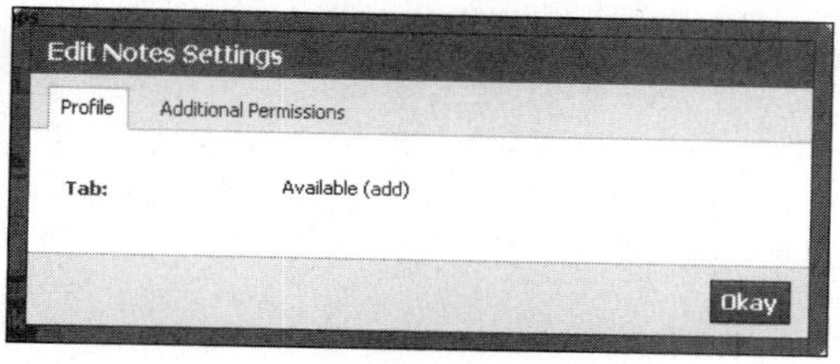

Figure 2-12: Click the link called Edit Notes Settings.

5. **On the Profile tab, click Add (next to Available, to the right of Tab).**

   The app is added to your featured apps area.

6. **Click the Additional Permissions tab, and decide whether you want to have this app post to your Timeline, too.**

   Figure 2-13 shows the Publish Content to My Wall check box. All of the Facebook-built apps have this additional permission check box. If you select it, whatever happens through this app, it creates a post on your Page. In most cases, you want to select this check box.

7. **Click Okay.**

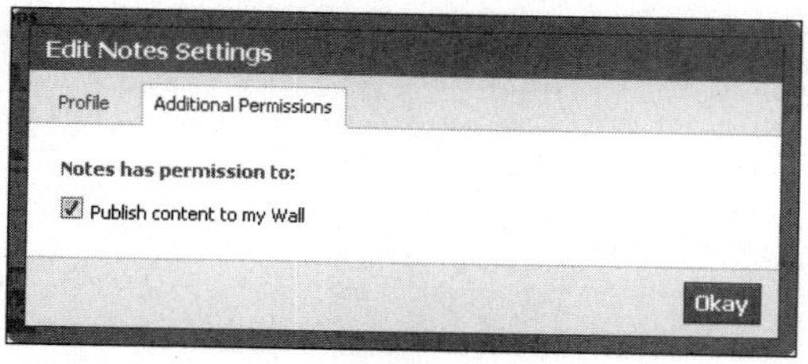

Figure 2-13: The Additional Permissions check box can be selected or not.

After you add any of these Facebook-built apps, you need to go back to your Timeline to see them. You do that by clicking the View Page button in the top-right corner of the Page.

Facebook doesn't give you the ability to change the image or the hyperlinked text at the bottom of these apps. The image is connected to the last item created with that app. The Photo app shows the latest uploaded or tagged image; the Notes app shows a lined paper image with some of the words on the note; the Video app shows a screen shot of your latest video upload; and the Events app shows the image you've uploaded to the latest event listing.

The hyperlinked text below these boxes is only Photos, Events, Notes, or Video. You can change the image for any custom apps you add, and you can change the hyperlinked text, too.

Adding custom apps

The next-most-important task in developing your Page is organizing and adding a few custom apps. We talk a lot about adding apps in Book V, Chapter 1, but here's a quick overview.

Right below the Cover photo are four featured apps. One of them is Photos, which is a Facebook app; because it's a Facebook app, you can't move it, hide it, or change the hyperlinked text. The latest photo you've uploaded or tagged with the Page name is what shows up in this box.

The next three spaces are available to place custom apps. In fact, there are 12 more spaces for custom apps (more on that in a moment), but only a total of four apps show in this featured space. You'll be able to edit and modify the hyperlinked text and the image on the app box and be able to change their order.

Depending on your business, the type of apps you set here can be different, but these are the three main types most businesses use:

- **Email Capture with a Free Gift:** If you already use an e-mail list service (such as mailchimp, iContact, or Constant Contact), check to see whether it has a Facebook integration you can use for this app box. If not, you can always grab the HTML code for your sign-up form and place it in this space, using Heyo's HTML app (`https://heyo.com`) or an HTML app from any other third party (Involver, WooBox, and so on).
- **Event Announcement:** If you have an event coming up, you don't have to use the Facebook Event app; you can create a nice Page for your event by using any third-party app that allows you to add an image or HTML code.
- **Sales Page:** If your sales Page is 850 pixels wide or less, you can use Heyo's iFrame app to pull the whole web page into Facebook. Almost every third-party app company has a system that pulls in a website and places it on an app Page in Facebook. Here's a great example of how that can look: `http://bit.ly/GoodExample`.

Figure 2-14 shows a Page that uses custom apps; one features a sales page (Watch!); another gathers e-mail addresses in exchange for a free gift (Sign Up!); and the third tells about an upcoming event (Online Class).

Figure 2-14: Here's a great use of custom apps.

Currently, people can see custom apps only when they view your Page on a computer. The mobile view of a business Page through the Facebook app doesn't show any custom apps. Also, if you create a post with a link to a custom app, and someone taps that link on a mobile app, he or she is just redirected back to the Page's Timeline or taken to the browser interface. We all hope that this changes in the future, as many custom apps are important to a business on Facebook.

Make sure that you explore Book V to see how to add custom apps to your Page and Book VIII to see how you can use these apps to market effectively on Facebook.

Posting status updates

Posting a few interesting status updates before you publish your Page so as to populate your Timeline encourages people to stick around after they find your business on Facebook. We suggest informational posts about the purpose of your Page, its history, and some introductory posts about you or your business. You should also include one post with a link to either your website or e-commerce site. Another good idea is to add at least one milestone to your Page, which we discuss a bit later in this chapter.

Posting to your Page is so important that we have an entire minibook devoted to that topic! Book III is a complete discussion of how to use this feature, but to get your Page ready to publish, you need at least a few posts.

On your Page, look for the publishing area, as shown in Figure 2-15.

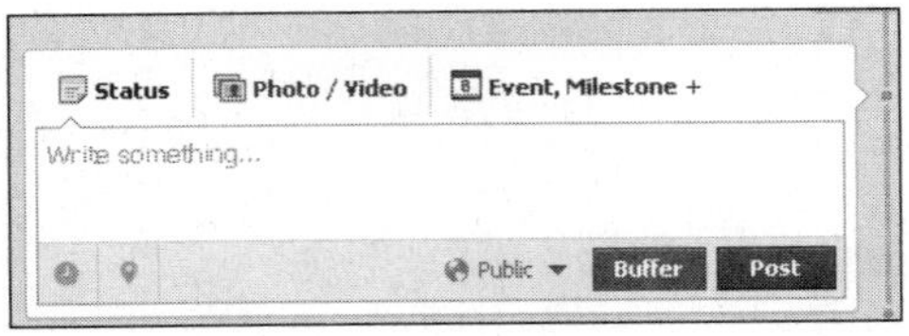

Figure 2-15: This is the publishing area for creating posts to your Page.

Follow these steps to create a simple post:

1. **Click inside the area that says Write something...**

   This step opens the publishing area. You see several icons along the bottom of this space for scheduling, adding a location, and targeting.

2. **Type something interesting.**

   A complete discussion about posting is in Book III.

3. **Click Post.**

   This post shows up on the Timeline. No one will see it until you publish the Page. After the Page is published, you need to create more posts so that they go out into the News Feeds of the people who have liked your Page.

If you created a Local Business Page, you also have the ability to create an offer. We talk about offers in Book III.

Publishing your Page

Before you can invite your Friends and promote your business on Facebook, you need to publish your Page. Here's how:

1. **Go to your Page's Admin panel.**
2. **Click the Edit Page button, and choose Manage Permission from the drop-down menu.**
3. **Clear the Page Visibility check box.**

   Now the Page is published. People can find it in a search, and it's open for people to like.

Editing and adding milestones

One of the best posts for a new Page is a milestone. In fact, when you created your Page, Facebook created your first milestone! When you look at your Timeline, you see that the very first post is a milestone. It may say *Founded on* (and then the date you created the Page). The first thing you want to do is edit this milestone. If it stays at this point in time, you won't be able to add any milestones in the past. Therefore, edit the date for this first milestone back before the milestones you want to add later.

Milestones are similar to Life Events on your personal account. They are similar in how they look and are placed on the Timeline structure. Whereas Life Events tell the story of your personal life, milestones help to tell the story of your business.

Creating milestones is fully discussed in Book III, Chapter 1.

Follow these steps to edit the first milestone:

1. **Find the first milestone.**
2. **Hover over the top-right corner, and click the pencil icon and the Edit link that appear.**
3. **Adjust the date to be as far back as you want.**

   You can also adjust the Milestone type (Opening, Started, Founded, Launched, Born, or Created).
4. **(Optional) Add the story, and upload a photo.**

   We love stories and photos, and Facebook does, too. Add them and make them as personal as possible, and you'll get a better response for the milestone. Ideal image size for a milestone is 843 pixels wide by 403 pixels long.

   You are on a mission to get Likes and comments so that Facebook values your posts and gives them a better EdgeRank. EdgeRank is discussed fully in Book IV, Chapter 2.
5. **Click Save.**

   Now you're free to add milestones to any date from this one to the present. You can't add a milestone to a future date.

If you don't see this starting milestone, when you try to create a milestone, Facebook asks you to create the first one first. Got that? Just go through the prompts, and remember to date it as far back as you can so that you can add other milestones that happened in the past.

Here's how to create the next milestone:

1. **On your Page, click inside the publishing area.**
2. **Click Event, Milestone +.**

   This step opens a menu with these choices: Event, Milestone, and Question.
3. **Click Milestone.**

   See Figure 2-16 for the areas you need to fill in.

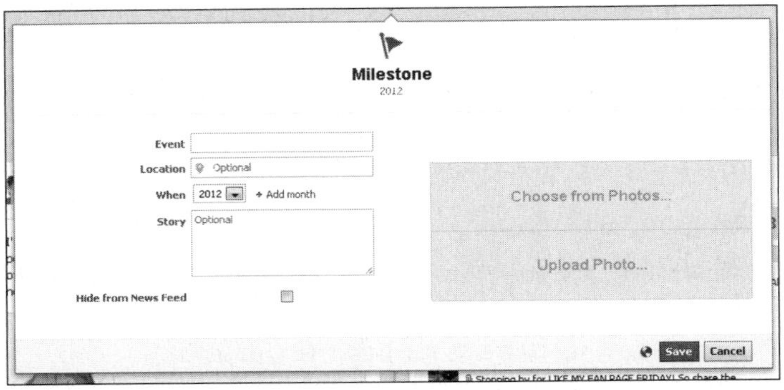

Figure 2-16: These are the fields for creating a milestone.

4. **In the Event field, add a title.**

   This becomes the title of the milestone. The large-font title at the top of this interface changes as you fill in this field. The flag icon doesn't change.
5. **(Optional) Fill in the location if it's important to the milestone.**
6. **Add the date.**

   When you add a specific date, the milestone will attach to the Timeline at that particular date.
7. **Type the story.**

   Adding a story makes the milestone much more interesting.
8. **Upload an image that goes with the milestone.**

   The ideal image size is 843 pixels wide by 403 pixels long.
9. **If you want to hide this milestone from the News Feed, select the Hide from News Feed check box.**
10. **Click Save.**

Milestones are formatted as highlights on the Timeline, which means that they span the whole Page from left to right.

Inviting your Facebook Friends

The next step is inviting your Friends to like your Page. We suggest customizing your Page as much as possible (with posts, photos, and apps) before inviting and sharing it, but if you feel that your Page is ready, inviting your Facebook Friends is next. Follow these steps:

1. **On the Admin panel of your new Page, click the Build Audience button (at the top).**

   When you click that button, a drop-down menu appears.

2. **Click the Invite Friends link.**

   A new dialog box appears, in which you can select your personal Facebook Friends to invite them to like your Page.

3. **To select a Friend, click that person's picture.**

4. **Continue clicking until you've selected everyone you want to share your Page with.**

   Notice the Filter drop-down menu. If you have a lot of Friends, you can filter certain selections (by location or shared group, for example) for easier selection, as shown in Figure 2-17.

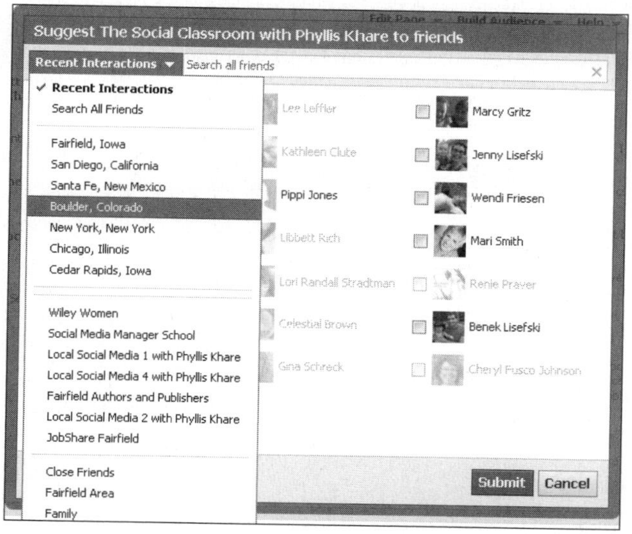

Figure 2-17: Inviting your Friends is easier if you use the Filter drop-down menu.

5. **Click the Submit button.**

   Your Friends get a generic-looking invitation delivered to their Notifications area.

If you opened a business account instead of a personal account to start your business Page (refer to the end of Chapter 1 of this minibook), you won't see this option to invite Friends listed at all.

Inviting e-mail contacts

Your contacts outside Facebook may be a gold mine of people who would benefit from your Page. With the help of the Invite Email Contacts dialog box, you can import the contact info for all the folks you know into a space where you can invite them to your Page.

There are a few things to note about this process:

- Only Admins of Pages with fewer than 5,000 likes can import their e-mail lists and invite people on those lists to like their Page, so invite your e-mail contacts before you reach that number.
- Facebook imports your contact file securely. Then you can suggest your Page to your contacts.
- If you use Gmail, for example, you need to export your contacts in CSV (comma-separated values) format and then upload the `.csv` file to Facebook.

To import your contacts, go to the Admin panel, and click Build Audience to access the drop-down menu; next, click the Invite Email Contacts link. Doing so brings up the Invite Email Contacts dialog box, which is shown in Figure 2-18.

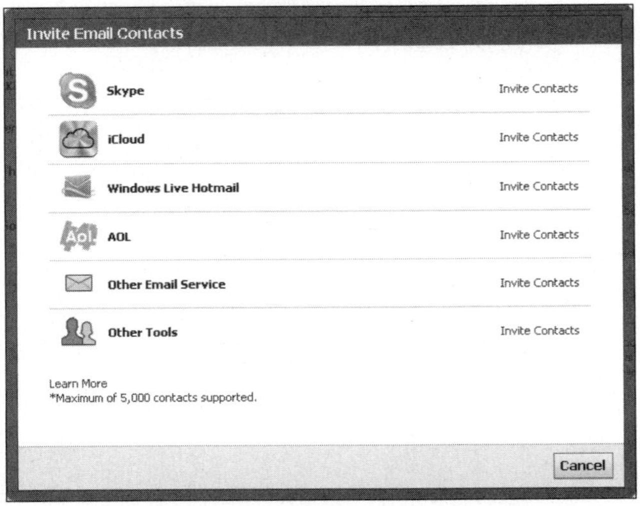

Figure 2-18: You can import your e-mail contacts to tell your Friends and contacts about your new Page.

The idea here is that you can either upload a contacts file you put together yourself or have Facebook search your iCloud, Skype, Windows Live, Hotmail, and AOL accounts to find people for you to contact who are already on Facebook. When you click the Invite Contacts link next to any of those services, you need to type your e-mail address and password, and then click the Find Contacts button.

To help you create a contacts file to upload, Facebook has created instructions specific to whichever mail system you use. When you click the Other Email Service link and type a Gmail address, for example, Facebook presents instructions for exporting your Gmail contacts in a file that Facebook can use.

Then you can select the people you want to invite to your Page. The preview shown in Figure 2-19 depicts how the invitation looks to those whose e-mail address matches a personal Facebook account, as you can see at the top; the bottom shows how it would look if it were sent to an e-mail address that isn't associated with a Facebook account.

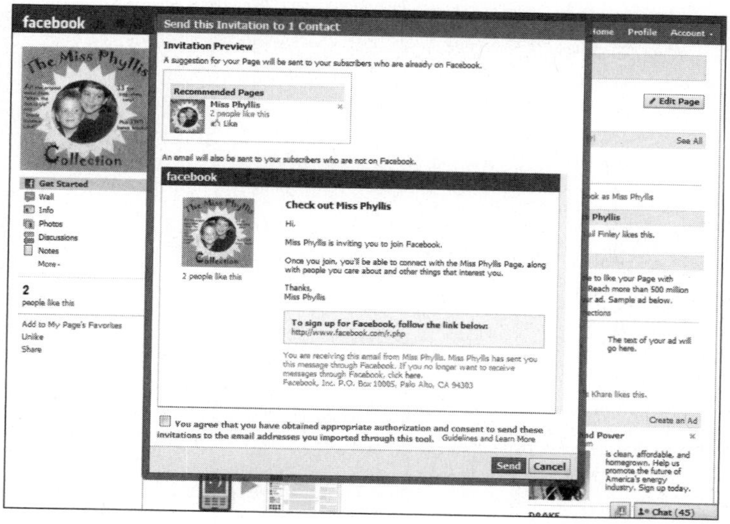

Figure 2-19: Facebook sends a message to your e-mail contacts and invites them to like your Page.

For users who are already on Facebook, this invitation shows up on the right side of their News Feed as an invitation from your Page. If users don't have a Facebook account, they get an e-mail suggesting that they join Facebook so that they can like your Page.

TIP

Facebook puts Page invitations in a fairly obscure place: `www.facebook.com/pages`. No one knows to go there, but Facebook has a very nice section on the right side called Page Invites with all the invitations that have been sent to you. Currently, it's the best place to go to see those invitations. Spread the word.

Sharing your Page

At the top of your Page, next to the Edit Page button you've been using, is another button called Building Your Audience. The third link below Building Your Audience is Sharing Your Page. This particular process looks the same whether or not you're an Admin of the Page, but non-Admins will access the Share link through the gear icon located below the Cover photo to the right. No matter where the link is found, when you click the link, the Share This Page dialog box (shown in Figure 2-20) appears. In this dialog box, you can create a nice invitation that you can post to your personal account Timeline, to someone else's Timeline, to a group Page, to another Page for which you're an Admin, or to a private Facebook Message.

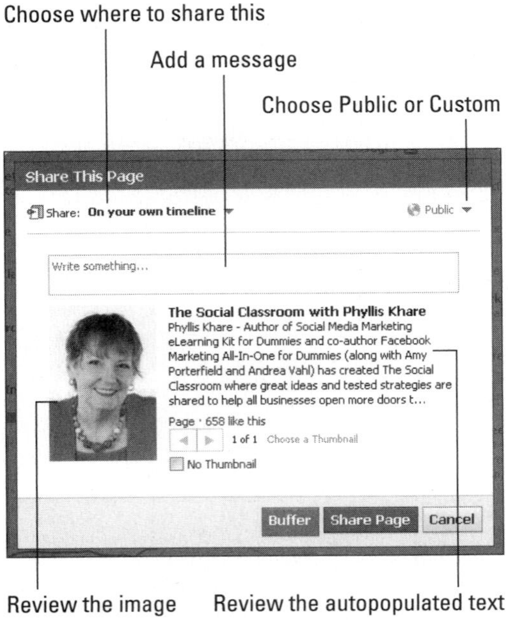

Figure 2-20: The Share This Page dialog box has a few things you need to check before you send out invitations.

Check out a few things before you send invitations:

- **Review the autopopulated text:** This text is pulled right off your Info tab — generally, the text in the Company Overview field. If you don't like what's written here, you have to go back to the Info tab and change the text there. Or you can click the text; an editor interface comes up, and you can type whatever text you want.

Other people will be using this Share function, so you want to enter the text that you want to show up here automatically so they don't have to edit it. Go back to your Info tab to fix the text if needed.

- **Review the image:** This image is the Profile image, not the Cover image. If you want something else to show up there, you need to change the Profile image for the Page. It is not editable from this Share interface.
- **Add a message:** Make sure that you list the benefits for liking the Page. You can create a nice, little message that's compelling. You can mention that you have contests and free events — whatever is appropriate for your business.
- **Decide where to Share:** You can share on your own personal Timeline, on a Friend's Timeline, in a group, on another Page for which you're an Admin, or in a private Facebook Message. Click the drop-down menu to choose which one you want.
- **Decide whether your shared update will be Public or Custom:** You can change the viewing filter by clicking the Public icon to reveal a drop-down menu and changing it to a Facebook Friends list or a custom list.

After you've reviewed the invitation, click Share Page.

Promoting this Page on your website

One of the best ways to have people connect with your business on Facebook is to place a *Like box* (a box that can be placed in your website's sidebar) on your website or blog.

To customize a Facebook Like box, go to `https://developers.facebook.com/docs/reference/plugins/like-box`. You can tweak the Like box's design to your heart's content. When you're done tweaking, you receive a code to place on your website or blog.

A complete description and instructions are in Book VII, Chapter 2, where all the Facebook social plug-ins (Activity Feed, Comments, Facepile, Like Box, Like Button, Live Stream, Login Button, and Recommendations) are explained.

To be clear, there are social plug-ins, and there are badges. A *badge* contains a link that takes people back to your Page, whereas a *social plug-in* allows you to click the Like button for a Page without leaving the website on which the box is placed.

You can create four types of badges for your website. Two types work with your Page: the Like badge and the Page badge. You can find the interface to create them at www.facebook.com/badges. We don't recommend using badges, however, they're not helpful in attracting more likes; they don't contain a built-in Like button, as Like *boxes* do.

Setting up your mobile phone

Facebook understands that you aren't always at your desk or computer when you need to post an update to your business Page. If you're on the go and need to share something with your fans, you can use your smartphone, and in this section, we show you how.

Return to your Page's Admin panel. Click Edit Page and then click Update Info. From the left menu, choose Mobile. Currently, you have four Mobile options:

- **With Mobile Email:** This option gives you the information you need to upload photos or post updates from your mobile e-mail account. Each Page can have its own Facebook e-mail address, which Facebook creates for you automatically. You can use this address to send e-mails that will post on your Page. If you want Facebook to send this e-mail address to you *in* an e-mail, click the Learn More button. This new interface lets you choose to have the e-mail sent to the e-mail address of your choice or to your phone. It also lets you refresh the e-mail to create a new one. You can refresh your e-mail only a few times. See Figure 2-21.

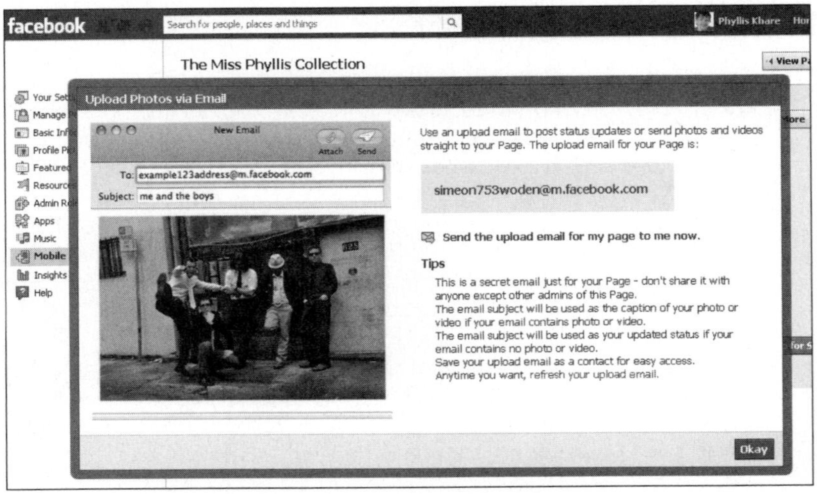

Figure 2-21: Facebook generates an e-mail address for your Page.

When you have the e-mail address in place and want to upload a photo, e-mail the photo to this address, and include a caption in the e-mail's Subject line. To update your status, write in the e-mail Subject line and leave the e-mail body blank.

- **With Mobile Web:** This option reminds you how to find your Page when you're using a mobile browser. Having a username set up simplifies this process. We talk about usernames in Chapter 1 of this minibook.
- **With the iPhone:** Facebook continues to update its official app for all iOS devices. If you want to post directly to your Page, it might be better to use the Pages app Facebook developed instead of trying to create a bookmark on your phone, as Facebook suggests in the text currently on this Mobile tab. As with all things Facebook, the text here might change at any moment. And there might even be a new bullet point for Android phones, or for the (hush-hush) Facebook phone!

TIP

If you have a smartphone with a Facebook app, it's probably easier just to open the app and post a status update inside the app. If you have an administrative team that will be posting to your Page, make sure that the team members get the mobile e-mail address.

Managing Missteps

You may discover that you made a mistake when you created your business Page. Maybe you created your personal Profile for your business instead of a business Page. Maybe you created the wrong kind of business Page and want to change it. Or maybe you created a personal Profile in your name, but most of your Friends are connected to your Profile because of the business you promote from this account. You can almost always fix your issue, but the sooner you realize and can correct your mistake, the better. It's always easier to change a Page when you have fewer connections.

Creating personal Profiles with a business name

A misconception that users have is that it's perfectly okay to create a personal Profile using a business name (first name O'Grady's, last name Cleaners, for example). This is completely against Facebook rules. If you committed that misstep, don't worry: It's fixable. If you've developed an extensive group of Friends under this name, you can either ask them to move over and like your new business Page or change the name of this account to your actual name and activate the Subscribe button.

Sorting out or deleting a personal Profile set up as a business

If you created a personal Profile with your business name, you can change the name of your account to your actual name, as long as you don't already have a personal account in your name. (If you already have a personal account with your real name, you'll need to ask people to move to your business Page and then delete this account.) Follow these steps:

1. **Go to your personal Profile's Account Settings by clicking the drop-down arrow next to Home in the top-right corner of your Facebook Page.**

   Or go directly to `www.facebook.com/settings`.

2. **Click the Edit link to the right of Name.**
3. **Change the name to your actual name.**
4. **Enter your Facebook password.**
5. **Click Save Changes.**

Alternatively, build your new, honest-to-goodness official business Page and then add a status message regarding the change to the original personal Profile you created for the business. The new status update should give your Friends the URL to the new business Page and explain that you created a new business Page to conform to Facebook guidelines. Tell them that you hope they'll join you over there and like the Page.

TIP

If you created this personal Profile under the business name and won't be changing the name to your actual name, you can also tell Friends that you'll be deactivating the current Profile Page and explain what they can find at the new business Page (such as coupons, special deals, updates, and so on). You'll likely need to post this status update several times before people migrate over. We suggest setting a deadline for moving to the new business Page so that your connections will know exactly when you'll deactivate the business-name Profile Page.

WARNING!

If you go this route, make sure to designate your *real* personal account an Admin of the business Page before you delete the rogue personal account. Otherwise, you won't be able to get back to the new business Page.

If you created a personal Profile in your real name but promoted your business from there, you can keep the original personal Profile as your personal account, activate the Subscribe button (as we describe earlier in this chapter), and post Public updates to subscribers.

Here's a sample of a post that Jane wrote, asking her Friends to move over to her business Page:

> Hi everyone, I have a new Page for my new CD of contemporary lullabies, "Midnight Lullaby." This project has been a long time coming, and I'm hoping you can check it out and click the Like button. Here's the link: `www.facebook.com/ladylullabymusic`. I plan to add many things to this new Page, but for right now please Like it, and I'll keep you posted from there. This new Page is where I will be spending my time on Facebook, so if you want to connect with me, please do it from there.
>
> Thank you!
>
> Jane (Jane Roman Pitt) `www.facebook.com/midnightlullabyCD`

She decided to keep her original personal Profile because it was under her name but moved all her posts about her business to her new Page. She had already created a vanity URL for her personal Profile with her CD's name, which couldn't be modified at the time.

If you set your personal account username to be your business name, you might be able to change it. Go to your Account Settings, and then General Settings. If you can change it, the interface to do so will be there. If you have already changed it once, you will not be able to change it again.

If you decide to delete your personal account with the business name, follow these steps, but remember that you have to have a personal account to have a business Page. So if you delete the personal account instead of changing the name to your name, you'll need to open another personal account before you open a Page.

REMEMBER

If you already have a personal account, you need to make sure, as noted earlier, that you assign your real account the role of Page Admin *before* you delete the incorrectly created personal account. Follow these steps:

1. **Log in to Facebook with the e-mail you used to create the personal account for your business.**
2. **Click the drop-down arrow in the top-right corner of your Page.**
3. **Choose Account Settings from the menu.**
4. **On the left menu choose General Settings.**

   On the bottom of this page you have the option to download a copy of your Facebook data. If you choose to do this, click the link and follow the steps to create an archive of this personal account's photos, posts, and messages.
5. **After you have downloaded the data (optional), go back to the left menu under Account Settings and choose Security.**

   On the bottom of this page you will see a link that says, "Deactivate your account."

   At this point, if you are sure you will not be needing this personal account, instead of Deactivating, you can completely delete it by going to `www.facebook.com/help/delete_account`.

   Otherwise, Deactivating leaves the door open to bring the personal account back at any time by logging in with the e-mail and password you had for this account. Deactivating hides all the data from this account, and keeps it in a drawer in Texas somewhere.
6. **If you decide to Deactivate, click the link on the Security tab and go through the process.**
7. **If you decide to Delete, go to** `www.facebook.com/help/delete_account`.

Now that you've deactivated or deleted your personal account with the business name, sign in to Facebook with your new (or regular) personal account, go to your new official business Page, and start interacting with your connections! Welcome them to your new space, and encourage them to interact with you.

Changing your business Page type or name

Sometimes, people make a business Page and realize that they've made a mistake. Maybe they chose the wrong type of business Page, or they want to change the name of the Page or the category that's associated with the Page. You can change the category or type of Page at any time, but you can change a business Page's name only if fewer than 200 people like the Page. Sometimes, Facebook allows Pages with more than 200 likes to change their name, but this seems to be a random event.

To make those types of changes, follow these steps:

1. **Log in to Facebook.**
2. **Go to your Page.**

   You can find your Page quickly by looking in the left menu while viewing your personal account news feed.
3. **In the Admin Panel, click Edit Page; then click Update Info.**

   You arrive at the Basic Information tab, shown in Figure 2-22.

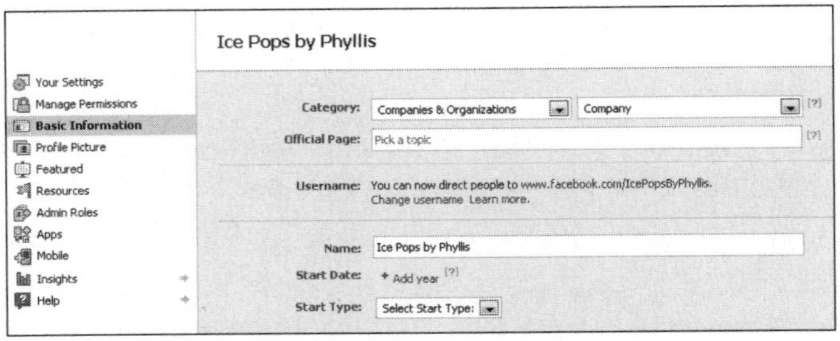

Figure 2-22: Change or modify a Page category or name here.

You can edit the category, subcategory, and name of your business Page. At the top of the Page, you see two drop-down menus, and you can take any of the following actions to make desired changes:

- To change the category of your business Page, click the first drop-down menu, and make your choice.
- To change the subcategory of your business Page, click the second drop-down menu, and make your choice.

- To change your business Page name, click inside the Name text box, delete the existing name, and retype the new name. The new name will appear as the title of your Page but won't change your vanity URL (username).

4. **Click the Save Changes button.**

Sometimes, when you change the Page category, the input fields change. If you go from People/Author to Books & Magazine/Book, for example, the fields automatically change to give you a different set of input fields.

If you have more than 200 likes but must change your business Page name, Facebook sometimes puts a link on the Basic Information tab where you can go through the process of changing it. The only other recourse is to delete the original Page and start from scratch. We sincerely discourage you from doing this because you'll lose all of your likes (connections) and will have to re-create your community from scratch. Also, changing your name after you have more than 200 likes may be confusing for your audience. If you must delete your Page, however, follow these steps:

1. **Log in to Facebook.**
2. **Find your Page name in the left menu.**

   If you don't see the name of your Page, click the More link to see the list of all your Pages.
3. **Click the Edit Page button.**

   You are in the editing area for your Page, with a navigation menu on the left side.
4. **Choose Manage Permissions from this navigation menu.**
5. **Click the Permanently Delete This Page link (just above the Save Changes button).**

   A confirmation dialog box appears, asking whether you really, *really* want to do this. After all, this deletion is permanent.

   WARNING! Any Admin can delete a Page that he or she administers. Please delete with caution, because you absolutely cannot reinstate a removed Page.
6. **Click Delete.**

   Your Page is history.

Chapter 3: Administering Your Facebook Business Page

In This Chapter

- **Interacting with Facebook as your personal Profile or as your Page**
- **Understanding what other people see when they visit your Page**
- **Learning how to use your Page Admin panel and editing dashboard**

Now that you're a Page Admin, Facebook has granted you an additional permission: You can view Facebook as yourself (that is, through your personal Profile) or as your Page (that is, through your business Page). This particular administrative perk can be a little confusing at first, but by the end of this chapter, you'll completely understand how and when to use this option.

As Admin of your Facebook business Page, you need to maintain it. An important part of maintenance is simply understanding how your Page looks to visitors and fans, what you can customize and control, and what Page elements are visible only to you when you're acting as the Admin and when you are viewing your Page "as" your Page. This chapter explains the elements of your business Page and then shows you how to use your Admin panel and administrative editing dashboard to control some of those aspects.

Viewing Facebook as Your Page

Now that you have a Facebook business Page, you have two separate Profiles with Facebook: your personal Profile and your Page Profile. Each Profile allows you to view Facebook, post status updates, and comment on other posts. But depending on which Profile you're using, you show up as either your personal Profile (you) or your Page Profile (your business).

In addition, each Profile has its own News Feed:

- **Your personal Profile News Feed:** Based on your Friends' status updates and the business Pages you've liked as your personal Profile
- **Your Page Profile News Feed:** Based solely on the Pages you've liked as your Page (which we explain in a minute)

In this section, we explain how and when you may want to use each of your Profile options. Before we do, though, you may find it helpful to see each of these Profile options in action. Start by changing your Profile view from personal Profile to Page Profile. To do that, follow these steps:

1. **Log in to Facebook as you normally do.**
2. **Click the Account drop-down arrow in the top-right corner of the page.**
3. **From the drop-down menu, choose the Page link that you want to use.**

   This menu is where you toggle among your personal and Page Profiles. If you're an Admin of several pages, you need to select the correct Page.

After you click the preferred Page link, you're taken directly to that Page. Now you're viewing your Page "as" your Page, not as your personal account with Admin privileges for the Page. This point is an important one to understand, and you may need to switch between your personal Profile and your Page Profile to see the differences.

When you change over to working as your Page, you should see your Page's Admin panel expanded to include these sections: Notifications, Messages, New Likes, Insights, and Page Tips. See Figure 3-1 for that view.

Figure 3-1: This Admin panel is available for every Page you create.

We go over all those sections later in this chapter. For now, we stick to the two different Profiles you have available and how those views look while you're on your Page.

We're sure that you're used to seeing your personal account News Feed. Well, a business Page can have a News Feed, too! Your Page Profile News Feed is based solely on the Pages you've liked as your Page. To see that News Feed, click the link in the top-right of the Page called Home. This feed functions just the same as your personal Profile News Feed, except that it's filled with posts from other Facebook Pages that you (as your Page) have liked. If you haven't liked any Pages yet as your Page, you won't have anything in this News Feed. You can't like a personal account as a Page, so this feed shows only Page updates.

How does a Page like another Page? The next section explains how. Right now, to switch back to your personal Profile, follow these steps:

1. **Click the Account link in the top-right corner of the page.**
2. **From the drop-down menu, choose Use Facebook as *your personal account name.***

   This menu is where you toggle your personal and Page Profiles.

There's one more little view that you need to understand. When you're on Facebook as yourself, and you go to your Page, you see a notification bar at the top of the page that looks like Figure 3-2. Notice the word *Voice* and the link to change to yourself. But wait! We can hear you say, "But I *am* myself!" This Voice notification and link replace what was previously called Posting Preference and was part of the editing dashboard. Facebook pulled it out to make it very obvious "who" you are while you're on your Page: your personal account or your Page. We know that this feature has a little Dr. Seuss feeling to it, but the more you test it, the more you'll understand it.

Figure 3-2: Change who (your personal Profile or business Page) will post on the Page.

TIP

Now that you've had a chance to see your Profile options and are comfortable switching between them, we have a few tips for you:

- If you're viewing Facebook with your Page Profile, and you go to another business Page for which you're an Admin, you won't be able to do any Admin stuff (editing, posting as that Page, and so on) until you switch back to your personal Profile.
- You can't post as your Page on anyone's personal Facebook Profile, but you can post as your Page on another Page.
- Try not to be too spammy by posting as your Page all the time. Yes, this option is a great way to promote your Page, but remember that Facebook is a social network, not a place to go dropping your business name everywhere!

Liking other Pages as your Page

If you've been on Facebook for a while, maybe you've already liked your favorite business Pages as yourself (that is, your personal Profile). If so, you know that when you like a Page, any status updates or shared content for that Page make their way into your News Feed. Liking a Page is one more way to keep up with the brands you enjoy.

Commenting as your business Page instead of yourself is one way to promote your own business Page and increase its visibility in new communities.

We encourage you to spend some time developing a strategy around which Pages you want to have associated with your own business Page. When you're choosing which Pages to like, it's a good idea to choose Pages that you think will fit with your audience's expectations. Liking the NFL Page, for example, would seem incongruous with your Doll Factory Page and wouldn't mesh well with your established community. On the other hand, that same community may appreciate a link to another business Page about restoring antique dolls.

If you're viewing a Page as your Page, and you prefer to comment as your personal Profile instead, you need to switch back to your personal Profile (by choosing your personal Profile from the Account drop-down menu). When you switch back, you're deposited on your personal Profile News Feed instead of the Page you were just viewing. You need to navigate back to that Page and then leave your comment as your personal Profile.

Follow these steps to like a Page as your business Page:

1. **Switch to your business Page, as noted previously.**
2. **Navigate to a Page you want to like.**
3. **Click the Like button at the top of the Page.**

   Note that this process is the same one you use when you like a Page as your personal Profile.

4. **(Optional) Post a comment.**

   Pages don't receive notification when a Page likes them, so it's nice to leave a comment as your Page to say hello. The Page owner will, however, be able to see that you've liked his Page as a Page when he looks through his likers and filters for Pages (more on that coming up). When you leave your comment, the posting name and thumbnail image are that of your Page Profile, not your personal Profile.

REMEMBER

When one business Page likes another business Page, that like doesn't count toward the total number of likes. Suppose that Blogging Basics 101 has 800 likes. If the Simply Amusing Designs Page decides to like Blogging Basics 101, the total number of likes on Blogging Basics 101 stays at 800 instead of increasing to 801. That way, the likes on a Page aren't artificially inflated by personal and business Profiles owned by the same person.

Using a strategy of liking certain Pages as your Page gives you a curated News Feed for you to view (as your Page). It's a bit like creating a list of the businesses you want to keep up with. The Home News Feed for your Page Profile can be a great place to view what other Pages are doing for marketing on Facebook, too.

Changing voice preferences

By default, your Facebook business Page settings are such that when you're on your own business Page, any post you make appears to be from your Page. (In other words, the Page image thumbnail and name are what people see for those posts.) You can change this setting and post as yourself (your personal Profile) on your own Page, too. Your Page may be for your magazine, for example, but you want to post as yourself — the publisher — for a particular reply or comment to a post. You need to change the voice by clicking the link shown in Figure 3-2, earlier in this chapter. Businesses have to decide how they want their Admins to post and comment on the Page. Some businesses "sign" their posts with their real names, and some switch between Page Profile and personal Profile, depending on what they're posting on the Page.

REMEMBER

How an Admin posts on a Page should be spelled out in a social media policy so that everyone is on the same page (pun intended).

Touring the Admin panel

The general layout of the Admin panel is shown in Figure 3-3. The panel has five sections, and you can expand each section by clicking the See All link to the right of its name. Also, you can Show or Hide the Admin panel itself by clicking the Show/Hide button in the top-right corner of the Page. In this section, we give you a quick tour of the Admin panel's sections.

Toggle between showing and hiding the Admin panel.

Figure 3-3: The Admin panel.

Notifications

The Notifications section sits in the top-left corner of the Admin panel. This section contains a chronological list of actions on your Page: likes, comments, posts to your Timeline, and so on. You can see at a glance the last five or six actions. You also see a red number if there are any notification actions that you haven't viewed yet, and you can click the See All link to open a list of all notifications. When you click any notification, the activity opens. If you click a notification about someone liking an image, for example, when you click the notification, you go right to that image and can view all the comments.

Messages

The Messages section, to the right of the Notifications section, is an inbox containing messages that people have left for your Page to answer. You can turn on the Message feature or turn it off. (In Figure 3-3, earlier in this chapter, the feature is turned on.) You need to make sure that you're aware of this section and either get e-mail notifications when someone leaves a message or check this section often so you can answer messages in a timely manner.

To turn the Message feature on or off, click the Edit Page button at the top of your Page, and on the Manage Permission tab look for the check box for Messages.

When you click the See All link next to Messages, you see a chronological list of all the messages (see Figure 3-4). Click the X to the right of a message to archive it. You can use the search box to find any unread messages.

Messages are private to the Admins of a Page. Posts left on your Page's Timeline are public. These are two different types of notifications you need to address as an Admin of your Page. Later on in this chapter, we have a more detailed explanation of Page Messages.

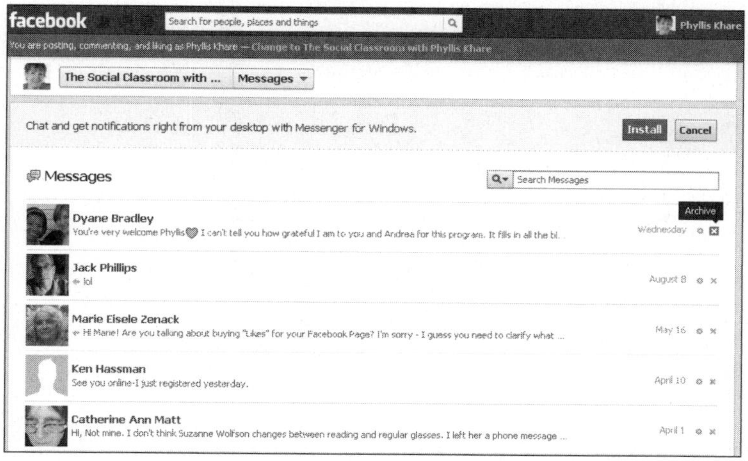

Figure 3-4: The Messages interface lets you archive or search for messages left for your Page.

New Likes

The New Likes section, below the Notifications section, lists a few of the newest people who have liked your Page. If you're viewing your Page as yourself as Admin, you can hover over the names in this section and Request to be a personal Facebook Friend, Subscribe to their Public updates, or send a Message (if they have that feature turned on for their personal Profile). If you are viewing your Page as your Page, you won't see those links to connect when you hover over their names.

When you click the See All link, a new interface opens, showing all the people who have liked your Page. Choose Pages that like this from the drop-down menu (see Figure 3-5) to see the list of Pages who have liked your Page. If you're viewing your Page as your Page, you can click those Page names to go to their Page and like the Page as your Page. If you are viewing your Page as yourself as an Admin, when you click the Page names and go to their Page, clicking the Like button is a personal like.

TIP

Check your new likes on a regular basis, and welcome new people to your Page by posting their first names or by tagging their business Pages. (Find out all about tagging in Book IV, Chapter 2.) Sort the new likes by Page; then like those Pages as your Page and leave comments.

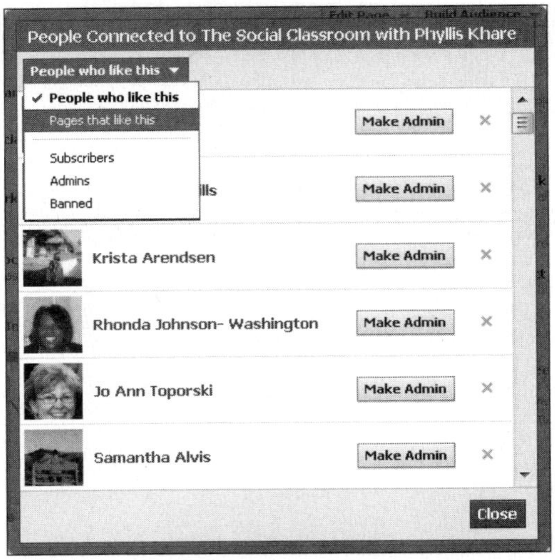

Figure 3-5: See who likes your Page.

Insights

The next section inside your Admin panel is Insights, which is Facebook's analytics section. It contains a wealth of information that you can use to better understand who your audience is and what it likes. Book IX, Chapter 2 covers Insights.

This section has a little graph that shows at a glance how your Page is doing in terms of number of Your Posts, number of people Talking About This, and Reach. Hover over the lines and dots to see more information.

When you click the See All link, you go to the full Insights interface, which is a very rich environment with five tabs, graphs, and data galore. If you're viewing Insights on a new Page, you won't have enough data to see any graphs yet. Make sure that you come back and view this section after you've collected Page likes and conversations.

Page Tips

Currently, the last section of the Admin panel is a space where Facebook can post things it wants you to see. On one day, for example, Facebook offered Phyllis a promotion for business cards from Moo.com; when she clicked the Next link, she saw a quick link that allowed her to create an ad for the Page. We can imagine this space being used for all sorts of announcements and promotional offers.

Understanding How Other People See Your Page

We think it's a good idea to give you an overview of some fully functioning Pages so you can see how business Pages look to the public. The best place to start is www.facebook.com/pages. Click any of the Pages listed, and note these Page features:

- ✦ Cover photo
- ✦ Featured apps
- ✦ Profile image
- ✦ Friends (mutual connections)
- ✦ About section
- ✦ Talking about This (number of people who are interacting with your Page)
- ✦ Likes (number of personal Profiles that have liked the Page)
- ✦ Message button
- ✦ View toggle
- ✦ Gear icon

Figure 3-6 has callouts for each item on this list so you can see how these elements appear on a business Page. The following sections explain these elements.

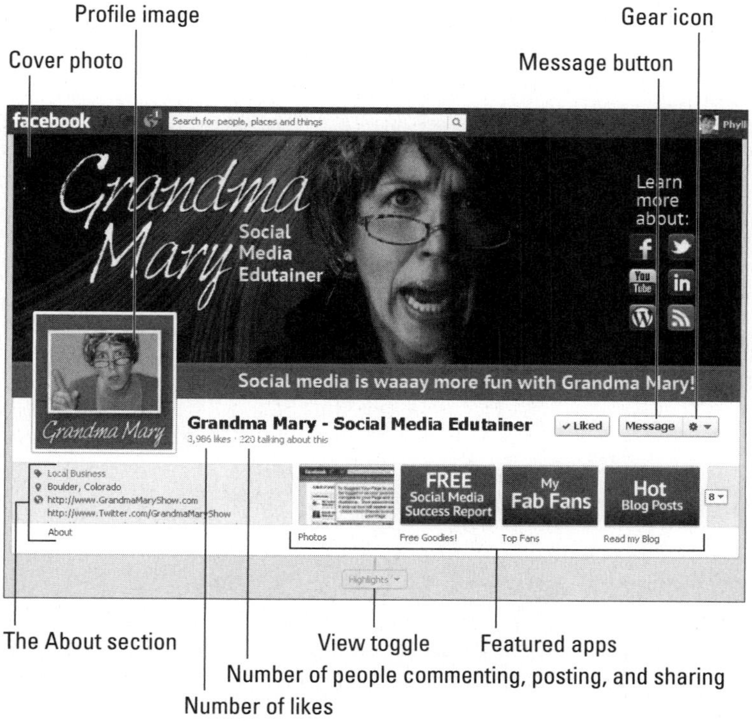

Figure 3-6: A business Page as seen by the public.

Cover photo

One of the biggest changes in Facebook Pages recently was the format change to Timeline. Now personal accounts and business Pages have the Timeline structure, and one of the most important components of the Timeline is the Cover photo. This image is 851 pixels wide and 315 pixels tall. There are several restrictions about what you can use in a Cover photo, as fully discussed in Chapter 2 of this minibook. The reason we're bringing the topic up again is to give you some ideas about using a Cover photo to your business advantage even with those restrictions.

We don't know whether you've noticed, but now when you hover over any account in the News Feed (personal or business Page), a box called the *hover card* pops up, showing you the Profile image, the Cover photo, and some text related to that account. The text that appears for a business Page is the category. New Media Expo does a great job of using a Cover image and a Profile image to create a great effect, as shown in Figure 3-7.

The hover card can be considered a free ad. If done well, like in the New Media Expo example, branding and information can be conveyed beautifully. Notice in the example how you see the date of the event, thumbnails of any Facebook Friends who are attending (social proof), an image of the excitement of attending (the Cover image), and a quick way to like the Page.

Check your Page's hover card by going to your Page and hovering over your own Page's name on a recent post. Does the hover card fully convey the qualities or products and services your business provides?

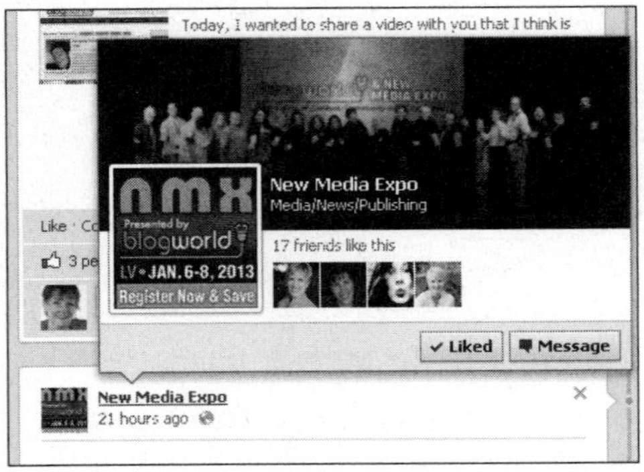

Figure 3-7: Here's a great example of why a Cover photo, Profile image, and page category are important.

Featured apps

If you have a brand-new Page and haven't added any Facebook apps or custom apps yet (more on that soon), your visitors see only one or two app boxes below your Cover photo: Photos and Likes (if you or someone else has liked the Page). You want to add apps as you develop your Page, and we show you how to do that in Chapter 2 of this minibook. You may want to add your e-commerce page, newsletter sign-up page, YouTube videos, and many more things.

Your visitors see these Featured apps on your Page and are able to click through all of them. If you have more than four app boxes, visitors to your site can expand or contract the apps by clicking the arrow to the right of the app boxes.

Keep two things in mind:

- ✦ Currently, you can't see any custom apps through the official Facebook mobile app.
- ✦ Most people don't know how to click the drop-down arrow to reveal the other apps.

Three highly functional apps probably are plenty to have in the beginning. As you create contests and other offers, you can add apps that contain that information.

Profile image

The Profile image is important for many reasons; its thumbnail is what accompanies your posts, it's on the hover card (previously mentioned), and you can use promotional text on it.

If you are branding your business logo, the Profile image is a great place to put it. If you are branding yourself, your lovely face needs to be in this position. If you have events, you can use the Profile image to promote the date and location (see the New Media Expo example in Figure 3-7).

Friends (Mutual connections)

Facebook has a section in the top-right corner of personal Profile Timeline that shows friendship connections. If you're viewing Facebook with your personal Profile and go to someone's personal Profile, you can see which Friends you have in common with that person, which photos you and that person tagged have in common, and Pages that both of you liked.

Facebook created a similar space for Pages. When you visit any Facebook Page, you see in the top-right corner (below the Cover photo and Featured apps) a similar space showing which of your personal Profile Friends have liked that Page too. You see this display only if you're viewing Pages as your personal Profile. If you switch over to viewing Facebook as your Page, that section disappears.

About section

Below the Cover photo is a little section that shows a little bit of text. This area contains some of the words you put in the About field on the Basic Information page when you started your Page. To adjust the text that shows up here, click the About area or the word "About" and you'll go to the Basic Information for your page. Hover over the top-right corner of About, click the hidden Edit button, and change the text in the About field. Click Save Changes when you are done.

Facebook collapses the text so that approximately 75 characters show.

Any web address you enter in the About field on the Basic Information page (if it contains the `http://` part) will be hyperlinked, so make sure that you type it in full so that people go to the correct page when they click the address.

Notice what's appealing in the About section on other Pages. Some Pages use the space to give viewers a quick explanation of the Page and to list a call to action. Here are a few good examples:

- **Gettin' Geeky (**`www.facebook.com/GettinGeeky`**):** A place where technology isn't so scary. The site is a place where visitors can learn together without feeling intimidated about asking questions. The site lets you post challenges and discover ways to use technology to build your business.
- **iPhone Life (**`http://iphonelife.com`**):** A site that helps you unleash the power of your iPhone, iPad, and iPod touch, covering topics such as the best apps, top tips, and great gear.
- **Mashable Social Media (**`http://mashable.com/social-media`**):** A site that covers the latest happenings in social media, with tips on using Twitter, Facebook, YouTube, Pinterest, and more.

The numbers

Two numbers are listed below the name of any business Page. These are public numbers that everyone can see:

- The first number is the number of people who have clicked the Like button at the top of the Page. This number doesn't include business Pages that have liked the Page — only personal Profiles that have done so.
- The second number is the "talking about this" number, which we discuss fully in Book IX. This number is the number of people who have interacted with your Page in any way, such as liking it, posting to your Timeline, commenting, or sharing one of your posts.

Note: If you have a local business and your Page is a Places Page (see Chapter 1 of this minibook), there's a third number, for check-ins.

All the Admins of your Page see these numbers as hyperlinks to the Insights interface, but visitors to your Page won't be able to click them. You can't hide these numbers or move their locations.

As you build the number of people who click the Like button, and you follow the suggestions in this book about creating a good community on your Page, you'll naturally find more interaction on your Page. You also have a better EdgeRank score (more about that in Book IV, Chapter 2) and, we hope, increased revenue or branding awareness — whatever main goal you chose for your Page (see Book I, Chapter 2).

Some Facebook consultants say that a good time to start running contests is when you reach more than 1,000 likes, as you should have plenty of entries then, but you know your niche better than anyone else. When you reach a milestone number, do something special for your Page community. Some Pages celebrate milestones at 100, 500, 1,000, 2,000 likes, and so on. Think up something special for each milestone. If you decide to give something away, make sure that you follow Facebook's guidelines for sweepstakes and contests. You can find all the info in Book VI, Chapter 2.

The likes

Below the Cover photo is a section called Likes. If you have checked the box under Manage Permissions, Post Visibility, there will be a box for Post by Others above the Likes section. In the Likes section, you and your visitors can see other Pages that your business Page has liked, as shown in Figure 3-8. This section shows up to five other Pages. Every time anyone refreshes your Page, the Pages listed are in a different order. Also, you can set your Admin dashboard to display five Featured likes. We show you how to do that a little later in this chapter.

Figure 3-8: A Page has liked these other business Pages.

You need to decide whether you want your visitors to see these Pages or not. Some businesses like to associate themselves with certain Pages to add to their reputations; others don't want to show anything that takes someone off their Page.

These Pages are not the ones that you liked as your personal Profile. Pages that you like as yourself (that is, as your personal Profile) are listed on your personal Profile's Info page.

Message button

You have the option to turn on or off the private Message button on your Page. If the button is turned on, you see it on the Page, as shown in Figure 3-6, earlier in this chapter. If the button is turned off, you won't see it.

This Message button functions just like a Private Message on your personal account. Your Page can receive private messages, too. You can think of Messages as a kind of e-mail inbox. That's the way Facebook wants you to look at Page Messages.

To turn on the Message button on your Page, follow these steps:

1. **Click Edit Page in the Admin panel.**
2. **Select Update Info.**
3. **Choose Manage Permissions from the left menu.**
4. **Click the Messages check box to activate the Message button on your Page.**
5. **Click Save Changes.**

When you have the Message button turned on, you need to check the Messages section of your Admin panel regularly. Reply to messages just as you reply to e-mails.

View toggle

Your visitors can toggle what they see on your Page by clicking a button below the Cover photo at the top of the Timeline, as shown in Figure 3-9. Facebook currently defaults a visitor to the Highlights view. Facebook uses an algorithm to rank posts you see in the Highlights view by an engagement formula called *EdgeRank*. We talk a lot about EdgeRank in Book IV, Chapter 2. Facebook loves to arrange things according to likes, comments, and other engagements, but a visitor has the option to change the view from Highlights to Friend Activity, Posts by Page, and Posts by Others.

Currently, changing the view toggle is a matter of educating people to click the drop-down list and choose what they want to see.

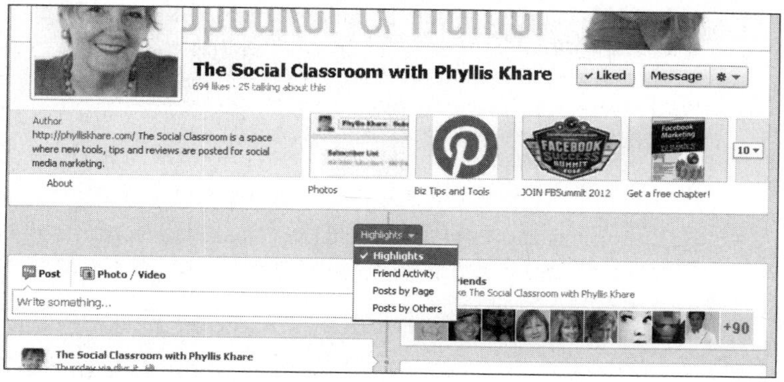

Figure 3-9: Toggle the Timeline view.

Gear-icon links

All Pages have a gear icon below the Cover photo, as shown in Figure 3-10. Click the icon to see a variety of links that we'll go through next. What regular visitors see through this gear icon on your Page and what you (and any Admin of any Facebook Page) see will be different. Also, if you're viewing your Page as your Page, you see a different view from the Admin view.

Figure 3-10: Clicking the gear icon drops down a list of handy links.

Hang with us, and we'll go through all the items you can see by clicking this gear icon:

- **Add to Interest Lists:** This option enables you to add the Page to a Facebook Interest List. Using Interest Lists can be a strategy to get your Page seen by a larger audience. Book VII, Chapter 1 discusses advanced marketing strategies. This Add to Interest link is seen by anyone on any Page.

- **Add to My Page's Favorites:** This is a quick link to add a Page to your Page's Favorites. You need to be on Facebook as yourself, not as your Page, and then click the gear icon on a Page that you want to add to *your* Page's favorites list. When you click the link to Add to My Page's Favorites, a new dialog box will open and you can add it or choose the Page you want it added to (if you are an Admin of several Pages) by clicking a drop-down arrow and selecting the preferred Page.
- **Remove from My Page's Favorites:** This link is only visible to Admins of *any* Facebook Page, this option removes a Page from your Page's Favorites. It also removes the Page from your Featured Pages, if applicable. Choosing this option isn't the same as unliking a Page.
- **Create a Page:** This is a quick link to go to the interface to create a new Page. Everyone sees this link.
- **Create an Ad:** You see this option only if you're an Admin of the Page. Visitors to your Page don't see it.
- **Share:** This option is by far the most important. You want visitors to your Page to choose it! Doing so brings up a post (that you can edit) that appears on their Timelines for all their Friends to see. (We talk about sharing in detail in Book IV, Chapter 1.) Go ahead and choose this option on any Page to see what happens. All the information in the post comes from particular fields on the Info link for the Page you're viewing. If the Page didn't put information in the Company Overview section (or other fields — again, review Book IV, Chapter 1), there will be no text, just the name of the Page hyperlinked back to the Page. You may want to adjust your own Page after seeing how it looks on someone else's Page.
- **View Insights:** You see this option, which takes you to Insights, only if you're an Admin of the Page. Visitors don't see it. We discuss Facebook Insights in Book IX, Chapter 2.
- **Unlike/Like:** If you've already liked the Page that you're viewing, you see an Unlike option. If you haven't liked the Page yet, you see a Like option.
- **Visit Help Center:** This is a quick link to the Facebook Help Center. You only see it on Pages where you are an Admin.
- **Send Feedback:** This option takes you to an interface where you can send a note to Facebook about the Page. This option is different from reporting a Page.
- **Report Page:** You can report any Page if you feel that it's breaking Facebook rules, and other people can report your Page if they feel that it's breaking Facebook rules. When you click this link, you bring up a dialog box that takes you through the process of reporting the Page. If you don't see this as a link, you can click the Visit Help Center link and search for Reporting a Page.
- **Privacy:** This link takes you to a page that outlines Facebook's privacy terms.

- **Terms:** This link takes you to Facebook's Statement of Rights and Responsibilities document.
- **Do you know the owner?:** If the Page you are viewing is a Places Page and the owner of the business hasn't claimed it yet, you will see this link. Remember, there are two steps when you create a local business type Page: creating the Page and claiming the Page. This is discussed in Book II, Chapter 1.
- **Is this your business?:** Same as above, if the owner hasn't claimed it yet, you will see this link. If you are viewing your own Page and you see this link, you need to click it to start the process of claiming it. Refer to Book II, Chapter 1.

If you created a limited *business account* (see Chapter 1 of this minibook), you see the Share option only on your own Page. You see Add to My Page's Favorites, Create a Page, Report Page, and Share on other Facebook Pages. And if you select Share, you will only be able to share on your Page(s) and not on your Timeline (because you don't have one) or on someone else's Timeline.

Editing Your Page

Now that you know how other people see your Page, you can see how it looks from the inside! This section explores all the ways you can edit your Page. You see where you add applications (apps), change the information people see about your Page, change your Profile image, and do many other things.

To start, click the Edit Page button at the top of your Admin panel, as shown in Figure 3-11.

You can click Update Info, Manage Permissions, Admin Roles, or Manage Notifications. It doesn't matter, because clicking any of these will put you on your Page's editing dashboard. You'll be able to choose the item you want in the left menu.

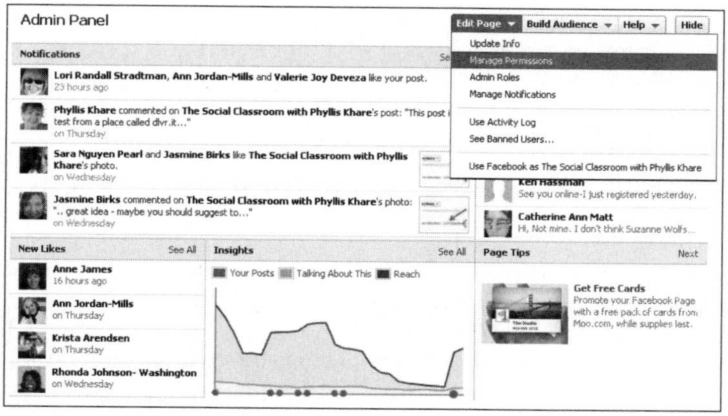

Figure 3-11: Click this button to find the interface for editing your Page.

You're looking at your business Page's administrative dashboard, as shown in Figure 3-12. This dashboard is where you edit and modify your Page. Notice the nice collection of navigation links on the left side. In the following sections, we walk you through each of these links, going from top to bottom.

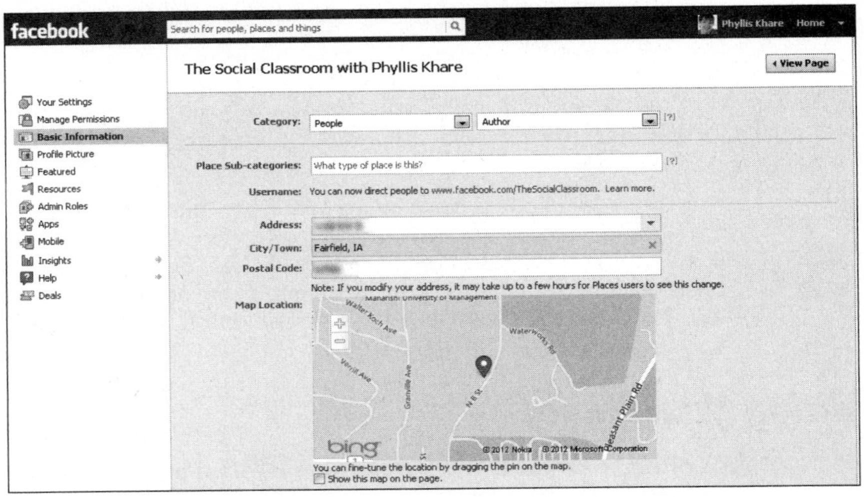

Figure 3-12: The navigation menu for editing your Page.

Your Settings

When you select the top link, called Your Settings, you see three sections:

- Email Notifications
- Pages Manager Mobile Notifications
- Onsite Notification

These are three ways to be notified when there is activity on your Page. Choose the ones that work best for you. Each Admin of the Page can choose the way he wants to be notified by visiting his editing dashboard and viewing Your Settings and selecting what he prefers.

Email Notifications

The Email Notifications section lets you decide whether you want to get an e-mail notification every time someone posts to or comments on your Page. All Admins of your Page need to adjust these settings to suit their preferences.

You want to know when someone posts or comments to your Page for a variety of reasons, but mostly, you want to be able to respond quickly to any concerns or questions. You also want to know if someone has posted anything considered spam so you can remove it quickly. Depending on your business, a quick response raises your online reputation, so you can use Facebook's e-mail notification or try a third-party system. The authors of this book are enjoying the Hyper Alerts (`www.hyperalerts.no`) notification system, for example.

TIP: Look for the link below the Email Notifications check box called View All Email Settings for Your Pages. See it? We suggest that you click it. When you do, you're taken to a page that shows all your e-mail notification settings. You may want to go through this page, as we were surprised by how many e-mail notification settings we needed to change, especially for apps.

Look for the Pages section, which has four check boxes:

- Makes You a Page Admin
- Suggests Page to You
- Weekly Page Updates for Admins
- Change Email Settings for Individual Pages

You can make your own decision about the first two options, but we suggest that you select the Weekly Page Updates for Admins option because it gives you a nice summary of the activity of all the Pages you Admin for the previous week. You can see this info in Insights (see Book IX, Chapter 2 for more about Insights), but in the meantime, these updates are good to receive. The updates are sent to the e-mail address you used to open your personal Profile with Facebook.

TIP: If you click Change Email Settings for Individual Pages, a dialog box appears, listing all the Pages you have created. You can select or deselect e-mail notifications for each Page in that dialog box.

Pages Manager Mobile Notifications

Checking this box will send push notifications to the Pages Manager mobile app when people post or comment on your Page. If you do not use this particular app, you can keep it unchecked.

Onsite Notification

If you prefer to have a Facebook Notification any time someone posts or comments on your Page, check this box.

You can check one, two, or all three of these notifications options if you wish.

Manage Permissions

Back on your Page dashboard, clicking the Manage Permissions link opens an editing page with options that determine how a person can interact with your Page. We want to explain each option on this page, because these options directly affect how first-time and loyal visitors see and network on your Page.

- **Page Visibility:** We discuss the Page Visibility check box in detail in Chapter 2 of this minibook. Selecting this check box hides your Page from the public until it's ready for viewing.
- **Country Restrictions:** When you leave this field blank, anyone can see the Page whether she is logged into Facebook or not. When you type a country's name in this field, you can select the country's name that is autosuggested. Then you have two radio button choices: Only show this page to viewers in these countries or Hide this page from viewers in these countries.
- **Age Restrictions:** The default setting allows anyone older than 13 to see your Page. If you need to restrict viewing to people older than 17, 18, 19, or 21, you can set that level by choosing it from the drop-down menu.

  If you're promoting a business connected with alcohol, the Alcohol-Related age restriction sets the minimum age based on the location of the user. Only users in Canada and South Korea who are 19 or older, users in Japan and Paraguay who are 20 or older, users in India who are 25 or older, and users elsewhere (including the United States) who are 21 or older can view your Page. Facebook makes the point quite clearly that you are ultimately responsible for who sees your Page, however.
- **Posting Ability:** This section has two check boxes: Everyone Can Post to the Page's Timeline and Everyone Can Add Photos and Videos to the Page's Timeline. Checking these boxes allows anyone to create a new post directly on the Page's Timeline. If you prefer to have people only be able to comment on the Page's own posts and not as a new post on the Timeline, then uncheck these two boxes. You can read Book IV, Chapter 2, where we discuss this more thoroughly.

  Sometimes, you want (or don't want) random visitors to be able to post videos or photos on your Page. You can always remove random spam posts, but you can nip spam in the bud by not allowing outside posts.
- **Post Visibility:** You can collect all the posts that others make on your Timeline by checking this box. Then you can decide whether you want to make these posts visible or hide them from the Page. After reviewing the posts, you can highlight any of them so they show up in the Highlight view.
- **Tagging Ability:** Check this box to allow people to tag photos they take with the name of your Page. Think this one through. If your business sponsors events or has products that are sold in stores, you want your fans to be able to take a photo and tag your Page so those photos end up in your Page's albums. But some people use this feature to get the attention of a Page or to spam the Page. To remove a tag, view the photo

and click the Options button at the bottom of the photo, and then select Report/Remove tag. Then select the radio button to remove the tag.

- **Messages:** When you check this box, people can message the Page just like they can message a person's personal Profile. We discussed this earlier in this chapter in the section, "Touring the Admin panel."
- **Moderation Blocklist:** You can add comma-separated keywords that Facebook automatically marks as spam if they show up in a post to your Page or in a comment on a post.
- **Profanity Blocklist:** The drop-down list gives you three choices; None, Medium, and Strong. We know that we should come up with a witty description here, but &*%@# if we can! Seriously, if you think that people might come by your Page and use profanity, choose Medium or Strong.
- **Delete *Page Name*:** The Delete *Page Name* option erases this Page. Keep in mind that you can't undo this action. Deleting a Page deletes everything — photos, posts, and so on. Make sure that you copy everything you want from the Page before you choose this option.

  If you delete a Page for which you had already set a vanity URL (and you want to use that particular URL for a new Page), that URL won't be available for at least 14 days after deletion. If it isn't available after that period, you need to file an infringement form with Facebook and ask to use it again. It may be easier to just hide the Page by selecting the Page Visibility check box at the top of the Manage Permissions section. Find the infringement form at `www.facebook.com/help/contact/?id=208282075858952`.

Basic Information

Remember all that work you did to figure out the type and category you wanted when you created your Page? Remember the Info editing? Well, if not, that's okay. You can edit everything on your Page's Info tab by clicking the Basic Information link on your administrative dashboard.

The fields you find on the Basic Information tab are specific to the category and Page type you selected when creating your Page. You can change the category and Page type for your Page by choosing new settings from the drop-down menus. The first drop-down menu allows you to choose a new category for your Page; the second drop-down menu allows you to choose a new Page type. Make sure that you click Save Changes before editing the fields, because those fields might change with the category change.

Fill in all the fields, remembering that you don't have to stick to what the fields are asking for. The Founded field, for example, allows you to have up to 260 characters, but you don't have to use that many. This is what one of our writers put in that space:

2010 The Year of Becoming Socially Congruent! We start with being congruent at your very core – who you are – then work our way out to the way you use social media to market what you do. All of the layers need to be congruent, like nesting triangles.

You can also add your Twitter username, website address, LinkedIn profile page, and any number of other things. If you include a web address, make sure to include `http://` so that the address will be hyperlinked.

When you create your Page, the URL is long and unwieldy because it contains your Page's ID number. It looks something like this:

```
http://www.facebook.com/pages/The-Social-Classroom-with-
    Phyllis-Khare/123451234512345
```

What you want is a vanity URL (or pretty URL). Facebook also calls it a username. You want it to look like this:

```
http://facebook.com/TheSocialClassroom
```

Currently, Facebook allows you to create a username right away for at least one Page. If you want to get a vanity URL for several Pages, Facebook may say that you must have at least 25 likes for your Page. If Facebook requests you to garner those 25 likes first, you need to ask your friends, staff members, or members of your large extended family to go to your Page and click the Like button after you have published the Page. However you get those likes, get them as soon as possible, because you want to be able to claim your nice-looking URL for other promotional activities noted in Book IV, Chapter 1.

When you set up your business Page, or when you've reached the requested 25 likes on your Page, navigate to the Basic Information tab from your administrative dashboard, or go directly to `www.facebook.com/username`.

WARNING!

You can use the Username page to set your personal Profile username, too. Make sure that you don't set your business Page name to your personal name! Notice the username page has two sections (see Figure 3-13): one for your personal name and one for your Pages. Your best bet is to set your personal account to your name (such as `www.facebook.com/phylliskhare`) and then set your Page URL.

You may choose a username that Facebook suggests or create your own. Click the Check Availability button to check available usernames. A Username Available box comes up, displaying several things to keep in mind about a username, such as making sure that you have the right to use the name you've selected.

Your username is already set
You can direct your friends to facebook.com/phylliskhare.
Each Page can have a username
Easily direct someone to your Page by setting a username for it. After you set your username, you may only change it once.
Page Name: The Technology Cheerleader
The Technology Cheerleader is not eligible for a username at this time. In the future, The Technology Cheerleader will be able to set a username. Learn more.
Check Availability
Learn more about Facebook usernames.

Figure 3-13: When setting your username for your Page, make sure you are selecting for Pages, not your personal account.

When you have something that you like, and it's available, click Confirm. Now you have a nice, neat URL for your Facebook Page. You can use this URL on everything, including letterhead, websites, and e-mail signatures. We go into great detail on how to use this URL in Book IV. In the meantime, put this URL in your next e-mail to your customers so that they can find you easily on Facebook.

Profile Picture

We show you how to add an image in Chapter 2 of this minibook. In case you haven't already added an image, you can upload a picture from your computer or take a picture with your webcam now.

Please take the time to create a very nice image to act as your Page image. The image can be 180 × 180 pixels. Review Chapter 2 of this minibook to get some good marketing ideas and to review the steps for modifying your thumbnail image.

Featured

The Featured tab has two parts: Likes and Page Owners. We describe both below.

Editing Featured Likes

The Likes section lets you feature up to five Facebook Pages in a section of your Timeline. You can specify which Pages you've liked as your Page will be shown there by selecting five of them as Featured. The steps for liking a Page as your Page and featuring a Page are outlined earlier in this chapter. Click the Edit Featured Likes button and select the check box next to the five Pages you'd like to feature on your Page. Any time you want to feature different Pages, just return to this tab and click the button again and check the five you want.

To have Pages show up in the Likes section of your business Page, follow these steps:

1. **Log in to Facebook as you normally do.**
2. **Click the drop-down arrow in the top-right corner of the page.**
3. **Choose Use Facebook as Page from the drop-down menu.**

   This menu is where you toggle between your personal and Page Profiles. If you're an Admin of several Pages, you need to select the correct Page and then click the Switch button.
4. **Navigate to the Page you want to include in your Like section.**
5. **Click the Like button at the top of that Page.**

When you return to your own business Page, the Page that you liked is listed in the Likes section of your own Page's Timeline. After you like more than five Pages, you need to decide which of these Pages you want to feature.

To adjust which Pages are featured on your Page, follow these steps:

1. **Log in to Facebook as you normally do.**
2. **Go to your Page.**

   You can do this next step as an Admin or as your Page.
3. **Click the Edit Page button at the top of the Admin panel and choose Update Info.**

   This step gives you access to your editing menu.
4. **Click the Featured link.**
5. **Click the Edit Featured Likes button.**

   Now you see all the Pages that you've liked as your Page.
6. **Select the five Pages that you want to feature.**

   If you don't want to feature any Pages, clear all check boxes.
7. **Click Save.**

As we explain at the beginning of this chapter, you can like Pages as your Page now, so if you have been on Facebook for a while and have liked certain business Pages through your personal Profile, you can log in as your Page and like those Pages as your Page.

Editing Featured Page Owners

The second section of the Featured tab, called Page Owners, raises the curtain on the Admins of the Page. Some businesses want to keep that information private; others want the world to know. This section is where you get to make that decision. When you Feature any or all of the Admins, the Admins have their personal-account thumbnail images and their names listed on the Page's Timeline.

Resources

The Resources tab has three sections (Develop Your Page, Connect with People, and Additional Resources) and 11 important links, which you should look at *very* closely. We give you a short overview here; all these links are very big subjects, and some have whole minibooks dedicated to them!

- *Develop Your Page*
  - **Best practices guides to make your Page engaging:** Click through to read Facebook's posts on its own Facebook Page about Pages.
- *Connect with People*
  - **Advertise on Facebook:** Yes, we have a whole minibook dedicated to this topic: Book VIII. For now, we just want to point out that you can find the navigation link to Facebook's advertising section right here. Clicking this link takes you directly to the interface where you can create an ad. Facebook helps you by autopopulating some of the fields, but everything is adjustable. This ad gives you the opportunity to reach hundreds or thousands of people, or a small, highly targeted number of people on Facebook.
  - **Select a Username:** This option is discussed in the "Basic Information" section, earlier in this chapter. You can start the process to create a vanity URL here or in the Basic Information tab, as the link there is identical. This step is a must-do for all business Pages.
  - **Invite Email Contacts:** We discuss this process in Chapter 2 of this minibook. You can upload a contact file or find your e-mail contacts that are already on Facebook and then invite your contacts to view and like your Page. After your Page is put together, you definitely want to come back to this link and complete this step.
  - **Use Social Plugins:** When you click the link, you see ten links to the different types of plug-ins you can create: Like Button, Send Button, Subscribe Button, Comments, Activity Feed, Recommendations Box, Like Box, Login Button, Registration, and Facepile.

    We highly recommend that you place a Like box on your regular website. The process for adding a Like box to your website is fully described in Book VII, Chapter 2.

A Like box allows people to like your Facebook Page without leaving the website they're viewing. If you have a website with a Like box installed in its sidebar, people who are reading your blog can click the Like button in the Like box, and they will be connected to (counted as fans of) your Facebook Page without leaving your website.

  - **Link Your Page to Twitter:** Clicking this link takes you to a page where you can attach your Twitter account to your Page, which means that anything you post on your Page also autoposts to Twitter with a link back to your Page.

- *Additional Resources*
  - **Pages Help Center:** This link takes you to Facebook's Help Center for Pages.
  - **Developer Help:** If you're a Facebook app developer, this is the quick link to the Help Center for developers.
  - **Best Practice Guide for Marketing on Facebook:** This link takes you to a nice overview of best practices for Pages.
  - **Brand Permissions:** When you click this link, you go to Facebook's Brand Permission Center — Usage Guidelines page, where you can read all about Facebook's trademark restrictions and see how to keep from crowding the Facebook logo in a way that Facebook doesn't appreciate.
  - **Learn about SEO for Your Page:** This link takes you to a video showing you the basics of search engine optimization.

Admin Roles

Admins are people who can administer your Page. There are five types of Admin roles, which we describe in this list:

- **Manager:** The *Manager* role is what you are when you create the Page. You and anyone else with this designation can edit and delete items on your Page, ban users, post status updates and comments, and send messages to fans. Everything you can do with your Page, Manager Admins can do, too.
- **Content Creator:** Anyone with the *Content Creator* Admin status can edit the Page, create a status update, create ads, and view Insights on your Facebook business Page, and it will look as though the Page made the update, not them personally (unless they change the voice, as discussed at the beginning of this chapter). The status update has the Page thumbnail image and the Page name listed. A Content Creator can do everything that a Manager can do except add or remove Admins.

- **Moderator:** The *Moderator* Admin status allows someone to reply to comments, ban and block people, send messages, create ads, and view Insights, but not to create a post on the Page.
- **Advertiser:** The *Advertiser* Admin status allows someone to view Insights and to create and manage ads on behalf of the Page.
- **Insights Analyst:** The *Insights Analyst* Admin status lets someone into the Insights interface and download data from that area.

TIP

Here are some quick points about being an Admin of a Page:

- You can have as many Admins and Admin types as you want.
- Always have at least one other person as your Manager Admin in case you're unavailable to make changes in other Manager roles.
- All Admins need to click the Your Settings link on the navigation menu to adjust the e-mail notification settings and must understand the voice process. By default, Facebook selects the e-mail notification check box for all activity on the Page. This setting means that all Admins receive e-mail notification whenever someone posts or comments on the Page unless Admins deselect it. We discuss this topic in the "Your Settings" section, earlier in the chapter.
- You can remove your Admin status (or have another Admin remove you). Then you view your Page just the way any fan of your Page does. You don't see the Admin panel, and when you post, you post from your personal Profile. You don't receive any e-mail notifications for the Page.
- Facebook requires each Page to have at least one Manager Admin. If you try to remove yourself as a Manager Admin before adding someone else, you won't be able to remove yourself.

Here are the steps for adding someone to your Page as any type of Admin:

1. **Go to your Page, and click the Edit Page button.**
2. **Click Admin Roles in the drop-down choices.**
3. **Type the name or e-mail address of the person you want to add as an Admin.**

   If you start typing the name, Facebook displays suggestions; just click a name to select it. You need to be a Friend of this person to be able to add him or her as an Admin this way.

   If you aren't the person's Facebook Friend, you can add the e-mail address that he or she used to open the Facebook account. The person receives a Facebook notification and needs to accept the invitation to be an Admin of the Page.

4. **Choose the Admin role from the drop-down menu.**
5. **Click the Save Changes button.**

   A security dialog box will come up where you have to enter your personal Facebook password.
6. **Enter your Facebook password as a security step and click Confirm.**

Now that person is added to the list of Admins for the Page.

Here are the steps for removing someone as an Admin of your Page:

1. **Go to your Page, and click the Edit Page button.**
2. **Click Admin Roles in the drop-down choices.**
3. **Click the X next to the name of the person you want to remove.**

   If you're removing yourself, click the X next to your name.

   You won't be able to edit your Page or gain access to Insights, ads, notifications, and so on when you remove yourself as an Admin. If you try to remove yourself as an Admin before adding another Manager Admin, you won't be able to remove yourself.
4. **Click Save Changes.**
5. **Enter your Facebook password as a security step and click Confirm.**

Apps

Apps (or applications) are developed by third parties, or by Facebook itself, to expand the functions of Facebook. Thousands of apps are available. You can connect an app to your Page to expand what people can do on your Page. Facebook doesn't have a functioning app directory for businesses at this writing, so if you want to take a more-focused approach, a nice place to explore all the apps that have to do with a business application is Appbistro (`http://appbistro.com`).

When you create a new Page, you need to activate a few apps right away, because they create important links that people will be looking for on your Page. These apps, developed by Facebook, are

- Photos
- Video
- Events (if your business will be having them)

Chapter 4 of this minibook explains all the steps for adding applications to your new Page.

Applications are so important to Facebook that we discuss them in all nine minibooks, especially Book V.

Mobile

When you select the Mobile link, you have the opportunity to create three kinds of mobile connections to your Page:

- **With Mobile E-mail:** We discuss your mobile e-mail options in Chapter 1 of this minibook, but to recap, you can send a post or upload a photo to your Page by using an e-mail address created specifically for your Page. Facebook puts your unique e-mail address in this section for easy reference. What you type in the subject line of the e-mail on your mobile phone becomes the update to your Page, or if you're uploading a photo, the subject line becomes the caption. Nothing that you type in the body of the e-mail shows up, so leave it blank.
- **With Mobile Web:** You can see how your Page looks on a mobile phone by typing its URL in the phone's browser. It's easier to type in a custom URL on a mobile device, so Facebook put a link for creating a Page username in this part of the dashboard. The link to create a custom URL is `http://facebook.com/username`.

  If you type **www.facebook.com/thesocialclassroom** on an Android phone, for example, you're redirected to `http://m.facebook.com/thesocialclassroom` (notice the `m`). It turns out that your phone is so smart, it knows when you're looking at Facebook on a phone, so it directs you to the mobile interface for Facebook. Your Page will look a bit different from how it looks on a computer, so make sure that you check it.

  You can also type **http://touch.facebook.com/*yourpagename*** to see how your Page will look to those who view it on a phone.
- **With the iPhone:** First, install the Facebook app on your iPhone or iPad; then log in. When you click the menu icon (a box with three horizontal lines), you see the Pages for which you're an Admin in the left navigation menu.

  TIP: We recommend that you get the Facebook Page Manager app. You can do a search in the App Store for it. It's really handy if you manage several Pages.

Insights

Clicking the Insights link on your administrative dashboard takes you directly to your Insights dashboard.

Insights is Facebook's analytics system. You can see who uses your Page, as well as see her interactions, age, and gender; where she lives; and her cats' names (well, no, not yet). You can also see very detailed graphs about the users of your Page and their interactions with it. Get acquainted with the Insights dashboard, because it can really help you see who your audience is and give you insight into what people respond to most on your Page.

There's so much to this wonderful analytics program that we dedicate an entire chapter — Book IX, Chapter 2 — to it.

Help

This link is your direct link to the Facebook Help directory. Even though this link is simply named Help, it links directly to the business Pages Help section rather than to some general Facebook help page. The page has many sections with a wealth of information to help you with your Page.

We feel that it's good to go straight to the horse's mouth (what does that mean, anyway?) when we have a question about Facebook. That's why this link to the Help section for Pages is handy to have on the editing menu.

Consider bookmarking these other sites for help reference:

- **AllFacebook:** `www.allfacebook.com`
- **Mashable:** `www.mashable.com`

Deals

If your Page is a Places Page (review Book II, Chapter 1) you will see a link for Deals on your dashboard menu. We explain Deals in great detail in Book VII, Chapter 4.

Chapter 4: Arranging What Your Visitors See

In This Chapter

- Finding your new Page
- Understanding how apps act as navigation links
- Changing the order of the apps
- Using the hover card as an ad

You and your Page Admins need to be very familiar with how your Page looks to visitors on Facebook. In Chapter 3 of this minibook, we discuss how to present yourself when new visitors arrive on your Page. In this chapter, we tell you how to move your apps around and switch up your Cover image for the best impact on the Page and in the News Feed.

Finding Your Page

The first question we get from marketers who are new to Facebook is, "How do I find my Page?" Facebook used to make it hard to find one's own Page, but it has since created a left-column bookmarks menu that contains links to everything you need, as shown in Figure 4-1. Click More to see the whole list. ***Note:*** You see this bookmarks menu when you're viewing your personal Profile's News Feed.

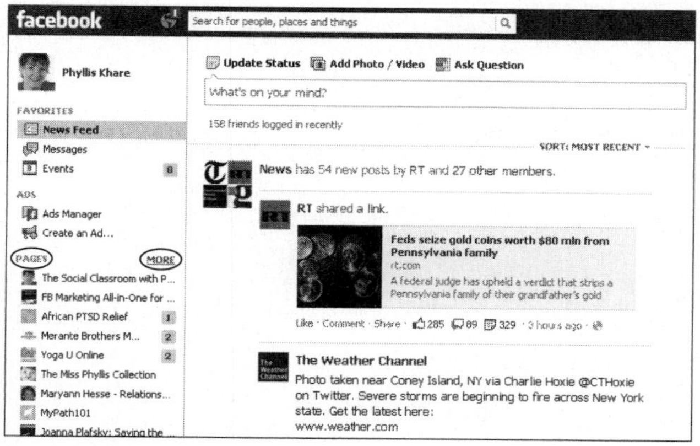

Figure 4-1: The bookmarks menu appears to the left of your News Feed.

You can find your Page easily by using any of the following options:

- **Look for the Page name in the left column of your personal account's News Feed.** Any Page that you created or serve as Admin for will be listed there, below the heading, Pages. If you are an Admin for more than four Pages, click the More link that shows up when you hover over the Page names. Doing so opens a new page with all your Pages listed.
- **Add the Page's username to the browser bar after** `www.facebook.com`**.** After you obtain a vanity URL (see Chapter 3 of this minibook to create one), you can add the username to the Facebook URL in your browser bar and then bookmark the URL on your computer for easy access. This is how an URL looks after you add the vanity URL: `www.facebook.com/`*`yourusername`*. Here are a few examples:

  `www.facebook.com/AmyPorterfield`

  `www.facebook.com/The SocialClassroom`

  `www.facebook.com/GrandmaMaryShow`
- **Use the Facebook search bar.** This search bar is at the top of every Facebook page. Start typing your Page's username, and Facebook displays it for you to select. If your business Page doesn't come up as you type, type the name of the Page completely and then click the See More Results link at the bottom of Facebook's suggestions list.

  You arrive on a search page that lists multiple Pages, people, groups, and so on with names similar to what you typed. You have the option of filtering these results via the options on the left sidebar. Those options are as follows:

  - All Results
  - People
  - Pages
  - Places
  - Groups
  - Apps
  - Events
  - Music
  - Web Results
  - Posts by Friends
  - Public Posts
  - Posts in Groups

To find your business Page, select the Pages option. You should see your Page's name. Click it to go to your Page.

TIP

The nice thing about this search interface is that you can see how the keywords in your Page name are showing up on Facebook and on the web; to do so, scroll down the Search Results page and see how those keywords show up in other people's posts (and in classic web searches). Select each of the filters (Pages, Groups, Events, and so on) to view the results.

Understanding How Apps Act as Navigation Links

In Chapter 3 of this minibook, we give you a little tour of a business Page and show you where everything is located. The boxes below your Cover image that you and your visitors see on your Page are actually *applications* (usually referred to as *apps*). Apps are add-ons that provide extra functionality to your Page. We explain them a bit in Chapter 3 of this minibook and more thoroughly in Book V. In this chapter, we show you how to move them around for the best impact.

As we note in Chapter 3 of this minibook, when you create your Page, the public sees only two apps: Photos and Likes (if at least one person has liked the Page). You can add some great apps to the app section right away, such as Events, Notes, and Video. These apps were developed and designed by Facebook, so they're in the queue (so to speak), ready to be added to your Page. In Chapter 3 of this minibook and in all the following minibooks (especially Books IV and V), we describe how to add custom-built links, such as Welcome links, store links, YouTube links, and hundreds of others.

Apps act as gateways. You can set up an app to take people back to

- ✦ Your website's home page
- ✦ Your product pages (not on Facebook)
- ✦ Your sales pages
- ✦ Your contest pages

Using a simple image and a link, you can create an app space to link anywhere.

You can also create a Facebook ad that goes right back to the app. If you have a webinar sign-up app, for example, you can create an ad that's linked directly to that sign-up interface. You can target the ad to your existing fans or use the app as a fan-gate, requiring a visitor to like your Page to get the webinar info.

If you have a contest, create an ad that links right back to that app on your Page. Design the app so that visitors need to click Like to see the contest rules and enter the contest. This is a fantastic way to garner more likes for your Page and to create buzz and excitement about your contest.

TIP

You should know that after their initial visit to your business Page, most people view your Page's updates only via their News Feeds and tickers; they will rarely visit your actual business Page. Facebook has added a new feature called the *hover card,* which shows your Cover image, Profile image, and Page category when a reader mouses over your Page name in his or her News Feed. We go over that topic in a moment. If you want your audience to visit your Page and explore your other apps, you need to provide strong calls to action in your status updates and provide a link directly to the app. Examples of a call to action include a request to like your Page, join an Event, or participate in a contest. To develop a stronger sense of community, bringing people back to your Page is an important goal.

Adding Facebook Apps to Your Page

The number of Facebook-developed apps that are available is getting smaller and smaller. Currently, four Facebook apps are available: Photos, Notes, Video, and Events. Generally, these apps appear on your Page by default. To make sure that your visitors can see all of them, follow these steps:

1. **Go to your Page, and click the Edit Page button in the Admin panel.**
2. **Click Update Info.**

   Your administrative dashboard opens.
3. **Click Apps in the left column.**

   The Apps tab shows all the apps you currently have connected to your Page.
4. **Find the app that you want to add to the apps section of your Page Timeline, and click the Edit Settings link below the name of the app.**

   A dialog box appears. For most default applications (such as Notes, Photos, and Events), this dialog box has two tabs: Profile and Additional Permissions. For other applications (both default and custom), this dialog box has only a Profile tab.
5. **Click the Add link on the Profile tab.**

   What you see next depends on the app you're adding. We note those variations later.

6. **Click the Additional Permissions tab (if it's there).**

   Decide whether you want the app to be able to post to the Page Timeline. For the Photos app, for example, click the permission box if you want photos to be posted to the Page Timeline each time you upload and publish a photo.

7. **Click Okay.**

   The app is listed in your Page's app section for all to see.

TIP

You can use these instructions to turn on any of the following Facebook apps.

Events app

If your business has Events, you may want to add this link by following the steps in the preceding section. Figure 4-2 shows a convention center's Events page. Notice that the interface has tabs for Upcoming Events and Past Events.

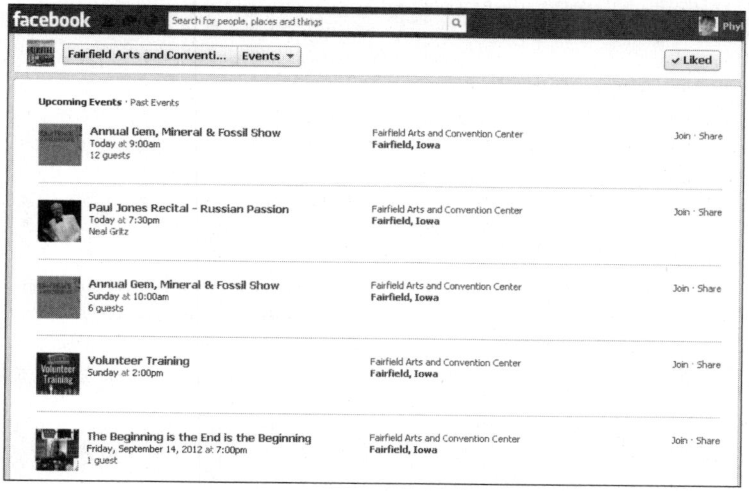

Figure 4-2: The Events application lists the Events that your business wants to showcase.

If you click an Event title, you're taken to that particular Event's Page. Using Facebook Events for marketing is discussed thoroughly in Book VI, Chapter 1.

Photos app

This application is automatically the first app in the app section for a new Page. Since Facebook has re-designed the whole photo interface (with a grid-style photos stream, and the ability to like and comment on the photo thumbnails), you want to make sure your photos are a great addition to your Page.

Having this app on your Page allows visitors to see the photos you've uploaded to your Page and photos that have been tagged with your Page's name (if you set that option in your Page settings). You can arrange your photos in custom-titled albums, but Facebook keeps your Profile images in one album called Profile Pictures (and you can't change the name of this album).

If you post a photo to the Page Timeline, Facebook puts it in an album called Wall Photos. You can't change the name of this album, either, but you can delete photos that end up in this album. We discuss photo uploading, arranging, album naming, and the world of images in Book IV, Chapter 1.

As we discuss in Chapter 3 of this minibook, you can prevent a liker from posting photos to your Page by making the appropriate setting in the Manage Permissions section of your administrative dashboard.

People who click the Photo app on your Page see your Page's Photos Stream. This is a tight grid of all the photos you, as your Page, have uploaded. There are three tabs at the top: Photos of the Page (photos that are tagged with your Page name), Photos (that you as your Page have uploaded), and Albums. Clicking the Photo app on your Page takes users to the middle tab — Photos. (Notice each photo has the interface to like the photo and comment without having to open the photo to full view.)

When users click the Album tab they see as the album thumbnails. If you hover over an album thumbnail a five-image slideshow starts inside the thumbnail space. It's a nice little touch to quickly see if this is the album you want to open.

When you click any album, another grid appears with the same set up of seeing the Like and comments interface on the thumbnails of the photos in the album. When you finally click on an individual photo, a lightbox opens. A *lightbox* is a dialog box that shows specific information — in this case, your photos, descriptions, and any comments. The lightbox has arrows on either side so that the visitor can move through the photo album one image at a time. Four hidden links show up when a visitor hovers over the bottom of any image: Tag Photo, Options, Share, and Like.

If you are an Admin of the Page, below the Options link you see several other links: Add Location, Change Date, Rotate Left, Rotate Right, Download, Make Profile Picture for Page, Delete this Photo, and Enter Fullscreen. Your visitors to your photos see only Download, Report This Photo, and Enter Fullscreen.

You can use photos like ads because you can upload an image of your promotional page or text and, in the description section, place the hyperlinked URL that people can click to buy a product or sign up for something. Figure 4-3 shows an example of how much information you can put in the description section. We spend some time on the marketing possibilities of photos in Facebook in Book IV, Chapter 1.

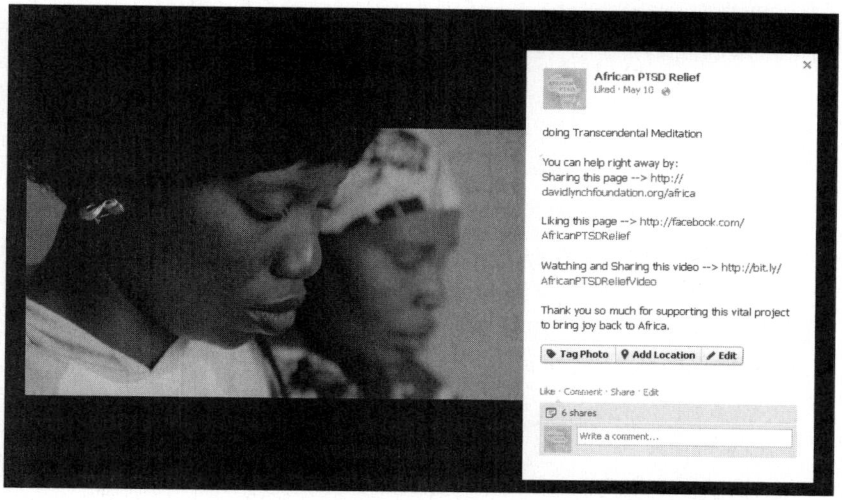

Figure 4-3: Notice the full description (on right) that includes links.

Notes app

A *note* is a public post and appears in the News Feed for all fans to see, and anyone tagged in the note receives a notification. The Notes app used to be the only place to publish a really long post, but now you can have an almost unlimited number of characters (currently more than 63,000) in a regular post, too. We like to think of a note as being similar to a blog post. You can title the note, upload a photo with it, and add some formatting (bold, italic, underline, bullets, numbering and quotations) to it. The people who are tagged receive a notification and can view the note. (They can untag themselves if they don't want to be attached to the note publicly.)

You can create a note and tag people and Pages to view it. You can tag your Friends and any Facebook Page. When you create a note, a notification appears in your Page Timeline and goes out to your likers' News Feeds for everyone to see.

You can consider the Notes apps as a blog, an additional blog, or a larger posting space. You can create a special type of conversation among you and your likers. This conversation space could be for people who are enthusiastic about a particular subject. If you've already added the Notes app to your app section (see the generic instructions in "Adding Facebook Apps to Your Page," earlier in this chapter), follow these steps to create and manage your notes:

1. **Click the Notes app in your Page's app section below the Cover image.**

   If you don't see the app, you need to add it to the app section (refer to "Adding Facebook Apps to Your Page," earlier in this chapter).

2. **Click the +Write a Note button in the top-right corner.**

   This button opens an editing space where you can create a title, type the text of the note, tag people and/or Pages, add a photo, preview, save a draft, and publish.

3. **Enter the title and body of the note.**

   You can use a few editing tools, such as bold and italic.

   A note can be really long. How long? We don't know exactly, but we've seen up to five pages' worth fit in there. So write away!

4. **Tag people and Pages.**

   To tag a person or a Page, start typing the person's name or the Page name in the Tag field. Facebook displays a list of your Friends and Pages. Click the ones you want to tag (see Figure 4-4).

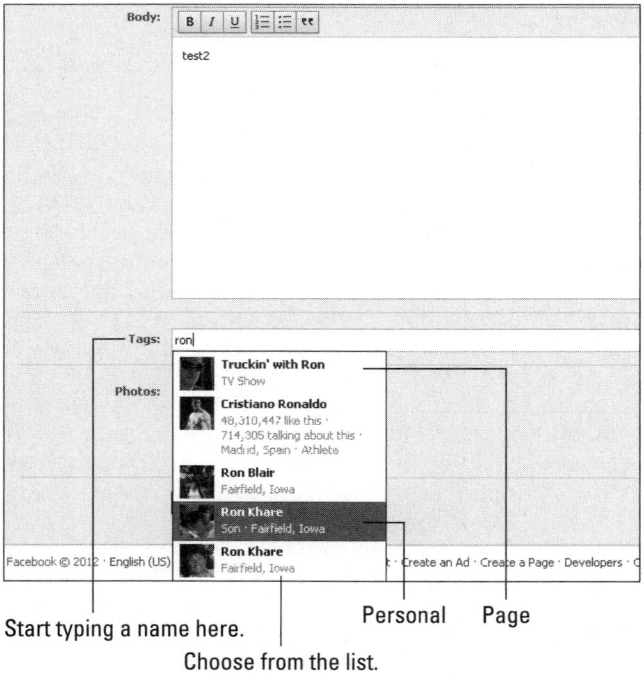

Figure 4-4: Tag a person or Page in your note.

5. **Click the Add a Photo link, find the photo on your computer, and upload it.**
6. **Click Publish, Preview, Save Draft, or Discard.**

   You can decide how to proceed with this step:

   - *Publish:* Your note is published to the world! The note shows up as a Page status update and appears in likers' News Feeds. Any people or Pages you've tagged are notified. Anyone can read and comment on your note.
   - *Preview:* When you click Preview, you see exactly how your note will look when viewed. It has two links at the top: Publish and Edit. You can edit the note by clicking Edit or go ahead with the publishing process by clicking Publish.
   - *Save Draft:* The next time you want to edit the note, look for the Notes app box. When you click that box, a Page Name Drafts link appears next to the Page's name. Click the Drafts link and you see a list of all your note drafts (see Figure 4-5). Just click the title you want to start editing. Non-Admins won't see the link to your drafts.
   - *Discard:* Discarding a note removes it from your drafts. Discard is a way to delete before something is published.

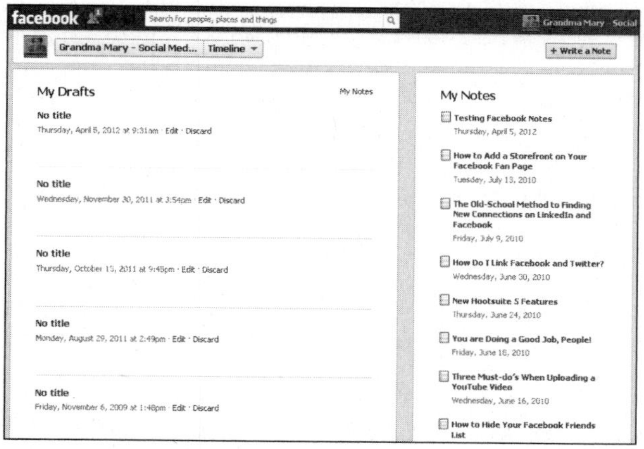

Figure 4-5: Click the Notes app box and then the link to your drafts to choose the Note to edit.

When your visitors click the Notes app, they go to an interface with your notes on the left and notes by other Pages they've liked on the right.

Many Pages use the Notes app to create a daily list of events in their stores or a daily webinar schedule with quick links to the Event pages. There are many ways to use this particular app.

Video app

Here's another app that you may need to think through before you add it to your Page's app section. Facebook's Video app may not be the best app for you to use on your Page. If your business uses a lot of videos, you may want to explore a few third-party apps before making a final decision to add this one. We discuss using the YouTube app for marketing in Book III, Chapter 1.

Here are a few points about the Facebook-built Video app:

- If you post a status update with a YouTube URL, the video won't show up on the Video page. You have to upload or record a video with the Facebook Video app for the video to be listed on the Video page.
- Facebook doesn't provide a lightbox interface for videos, the way it does for photos.
- If people share your Page's video by posting it to their Timelines, users have the option to like your Page by clicking a Like button in the corner.

One of the most interesting features of the Facebook Video app is that it allows you to record and post a video directly from your webcam. Right there — right now — with your pajamas on! Seriously, though, if your business has updates that need to be posted quickly, you may want to try this feature. Facebook lets you record up to 20 minutes of video. Click the Video app on your Page and then click the +Add Video button in the top-right corner of the page. When the Add Videos page appears, instead of clicking the Upload button, click the Record button. The procedure is discussed in Book III, Chapter 1.

Changing the Order of Apps on Your Page

All apps on your business Page, except Photos, can be rearranged from side to side and top to bottom. Four apps, called Featured apps, are visible. When you click the down arrow, you see up to 12 more apps, and called Favorites. You can add and remove apps from Favorites. To rearrange the order of the apps, follow these steps:

1. **Click the down arrow next to your apps to expand all the apps you have available.**
2. **Mouse over the app you want to move.**

   You see a pencil icon in the top-right corner of the app, as shown in Figure 4-6.

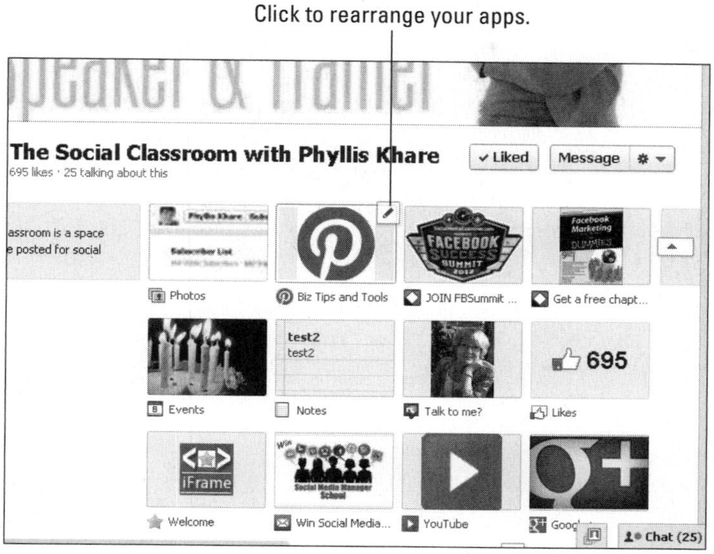

Figure 4-6: Hover over an app to reveal the pencil icon.

3. **Click the pencil icon.**

   A drop-down menu appears.

4. **From the drop-down menu, choose the app to swap.**
5. **Click the arrow next to your apps again to see how the new lineup looks.**

   You may need to repeat this process several times to get the apps in the positions where you want them.

After clicking the pencil icon, you can also choose Remove from Favorites to make the app box disappear. You can still get to the apps you've removed; see Chapter 2 of this minibook for details.

Using the Hover Card as an Ad

A nice little feature that Facebook has added recently is the hover card (see Figure 4-7). A *hover card* is a little pop-up box that contains a quick view of information about a Page or person (including the Cover photo, Profile image, or Page category) when you hover your cursor over the person's or Page's name in your News Feed.

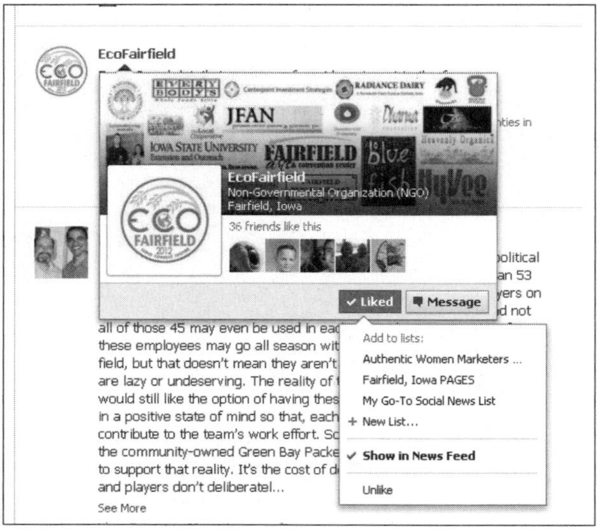

Figure 4-7: Hover cards give you a quick view of information about a person or Page.

Notice how many things you can do from a hover card:

- ✦ Like or unlike a Page
- ✦ Request to be a Friend or subscriber
- ✦ Add to an Interest List or create a custom list for the person or Page
- ✦ Message the person or Page
- ✦ Select to show in the News Feed or not

The nice thing about a hover card is the overall impression it gives. See Figure 4-8 for a well-done Page design with a really nice hover card that works as an ad without being an ad!

Figure 4-8: This hover card for New Media Expo looks like a wonderful ad without being an ad.

To create beautiful hover cards like the one shown in Figure 4-8, do the following:

- ✦ Make sure your Page's Cover photo is an inviting image that conveys the spirit of your upcoming event.
- ✦ Create and upload a new Profile image that includes the dates and location of the upcoming event.
- ✦ Check your Page type under Edit Page, Update Info. Change the category in the fields provided.

Once you have completed these tasks, hover over your own Page's name in the Timeline and see how your hover card looks.

Chapter 5: Using Your Personal Profile to Support Your Business

In This Chapter

- Finding out whether you should turn on your Subscribe button
- Understanding how to post publicly
- Posting business milestones on your personal Profile
- Changing your Public Timeline to support your business
- Using personal Cover photos that support your business

We deliberately crafted the title of this chapter. Notice the word *support* in the title. We're not suggesting that you turn your personal Profile into a straight-up business Page. Please make sure that you understand the difference between a personal Profile and a business Page by reading all of this minibook!

What we're saying is that you can use your personal Profile to support your business in some very specific ways, such as finding out if the Subscribe button is right for you, understanding the difference between a Public post and a Friends post and how you can use photos on your personal Profile that support your business without breaking any Facebook rules.

Facebook realized that there are people in this world who are best served by a modified personal Profile instead of a business Page. These people are considered to be public figures. Are you a public figure? Maybe you are but don't realize it!

Determining Whether the Subscribe Button Is for You

The Subscribe button is something you can *turn on* inside your personal Profile so that people can *subscribe to* your *public updates.* We describe each of these terms in this list:

- **Turn on:** You can switch this system on, and you can switch it off. (You need to make a few adjustments when you turn it on.)
- **Subscribe:** This is a one-way connection inside Facebook. You can subscribe to someone without being his or her Friend. You and your Friends are subscribed to one another. If you are subscribed to someone, but they aren't subscribed to you, you see their Public posts, but

they don't see yours. Once you turn on your Subscribe button anyone, anywhere in the world can subscribe to your Public posts.

- **Public updates:** You can post an update that is designated as Public, which means that anyone can see it, including your Friends and those who have subscribed to you. And as an added bonus, if someone has requested to be your Friend and you haven't responded, he is automatically a subscriber and will see your Public posts.

The *biggest pro* for turning on the Subscribe button is that there's no limit on the number of subscribers you can have. (In comparison, the Friend limit on Facebook is currently 5,000.) You can go through your Friend list and unfriend people you don't really know, and they will automatically become a Subscriber. This cleans up your Friends list. The *biggest con* for turning on the Subscribe button is having to create Public posts. Public posts are generally different from what you might be used to posting on Facebook. The public is not so interested in your cat, but it might be very interested in your work with the Humane Society. There is a difference in those two kinds of posts, and you'll need to remember to make both.

So now you need to determine whether you are a public figure and whether you should go through the process of turning on your Subscribe button. Through this process, you also see whether you need to have both a personal Profile with the Subscribe button turned on *and* a business Page. Table 5-1 shows the different available features for a personal Timeline with the Subscribe button and a business Page.

Note: Turning on your Subscribe button is available only to those over the age of 18.

Table 5-1 Which Facebook Features Do You Need?

Available Features	*Personal Timeline + Subscribe Button*	*Business Page*
Use for both Friends and a bigger audience	X	
Quick mobile updating	X	
Timeline applications (personal)	X	
Interest Lists/Groups/Chat	X	
Privacy settings	X	
Timeline layout	X	X
Facebook Insights		X
Multiple people can Admin		X
Custom tabs and apps		X
Target Updates by Location/Language		X
Promote with Ads and Sponsored Stories		X

Here is a series of questions to ask yourself to determine whether the Subscribe button is right for you. Keep count of how many questions you answer "Yes." By the end of the quiz, it will be obvious whether you need to continue reading this chapter!

- **Do you consider yourself to be a public figure?**

  Public figure is a slippery term. Facebook says that authors, magazine and newspaper writers, politicians, actors, and radio and TV personalities are public figures, but there are other definitions too.

- **Do others consider you to be a public figure?**

  When others think of you, do they think "public figure"? You may be a spokesperson for some type of event (local, regional, or national), or you may represent a topic (such as a conversation in your business niche or a nonprofit organization).

- **Are you considered to be an expert in your field?**

  Do people seek you out when they have a question about your business niche? Do you speak about your business niche at events?

- **When people look at you, do they think of your business?**

  Most small-business people carry both sides of their lives — business and personal — with them wherever they go. If you're walking down the street, and someone says "Hi," does he or she also ask you about your family or your business or both?

- **Do you like to share things that are business related?**

  Look back at your personal posts on Facebook for the past year. How many of them are related to your business niche? Would you share more of those types of posts if you felt that people wanted to see them?

- **Do you have people who want to be your Facebook Friends but are really business contacts?**

  Have people who you don't know personally asked to be your Friends? Have you ignored a bunch of people who've asked to be your Friends?

- **Are you branding yourself?**

  Are you setting yourself up to be a public figure in the future? Do you want to be a public figure?

- **Are you and your products the same thing?**

  Do you sell information products that feature you as the expert?

- **Are you branding your company to include you?**

  Apple=Steve Jobs. Is that the kind of relationship you have with your company?

Don't turn on your Subscribe button if you answered most of the questions "No."

Do turn on your Subscribe button if

- ✦ You answered most of the questions "Yes."
- ✦ You're branding yourself.
- ✦ You're branding your products, and people think of you and your products together.

If you're branding your company, you don't *have* to turn on your Subscribe button. If you enjoy your business and have a great passion for it, though, consider turning on the button so that you can expand your territory of influence.

We show you how to turn on your Subscribe button in the next section. Anyone can turn on his Subscribe button. (Even people who answered "No" to all the previous questions.) You can turn it on to test it out and turn it off if it doesn't work for you.

Turning On Your Subscribe Button

Now that you have an answer to the question about whether to turn on your Subscribe button — and the answer is yes — you have to understand some important points about the Subscribe system, which can be very confusing at first.

The word *subscribe* is the word that Facebook uses to explain a *connection.* You and your Friends are subscribed to one another. You're still called Friends, but the *function* is being subscribed.

After you go through the process of turning on your Subscribe button, you won't be able to see the Subscribe button on your Timeline. This aspect is the most frustrating part of teaching people how to turn on the button! Just trust us on this one. The button is there; you just can't see it if you're logged in as yourself.

The easiest way to turn on your Subscribe button is to go to `www.facebook.com/about/subscribe%20` and click the big green Allow Subscribers button shown in Figure 5-1. And then read the next section to understand the setting options.

Another way to turn on your Subscribe button is to follow these steps:

1. **Click the drop-down arrow at the top-right of any Facebook page and click Account Settings.**
2. **In the left sidebar, click Subscribers.**

   Now you are on a page with several sections. The top section is called Allow Subscribers.

3. **Select the check box to allow subscribers.**

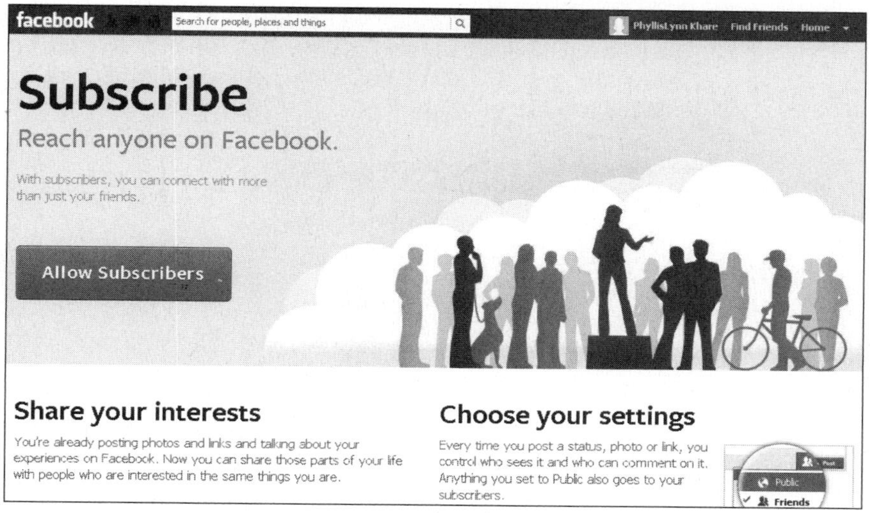
facebook
Search for people, places and things
PhyllisLynn Khare
Find Friends
Home
Subscribe
Reach anyone on Facebook.
With subscribers, you can connect with more than just your friends.
Allow Subscribers
Share your interests
You're already posting photos and links and talking about your experiences on Facebook. Now you can share those parts of your life with people who are interested in the same things you are.
Choose your settings
Every time you post a status, photo or link, you control who sees it and who can comment on it. Anything you set to Public also goes to your subscribers.
Public
Friends

Figure 5-1: Click the Allow Subscribers button to start the process of turning on your Subscribe button.

No matter how you turn on your Subscribe button, you need to continue the process and edit your settings for comments and notifications. We will get to that in the next section. Here are a few interesting points about the Subscribe button:

✦ When subscribers click your Subscribe button, they can choose (as shown in Figure 5-2) which types of your public updates they get: Life Events, Status Updates, Photos, Games, Comments and Likes, Music and Videos, and Other Activity.

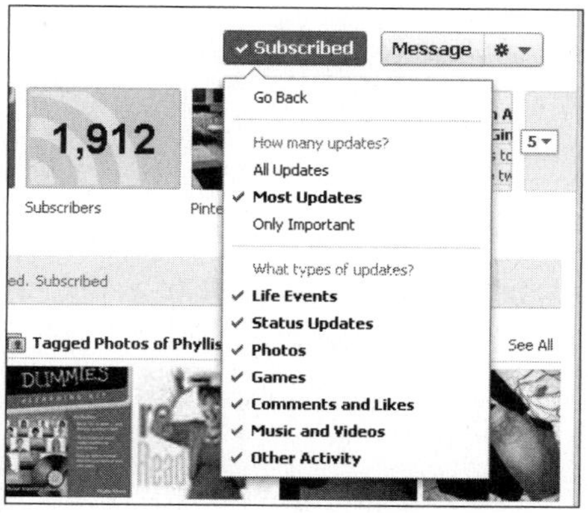
✓ Subscribed
Message
1,912
Subscribers
Go Back
How many updates?
All Updates
✓ Most Updates
Only Important
What types of updates?
✓ Life Events
✓ Status Updates
✓ Photos
✓ Games
✓ Comments and Likes
✓ Music and Videos
✓ Other Activity
Tagged Photos of Phyllis
See All

Figure 5-2: Subscribers choose which updates appear in their News Feeds.

- Only people who allow subscribers have a Subscribe button on their Profiles. If you don't see the button on a person's personal Timeline, you can't subscribe to his updates without being his Friend. You see the Add Friend button instead. Sometimes, you see two buttons: Add Friend and Subscribed, as shown in Figure 5-3. When both buttons appear, you know that you've subscribed to this person's Public updates, and you can make a Friend request.

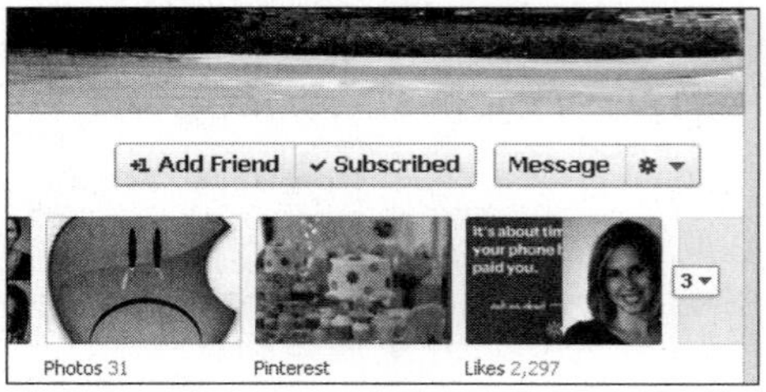

Figure 5-3: Sometimes, you see Add Friend and Subscribed buttons.

How do people subscribe to *your* updates? After you allow subscribers, a Subscribe button shows up on your Profile. Someone would need to visit your Timeline to click the Subscribe button, or click the Subscribe button if your Profile shows up in the ticker, or if Facebook decides to suggest you in the right column above the ads the Subscribe button is there, too. Facebook might change these ways, or add to them in the future. Facebook has also created a nice interface (`www.facebook.com/subscriptions/suggestions`) where you can see all the people who have turned on their Subscribe button.

Subscribers can see only the things on your personal Profile that you share publicly. We show you how to see which things are public on your Timeline in the "Adjusting Your Timeline for Public Viewing" section later in this chapter.

TIP

Avoid heavy sales-type marketing techniques in your Public posts. Even though the subscribe system is like having an opt-in newsletter, you still need to remember that Facebook is a social platform.

Editing the Subscribe Settings

After you turn on your Subscribe button, you need to adjust the settings for Comments and Notifications. Both settings are important, and we explain them both in this section. You can go back and change these settings at any time, so don't stress about them too much at this point. See how everything goes; you'll know what you need to change over time.

When you click the green Allow Subscribers button (refer to Figure 5-1) to turn on your Subscribe button, you see a new dialog box with the following settings to adjust:

- **Subscriber Comments:** Who can comment on your public updates? The drop-down menu lists Everyone, Friends of Friends, and Friends. Think about your choice. If you create Public posts, you want your Subscribers to be able to comment on them, so choose Everyone.
- **Subscriber Notifications:** Notifications tell you when new people subscribe to you, like one of your posts, and so on. You can decide whether you want notifications from Friends of Friends, Everyone, or No One. You can choose Everyone and see how things go. You can always come back and adjust these settings. We show you how to do that in a moment.
- **Username:** If you haven't set your personal Profile username yet, you can click the link and go through the process of creating a nice URL.
- **Twitter:** You can connect or disconnect your personal Profile to your Twitter account here. You can also set it at `http://facebook.com/twitter`.

After you adjust these settings they are automatically saved.

To adjust these settings at a later date, click the Subscribers box on your personal Profile (below your Cover photo) and then click the Settings (gear) icon. The Edit Subscribe Settings dialog box appears, as shown in Figure 5-4. This dialog box allows you to adjust the settings at any time.

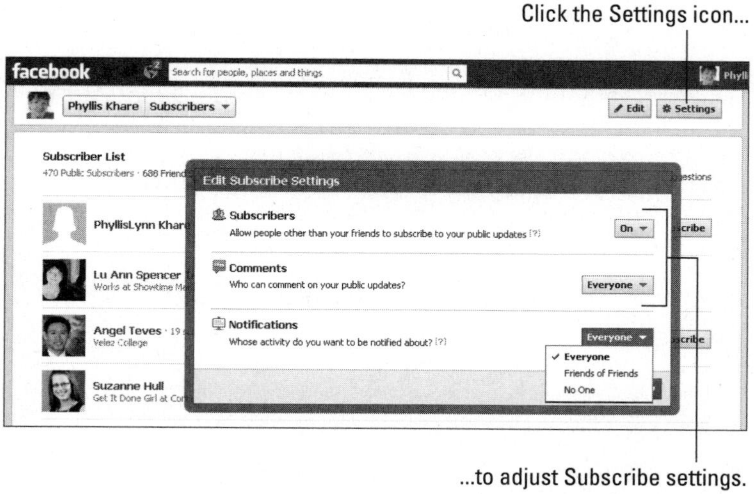

Figure 5-4: Revisit subscribe settings here.

Another interesting fact: After you turn on your Subscribe button, if someone asks to be your Friend, and you ignore her, that person automatically becomes a subscriber and is able to see your public posts.

Seeing How to Post Publicly

Now that you've turned on your Subscribe button, and people are starting to subscribe to you, you need to remember to post publicly the kinds of things that will support your business.

Because this is a post from your personal Profile, add your personal take, your personal feelings, and your personal experience to the post. The following list offers some examples of types of Public posts:

- **Posts of public photos:** If you have a new product coming out, post a picture of yourself holding it, and in the description of the photo talk about your *personal* experience with that product. Did it take a long time to develop? Did development involve some twist of fate? Did you have a personal "Aha" moment about it? What was the personal connection?
- **Links to articles:** If you're being featured in an article, post the link to the article, and in the post, talk about what it was like to be interviewed. What did the interviewer leave out? Did you like how the interviewer worked?
- **Release of new product:** You've developed a new information product. Don't be blatant about it, but don't just post a discount code! Talk about your personal reasons for developing the product. Talk about the process of creating something new. People will click through if your post resonates with them.

Figure 5-5 shows where the posting icon is located. You need to make sure that you select Public (the option with the globe icon).

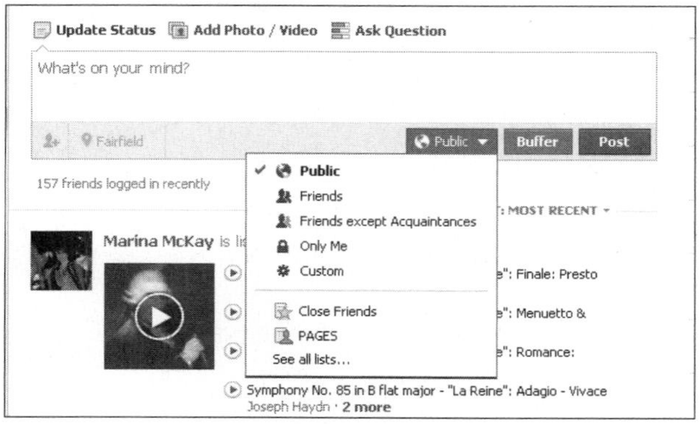

Figure 5-5: Set the posting icon to Public (globe icon).

You can change the icon when you're posting on your Timeline and in the News Feed view. Just remember to check the icon before you post. You can change the icon on your mobile phone with the same process of using the drop-down menu and selecting the globe.

TIP: If you need to change the setting from Friends to Public, or vice versa, just click the drop-down arrow on the post, and choose the setting you intend to use.

Sometimes, the way you posted the last time is the default for the next time you post. This situation happens a lot when you post from a mobile device. You can make sure that the default is always Public or always Friends by going to your Privacy Settings (see Figure 5-6) on your computer and setting your preferred default. If you tend to post things from your phone that need to be public, choose Public as the default.

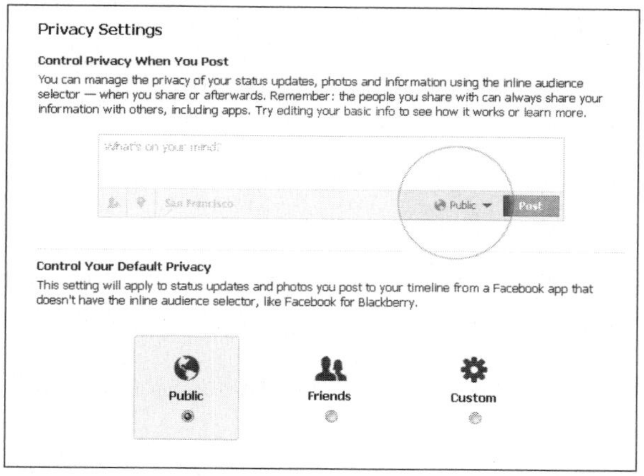

Privacy Settings
Control Privacy When You Post
You can manage the privacy of your status updates, photos and information using the inline audience selector — when you share or afterwards. Remember: the people you share with can always share your information with others, including apps. Try editing your basic info to see how it works or learn more.
What's on your mind?
San Francisco
Public
Post
Control Your Default Privacy
This setting will apply to status updates and photos you post to your timeline from a Facebook app that doesn't have the inline audience selector, like Facebook for Blackberry.
Public
Friends
Custom

Figure 5-6: Choose the default setting for your posts from your computer and mobile phone.

Marketing Basics with a Personal Profile

This section title might bring up all sorts of comments, such as, "You can't market on a personal account." That's completely true. But you can support your marketing by allowing people into your business world through your personal experience of your business. There's an art to sharing and marketing appropriately through a personal account. As stated at the beginning of this chapter, if you wrap your posts in deeply personal impressions, being human and being transparent, you can open this personal-account door to more potential customers.

As with all social accounts, learning how to be an attraction-based marketer will serve you well. Some of the tenets of attraction-based marketing are

- **Giving content freely:** Figure out how much of your business content can be used freely, without links to your blog or as a tease. Give help to those who need it. This technique does two things: shows that you have expert understanding of your niche and shows that you're a nice person. Both of those aspects are highly attractive in a business sense.
- **Being human:** Some of the most successful people in almost any business are the ones who let you into their thinking, emotions, and experiences. They tell you when they were wrong and when they nailed something. They're accessible and friendly.
- **Being hooked up:** Make all the important links back to your products and services easy to find. Make it extremely easy for someone to read your posts and then find your website or product pages. The About section on your personal account needs a really good review to make sure that people can click over to your site from there. If you also have a business Page, you need to make sure that the Work section of your personal account actually links to your Page, not to a phantom Interest Page. Review Book II, Chapter 2 for that discussion.

If you've turned on your Subscribe button, you can do all the things we suggest in Book II, Chapter 2, including these:

- Add your personal Facebook URL to your letterhead and e-mail signatures.
- Make an announcement via your other social accounts.
- Mention the Subscribe button in all interviews and promotional materials.
- Put your personal-account URL on your business card.

If you get some traction with people subscribing, you may find yourself on this page:

`www.facebook.com/subscriptions/suggestions`

Make sure that you visit that page and subscribe to other people in your industry or in a niche that provides you customers. After you subscribe to those updates, comment and enliven conversation like this:

1. **Subscribe to excellent connections in your business niche (especially bloggers and media writers).**
2. **Post only excellent comments — not flippant, throwaway comments.**
3. **Always reply to comments, both on your Timeline and on the other person's Timeline.**

Many of the people you subscribe to may be A-list people, in that every time they post, hundreds of people comment. Phyllis subscribes to some Internet rock stars, including Mari Smith and Robert Scoble. Robert responds only to what he would call intelligent questions. The lesson is this: Don't just post "I agree" or "Good post."

Understanding Friend Subscribers and Public Subscribers

After you turn on your Subscribe button, you have three types of subscribers:

✦ **Public Subscribers:** These are people who have subscribed to your Public posts. If you ignore a Friend Request, they automatically become a subscriber and will see your Public posts.

✦ **Friend Subscribers:** These are your Facebook Friends. You are subscribed to each other. When you create a Public post, your Friends will see it, too. When you create a post and change the viewing icon to Friends, only people in this category will see the post.

✦ **Subscribers via Lists:** Anyone on Facebook can create an Interest List. An Interest List is a list of people and Pages you collect together. You can put all the TV Show Pages on one list, all the Natural food chefs in another, and so on. Then you can click the name of the List in the left sidebar (on the News Feed view) and just see the posts from the people and Pages on that List.

  If someone puts your personal Profile on a List and shares the List, people will be able to subscribe to the List. When that happens, you gain another number in this category. Even though they're subscribing to the List, Facebook gives you the added number. You can find Interest Lists to follow at `www.facebook.com/addlist`.

TIP

Create your own Interest List in your business niche and add yourself to the List. Then Share the List and watch your numbers go higher.

To see who is in each category, click the Subscribers app box on your personal Timeline. You go to your Subscriber page. Figure 5-7 shows three numbers that are hyperlinked. Click each number to see the people in each category.

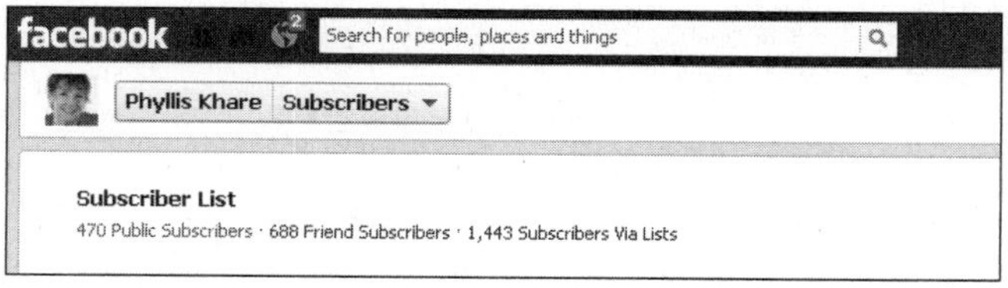

Figure 5-7: See who has subscribed to your public updates.

If you have been put on an Interest List, you see the name of the List and numbers that are hyperlinked to those people. See Figure 5-8 for a list of several numbers and information to explore.

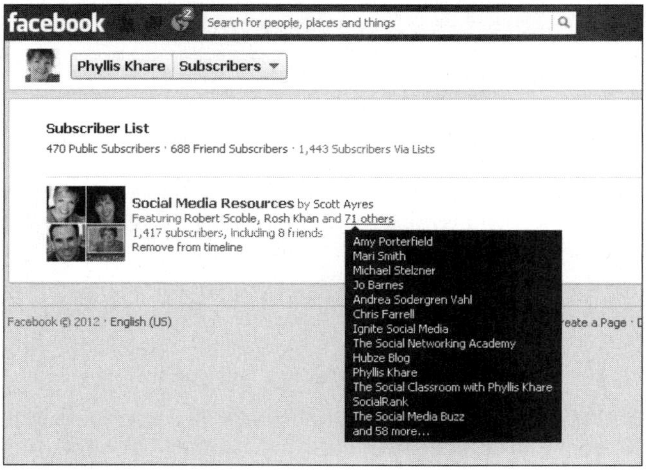

Figure 5-8: Explore the hyperlinked numbers for more information about the subscribers.

Adding Public Life Events to Your Personal Profile

This step is very important. Some people call the personal Timeline the ultimate résumé because of the wonderful Life Events feature. This is basically the same thing as adding milestones on a business Page except that this interface is really detailed. (We discuss milestones in great detail in Book III.) Life Events can go all the way back to when you were born! Now you can add as many life events as you want, in many areas, but in this section, we focus on using life events to support your business.

You can add life events when things like these happen:

- ✦ You get a book deal.
- ✦ You publish an article.
- ✦ You win an award.
- ✦ You gain special recognition from your industry.
- ✦ You launch a new product.
- ✦ Your business reaches a financial milestone.
- ✦ You are featured in a local paper or magazine.

You can add all sorts of things to this list. Focus on adding these life events, and make sure to make them Public. You can't add things with future dates, by the way. Don't make Life Events one big infomercial! Add your personal experience to each post, in your authentic human voice. And don't post all your life events at one time; spread them out over a few weeks.

Here's how to create a Life Event on your personal Timeline:

1. **Go to your personal Timeline.**
2. **In the posting box, select the Life Event tab.**

   You see a set of options; Work & Education, Family & Relationships, Home & Living, Health & Wellness, and Travel & Experiences.
3. **Click the category of Life Event you want to post.**

   Subcategories appear in a submenu, as shown in Figure 5-9.

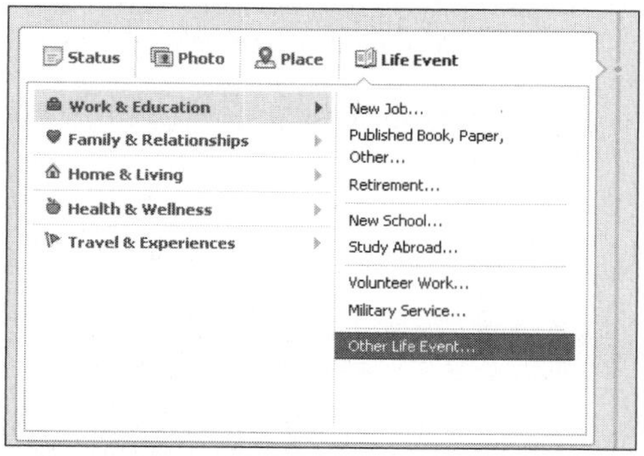

Figure 5-9: The Life Event interface is very detailed.

4. **Choose the subcategory that matches what you want to post, or choose Other Life Event.**

   All the subcategories have Other Life Event as an option. When you choose it, you get to create a custom title for the Life Event. In most cases, you want to choose Other Life Event for this reason.
5. **Fill in the fields.**

   Each subcategory has slightly different fields to fill in. Fill in as much information as you can. Make sure you adjust the date fields to be the date of the Life Event.
6. **Upload or choose a photo.**

   Always upload or choose a photo. A photo really makes a Life Event pop on the Timeline.
7. **Make sure that the viewing icon is set to Public.**

   The whole point of this task is to create items that the Public and your Public subscribers can see on your Timeline. The Public icon is the globe.
8. **Click Save.**

   Now your Life Event is placed on your personal Timeline on the date you set for it. Go look. Life Events are wonderful to view on a Timeline.

Adjusting Your Timeline for Public Viewing

If you've placed Life Events that support your business on your personal Timeline, you'll want to see how your Timeline looks to the public. You can view your personal Timeline as though different types of people are viewing it: the Public or a particular Friend.

To do that, click the gear icon and choose View As from the drop-down menu (as shown in Figure 5-10); then click the Public link and look through your entire Timeline to see what Joe Public sees. If you see anything that you don't want the public to see, you need to go back to your Timeline and change who can see a particular post. For example, when viewing your Timeline as the Public, if you find a post that you meant just your Friends to see, click the Back to Timeline button (at top of the Page) and find that particular post; find the globe icon (to change view settings), click the drop-down arrow, and choose Friends instead of Public.

Figure 5-10: The View As option lets you see how your personal Profile looks to the public.

Click the gear icon again, choose View As, and this time type a Friend's name in the Enter a Friend's Name text box (in the upper-left area of the Page); now you see how your Timeline looks to him. Think about your business and how your subscribers will see your account. Use this system of checking what's public and what's for Friends to clean up your Profile. If you're using your personal Profile to support your business, make sure the Public view does just that. Change the view settings to fit the types of posts you make on Facebook.

Uploading a Cover Photo that Supports Your Business

Facebook doesn't want you to think of your Page's Cover photo as a billboard; it wants you to think of the Cover photo as a view of the spirit or soul of your business. The same idea applies to the Cover photo for your personal Profile.

Figure 5-11 shows some personal Profile Cover photos that support a business. The top image depicts Amy Porterfield's Cover photo on her personal Profile; it shows both sides of her life. You get a true sense of Dabney Porte's business spirit in her Cover photo, shown in the middle image. Phyllis Khare's Cover photo on her personal Profile (bottom image) shows her personality clearly and matches the branding on her business Page.

Figure 5-11: Use a Cover photo that conveys who you are without breaking Facebook's rules.

Book III

Adding the Basics to Your Facebook Page

The 5th Wave By Rich Tennant

"Here's an idea. Why don't you start a social network for doofuses who think they know how to set a broken leg, but don't."

Contents at a Glance

Chapter 1: Posting to Your Page

In This Chapter

- Exploring the best practices for your posts
- Becoming a pro at attachments
- Targeting your updates

The most critical aspect of your Facebook presence is your posts. What you put on your Wall is the showcase of your business. After a Facebook user likes you, he most likely won't go to your Page very often; typically, a user sees you only as an update in his News Feed. So you have to be interesting, engaging, responsive, useful, and fun. No pressure, right?

You want your posts to establish you as an authority and expert in your field, and this chapter tells you what types of material you can use to accomplish that goal.

Never forget, however, that Facebook is a place where people come to be *social*. It's like a big cocktail party where people are having fun talking, so don't be a wet blanket and talk only about the big sale you're having. You don't want to be that irritating sales guy at the networking event whom everyone avoids — or, worse, "un-likes"!

Helpful tips, useful information, links, and photos can go a long way toward making your Page engaging and popular. To that end, in this chapter, you find out how to post text updates, photos, links, and videos. You also discover how to target your updates to specific members of your community.

Posting Updates to Your Timeline via the Publisher

To post an update to your community, you do so in what's called the Publisher. The Publisher is located on your Timeline and contains the prompt "What's on your mind?" See Figure 1-1.

The function of the Publisher on your Page is very similar to that of the Publisher on your personal Profile. When you post a status update to your personal Profile, however, it goes out to the News Feed of all your Friends, whereas an update to the Timeline on your Page goes out to the News Feed of all those who like you. Then your Page's status update shows up in the News Feed, just as a person's status update shows up in the News Feed of Friends.

Figure 1-1: The Publisher is where you post information to your Timeline.

Your update also appears in people's tickers (the scrolling real-time updates on the right side of the home page of your personal Profile). For more information on the Ticker, see Book II, Chapter 1. Realize that when you post to your Page Timeline, your post shows up in people's News Feeds along with all the other posts of their Friends and Pages they like. Don't refer to previous posts or things on your business Page that people can't see right then. If you want people to come to your Page to see those things, make sure that you tell them to come to your Page. Also make sure that each post can stand alone as a complete thought.

Be aware that not every single post on your Page will be seen by every single fan. Not every post actually makes it into your fans' News Feeds. You can actually see how many of your fans potentially saw your post after you post it. Facebook determines whether or not your post goes into your fans' News Feeds based on their EdgeRank algorithm. Find out more about EdgeRank and getting your posts into the News Feed in Book IV, Chapter 2.

How long to make your post

Facebook extended the length of the status updates not too long ago to a whopping 63,206 characters! It's almost a small blog post. ***Note:*** After you type around 240 characters (depending on word structure), your post will be cut short, and a See More link appears, as shown in Figure 1-2.

Keep your post short so that people can easily read it and not miss anything valuable if they don't click the See More link.

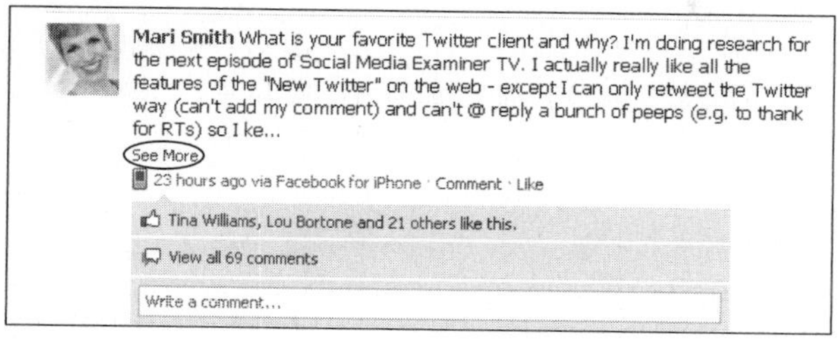

Figure 1-2: A long status update is truncated in the News Feed, but the whole post is still there.

How often to post an update

One of the most frequently asked questions is, "How often should I post?" The answer will vary depending on your goals and comfort level. Some people worry about "bothering" their community with too many posts, or they worry that some people will un-like or hide their Page if they post too much. We can assure you that most of your community members won't mind your posts if you're doing them in the right way. That's why it's important to provide value.

Also, many people aren't on Facebook all the time and may not see your posts. Depending on how many Friends a user has or how many Pages a user likes, your post may go through a News Feed fairly quickly.

If you have one person who likes your Page and has ten Friends who post one update per day, and your Page is posting five updates per day, you'll be very visible, occupying one third of the daily News Feed. But if you have a person who likes your Page and has 500 Friends who post one update per day, your updates will just be 1 percent of the daily News Feed, and that person may miss your posts. Bottom line: Don't worry about posting too often. People will miss your updates, and you want to continue to stay visible.

Studies have shown that posting two to five times per day is ideal. If that sounds like too much, at least try to post once a day during the week. Weekends can also be a great time to post, as people are checking on Facebook, and there may not be as many other Pages posting on the weekends. But you also need to take a break every once in a while!

What types of material to include

When you go to create a post, think about your community. What do its members need? What's in it for them? Think of yourself as the funnel that guides the best information to your community — and that will be what keeps your community coming back for more. Also realize that you're participating in a conversation. Just as you do at a cocktail party, you want to respond when people comment on your post. Don't just post and run. (And don't post when you've had too many cocktails; you may regret it in the morning!)

Be sure to vary the types of material you post, too. Following are types of posts that you can use to market yourself as an expert, have fun, and plug your business all at the same time without being annoying:

- Pictures of a great event you had
- Video of behind-the-scenes happenings at your business
- Questions that engage your audience and allow you to do some market research
- Links to blog posts that solve people's problems within your niche

  TIP: Don't worry that you're giving information away for free. Your community will appreciate the information and look to you when they need help that they can hire you for.
- Controversial news stories within your niche that will spark conversation
- Events you're hosting that will benefit your community
- Links to resources that are helpful for your niche

Again, this is just a partial list of post types. How do you use these types to market your business? You establish yourself as the go-to person for your market. You notice that these posts aren't all about you and what you're selling, but you're continually popping into the News Feed and reminding your community that you're there. You're branding yourself as an expert in your business.

Including Attachments

You may have noticed icons above the Publisher (refer to Figure 1-1). You use these icons to attach items to your post. The icons are, from left to right, Status, Photo/Video, and Event, Milestone +. If your Page is categorized as a Local Business, you may have Offer, Event + as the last selection. The plus sign (+) means that additional options for attachments are available when you click that selection, as shown in Figure 1-3.

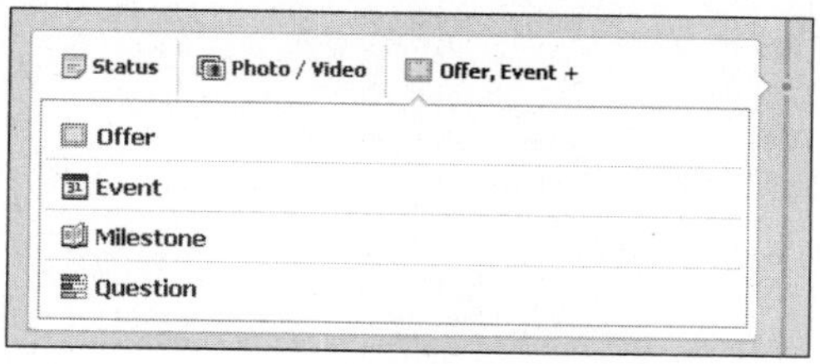

Figure 1-3: Click the + symbol to see additional types of attachment.

We recommend varying your posts so that you use these attachments frequently. People like multimedia, and your status updates will be more visible when you use these features.

Updating status and posting links

Posting a status update is relatively straightforward, especially if you've been using your Facebook personal Profile for any length of time. All you do is start entering your text in the Publisher (shown in Figure 1-1) and click Post.

If you'd like to add a link to a website, all you need to do is to copy the website's address (or type it in yourself) into the Publisher area. When you post a link, you can use the 63,206 characters of the status box, or Publisher, to introduce the link and entice people to click the story. (There's no need to be quite that verbose; a short introduction or comment is just fine.)

After you add the link to the Publisher, the website is represented as a title and a short description next to a thumbnail image, as shown in Figure 1-4. These items are pulled in from the website itself. You can edit this information by clicking the title or description. You also may have a choice of the thumbnail image to post, or you can click No Thumbnail if the image doesn't match the story.

To add a link with your status update, follow these steps:

1. **Copy the URL from the website you want to put into your post.**
2. **Paste the URL into the Publisher or just type the address into the Publisher.**

   You see the website information, as shown in Figure 1-4.

Figure 1-4: When you add a link, Facebook brings in the description and a picture.

3. **Adjust the information as necessary by selecting a thumbnail (or No Thumbnail), modifying the description of the site by double-clicking the description, and modifying the title of the site (by double-clicking it).**
4. **Add some scintillating text to the Publisher right before the website address.**

   (You can add it after the address, but we recommend the text before it.)

   This text might be a short description of, or plug for, the site you're linking to. The purpose of the text in this post is to give your community a reason to click the link.
5. **Click the blue Post button to post this status update with your link to your Wall.**

As mentioned in Step 3, you may be able to choose among several thumbnail images to go with your link. The images are pulled from the site and might include images from advertisements on the website's sidebar, so the images may not match the story. If you can't find an image that matches the link, you can select No Thumbnail.

TECHNICAL STUFF

The title and description are pulled in from the meta title and meta description on the website. Depending on the site, these items may not even match the story on that site that you're trying to promote. The webmaster of the site has control of the meta title and description, but you can edit what shows up in your post by clicking the Title and Description before you attach the link.

Here's another thing you can do when posting a link. After you have the link *attached* — meaning that the picture and description are shown as in Figure 1-4 — you can remove the link in the Publisher area. Then the post won't have a clickable link in the text area, but if people want to read the story, they can just click the title, picture, or description that's attached, and they're taken to the website. You may want to use this option if the link is really long (or if it looks messy). All you need to do is to backspace or delete the link before you click Share. If you want to have a highlighted, clickable link in your text area, just leave the link in the Publisher.

Note that you can also add a location to your status updates. You can do this by clicking the Place icon in the bottom-left corner of the Publisher. When you click this icon, you can add a Facebook Place or Facebook Page name. This can be like your Page "checking in" at a Place to let people know where you are at. We see limited benefit from this feature, but it is available.

A different way to post a link is to post it with a photo. Sometimes, posting a photo with a link gets more attention than posting just a link, because the photo shows up larger in the News Feed. See the next section, "Attaching photos," to find out how to post photos with a link.

Don't post links only to your own website, though. Vary your content so that you become a funnel of information on the web for your community. So where do you find these interesting links to post? Here are several ways to attract interesting material so that you can share it with your community:

- **Google Alerts:** Get e-mail updates of the latest relevant Google results based on keywords in your niche. All you have to do is go to `www.google.com/alerts`, enter keywords you want to monitor, and then you can select how frequently you want to receive them (once a day, once a week, or as it happens).

  We also recommend adding the name of your company as a keyword (unless it's a common name) so that you can monitor if there is some blog post or news about your company posted on the web that you need to be aware of.
- **Google Reader:** Subscribe to other interesting blogs in your niche via an RSS feed, and check in with your blogs each day to find interesting posts. Sign up at `http://reader.google.com`.
- **Alltop:** This site is a gathering of interesting blogs on various topics, arranged by topic and most recent posts at `http://alltop.com`.
- **Other fan Pages in your niche:** Make sure to be a fan of "competitor" fan Pages to see what those folks are doing. It's okay to repost a link if it's an interesting bit of news.
- **Twitter:** A lot of interesting links are on Twitter (`www.twitter.com`). Follow the top people in your niche, and when you find something newsworthy, post it to your Page.

Sometimes, a link doesn't post correctly and doesn't pull any metadata or website information in with the link. In that case, you can try to debug the link in the Facebook Developers area before posting. Just go to `http://developers.facebook.com/tools/debug`, paste the link into the Debug field, and click Debug. You get information on why the link may not have been working, but usually, there's nothing you need to do with this information. Just go back to your Facebook Page and try pasting the link into your Publisher again. This works 99 times out of 100!

Attaching photos

Attaching photos is a great strategy for getting more interaction with your audience and marketing your brand, because people love multimedia. A photo is more noticeable than just a status update because it takes up more space in the News Feed. Disney Pixar posts a lot of photos of its movies with a little caption to engage. Take a look at Figure 1-5 for an example.

Figure 1-5: Disney Pixar gets thousands of likes and hundreds of comments on each photo posted from its movies.

If you're a speaker, a photo of you speaking at an event will market your business in a more exciting way than if you just post an update saying, "Spoke at an event with business owners today." The great thing is that you can "show and tell" — that is, post the status and show the picture.

Or suppose that your business is a restaurant. You can post pictures of your food, kitchen, busy Friday-night crowd, and so on. The possibilities are endless! Spend some time thinking of all the picture posts you can have about your business.

To attach a photo, just click the Photo/Video icon in the Publisher. Then you have the choice to upload a photo or video, record a video with your webcam, or create a photo album, as shown in Figure 1-6.

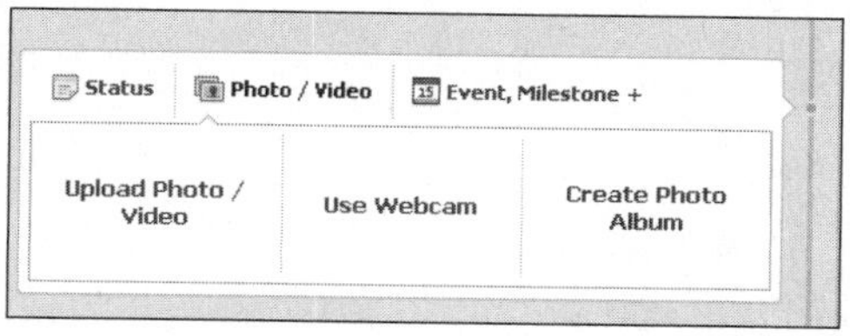

Figure 1-6: You have several choices for uploading your photos.

You can also post a photo as a link from a third-party site such as Flickr or TwitPic. When you upload a photo to the Publisher as an attachment, however, it's stored in your Photo tab for people to reference easily later. If you share a photo from Flickr as an attachment, it's just a Timeline post that will be harder to get back to and enjoy.

Another tactic is to post a photo or screen shot and then add other interactive things, such as a link to a website and tags for other Pages. Whenever you add a photo, you can always add a tag and a link within your status update that goes with the photo. The benefit of posting your update as a photo is that it appears larger in the News Feed. In Figure 1-7, you see that Mari Smith added an actual photo from the article she's talking about and then included the link to the article, as well as a tag for the Page. Learn more about tagging other Pages in Book IV, Chapter 2.

You may have multiple photos to post on a certain topic at one time. In that case, you should select the Create Photo Album option after you select Photo/Video (refer to Figure 1-6). When you do, you'll be able to select the photos on your computer, and as they upload, you can add more. You have the opportunity to add captions, tag the photos, and select an album cover before you post the photo album. The photo album posts at one time, with multiple photos showing up in the News Feed.

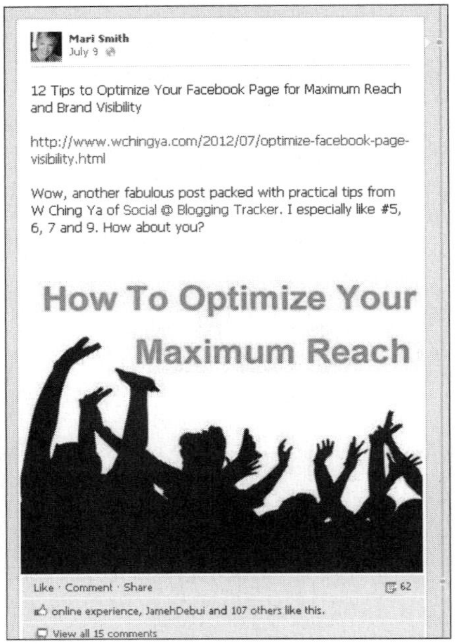

Figure 1-7: Add a photo and then include a link and/or tags to other Pages.

Attaching video

Video is a powerful tool to help your audience get to know you. You can easily upload a video to Facebook, and you can even record one on the fly from a webcam to post right away. When you click the Photo/Video icon in the Publisher, you're given the choice to upload a video from your computer or record a video with a webcam (refer to Figure 1-6).

Upload a video shorter than 20 minutes, less than 1024MB, and made by you or your Friends per Facebook terms. Again, you always want to abide by Facebook's Terms and Conditions; otherwise, your Page will be in danger of being shut down.

You can upload video files in many formats, but MP4 format works best. You can find the entire list of supported video formats here: `www.facebook.com/help/?faq=218673814818907`. After you select the video that you want to upload from your computer and type a comment about the video, click the Post button. Facebook opens another browser window to show the progress of your video upload, and you're alerted when the upload is complete, as shown in Figure 1-8. Don't close this window until the process has completed.

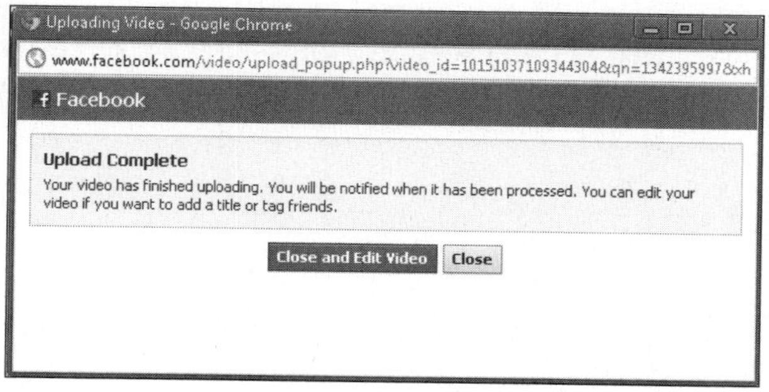

Figure 1-8: A new browser window appears when your video upload is complete.

TIP

The video upload process can be slow; sometimes, it can stall. Files in MP4 format typically work best.

When the video is done uploading, click the Edit Video button to edit some of the details in the screen shown in Figure 1-9.

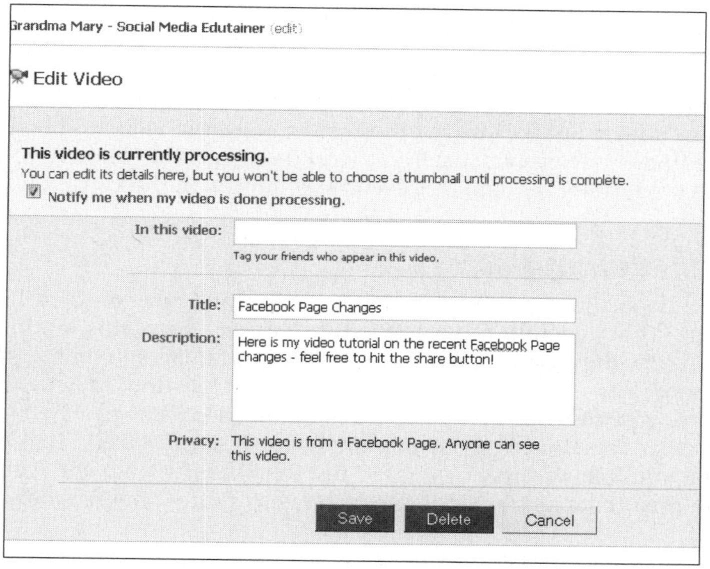

Figure 1-9: Edit the details of your uploaded video.

Uploaded videos can play right within the Facebook status update and will stay in your Videos area for your community to reference later.

Another advantage to uploading videos directly to Facebook is that when nonfans view your videos on Facebook, they see the Like button for your Facebook Page in the top-left corner of the video screen, as shown in Figure 1-10. This is a great way to make it easy for people to like your Page.

Figure 1-10: A Like button appears in the corner of your video to let your nonlikers connect with you easily.

You can also post videos by posting a link to a third-party video site, such as YouTube or Vimeo. Most of these sites allow the video to be played within the update. These videos aren't stored on your Facebook Page for people to see later, however, and there's no Like button in the corner.

Scheduling posts

Facebook allows you to schedule posts in the future or to add posts to the past (although milestones are better for that). As of this writing, you can schedule only status updates (with or without links in them), photos, and videos. You can't schedule Event postings, Questions, Offers, or postings of Photo albums. You also cannot schedule a post that you are sharing from another Facebook Page. If you find a great post or image from another Page that you follow, and you want to use the Share button, you cannot schedule the post to be shared later — you have to share it immediately.

To schedule a post, just follow these steps:

1. **Complete your post just as you would if you were to post it immediately.**
2. **Click the clock symbol in the bottom-left corner of the Publisher.**

   The Date drop-down menus appear, shown in Figure 1-11, where you can specify details exactly when you want to have the post scheduled.

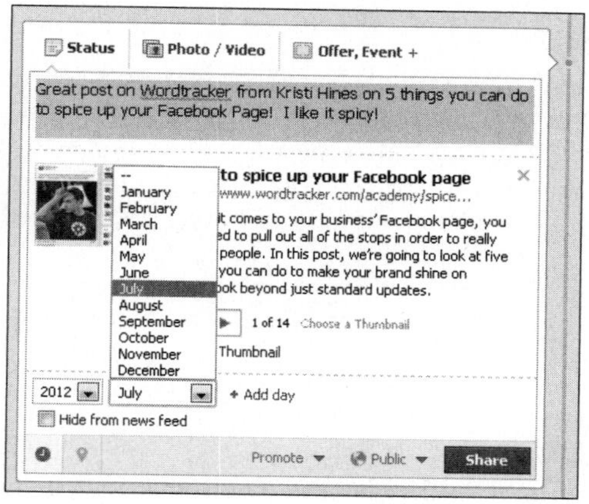

Figure 1-11: Click the clock symbol in the bottom-left corner of the Publisher.

3. **Add the year, month, day, and time that you would like the post to be published.**
4. **Click the blue Post button to schedule your post.**

Your post is scheduled. To view the post, check your Activity Log, which you access from your Admin Panel. Click the Edit Page button, and choose Use Activity Log from the drop-down menu. You see your scheduled posts, as shown in Figure 1-12.

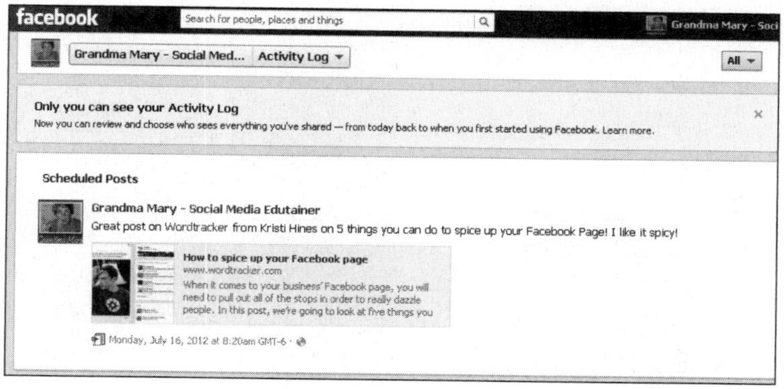

Figure 1-12: View your Activity Log to see your scheduled posts.

From here, you can delete your scheduled posts by mousing over the upper-right corner area of your post and clicking the X that appears. But you cannot edit your scheduled post. If you need to change anything, you need to repeat the preceding steps and reschedule the post.

Scheduling Events

You can also post an Event directly from the Publisher. A word of caution, however: Every time you use the Event option to publish, you're creating a brand-new Facebook Event. To create a new Event from the Publisher, just click the Event, Milestone + icon (or the Offer, Event + icon, depending on what you have). A pop-up window appears; you can create your Event in this window.

See Book VI, Chapter 1 for more information on creating and marketing your Facebook Event.

Adding milestones

Milestones are big events in your company's history that you want to highlight. Milestones appear slightly different from traditional updates, as shown in *The New York Times's* milestones for 1912 (see Figure 1-13). Milestones are a great way to showcase awards, new products, and other momentous occasions.

Figure 1-13: Milestones from *The New York Times.*

When you publish a milestone, it's placed in the appropriate area of your Timeline. You can add a photo, if you want, or just a status update about what happened at that time. Milestones are great for letting people know more about the history of your business and can be fun for people to discover on your Timeline. They can give people a reason to hang out on your Timeline longer.

People can navigate to your milestone or periods of time on your Facebook Page by using the months and years chart on the right side of your Timeline. Go to any Page and have fun with this feature by jumping around to see the posts at that point in the Page history. Try this with `www.facebook.com/cocacola` to see the history of Coca-Cola, for example.

To add a milestone to your Page, simply click the Event, Milestone + icon (or the Offer, Event + icon, depending on what you have). In the pop-up window that appears, you can fill in the details of your milestone, as shown in Figure 1-14.

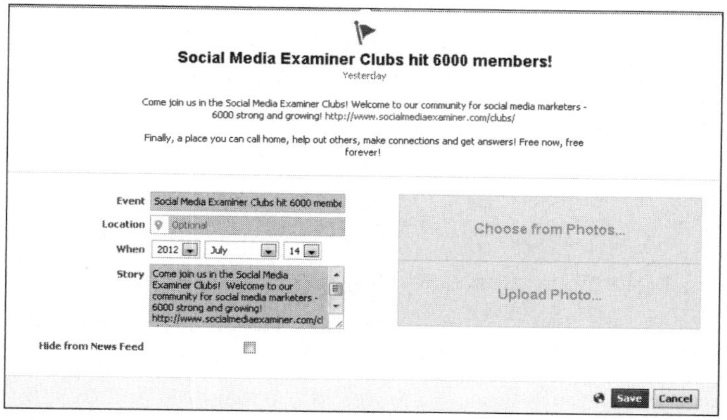

Figure 1-14: Fill in the details of your milestone.

Your milestone is published in your News Feed (which is also a fun way to tell your audience about cool things that are happening). If you have several milestones to add, space the milestones out so that you don't have so many posts at the same time, or select the Hide from News Feed check box so that it posts on your Timeline but doesn't overwhelm your audience.

Posting questions

Questions can be a great tool to get interaction from your audience. People love to give their opinion or chime in with their experience, as shown in Figure 1-15, in which 356 people answered the question posed.

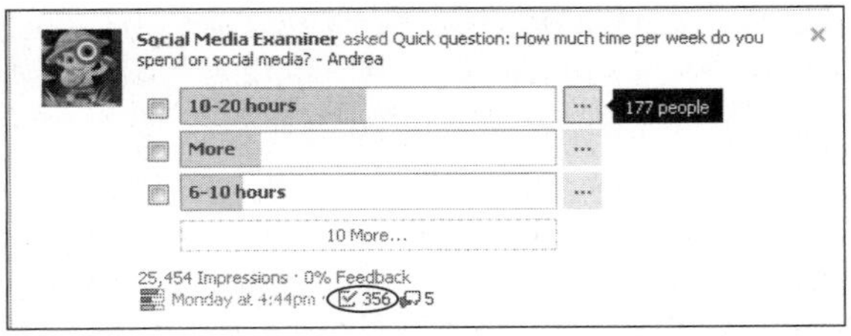

Figure 1-15: Questions can get a lot of response from your community.

You can also do market research, albeit unscientifically, with these questions. As you can see, we found out that 177 people of the 356 responses spent 10–20 hours per week on social media, which wasn't what we had expected.

The questions are in the form of poll answers, and you can choose to limit your answers to ones that you allow, or you can let your community members add their own selections. To use the Questions feature, follow these steps:

1. **From the Publisher on your Facebook Page Wall, click the Event, Milestone + icon (or the Offer, Event + icon, depending on which you have).**

   A drop-down menu appears, with posting options.

2. **Select Question.**

   A box appears in which you can type your question.

3. **Type your question in the top box.**

4. **Click Add Poll Options in the bottom-left corner and type possible answers to the question in the boxes.**

   As soon as you type an answer in the last box, another box appears below your box showing Add an Option (see Figure 1-16) to give you more possible answers.

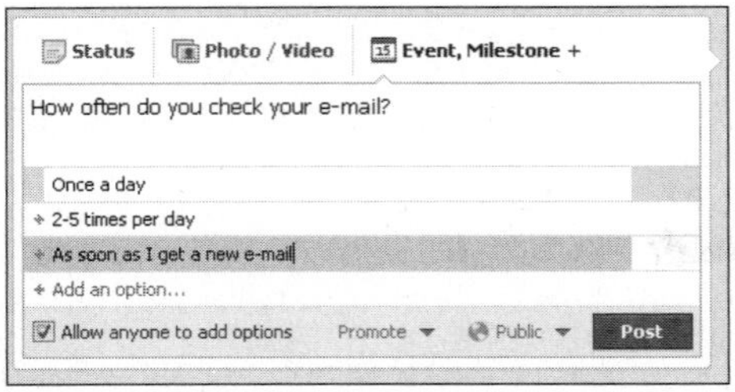

Figure 1-16: Type your question and poll options in the appropriate boxes.

5. **Add as many poll options as you want.**

   When you're done adding options, you see an extra empty box that doesn't appear in the final question.

6. **If you don't want to allow people to be able to add options, deselect the Allow Anyone to Add Options check box.**
7. **Click the blue Post button.**

   Your question is posted.

This question will appear in the News Feed and the ticker of everyone who likes your Page. Questions are also very viral, meaning that when people answer a question, their answer appears in their News Feed for their Friends to see, and then it can be answered by their Friends as well.

You may wonder whether to allow people to add their own options to answer the question. Sometimes, people enjoy putting in their own options and trying to add something clever. But you may want to get clearer responses for research purposes, so you may not want to allow additional responses.

Questions also have their own Wall on which people can comment. To see this Wall, you have to click the question's hyperlink on your Wall. As shown in Figure 1-17, a pop-up window appears, showing more details about the question.

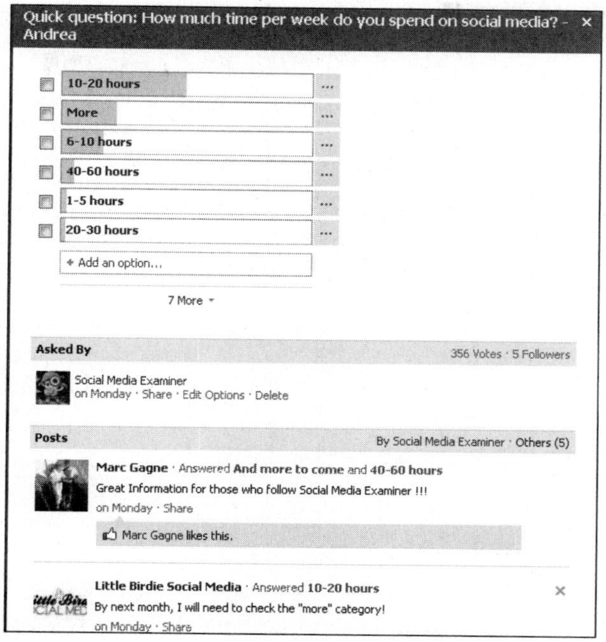

Figure 1-17: The pop-up window with all the details on the responses to the question.

Here's what you can see and do in the pop-up window:

- ✦ Responses (in order of number of votes) appear. If you allowed additional responses, you also see what people added.
- ✦ The number of votes appears when you mouse over the bar graphs.
- ✦ Click the three dots to the right of the bar to see another pop-up window with a list of all the people who voted for this option.
- ✦ If all the options can't be displayed, you can click the hyperlink to show the additional options (refer to Figure 1-17, which shows the 7 More hyperlink to indicate there are additional answers).
- ✦ Below the responses, you can see who asked the question, how many total votes the question received, and how many people are following the question. When people follow a question, they receive a notification whenever one of their Friends also answers the question.
- ✦ Below the Posts heading are all the people who have posted an additional response to this question. Each question has its own page on which people can discuss the question, so you may have the answers in the form of a poll, but people can elaborate on their responses on the page.

Using Facebook Offers

Posting a Facebook Offer is also done through the Publisher. A Facebook Offer is like a coupon that people claim and then redeem either at your place of business or online. After you post your offer, it goes out into the News Feed, and your fans can click it to claim it. When they claim it, they add their e-mail addresses to the form, and the offer is sent to them. The great thing about offers is that they can be very viral. When someone claims your offer, your offer posts to that person's News Feed for all of his or her Friends to see and possibly claim themselves as shown in Figure 1-18.

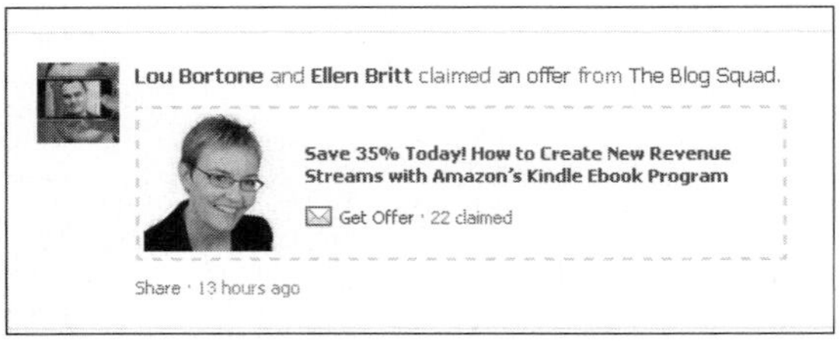

Lou Bortone and Ellen Britt claimed an offer from The Blog Squad.
Save 35% Today! How to Create New Revenue Streams with Amazon's Kindle Ebook Program
Get Offer · 22 claimed
Share · 13 hours ago

Figure 1-18: A claimed offer in the News Feed.

Facebook Offers are now available for online and local businesses but do cost money to run. The first offer is free, and then you have to pay to use

Facebook Offers. Find out how to set up the offer and some of the best practices in Book VII Chapter 1.

Targeting Your Updates by Location and Language

A little-known trick that you can do with the Publisher is to target your updates to certain members of your community. As of this writing, targeting is still being rolled out to all Pages and you may not yet have access to this feature. But it is scheduled to roll out to all Pages with 100 likes or more. You can target your updates by the following options:

- **Gender:** Men or Women
- **Relationship Status:** Single, In a Relationship, Engaged, or Married
- **Educational Status:** In High School, In College, College Grad
- **Interested In:** Men or Women
- **Age:** Select a range between 13 and 65
- **Location:** Country, Region or State, City
- **Language:** Type in the language

When you select the targeting, only those likers whom you specify in your target will see your status update in their News Feeds. This can be very helpful when you are posting something where you want a certain demographic to respond or if you have a local event. If you have an Event happening in San Francisco, you can update only the people who live near there — meaning that your community members in New York won't see those posts in their News Feeds.

To use this feature, follow these steps after you type your status update:

1. **Click the Target icon button to the right of the clock icon in the Publisher, as shown in Figure 1-19.**

   You then see an additional link to Add Targeting.

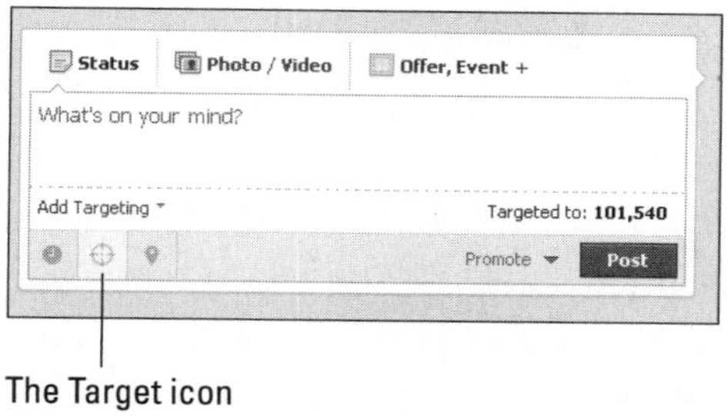

Figure 1-19: Click the Target icon to enable the targeting options.

2. **Click the Add Targeting link.**

   A drop-down menu appears that allows you to select which options you want to choose to target, as shown in Figure 1-20.

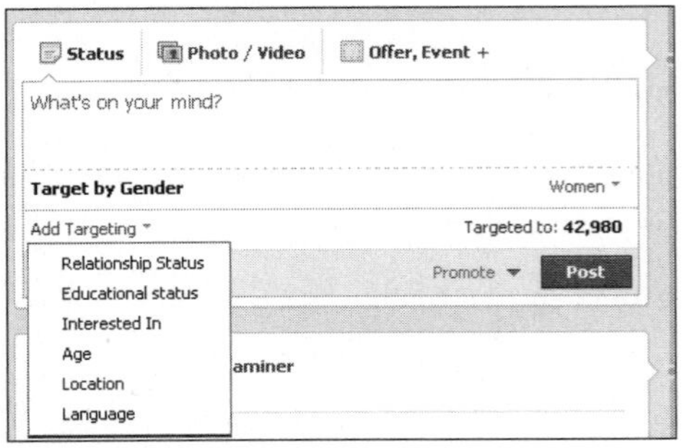

Figure 1-20: Choose a specific audience for your status update.

3. **Select which demographic you want to target from the drop-down menu.**

   You see the selection listed as shown in the Target by Gender field in Figure 1-20.

4. **Use the drop-down menu next to the demographic to select which part of the demographic you want to target.**

   For example, in Figure 1-20, Women have been selected.

   If you select Target by Location, a pop-up box appears and you can select the radio buttons as shown in Figure 1-21 for Country, Region or State, or City. You can select many countries to target, many states or regions within one country, or many cities within one country. Once you have made all your location selections, click Choose Locations.

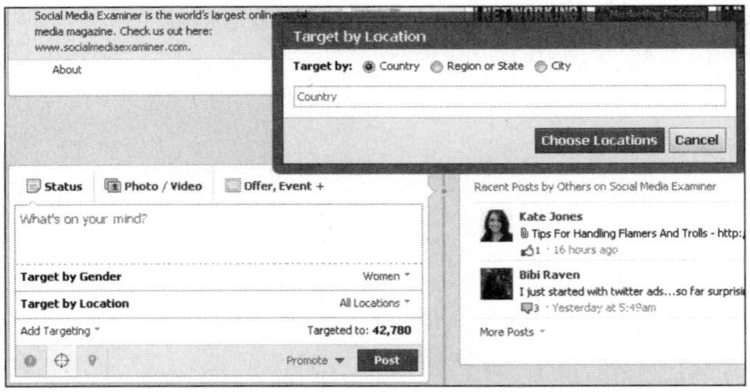

Figure 1-21: You may choose to target regionally.

5. **Click the blue Post button after making all your targeting selections and writing your post in the What's on Your Mind? box.**

   Your post will then go out into the News Feeds of only those targeted fans of your Page. The post will not show that it has been targeted but you will be able to see it has been targeted if you mouse over the "world" icon on the post when it is on your Timeline. You will see the exact demographic that you selected in the targeting options listed in a small pop-up.

   TIP: In Figure 1-21, notice that the number of people in the targeted demographic are listed in the post. You may want to use the targeting option just to see more about your demographics.

Promoting posts

In the Publisher, you have the option to promote a post. A *Promoted Post* is a way to pay to have that particular post pushed out to more of your fans. You pay a set fee to get your post shown in the News Feeds of more of your fans than would have seen it organically. You can do this as you get ready to post your update or after the fact.

Learn more about Promoted Posts in Book VIII, Chapter 2.

Pinning and highlighting posts

After you publish a post, it's time to have a little fun by highlighting certain posts or by pinning a post to the top of your Timeline for a certain period to draw more attention to it.

When you highlight a post, the post spans the width of your Timeline. Kia Motors does a great job of highlighting a photo in the post, as shown in Figure 1-22.

To highlight a post, you first have to post it; then mouse over the top-right corner of the post to reveal the star shown in Figure 1-23. Just click the star to highlight the post.

Figure 1-22: Use highlighted posts to emphasize something on your Timeline.

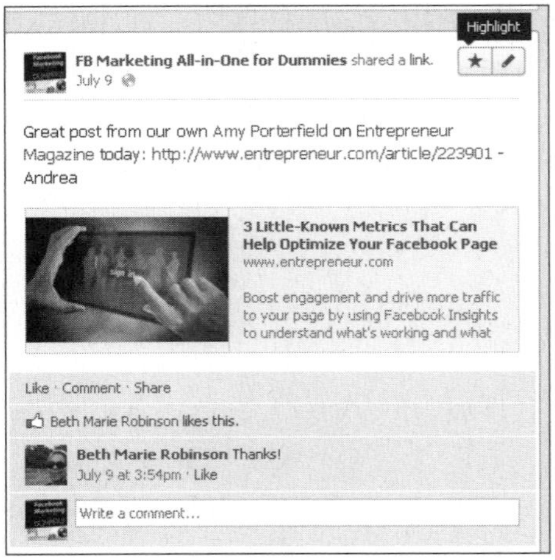

Figure 1-23: Mouse over the top-right corner of a post to find the star.

Note: Highlighting a post doesn't affect how it shows up in the News Feeds of your fans. It affects only how the post is displayed on your Timeline.

Pinning a post to the top of your Timeline can be a great way to draw attention to one of your posts for people who visit your Page. You can pin a post for a total of seven days. Then the post automatically returns to the area of your Timeline where it belongs.

You may decide to pin a promotion to the top of your Page, a question, or a video. Try it to see how it works for you. To pin a post to the top of your Page, just follow these steps on any published post:

1. **Mouse over the top-right corner of the post to reveal the pencil icon (refer to Figure 1-23).**
2. **Click the pencil icon.**

   A drop-down menu appears.
3. **Select Pin to Top.**

   Your post appears at the top of your Timeline with a small orange flag on it indicating that it is a pinned post. To unpin it, click the pencil icon in the top-right corner of the post and then choose Unpin from Top.

Chapter 2: Facebook Apps 101

In This Chapter

- **Defining Facebook apps**
- **Adding, rearranging, and deleting apps**
- **Customizing the app photo and title**
- **Exploring the Facebook App dashboard**

You may have seen customized tabs or apps on some Facebook business Pages. The apps appear below the Cover photo of a Page and can have a wide range of functions. You can use apps to showcase your other social sites, have a storefront, give a coupon, run a contest, and much more! Apps can also help contribute to the branding of your company and make your Facebook Page come alive.

The term *Facebook apps* encompasses a wide range of products. When someone refers to a Facebook app, he can mean everything from Facebook games like FarmVille to Facebook Events and highly customized apps that can be mini websites within your Facebook Page.

In this chapter, you learn about the apps — sometimes referred to as tabs — that can appear on your Facebook Page. (We use the terms *apps* and *tabs* interchangeably in this chapter.) You discover the basics about how to install apps and how to move them so that they're featured more prominently. In Book V, we cover Facebook applications in much greater depth and discuss a wide range of specific apps to enhance your Page.

Defining Apps and Understanding Facebook Installed Apps

Facebook has developed four apps that are installed on your Page when you create it:

- **Photos:** Organized into Albums, Timeline Photos, and photos posted by fans
- **Events:** Upcoming and past events (covered in depth in Book VI)
- **Video:** Videos uploaded directly to Facebook
- **Notes:** Mini blog posts with photos or other text

Only Photos appears on your Timeline when you start your Facebook Page. The Video and Notes apps are in your Facebook dashboard under Apps.

The apps that Facebook has created can't have custom names or custom Cover images. The Photos tab defaults to the last photo that was uploaded, and the Events tab defaults to a photo of the most recent event or the event that is coming up soonest. Notes and Video show snapshots of the notes and videos that you've uploaded most recently.

If you want any other apps on your Facebook Page, you have to install them. Facebook has created the four basic apps, but any other app has been created by an independent developer or third party. All Pages are capable of displaying 12 Facebook apps. You can have more installed, but only 12 will appear on your Page for your fans to view, and Facebook displays only the first 4 apps on the top row when someone navigates to your Page. Although your fans see only the first 12, you will be able to see and access all your apps as an admin; the apps appear under your Cover photo.

It's fun to look at all the ways you can spruce up your Page with apps. Pages are using apps in different ways, and the apps can be very engaging. Look at the interesting examples in Figures 2-1 and 2-2.

Figure 2-1: Macy's has a variety of useful apps.

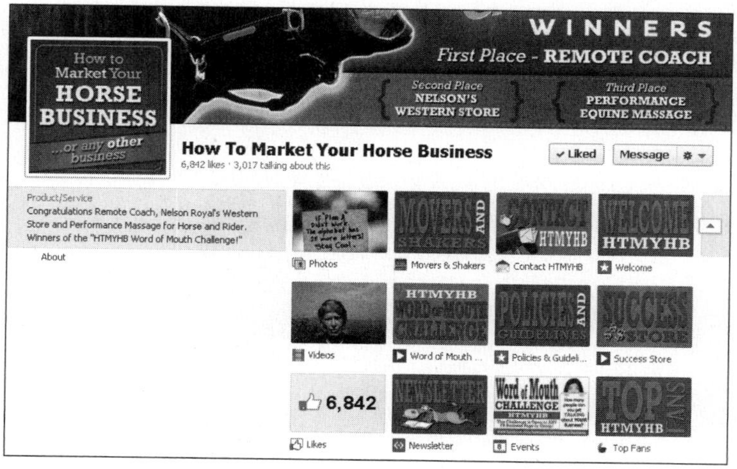

Figure 2-2: How to Market Your Horse Business uses app tabs for added branding.

You can adjust the apps that appear in the first row, but the Photos app is always in the first position and can't be moved. (Technically, you have three available "featured" apps.) To see any additional apps, the user needs to click the down arrow next to the four featured apps, as shown in Figure 2-3. The number with the arrow indicates how many apps are "hiding."

Click to see more apps.

Figure 2-3: Click the down arrow to see more apps.

When you click the photo of the app, you're taken to the associated tab within your Page. If you click the Macy's Is Hiring! tab shown in Figure 2-1, for example, you're taken into the app, which is a mini website that allows people to search for jobs, as shown in Figure 2-4. You can see that you're on the Macy's Page because the tab Macy's Is Hiring! is in the top-left corner. To navigate back to the main Macy's Facebook Page, just click the Macy's box.

Figure 2-4: An interactive Facebook tab on Macy's Facebook Page.

Some apps that you find may not have been updated recently or may be a bit difficult to work with. All the third-party apps covered in this book work well, but so many apps are out there that it's important to be aware of the potential pitfalls!

Many times, the Facebook apps that appear on a Facebook Page are called *tabs,* and these terms are used interchangeably in this chapter.

Adding an App to Your Page

Installing a new app can be a different process for each app, because all but the four Facebook-created apps were developed by third parties. As we discuss each app in this book, we take you through the appropriate steps, but it helps you to have general knowledge of how apps work:

1. **Navigate to the app you want to install.**

   (You see in Book V how to find appropriate apps to install.) Usually, you install the app from within Facebook, but sometimes, you have to navigate to the app's website, configure the app there, and then install it.

2. **Give the app permission to access your information and permission to post to your Page.**

   Usually, you must be logged in as your *personal Profile* rather than as your Page, as shown in Figure 2-5. This process may make you nervous, because you know that you want to add the app to your Page, not your personal Profile. But rest assured — you'll be able to specify where the app is to appear!

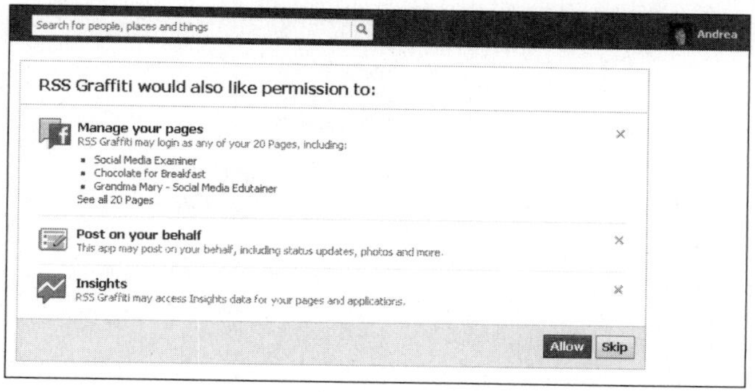
Search for people, places and things
Andrea
RSS Graffiti would also like permission to:
Manage your pages
RSS Graffiti may login as any of your 20 Pages, including:
Social Media Examiner
Chocolate for Breakfast
Grandma Mary - Social Media Edutainer
See all 20 Pages
Post on your behalf
This app may post on your behalf, including status updates, photos and more.
Insights
RSS Graffiti may access Insights data for your pages and applications.
Allow
Skip

Figure 2-5: You must give permission for an app to post to your Pages from your personal Profile.

3. **Choose the Page where you want to add the app, as shown in Figure 2-6.**

   This process can be a bit different for each app, as you see throughout this book.

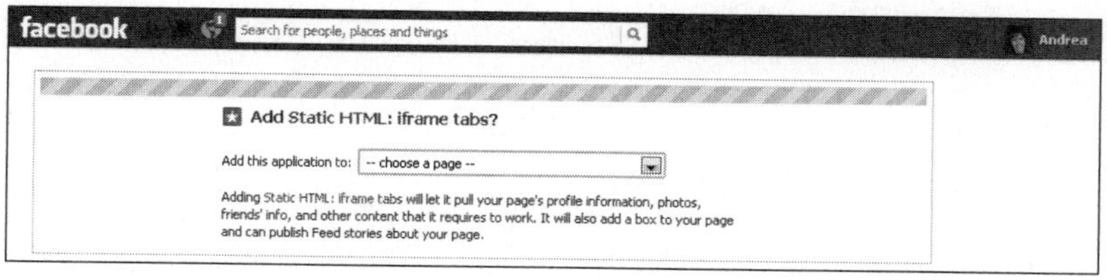
facebook
Search for people, places and things
Andrea
Add Static HTML: iframe tabs?
Add this application to:
-- choose a page --
Adding Static HTML: iframe tabs will let it pull your page's profile information, photos, friends' info, and other content that it requires to work. It will also add a box to your page and can publish Feed stories about your page.

Figure 2-6: You have the chance to add the app to your Page.

When you complete these steps, the app appears in the Apps area below your Cover photo on your Facebook Page.

As we mention earlier in this chapter, you can have more apps installed on your Facebook Page, but only the first 12 (the first 3 rows of apps) will be visible to anyone visiting your Page. As the administrator of a Page, you are able to see *all* your apps, as mentioned previously and as illustrated in Figure 2-7. Just remember that your fans can see only the first three rows. To make an app appear in the first three rows, you need to swap some apps; for details, see the next section, "Rearranging the Positions of Your Apps."

Also, you can have more apps that are not shown underneath your Cover photo but are installed on your Page. To access those apps, go to your Page dashboard and click apps in the left sidebar. See the "Finding Apps in your Page Dashboard," section, later in this chapter.

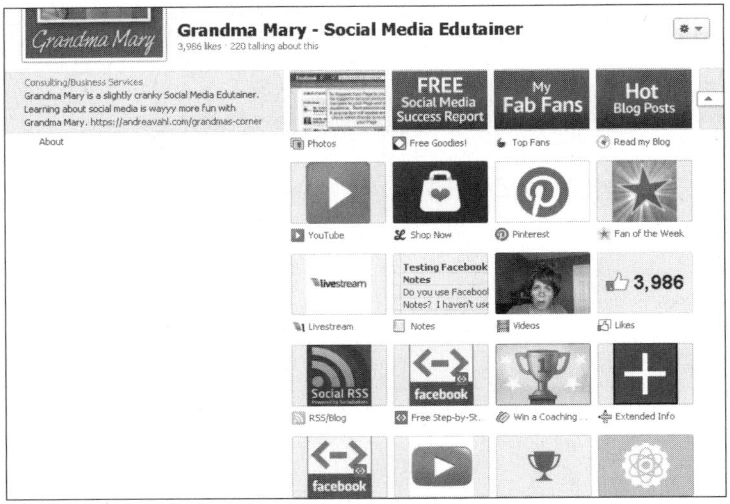

Figure 2-7: As an Admin, you can see all your apps.

Rearranging the Positions of Your Apps

The most visible apps are going to be the ones in the first row, so you need to make them count! Put your best apps in the first row. (Because the Photos app is fixed, you have only three apps to work with in that row.) Then, of course, put any other apps you want to showcase in the next two rows. Many people don't have more than 12 apps, but if you enjoy trying new apps, you can have more than the allotted 12.

Also note that you can't move the Facebook Likes tab below the first three rows of apps to hide it. That tab is visible on every Facebook Page and can't be hidden.

To swap the positions of the apps on your Facebook Page, follow these steps:

1. **Click the down arrow next to your apps to expand all the apps you have available.**
2. **Mouse over an app that you want to move.**

   You see a pencil icon in the top-right corner of the app.
3. **Click the pencil icon.**

   A drop-down menu appears.
4. **From the drop-down menu, choose the app that you want the selected app to swap places with.**

Deleting an App from Your Page

When you add an app to your Page, it doesn't have to live there forever. You can delete it completely or just "hide" it so that it doesn't appear on your Timeline. Use the pencil icon on any of the Apps to remove an App from your Favorites to take it off your Timeline. You can see all the steps on how to do this in Book V, Chapter 1.

TIP

If you have an app that isn't functioning correctly, it's good practice to remove this app so that anyone who's clicking around on your Page doesn't stumble across it.

Customizing the App Title and App Photo

Two of the key parts of the apps you add to your Page are the app title and the app photo. The apps you install have a default title and photo, which usually aren't that interesting. As you have observed from Figures 2-1 and 2-2 showing the app photos, customizing these elements can enhance your branding, draw attention to the app, and give your page a professional look.

As you know, Facebook prohibits any call to action in your Page Cover photo, but your app titles and photos can have a call to action in them. Click Here, Free Report, and Get a Coupon, for example, are all valid and intriguing app titles.

The app photo is 111 pixels wide by 74 pixels tall, which isn't enough space for a very detailed photo. But even having a colored background with some interesting text, as shown in Figure 2-2 earlier in this chapter, is a good strategy.

To change your app title and app photo, follow these steps:

1. **Click the down arrow next to your apps to expand all the apps you have available.**
2. **Mouse over the app you want to edit.**

   You see a pencil icon in the top-right corner of the app.
3. **Click the pencil.**

   A drop-down menu appears.
4. **Choose Edit Settings from the drop-down menu.**

   A pop-up window appears, as shown in Figure 2-8.

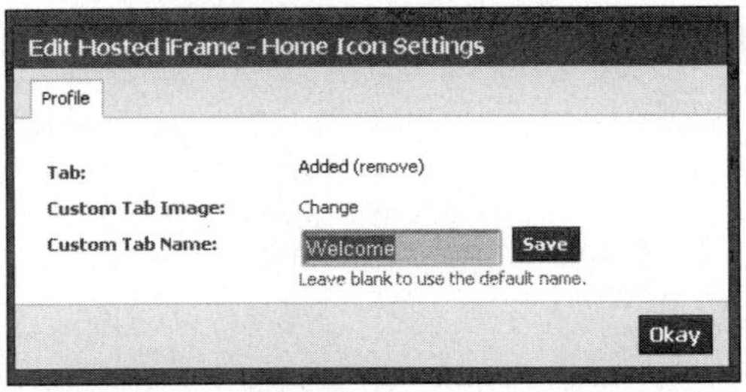

Figure 2-8: Change the tab name and the tab image.

5. **Type the Custom Tab Name you want to use and click Save.**

   Only the first 15 characters appear on your Page; then the name is cut off.

6. **Click the Change hyperlink next to Custom Tab Image to change the tab image.**

   You're taken to a new browser window, where you can upload a custom image.

7. **Click the Change hyperlink.**

   A pop-up window appears, allowing you to choose a file. The image must be 111 × 74 pixels (or an even multiple of that ratio); otherwise, it will be resized.

8. **Navigate to the file you want to upload, and click Open.**

   Your image appears in the Image section, as shown in Figure 2-9.

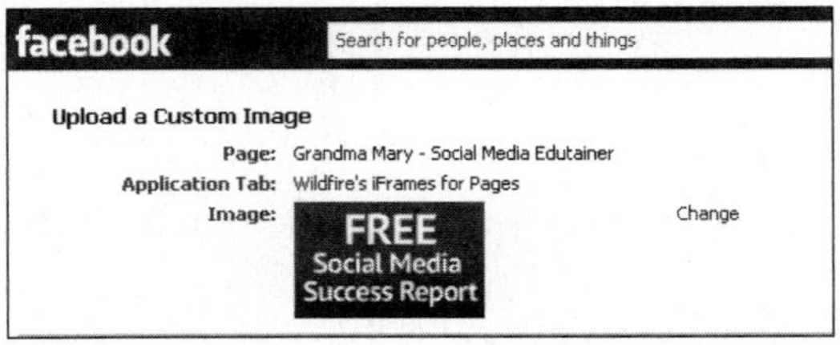

Figure 2-9: Upload a custom image.

The photo has been changed, and now you can close the new browser window that was opened and navigate back to your Facebook Page (the other browser window should still be open). To see the change in effect, just refresh your Page in the browser window.

Finding Apps in Your Page Dashboard

As mentioned earlier in this chapter, the Photos tab is the only one that appears on your Facebook Page when you first get started. But you do have other Facebook apps installed on your Page. You just need to know where to look for them. To access all your apps, follow these steps from your Facebook Page Admin Panel:

1. **Click Edit Page.**

   A drop-down menu appears.

2. **Select Update Info.**

   You are taken to your Page dashboard.

3. **Select Apps from the left side-bar menu.**

   You now see all your apps that you have installed on your Page (see Figure 2-10). If you have not installed any yet, you will see the Facebook Apps: Photos, Events, Video, and Notes.

Learn more about adjusting, deleting, and adding the apps from the Page dashboard in Book V, Chapter 1.

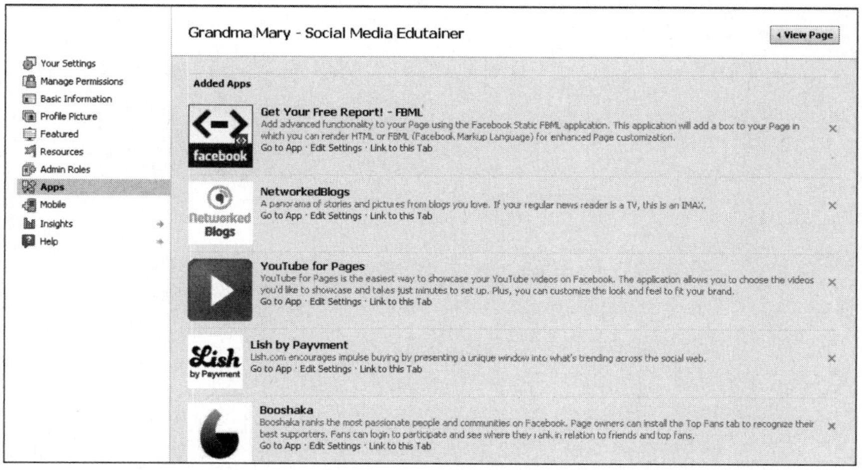

Figure 2-10: Viewing apps from your Page dashboard.

Chapter 3: Importing Your Blog Posts into Your Facebook Page

In This Chapter

- **Obtaining the web address of your RSS feed**
- **Deciding which Facebook application to use to import your blog**
- **Installing and configuring the NetworkedBlogs application**
- **Looking at Social RSS**
- **Exploring RSS Graffiti**
- **Using the dlvr.it tool**

If you have a blog, the easiest way to add new content on your Facebook Page is to import your blog posts. Easier yet would be getting this job done automatically.

You're in luck, because several Facebook applications (and some web-based tools) are available for doing just that. When you post something new on your blog, the application automatically creates a new entry on your Page, which in turn goes out to the News Feeds of people who like you. This automation means one fewer task for you after you post a new blog entry.

In this chapter, we tell you how to use four of the most popular applications for importing blog posts to your Facebook Page. Each application requires your RSS feed's URL, so the chapter starts by telling you how to find that URL.

Importing your blog automatically saves you time and hassle. Luckily, you have lots of choices how. Try one. If it doesn't work for you, you can always stop that application and install a different one.

Getting the Address of Your RSS Feed

No matter what blog-import application you decide to use, you need to know the web address, or *URL,* of your blog's RSS feed. *RSS,* which stands for *Really Simple Syndication,* is a standard used on the Internet to pull information from websites in an organized manner. It pulls only the text, leaving all the fancy graphics that appear on your blog behind.

The address of your RSS feed is typically something like this: `www.YourWebSite.com/feed`. Depending on how your website is set up, though, this address could be something quite different. If you don't know the address of your RSS feed, check with your web developer. If that's not an option, here's a handy trick for discovering your feed address.

On Internet Explorer

If you're using Internet Explorer, follow these steps to find your RSS feed address:

1. **Go to your website or blog in Internet Explorer.**

   Right above the website, you should see the RSS icon in orange, as shown in Figure 3-1. If the icon is gray, the browser can't find an RSS feed on your site, and you need to contact your web developer.

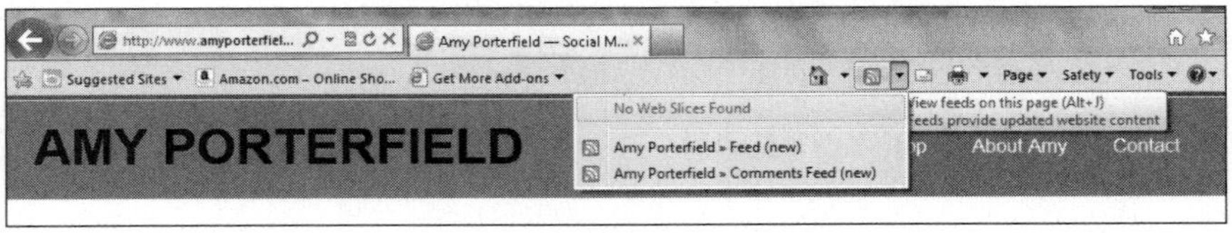

Figure 3-1: The RSS icon appears in orange right above your website.

2. **Click the main RSS feed listed (if you see more than one).**

   In Figure 3-1, Amy's blog also shows the Comments feed for all the comments posted on her blog. You'll be taken to the view of the RSS feed, and the address for that feed displays in the browser address window.

On Firefox

If you're using Firefox, follow these steps to find your RSS feed address:

1. **Go to your website or blog in Firefox.**
2. **Click Bookmarks in the menu bar.**

   A drop-down menu appears.
3. **Mouse over the Subscribe to This Page option.**

   A submenu appears.

4. **Click the main feed.**

   The RSS feed opens in a new window, and the address of the feed displays in the browser's address bar.

In HTML code

Another handy trick for finding the RSS feed is looking at the HTML code of the website. You can do this in any browser, although the steps may vary, depending on your browser. In this section, we offer the steps for several browsers.

If you're using Firefox

1. **Go to the website or blog.**
2. **Right-click anywhere on the page.**

   A drop-down menu appears.
3. **Choose View Page Source.**

   A new window opens, showing the HTML code.

If you're using Internet Explorer

1. **Go to the website or blog.**
2. **Click Page on the menu bar.**

   A drop-down menu appears.
3. **Choose View Source.**

   A new window opens, showing the HTML code.

If you're using Google Chrome

1. **Go to the website or blog.**
2. **Click the wrench icon in the top-right corner.**

   A drop-down menu appears.
3. **Choose Tools.**

   A drop-down menu appears.
4. **Select View Source.**

   A new tab opens, showing the HTML code.

If you're using Safari

1. **Go to the website or blog.**
2. **Click the page icon in the top-right corner.**

   A drop-down menu appears.
3. **Choose View Source.**

   A new window appears, showing the HTML code.

When you've opened the tab or window containing the HTML code in any of the browsers, press Ctrl+F (⌘+F on a Mac) on your keyboard to search for a phrase. Enter **rss** to find the RSS feed address. Using Amy Porterfield's website as an example, you find the following when you search on the term *rss*:

```
<link rel="alternate" type="application/rss+xml" title="Amy Porterfield | Social
    Media Strategy Consultant RSS Feed" href="http://amyporterfield.com/feed/" />
```

The RSS feed address is right after the `href=` term and is `http://amyporterfield.com/feed/`.

Introducing the Facebook Blog-Import Applications

After you have the address of your RSS feed (as we discuss in the previous section), you're ready to begin using one of Facebook's applications to import your blog. But which one? Here's a list of some ways to import your blog into Facebook automatically:

- NetworkedBlogs application
- Social RSS application
- RSS Graffiti
- dlvr.it

These applications were developed by third parties (not Facebook). All these applications have some benefits, and deciding which one to use is a matter of preference. As a metric, the number of users can indicate popularity. NetworkedBlogs has more than 1.9 million monthly users, Social RSS has more than 788,000, and RSS Graffiti has more than 395,000. The Facebook Notes app doesn't have a use statistic available.

To help you decide which application is right for you, the following sections describe each application, show you how easy it is to set up, what features it has, and what the imported posts look like. All these applications are free, although Social RSS has a paid option that provides a higher level of service.

Using the NetworkedBlogs Application

NetworkedBlogs is the most popular method of importing your blog posts into your Page automatically. You import your blog into both your Page and your personal Profile. After you import your blog, a tab appears on your Page that contains your previous posts for people to reference; see Figure 3-2.

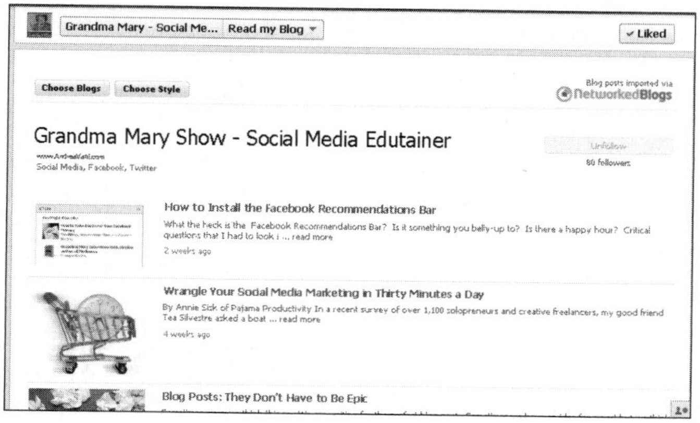

Figure 3-2: Your blog posts are stored on a tab when you use Networked-Blogs.

Clicking one of these links takes a viewer directly to that blog post. Each post is also posted on your Timeline automatically (if you choose automatic posting), and the post looks similar to the one shown in Figure 3-3. The first few lines of the blog post, as well as a picture from the post, are pulled in automatically. You can tell where the post came from by the note below it ("via NetworkedBlogs").

Figure 3-3: See where the post came from.

If you don't have a picture embedded in your post, the NetworkedBlogs application displays a screen shot of your whole blog as the thumbnail picture next to your Timeline post.

Registering your blog on NetworkedBlogs

The NetworkedBlogs application can be a little tricky to navigate, but it has a good frequently asked questions (FAQ) section that can help you through the process. Your first step is to register your blog by following these steps:

1. **Log into Facebook as your personal Profile.**
2. **Go to** `http://apps.facebook.com/blognetworks`**, and click Log In.**

   You may have to click Log In with Facebook one more time in a pop-up window.

   You're taken to the NetworkedBlogs application page, which is actually outside Facebook. You are now at `www.networkedblogs.com`. You may also have to click through a couple of pages that ask you to follow some initial blogs. You do not have to do this, and you can click Next at the bottom of the Page.
3. **Click the Register a Blog link at the top of the page.**

   A new page appears.
4. **Enter the home page of the blog, and click Next.**

   You're taken to a page where you fill in the information about your blog, as shown in Figure 3-4.

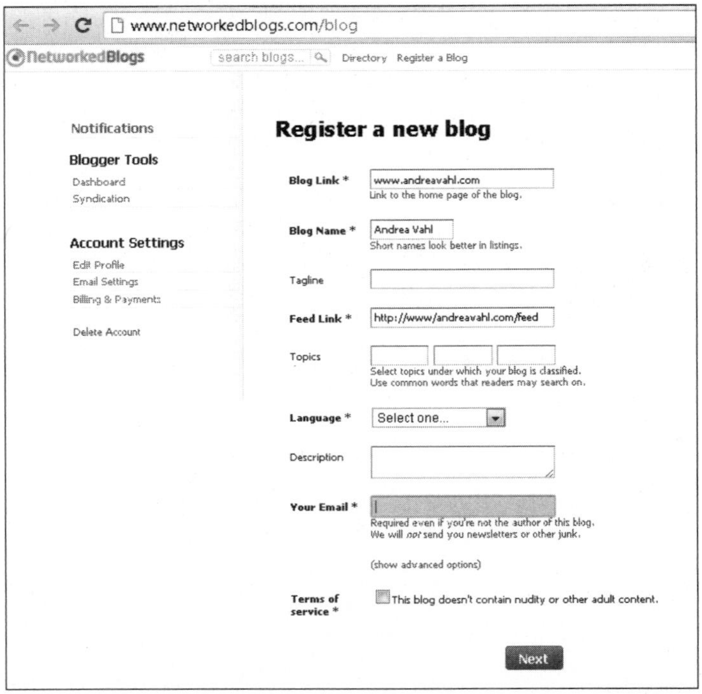

Figure 3-4: Fill in this information for your blog.

The starred items in Figure 3-4 are mandatory; everything else is optional. You can edit any of this information later. Use these tips for filling in this information:

- *Blog Link:* The link to the home page of the blog.
- *Blog Name:* The title of your blog. Keep it short.
- *Tagline:* A little more space to tell people what your blog is about.
- *Feed Link:* The RSS feed link for your blog (refer to "Getting the Address of Your RSS Feed," earlier in this chapter).
- *Topics:* Three keywords that indicate what your blog is about. These keywords can be any keywords that people who use the NetworkedBlogs app might use in searching for blogs that they're interested in.
- *Language:* The language your blog is written in.
- *Description:* A description of your blog. What you enter here shows up in the NetworkedBlogs directory, so make it interesting, and tell people why they'd want to read your blog.
- *Your E-mail:* For Networked Blogs verification. You don't receive e-mail from NetworkedBlogs.
- *Terms of Service:* An agreement that the blog doesn't contain nudity or other adult content.

5. **Click the Next button at the bottom of the screen (refer to Figure 3-4).**

   A new screen appears, asking whether you're the author of the blog for which you just entered information.

6. **Click the Yes button.**

   Another screen appears; this one determines which method you want to use to verify that you're the owner of your blog.

7. **Choose which method you want to use to verify your ownership of the blog: Ask Friends to Verify You or Install the Widget.**

   You can have your Facebook Friends verify that you own the blog; if you select that option, you can select nine Friends and send the request for verification to them. The problem with this option is that not everyone sees that request in his or her notifications (people don't always know to look there), so your verification can take a long time. The better option is to use the widget to verify ownership, if you can.

Verifying ownership of your blog

If you select the Ask Friends to Verify You option, a screen listing all your Facebook Friends appears, and you can select who gets a request to verify that you own your blog. After you select the Friends who will verify the ownership of your blog, you're done. You can move to the next section on setting up syndication.

If you choose the widget to verify ownership, you just need to install this widget temporarily until the NetworkedBlogs application verifies that you put the widget on your blog (you get a notification); then you can remove it. You may choose to keep the widget to promote the fact that you're part of NetworkedBlogs. If you keep the widget on your website, people can click the Follow This Blog button to follow your blog through the NetworkedBlogs app.

If you opt to install the widget, you're taken to the screen shown in Figure 3-5.

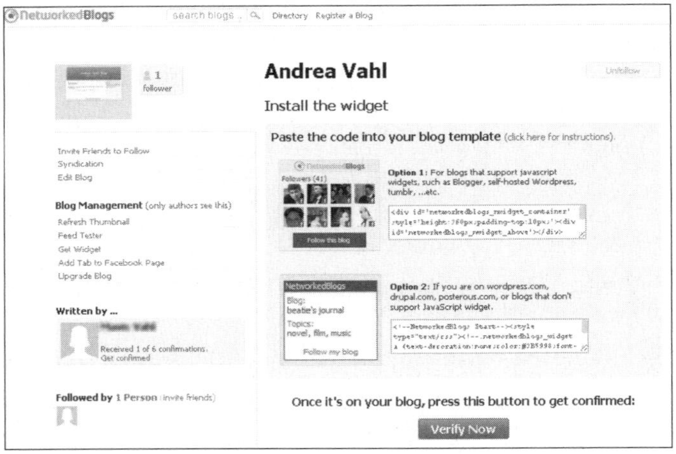

Figure 3-5: Choose Option 1 or Option 2.

Continue by following these steps:

1. **Choose Option 1 if you have a self-hosted WordPress blog or Tumblr or Blogger; choose Option 2 if you have your blog on WordPress.com, Drupal.com, or Posterous.com.**

   The code in Option 1 is for sites that allow JavaScript; the code in Option 2 is for sites (such as WordPress.com) that don't allow JavaScript.

   TIP

   A self-hosted blog typically is on a site where you pay for hosting. The WordPress.com, Blogger.com, Drupal.com, and Posterous.com sites will host your blog for free, but they have some limitations.

2. **Highlight the code for the appropriate option, and copy it (by pressing Ctrl+C on a Windows PC or ⌘+C on a Mac).**
3. **Click the blue Click Here for Instructions link (next to Paste the Code into Your Blog Template in Figure 3-5).**

   A new window appears, displaying instructions for different platforms.
4. **Follow the instructions to install the code.**
5. **Click the blue Verify Now button.**

   If you installed the widget correctly, you get a Verification Successful message.

   Your verification is complete. You can remove the NetworkedBlogs widget or badge, if you want.

Setting up syndication

Syndication tells NetworkedBlogs where you want your new blog posts to be posted in Facebook (and NetworkedBlogs can automatically tweet your new post, too). Syndication is a great tool to help you automate sending your blog content to Facebook and Twitter.

To set up your syndication, follow these steps:

1. **Click the Blogger Dashboard link in the top-right corner of the NetworkedBlogs application.**
2. **If you're using the application for the first time, click the Grant Permissions button.**

   A pop-up window appears, asking you to allow the NetworkedBlogs app to post on your behalf and access your data. This request can look daunting, but the app is reputable.
3. **Click Allow.**

   You see your Blogger dashboard.
4. **Click Syndication in the left sidebar.**

   You see a drop-down menu with your blog and the places you want to send your post listed.
5. **From the drop-down menu, choose the blog you want to configure.**
6. **Add Facebook targets and/or Twitter targets, as shown in Figure 3-6.**

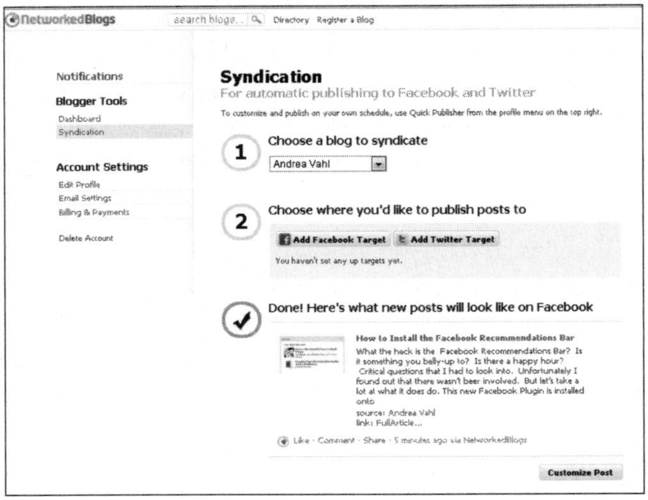

Figure 3-6: Click Add Facebook Target to select your Facebook Profile or Page.

You can also customize the post by clicking the Customize Post button at the bottom of the Syndication page (refer to Figure 3-6). You can specify whether to include an image; we highly recommend that you do. You can also choose whether you want to hide the NetworkedBlogs toolbar when people navigate to your post from the NetworkedBlogs link. The toolbar can make it easier for people to share, but the choice is up to you.

TIP

If you get stuck, the NetworkedBlogs application has a decent support page at `www.networkedblogs.com/help`.

After you successfully configure your NetworkedBlogs application and post a new blog post, the application automatically sends the post to your Page or personal Profile (depending on how it's configured). The post usually appears within a few minutes after you post to your blog, but we've seen it take as long as an hour. Just be patient if you don't see it right away.

TIP

If you find that your blog post isn't updated in the NetworkedBlogs application, you have to click a Pull Now button to find any new blog posts on your blog and bring them into the application. To do so, go to the Blogger dashboard, click the name of your blog on the dashboard, and then click the Pull Now button shown in Figure 3-7.

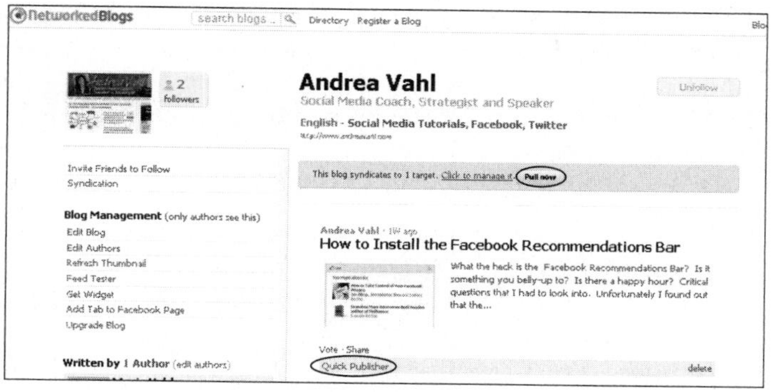

Figure 3-7: Click Pull Now if your blog post hasn't been brought into the application automatically.

Reposting a blog post with NetworkedBlogs

You can repost any of your old blog posts by clicking the Quick Publisher link below the post (refer to Figure 3-7). Just follow these easy steps:

1. **Click the Quick Publisher link.**

   A pop-up window appears.

2. **Select the target (where you want to send the blog post) by clicking the Publish To field.**

   You can select multiple targets.

3. **Select the post to send by clicking the Attach a Post from My Blog button.**

   A drop-down menu appears, listing your blog posts, as shown in Figure 3-8.

4. **Choose one from the list and then click the blue Publish button.**

   The post is sent.

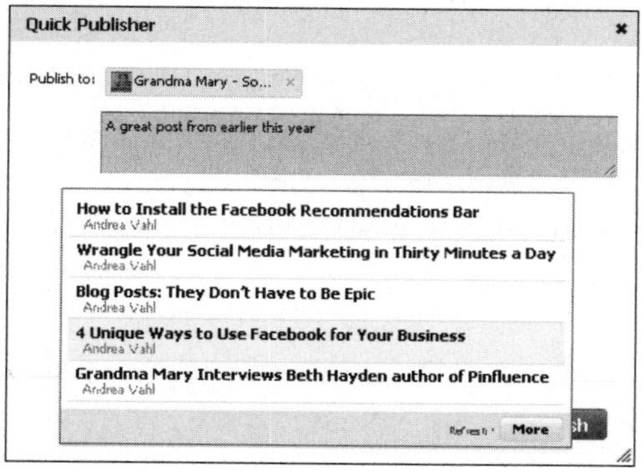

Figure 3-8: Select which blog post you want to send out to your networks in the Quick Publisher.

TIP

We recommend reposting some of your blog posts from time to time if they're still relevant and helpful to your audience. New people who are coming to your Page won't have seen all the posts when they first came out. Even longtime members of your community may have missed a post or didn't have a chance to read it, so they'll welcome the opportunity to view helpful posts. As long as you use the reposting feature prudently, it's a good thing to do occasionally.

Many people ask whether they should post their business blog to their personal Profile as well as their Page. Our recommendation is that you should do so unless you feel very strongly about "bothering" your Friends and family members. You probably aren't posting to your blog that often, and your Friends and family should know what you're doing in your business. Many referrals can — and should — come from your Friends and family, and seeing a blog post may spark a connection for them to share your post with one of their Friends.

Adding the NetworkedBlogs tab to your Facebook Page

NetworkedBlogs allows you to add a tab to your Facebook Page to display your blog posts, as shown in Figure 3-2, earlier in this chapter. This tab gives your Facebook fans easy access to your blog from Facebook without having to go anywhere.

Some people decide to use only NetworkedBlogs as a way to import their blog posts onto a Facebook tab, and they do not use NetworkedBlogs to automatically post to their Page. Manually posting your new blog post to the Timeline gives you more control of how the post looks and of the commentary that goes along with the post. Ultimately, you have to weigh the benefit of automation against the benefit of manually posting something that could be a bit more engaging because of the personal touch you add.

Adding the tab to your Page is easy. Follow these steps:

1. **In NetworkedBlogs, click Blogger Dashboard in the top-right corner.**

   Alternatively, go to `www.networkedblogs.com/dashboard` when you're logged in to the NetworkedBlogs app. You see your blog listed.

2. **Click Add to Facebook Page below the name of your blog in the center of the page.**

   A pop-up selection window appears.

3. **Choose the appropriate Page from the drop-down menu.**
4. **Click Add Page Tab.**

   You see a message that your Page has been added.

Now when you navigate to your Page, you see the Blog tab in your Apps area. You can change the position of the tab and the app photo as outlined in Chapter 2 of this minibook.

Getting more readers by increasing your ranking inside the app page

Within the NetworkedBlogs application, you can follow other blogs. When you do, those blogs appear in your NetworkedBlogs News Feed when you click Home within the NetworkedBlogs app (just under the NetworkedBlogs logo). Oh, no! Not another news feed! Yes, but this news feed can be helpful for keeping track of the blogs that you want to follow.

You can also increase your blog's readership by trying to increase your ranking within the NetworkedBlogs application. The more followers and high ratings you have, the higher your blog is listed in NetworkedBlogs's Browse area for your topic — another place that can bring more attention to your blog and your business.

Begin by browsing the blogs within NetworkedBlogs by topic: Click the Directory link at the top of the page; then select topics you're interested in on the left side of Top Blogs. The more followers and ratings you can get, the better your chance of coming up in the top 50. To get more followers and ratings, start by asking your Facebook Friends to follow and rate your blog within the NetworkedBlogs application.

Installing Social RSS

Another Facebook application that you can use to import your blog posts automatically is Social RSS. Social RSS is a little easier to set up than NetworkedBlogs is, but the free version may not work for you if you're posting more than three times per week. See "Deciding when to upgrade to paid service," later in this chapter, for more information.

To start using the Social RSS app, follow these steps:

1. **Log in to Facebook as your personal Profile.**
2. **Go to** `http://apps.facebook.com/social-rss`.

   You see information about the app, including how it will appear on your Timeline.
3. **From the Who Can See Posts This App Makes for You on Your Facebook Timeline drop-down menu, choose Everyone.**

   You want everyone to see your blog posts!

4. **Click the blue Go to App button.**

   You see a Request for Permission screen to allow Social RSS to access your basic information.

5. **Click Allow.**

   You see the Social RSS initial screen, listing the terms of use. Scroll down until you see the feed settings.

6. **From the drop-down menu, choose the Page to which you want to add an RSS feed.**

   A configuration screen appears, as shown in Figure 3-9.

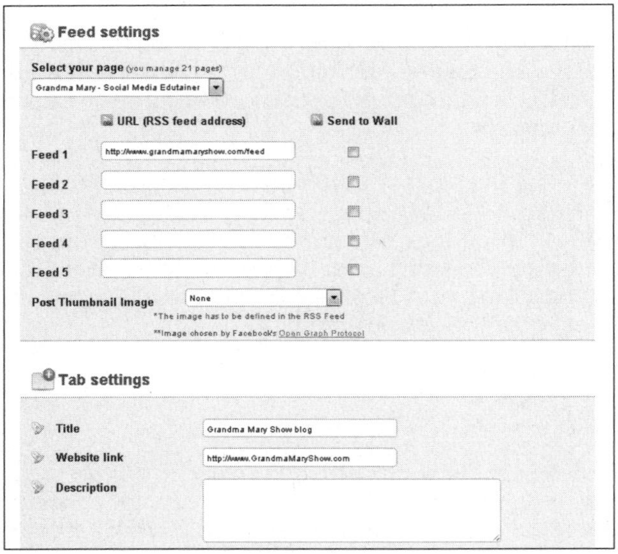

Figure 3-9: Configure the Social RSS application here.

7. **Below the URL heading, enter your RSS feed's address in the Feed 1 box.**

   Refer to "Getting the Address of Your RSS Feed," earlier in the chapter, for more information about this address. Notice that you can bring in multiple RSS Feeds with this app from here using the Feed 2 through Feed 5 boxes.

8. **Select the Send to Wall check box if you want your feed to be posted to your Timeline automatically.**

9. **From the drop-down menu, choose the thumbnail image you want to post.**

10. **Scroll down to and configure the tab settings.**

    These settings are for the tab that appears on your Page. Here's some information about what to put in each field:

    - *Title:* The title of your app as it appears below the app photo on your Page. If you're pulling in multiple RSS feeds with the Social RSS app, all the feeds will appear on the same Page. If you're pulling in just your blog, you can title the app *Blog.* If you have multiple feeds coming in, you may want to call the app *Industry News* (or whatever characterizes those streams best).
    - *Website Link:* Your website address for people to click.
    - *Description:* A brief paragraph about your blog or the set of RSS feeds. This description appears at the top of the page of posts.
    - *Timezone:* Your time zone.

11. **Click the Update button at the bottom of the page.**

    A pop-up window appears, saying that your feeds have been successfully updated. The window also promotes the Social RSS app's paid service. The free service lets you import just one post per day; the paid service lets you import new articles each hour.

Figure 3-10 shows what a post looks like when it's automatically imported into your Timeline.

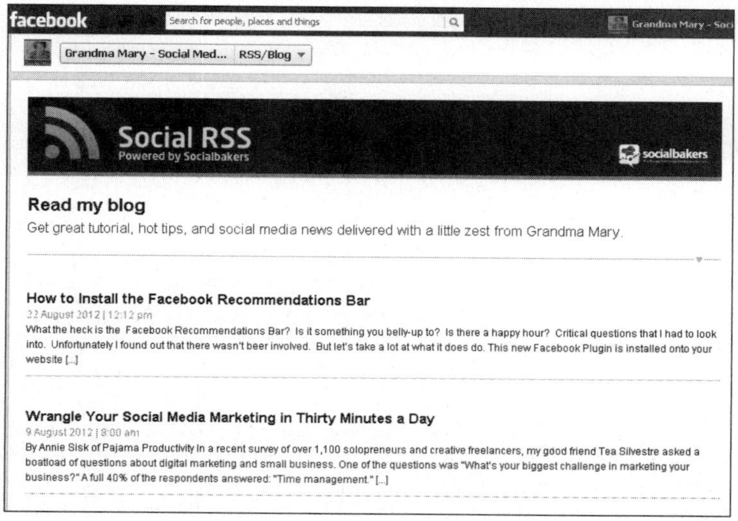

Figure 3-10: An example of the Social RSS tab.

Using Social RSS

After you configure Social RSS, it automatically adds your posts to your Page Timeline (if you selected that option) and to your RSS/Blog tab on your Page. You can always edit the settings or add more feeds from other places.

You also can add a feed to your personal Profile from the Social RSS application. Just choose User Profile Wall from the drop-down menu in the Social RSS configuration area.

Beyond that, Social RSS doesn't have too many other features unless you upgrade to the paid service (described next), which gives you some added statistics.

Deciding when to upgrade to paid service

The Social RSS application, `http://apps.facebook.com/social-rss`, offers a paid service ($24 per year, as of this writing) that grants you more posts per hour (up to five per feed per hour, with a maximum of five feeds). By comparison, the free Social RSS currently allows for one post to your Timeline per day. If you're using this application for multiple feeds that post every day, it's not going to work. If you're using Social RSS to bring in your own blog to Facebook, the free option will probably work just fine because most people aren't blogging more than once per day.

Social RSS has been acquired by Socialbakers, and its pop-up window advertising the full-service option appears right after you configure the feed. Socialbakers also advertises its Facebook analytics program within this app and provides a 14-day trial on its analytics.

Using RSS Graffiti

Another Facebook application that you can use to post your blog entries automatically on your Facebook Timeline is RSS Graffiti. This app doesn't limit you to importing only blog posts: You can use it to bring in any RSS feed from anywhere, much as you can with Social RSS. You can also use RSS Graffiti to post in Facebook Groups. You can control how many posts per day are pulled in, just in case the RSS feed you enter has more posts than you want to share with your community.

Adding RSS feeds can help you add content to your Page. You may want to use RSS feeds to import industry news or other helpful blogs. You can search some of the RSS-feed directories that are available, but you're better off bringing in a feed from a site that you know, like, and trust.

RSS Graffiti is highly configurable. You can configure the post style, the scheduling of updates, and the times when the messages are posted. All these features translate into many settings, all of which you can change. Most of the settings can be left at their default values.

REMEMBER

One thing that RSS Graffiti doesn't have is a tab that you can add to your Page. It only posts the RSS feed on your Timeline. If you want a place to show your most recent blog posts on your Facebook Page, we recommend using Social RSS or NetworkedBlogs.

To get started with RSS Graffiti, follow these steps:

1. **Log in to Facebook as your personal Profile.**
2. **Go to** `http://apps.facebook.com/rssgraffiti`**.**

   You see information about the app and how it will appear on your Timeline.
3. **From the Who Can See Posts This App Makes for You on Your Facebook Timeline drop-down menu, choose Everyone.**
4. **Click the blue Go to App button.**

   You see a Request for Permission screen, asking you to allow RSS Graffiti to access your basic information.
5. **Click Allow.**
6. **If you see a pop-up window, click Go to Permissions.**

   You're taken to the RSS Graffiti dashboard.
7. **Click Add New Publishing Plan.**

   A window appears, allowing you to name your publishing plan.
8. **Type a name in the text box, and click Create Publishing Plan.**

   A configuration area appears, as shown in Figure 3-11.

Figure 3-11: Select the source (RSS feed) and the target (Page or Profile).

9. **Click the Add New button next to Sources.**

   A pop-up window appears, allowing you to add your RSS feed.

10. **Add the address of your RSS feed (refer to "Getting the Address of Your RSS Feed," earlier in this chapter), and click Add Source.**

    A pop-up window appears, allowing you to configure the RSS feed, as shown in Figure 3-12.

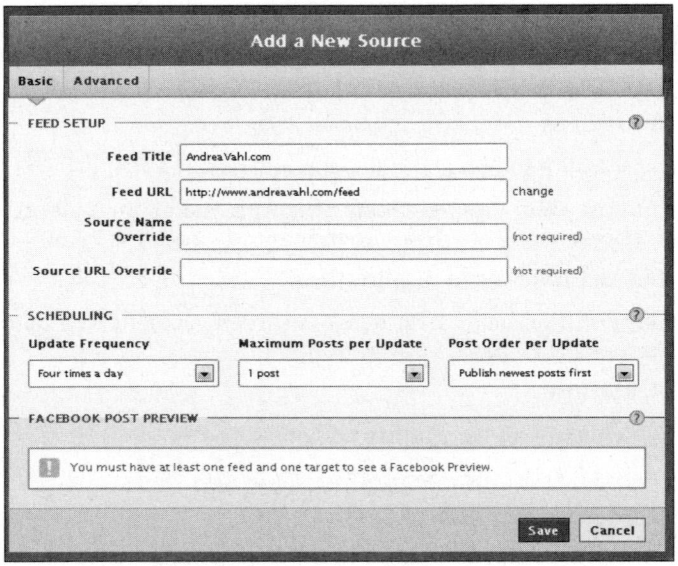

Figure 3-12: Configure your settings.

As we mention earlier in this chapter, you can configure many features of RSS Graffiti, but the default settings work well for most people, and you can skip to Step 11.

Or, if you want to customize your settings, you can read a little bit more about what each of the settings means here:

- *Source Name Override:* Change the name that appears when you post the article or blog post.
- *Source URL Override:* Override the URL that points to the website. Leave this field blank to use the feed's URL.
- *Scheduling:* Change the update frequency and maximum posts per update, and specify whether you want the newest posts to post first.

On the Advanced tab, you can set these options:

- *Format Message:* Add messages to each post, using these options. You may choose to add a static message such as *New Post from My Blog* or something similar.
- *Filtering Options:* Set the date and time after which posts can be published on your Timeline. Older posts won't be published unless you change this option. You can indicate how long a post must be up (in minutes) before it's posted to your Timeline by setting the Eligibility Age option. You may want to use this option if you sometimes make minor edits in posts shortly after you publish them. That way, you have a buffer of time before the story is posted to your Facebook Timeline.

11. **Click Save after you've configured your source RSS feed.**

    The pop-up window disappears, and you see the name of the feed in the Sources area (refer to Figure 3-11).

12. **Click Add New next to Target.**

    A pop-up window appears, showing your available Pages and groups.

13. **Select the Page.**

    You can also choose to publish on behalf of the Page or your personal Profile, but for now, accept the default selection of the Page.

14. **Select the post style.**

    You can choose Standard, Compact, or Status Updates. A preview window appears next to each selection. Choose what works best for you by selecting the appropriate radio button.

15. **Click Save Changes.**

    Your publishing plan is finished, and your posts will start updating when you make a new blog post.

Be careful about adding just any RSS feed to your Page. After all, you don't control that content, and you may not agree with a post that's brought in.

Using the dlvr.it Tool

dlvr.it is a great tool that you can use to automatically post your blog or any RSS feed to Facebook and Twitter. It's a cinch to set up, and it offers analytics on the posted articles, which is a nice feature for helping you track clicks. You can also use the tool to schedule any post (not just a post from your blog) for later.

Signing up and getting started are easy. Just go to `http://dlvr.it`, and follow these steps:

1. **In the appropriate fields on the main page, enter your e-mail address and a password of your choice.**
2. **Click Sign Up.**

   You're taken to a page where you can to add your RSS feed, as shown in Figure 3-13.

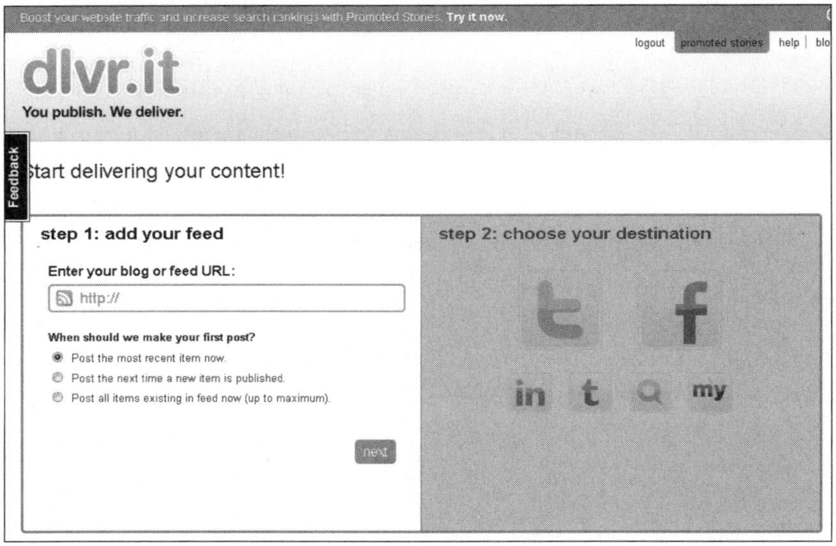

Figure 3-13: Add your RSS feed.

3. **Enter the RSS feed of your blog.**

   Refer to "Getting the Address of Your RSS Feed," earlier in the chapter.
4. **Select the appropriate radio button to indicate whether you want to post your first item now or the next time a new item is published, or to post all items in the feed.**
5. **Click Next.**

   The Step 2: Choose Your Destination section is highlighted.
6. **Click the Facebook button.**

   The application detects whether you're logged in to Facebook, and if you're not, it prompts you to log in to your account.

7. **From the drop-down menu, choose the Facebook Page where you want to post your blog.**
8. **Click Continue.**

   You get a message that the *route* (the automated posting from your blog to your Facebook Page), has been added, and you see your new route, as shown in Figure 3-14.

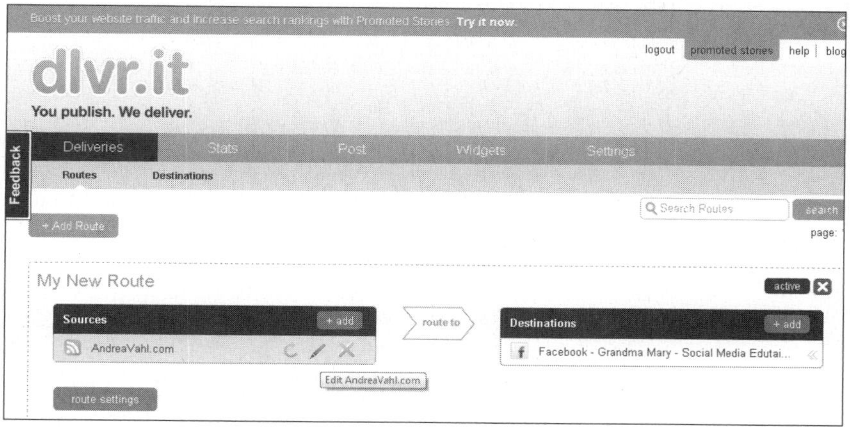

Figure 3-14: Your dlvr.it route.

You can add more routes (to Twitter, LinkedIn, or your Facebook personal Profile), if you want, by clicking the Add Route button.

Note that if you mouse over your Sources or Destinations (refer to Figure 3-14), you see a pencil icon; click that icon to see advanced settings. These settings give you much more control of when your blog posts are posted, what text is displayed, what filters you can add to the RSS feed, and more. These settings are beyond the scope of this book, but Figure 3-15 shows you a snapshot of the types of customization that are available.

REMEMBER

Don't worry about duplicating content. Some people ask whether they should post on their blog and then repeat that information on their Facebook Page and on Twitter, and maybe also send out a newsletter with the link to the post. Don't worry that people are going to get sick of that post. Most likely, they see it in only one or two places unless you're posting the same thing over and over. After all, you're trying to get the word out about your blog post, and people need multiple opportunities to read it.

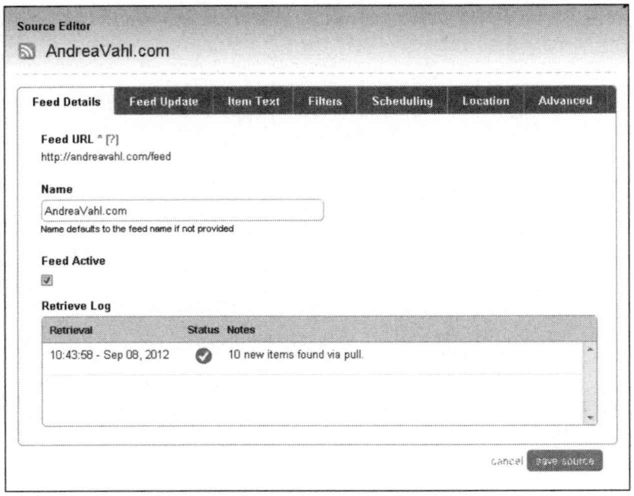

Figure 3-15: Advanced settings for the RSS feed gives you many customization options.

Chapter 4: Connecting Your Page to Twitter

In This Chapter

- **Connecting to Twitter in various ways**
- **Using HootSuite and TweetDeck**
- **Exploring other posting tools**
- **Adding a Twitter tab to your Facebook Page**

You likely know what Twitter is and how to use it. You may not have heard of HootSuite and TweetDeck, though, or know how to use them to your advantage when you coordinate your social networks in tandem with Facebook marketing.

Bottom line, in this chapter, we show you the benefits (and a few considerations) of connecting your Facebook presence with Twitter to complement and diversify your Facebook marketing campaigns. And, yes, we also show literally how to connect these so you can put them to best use.

TIP

Some of these third-party applications may not get the same visibility as a traditional post that you put straight on your Wall. Posts that come into Facebook via Twitter and the other apps mentioned here are sometimes hidden with other posts coming in from the same application, but at this writing, we did not find that to be the case. Watch your News Feed to see how the posts are being shown.

To Connect or Not to Connect

So do you want to tweet everything you post to your Page, post to your Page from Twitter, or update simultaneously? More important, should you? First, consider the implications of linking the two accounts.

Most social media thought leaders agree that posting in both Twitter and Facebook all the time isn't a good idea, because your Facebook community is different from your Twitter community; it expects different things. Twitter typically has more quick interactions and conversations, whereas a Facebook community expects fewer updates and more threaded conversations.

Also, if you're participating on other social media sites, we recommend connecting them with your Facebook Page, because people on Facebook may not be aware of where to find you on YouTube, Twitter, or LinkedIn. And adding your other accounts can give your users a richer experience through SlideShare presentations and YouTube videos (find out more about adding these apps in Book V, Chapter 1).

To help you coordinate all your social networks, consider using tools like HootSuite and TweetDeck to simplify your life by creating a single dashboard that lets you monitor your various social profiles and update from one place. We show you how to use both of these tools in this chapter.

Connecting Facebook and Twitter

How to connect Twitter and Facebook? Let us count the ways! There are many ways to link your Facebook Page to your tweets. (For those of you who aren't familiar with Twitter, a *tweet* is equivalent to a status update in Facebook, but only 140 characters long.) Here are some of the options for connecting Facebook and Twitter, each of which we cover in detail:

- **En masse:** Send every post on your Facebook Page to your Twitter account automatically.
- **Selectively:** Selectively post from Twitter to your Facebook account by adding a hashtag to the tweets that you want posted on your Facebook Page. Keep reading to see what a hashtag is and how it works.
- **Both:** Update Twitter and Facebook simultaneously *and* selectively by using HootSuite or TweetDeck.

Linking your Facebook Page to Twitter

If you want to send everything that you put on your Facebook Wall to Twitter, you can do that easily and automatically through Facebook. This isn't a bad thing to do, because typically, you're posting to your Facebook Page less frequently than you post to Twitter. Also, the Twitter community accepts more-frequent posts than the Facebook community does.

REMEMBER

Just keep in mind that Facebook status updates can be 60,000 characters long — way longer than the 140-character limit of a tweet. In a bit, we'll show you how to handle that limitation.

Sending all your Facebook updates to Twitter can be a good way to connect your community on Twitter to your Facebook Page. Just be mindful that some people don't like the duplication with Twitter and Facebook: If you're going to tweet, just tweet as Twitter was meant to be used, without trying to fit more than the original 140 characters into your tweets.

That said, you must decide what is right for you and your brand. Automation between Facebook and Twitter can be a good thing for the following reasons:

- ✦ Saves you time
- ✦ Adds more content to your Twitter feed
- ✦ Can bring your Twitter community to your Facebook Page

To make the connection, log in to your Facebook personal Profile. (Logging in as your Page doesn't work with these steps.) Once you are in the application, you will specify the Page where your tweets will be sent. Just follow these steps:

1. **Go to** `www.facebook.com/twitter`**.**

   You can open a new window in your browser or just type the URL in your browser window. You see the screen shown in Figure 4-1, displaying all the Pages of which you're an admin.

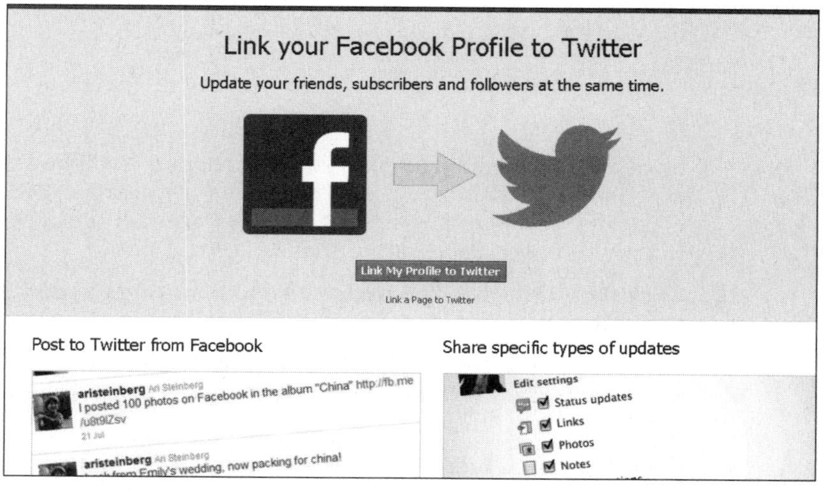

Figure 4-1: Send your Facebook Page updates to Twitter.

2. **Click the Link a Page to Twitter hyperlink just below the Link My Profile to Twitter button.**

   You are taken to a screen that shows the Pages where you are an Administrator.

3. **Click the Link to Twitter button next to the Page you want to link.**

   You go to Twitter to authorize this action; what you see is shown in Figure 4-2. If nothing happens when you click the Link to Twitter button, your pop-up blocker may be blocking the access to the site, and you may need to allow access.

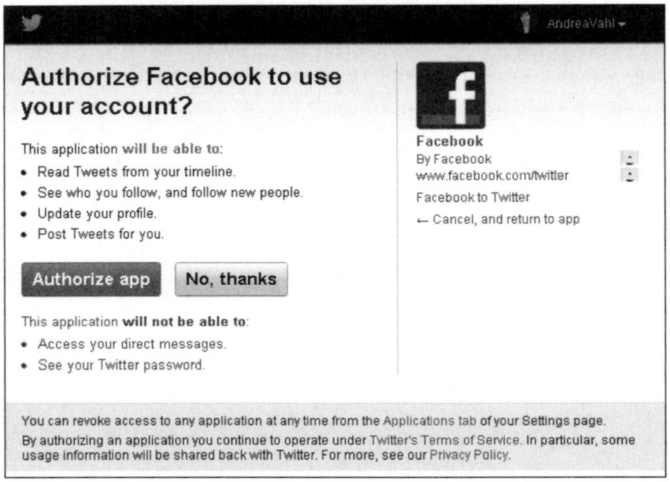

Figure 4-2: Twitter requires that you authorize the postings from your Page.

TIP: If you're not logged in to your Twitter account, you'll be asked to log in at that time to authorize the postings. But if you are logged into Twitter, make sure you're logged in to the Twitter account that you want to link to that Facebook Page, rather than a different one!

4. **Click the Authorize App button to allow posting to your Twitter account.**

   You're redirected to Facebook, where your Page is now confirmed to be linked to Twitter, as shown in Figure 4-3. You can select exactly the types of posts you want to tweet.

5. **Clear the check boxes of the items you don't want to send to Twitter.**
6. **Click Save Changes.**

TIP: If you ever decide to stop tweeting your Page posts, just go back to `www.facebook.com/twitter`, and click the Unlink from Twitter link to stop the tweeting. You can also use this link to change the settings of what is tweeted out, as shown in Figure 4-3.

Figure 4-3: Your Facebook Page and Twitter are now linked, and you can select what to send to Twitter.

Seeing what happens to too-long tweets

As we mention earlier in this chapter, status updates in Facebook are potentially longer than the ones allowed in Twitter. So what happens if you post something in Facebook that's too long to tweet, but you have Facebook and Twitter linked? Well, Facebook automatically cuts off the tweet and posts a link to the actual Facebook update so that someone could click it to read the entire post.

Figure 4-4 shows a too-long tweet that was sent from a Facebook Page.

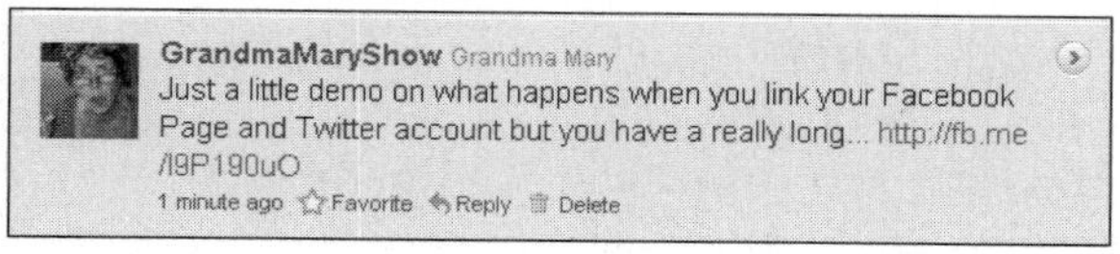

Figure 4-4: A too-long tweet sent from Facebook.

Someone following the post on Twitter who wants to read the rest of that sentence just clicks the link at the end of the tweet to be taken to the Facebook update, as shown in Figure 4-5.

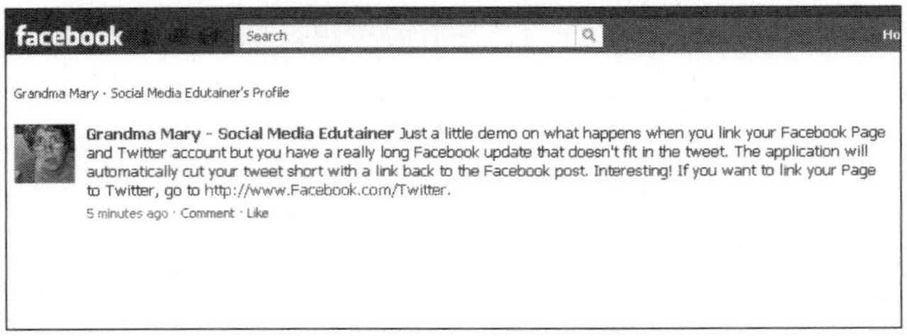

Figure 4-5: The whole status update is now visible within Facebook.

Notice in Figure 4-5 the two links that the person viewing the tweet could click to go to your Facebook Page:

- The link preceding the status update that reads `Grandma Mary - Social Media Edutainer`
- The link above the status update — in this example, `Grandma Mary - Social Media Edutainer's Profile`

Using Twitter Tools to Update Facebook

You can send your updates from a Twitter tool — or Twitter *client,* as it's sometimes called — to update your Facebook Profile or Facebook Page. This is a great idea if you are on multiple social sites and want to update some of them at the same time. Two of the most popular Twitter tools are HootSuite and TweetDeck. Both are designed mainly for Twitter, but you can also use them to update multiple other social media platforms at the same time, such as LinkedIn, Facebook, MySpace, and Foursquare.

TIP: Don't post a lot of Twitter-specific lingo to your Wall, such as messages with `@reply` or tweets with hashtags in them. Your Facebook community may not be on Twitter and won't understand all the symbols and messages.

Exploring HootSuite

HootSuite is a free, web-based app you use to manage multiple social media accounts. Because it's web-based, you can run the application from its website and have access to it from any computer. By comparison, TweetDeck is a program that you download onto your computer and run from your desktop. It's also worth mentioning that HootSuite and TweetDeck both have mobile apps for your smartphone.

Walking you through the entire setup of HootSuite and TweetDeck is beyond the scope of this book, and the installs are pretty intuitive. We just want to show you how you can align your Facebook accounts with these applications and how they work.

TIP

HootSuite is a free app, but it does have some nice perks if you upgrade to its paid Pro Plan at $5.99 per month. The Pro Plan includes features such as the ability to adding more than five social media accounts, the ability to have a team member monitor the same social media accounts, and Google Analytics integration.

To start using HootSuite, go to www.hootsuite.com. Enter your name and e-mail address, choose a password, and then click the Sign Up Now button to get started and walk through the configuration steps.

With HootSuite, you can add multiple social profiles by clicking your picture icon in the top-left corner of the page and then selecting Add a Social Network in the boxes on the lower part of the tab, as shown in Figure 4-6.

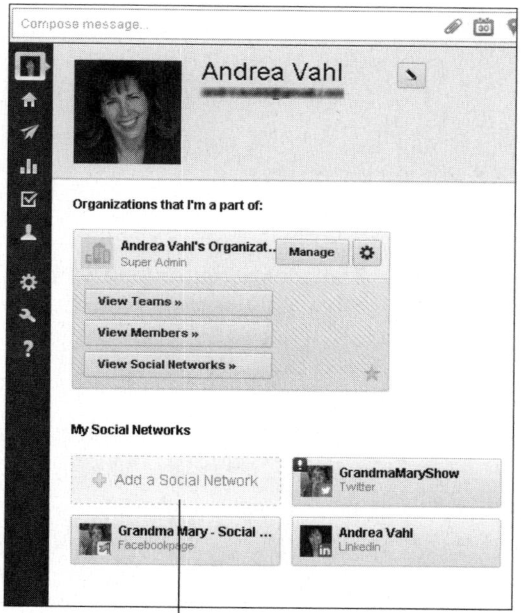

Figure 4-6: Add social profiles to HootSuite here.

A dialog box like the one shown in Figure 4-7 appears; you can add your various social profiles by selecting the sites on the left side of the dialog box, as shown in the figure. With the HootSuite tool, you can update Twitter, Facebook, LinkedIn, Google+, WordPress, MySpace, Mixi, and Foursquare. You can add your Facebook personal Profile, as well as any Facebook Page that you administer. Having your personal Profile and Facebook Pages all in one place with HootSuite means that you can do all your updating in one place. You can also see your News Feed and comments within HootSuite.

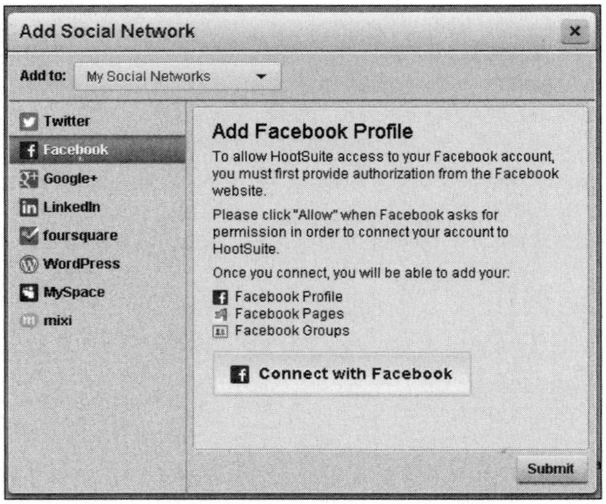

Figure 4-7: Configuring your social networks in HootSuite.

Figure 4-8 shows what the HootSuite dashboard looks like. The Compose Message field (top-left corner) is where you enter your status update for Twitter, Facebook, LinkedIn, or some combination of all these websites.

Figure 4-8: The HootSuite dashboard.

Next to the Compose Message field is a series of icons, all indicating the social media profiles that you can update at the same time. In Figure 4-8, left to right, are social media profile pictures with small icons for Twitter, Facebook, Facebook Page (a flag), and LinkedIn. The icons appear in the bottom-right corner of the pictures.

Suppose that you want to post a message and send it to your Facebook personal Profile, your Facebook Page, Twitter, and LinkedIn at the same time. You could click to select each of those profiles, enter your message, and then click Send Now to update all your profiles simultaneously, as shown in Figure 4-9. Notice that you see a Facebook preview link below your post when you check any of your Facebook Profiles. This preview link gives you the ability to customize the photo you attach to the post, just as you can do when you post a link in Facebook directly. Make any adjustments to the post and then click Send Now.

Figure 4-9: Click the profiles you want to update with the same message.

HootSuite can also schedule your status updates. If you're going to be gone for the day or for a vacation, you can schedule a few updates to post to your social profiles when you're gone. HootSweet!

TIP

Scheduling updates is good for your business so that you aren't completely out of sight while you're gone. Many businesses even let their community know that they will be gone but will be posting useful content or some of their best past blog posts. This technique is a good practice, because your community members will know not to expect immediate return messages if they respond to a posting.

To schedule a post with HootSuite, compose your message just as you would a normal message; select the social media profile(s) to which you want the message to be sent; and then click the calendar icon below the update window, shown in Figure 4-10, to choose the time and date to send the message.

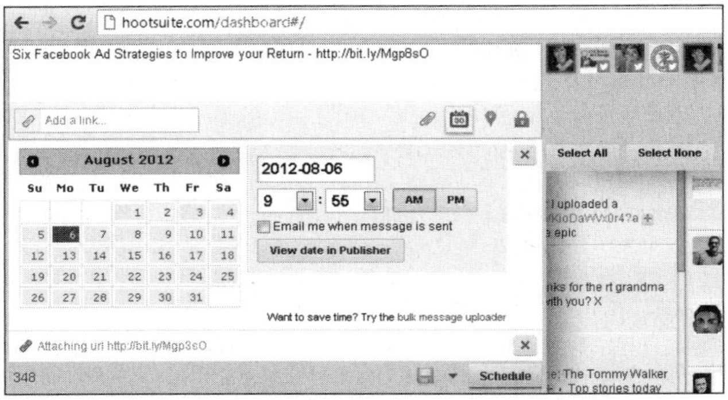

Figure 4-10: Click the calendar icon to schedule your message.

After you have the time and date set, click the Schedule button, which replaces the Send Now button.

Using TweetDeck

TweetDeck is another great (and free) option for updating and connecting your social media accounts. As we mention earlier in this chapter, it runs on your computer (and also has a mobile app). Just go to `www.tweetdeck.com`, and click Download TweetDeck to download the application and go through the setup process. You also need to download the Adobe AIR application, if you don't have it already. The setup process walks you through everything you need.

Figure 4-11 shows a screen shot of the TweetDeck application. The What's Happening? box (top of the screen) is where you put your updates. The social media profiles are across the top; click the names to update several profiles simultaneously. To send your post, just press the Enter or Return key on your keyboard after you're done typing your update in the window. You can also click the Send button on the right side of the screen, below the update window.

To add social media accounts to TweetDeck, click the dotted line box to the right of the other social sites listed above your update section (with the + symbol and the silhouette, as shown in Figure 4-11) and then click Add New Account in the pop-up window, as shown in Figure 4-12.

With TweetDeck, you can add social media profiles for the sites where you participate, including Twitter, Facebook, LinkedIn, MySpace, and Foursquare.

Figure 4-11: The TweetDeck application.

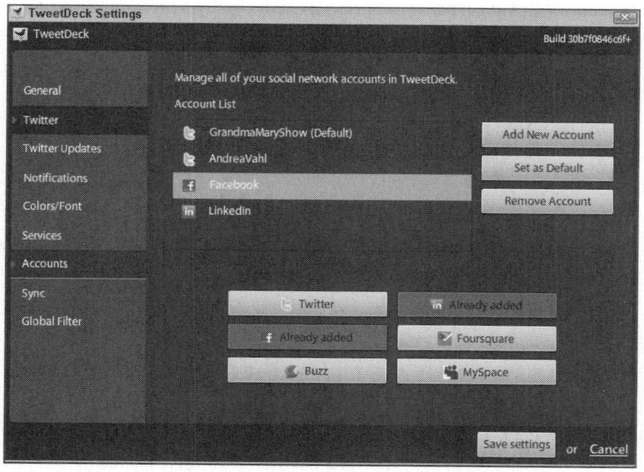

Figure 4-12: Add social media accounts by clicking the Add New Account button in the Settings box.

TweetDeck has a link shortener built into the update window. When you insert a URL into your post, TweetDeck automatically shortens your link. You can also schedule your updates just as you can with HootSuite.

To schedule a post, click the clock icon in the bottom-right section of the update window. A pop-up box appears, as shown in Figure 4-13, to allow you to schedule the post.

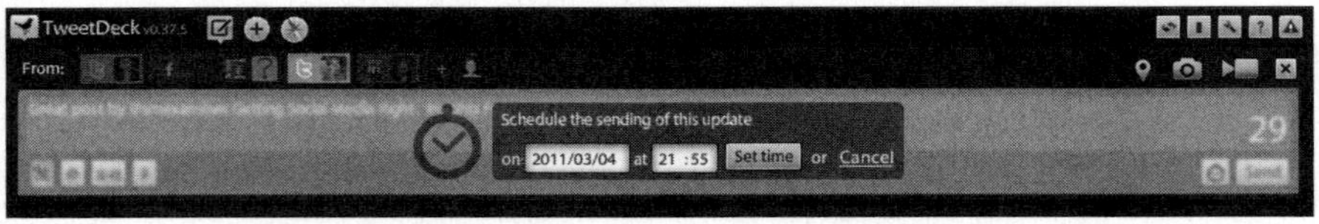

Figure 4-13: Schedule your updates in TweetDeck.

Using other posting clients

Other clients are available that will post to your Facebook personal Profile, your Page, and other social media profiles from one place, including these:

- **SocialOomph:** This web-based tool (available at `www.socialoomph.com`) focuses on Twitter, but the paid version lets you update Facebook personal Profiles and Pages.
- **Buffer:** This tool, available at `www.bufferapp.com`, schedules your posts to your sites based on times that it determines are the optimal times to share content for your audience. So if your audience is more active in the evening, your posts will be sent out in the evening. You load your "buffer" with content, and the application drips the posts out at the appropriate times. You can post to both Facebook and Twitter.

Keep in mind that we've included only a small sample of the posting clients that are available. More are being added every day! Some of these clients have analytics that track your followers, keywords, and retweets or give you the ability to schedule your updates in the future. Some have free features; others are available for a subscription price.

Adding a Twitter Tab to Your Facebook Page

Another thing you can do to connect Facebook and Twitter is add a custom tab to your Facebook Page that shows your recent tweets. (We cover adding applications more extensively in Book V.)

Adding an application like this can be a good way to add a little pizzazz to your Page and to let people know about your Twitter profile. You can use a few applications to showcase your tweets, but Involver is one of the best, and it's free.

To install the Involver Twitter application, just go to `www.involver.com/applications`, and follow these steps:

1. **Click the Free Install button next to the Twitter application, as shown in Figure 4-14.**

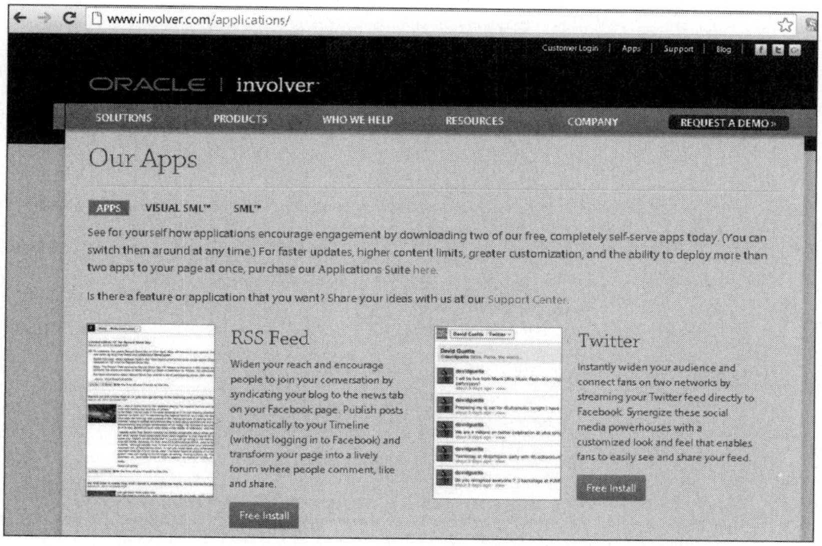

Figure 4-14: Add the Twitter application to your Page.

You're taken to Facebook to select the Page on which to install the application, as shown in Figure 4-15.

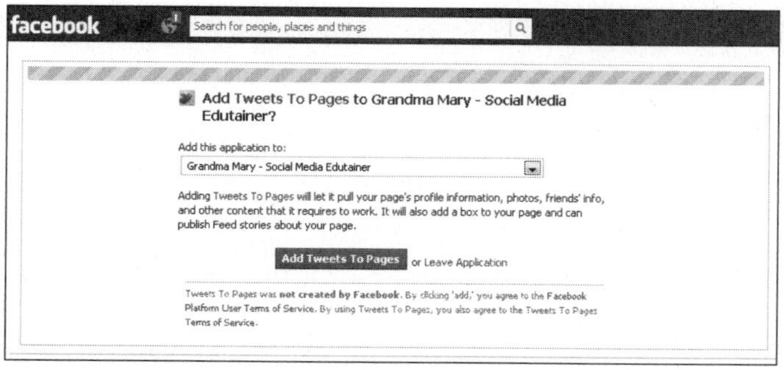

Figure 4-15: Select the Page where you want to install the Twitter app.

2. **From the drop-down menu, choose the Page where you want to add the Twitter app.**
3. **Click Add Tweets to Pages.**

   You're taken to a screen where you give the app permission to post on your Page.
4. **Click Go To App.**

   You are taken to a permissions page to allow access to your fan Pages.
5. **Click Allow.**

   You're taken to a page where you enter your company name and phone number. This information is only for Involver, and you don't need to worry; your information is safe.
6. **Enter your information, click the box to indicate that you've read the terms (after reading them, of course!), and click Save Changes.**

   Next, you're asked to authenticate with your Twitter account.
7. **Click the Please Authenticate with Twitter link.**

   If you haven't logged in to Twitter in another browser window, you're asked to log in now. If you've logged in to Twitter in another window, you see a Sign In window with your account information in the top-right corner.
8. **Click Sign In.**

   The next page contains the information you need to configure the app, as shown in Figure 4-16.

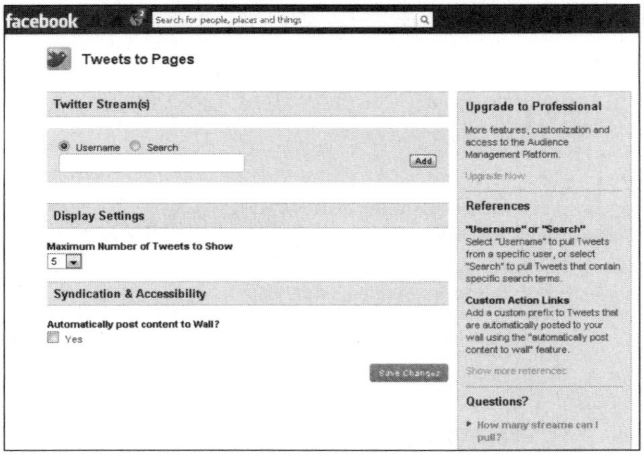

Figure 4-16: Configure what you want to display in your Twitter app.

9. **Enter your Twitter username in the text box, and click Add.**

   It is not necessary to add the @ symbol in the text box. Just add your Twitter username.

10. **Select how many tweets you want to display on your tab, and click Save Changes.**

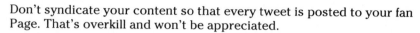

    Don't syndicate your content so that every tweet is posted to your fan Page. That's overkill and won't be appreciated.

    Your changes are saved, and your Twitter tab is added.

The tab may not show up for a little bit, but you can see your Twitter tab in your list of apps below your cover photo on your Page. You may want to switch the order of the applications or include a custom Cover photo. See Book V, Chapter 1, for information on how to do this.

Chapter 5: The Fine Print: Legal and Other Considerations

In This Chapter

- **Finding the fine print**
- **Complying with the Federal Trade Commission**
- **Posting content for regulated industries**

Remember when you signed up for Facebook, and you selected the box that said you agreed to Facebook's Terms and Policies? You sat down and read all that fine print right then and there before agreeing, right? Surrre, you did. As most of us do, you probably just clicked OK or Agree or whatever you needed to do to get into the site as quickly as possible.

The good news is that the Facebook Terms and Policies are fairly manageable, with no online bullying, no virus uploading, and no general law-breaking. But don't overlook point 1 in the Safety section:

> You will not send or otherwise post unauthorized commercial communications (such as spam) on Facebook.

That's vague at best. Allow us to explain a bit better in this chapter, with some guidelines for staying on the right side of Facebook — and U.S. federal — law as you embark on your Facebook marketing endeavors.

Digesting Legal Considerations

The first step in figuring out the legal considerations is finding them! The main site for the Facebook Terms and Policies is `www.facebook.com/policies`. Within this page, you can find links to many other lists of terms and policies, such as Ads and Sponsored Stories, Pages, Promotions, and Platform Policies (for Developers).

Facebook does monitor these Terms and Policies, although not always thoroughly, because after all, it can't be everywhere at once. And yes, Facebook will indeed disable your account if you violate these terms.

We've frequently seen enforcement against spam. You may (or may not) know, however, that you can send messages to people who aren't your Friends. This ability is helpful sometimes, if you need to get a private message to someone who likes your Page but who isn't a personal Facebook Friend. The problem with sending messages to people who aren't your Friends on Facebook is that you don't know how much is too much. Facebook doesn't specify how many messages you can send without getting banned. Typically, you aren't going to be sending many messages to people you aren't Friends with, so you should be riding on the right side of Facebook law.

If you go to the Profiles of people you aren't Friends with, you see a Message button if they've allowed people who aren't their Friends to message them. If you click the button, you can send a message even though you aren't Friends with that person. In Figure 5-1, you see a profile of someone named Angela, and you can see that we're not Friends with Angela. We can't see some of her personal information — but we can send her a message.

Figure 5-1: Send a private message from your personal account.

If you send a message to too many people you don't know, though — especially if the message contains a link to a website — you'll get a warning from Facebook. If you continue sending messages like this, your account will be disabled. Not good. So the message here is that you can send messages to people you don't know, but don't send too many simultaneously. We recommend sending ten or fewer messages a week to people you don't know if you need to contact people you aren't Friends with on Facebook.

REMEMBER

You can't send any Facebook messages actively as your Facebook Page. You can only respond to Facebook messages that come into your Page if you have the Message button activated. (See Book II, Chapter 3 for more information on the Message button.) You can send Facebook e-mails only through your personal Profile, in any case — to Friends or non-Friends.

Pages have also been shut down for violating the Promotions Policies. So if you are going to run a contest, sweepstakes, or have some type of promotion on your Facebook Page, make sure you read through the Promotion Policies. The one that gets violated the most is the first one listed in the Promotions section: Promotions on Facebook must be administered within apps on Facebook.com, either on a Canvas Page or a Page app. See Book VI for more information on running a Facebook contest the right way.

REMEMBER

You are also responsible for following the applicable local laws for running a contest in your geographic region. Consult with a lawyer if you have questions about running your promotion or contest.

Facebook's Advertising Guidelines are fairly extensive, and we recommend reviewing them before you run an ad (`www.facebook.com/ad_guidelines.php`). Although you won't violate any laws and your Page won't be shut down if you go against these guidelines, you will save yourself some time by starting your ad the right way.

Understanding U.S. Regulations on Testimonials and Reviews

Businesses often use their Facebook Pages to sell their own products or possibly to market other people's products and get a commission on the sale of those products. Using testimonials and reviews can help sales because people like to see *social proof* of a product. (If one person likes it or gets good results, maybe you will, too.) Testimonials and reviews are good marketing tools. But you do need to be aware of some of the Federal Trade Commission (FTC) regulations concerning reviews and testimonials if you intend to use them in your marketing efforts. The FTC's job is to protect consumers from fraudulent business practices and general marketing sliminess.

In October 2009, the FTC released updated guidelines for how advertisers are allowed to show testimonials and reviews. You can find the new regulations here:

`www.ftc.gov/os/2009/10/091005endorsementguidesfnnotice.pdf`

We're guessing that no one is very eager to read this 81-page legal document, but you do need to be aware of the changes as a result of these guidelines that could affect the way you do business.

One of the big unknowns in all these regulations is how they will be enforced. The FTC can't monitor every Facebook Page, website, and e-mail sent out, of course. But as with every rule, law, or terms set forth by a governing body, it's best to try to comply from the beginning. All it takes is one disgruntled customer to bring infractions to light, and no one wants to end up with some hefty fines from the FTC.

The first change that may affect you is the disclosure of material connections between you and a company whose product you're promoting. If you're familiar with affiliate marketing, this change can affect what you might post on your Page. In *affiliate marketing,* a business compensates someone for sales brought in by that person's marketing efforts. The person promoting the company's products is typically compensated with a percentage of each sale, like a commission. Many companies, including Amazon, have affiliate programs to encourage sales through this independent sales force.

But the new FTC guidelines, noted here, state that you need to disclose a material connection between you and a business that may compensate you for promoting its product:

> **255.1 Consumer endorsements**
>
> (d) Advertisers are subject to liability for false or unsubstantiated statements made through endorsements, or for failing to disclose material connections between themselves and their endorsers. Endorsers also may be liable for statements made in the course of their endorsements.

Many people comply with this regulation by stating that the link is an "affiliate link" when they promote a product or program. This practice is compliant with the FTC guideline. An example is shown in Figure 5-2.

A fine mess to not get yourself into

The FTC fine is rumored to be $11,000 per infraction, but Richard Cleland, assistant director of the agency's Division of Advertising Practices, said this: "That $11,000 fine is not true. Worst-case scenario, someone receives a warning, refuses to comply, followed by a serious product defect; we would institute a proceeding with a cease-and-desist order and mandate compliance with the law. To the extent that I have seen and heard, people are not objecting to the disclosure requirements but to the fear of penalty if they inadvertently make a mistake." Richard goes on to say that there is no penalty for a first infraction, which is good news. That tempers the fear a bit, but as we mention in this section, you should follow the FTC guidelines from the beginning to avoid any issues.

Figure 5-2: Promoting affiliate links to products.

Here's another way to be compliant: Post an explanation of the product being promoted, as well as a link to a site where someone could buy the product, and make a statement such as, "This is an affiliate link, but I don't promote anything I don't believe in wholeheartedly." (Grandma Mary states her case in her own unique way in Figure 5-2.) Your audience will understand that sometimes you bring them products that fit their needs, much as you do your own products. As long as you aren't continually selling to them, they don't mind. Some people disclose that a link they're posting isn't an affiliate link, so that it's clear that they aren't making any money by promoting this product.

Many people "endorse" a product with which they are affiliated, and you need to be careful about what you say about a product as you post about it.

> **255.2 Consumer endorsements**
>
> (b) An advertisement containing an endorsement relating the experience of one or more consumers on a central or key attribute of the product or service will likely be interpreted as representing the endorser's experience is representative of what consumers will generally achieve with the advertised product or service in actual, albeit variable, conditions of use. Therefore, an advertiser should possess and rely upon adequate substantiation for this representation. If the advertiser does not have substantiation that the endorser's experience is representative of what consumers will generally achieve, the advertisement should clearly and conspicuously disclose the generally expected performance in the depicted circumstances, and the advertiser must possess and rely on adequate substantiation for that representation.

This means that you need to be careful about making claims relating to your product. If you have a weight-loss or health product, you can no longer say something like this: "Tim lost 100 pounds in his first 2 weeks with our product. Results not typical." Even if this claim were true, the FTC would like a clearer representation of expectations for your product. The reasoning is that consumers tend to ignore the "Results not typical" warning, and the FTC's job is to protect consumers. A good addition to the preceding statement would be something like this: "Typically, our clients lose an average of *x* pounds over *x* time."

Meeting Content Compliance for Certain Industries

Certain industries have more regulations than others regarding what they can share online. Some industries follow specific regulations outlined by law, and other companies follow self-created policies relating to social media and online activities. If you're in one of the following industries, you have some form of guidelines relating to online activity:

- **Finance (investments, mortgage lending, banking, and so on):** Any financial institution needs to be cautious about what information it shares. Financial institutions are expected to keep records of customer communications, which could include online social media communications, and they need to be concerned about sensitive customer-confidentiality issues when interacting with clients.
- **Insurance:** Insurance agents are allowed to give advice only to people in the state in which they're licensed. This can pose a problem on a Page used by people from other states, because you can restrict who likes your page by country, but not by state. If you're an insurance agent, make sure that your posts avoid giving straight insurance advice.
- **Public companies:** Publicly traded companies need to be cautious about making any forward-looking statements. The Regulations Fair Disclosure policy, introduced in 2000, states that all publicly traded companies must release information to investors and the public at the same time. If this policy isn't followed, insider-trading or selective-disclosure charges could be filed.
- **Pharmaceuticals:** Pharmaceutical companies need to worry about claims being made online and also about outlining adverse effects of their products. This restriction could include any statements made within the company's Facebook community itself.
- **Health care:** Health care industries have to be careful about patient confidentiality, which includes the fact that a patient–doctor relationship exists. They also have to beware of giving medical advice. Figure 5-3 shows a Page of Dr. Karen Becker, who is a veterinarian. Her About page clearly states that she can't give out advice. We recommend that you make a similar statement or include a link to your disclaimer on your website.

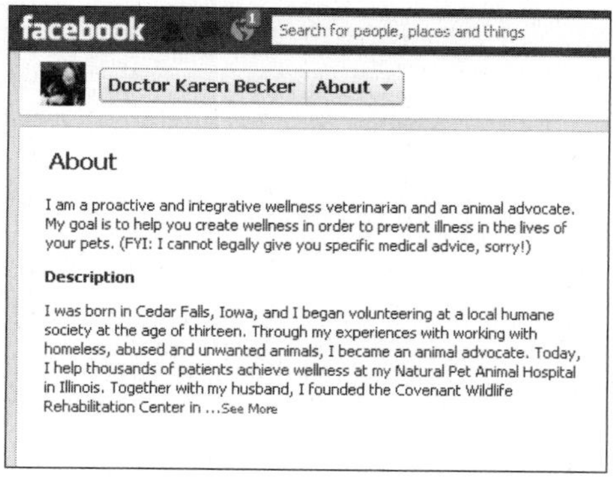

Figure 5-3: In your About area, indicate if you can't give specific advice.

If you're in one of these industries, you're probably aware of regulations and guidelines already set forth by the governing bodies related to your industry. This section is just a gentle reminder to be aware of your Facebook posts, tweets, and comments on the web.

Bottom line, you can still have a Facebook Page to connect to your community, but you may have to keep your posts slightly more social. You can post about things you are doing in the community and things that are happening in the office, ask fun questions, and do other things to promote your business in a general way.

Book IV

Building, Engaging, Retaining, and Selling to Your Community

The 5th Wave By Rich Tennant

"Hello—forget the company's financials, look at the CEO's Facebook page under '25 Things the SEC Doesn't Know About Me.'"

Contents at a Glance

Chapter 1: Building Visibility for Your Page

In This Chapter

- **Letting everyone know where to find you on Facebook**
- **Sharing and suggesting your Page with your existing customers and connections**
- **Sharing photos to attract people to your Page**

Books II and III explain how to design a functional Facebook Page. In this minibook, you find some practical ways to increase the visibility for your Page by letting people know where you're located on Facebook and learning how to share and suggest your Page to Friends.

Imagine that you open a new storefront. You want to send out notifications to everyone on your lists, both existing and potential customers, so they can find you. You need to do the same for your Facebook Page.

Some of your existing customers and connections are already on Facebook, but some (depending on your customer demographics) are not. At the ready are Facebook's built-in systems for attracting people to your Page and some time-tested offline strategies to bring people not on Facebook to your Page.

REMEMBER

A Facebook business Page is completely public, which means anyone can view it whether or not he or she has a personal Profile on Facebook. People without personal Profiles won't be able to like, comment, or share anything on your Page, but they can view all your posts and photos.

When you open the doors to your new Facebook location, you'll be stepping into a new type of marketing, one based on conversation, content, value, and sharing. The next few pages contain ideas you can use right away to add Facebook to your existing company materials and website, as well as some basic techniques using the Facebook Photo Album that are sure to attract people to your Page.

Inviting Your Existing Customers and Connections to Your Page

Think of your Facebook Page as a new bricks-and-mortar space. It has an address and is open 24/7. You just moved in, and it's time to let people know about it. The point is to build a bit of a buzz about your new place so people will like the Page and share it with their Friends.

Some businesses create a Page launch day. This way, they can make a big splash with their entry on Facebook. Others go slowly and build their presence on Facebook over time. Pick the way that suits you and your business, but make sure you do all the following (that apply) to invite your existing customers and connections.

REMEMBER

You might be able to get your vanity URL right after you create your new business Page, or you might need to have at least 25 people like your Page to be eligible for a vanity URL. Plan ahead, and if you need to, get your 25 people right away so you can use a more elegant Facebook address — such as `www.facebook.com/SociallyCongruent` — on your hard-copy materials. See Book II, Chapter 1 for how to secure a vanity URL.

A vanity URL doesn't contain numbers like this:

```
http://www.facebook.com/Pages/manage/?act=40641063#!/Pages/
    Socially-Congruent/147368801953769?ref=ts
```

Changing your hold message

If your business has a phone on-hold system, update it and add your Facebook address. Here are several great (made-up) examples:

> Thank you for calling. We're so sorry you have to wait. Waiting makes me cranky, but if you are at your computer why don't you go check out my new Facebook Page! Go to Facebook dot com forward slash Grandma Mary Show that's all one word GrandmaMaryShow. Show me some love and "like" me! Now back to the lovely hold music.

> Thank you for calling. If you are listening to this hold message maybe we are out brewing some tea! If you're like many of our customers — you have Facebook up and running — find Planetary Teas and see what's steeping there.

> While you're holding, you might as well go over to my Facebook Page (yes, I'm on Facebook). In fact, you might find a discount or two over there that might come in handy when I pick up your call! Go to Facebook-dot-com-forward-slash-Ellen-Finkelstein.

Adding your Page address to your e-mail signature

Most businesses want to add their Page name to their e-mail signature right away. You don't have to have your vanity URL yet to do this because you can hyperlink a long URL to simple text. In case you don't have a signature yet, we show you how to fix that, too.

Follow the instructions for the e-mail client you use to create an e-mail signature that promotes your Page.

If you use Microsoft Outlook 2007, follow these instructions. Other versions of Outlook will be similar, but it's always good to check Outlook's tutorials on how to modify your e-mail signature.

1. **Open Outlook, and sign in to your account.**
2. **Choose Tools⇨Options.**
3. **On the Options dialog box that appears, click the Mail Format tab.**
4. **Click the Signatures button.**

   Doing so pulls up the Signatures and Stationery dialog box. Make sure that you're on the E-mail Signature tab, as shown in Figure 1-1.
5. **Either select an existing signature to edit or click New to create a new signature, as shown in Figure 1-1.**

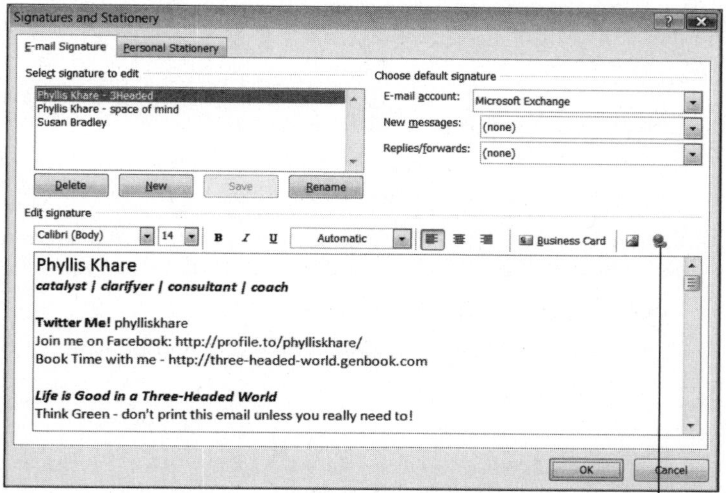

Figure 1-1: On this E-mail Signature tab, you can either edit an existing signature or create a new one.

Click to add a URL to your signature.

- *Editing an existing signature:* Select the existing signature, enter your new text, select it, and click the Hyperlink icon (refer to Figure 1-1), as noted in Figure 1-1. This pulls up the Insert Hyperlink dialog box. Type your Facebook Page URL in the address field and then click OK.
- *Adding a new signature:* Click New and a dialog box opens, allowing you to give this new signature a name. Name it and click OK. Then design your signature in the editing box. Again, to add a hyperlink to your Facebook Page name, type the name of the Page, select it, click the Hyperlink icon, and add the URL in the Address field.

6. **Click OK.**

When you create a new e-mail message, your existing signature autopopulates in the new e-mail. To change the e-mail signature from within the message, click the Insert tab in the new e-mail window, select Signatures from the Ribbon, and click the name of the new signature. Outlook replaces the signature in the new e-mail message with the one you choose.

If you use Yahoo!, follow these steps to add a hyperlink to your e-mail signature:

1. **Open Yahoo! Mail, and sign in to your account.**
2. **Click the Options link (in the top-left corner of the page) and then choose Mail Options from the menu that appears.**
3. **Click the Signature link (on the menu on the left side of the page).**

   You are now on the signature-creation page. Use the drop-down menu to toggle to Rich Text if the menu defaults to Don't Use a Signature or Plain Text.
4. **Design your signature, and type the text you want to hyperlink to your Facebook Page.**
5. **Select the text to hyperlink to your Facebook Page.**
6. **Click the Hyperlink icon, type your Facebook URL in the Insert Link To field (see Figure 1-2), and then click OK.**
7. **Click Save at the top of the page.**

   REMEMBER: Yahoo! supports only one signature per account at this time.

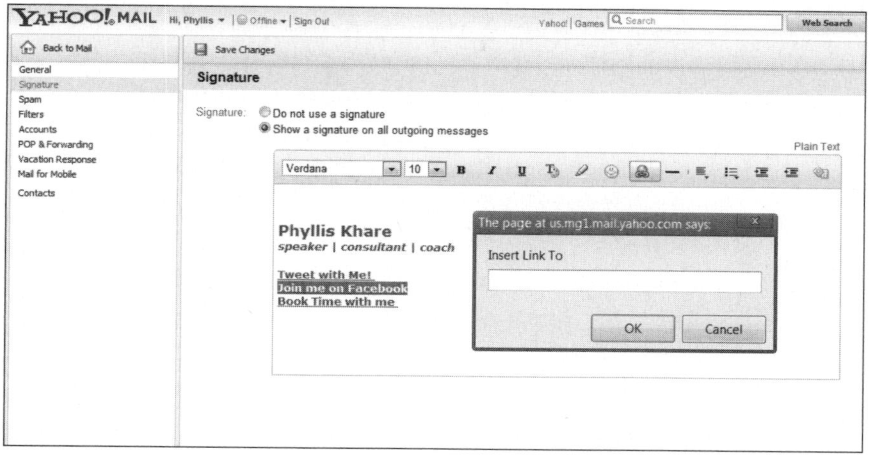

Figure 1-2: The Yahoo! Signature page makes it easy to add your Facebook link.

If you use Gmail, you design your signature a little differently than you do in Yahoo! and Outlook. The good news is that you can add an image to your signature; however, you can't upload it from your computer. You need to host images in the cloud — which means using a service such as Flickr, or even Facebook, to store the images online.

1. **Open Gmail, and sign in to your account.**
2. **Click the Options icon (it looks like a gear) in the top-right corner of the page.**

   Note: The Gmail Options link may look different, depending on which browser, and which version of that browser, you're using. The link may be labeled Settings.

   The Settings page appears and defaults to the General tab.
3. **Find the Signature section (about halfway down the page), and select the e-mail address to which you want to add the Facebook address.**

   TIP

   If you have only one Gmail address, you won't see a drop-down menu.

   You can have as many signatures as you have Gmail addresses.
4. **Design your signature with your name and contact info.**

5. **Enter the name of your Facebook Page, select it, and click the hyperlink icon.**
6. **Type or paste your Facebook Page URL in the Web Address field.**

   If you type the URL in your signature (for example, **`https://www.facebook.com/GrandmaMaryShow`** instead of **Grandma Mary Show**), the URL information is autopopulated when you click the hyperlink icon.
7. **Click OK.**
8. **(Optional) Add an image (a photo or logo image) to your signature:**

   a. *Click the Image icon (the one with the land-and-sky image).*

   b. *In the Add an Image dialog box that opens, enter the image's URL.*

   This is what makes Gmail's signature program different from the others. You can't just upload an image from your computer. The image has to exist somewhere online. Gmail will connect to that address online and pull it into the signature each time you send an e-mail.

   If the image you want to use exists only on your computer's hard drive, you can upload it to your Facebook album or to an image site such as Flickr. After you upload it, right-click it (Ctrl-click on a Mac) and then choose Copy Image URL (or Copy Link Address or Copy Image Location) from the menu that appears.

   c. *Paste the URL in the Image dialog box, shown in Figure 1-3.*

   A preview of the image is there for you to check.

   d. *Click OK.*

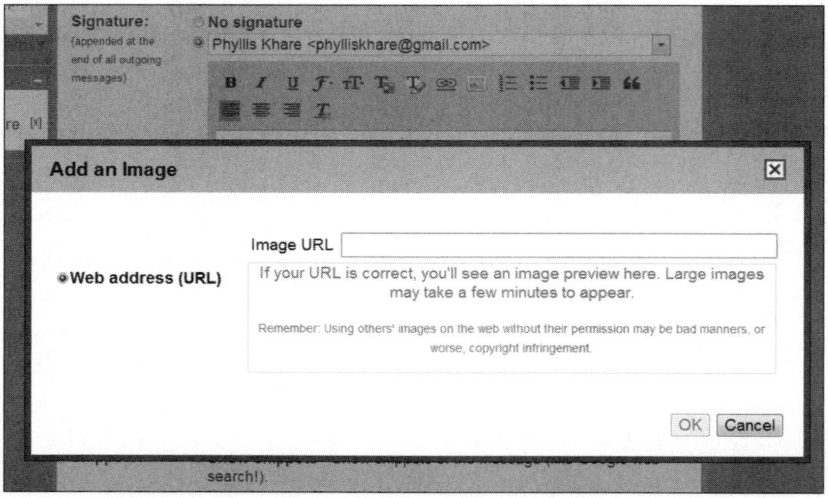

Figure 1-3: Add the image URL, and it loads automatically in each e-mail you send.

All images online have an address or URL. You can use any image on your website or any image hosted on Facebook, or photo-hosting sites such as Flickr.

Using other people's images could be an infringement of copyright. Use only those images for which you have permission to use.

9. **Click Save Changes at the bottom of the page.**

Figure 1-4 shows a full signature example, including an image, created with Gmail.

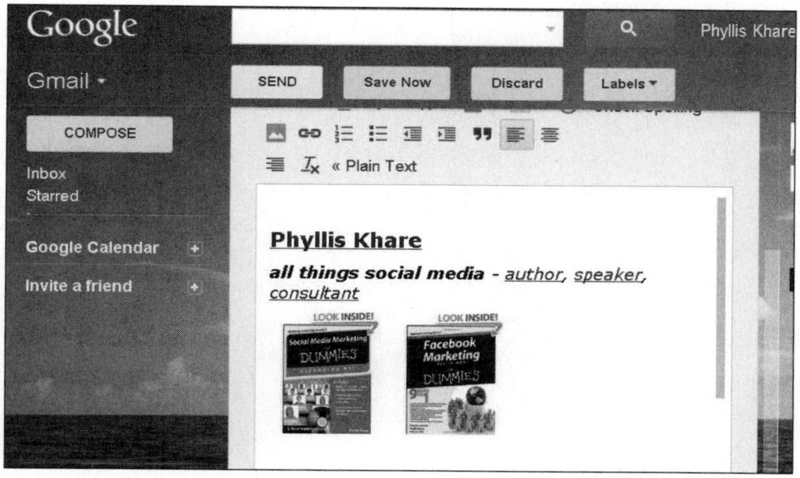

Figure 1-4: Signatures with added links and an image.

You can add some simple text to your signature with the link spelled out (not hyperlinked), as follows:

> You might Like Us on Facebook, too.
>
> `http://facebook.com/`*`yourcompanyname`*
>
> Do you hang out on Facebook? Come say hi at `http://facebook.com/`*`yourcompanyname`*

You can also use an Internet browser extension or application to create a signature that contains a Facebook icon linked to your Page. The best one we've found that works in all major browser-based e-mail is WiseStamp. When you go to `www.wisestamp.com`, the site figures out which browser you're using and shows you the correct download link. Then just follow the instructions provided.

Figure 1-5 shows an example of a WiseStamp signature. When your e-mail recipients click the Facebook icon, they go straight to your Facebook Page.

Figure 1-5: Use WiseStamp to create a memorable signature.

Including your new Facebook address on hard-copy mailings

Some businesses dedicate a hard-copy mailing to their customers to tell them about their new Facebook Page. You can include the announcement in a regular mailing or create a special one, but if your customers read what you send them in the mail (postcards, brochures, newsletters), you need to make the announcement in that medium, too.

Many companies are now including in all their hard-copy mailings a small social connection area that shows their online connections, including their website address, YouTube channel, Twitter username, LinkedIn company page address, and more. Figure 1-6 shows a great example from a hard-copy magazine.

Figure 1-6: A social media connection bar in a magazine.

Updating your letterhead and stationery

You need to have your vanity URL before you update your letterhead. As we discuss earlier in this chapter, you may need 25 people to like your Page to be eligible to get one. Then you can add an elegant URL, like `www.facebook.com/SociallyCongruent`, to your stationery, as shown in Figure 1-7.

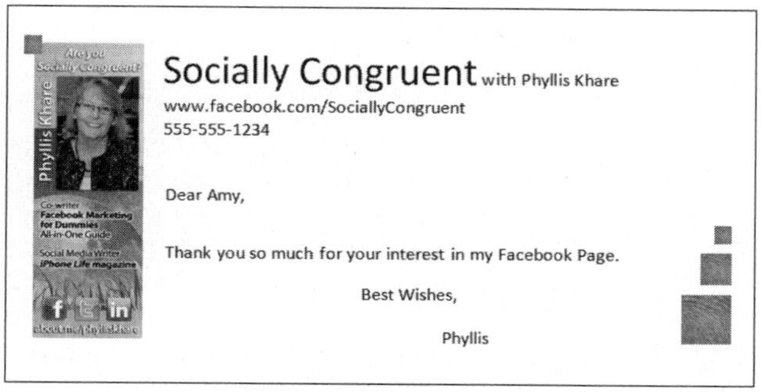

Figure 1-7: A Facebook address can be added to any letterhead design.

Including a Facebook icon on your web page

Web pages now commonly feature a Facebook icon. In fact, a website without one seems to be missing something. You eventually want to integrate everything Facebook has to offer with your website. See Book VII (on advanced marketing) for everything Facebook offers. For now, a simple first step is to connect your website to Facebook.

Putting a linked Facebook icon on your website or blog is very easy. All you need are your Facebook Page URL address and an image of the icon you want to use. You can even do this before you secure your vanity URL. You can have a graphic designer create an icon image for you or use an existing one, as shown in Figure 1-8.

Figure 1-8: Standard Facebook icon images you can use.

A great source of Facebook icon images is Iconfinder (`www.iconfinder.com`). Enter **Facebook** in the search bar and then select the icon you prefer. The drop-down menu gives you three options: No License Filtering, Allowed for Commercial Use, and Allowed for Commercial Use — No Link Required. We suggest option 3 because it's the simplest to use.

After you select the appropriate category, find an icon that blends well with your website. Select it and then select the size you need. If you don't know what size you need, download all the sizes and save them to your computer. Then you need to send these images to your webmaster to place on your website or do the job yourself.

If you're using a WordPress, Joomla, or Drupal template for your website, you may find that Facebook icons are built into the template offerings, and all you need to do is add your Facebook Page address to activate the icon on your website. Many plug-ins for those systems allow you to add a Facebook icon and link it to your Page. You need to explore your website-creation system and see whether this feature is available.

If you're using an HTML system to create your website, you can create your own linked image and then upload the new HTML page with the new icon (with the link code) to your server. If that last sentence made no sense to you, you need to talk to your webmaster or website designer.

Linking to your Page from your personal Profile

If your Page is a service that you offer, go back to your personal Facebook Profile, and add a little bit to your About tab about your new Page's location. If your business is something that you want to keep completely separate from your personal Profile on Facebook, you can skip these steps. Book II, Chapter 2 covers how to edit your About tab.

To link to your business Page from your personal Profile, follow these steps:

1. **Click your name in the top-right corner of any page on Facebook.**

   This step takes you to your personal Timeline.

2. **Find the About link below your picture, and click it.**

   You're in an interface where you can edit all the bits and pieces of your personal account.

3. **Click the Work and Education Edit button.**

   You can use the Work and Education section to add your new Page address.

4. **Type the name of your new business Page.**

5. **When you see the Page come up in the suggestions, click it to add it to your Work section.**

   Fill in your position and any other important information (address and so on).

6. **Click the Add Job button.**

7. **Click the Done Editing button.**

Figure 1-9 shows how the editing space looks on the Timeline.

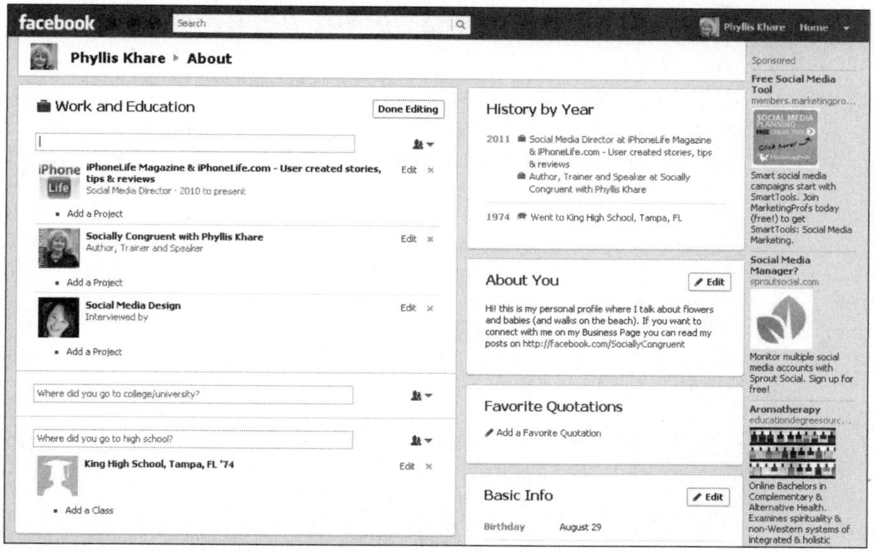

Figure 1-9: This screen is where you add your business Page location on your personal Timeline.

Make sure that the viewing option is set to Public so that people will be able to see your Page linked and be able to click through to it. You can change the icon by clicking the drop-down arrow while you're in Editing view and selecting the world icon (Public).

Another creative idea is to put your business Page URL on your personal Profile's Cover photo. You have to do a little photo editing, but the result will help move people over to your Page. Or you can put your website address on the image, as in Figure 1-10.

Figure 1-10: This is how you can modify your personal Cover image to show people where you want them to find you.

Inviting your other social networks to visit your Page

Maybe you've been active on Twitter or various niche social media sites, and now you want to invite the people you've met there to visit your Page. You can get people to click the link to check you out, but you want them to like you, too.

A good way to develop a flow to your Page, so that people are asking questions or commenting on your posts, is to invite your most engaged members of your other social networks to join you on Facebook.

Here are some examples of how you can connect your Facebook Page with other social media:

- **Twitter:** Add your Facebook Page link to any Direct Messages you already have going out to new followers.
- **LinkedIn:** Add your Facebook link to any message you send, and make sure that it's listed on your Profile.

✦ **YouTube:** Add your link to any YouTube channel in the info section, and to the first line of each video's description section. You can also use the LinkedTube service (`www.linkedtube.com`) to create a clickable link right on the video itself.

Every social media system has a place to add links; be sure to go to each one you already use and add your new Facebook Page address.

After you add the link to your Page on your other networks, you can start to invite people to your Page through your regular posts and updates. One of the attractive things about a Facebook Page is that you can have a longer conversation than the 140-character limit in Twitter, so your Twitter followers might enjoy a longer conversation with you on Facebook.

TIP

On a regular basis, create a post that links back to your Page on all your other social networks. You can also post the direct links to any photo or album you've created. See the upcoming section "Sharing your albums and photos." This is a nice way to invite people to see your Page and (ideally) stick around and like it.

Growing your Page manually or buying automatic fans

The debate between growing your Page manually and buying automatic fans is a controversial subject. As much as we'd like to take the middle ground on this, we recommend that you grow your Page manually, organically. It's always better to have people on your Page who are real, engaged fans of your product or service rather than to pay companies for any "Get fans fast!" services you hear about or see online.

Think creatively about contests, games, applications, and other forms of Page building rather than buying your way into Facebook fame. See Books V–VIII for those strategies.

Sharing Your Page with Your Friends on Facebook

You have several ways to invite your Friends to like your Page:

✦ As a Page administrator, you can use the Invite Friends link in your Admin panel.

✦ As an admin, you can invite your e-mail contacts to like your Page.

✦ You and everyone else can share the Page. Sharing a Page puts the invitation in the sharee's Notifications.

If you don't want any of your Friends to be invited to be connected to this Page, you can skip inviting and sharing.

Still, you may want to go through the steps to share your Page because these steps are the same ones you'll want your supporters to duplicate to show your Page to their Friends. Understanding how Sharing works allows you to craft the best message to solicit your Friends' help in expanding your reach.

There are countless other ways to bring people other than your Facebook Friends to your Page, but these ways are built into Facebook's own system and can be used effectively to create momentum toward an engaged community for your business. After you have a few friendly faces who have liked your Page, you can start to use some of the advanced marketing ideas in Books V–VIII.

Inviting Facebook Friends to your Page

Facebook recently changed the process for inviting your Friends to like a Page. Now only the Page admins can use the Invite Friends feature. Everyone else needs to use the Share feature.

As an admin, to invite your personal Facebook Friends to your business Page, follow these steps:

1. **Go to your Page, and look above the Admin panel.**
2. **Click the Build Audience drop-down menu, as shown in Figure 1-11, and choose Invite Friends.**

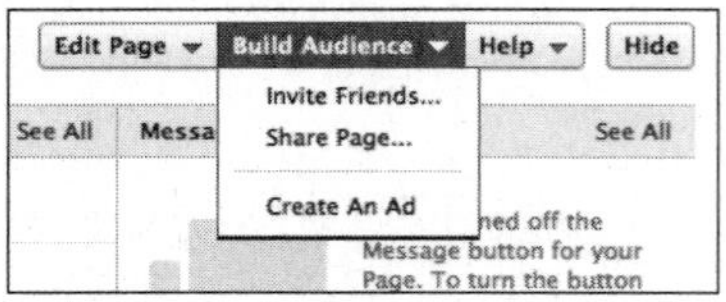

Figure 1-11: The Build Audience drop-down menu.

3. **In the dialog box that appears, search for and select your Friends.**

   You have several ways to do this:

   - From the Search All Friends drop-down menu, choose Recent Interactions, a geographic location, membership in a shared group, or members of your Friends lists (see Figure 1-12).
   - Type a person's name.
   - Click a person's Profile image to select that person.

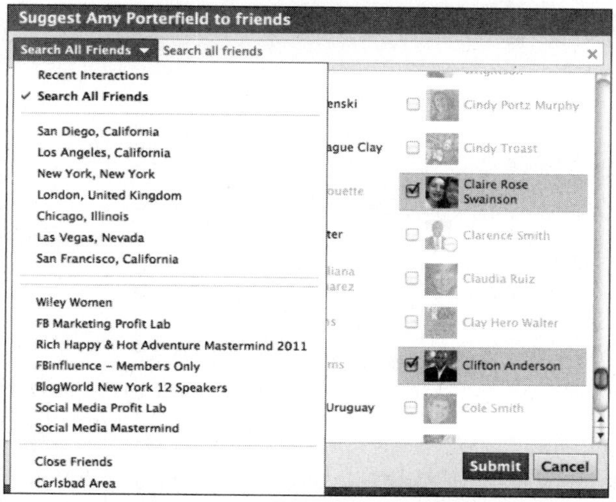

Figure 1-12: Use the drop-down menu to find people you want to invite to like your Page.

4. **Click Submit.**

   When you have selected everyone you want to invite, click Submit and the invitation will be sent.

If a person's Profile picture is grayed out, that person has already been invited to like the Page.

REMEMBER: You know your Friends. Don't overdo inviting, because getting an invitation week after week for the same Page, either through Suggesting or Sharing or posting, can be really irritating. To find other ways to attract your Friends to your Page, keep reading this book!

REMEMBER: Friends lists are created in your personal Profile. You can't create any business Page lists. One time when a Friends list is important for your Page is when you're asking your Friends to like your Page by using the Share or Invite link.

Currently, you don't get a chance to add a personal message to a Friends invitation. Your Friends can ignore the message, click the link that takes them to your Page and click the Like button there, or click the Like link in the notification.

Sharing your Page

The other main way to invite your Friends to your new Page is to choose Share Page from the Build Audience drop-down menu, as shown in Figure 1-13. When you choose the Share Page option, the resulting dialog box gives you the option to post it to your personal Timeline, in a Friend's Timeline, in a group, on your business Page, or in a private message.

You should post an invitation to your Friends in many ways — on and off Facebook — to have them connect to your new Page.

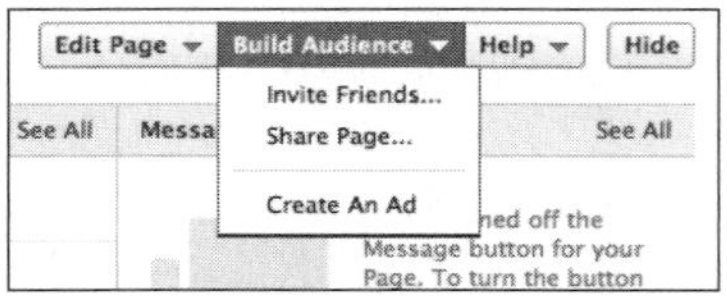

Figure 1-13: Invite Friends to like your Page.

Choosing Share Page initiates something very important: It pulls up a window that autofills with some of the information from your Page's Info section. The items included are defined by the type of business category you choose, as discussed in Book II, Chapter 1. If you filled in your Info fields fully, you see a description of your business, including your Page's Profile image, all ready to send.

Anyone sending a Share invitation can edit the title and the information by clicking in those fields and typing something new.

You can add a comment in the status box above the invitation. After you craft the new status-box text, you can decide to whom to send the invitation.

If you are posting to your own Timeline, you can also change who can see the Share post by clicking the Post Privacy Setting drop-down (see Figure 1-14) and deciding whether everyone, just Friends, or others can see it. You have several choices, and you can also select Custom and then set who can and who can't see this invitation.

Figure 1-14: Set who gets to see your Share Page message.

The next few figures show examples of what the Share invitation will look like, depending on which business category you chose for your Page.

The first example shows someone who chose Product/Service. It populates the invitation only with the Company Overview text from the Basic Information page, as shown in Figure 1-15. Look how much information can be sent!

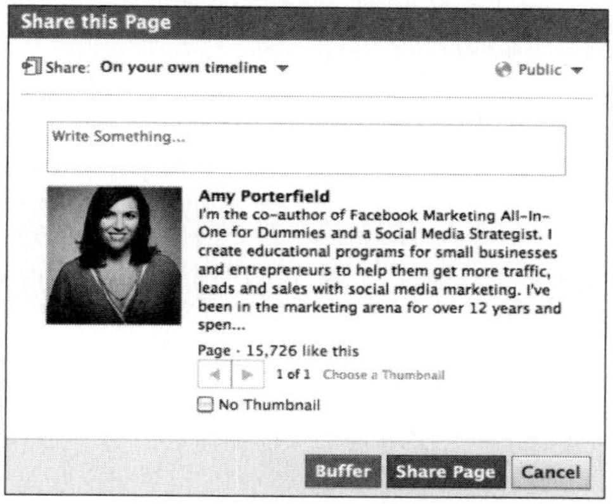

Figure 1-15: Only the Company Overview is used in the invitation from a Product/Service type of Page.

In the second example, the category is Public Figure, which populates the invitation only with the Personal Information from the Basic Information page, as shown in Figure 1-16.

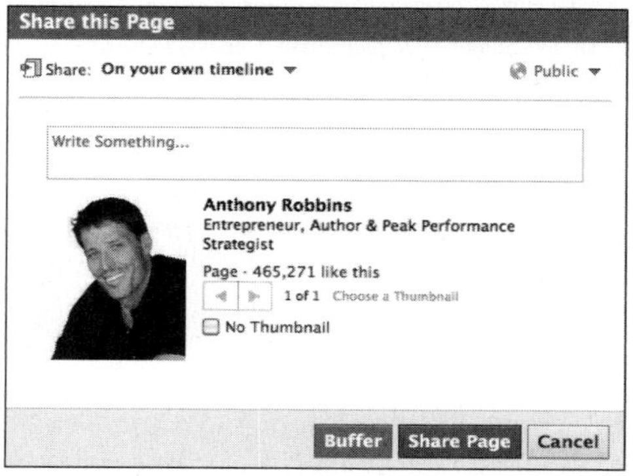

Figure 1-16: The Personal Information field is used in the invitation for Public Figures.

Figure 1-17 shows what is pulled up for a Page with the category Musician/Band. It populates the invitation only with the Biography part of the Basic Information page. If you don't put anything in the Biography field, the invitation pulls information from the Members field. You may need to experiment with where you place text on your Basic Information page so that your Share Page invitation contains the text you want other people to see.

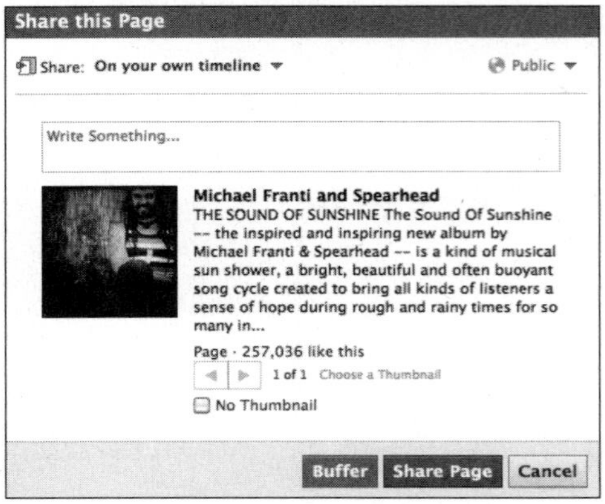

Figure 1-17: The Biography section might be used for a musician.

In the next example, a TV show, the invitation populates only with the Plot Outline text of the Info link, as shown in Figure 1-18.

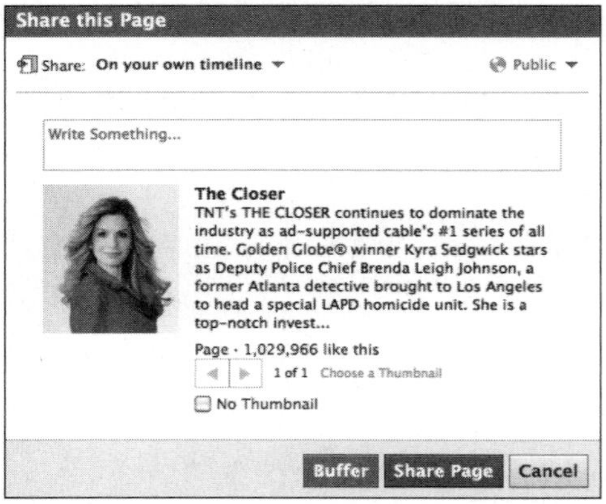

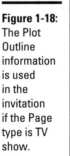

Figure 1-18: The Plot Outline information is used in the invitation if the Page type is TV show.

The people who end up sharing your Page this way usually don't know they can edit the Title and Information fields. They don't know they have control of the information that populates the invitation, so you can see why it's important to have the right category and to fill in the Basic Information section fully.

Sending requests to promote your Page

It's perfectly okay to privately message some of your closest Friends and business partners to ask them to share your Page with their Friends on Facebook. You can call them on the phone (imagine that!), e-mail your new Facebook address link to them, give them a handwritten invitation over drinks (it's been done), or use the built-in instant messaging (chat) system that Facebook offers. If your Friends like using the chat system, you can have a nice little conversation with them about your new Page.

You can see which Friends are online by clicking the Chat menu in the bottom-right corner of any Facebook Page. A green dot appears next to a Friend who is online and available to chat, and a phone icon appears next to a Friend who has her phone connected to her Facebook account. If you click on someone with the phone icon, the regular chat message box opens up, but the message is delivered to the phone. On Profiles and anywhere else on the site, clicking a chat icon starts a conversation with that person.

To send a chat message, simply type your message and then press Enter or Return.

Finding and thanking your key enthusiasts

Acknowledging the people who spread the word about your Page is always a good idea. You can offer an incentive or reward for their efforts. The trick is figuring out who is helping you out! Currently, the only way is to ask. So take the bull by the horns, pop the question in the form of a Page update, (such as "Who has shared this Page today?"), and offer discount coupons or codes as rewards.

We've seen many creative ways of thanking enthusiastic supporters. The folks behind one Page we know offer free, live training to anyone that evening if they can get their like count up over a certain number. If they can add 50 new likers to their Page by 5 p.m., everyone is invited to free training in using iFrames to create a video tab! This strategy has been very effective for this business.

Adding Photos to Attract People to Your Page

No matter whether you have a physical product or are in a service industry, photos sell and attract. You have many ways to use photos to invite people to your Page and to keep them actively engaged.

Collect many high-quality photos of your product, or shots of your service, or anything that relates to your Page's focus. Continue to collect these photos, and make sure to post them on a regular basis. More than 2.5 billion photos are uploaded to Facebook every month, and Facebook continues to be one of the best ways to market, no matter what other social media platform you're on.

Read the information in this section to develop a marketing strategy using photos in Facebook.

Creating a marketing strategy with your Cover photo

The new Timeline format features a large Cover photo, which we talk about in Book II, Chapter 2. Here, you need to think about how to really use this large image to your business advantage.

As we discuss further in Book II, Chapter 2, Facebook is very clear about not having this image turn into an ad or a billboard. Facebook wants to keep it kind of an artistic experience, which can be a challenge for some businesses. Here are some ideas to jump-start your creativity:

- **Highlight your fans.** Mari Smith does an excellent job of executing this marketing idea. You can see her images through time where she highlights a single fan or all her fans. You can go directly to her Cover Photos album here: `http://on.fb.me/MariCoverPhotos`.
- **Show happy customers.** If you have images that convey satisfaction with your product or service, there's no better way to use the Cover photo space. A nice example is `www.facebook.com/CrustPizzeria`. If the happy faces are not currently Crust Pizzeria's Cover photo, click Photos and then click Cover Photos to see the Cover photos that show the happy customers.
- **Issue a call to action.** This strategy is a fine line to tread, but it can be done. You can look at Amy's Cover photos for a few good examples here: `http://on.fb.me/AmyCoverPhotos`. You can't use the words "Click Here" or "Go to This Website," but you can put the title and date of an upcoming webinar on the image, as Amy has done.

Creating a marketing strategy with photo albums

Consider your business before you click the photo-upload link. Think about what would be interesting to people who already know you and what would be interesting to those who have never heard of you. Use the photo system in Facebook to its fullest, keeping in mind best practices for your niche or industry.

Take a moment to think of some really interesting Photo Album names that would promote your business. You always have the Album called Profile

Pictures and Cover Photos, which will always contain all the photos you use for your Profile image and Cover images, but you can name every other album that you create.

If you're selling a physical product, for example, create an album called Happy Customers, and upload shots of happy customers using your product. Create an album called Found in Chicago for photos of your product on the shelves of a store in Chicago. You could use this idea in a contest; see more in Book VI on making Facebook come alive with events and contests.

If you're selling a service, create an album called Here I Am, *Doing It* (replace *Doing It* with your service), and upload photos of your staff doing their work, or showing you providing a session of your service. How about creating an album called Award-Winning for photos of your awards and achievements?

TIP

Your business might use humor to attract a strong group of fans — that is, likers. If you think that putting up a picture of your dog and labeling him the Acting CEO works for your customer base, go ahead and have fun with it! The people who really like your Page will most likely share these photos, so make them relevant to your business. They can be funny — and goodness knows that we all could use a laugh.

Uploading photos to your Facebook Page

Uploading photos to your Facebook Page involves the same process as uploading to your personal Profile, except that you start from your Page.

Uploading photos to Facebook is a snap. Here's how:

1. **Log in to your personal Facebook account, and go to your Page.**
2. **Click the Photos app box below your Cover photo.**
3. **On the new page that appears, click the Add Photos button on the top-right side of the page.**

   Yet another new page appears.
4. **Click the +Select Photos to Upload button.**
5. **In the dialog box that appears, browse your computer for and select the photos you want to upload.**

   You can select multiple images by Ctrl+clicking on a PC or ⌘+clicking on a Mac.
6. **While your photos upload, fill in a name for your album (use the strategies described in the preceding section), the location, and the quality.**

7. **Add a description.**

   This step is very important because this text stays with the photo no matter where it's viewed. Try to incorporate your full website address, or full Facebook Page address. These addresses will be hyperlinked and clickable.

   Include the `http://` part of your URL, your product name, or contact info in the caption field to make the link clickable, like the one shown in Figure 1-19.

8. **When the photos are loaded, click the Post Photos button.**

   The album of photos appears on your Page's Timeline.

Figure 1-19: Adding an http:// link is a vital marketing step.

You also want to designate a photo to be the album cover, which you do by following these steps:

1. **On your Page, click the Photo app and select the album you want to work with.**

   You can only set the cover for albums you've created. You can't set a Cover photo for the Cover photos album or Profile pictures.

2. **Click Edit Album.**

   All the images in the album are in view.

3. **Hover over the image you want to designate as the Cover.**
4. **When a small drop-down arrow appears in the top-right corner of the image, click it and choose Make Album Cover.**
5. **Click Done.**

TIP

Use Adobe Photoshop or other photo-editing software to create beautifully designed photos that will become your album covers. Upload these photos and select them as the Cover, and you create something very clear and easy to select when viewing and sharing.

If you already have a photo album created and want to add more to that particular album, follow these steps:

1. **Log in to your personal Profile and click your Page's name in the left sidebar.**

   You're taken to your business Page.

2. **Click the Photos app box below your Cover photo.**
3. **On the new page that appears, click the album to which you want to add photos.**

   The album's thumbnail images appear.

4. **Click the Add Photos button in the top-right corner of the Page.**
5. **In the dialog box that appears, browse your computer for the photos you want to upload.**
6. **Follow Steps 5–8 in the steps list at the beginning of "Uploading photos to your Facebook Page."**
7. **Follow the steps in the preceding list to designate a Cover photo.**

Sharing your albums and photos

The marketing strategy behind sharing your albums and photos is something that you need to sit down and design. Maybe every Friday you send out a new album, or every Tuesday you post an image of your products that you found around town or in another city.

You can also share this album or individual pictures again, after publishing, from two places:

- **Your business Page Timeline:** If you see your album or photo on the Page Timeline, you can click the Share link below the photo, as shown in Figure 1-20.

  You can put a call to action in the Message field when you share, asking people to share the album with their Friends.

- **The album itself:** The second way is to go through the album, which we show you in the next set of steps.

Figure 1-20: You can click the Share link below the photo album posted on your Timeline.

To share an album (or individual pictures) after publishing, follow these steps:

1. **Go to your Page, and select the Photos app box.**
2. **Select the album you want to share.**
3. **Click the Share link below the images.**
4. **Choose where to share the album by clicking the drop-down arrow shown in Figure 1-21:**
   - On Your Own (personal) Timeline
   - On a Friend's Timeline
   - In a Group
   - On Your Page
   - In a Private Message

Figure 1-21: You can share your photo album in several ways.

If you share in a private message, the link to the photo or album will go to the recipient's Messages section. You can also send the album to folks outside the Facebook platform by using an e-mail address, but they will need to join Facebook to see the picture(s). See the following section for more details.

5. **Select a viewing option: Public, Friends, Friends except Acquaintances, Only Me, or any of your personal lists.**
6. **Click the Share Photo button.**

Sharing with people other than your personal Friends on Facebook

You can send any photo or album directly to anyone other than your personal Facebook Friends by following the steps in the preceding section, except this time instead of selecting to send it to your own Timeline, choose In a Private Message from the drop-down menu and type an e-mail address rather than a Facebook name. Facebook sends an e-mail with a link to the photo. ***Note:*** If the person you send it to is on Facebook, he'll be able to view it. If he doesn't have a Facebook account, the link will take him to a Page with the message that he can't view the photo unless he joins Facebook.

You also have a direct URL to each album that you can send to anyone, and those people will be able to view it. Or you can post anywhere online. To find this direct URL, follow these steps:

1. **Go to your Page and select the Photos app box.**
2. **Select the photo that you want to share.**
3. **Make sure that you're viewing the photo (it will be in a lightbox setting).**
4. **Copy the URL of the image from the browser bar.**
5. **Paste the URL in an e-mail message.**
6. **Send the e-mail.**

   If the person to whom you sent the URL to doesn't have a Facebook account, she can view the photo anyway as long as you have viewing set to Public. An invitation to join Facebook will be there too.

Chapter 2: Engaging and Retaining Your Community

In This Chapter

- **Engaging people to keep them coming back to your Page**
- **Understanding and making the most of the News Feed**
- **Learning the art of responding to comments**
- **Banning and removing people and comments as a last resort**

Engagement is the Holy Grail for Facebook Pages. To engage your target audience, you need to be clear about your purpose and branding, and let your own personality (or your brand's) shine through. Best practices dictate that you can post almost anything to your Page as long as you connect it to your particular focus and adhere to the express purpose of having conversations with current and potential customers.

If your Page is about sustainability practices, for example, you might post a picture of your children adding to the compost bin or chasing the chickens running around in your yard. By contrast, posting a video of your favorite *American Idol* contestant on your sustainability Page is not in line with that particular focus (unless, of course, that person raises chickens and sings about them in the video).

In Book II, Chapter 3, we explain how to use the regular posting features, status updates, video posts, audio, events, and other aspects of posting. In this chapter, we explore how to use those features to engage your community even further.

Specifically, we tell you how to use questions, milestones, and images to create conversations on your Page. We also explain why you need to understand Facebook's EdgeRank (how it affects who sees what on your Page) and how to create posts that will give you more views and engagement.

We explain the difference between what your visitors see when your Page has Highlights selected and how that changes when they select Posts by Others, Posts by Page, or Friend Activity, and how that all ties into Admin settings for your Timeline. Finally, we show you how to remove unpleasant guests from your Page.

Creating Posts and Updates That Engage Your Readers

Some types of posts resonate with your audience better than others. In the beginning, you might want to try a variety to see which ones work the best. After you discover the formats that your audience responds to most favorably, you can post in those formats on a regular schedule so that people expect and even look forward to your posts. Doing so sets the stage for the conversations to start.

If every Friday you post a coupon code or Facebook Offer (review Offers in Book III), a clue to a treasure-hunt contest, or a free training ticket, people will start to remember and look for your posts on those days.

Facebook has more than 42 million Pages with 10 or more likes (as of March 31, 2012), but the great majority of these Pages are still trying to figure out how to attract an audience, authentically engage the people who might like them, and develop increased revenue. Many brands, on the other hand, have well more than 1 million likers and have figured out the best ways to engage their particular base so that a viral effect starts and they recruit even more people to their brand or cause. How do they do it? They use several strategies, detailed in the following sections, that you can try.

Asking questions

We discuss two types of questions here. One type is a regular question that you ask in a regular status update; the other uses Facebook's Question tool. We discuss exactly how to create a Facebook Question in Book III, Chapter 1, but in general, asking questions might be a great way to engage your audience.

Asking questions or inviting your audience's opinion on something instantly creates a personal connection. People like to tell you their opinion on subjects that are dear to them. Your most enthusiastic Likers have an opinion about your brand, your marketing message, or your community involvement (or lack of it). Asking them to express those opinions can open the door to lots of conversation and involvement.

But which system do you use to ask the question? If you want the question to find its way into the News Feeds of the people who have liked your Page, we suggest using a simple question as a regular post. If you want the question to find its way outside your Page connections, use the Facebook Question tool in the status box (as we describe in Book III, Chapter 1).

Some companies are finding that combining questions with video can create an even stronger engagement than using just one or the other. In a great article called "4 Easy Ways to Engage your Facebook Fans," posted on one of the best resources for social media marketing, Mashable.com (`http://mashable.com/2010/03/19/facebook-fan-engagement`), you can find many detailed examples of techniques for engaging an audience, one of which is including questions when you post a video. One company found that it received 100 times more media impressions (people sharing the videos) when people also responded to a question about the video.

Here are some engaging ways to ask a question:

- Find a topical news story that connects to your business, and ask what people think about it. Post the question with the news video for a bigger response.
- Pose a question you get from your potential customers, and ask your enthusiasts how they would answer it.
- Ask a simple question, such as "Who wants a coupon?"
- Use fill-in-the-blank questions. The Life is Good Facebook Page (`www.facebook.com/lifeisgood`), for example, asked this question: "A positive life lesson I'd like to share is ____________." There were more than 1,300 comments and more than 500 likes in just a few days! Some of the most popular fill-in-the-blank questions require just a one or two word response. Like, "Chocolate – Dark or Milk?"

REMEMBER: The prospect of receiving discounts is always one of the top two reasons for consumers to like a brand on Facebook, so asking the question "Who wants a coupon?" usually gets a good response. Creating coupons for your Page is discussed in Book VI, Chapter 2.

TIP: If you can, always ask a question that has a simple answer. Don't ask your audience to write a detailed evaluation of something. Instead, ask a question that has a one- or two-word response.

Polling your audience

You may find that polling your audience creates a higher level of engagement with your Page than many other types of strategies do. By taking a poll, you may discover audience preferences that will direct your promotions and communications in a different direction from the one you thought you'd need to go. Your customers and potential customers are the ones you need to serve, and using polls helps you gather insight into what they really want.

So what's the difference between a Question and a Poll? Questions are for engaging your audience (share your positive life experience) whereas with a poll, you gather information about what your audience wants/needs from your business.

A Poll has precreated answers that someone can just click. A Question allows for a variety of answers. Facebook's built-in Question tool is like a Poll, although you create the answers that someone can just click. You can also open the built-in Facebook Questions up to other responses, but in general, it acts more like a Poll.

Here are a few tips for creating a simple poll:

- Make it short.
- Make each question simple and direct.
- Make sure to post the results quickly so that people can see that their opinions have registered.
- Draw some conclusions, post them, and ask the responders whether you drew the right ones — an excellent way to re-engage them in conversation.

You can ask several kinds of Poll questions:

- Pose Yes/No questions to your audience.
- Present your audience multiple-choice questions.
- Ask your audience to rank a list of items.

Promoting your fans and enthusiasts

Back when Facebook used the "fan" and "fan Page" vocabulary, it was a bit easier to write about the people who connected to your Page. Now you have to make "liker" sound as though it's a normal thing to say. For the purpose of this section, we're revisiting the use of the word *fan* because it more aptly describes the person who, on his or her own, promotes and shares your content with a wider audience. Such a person likes you — she really likes you!

Nothing in marketing is more powerful than word-of-mouth promotion. We all know that. How do you find and encourage people to open their mouths and speak favorably on your behalf? First, acknowledge them. You know how it feels when you've been acknowledged for something you've done. You can give that feeling to someone else on your Page in a variety of ways:

- Ask your fans whether they've volunteered for any charities or donated toward one. Then challenge your fans to match that goodwill, or write a blog post about the charity and mention your fan by name.
- Publicly thank, by name, the people who are sharing your posts with others.
- Have your Page be a place for fans to share what they do by dedicating a day to those posts. If your Page is dedicated to sustainability, be a forum for fans to share their best resources. Have a Resource Wednesday, a Sharing Saturday, or whatever suits your Page.

Many Pages use a Fan Page Friday concept, similar to Follow Friday on Twitter. Figure 2-1 shows how that looks on Grandma Mary's Page (`www.facebook.com/GrandmaMaryShow`).

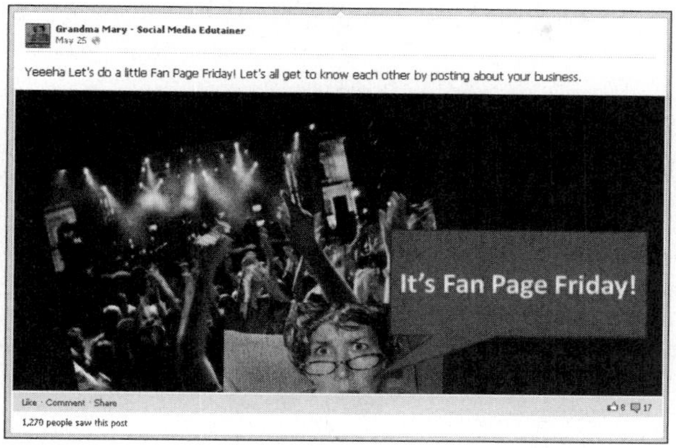

Figure 2-1: Fan Page Friday is a time-tested strategy for developing your Page.

Tagging key players in updates

How do people know you've thanked them on your Page? If they happen to see your status update come through their News Feeds, they'll see their names. But what if they don't catch your update in the News Feed? If you tag them by using the @ system, they see the post on their personal Timelines and get Notifications that they've been tagged in a post by you. This works for your Friends and Pages that you like.

Keep these things in mind:

✦ If you're posting as the Page, you can't tag Friends or individuals in the main Status Update (but you can tag other Pages).

✦ If you're posting as yourself, you can tag Friends, individuals, or Pages.

The problem is that if you post to your Page as your personal Profile instead of as your Page, that update doesn't show in the News Feed for anyone not associated with your personal Profile. That means fans of your Page that aren't connected to your personal Profile won't see that update. However, if you post to your Page as your Page and a fan responds, you can then type a response to that person and tag them.

To tag a Friend or Page in a post, follow these steps:

1. **Type the @ symbol in the Status Update box on your Page and then start typing the name of the Friend or Page you want to tag.**

   Make sure not to put a space between the `@` and the name you type; see how `@Amy` appears in Figure 2-2.

   A list of all your Friends and Pages with that name appears.

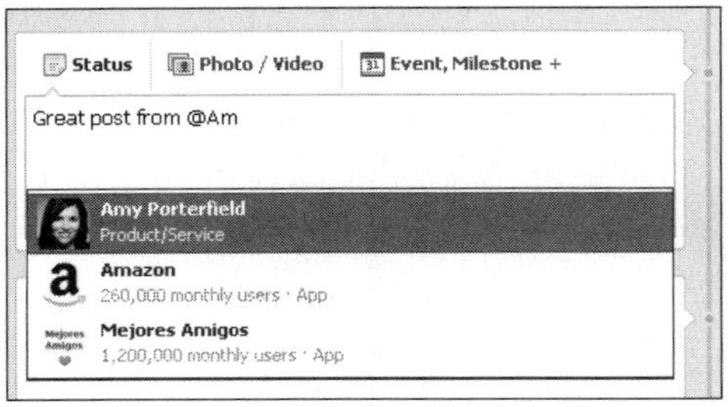

Figure 2-2: Use the @ symbol to put a hyperlinked Page name in the status update.

2. **Click the correct name or Page name.**

   The name you click appears in the status-update box, hyperlinked to that person's personal Profile or Page.

3. **Finish crafting the message.**

4. **Click Share.**

   The person or Page sees your message on his or her Timeline and notifications.

Using public posts to thank people

Key players are your cheerleaders, enthusiasts, and walking advertising system. On Facebook, these key players can influence hundreds, even thousands, of people with their comments. Most of us take our friends' recommendations more seriously than those of strangers whom we may have found searching online. After you establish who *your* key players are, thank them, and encourage them to interact even more.

Through your Insights dashboard, you might find that women 24 to 34 years old are your highest viewing demographic. Thank the members of that age group, too, by providing something that is valuable to them generally. You might create a post that provides a link to something they value, such as discount codes for diapers, as a way to thank them for being part of your Page.

If you find through your Insights dashboard that a huge number of people from California visit your Page, say hi to them and thank them. You could say, "Hi to all the people in California who have liked this Page! Post a picture of you outside on your favorite hiking trail with our Brand Z hiking shoes!"

You can find a textbook case of using questions, polls, and acknowledgement on the NFL Page (`http://facebook.com/NFL`). Just scroll through the posts to see the mix of video, polls, questions, discounts, and giveaways. Most important, note the number of people who liked the post; also note the number of comments generated by that post. You can see many of these things in Figure 2-3.

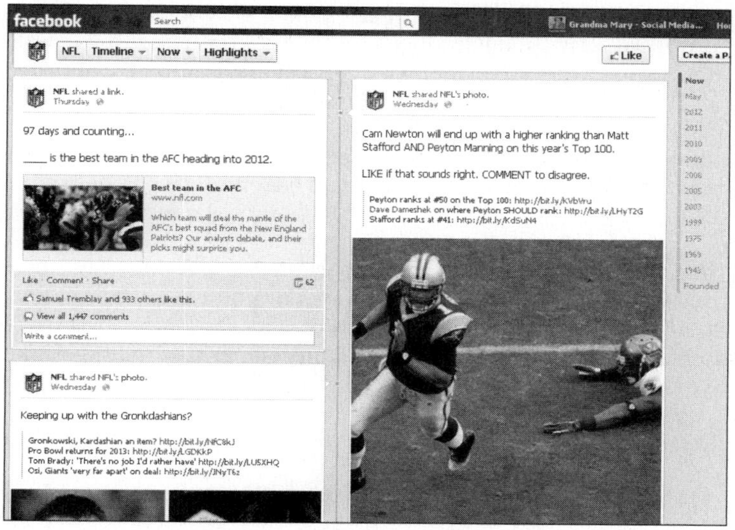

Figure 2-3: A variety of posts engage the fans of the NFL Page.

Creating incentives for repeat visits

The majority of the close to 1 billion people on Facebook go through a process that may look a little like this: They log in and see the News Feed (the one that Facebook aggregates for them, which might not include your Page posts). Next, they scan the top 15 or so posts and maybe click through or comment on a few posts. They try to remember where Facebook hid a Friend's birthday list, and they generally surf around. They don't look at the ads on the side of the Page (that you spent money for). They quickly go to their favorite game, look at the clock, and realize the enormous amount of time that just got sucked out of their lives!

Another scenario for a smaller percentage of people looks like this: They log in, and they know how to click the Sort link to see either Top Stories or see more Recent Stories. They scan through the ticker commenting, liking, and sharing posts with their Friends. They notice the ads on the side and ask, "How did I get targeted for this one?"

Another scenario that we've found for a younger demographic (20–35-year-olds) looks like this: They don't need to log in, because they never log out; they check Facebook via their phones pretty much all day. They filter their view to see only status updates, and that's all they view — period.

TIP: Currently, more than 400 million active Facebook users access Facebook through their mobile phones (and devices). According to Facebook, these people are twice as active on Facebook as nonmobile users are. Make sure that you view your Facebook Page through your phone so that you can see what those people see. View it with the direct browser link at `http://m.facebook.com` and through iPhone and Android applications.

So, looking at these three scenarios, how do you get people to not only view your Page after they initially like it, but also return regularly? Do they need to return to your Page? Can you send everything you want them to see in a post? You need to ask these questions about your business.

Human nature is often predictable. People like incentives. According to research, and especially research on Facebook, we like discounts, coupons, competition, acknowledgement, and personal conversation.

Take the time to measure and note your audience demographics. Note whether your readers prefer coupons or contests. (If you don't know, ask them!) Pay attention to what kinds of status updates they respond to and then do more of what's working. Think "incentive" all the time. Find things that activate those human qualities that foster engagement.

Here's a list of actions to try, based on all the information so far in this chapter:

- **Ask questions.** Use both types (see "Asking questions," earlier in this chapter) to see which works best for you. Encourage conversation by responding to all questions with an answer and another question.
- **Give things away.** Give coupons, discount codes, e-books, and other stuff related to your business. Make giveaways a regular activity to encourage return visits.
- **Acknowledge people.** Reward your community through activities such as Fan Friday, charity support, and random acts of thanking.
- **Use Facebook-approved contests.** We cover contests in detail in Book VI.
- **Respond quickly.** People are impressed when an actual human responds to a customer question or comment.
- **Share the best.** Share your best videos, best tutorials, best resources, best quotations — whatever is appropriate for your business to share.

You know what motivates *you* to seek something out. Analyzing your own behavior can lead to insights about what may work on your Facebook business Page.

Developing a posting schedule

One aspect of engaging readers is how often you post. Good social media consultants tell you to post at the rate your audience expects.

Your audience's expectations for your rate of posting depend on what you post. If you post breaking news in your field, for example, your audience depends on you to disseminate information as it becomes available. This can make for frequent posting.

Here are some examples to show how other Pages handle frequency of posting:

- **Mari Smith,** a well-known social media speaker, directly posts 5 to 10 times per day with as many as 15 or more comments on Timeline posts on her Page (`www.facebook.com/marismith`).
- **iPhone Life magazine** (`www.facebook.com/iphonelifemagazine`), an online and hard-copy magazine for iPhone enthusiasts, posts three to eight times per day.
- **GeekBeatTV** (`www.facebook.com/geekbeattv`), a channel of the well-known Internet TV Station Revision3, posts once or twice per day with lots of comments.
- **NPR** (`www.facebook.com/NPR`) posts as often as hourly.

Here are some examples of how often small businesses with a local reach post:

- **Noah's Ark Animal Foundation:** This no-kill shelter in Fairfield, Iowa, has a mission to rescue, protect, and find loving homes for stray and neglected dogs and cats. It posts once a day and has a wonderful adoption strategy, using beautiful photos and videos of its dogs and cats. It sponsors Meow Mondays, Woof Wednesdays, and Foster Fridays. In between, it posts news about its dog-park project.

  `www.facebook.com/NoahsArkIowa`
- **Finnywick's:** This local toy store, also in Fairfield, Iowa, posts only once per week and highlights a new toy that has just arrived.

  `www.facebook.com/Finnywicks`

REMEMBER

Large and small businesses use a variety of posting schedules and strategies. Figure out what's unique about your business, what your fans want to see, and how often they want to see it. Put all that together on your Page.

Targeting Your Posts to Be Seen

To know how to send your posts, you need to understand how Facebook decides where to post them. The three areas where they can show up are the Top Stories feed, the Most Recent feed, and the ticker. Posts could also show up in any custom list someone has created through a personal Profile.

The Top Stories feed aggregates the most interesting content (from Pages and Friends) based on a Facebook algorithm called *EdgeRank,* and the Most Recent feed shows you the posts of your Friends and Pages you've liked and have conversations with on a regular basis in chronological order. The ticker (which appears to the right of the News Feed) is where Facebook puts *activity stories* — actions such as someone liking a Page, subscribing to a personal Profile, commenting on a photo, and so on. Personally, we find the ticker to be full of wonderful things, as you can see in Figure 2-4.

Figure 2-4: The ticker shows activity stories to a wider audience.

Facebook's own research says that 95 percent of users view only the Top Stories feed. From our experience, we can tell you that most people don't know that Facebook's EdgeRank decides which posts will show up in Top Stories.

Try to educate your fans to click the name of your Page when they see it in the News Feed and then hover over the liked link to make sure that Show in News Feed is selected (as shown in Figure 2-5).

Figure 2-5: Let your fans know to select Show in News Feed.

In the Facebook iPad app, you also see a drop-down menu where you can further filter what you see: only posts by Pages, only posts with links, only posts with photos, only status updates, or any custom Friend lists.

What does this mean for your Page? First and foremost, you need to understand what EdgeRank is so that you can deliver your updates in the best way for your likers to (potentially) see them. You also need to educate your fans about how they can adjust what they see in their News Feed by clicking the Sort arrow and changing it from Top Stories to Most Recent.

Understanding EdgeRank

You want more than anything for your Page to have high visibility and to show up in people's Top Stories feeds. A Page with high interaction gets better EdgeRank and ends up in the Top Stories feed, which means that more people will see your posts. The formula Facebook that uses to determine the visibility of a Page is EdgeRank, which is based on three factors:

- **Affinity:** How often two people interact on Facebook. Affinity scores increase the more often you (or your Page) and a person exchange messages, Timeline posts, comments, and links. The more often a person who likes your Page posts, the better the affinity exists between your Page and that person, and the more likely your Page posts are to show up in that person's Top Stories feed.
- **Weight:** How many comments and likes a post gets. Weight value increases the more comments, likes, and other variables a post has, based on what Facebook is weighing at the moment. Places, video, and photos seem to have the most weight.
- **Decay:** How old the post is. Decay weakens the EdgeRank automatically as your post grows older in the Timeline; as time increases, value decreases.

TIP

Like and make a comment for each post made on your Page to engage conversation. You can comment as yourself (if you've selected that option) or as the Page. Commenting as both is good unless it seems odd to do so. This one action (commenting) will help increase the Weight value.

If one of your likers clicks the Share link for one of your posts and likes it, too, the shared post has a better chance at showing up in the Top Stories feeds of his Friends (those who have the highest affinity scores with the sharer). Whew — did you get that? That's just the tip of this algorithm.

We don't explain how EdgeRank is formulated (because it's fairly complicated), but we can explain a few strategies to help boost your Page's score. You can also read this very good article on EdgeRank and strategies to maximize your Page's visibility:

```
http://www.socialmediaexaminer.com/6-tips-to-
   increase-your-facebook-edgerank-and-exposure/
```

Using EdgeRank optimization strategies

Here are some EdgeRank optimization strategies:

- Encourage people to like your posts. Ask them directly — as in "Like this post to show your support for. . . ."
- If you have a Facebook Places Page, consider merging it with your regular Facebook business Page to increase the weight, or relevance, of what is posted. Before you do that, please see Book II, Chapter 1.
- Be sure to post photos, videos, and use Facebook Questions on a regular basis because they have more weight in the formula. Even better is having your likers post their photos to your Page's Timeline.
- Post when your audience will see the posts. Are they looking at Facebook daily or only on the weekend? Post when they're online and looking. (Find out in Book IX how to determine when your fans are seeing your posts.)

✦ Ask your closest Friends and key players to make comments on your Page as much as possible, and return the favor to start the conversation rolling and help shy people feel safer about commenting.

Following these easy strategies will help boost your EdgeRank and help deposit your posts in your likers' Top Stories feeds. It may also be helpful to educate your Friends and likers about how this system works. Many people have asked why they don't see posts from certain Pages and people. EdgeRank is the reason.

Creating and Participating in Conversations with Your Audience

Creating and participating in conversations is why we're on Facebook. Having an authentic conversation that involves and motivates people feels good and draws more people to the conversation. All the writers of this book have found new and wonderful people through personal conversations on Facebook.

When you can converse with someone about a customer-service issue or tell someone through a post how happy you are with that person's product, and he or she responds to you quickly and treats you with respect, a bond is created that will bring you back to that business again and again. The business is counting on this reaction, and that's why so much attention is being given to the art of conversation in Facebook.

Revisiting the settings for posts to your Timeline

When you create your Page (see Book II, Chapter 1), you make the decision to have the posts on the Timeline be just your own or open for posting by the public, as well. Most Page creators select the Everyone options because those options encourage conversation; anyone can post something. If you don't select those options, people will be able to comment only to something already posted by the Page.

After you start to have conversations with people on your Page, you might want to modify those original settings. To review and possibly change those settings, follow these steps:

1. **Go to your Page, and open the Admin Panel at the top.**
2. **Click Edit Page.**
3. **Click Manage Permissions in the left sidebar.**
4. **On the resulting page, make your Posting Ability, Post Visibility, and Tagging Ability selections (see Figure 2-6).**
5. **Click Save Changes.**

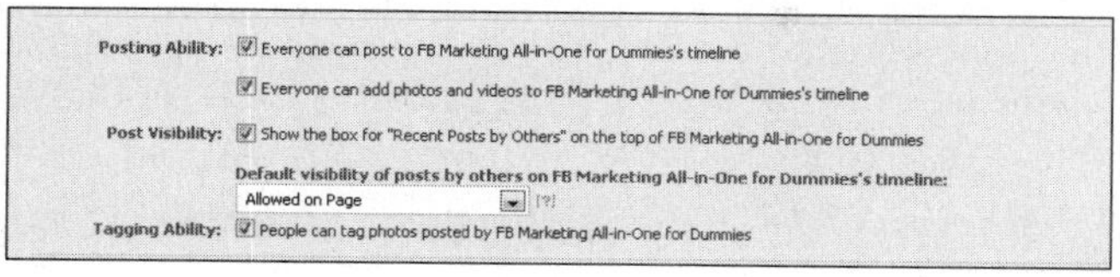

Figure 2-6: Modifying the Timeline posting options.

Understanding the different views people see on your Page

It would be a wonderful thing if we all saw the same thing on a Facebook Page, but because of EdgeRank and the four toggle views (Highlights, Friend Activity, Posts by Page, Posts by Others), we don't. What Joe sees on the Grandma Mary Facebook Page is a little different from what Jesse sees because of the different interaction (EdgeRank) they've developed with the Page and Grandma Mary. By understanding all the different views a person can have on *your* Page, you'll be more educated about how to generate and participate in conversation with them. Figure 2-7 shows where people can toggle the view of a Page from Highlights to Friends Activity, Posts by Page, or Posts by Others.

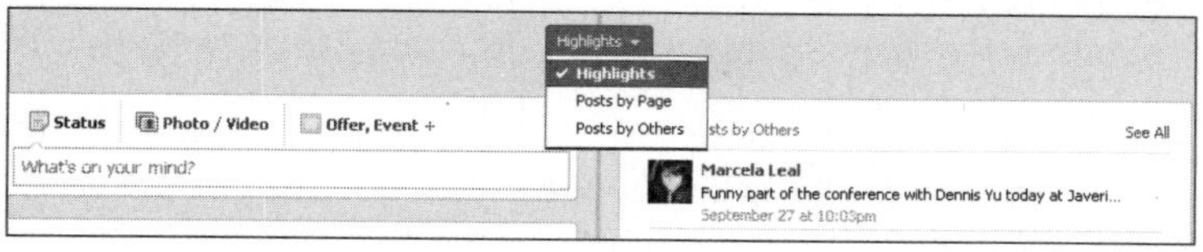

Figure 2-7: Toggling the view.

Facebook defaults the Page view to Highlights; highlights are determined by Facebook. They're collections of posts that have the most interaction, posts that you've highlighted, and photos. The viewer can toggle the view to Posts by Page to be able to view the posts the Page has created in chronological order.

If you prefer that people see your posts in chronological order, you need to educate them about how to toggle the link at the top of the Timeline to Posts by Page. Some Pages occasionally create a post to remind people how to toggle the view. Here's some suggested text to use for that post:

> You can view the posts on this Page in chronological order by clicking Highlights (right below the Timeline Cover photo) and choosing Posts by Page.

If you allow others to post on your Page's Timeline, you can toggle the view to see only those posts by selecting Posts by Others. By toggling to Friend Activity, you see only posts by your personal Friends on this Page.

Being responsive and allowing conversation

If the Holy Grail of Facebook marketing is engagement, being open to all types of communication is the way to go. Regardless of whether your fans select the Timeline view to be Highlights or Posts by Page, you still need to comment, ask questions, be responsive, and generally be available to the people who like your Page.

The best way to be aware when people interact with your Page is to monitor your Notifications section in your Admin Panel and the Posts by Others view (or box).

TIP

Many businesses use this conversational quality in Facebook to nurture a community of people whom they can run ideas by or test new products on via giveaways. By having a friendly, responsive Page, you can realize many opportunities for testing and expanding your business.

Also, as the admin of your Page, you get to direct the conversation but also should be open to the conversation going in a different direction from what you anticipated. More than anything, people on Facebook are looking for a community of like-minded people, and your Page can be that place for them.

Even if you have a controversial subject on your Page, you gain respect by behaving like an adult when you need to be responsive. Allow the conversation to flow, but also moderate, remove, or report users and Pages if things get out of hand.

Keeping the Conversation Civil

Most of the time, the conversation on Facebook is fun and enjoyable. Occasionally, however, someone decides to post things on your Page that aren't congruent with your business. In other words, they post spam or rude and derogatory statements.

We hope that you never need to remove or ban someone from your Page, but you have a responsibility, as the admin of your Page, to keep the conversation going in a positive direction and in line with what your Page is all about.

You need to understand the four types of posts to your Page and also how you can delete, hide, or report them:

- **If you want to remove a post that *you* posted:** Click the hidden pencil icon to the right of the post and then choose Delete or Hide from Page.
- **If you want to remove a post from your Page in which your Page was tagged:** Click the pencil icon and then choose Hide or Report/Mark as Spam. You can't delete this type of post, though, because it was created by someone else. The best you can do is to hide it from people who visit your Page or report it.
- **If you want to remove a post that was posted directly on your Page (not tagged):** Click the X and then choose Hidden from Page, Delete, or Report/Mark as spam.
- **If you want to delete a comment:** Hover over the comment and click the X that shows up on the right side. Then select one of the options: Delete, Hide Post, or Report as Abuse.

After you delete a post, you can't undo the action, so be sure that you really want to delete it before you click the Delete button. The person who created the post isn't notified that the post was removed. The only way that person will know that it was deleted is if she comes back to your Page to look for it and can't find it.

Note: Deleting a post doesn't ban the poster from posting again.

Reporting a poster

Deleting or hiding a post is one thing; using Report/Mark as Spam takes it up a notch. This process is for posts that cross the line into spam, abuse, or use of violent words.

Anyone can create a new Facebook account, like your Page, and again post inappropriate comments. You need to be vigilant about keeping an eye out for the bad apples in the barrel.

Following are two ways to ban a user or a Page from posting to your Page. If you have a few likers, the first way is really easy to use. If millions of people have liked your Page, the second way is the only way to go.

Banning someone when you have a small following

If you have only a few likers and want to ban someone or another Page from your Page, go to your Page and follow these steps:

1. **Open the Admin Panel, and click the See All link in the New Likes box.**

   A dialog box with a list of all the users who have liked your Page appears (see Figure 2-8). You need to find the name of the offending person.

2. **Click the X to the right of the user you want to ban.**
3. **In the dialog box that appears, select the Ban Permanently check box.**

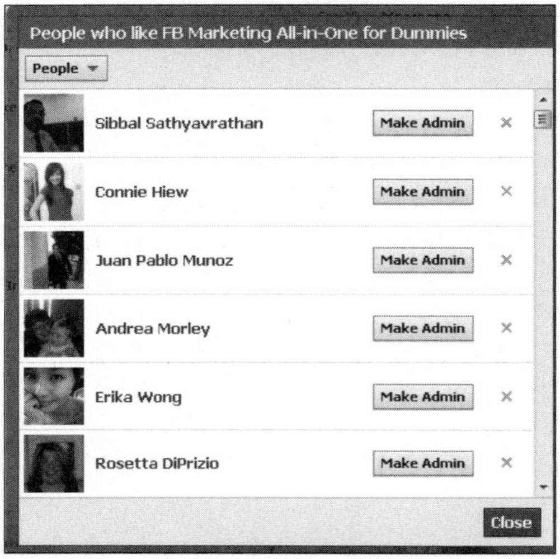

Figure 2-8: Find the name of the offending person through your Like box to ban them from your Page.

4. **Click Okay.**

   Now this person or Page won't be able to re-like your Page and post again unless he creates a new account with a different name.

Banning someone when you have a large following

The other way to ban a person or another Page from your Page — especially if a large number of people like your Page — is to ban her directly from an offending post that she made. Follow these steps:

1. **Put your cursor on the right side of the offending post, and click the X.**

   A drop-down menu appears, with the six options shown in Figure 2-9: Default (Allowed), Highlighted on Page, Allowed on Page, Hidden from Page, Delete, and Report/Mark as Spam.

Figure 2-9: Report a post as abusive and ban the person who posted it.

2. **To ban someone from your Page, select the Report/Mark as Spam option.**

   You will see a confirmation in the Timeline with two links: Undo or ban this person from posting publicly. If you made a mistake, better to click the Undo link right away, as you will not be able to undo at a later date.

Sometimes, a post crosses the line and becomes what you consider abusive. Facebook describes *abusive* as spam or scam; hate speech or personal attacks; violence or harmful behavior; or nudity, pornography, or sexually explicit content.

If you need to report a post as abusive, follow the steps for deleting a single post, choose Report/Mark as Spam, and then ban the user. After you submit the post, Facebook investigates the report and decides whether it needs to ban the user or the Page from Facebook.

Remembering that users can block your posts too

Just as you can block or ban users from posting on your Page, users can turn the tables on you by blocking your posts from their News Feeds and/or reporting your Page!

Not too long ago, Facebook rolled out a new feature that enables fans of your Page to hide your posts from their view (without un-Liking your Page). When someone sees your post in his News Feed, a hover card pops up; he can then hover over the Liked button in the bottom-right corner and deselect Show in News Feed. This action effectively removes your posts from his view unless he visits your Page directly.

Deselecting Show in News Feed keeps the user as a liker of your Page but leaves your posts out of his News Feed completely. You can find out how many people (but not specific names) have hidden your Page's posts in your Insights dashboard. A complete description of the Insights dashboard is in Book IX, Chapter 2.

Last, but certainly not least, anyone can go to your Page and Report it. When you click the drop-down menu to the right of the Message or Like button on any Page, you see options that let you un-like the Page or Report it (see Figure 2-10). If users report your Page, Facebook investigates you and your Page for any violations.

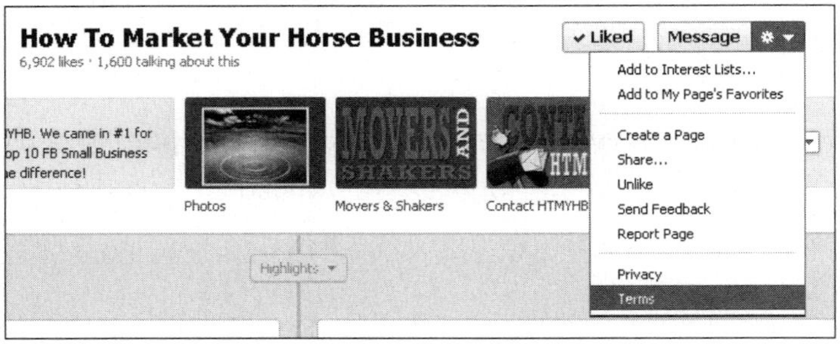

Figure 2-10: You can Report a Facebook business Page by using the drop-down menu.

Chapter 3: Better Engagement with the Help of Facebook Like Links and Buttons

In This Chapter

- Understanding the Facebook Like link and button
- Seeing the implications of using the Like button code outside Facebook
- Discovering how to create a simple Like button code for your website

This chapter explains both the Like *link* and the Like *button* and how to use them to engage your audience on Facebook and outside the Facebook environment. A fuller discussion of the enormous implication of using this Facebook integration tool occurs in Book VII, Chapter 2.

The Button versus the Link

You will see the Like interface on Facebook itself in two ways. One way is as a link, which appears at the bottom of posts on Facebook. See Figure 3-1 for an example of a simple link on a Facebook post. The other way is as a button, as shown in Figure 3-2; buttons appear at the top of a Facebook Page.

Figure 3-1: The Like link.

Figure 3-2: The Like button.

This is a Like button.

By now, if you've spent any time on Facebook — or on the Internet, for that matter — you'll have run across the Like link and button in many places.

Here are a few places where you'll find them:

- As a link at the bottom of each post in your Facebook News Feed
- As a link on the bottom of each comment from any post in your News Feed
- As a link on Facebook Ads
- As a button at the top of any Page you haven't liked yet
- As a button on blog posts outside Facebook
- As a button on a Facebook box on websites outside Facebook

The Like *link* is generated automatically for you in Facebook posts and comments. The Like *button* is also automatically generated on your Facebook business Page and can be manually placed on any type of online interface to which you can add HTML code. The Facebook Like button installed on your website allows people to share content from that site with their Friends back on Facebook.

In the next section, we give you a simple overview of where you might see the link and button, how these elements differ, and why both are important to you as a marketer on Facebook.

Answering Common Questions

If you're new to the Facebook environment, you may have questions about what happens when Like buttons and links are clicked. In this section, we present and answer a few common questions. We hope this section helps you understand what your fans will experience when they click the Like button at the top of your Facebook Page or your website's Facebook Like widget. It should also help you understand what happens when fans click any Like link on your Page posts or any ads you create.

Facebook marketing doesn't work fully unless you have a group of people who are connected to your Page. They get connected through liking your Page. All the fun stuff you can do on Facebook for marketing really depends on this liking aspect. Without liking, none of those social-sharing advantages can fully come into play. You can make liking your Facebook Page easy by placing the Facebook Like button in as many places as possible! On the following pages, we provide questions and answers that explain how fans can use the Facebook Like link and button. This Q&A can also help you determine which design and marketing options are best for you.

Q. What happens when someone clicks the Like link on one of your Page posts?

A. As shown in Figure 3-3, a Like link will always be there when you post on your Page.

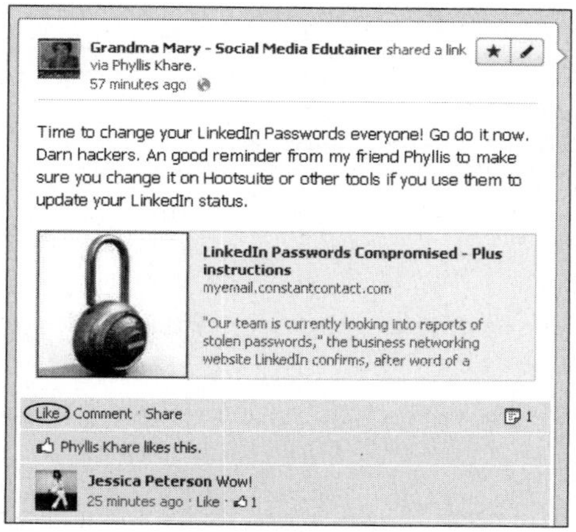

Figure 3-3: There are many reasons to click the Like link on a post.

When people click the Like link on a post on your Page, engagement on your Page increases, thereby adding to a better EdgeRank for your Page.

If several people like the post, Facebook tallies the number of likes and puts that number next to a thumbs-up icon on your post, as well as wherever the post shows up on a fan's News Feed. If someone clicks the thumbs-up icon, the comments open; if he or she clicks the thumbs-up icon again, a box displays the names of the other people who liked the post.

When you view your Page as the admin and click the Notifications box in the Admin panel, you see who has liked a post on your Page. Click the See All link to see all the notifications for the past week.

You can also scroll through the posts on your Page, click the numerical notation, and like any Pages (as your Page) by clicking the Like button next to their names. (If you've already liked a Page, there won't be a Like button.)

Each time someone clicks the Like link on a post, the post has a better ranking from Facebook. See our explanation of EdgeRank in Book IV, Chapter 2, to see how the Facebook algorithm comes into play when people click the Like link on a post.

The notification of the like also shows up in the ticker. This is a great thing because it expands the reach of the like. People may notice it and click through to your Page, or they may click the Like button for your Page right there through the ticker. See Figure 3-4.

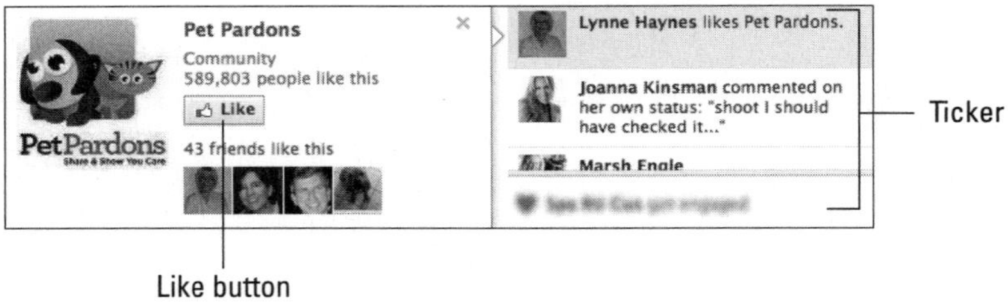

Figure 3-4: People can click Like in the ticker.

Q. What happens when someone clicks the Like link on a comment on one of your Page posts?

A. As shown in Figure 3-5, each comment has a Like link, too.

Figure 3-5: Liking a comment that someone posts on your Page acknowledges that you've read it.

Again, clicking the Like link for a comment adds to the engagement on your Page — and you want that! Clicking the Like link below a comment that someone has left on your Page acknowledges that you've read it — and liked it! That person gets a Facebook notification (which he can find by clicking his Notification icon) in his personal account that you liked the comment.

Q. What happens when someone clicks the Like button at the top of any Facebook Page?

A. As shown in Figure 3-6, the Like button at the top of a Page tells you that you haven't liked the Page yet.

Figure 3-6: This is the Like button you want people to click!

This Like button is one of the most important on Facebook. It's the button you want people to click!

After users click the Like button at the top of your Page, several things happen:

- ✦ Your Page appears in the Activity section of the users' personal Timelines.
- ✦ A notification goes on users' Timelines that they liked your Page (unless they modified their privacy settings to disallow those types of postings on their Timelines).
- ✦ The users potentially see your posts in their News Feeds. (This big topic is discussed more thoroughly in Chapter 2 of this minibook.) And a notification that you liked the Page shows up in the ticker, as noted earlier.
- ✦ You can target your ads to users who have liked your Page.

When a person likes your Page, they join your community. Each person who joins your community is a *connection* (in Facebook speak). Your connections consist of the people with whom you'll have conversations and who'll be spreading the word about you, your product, or your brand. Those people are connected to your Page through the act of liking it. You have gained permission, by their liking of your Page, to communicate with them through your posts. Now your posts will hopefully find their way into their News Feeds, and you'll be able to target any ads to all your likers or subsets of them — a very good thing.

Note: Before, people couldn't like, comment, or post without having liked the Page. Now, though, anyone can like a post, comment on a post, and share a post without having liked the Page. *This is a very big change for Facebook businesses.* You absolutely want people to like your Page because of the benefits we listed earlier, but now the door is open, and anyone can come in and engage with your Page without liking it first.

Q. What happens when someone clicks the Like link on your Facebook Ad?

A. As shown in Figure 3-7, a Facebook Ad can have a Like link or no link at all. If no link appears below the ad, the ad is notifying users of an Event, or it links to a site outside Facebook through the hyperlinked title of the ad.

When a user clicks the Like link on an ad, that user immediately becomes a liker of the Page that the ad is representing.

Figure 3-7: Some Facebook ads have a Like link; some don't.

You can verify this process for yourself by clicking the title of an ad and seeing that you haven't liked the Page. Then go back to the ad and click the Like link, return to the Page (are you still with us?), and refresh it. You should then see that you're included in the group of likers for that Page.

So, in other words, the Like link on an ad is the *same thing* as the Like button on the top of a Page. Clicking the link on the ad and clicking the Like button on a Page do the same thing.

The added benefit of having a Like link on an ad is in having the opportunity to explore the analytics of who liked the ad and draw some conclusions about the community you're developing. We delve into ad analytics in Book VIII.

Q. What happens when someone clicks the Like button on your individual website or blog posts?

A. The blog post shown in Figure 3-8 has a Like button so that readers can show their support of the post. The Like button on your blog post can be configured to allow users to post a comment to Facebook without leaving your blog. You can install a similar button by inserting code on your website, or using a Like button plug-in in WordPress.

Figure 3-8: Don't make users leave your blog to post comments to Facebook.

When someone clicks a Like button on a blog post, she's liking the post, not the Page (or the website). When a user clicks a Like button on your website or blog, a short summary of the content — called a *story* — with a link back to the content on your site, is posted to her Facebook Timeline. The user can choose to have the story post on someone else's Timeline, to one of her groups, or as a private message. The story also appears in the News Feed, with the potential to be seen by all the user's Friends.

Sometimes, a website owner changes the text on this button to read `Recommend`, but it does the same thing (as noted earlier) as if it read `Like`. You can also modify the code to allow someone to post a comment as he likes the post (refer to Figure 3-8).

Depending on which code you use (more about that in Book VII, Chapter 2), users have the ability not only to like your post (and have that notification show up in their News Feeds), but also to make a comment that will show up on Facebook, all without leaving your website.

> **Q. What happens when someone clicks the Like button on a Facebook Like box widget on your web page?**
>
> **A.** A Like box is shown in Figure 3-9. If you include a Like box widget on your web page or blog (discussed in Book VII, Chapter 2), your website or blog page has a direct link to your Facebook business Page. This means that when a user clicks a Like button on your Page inside the Facebook Like box widget, a connection is made between your Facebook Page and the user. Clicking that Like button in the Like box is the same as clicking the Like button at the top of your Facebook Page.

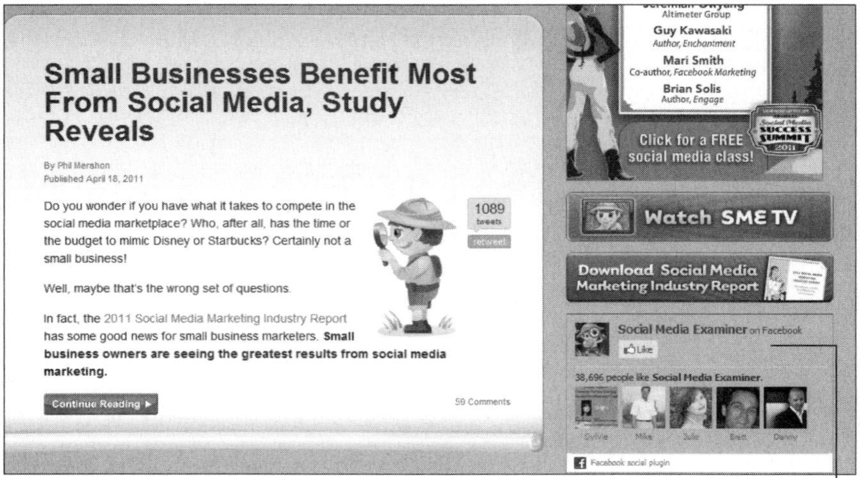

Figure 3-9: Clicking the Like button in a Facebook Like box (widget) on your website is like clicking the Like button on your Facebook Page.

A Facebook Like box

Your Facebook Page now appears in the Activity section of the user's personal Profile Timeline, and the user sees your posts in her News Feed. Your Facebook Page will show up in the same places that Facebook Pages show up around Facebook (such as through a search), and you can target your ads to those people who clicked that Like button.

Clicking the Like button on a Like box on a website gives the same benefits to the Page owner as clicking the Like button on the owner's Facebook Page.

Placing the Like Button Code

The Like *link* is generated automatically for you in Facebook posts, comments, and ads, and on your Facebook business Page.

You can place the Like *button* on pages outside Facebook by generating HTML code and then inserting it into your website's code so that it's part of every blog post you make, as shown in Figure 3-10.

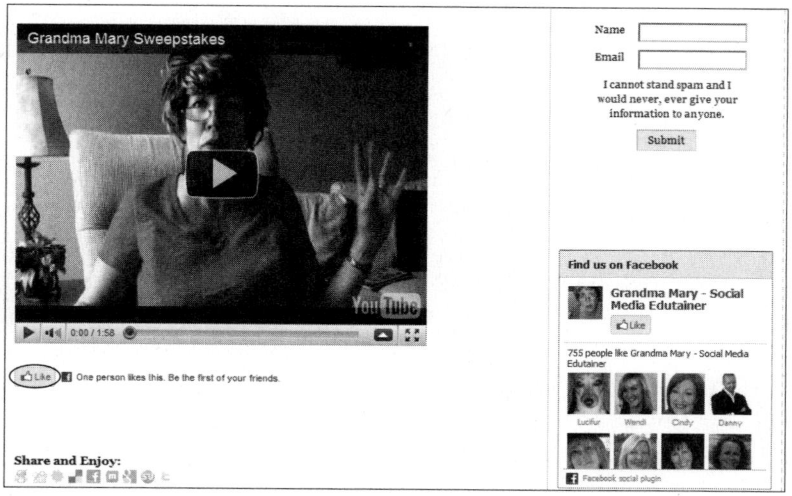

Figure 3-10: This is how a Like button looks on a blog post.

If talking code zips your Geek Meter up to Overwhelm level, take a minute to read the very simple instructions in the following section to see whether you can figure them out. If not, talk to your webmaster; have him or her generate the code and place it for you.

TIP

If you have a WordPress blog or website, plug-ins are available that do the same thing as this Facebook generator. An easy one to use is the Facebook Like Button Plugin for WordPress, available here:

```
http://wordpress.org/extend/plugins/fblikebutton
```

All the steps to install this widget in WordPress may be found in Book VII, Chapter 2.

Generating the Code for a Like Button

The following steps create code for a Like button. We're not going to go into the deeper development of code with Open Graph Tags, which would provide you additional analytic data from liking activity. In fact, we're going to go through only what Facebook calls Step One:

1. **Go to** `http://developers.facebook.com/docs/reference/plugins/like`.

   You're on the page that generates the code for your Like button.

2. **In the form, enter the URL of the web page where users will like your posts.**

   Type the complete URL of your website, including the `http://` part.

3. **Decide whether you want to include the Send button with your Like button.**

   We suggest that you select the box to include it.

4. **Choose your layout style from the drop-down menu.**

   The three choices are standard, button count, and box count. You can click each one to see a preview.

5. **Type in the width you want to use for your Like button.**

   Choose a width that complements the layout of your website or blog. The default size — 450 pixels — works for most sites.

6. **Select the Show Faces check box if you want to show the Profile images of the people who like your post.**

   The faces show up on the standard button style only and appear next to the button. Having the faces of visitors' Facebook Friends on a blog post helps build social trust and encourages them to like something if they see that their Friends have already liked it. Note that users see only the faces of their Friends, not of everyone who liked the post.

7. **From the drop-down menu, choose which verb (Like or Recommend) you want to display in the button.**

   Some people suggest that you choose Like most of the time because it's more widely recognized by Facebook users.

8. **Choose the color scheme for your button from the drop-down menu.**
9. **Choose the font for your button from the drop-down menu.**
10. **Click Get Code.**

    A dialog box pop ups, displaying two code boxes. You can choose iFrames code or XFBML code.

XFBML code is more versatile, but you need to know how to use the JavaScript SDK. The XFBML code allows you to resize the button height dynamically — and, with a bit of code tweaking, to know in real time when someone clicks the Like button. XFBML creates a comment box to allow people to add a comment to the like. You may have seen on other blogs that when you click the Like button, a little text field opens that gives you a chance to type a comment (refer to Figure 3-8). If users do add a comment, the story published back to Facebook is given more EdgeRank!

Modifying code takes a little expertise. If you enjoy working with code and are a do-it-yourself kind of person, Facebook has some support and training for you at `http://developers.facebook.com/docs/reference/javascript/`.

If you aren't concerned about the deeper analytics of tracking and just want people to like and share your posts on Facebook, you can configure the code from the preceding steps and copy either the XFBML or iFrames code that's generated.

11. **Copy the code you want.**

    Now you can place the code on your website or give the code to your webmaster to place on your site.

Chapter 4: Expanding Your E-Commerce Products and Services to Facebook

In This Chapter

- **Creating a new storefront on Facebook to feed into your existing e-commerce store**
- **Opening a self-contained store exclusive to Facebook**
- **Creating a self-contained News Feed store**
- **Exploring e-commerce app options**
- **Installing third-party e-commerce apps on your Page**
- **Using Facebook offers to drive engagement**

Nothing says "engagement" like shopping. By providing your loyal enthusiasts a way to buy your products and in the same stroke share the news of their purchase with their Friends on Facebook, you could start momentum toward brand awareness with the potential of increased revenue. If we remember correctly, that's one of the main reasons to have a Facebook Page in the first place! It all comes back to social proof. If you have *social authority,* that means you have a reputation for being the expert (or the best provider) on the subject of your business on social media platforms. *Social proof* (or *social trust*) happens when people try your products or services because they see their own Friends and connections liking your products and services (because you have established yourself as the social authority on those products and services).

In terms of Facebook, social trust is built when people see that their Friends have already said, in effect, "This is good." Imagine this scenario from your customers' perspectives. If they look at one of your hats for sale on your regular website, and you have Facebook's Open Graph application programming interface (API) implemented, or they click your Facebook Page shopping link, and right next to the Add to Cart button, they see thumbnail images of four of their Facebook Friends who already bought the hat, it brings social proof (trust and authority) and better customer engagement to your store. (Also, we hope it creates another sale for you!)

Here's a comment that we read on a shopping site on Facebook: "I like that I can still chat with my Facebook Friends while shopping in the same window. Easy way to get their input on my potential buys!"

This kind of social proof and real-time interaction leads to sales, which is why the largest corporations in the world are now on Facebook. There are four basic ways to connect your e-commerce to Facebook: a storefront, a store, a News Feed store, and offers. In this chapter, we explore the world of social shopping and all the ways you can add your e-commerce to the Facebook environment.

Understanding Facebook E-Commerce

You should consider using your Facebook Page as an e-commerce store because

- The average user spends about 1.2 days per month on Facebook, and that number is growing.
- Facebook is becoming *the* hub of all kinds of activity, including shopping.
- Free shopping applications make it easy for anyone to have an online storefront or store.
- Engagement goes up when you offer discounts, coupons, or other exclusive deals as Facebook shopping incentives.

REMEMBER

Potential customers on Facebook like to stay on Facebook. They might see in their News Feeds that one of their Friends has liked your Page and then go explore what you have to offer. Keep in mind that people may spend more money if it's easy to stay and shop on your Facebook Page or right there in the News Feed!

Facebook offers four types of shopping interfaces:

- **Storefront:** The storefront appears in an app on your Page (those boxes below your Cover photo) and is a place to browse products. When visitors click the Buy button, they're whisked away from Facebook to the company's website store to complete their purchases.
- **Store:** This is a fully functioning store where shoppers can browse goods and purchase them without leaving the Facebook environment.
- **News Feed Store:** This is a new type of interface where the store is in a News Feed post. Moontoast is an app company providing News Feed store apps, so make sure that you read about Moontoast later in this chapter, in the "Finding E-Commerce Apps that Fit Your Needs" section.
- **Offers:** This built-in Facebook function allows you to create an offer (discount or code) that people can claim and then use at your store or on

your site. It's a great stand-alone feature or a complement to your other e-commerce solutions. Currently, offers are available only after your Page has more than 400 likes. You can find the Help section for offers here: `https://www.facebook.com/help/offers`.

Using the Featured Apps Space for Your Store

Facebook gives you three of the four featured app spaces on a Page. You can use all of these for your e-commerce, if you'd like. If you have several types of products, you can use each app for each different product type. Your consultation services can be one of the apps, your e-books are another, and the third contains all your affiliate products.

Using apps for your e-commerce has both pros and cons.

Pros:

- ✦ You can replicate, or pull in through an RSS feed, an entire page from your e-commerce website. (You can use the Heyo app, covered later in this chapter, for this purpose.)
- ✦ You can create a call to action on the app image, such as *Buy Tea HERE!* or *Free tea with every order!* (You can change the image and the hyperlink for each app.)
- ✦ You can create an entire sales page using your own HTML code and direct people to your e-commerce site. (You can use the Static HTML app by Involver for this.)

Cons:

- ✦ Currently, you can't view apps in the Facebook mobile app (but you can if you use the browser view of Facebook).
- ✦ Currently, if you copy the URL from the app page and post it in the News Feed, you still can't see it from the mobile app.
- ✦ Generally, people don't visit a Page; instead, they prefer to scan through their News Feeds. (You do this yourself, don't you?)

In the following sections, we offer strategies you can use to mitigate these cons and turn lemons (mobile view of custom apps) into lemonade (more clicks).

Posting product images

Whether or not you use custom apps for your e-commerce, also post the images of your products. In the descriptions of the images, remember to include the `http://` link to the website where visitors can purchase the products.

Facebook gives you a boatload of character space in an image description but shows only the first 400 characters before the See More link. (We tested this limit and made it to 6,000 characters with no end in sight.)

If you create an album with your products, you can also send the link to the album to your e-mail lists and other off-Facebook promotions.

By posting an image, you bypass the mobile problem. All images are viewable in the current official mobile Facebook app.

Another reason why we're talking about images in this section is that Facebook restricts that first app space to images. You can use that restriction to your advantage by uploading product images to fill that space on a regular basis. You can also upload images of your ads and design them to fit the size limitations of the app.

Posting off-Facebook URLs

Because these featured app spaces don't show up in a mobile app, you can always post the URL of your e-commerce site in a regular post. The people viewing this post from a mobile app will be directed to your e-commerce site through a browser. As long as your e-commerce site looks great on a mobile device, you're good to go!

If your e-commerce is hosted on your own website, consider using a mobile theme so that visitors to your site see an interface that's configured for mobile viewing. Interfaces configured in this way are quite smart, as they can tell when a visitor is viewing from the site on a computer or a mobile phone and then show the appropriate view.

Posting an offer

We talk about using the built-in Facebook offers in Book II, Chapter 1, and in Book IX. We also discuss the topic briefly at the end of this chapter as a reminder of what wonderful features offers are. Facebook offers show up in News Feeds and are completely accessible through mobile phones. Using offers is a good marketing tactic because people generally prefer to scan through their News Feeds instead of clicking on ads or going to your Page.

Using PayPal to Accept Payment

We're just about ready to explain how to choose and install a storefront e-commerce app. First, you may need to create a PayPal account for your business, because most apps use PayPal for payment. The main benefits of using PayPal are that many of your users already have PayPal accounts, and those who don't can use a credit card with the PayPal interface. The benefit for your company (besides being able to accept credit cards) is that you don't need to open a bank merchant account to start collecting payments.

Setting up a PayPal account is quick and easy, but verifying the bank account that you associate with PayPal can take several days. After you have your PayPal account set up and verified, you can start the process of installing and connecting any third-party shopping application (which we discuss in the very next section!).

If you need assistance in setting up a PayPal account, go to `www.paypal.com`, and click the Business tab.

Finding E-Commerce Apps that Fit Your Needs

You can integrate many storefront applications into your Facebook business Page. In this section, we show you how to find these apps and choose the one that's right for your business.

Many of the hundreds of stand-alone Internet shopping sites (such as eBay and Etsy) are realizing that they need to integrate their sellers' stores with Facebook to stay current in the space where potential customers are already spending their time and money.

You can add your e-commerce products and services to your Facebook Page in many ways. The few we present in this section can get you started. The only limit is your imagination.

If you're a retailer or are considering promoting a product or service, you should check with the e-commerce system you're currently using to see whether that system already has a Facebook integration application.

Go to Appbistro (`http://appbistro.com`) to find applications that are best suited for your type of business. Appbistro is a treasure chest full of applications you can try out on your Page. We consider it to be a kind of yellow pages for Facebook applications.

If you're starting from scratch, though, you have many ways of finding the right e-commerce app for your business on Facebook:

- Search Facebook for *"e-commerce"* and explore the applications listed in the search results.
- Note which storefront apps other companies are using on their Facebook Pages.
- Search `www.allfacebook.com` or `http://mashable.com` for articles on Facebook shopping applications.

Or you can just test the ones listed in the sections that follow. We tested all of them before choosing the ones that fit our various businesses. After you select the application that you want to use, it's easy to put the app on your

Page, as most systems take you through the process step by step. First, though, we need to talk about some of your options.

Storenvy

Storenvy (`www.storenvy.com`) is a storefront application. It has a marketplace of independently owned stores. You can open an online store for free, and the Storenvy Facebook app lets you put an interface on your Facebook Page. When people click to buy your products, they go to your page on the Storenvy site. The application requires no setup fees, no monthly fees, no listing fees, and no transaction fees. You can have an unlimited amount of products, display up to five images per product, and fully customize your store. See Figure 4-1 for an example of a Storenvy e-commerce interface on Facebook.

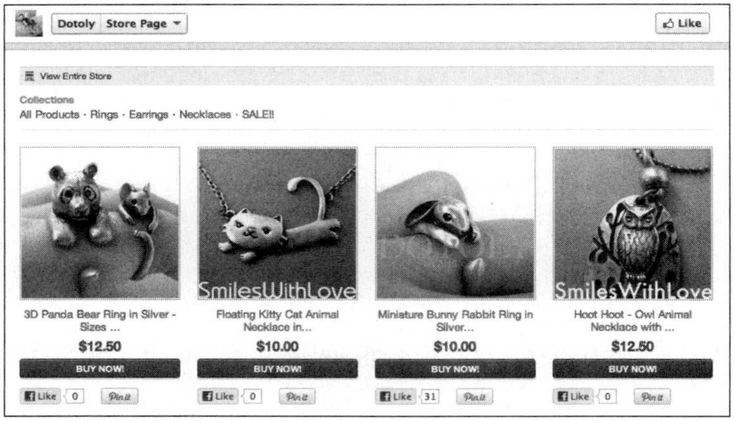

Figure 4-1: A Storenvy e-commerce interface on Facebook.

Payvment

Payvment (`www.facebook.com/payvment`) is a professional-grade store application that you can add to your Facebook Page. You can open a store for free. There are two other monthly pricing levels.

Payvment has a Facebook shopping-mall interface (`https://apps.facebook.com/shoppingmall`) filled with all its merchants. You can put items from different merchants in one shopping cart and pay one time. You can easily like and share items with your Facebook Friends.

If a customer leaves your Payvment store on your Facebook Page without purchasing the items in his cart, those items remain in his cart so that the next time he goes to purchase something anywhere on Facebook (using that same Payvment app on someone else's Page), those items will still be in the cart, queued up for purchase!

See Figure 4-2 for an example of a Payvment e-commerce interface on Facebook.

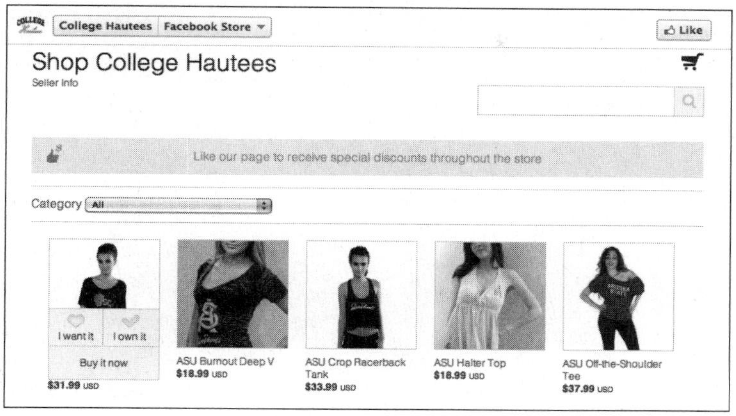

Figure 4-2: A Payvment e-commerce interface on Facebook.

ShopTab

ShopTab (`www.shoptab.net`) is a storefront application that's easy to set up. To use ShopTab, upload your products to the ShopTab website and then add the ShopTab application to your Facebook Page. ShopTab allows people to look through your products on your Facebook Page, but when users click to buy a product, they're taken to the ShopTab website to complete the purchase.

This application doesn't have a free version, but it does have a free trial.

Etsy

Thousands of artists and crafters are listed with Etsy (`www.etsy.com`) on Facebook Pages. Etsy recently retired its My Etsy app; instead, it has designed a way for users to post directly to the Facebook Page News Feed from the Etsy page. This method keeps products in the News Feed instead of on a stand-alone app page. This is a good thing, because most people view just the News Feed, and with the higher number of customers using mobile devices to purchase products, the News Feed is the best place to showcase items.

Currently, the Facebook mobile app doesn't show any custom app pages, so posting directly as an update is a good alternative to consider. See Figure 4-3 for an example of an Etsy e-commerce interface on Facebook. Notice, though, that this process doesn't place a Share link on the post. Someone would need to click through to the product to Share the item on Facebook.

Figure 4-3: An Etsy e-commerce interface on Facebook.

Moontoast

Moontoast (www.moontoast.com) has completely redesigned its function. More and more e-commerce solutions are focusing on the News Feed and not so much on a custom app page. Moontoast has developed a post that allows you to purchase right from within the News Feed. Figure 4-4 shows a Moontoast interface in the News Feed before (top) and after clicking.

Tinypay.me

Tinypay.me (https://tinypay.me) is another service you can use to create a link back to an e-commerce site. To use this service, you create a product page on Tinypay.me, and the Tinypay.me website creates an embed code that you can place on your Facebook business Page, using the Involver Static HTML iFrames app (more on that coming up). You can also just post the product's URL in a Facebook Page status update and forgo the application process completely!

Tinypay.me acts like a storefront because clicking the link takes the user to a page off Facebook where she can buy your product. This service is very easy to implement. See Figure 4-5 for an example of a Tinypay.me e-commerce interface on a Facebook Page, and see Figure 4-6 for how the app interface looks (where you paste the HTML embed code). Please note that the Page owner also included code for a table, so the items are arranged nicely on the Page.

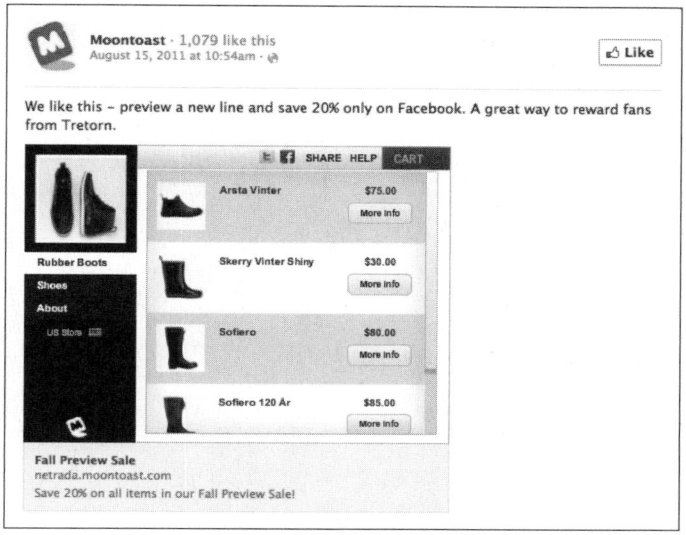

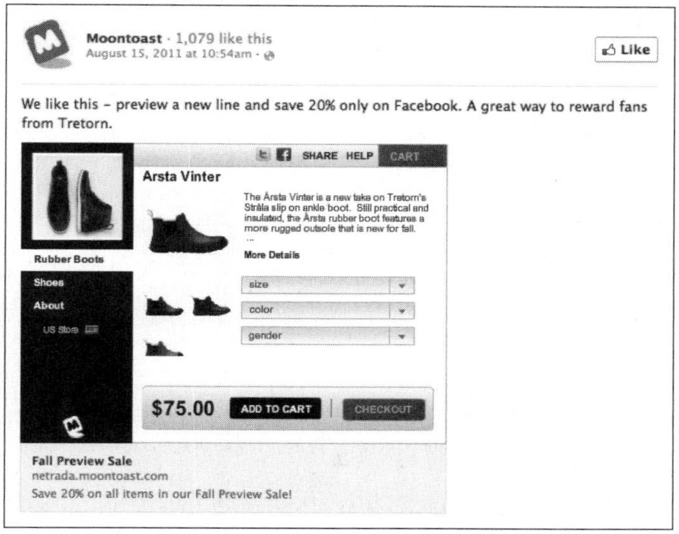

Figure 4-4: A Moontoast e-commerce interface on Facebook, before and after clicking.

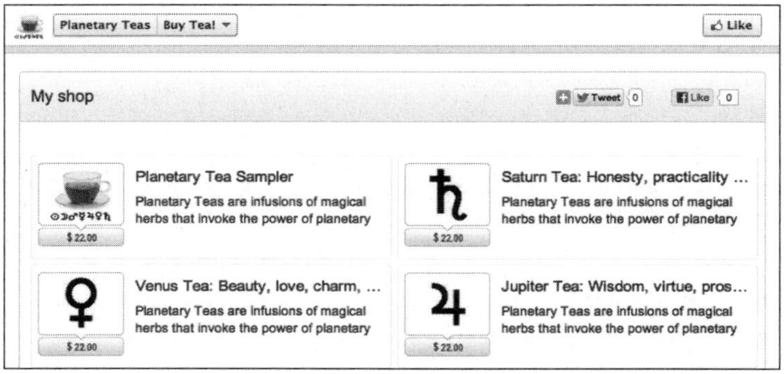

Figure 4-5: A Tinypay.me e-commerce interface on Facebook.

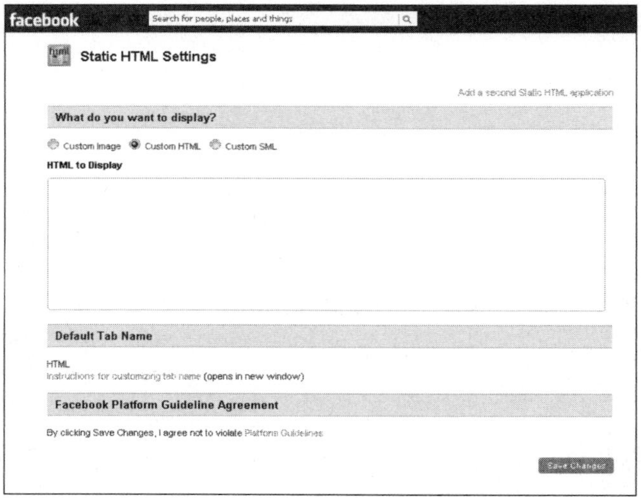

Figure 4-6: This is where you paste the embed code in the Static HTML app by Involver.

REMEMBER

The Static HTML App by Involver converts the HTML code to an iFrame format that you can use to paste HTML from your store.

TIP

Here's an important thing to think about when choosing the best shopping interface for your business: Are your customers looking for and buying products on Facebook using their iPhones or iPads? Many of these storefront apps use Adobe Flash, and as of this writing, Apple does not allow Flash on any of its iOS devices. This is why many businesses are now using apps that post directly to the Facebook News Feed instead of to a custom app page.

Installing a Facebook E-Commerce Application

In the "Finding E-Commerce Apps that Fit Your Needs" section, earlier in this chapter, we list many excellent e-commerce store applications that are currently available for integration with your Facebook Page.

All Facebook third-party app companies make it really easy to install an app on your Page. When you decide on the app you want, the app will provide step-by-step instructions for the installation process.

You still need to adjust the hyperlink text below the app box and the app cover image, and those instructions are fully explained in Book II. If you're installing a storefront application (that is, one that allows visitors to browse your products but requires them to complete the purchase at another website), you need to go to the website for that application and enter the products you want to sell in your store. Then your product information will be fed to the Facebook app link.

If you're installing a complete store application, you can load product information right there on Facebook or on the application's website. Then your customers can view product information and purchase those products on Facebook.

If you're using a News Feed store (like the one offered by Moontoast), follow the instructions to create those great News Feed store posts.

Creating a Link to Your Website Store on Your Page

With a Facebook Page, you have many opportunities to link back to your existing e-commerce website without installing an application. You can

- Create status updates with the specific URL of any products you mention.
- Upload promotional videos with links back to your website's store.
- Highlight your store URL on your Page's Info tab.
- Include your store's link in your business Page's Profile image description (not on the image itself).
- Implement any of the other strategies we discuss in Books II and III.

A very good way to connect an e-commerce site to Facebook, however, is to create a storefront link that takes you back to your regular website e-commerce Page, and we discuss that in the next section.

You can link to your My Etsy e-commerce page, eBay page, Amazon e-store, Tinypay.me pages, or any site where you sell your products. Just remember that many of these sites offer their own Facebook apps, and creating a storefront link with their official applications might look (and perform) better than just a link back to your website's storefront.

Using Other Applications to Create a Custom Link for Your Storefront

You can use several applications to create a custom app box on your Page that will link to your e-commerce website. Here are a few to explore. The following aren't considered to be shopping applications; they offer ways to create custom links for your Page that can be used for anything, including links to your e-commerce web pages.

Pagemodo

Pagemodo (`www.pagemodo.com`) is priced from free to $33 per month for enterprise businesses. It has a very easy-to-use interface with many templates to choose among. You can customize your template with images, links, videos, hidden codes, and many other things. Hidden codes are also called *reveal codes.* After someone clicks the Like button on your Page, new text (coupon codes, videos, and all sorts of other things) are revealed. To edit how this page looks, you go to your account interface on the Pagemodo website. Pagemodo has a one-page, three-custom-apps price for $3 to $6 per month. Those three apps could be a reveal coupon code, a products page and an HTML page.

TabSite

TabSite (`www.facebooktabsite.com`) is priced from free to $25 per month. The free version doesn't give you access to all the apps (TabSite calls them widgets), but it can create a basic custom app (widget). The editing interface for a TabSite tab is reminiscent of a Microsoft Word document, as you see in Figure 4-7. After you create and install your TabSite app on a Facebook Page, a new Welcome app appears in your custom apps. Then you can move it to the position you want (Featured or Showcased). See Book III, Chapter 2 and Book V, Chapter 1, for all the details on how to move app positions.

Heyo

Heyo (`https://heyo.com`) is a great interface that we're very excited about. It led the way with drag-and-drop applications onto a canvas. You don't have to know any kind of code to create a beautiful custom e-commerce storefront. The interface was built with noncoders in mind. Heyo comes in a free version as well as several paid versions.

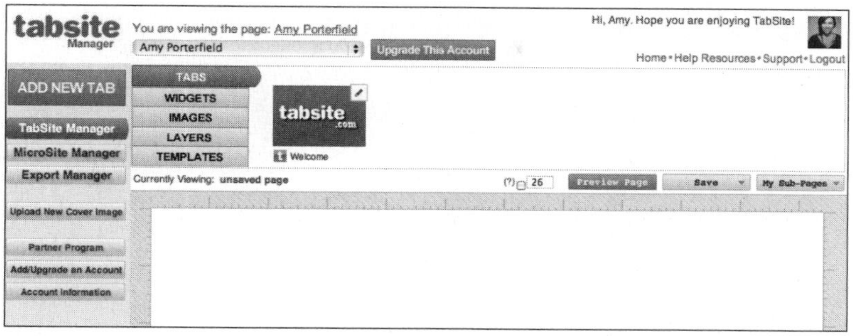

Figure 4-7: The editing interface for a TabSite tab.

BandPage

BandPage (`www.bandpage.com`) is an option to consider if you have a band or are a musician. This app offers a fully customizable storefront link for your music. BandPage connects your SoundCloud e-commerce site to this link for easy purchasing.

Posting Facebook Offers

We're taking a moment here to explore using Facebook offers because the feature is great for e-commerce, especially if your business is a local business.

If your business has store hours and a physical address, and you have more than 400 likes, you might have heard you can create an offer for your Page. We discuss local business Page types fully in Book II, Chapter 1 and offers in great detail in Book VII, Chapter 1. Here's a summary of the great features that offers bring to your business:

- Offers reach more people who have liked your Page than regular posts do.
- Offers have a three-day life span without your having to repost.
- Claimed offers are another level of engagement to build a loyal group of fans because fans need to either bring the offer into your place of business or present it to you at time of payment.
- Offers are essentially free News Feed ads.

We show you how to create and post an offer in Book VII, Chapter 1.

Consider pinning the offer to the top of the Timeline for visitors to see right away. You can also use Promotions to get the offer in front of more people or run a Sponsored story ad — all of these are discussed in Book VII, Chapter 1.

Chapter 5: Building Visibility for Your Personal Profile

In This Chapter

- **Getting people to Subscribe to your posts**
- **Directing the offline world to your personal Facebook Profile**
- **Using a personal Profile Cover image that supports your business**
- **Using Public photo albums and milestones to spread the word about your business**
- **Supporting your business by posting life events on your personal Profile**
- **Highlighting your business by rearranging apps**

Can you count how many things have changed with Facebook in the past year? Some of the most important changes happened in personal Profiles. Beside the transition to Timeline, Facebook opened the door for people who are considered to be public figures to be able to post to Subscribers with their public updates. This is big. We introduce this topic in Book II. In this chapter, we look at a few specific things you can do with building, engaging, retaining, and selling to your community by using your personal Profile.

If you made the decision to turn on your Subscribe button (refer to Book II, Chapter 5), you can do some specific things to encourage people to Subscribe to your personal Profile instead of asking them to be your Friend. All those things we discuss in Book II — about connecting your offline world to your business Page — come into play when we focus on your personal Profile.

The most important thing to remember when using your personal Profile to support your business is to keep the public posts and public images as personal as possible. In other words, you can post the same thing on your Page and your personal Profile, but as you may expect, the tone and perspective need to be more personal in the latter.

Because personal Profiles have Timeline Cover photos, too, you can develop a way to support your business with some specific shots woven between your more personal photos. We discuss how to make a photo album Public and how the visitors to your personal Profile will see your Timeline. Make sure that you review Book II, Chapter 4 for basic setup information.

Inviting People to Subscribe instead of Friend

In Book II, Chapter 4, we discuss how to modify your settings so that only Friends of Friends can ask to be your Friend and everyone else will see only the Subscribe button. Having the Subscribe button on your personal Profile is a passive way to get people to subscribe to your public posts instead of requesting to be your Friend. What about some active ways? Here are a few ideas to try:

- **Change your wording.** When you're out at events, instead of saying "Friend me on Facebook," say "Subscribe to me on Facebook."
- **Educate your audience.** Explain why being a Subscriber is a good thing, because your public posts are what people want to read anyway.
- **Ignore Friend requests.** People who ask to be Friends are automatically Subscribers. Ignore their Friend requests, and they'll still see your Public posts.

At some point, you may find that a lot of people are subscribed to your personal Profile. This may mean that you're being "suggested" by Facebook. You can see the whole list of people who have their Subscribe button turned on here: `www.facebook.com/subscriptions/suggestions`.

Occasionally, you see suggested people in the right column of your own News Feed.

Connecting Your Personal Profile to Your Offline World

Chapter 1 of this minibook includes a section on connecting your business Page to your offline world. That content can be applied to your personal Profile. Reread that section, but replace *business Page* with *personal Profile*. Also consider these highlights:

- **Change your phone hold message.** Say "Subscribe to me on Facebook."
- **Add your personal URL to your e-mail signature.** All the how-tos are in Chapter 1 of this minibook. Just change the URL you use to the personal Profile one, and you're good to go.
- **Include your personal Profile URL on hard-copy mailings.** If you have fliers, posters, hard-copy newsletters, and the like, include your personal Profile URL, and include the sentence "Subscribe to me on Facebook."
- **Update your letterhead and stationery.** As in the preceding item, use your personal Profile URL.
- **Modify your website's Facebook icon.** On your website, use your personal Profile URL as the link to the Facebook icon. If you have text with your icon, use *Subscribe* instead of *Friend*.

The most important point is this: If you're using your personal Profile to support your business, make sure that you let people know about the Subscribe button located on your personal Profile Timeline! Don't assume that they understand it or know how it works; just make it easy for them to click it and see your public updates.

Creating a Cover Photo Strategy

In Chapter 1 of this minibook, we talk about creating a strategy using the Cover photo on your business Page. The same strategy can be applied here, except that the nature of the images can be a little more personal. Here's a link to some fine examples to help you design your own:

`www.amyporterfield.com/2012/06/facebook-timeline-covers`

To create a personal Profile Cover photo that will support your business, you need to remember these points:

- **Include your face in the image.** Faces are much more interesting than the best logos, and authentic action shots are very interesting to people on Facebook. Images work better than almost any other type of posts, so use this knowledge to rock the Cover photo.
- **Reference your business in the image.** You can have your storefront on the image, a shot of the inside of your store, or one of your products being held by you. All these images are perfectly okay to use as a Cover photo.
- **Happy customer faces need model releases (so have them handy).** Not many people realize this, but if you're taking pictures of someone else, it would be prudent to have a model release — something that the person signs, saying that he knows his image will be up on Facebook.
- **Don't include any calls to action.** Think artistically about your image. Make it charming, attractive, and informative. You can't have text on the image that says *Try our hot dogs! 10% off your next order!*

You can see a nice way of presenting your whole life in Figure 5-1.

Now let's discuss some strategies you can use to have your personal Profile support your business. Do you have business events? Or does your business sponsor events? Both types of event provide opportunities to take photos that can be used in your Cover photo strategy. You can change out the image as the event progresses, or take a shot that shows your happy face and the event sponsors logos in the background.

Figure 5-1: Create your personal Profile Cover photo to span your personal and public lives.

Do you have new products? Are you intimately involved with the development of new products? An image of you working on a product would be a perfect Cover photo for a personal Profile.

Do you travel with your business? A shot of you at an event or on the beach after the event are good ways to promote without promoting. Great airplane shots of the clouds or the food you're eating in a restaurant in Singapore, with a description of where you are and what you're doing, are excellent uses of the Cover photo. Most people put these types of photos in an album, but consider them for the Cover photo too.

Making Photo Albums Public

You can implement this strategy right away. Think about the images you have that show you doing something in your business, such as holding a product or shaking someone's hand. You also may have images of the outside of your store, the inside of your store, one of your products, or a crowd of people at your last event. We could go on and on.

When you have a collection of these types of photos, you can create an album and upload the photos to it. Then you have a URL that will take people right to the album. Because you're making this folder Public, anyone, whether or not he or she has a Facebook account, will be able to view the photos.

Here's how to create a Public Album from scratch. Go to your personal Profile, and follow these steps:

1. **In the Update Status box, click the Photo icon.**
2. **Click the Create Photo Album option.**

   This option pulls up your computer files so you can choose the images you want to upload.
3. **Click Open to start the upload process.**
4. **Create a name for the album, and enter a location (optional) and also a date, if appropriate. (See Figure 5-2.)**

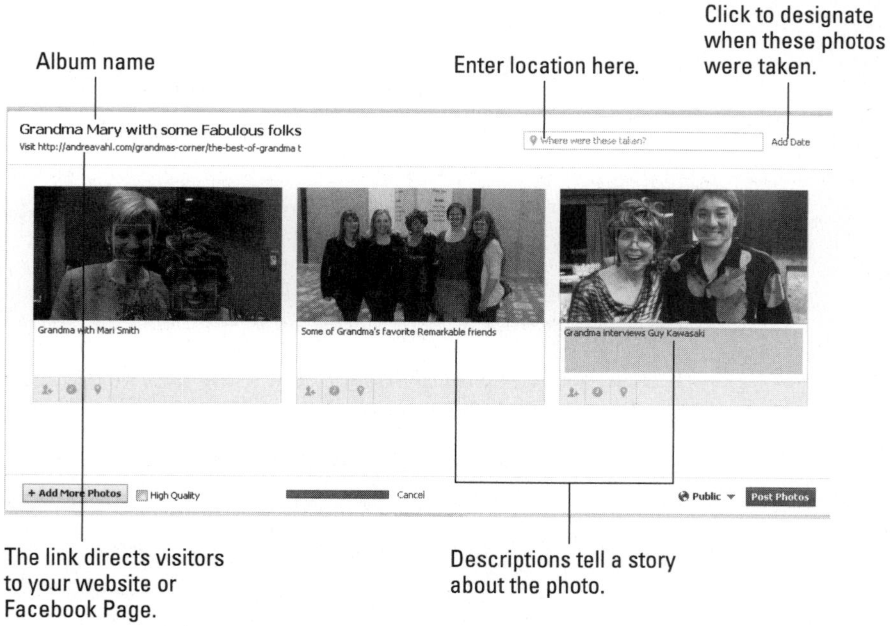

Figure 5-2: Give the new Public album a name and description.

5. **Fill in the description for each photo as fully as you can.**

   Always include an `http://` link to direct people to your website, product page, or your Facebook business Page, if it's relevant to the image.
6. **From the Sharing (world icon) drop-down menu in the bottom-right corner of the page, choose Public. (See Figure 5-3.)**

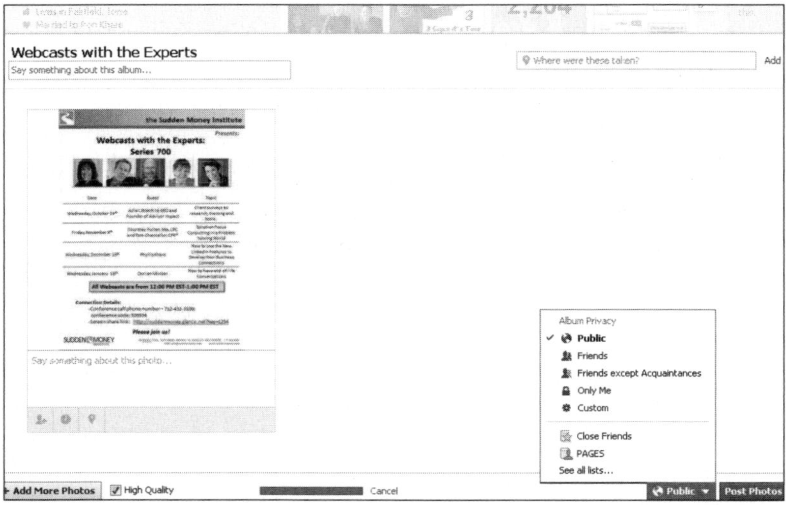

Figure 5-3: Make sure that you find the icon that will make the album Public.

7. **Click Post Photos.**

   This step publishes the whole album at one time as a Public post. Every Public subscriber and personal Friend will be able to see this album.

If you already have an album that you're using for these types of public photos, follow these steps:

1. **Go to your personal Profile Timeline, and click the Photos box.**
2. **Click the Album you want to add photos to.**
3. **Click the Add Photos button in the top-right corner of the page.**

   This step pulls up your computer files so you can choose the images you want to upload. You can select as many as you want by pressing Ctrl+Enter on a PC or ⌘+Return on a Mac.
4. **Click Open to start the upload process.**
5. **Put information in the description area, and include an `http://` link.**

   Including a clickable link gives the viewer the ability to take the next step: go directly to a blog post, a website, or a product page.
6. **In the bottom-right corner of the page, choose Public from the Sharing (world icon) drop-down menu.**
7. **Click Publish.**

At the bottom of the page, you see a very long URL. This is the URL you can use to direct people to this album (see Figure 5-4).

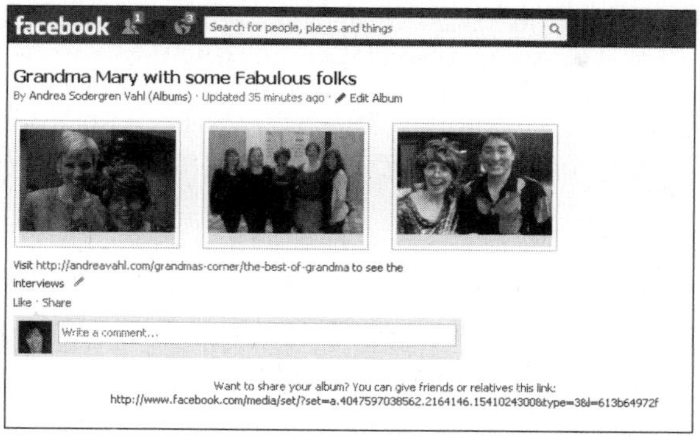

Figure 5-4: The long URL at the page's bottom directs people to this album.

Using Life Events to Support Your Business

We discuss how to use milestones for your business Page in Books II and III. You can use *life events* (which are the same things as milestones, only with a different name) in your personal Profile to support your business, too.

Think about all the milestones you have for your business and then put a personal spin on them for life events in your personal Profile. You need to use a few little tweaks to use this business-supporting process in your personal Profile. Whether or not you have a business Page, you can add these types of life events to support your business.

On a business Page, when you select milestone, you can immediately name the event, whereas in a personal Profile, you have several categories you can choose among to create a life event: Work & Education, Family & Relationships, Home & Living, Health & Wellness, and Travel & Experiences. Each of these categories has several options, always including Other. Figure 5-5 shows options for Work & Education. Choosing Other enables you to name your life event whatever you want.

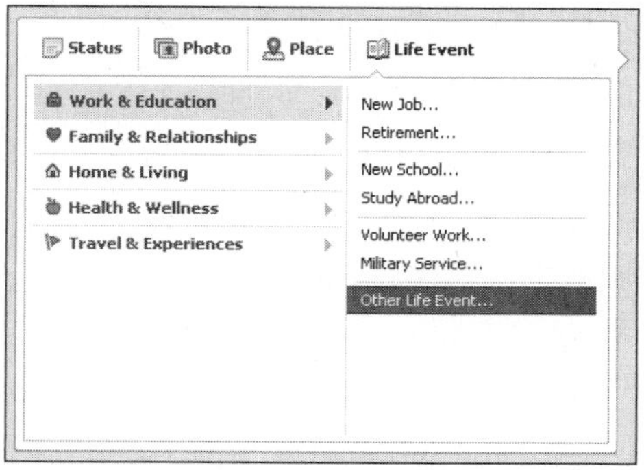

Figure 5-5: You can use the built-in titles for a life event or choose Other Life Event.

Using life events to support your business is actually pretty simple: You take a business event and make it personal by choosing the Work & Education category, selecting Other Life Event, and typing a name in the Event text box. Table 5-1 shows a couple examples. These life events can support your business in a completely appropriate way in your personal Profile.

Table 5-1 Presenting Business Milestones as Personal Life Events

Business Page Milestone	*Equivalent Personal Life Event Name*	*Accompanying Images*	*Other Tips*
Opened business	Opened My First Business	You cutting the ribbon, opening the door, and so on	Write in first person. Share your personal feelings.
Article in national magazine	Honored to Be Featured in This Cool Magazine	The article or the magazine's front cover next to your smiling face	Write in first person. Share a bit of the interview process.

Adjusting and Adding Apps

Personal Profile apps don't have the functionality that business Page apps do. You can change the order of apps, but you can't change the hyperlinked text below the apps, and you can't change the images. Despite those differences, you can still use apps to support your business.

Just like on a business Page, four featured app boxes appear below your personal Profile Cover photo. On a personal Timeline, however, you can adjust the placement of just two of those four spaces: You can't move Friends and Photos. To change the app placement, click the down arrow to the right of the featured apps, click the pencil icon of the app you want to move, and then swap with another app. (Review Book II, Chapter 4 for the process of arranging apps.)

Think about the types of apps that would support your business. You can peruse the available ones here: `www.facebook.com/about/timeline/apps`.

Here are a few that we recommend:

✦ **Pinterest:** To create an app for Pinterest, you have to start on Pinterest itself. Go to your Pinterest settings, and connect your Pinterest account to your Timeline. Consider turning on both options shown in Figure 5-6:

- *Log in with Facebook*: This just makes it easier to log into Pinterest.
- *Publish Activity to Facebook Timeline:* This option posts an update whenever you do an action on Pinterest.

After you turn on the Publish option, an app box will be on your personal Profile Timeline. It will contain your Pinterest pins, comments, and likes.

Figure 5-6: Start at your settings on Pinterest to create an app on your personal Timeline.

✦ **Spotify and/or SoundCloud:** If your business is in the music field, consider using Spotify to showcase your likes and SoundCloud to showcase your own music. Again, start with a personal account with Spotify or SoundCloud, and connect it to your personal Timeline.

✦ **RunKeeper or Map My Fitness:** If your business is in the fitness field, consider using one of these popular apps to showcase your own workouts.

✦ **TripAdvisor:** Do you travel for your business? Add this app to let people know where you are and what you're doing or where you want to go.

In all cases, make sure that you set the Posts on Your Behalf option (see Figure 5-7) to Everyone for widest impact.

Figure 5-7: Set the Posts on Your Behalf option to Everyone.

Book V

Understanding Facebook Applications

Contents at a Glance

Chapter 1: Customizing Your Page with Facebook Apps

In This Chapter

- **Grasping the importance of Facebook apps**
- **Discovering Facebook-developed and other installed apps**
- **Using Appbistro and the Search box to find apps**
- **Adding and deleting apps**
- **Exploring ways to use apps for marketing**

An *app,* or *application,* is how you can expand the way Facebook interacts with your audience. iPhones and other mobile phones have educated most people about what an app is. "There's an app for that" has been a well-known phrase for years. Thousands of apps can be used on mobile phones, and developers have built hundreds of applications for use in Facebook.

We need to make a distinction between the apps we discuss in this chapter and the new "social," or Open Graph, apps that have recently been introduced for your personal Profile (such as Spotify, Netflix, and Foodily).

If you need a true 101 introduction to apps and how apps work with your personal Facebook account, Book III, Chapter 2, provides that. The apps in this chapter make your *business* Page more interesting and functional. Social apps connect through *personal* accounts, and activity through those apps shows up on people's News Feeds and tickers.

You, as a business owner, can develop an app. That subject is a big one, which we expand on in Chapter 2 of this minibook. For now, we focus on business Page apps.

Understanding How Facebook Users Make Use of Apps

The App Center hosts more than 600 apps that are geared to personal accounts, and more than 70,000 apps not listed in the App Center are available for your Facebook business Page. Apps are the engine that drives the Facebook experience.

There seem to be three camps of Facebook application users:

- Those who are there for personal conversations and ignore or block many applications
- Those who are there to enjoy the applications and play games
- Business owners looking for ways to drive eyeballs to their Pages by using appropriately targeted applications

You're free to place as many existing apps on your Page as you want, or create custom apps (see Chapter 2 of this minibook).

If you view Facebook on an iPad, iPhone, or iPod touch, check whether your apps use Adobe Flash (such as the Scribd app from Involver); if so, you won't be able to view the content on those devices. Keep this fact in mind while you build your Page. Test all the apps you install on your Page on all platforms: iOS, Android, web, and so on.

Introducing Apps Developed by Facebook

Facebook Page apps are what make your Page unique and interesting. If all the content that you present on your Page is Timeline, Info, and Photos, it looks as though you haven't put any attention into presenting your business. On the other hand, you want to be very discerning about which types of apps you put on your Page. Having too many bells and whistles isn't charming either!

You can find apps developed by Facebook itself, as well as by third-party developers. The ones developed by Facebook are Photos, Notes, Events, and Video. These apps are really easy to activate on your Page, as we show you in this chapter. We like to call them "ready-to-go" apps because you don't need to go outside your Page to find them.

Some people are confused about the difference between the apps we recommend installing on your business Page and the apps listed in the App Center — which is where you find apps for your personal Profile. We describe the App Center in the nearby sidebar, and you may want to connect a few personal sites to your business Page to support your particular type of business. Pinterest, Foursquare, TripAdvisor, and ReverbNation come to mind. You can connect these to your business Page using a third-party app, or visit the site itself for Facebook connect details.

Exploring the App Center apps

Facebook has developed a space called App Center. It appears in the left sidebar when you're looking at the main News Feed page. When you click App Center, you see an interface with three tabs:

- **All:** Obviously, this tab is where you can see all the apps.
- **Web:** This tab lists apps that you can connect to your personal Profile that will work and be functional if they're interfacing with a computer.
- **Mobile:** Go here to find apps that work with the mobile Facebook app.

Then you see several filters: Games, Entertainment, Facebook, Lifestyle, Music, News, Photos & Videos, Sports, Travel & Local, and Utilities. You also see the Requests link. If a number appears next to it, someone has requested that you use the app with him or her. (Birthday calendar, anyone?)

The apps that are in App Center generally are ones that are connected to your personal Profile. If you have your Subscription button turned on, and one of these apps supports your business, you can enjoy it through App Center. If you're interested mostly in apps that function on your business Page, App Center isn't the place to look.

As a new Page owner, you already have a few ready-to-go apps in play, as we mention earlier. You find them by following these steps:

1. **On your Page, click the Edit Page button on the Admin panel.**
2. **Click Update Info.**

   Your Page dashboard appears.
3. **Click Apps on the sidebar of your dashboard.**

   The screen shows you all the apps that are currently available to be installed on your Page, as shown in Figure 1-1.

Click the Apps link to see which apps are ready to be installed on your new Page. A new Brand or Products Page with Product/Services as its main category, for example, has these apps available:

- Events
- Photos
- Notes
- Video

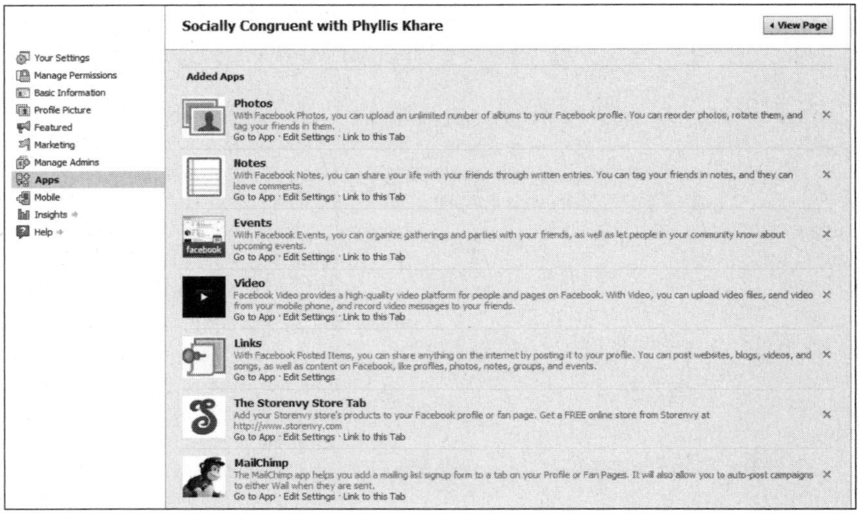

Figure 1-1: The list of apps added to your Page. Edit Settings to install them on your Page.

Each app has one, two, or sometimes three links below it: Go to App, Edit Settings, and Link to This Tab, as shown in Figure 1-2. We describe the links in this list:

- **Link to This Tab:** If you click the Link to This Tab link, a dialog box opens, displaying the direct URL to that particular place on your Page. So, for example, if you want to provide visitors a direct URL to your Static HTML tab, you can look for the Static HTML application, click the Link to This Tab link, and then copy and paste the URL in a message to send someone directly to that place on your Page.

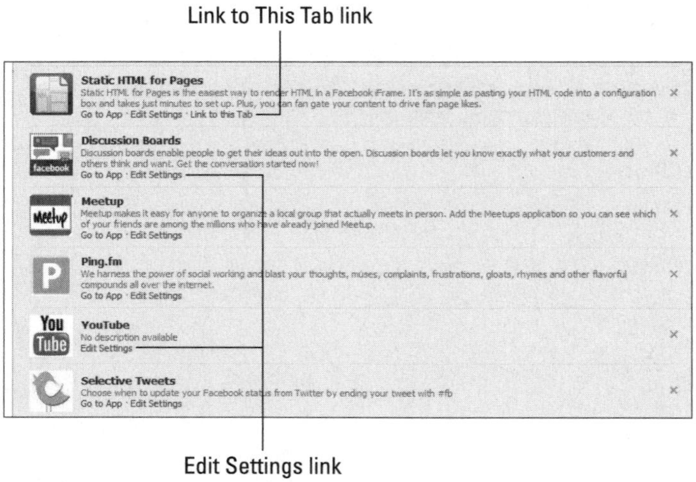

Figure 1-2: Below each app name are two or three links.

- **Edit Settings:** If you click the Edit Settings link, a dialog box appears, offering you the option of adding the app to or removing the app from the application group shown below your Cover photo. Facebook-built apps do not give you the ability to change the text of the link, but custom apps do, as shown in Figure 1-3.

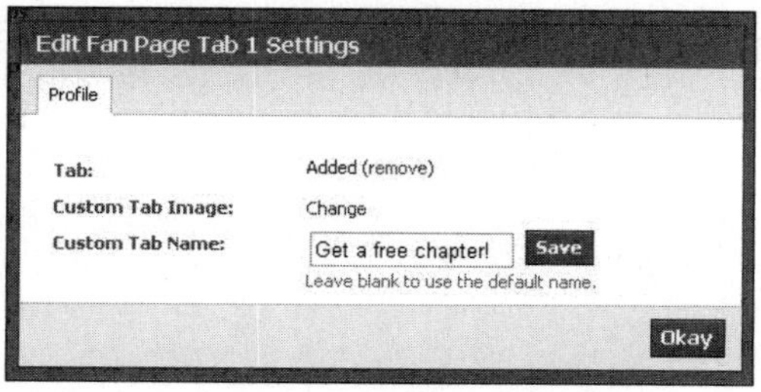

Figure 1-3: Click Edit Settings to add or remove an app tab, or to customize certain aspects.

- **Go to App:** If you click the Go to App link, you go directly to the editing page for that app or to a page where you can set options for the app. If you click the Go to App link for the Photo app, for example, you go directly to a page where you can set options for allowing fans to add their photos to your Page. If you click the Go to App link for the Events app, you go directly to the page where you can start creating an Event, as shown in Figure 1-4.

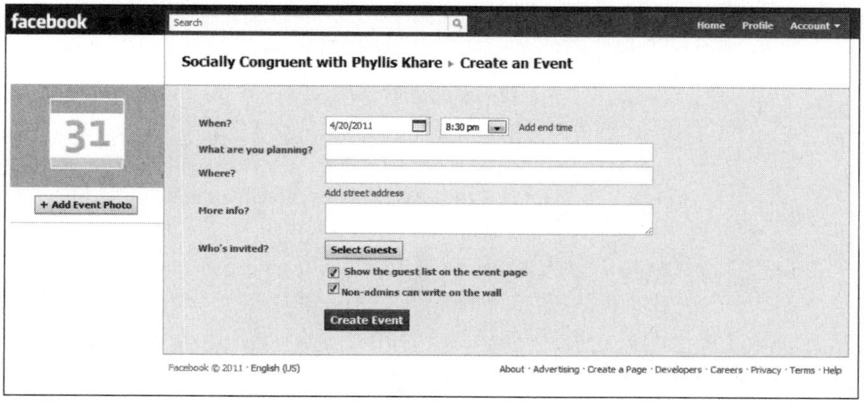

Figure 1-4: Click Go to App to view the creation/customization page for that app.

TIP

You should go through all the apps already listed on your Page's Apps dashboard and decide whether you want to have them as app boxes on your Page. Pages come with the Photos app box on the Page Timeline. Once you have someone (or yourself) click the Like button for the Page, you will have another app box called Likes. If you want any more of the apps that are available for your Page, you have to add them by clicking the Edit Settings link below each app you want to include and then clicking Add. Or, in Timeline view, click the plus icon (+) on one of the empty app boxes, and select the app you want. This process is described fully in Book II, Chapter 3.

Finding and Adding Apps to Your Page

The Facebook App Center is where you find apps for your personal Profile. If you want to use business apps on your Page, you need to find them somewhere other than the App Center. Many people prefer to find and install Facebook apps from Appbistro (`http://appbistro.com`), which we discuss next. Throughout this chapter, whenever we suggest that you look for an app, you can go to the Appbistro site, which is a very user-friendly place to find and install a business app.

Finding apps through Appbistro

You want to find apps to install on your Page, but what if you don't even know what to search for? We know of only two work-arounds at the moment: Go to Appbistro and browse the categories to find the app you want to install on your Page, or check out the suggested apps we list here and in almost every chapter of this book!

Before you add an app to your Page, take a moment to consider whether or not it is truly useful. Book I, Chapter 2 covers creating a marketing plan. Revisit your plan to make sure you're adding only those apps that you really need.

Follow these instructions to find an app through Appbistro and install it on your Page:

1. **Go to** `http://appbistro.com`.

   You're prompted to connect Appbistro with your Facebook account. You have the option to do this or just browse. We suggest that you connect it to this; it will make the application installation process easier down the road.

2. **On the left menu, click the category of the type of app you want to put on your Page (Contact Form, Coupons, eCommerce, Polls, and so on).**

   As shown in Figure 1-5, you can browse by app type or by Page type. The large button below an app's title designates whether the app is free or one you have to pay for.

3. **Find an app you want to install, and click it.**

   Read the description of the app before you install it on your page.

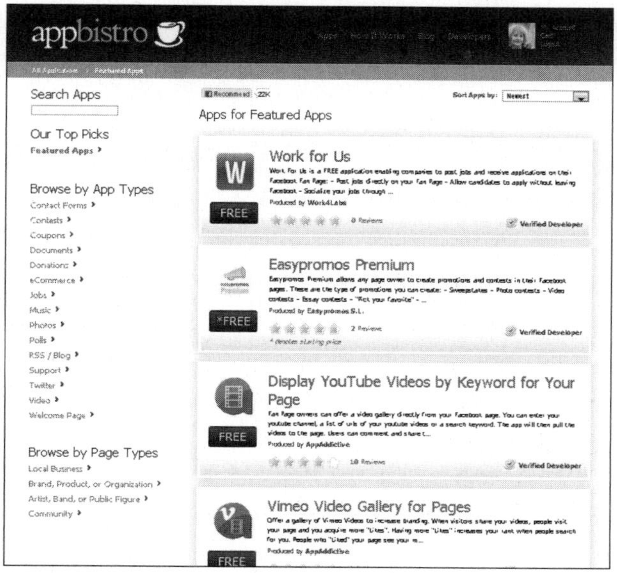

Figure 1-5: Browse through the apps, and find the one you want to add to your Page.

4. **Click the Install on Facebook button.**

   The Request for Permission dialog box appears.

5. **Click the Allow button to connect the app to your business Page (see Figure 1-6).**

   A new dialog box appears.

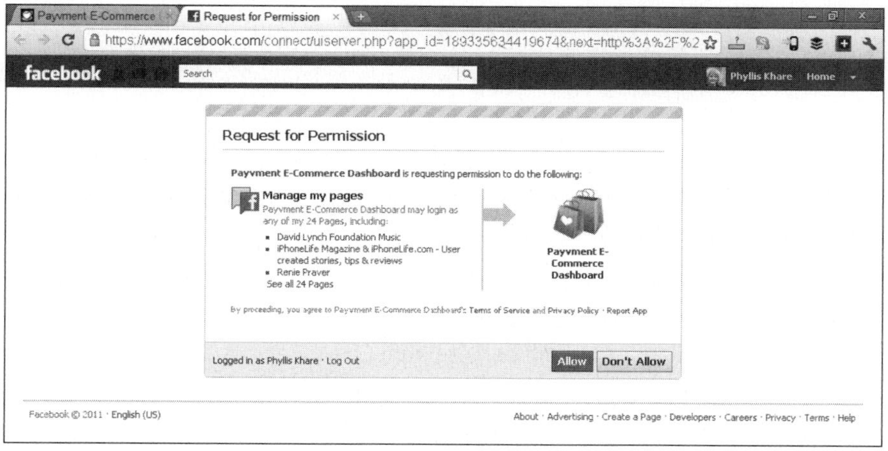

Figure 1-6: Allow permission to access your account.

6. **Choose the Page to which you want to add the app (see Figure 1-7).**

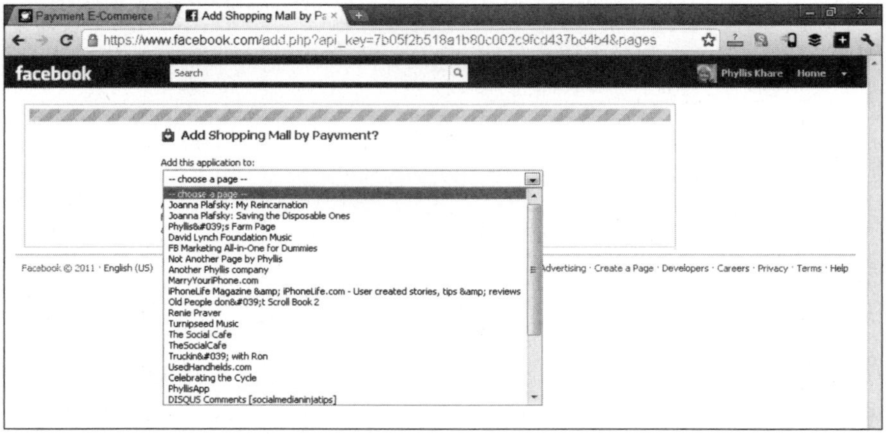

Figure 1-7: Choose the Page you want to add the app to.

Adding apps through Appbistro

Now that you've added an app through Appbistro, there are a few more steps to customize it for your Page.

1. **On your Page, click the Edit Page button at the top of the Admin panel.**
2. **Choose Update Info.**

   You're taken to your Page dashboard.
3. **Click Apps on the sidebar of your dashboard.**

   The next screen shows you all the applications installed on your Page. Remember that an app that's installed may not be active until you click Edit Settings for the app. When an app is active, it appears in your app boxes below your Page's Cover photo.
4. **Scroll down the list to the new app you just added to your Page.**
5. **Click the Edit Settings link below the app you just added.**

   A new dialog box appears.
6. **Click the Add link (if necessary), and change the text for the new link in the Custom Tab Name field.**

   Facebook still calls this link a tab.
7. **Click the Change link next to Custom Tab Image to upload a new image for this app. A new tab will open.**

   A new interface will open and you can browse your computer for the image you want to use. Select the image you want.

8. **Go back to the original tab, click Save, and then click Okay to close the dialog box.**

9. **Click the Go to App link.**

   This link takes you back to the app's interface or to an interface on your Page (depending on the app) where you can modify what will end up on the Page.

Go back to your Page, and see if the new app box is there. If you don't see it in the Featured app space (top row of apps), click the drop-down arrow, and find it. If you want it to be in the top row, hover over the app, and click the pencil icon. Then select the app you want it to swap places with.

Finding and adding apps through the search box

If you've seen or know about an app that you want to install on your page, you can use the search function to find it, and then follow these steps to install it on your Page:

1. **In the search box in the top-left corner of the screen, enter the name of the application you want to install on your Page.**

   The search function brings up everything that has the name you're searching for: Pages, Apps, people, and so on. Make sure that you find the one that's in the Apps category.

2. **Click the application's name.**

   You're taken to the application's Page. Depending on the app, you may see a page with just the one application or a page with all the apps available.

3. **Click the Add to Page button, as shown in Figure 1-8.**

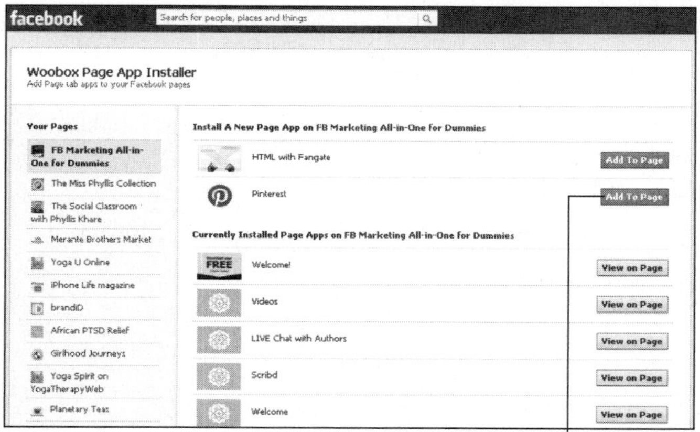

Figure 1-8: Find the Page that you want to add the application to and click the Add to Page button.

4. **If necessary, give the app more authorization, as shown in Figure 1-9.**

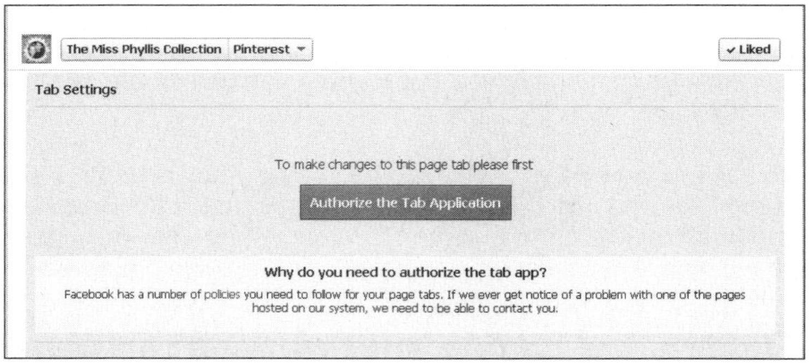

Figure 1-9: Authorize the application.

5. **Go to your Page, and click the drop-down arrow next to the Featured apps list below your Cover photo.**
6. **Click the pencil icon on the app you just added.**

   You see the pencil icon when you hover over the app box.
7. **Click the Edit Settings link below the app you just added.**

   The dialog box shown in Figure 1-10 appears. In this dialog box, you can change what appears as the app name, as well as what image appears for the app.

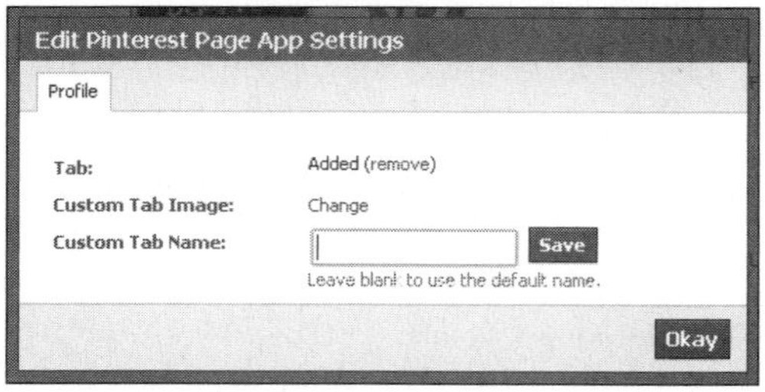

Figure 1-10: Change the app name and upload a custom app image.

8. **Type the text for the link in the Custom Tab Name field.**

   Facebook still calls this link a tab.

9. **Click Save.**
10. **(Optional) Click Change next to Custom Tab Image. A new tab opens on your computer.**

    A new interface opens, and you can browse your computer for the image you want to use. Select the image you want. You can upload a custom image for the tab box (see Figure 1-11).

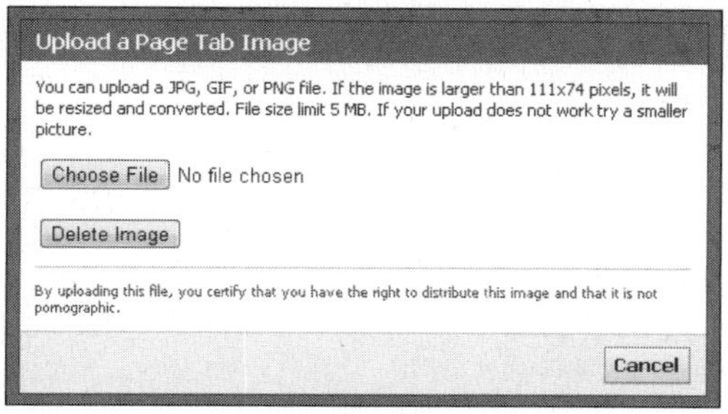

Upload a Page Tab Image
You can upload a JPG, GIF, or PNG file. If the image is larger than 111x74 pixels, it will be resized and converted. File size limit 5 MB. If your upload does not work try a smaller picture.
Choose File
No file chosen
Delete Image
By uploading this file, you certify that you have the right to distribute this image and that it is not pornographic.
Cancel

Figure 1-11: Upload a custom image for the app box.

11. **Go back to the tab with the original edit settings (refer to Figure 1-10), and click Okay.**

REMEMBER

Mobile viewers using a Facebook app may not be able to see some of your applications. Always see whether you can view applications on your mobile phone to make sure that other mobile-phone users can see them too.

Deleting Apps from Your Page

Sometimes, you have an app that just doesn't click with your audience. If that's the case, don't worry: Applications are very easy to remove from your Page.

You can remove the app from your Page but still have it available on your list of applications, and/or you can remove the application from your Page.

To remove the app box from your Timeline but still have the application in case you want to use it in the future, follow these steps:

1. **On your Page, click the drop-down arrow next to your Featured apps.**
2. **Click the pencil icon on the app you want to remove.**

   Another drop-down menu appears, listing the options shown in Figure 1-12.

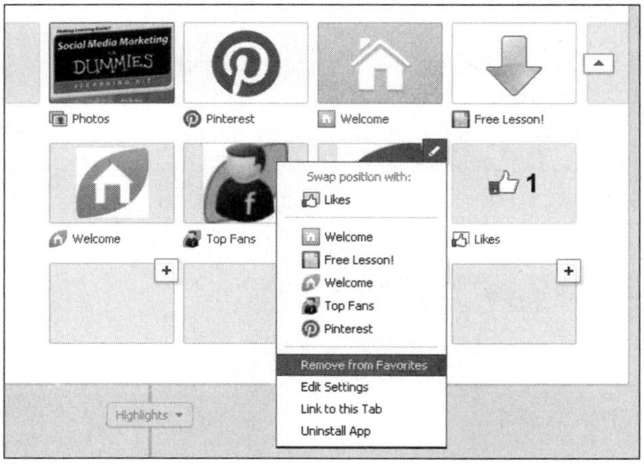

Figure 1-12: Choose Remove from Favorites to remove an app from your Timeline.

3. **Click Remove from Favorites.**

   The app no longer appears on your Timeline.

To fully remove the application from your Page, you can follow the preceding steps and choose Uninstall App in Step 3, or you can follow these steps:

1. **On your Page, click the Edit Page button in your Admin panel.**
2. **Click Update Info.**

   You're taken to your Page dashboard.
3. **Click Apps on the sidebar of your dashboard.**

   The next screen shows you all the applications you currently have installed on your Page.
4. **Find the app that you want to remove.**

   You may need to scroll down to find it.
5. **Click the X to the right of the application, as shown in Figure 1-13.**

   This step removes the application from your Page. If you want to use it in the future, you need to start from the beginning and add it to your Page again.

Click to remove an app.

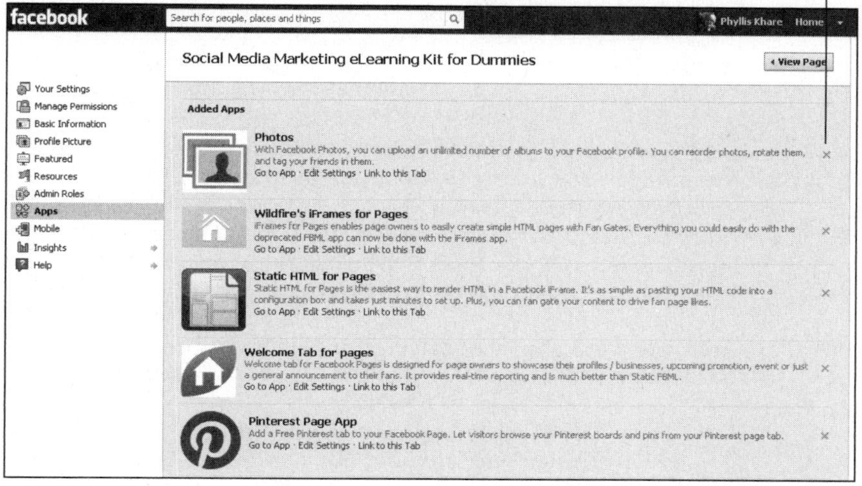

Figure 1-13: Click the X to remove the app from your Page.

Using Apps for Marketing

Of the tens of thousands of apps on Facebook, a few really good ones rise to the top. You may find these apps useful by connecting them to your Facebook business Page.

The most important place for an app is in one of the four Featured app spaces on your Page. Facebook's Photos app takes up one of those four spaces. You can't move or modify the text for the Photo app, but the other three are in your court.

Book II, Chapter 2 discusses which type of apps truly support a business. Think about your business, and figure out the best use for these featured spaces. Many businesses use them for these three things:

- **E-mail capture:** This is a vital process for businesses.
- **Webinar sign-up:** Use the sales page information for this type of app, or add upcoming event information (your company is a sponsor for a community event, for example).
- **E-commerce:** You can re-create your off-Facebook e-commerce website pages for viewing right on Facebook.

In this section, we highlight a few apps that we like to suggest to Page owners.

Contact forms and e-mail forms

You may already have an e-mail capture system set up on your website. Maybe you give something away in exchange for an e-mail address. Many e-mail systems such as AWeber.com have a Facebook app that you can access right from your accounts with those systems.

Check with the e-mail list system you're using to see whether it provides an easy way to add your e-mail capture form to your Facebook Page. If you're using systems such as MailChimp, Constant Contact, or iContact, you can use the way they provide, or just copy the form code and paste it in an iFrame or Static HTML app, re-creating the same thing you have on your website. The trick is using an app where you can paste this HTML or iFrame code.

Here are a few apps you can use for e-mail capture if you don't use the provider's app:

- **Heyo:** The free account (at `http://heyo.com`) allows you to completely design one app box. You can add images and all sorts of Like and Share buttons, and there's a space where you can paste the HTML code from your e-mail service. You can use this app as a fan-gate, too.
- **Woobox:** Sign up at `http://woobox.com`, to try the HTML fan-gate app, and use your e-mail capture HTML.
- **Contact Tab:** This particular contact app (available at `https://apps.facebook.com/`) contains a place to display all your social accounts, company information, a map to your business (Bing or Google), and a header image.
- **Contact Form:** You can use the free version (available at `www.facebook.com/contact.form`) and then upgrade to the paid version if you'd like to add a custom footer and get other little perks. You can see a nice use of this app at `http://bit.ly/FanPageFocus`.

You can also use any of these suggested apps to create a page for a webinar sign-up form. You can see how the app boxes look on Amy's Page shown in Figure 1-14. Notice the regular e-mail sign-up app box and the webinar app box.

Discussion-board apps

Facebook retired its own Discussion app a while ago, but some businesses still want to have some sort of forum or discussion board available to their communities. Here are two apps to explore if you need this type of app:

- **SocialAppsHQ:** The free account (at `http://socialappshq.com`) allows you to add a discussion app to your Page Timeline. This company also has several other really interesting apps for you to explore.

- **Forum for Pages:** This free app (at `www.facebook.com/forumforpages`) has ads in the left column; the paid version doesn't. The user interface is very clean and large.

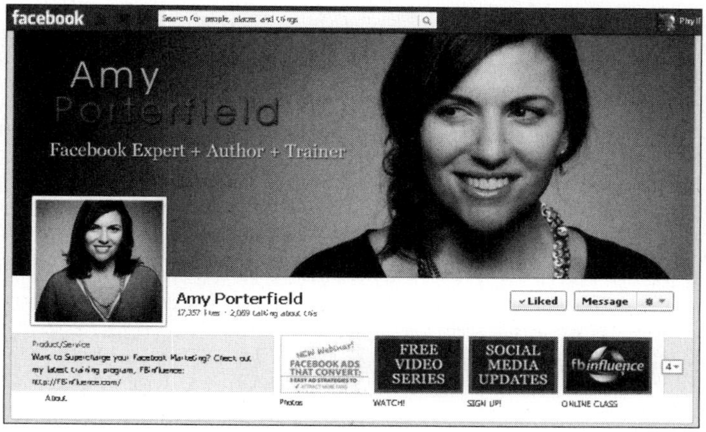

Figure 1-14: You can use the same app for different purposes.

Video apps

Almost every app company that we've suggested so far has an app for adding your YouTube videos to your Page. Generally, you add the username of your (or anyone else's) YouTube channel, and the app pulls the videos to your Facebook Page. Some apps allow you to select a particular playlist instead of pulling in the entire channel.

If you use Vimeo for your videos, we have an app for you, too. Check out Tabfusion below.

We don't recommend using the built-in Facebook app Video, for two reasons: Facebook might retire it at some point (and you could lose your videos), and other apps look better on a Facebook Page. If you upload videos directly to Facebook, they automatically go in the app box called Video.

Here are a couple of companies that have good YouTube apps:

- **Involver:** One of its free apps (at `www.involver.com/applications`) is the YouTube app. You can see it in action on Grandma Mary's page (we're especially fond of Grandma Mary), at `http://bit.ly/GrandmaMaryYouTube`. But Involver has other good apps for a business Page, as discussed in the nearby sidebar.
- **Tabfusion:** Tabfusion has three video apps: one for YouTube, one for Vimeo, and one for Blip.tv. This is app (at `http://tabfusion.com/applications.php`) charges for its services, so you need to consider that fact before choosing to use those apps. See `http://tabfusion.com/pricing.php`.

Finding apps with Involver

One way to find really good apps for your business Pages is to use Involver (www.involver.com/applications). Involver has many apps that are quite relevant to a Facebook business Page, including an RSS feed, the YouTube channel, Photo Gallery, and File Sharing (which is a great way for authors to give away chapter previews or book teaser copy). An app of note is Scribd. You upload a PDF file to www.scribd.com, and then it's automatically available on the app for viewing, sharing, downloading, e-mailing, and more — all from your Facebook Page. Make sure that you test the apps you're interested in. Some are better than others, and some have costs associated with them. You can read more about Involver in Book III, Chapter 4.

TIP

If your business uses video as a marketing device, try to find the best interface by testing and looking at samples to find the right fit. You can always hide or delete an app and try something else.

Pinterest apps

Currently, you can't pin items from Facebook to Pinterest, but you can pull in your pins and boards from Pinterest through an app to post on your personal account and/or your business Page.

Our favorite app for Pinterest is Woobox (http://woobox.com/pinterest). You can see an example of how it looks on Facebook at http://bit.ly/PinterestApp. The interface for configuring this app is very easy to understand and use, as you can see in Figure 1-15.

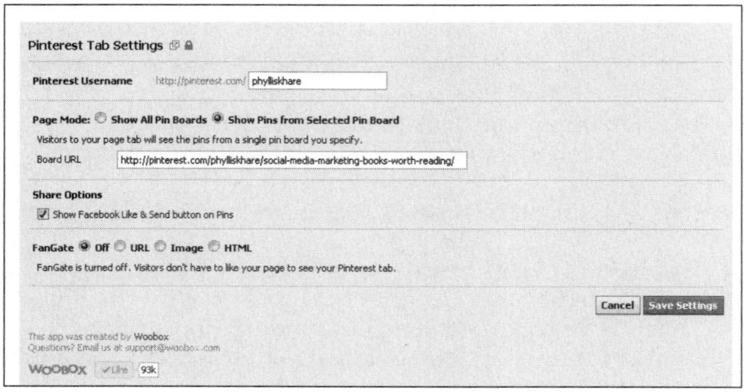

Figure 1-15: Setting up the Woobox Pinterest app is easy.

Google+

The Google Plus Tab for Pages app (`https://www.facebook.com/googleplustopages`) is extremely easy to use. The app pulls in all your Google+ posts and puts them on a tab on Facebook, as you can see in Figure 1-16. Any visitor can click the +1 (Google+'s equivalent to liking) next to any post.

Figure 1-16: People can +1 your Google+ posts right on Facebook.

Social RSS

Social RSS (`https://apps.facebook.com/social-rss`) recently redesigned its services. This app allows you to add your blog or any RSS feed to your Page. It can be really handy if you want to pull in specific posts from all over the Internet, not just your blog. If you want to post your tweets to your Timeline, for example, you can add your Twitter RSS feed to this app. This app is also discussed in Book III, Chapter 3.

Your existing business services

Many of the services that you may already be using outside the Facebook environment have apps, including these:

- Eventbrite: www.eventbrite.com
- MailChimp: http://mailchimp.com
- SurveyMonkey: www.surveymonkey.com
- PayPal: http://paypal.com

Go to these websites, and look for any Facebook integration. Some of these services have actual Facebook apps; others give you code to place in an app like Static HTML, which creates a nice link on your Page. See Book V, Chapter 2 to find out how to use Static HTML.

Other apps

Here are a few more you might want to explore for your personal account, with the Subscribe button turned on (refer to Book II, Chapter1), or your business Page.

- **Goodreads** (https://apps.facebook.com/good_reads) is an app for your personal account. The app corresponds to the Goodreads website (www.goodreads.com). You can add your own books and those that you'd like to recommend to others. The dedicated link creates a nice Timeline view of the books you want to discuss or share. This particular app is best for your personal Profile if you have the Subscribe button turned on.
- **Band Profile** (www.facebook.com/rn.mybandapp) currently has more than 8 million active users on Facebook! This app, powered by ReverbNation (www.reverbnation.com), creates a link called Band Profile and pulls info from your account at ReverbNation. People can join your fan list or mailing list, share and play your music, watch your music videos, see where your next show will be, and see your fans. In other words, it's a complete site for your music on your Facebook Page.
- **Tinychat** (http://apps.facebook.com/tinychat) has been a popular tool for Twitter users for a few years. Its Facebook app allows you to open a video chat within your Facebook Page and host discussions. You can send notifications to your personal friends or e-mail them a link they can use to connect. From a marketing perspective, consider using this app to create a weekly event in which you chat with your customers or clients, or an impromptu chat when something topical that relates to your business comes up. Currently, this app is best for a personal account with the Subscribe button turned on.

- **Zillow real estate apps** (`www.zillow.com/webtools/facebook-apps`) is a nice collection of apps you can use to add Listings, Reviews, Local Info, and a Contacts tab.
- **eListit** (`https://apps.facebook.com/elistit`) is connected to the website `http://elistit.com`, where real estate agents can advertise their businesses; network with other agents; get recommendations from clients, friends, and family members; and post their business Profiles (including listings, agent network, blogs, and endorsements) to a Page.
- **Livestream** (`https://apps.facebook.com/livestream`) is a live-video app that's used by some very active social media marketers and by Facebook itself for its live events. If using video appeals to you and your business, check out a fuller use of the Livestream app in Book VIII.

REMEMBER

As we mention early in this chapter, you should choose the apps that are most appropriate for your business. Also, don't overload your fans with needless clutter on your Page. Choose wisely. Revisit Book I, Chapter 2 to review the process of creating a marketing plan.

Facebook's mobile app

Facebook has an app for your mobile phone. The interface is optimized for mobile-phone viewing, which means that you'll find pluses and minuses about viewing Facebook business Pages through the mobile Facebook app. When using the mobile Facebook app on an Android or iOS device, for example, and you go to a business Page through a link in the News Feed, you see only two tabs: Timeline and Photos. All the apps that you've added, along with any custom-designed links you may have built for your Page, are unavailable for viewing on a mobile phone (currently). Take a good look at your demographics. Are your visitors viewing your Page only on mobile phones? If so, keep that fact in mind as you build your Page. You may need fewer apps and more posts to your Timeline.

Chapter 2: Using iFrame Apps to Create Custom Tabs

In This Chapter

- **Reviewing custom tabs**
- **Defining iFrames**
- **Touring the Facebook Developers site**
- **Creating your own iFrame application**
- **Letting someone build your iFrame application**
- **Using third-party applications to create your custom tab**

Do you have a vision for a special tab on your Facebook Page and haven't been able to find an app that did exactly what you wanted? Maybe you want a certain function or a layout that you haven't been able to find? That's when it's time to create your own custom tab! Luckily, plenty of options are available to help you create exactly what you need.

You can also have a "fan-gated" tab on your Page, which means that people must become fans before they can see the content. This tab is also known as a *reveal tab* where the initial graphic tells people that they must click Like before they can see what's below the image. These kinds of tabs are great at helping convert your visitors to fans, because they usually offer something good in exchange.

If you've been on Facebook for a long time, you may remember when custom tabs were allowed to be default landing tabs, so that someone who hadn't liked your Page yet got a customized message. This feature is no longer available, but with some ingenuity and some attractive tab cover images, you can attract people to your tabs and engage them. See Book III, Chapter 2 for more information about changing your tab cover photos.

These custom tabs are sometimes called iFrame apps because they use an iFrame to pull in your designed content. In this chapter, you discover what iFrames are, how to create your own iFrame application, and how to add it to your Page. We also introduce third-party applications that make creating a custom tab easy if you aren't comfortable coding your own iFrame (or don't have the resources to do so).

TIP: We cover the Facebook Developers site in depth in this chapter, and it's not for the timid. Feel free to skip that section and go to the middle of the chapter, where we list some resources for hiring someone to write the code for you. Or move on to later in the chapter, where we cover simple third-party applications.

Looking at Tabs

Tabs on Facebook, as you may have seen, can be highly customized, with branding and links that highlight a company. These custom tabs usually have a strong call to action (such as *Like our Page!*) and some fun and practical links (such as a video message, a newsletter sign-up link, or coupons for fans). The world is your oyster! Using a custom tab within your Facebook Page can further enhance your brand and make your Facebook Page stand out. Figures 2-1 through 2-3 show some examples of custom tabs.

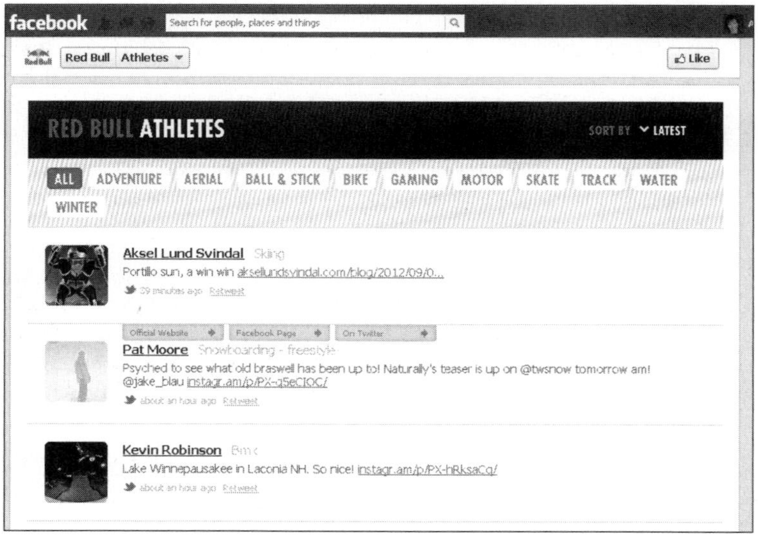

Figure 2-1: Red Bull has a tab that posts the most recent tweets by its athletes.

Figure 2-2: The Big Brand System uses its custom tab to get subscribers for its e-mail list.

Figure 2-3: The Visit Sheridan, Wyoming Page uses a reveal tab to entice people to click Like first.

Defining iFrames

iFrame — which stands for *Inline Frame* — is an HTML document embedded inside another HTML document on a website. An iFrame pulls the content from one website into another. So in the context of Facebook, an iFrame pulls the content of another website into an area on your Facebook Page.

iFrames are very powerful because anything that you can create on a website you can bring into your Facebook Page, creating a unique and rich experience for your community. To use iFrames on Facebook, you need to have a place on the web to put your content. By this, we mean that you need to have a server or host website where you can upload your photos, files, or whatever you'll be displaying on your custom tab. If you don't have a place to which you can upload your content, skip to "Using Third-Party Applications," later in this chapter. That section is where we introduce several third-party applications that can host your content for you.

iFrames have been used on the web for a long time but are a relatively new way to create a custom tab or other content on Facebook. Previously, people created a custom tab on a Facebook with an application called Static FBML (Facebook Markup Language). This application is no longer available, but we mention it because you may see references to Static FBML within Facebook and on other websites.

Outlining the Options

For Facebook Pages, you have three choices:

- ✦ Build an iFrame application from scratch.
- ✦ Hire someone to build the application for you.
- ✦ Use a third-party application.

The following sections explain some of the considerations involved with each option.

Building an iFrame application

Building an application sounds daunting, but the process can be broken down into several easy steps. We walk you through the specifics a little later in the chapter, but for now, here's an overview of the steps for building an iFrames application:

1. Become a verified Facebook Developer.

   This simple process requires a mobile phone (that can receive text messages) or a credit card (for verification purposes only).

2. Design the content for your Facebook app.

   Typically, this content is designed in an HTML editor such as Adobe Dreamweaver.

3. Upload the content for your Facebook app to your website.

   You may need to use an FTP (File Transfer Protocol) program to upload the HTML document and necessary images to your server.

4. Configure your Facebook application.

   You configure your application in the Developer area of Facebook.

5. Install the application on your Page.

When you create and install your own iFrames application, it shows up below your Cover photo with your other tabs.

REMEMBER

You need your own Secure Sockets Layer (SSL) certificate on your website to host your uploaded content for your Facebook app. SSL, which allows information on the website to be securely encrypted, is typically used when processing payments on a website. Facebook requires that any app have the content hosted by a secure server. An SSL certificate isn't too expensive; typically, it costs around $50. If you don't have an SSL certificate, Facebook provides free hosting through a partnership with Heroku. You can read more about this partnership at `http://developers.facebook.com/blog/post/558/`.

Although building your own application can be challenging, it has some advantages, as follows:

- ✦ You have complete control of your application (no extra references to third-party applications).
- ✦ Developing your own application is free (unless you hire someone to help you do the development). Many third-party applications cost money.
- ✦ You don't have to worry about something happening to the third-party application where you have your content stored (say something goes wrong in the third-party application or it goes out of business, then your custom tab may not work properly).

Hiring someone to build the application for you

If you aren't savvy about HTML and are trying to do something fairly complicated (such as embedding videos or an opt-in form), you may want to hire an app developer to do the work.

To find an app developer, check within your own network first. You may be surprised to find that some of the website developers you may know can easily create an app for you, depending on your needs. Try doing a search on LinkedIn for Facebook app developers among your connections.

You can also look at sites such `www.elance.com` and `www.odesk.com`, which have a huge supply of freelancers who can help you out. Many of these developers have references and examples of their past work available. You can post your requirements, and the freelancers can bid on the project. You choose the freelancer who's the best fit for your needs.

Using a third-party application

Third-party applications are applications created by another company (that is, a company other than Facebook) to simplify the process of creating custom content on Facebook. The idea is that you can use a third-party application to create your Page and then add the app to your Facebook Page. You don't need to code anything, and you don't have to upload files to your website.

Many of the apps have a drag-and-drop design interface to make designing your app a snap. Be aware that many apps are available, and more are being developed every day. Do your homework before you settle on one app, because there may be something new tomorrow that's a better fit for your needs.

Here are some of the applications that you can use to create a custom tab. We discuss these applications later in the chapter.

- **Heyo:** `www.heyo.com`
- **Static HTML for Pages:** `www.facebook.com/StaticHTMLapp`
- **North Social:** `www.northsocial.com`
- **ShortStack:** `www.shortstack.com`
- **Static HTML: iFrame Tabs:** `www.facebook.com/apps/application.php?id=190322544333196`
- **TabSite:** `www.tabsite.com`
- **FanPageEngine:** `www.fanpageengine.com`

REMEMBER

Third-party applications are developed by independent people or companies not connected with Facebook, and these applications may or may not work well. Occasionally, you'll come across some applications that are developed but then aren't updated, or you'll find that some applications don't work well from the start. If you're at all concerned about a particular application, we suggest visiting the website of the company that developed the app and noting which other companies are using the app. Many times, a website has links to the Facebook Pages that are using the company's applications so that you can see the apps in action and get an idea of how they work, as well as gauge the applications' popularity. All the apps that we cover in this chapter work very well; we just want to remind you to use caution when discovering new apps that may be available.

Exploring the Facebook Developers Site

The Facebook Developers site is where you begin your journey of creating your own application. To get to the site, log in to Facebook as your personal Profile and then go to `www.facebook.com/developers`. The Facebook Developers home page offers links to several areas of the Developers platform: Build for Websites, Build for Mobile, and Build Apps on Facebook. You can also link to the blog, the App Center, and other sites, as shown in Figure 2-4.

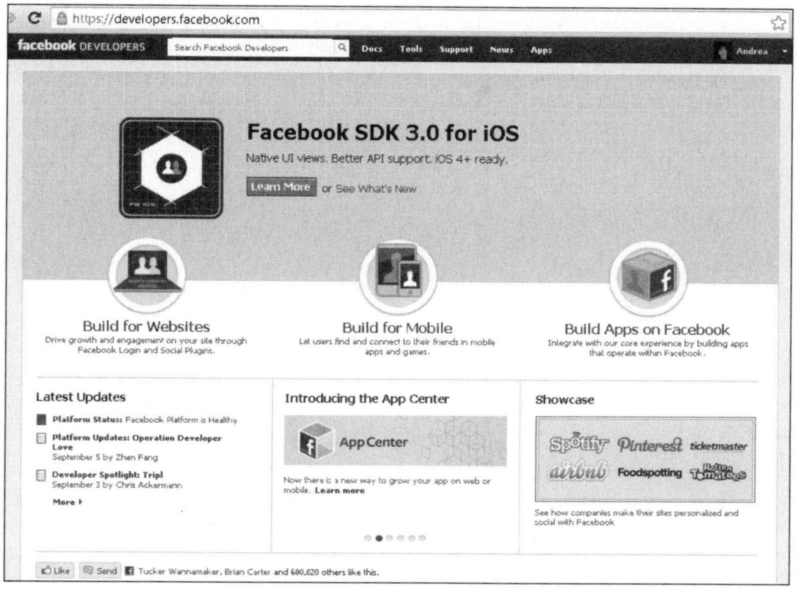

Figure 2-4: The Facebook Developers site.

Here are some of the elements of the Facebook Developers site that you can access from the top navigation menu:

- ✦ **Docs:** Click this link to find information about creating code for the Facebook plug-ins, creating applications, and so on.
- ✦ **Tools:** Access debugger tools, the JavaScript Test Console, and more. You won't need most of these tools for a simple Facebook app.
- ✦ **Support:** Get information about bugs, technical Q&A, and more.
- ✦ **News:** Get the latest updates from the Developer Blog.
- ✦ **Apps:** Navigate to the apps you've created here.

Becoming a Verified Facebook Developer

Applications can be malicious and often created to spread spam messages and viruses. To combat developers of these types of applications, Facebook requires some method of developer tracking. To become a verified Facebook Developer, you need to verify that you're a real person by providing a mobile phone number (that can receive text messages) or a credit-card number.

The verification process (and the pop-up boxes you see) can vary from person to person depending on when the user joined Facebook. Some people were required to verify their account with a mobile phone number when they joined Facebook; others weren't. Also, if you've never set up an application before, your app creation might fail, as shown in Figure 2-5. So if you see the App Creation Failed message when creating your app (in the upcoming "Creating an iFrame Application" section), come back to the steps that follow to verify your account.

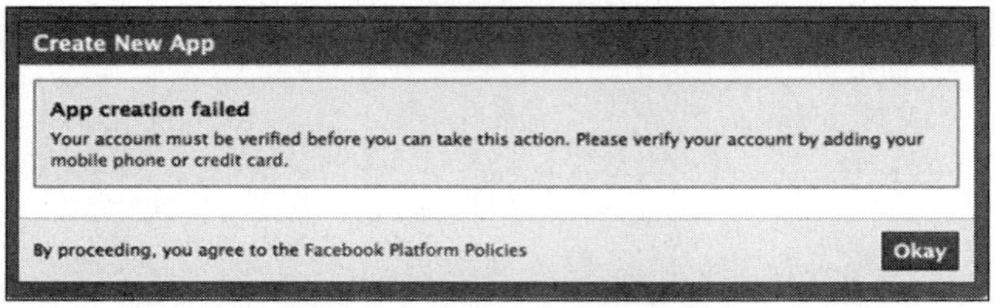

Figure 2-5: You might need to verify your account to become a Facebook Developer.

Verifying with a mobile phone number

If you want to verify your account with a mobile phone number, follow these steps:

1. **Click the Mobile Phone link (refer to Figure 2-5).**

   A pop-up window appears, asking for your country code and cellphone number.

2. **Select your country code and cellphone number.**
3. **Click the Continue button.**

   You receive a text message with a string of letters or numbers, which is your confirmation code. On your computer, you see a box for your confirmation code.

4. **Enter the confirmation code, and click Confirm.**

   You're now a verified Facebook Developer, and you can create an iFrame application.

TIP: The mobile phone verification process may not work well outside the United States. People have reported having trouble receiving the text message, so if you're outside the United States, you may want to use the credit-card option.

Verifying with a credit card

If you don't have a phone that can receive text messages, you need to verify your account by adding your credit card. Here's how:

1. **Click the Credit Card link (refer to Figure 2-5).**

   You're taken to a new window and Facebook asks you to reenter your Facebook password.

2. **Reenter your password and click the Continue button.**
3. **Type your credit-card information in the text box.**
4. **Click the Save button.**
5. **Click the Send button.**

You're now a verified Facebook Developer, and you can create an iFrame application.

Creating an iFrame Application

So you've decided to try your hand at creating your own iFrame application. Excellent! Although creating an iFrame app isn't terribly difficult if you're familiar with basic CSS and HTML code, you need to have a few things ready before you begin.

First, you need to create the web page on which you'll be displaying in the iFrame. Creating a web page is beyond the scope of this book, but you need to create a page 810 pixels wide to fit into the Facebook iFrame space.

The possibilities for your web page are literally endless. You can have a simple design with just an image or something more elaborate, such as a mini store. Here are some possibilities:

- A single image (very easy to code)
- Several images fitted together that allow for links
- Embedded video
- An opt-in box for your newsletter with additional photos, video, or both
- Photos or video combined with Facebook comments so that people can interact with your Page

TIP

If you create a web page wider than 810 pixels, it won't fit into the space on your Facebook Page and will have scroll bars on the bottom.

After you have your web page created and you've become a verified Facebook Developer, you're ready to create your iFrame app. Log in to your personal Profile, and follow these steps:

1. **Go to** `www.facebook.com/developers`.
2. **Click the Create New App button in the top-right corner.**

   The Create New App dialog box appears, as shown in Figure 2-6.

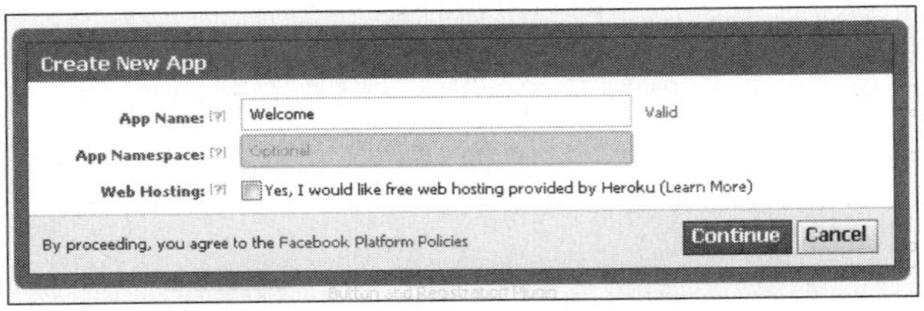

Figure 2-6: Name your app.

3. **Type the name of your app in the App Name text box.**

   The name you enter will appear on the tab of your Page. You don't need to fill out the App Namespace field.

4. **(Optional) Choose to get free web hosting if your site doesn't have an SSL certificate.**

   Facebook has partnered with Heroku to provide hosting for free.

5. **Click the Continue button.**

   You're taken to the Security Check Page.

   At this point, you might see the App Creation Failed message and you must complete the verification process with your mobile phone or credit card. Refer to the earlier section, "Becoming a Verified Facebook Developer, if necessary.

6. **Type the security-check text in the text box.**

7. **Click the Submit button.**

   You're taken to the application's Settings page, as shown in Figure 2-7, landing on the Basic tab.

   TIP: Many of the fields on this page are for games or other Facebook applications designed to be used by many Facebook users; they're optional for someone who is developing a custom tab with iFrames. For the purposes of an iFrame custom tab, you have to fill out only the information on the Basic tab. We explain which fields you need to worry about and which ones you can skip.

8. **Fill out the information for your application as follows:**

   - *Display Name:* The name of your application that is displayed to users. This entry is the title of the tab and is populated with the name you provide in Step 2.
   - *Namespace:* The Canvas Page URL name, which must be unique. The Canvas Page is the unique name of your URL for the application on Facebook and is in the form `https://apps.facebook.com/`*`Your_App_Namespace`*. (***Note:*** This setting is optional for Page tabs.)
   - *Contact Email:* Primary e-mail address for communication related to your application. This field should be populated by your Facebook login e-mail address, but you can change the address if needed.

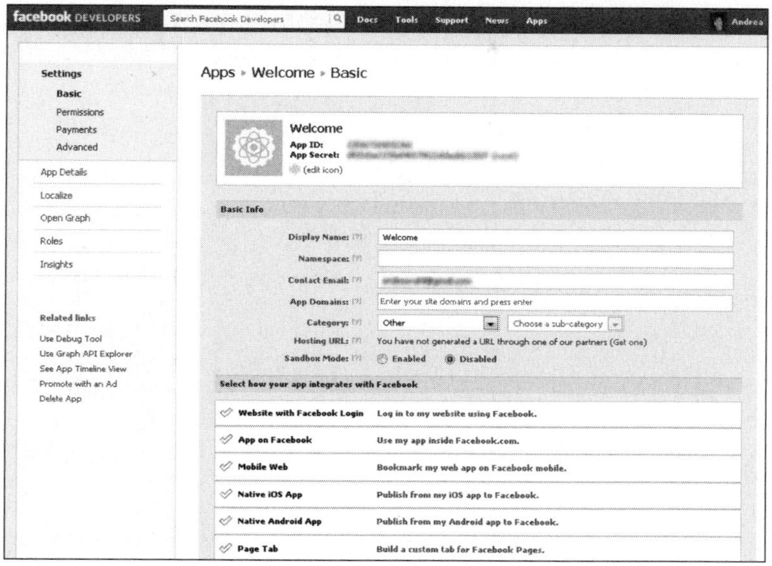

Figure 2-7: Edit your application.

- *App Domain:* The URL of the website where you'll have the application. (***Note:*** This setting is optional for Page tabs.)
- *Category:* The category that best fits your application (optional and directed toward other apps).
- *Hosting URL*: The URL address given to you by Facebook's partner Heroku if you are using its hosting option.
- *Sandbox Mode*: If enabled, only app developers can use and see your app. Switch to Enabled if you want to keep your app private while you develop it. There's no need to make a custom tab private because it won't be installed on your Page.

Then select how your app will integrate with Facebook. Each option requires you to enter additional information when you click the check mark next to it. The options are

- *Website with Facebook Login:* You want to allow people to log in to your website using Facebook.
- *App on Facebook:* You want to build an app on Facebook.com.
- *Mobile Web:* You have a mobile web app.
- *Native iOS App:* You have a native iOS app.
- *Native Android App:* You have a native Android app.
- *Page Tab:* You want to build a custom tab for Facebook Pages.

9. **Choose Page Tab by clicking the check mark next to the Page Tab option.**

   You see the fields shown in Figure 2-8.

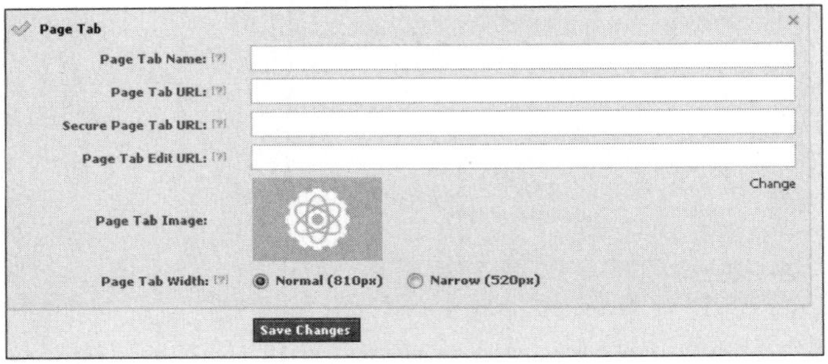

Figure 2-8: The Page Tab fields.

   Here are the descriptions of these fields:

   - *Page Tab Name:* This field is the title of the tab and is populated from the Display Name entry. If it isn't autopopulated, enter the text used in the Display Name field.
   - *Page Tab URL:* Facebook pulls content for your tab from this URL. This URL is the full path to the web page that you want to have displayed on your Facebook Welcome Page.
   - *Secure Page Tab URL:* The content of your tab needs to be hosted on a secure website that has an SSL certificate. The URL starts with `https` to indicate that it's secure and is in the form `https://www.`*`yourwebsitename`*`.com/folder/index.html`. If you are using the Heroku option, enter the URL you received from Heroku.
   - *Page Tab Edit URL:* This URL is given to Page Admins to edit or customize the Page Tab app. This setting is optional.
   - *Page Tab Image:* You have the opportunity to upload your image for your app Cover photo.
   - *Page Tab Width:* You can choose a Normal width of 810 pixels or a Narrow width of 520 pixels centered on the tab.

10. **Click the Save Changes button.**

   The Page Tab has been created. If you click the Apps link at the top of the page, you see all your apps listed, as shown in Figure 2-9. The app is available to you to edit at any time. Your next step is to navigate to the App Profile Page, where you can install this app on your Facebook Page, as we explain in the next section.

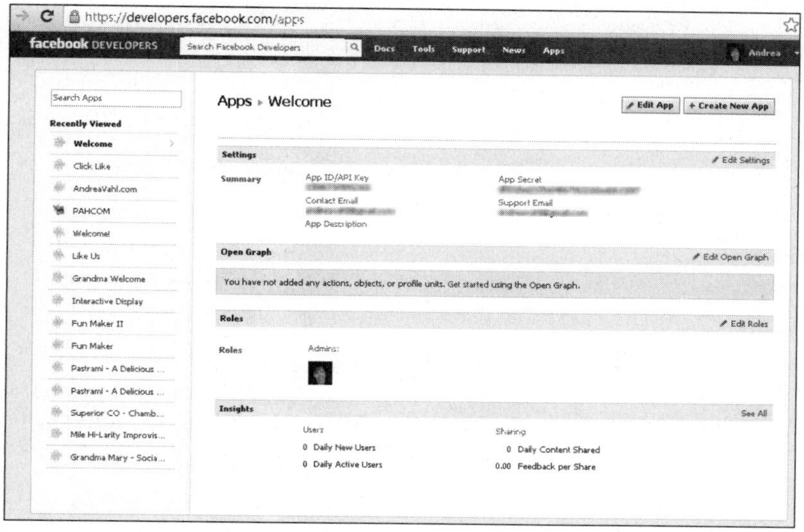

Figure 2-9: Your iFrame Page Tab has been created.

Installing the iFrame application on your Facebook Page

After you create your iFrame app, you need to install it on your Facebook Page. You can complete the ten steps in the preceding section, or you can go to the Developer page at `https://developers.facebook.com/apps`, select your app in the Recently Viewed section of the left sidebar, and then click the Edit App button in the top-right corner (refer to Figure 2-9).

To add the application to your Facebook Page, find your 15-digit app ID/API key at the top of the App page and then follow these steps:

1. **Type the following URL in your browser window, using your app ID and replacing *YOUR_APP_ID* with the 15-digit app ID/API key:**

   https://facebook.com/add.php?api_key=*YOUR_APP_ID*&pages=1.

   You're taken to the site where you add your app to your Page, as shown in Figure 2-10.

2. **From the Add This Application To drop-down menu (see Figure 2-10), choose the Page where you want to add your app.**
3. **Click the Add *"App Name"* button.**

Now your iFrame app is added as a custom tab to your Page. You can navigate to your page and change the position of your tab just as you would any tab.

facebook
Search for people, places and things
Add Welcome to Go Big Productions?
Add this application to:
Go Big Productions
Adding Welcome will let it pull your page's profile information, photos, friends' info, and other content that it requires to work. It will also add a box to your page and can publish Feed stories about your page.
Add Welcome
or Leave Application
Welcome was not created by Facebook. By clicking 'add,' you agree to the Facebook Platform User Terms of Service. By using Welcome, you also agree to the Welcome Terms of Service.

Figure 2-10: Select the Page where you want to add your app.

Using Third-Party Applications

If you're not an experienced HTML coder and don't want to mess around with creating an iFrame app, there's still hope! Several third-party applications exist to make installing an iFrame app easier.

Many third-party applications host your content for you, which means that you don't need to have your own web host or server. (We go deeper into these applications and their capabilities later in this section.) Many apps give you the option of uploading an image or HTML code. If you're good at coding a web page, you can use this space to create a mini web page, and the code is hosted by the app. If you're using HTML to code a mini web page, you have to host the images that you're putting on the Page.

Many of these applications allow you to have *fan-only* content. (Some call this content the *reveal tab* or *fan-gating*.) This feature allows you to have one image on top of some hidden content, and visitors can't see the hidden content until they click Like (refer to Figure 2-3, earlier in this chapter). If they like your Page already, the hidden content is available to them at any time.

Here's what you need before using a third-party application:

- **Custom image:** This image can be in any picture format, and it must be a maximum 810 pixels wide. There's no limit to the height, but if you want the image to appear "above the fold" on computer screens, don't make it higher than 500 pixels. Many apps also have a 520-pixel option that centers the image on the tab.

  You can create a custom tab that shows only this image. Or you can add fan-only content, which requires another image with the same dimensions or HTML code that displays a web page hidden below the image.
- **HTML code:** You can use this code to display a mini web page. You can use the HTML code alone or use that code below a custom image for fan-only content.

TIP

You can tell what application was used to create a custom Page by the icons below the tab Cover photos. If you see a star that matches the icon on the Static HTML: iFrame Tabs Page, for example, the Page owner used this app to create the Page. This information is useful sometimes if you're spying on the competition to see what they're doing.

Setup of the apps is left to the user, but you can see a bit about the back end of the apps and their capabilities.

Heyo

Heyo has a drag-and-drop design process that makes it very easy to add different elements to your custom tab without knowing how to code HTML. Because of the flexibility and configurability of Heyo, we don't cover all the steps here. Heyo has some nice video tutorials on its website. Free and paid options are available; you can find out more at `https://heyo.com`. Figure 2-11 shows an example of a custom tab created with Heyo.

Figure 2-11: A custom tab created with the Heyo application.

In the dashboard area of Heyo, you can select different widgets to add to your custom tab, add a background, or use a template to get started. The Heyo dashboard is shown in Figure 2-12. When you have the custom tab in show-worthy condition, you can publish that tab to your Page.

Figure 2-12: The Heyo dashboard.

Static HTML for Pages

Involver's application is called Static HTML for Pages, and the best place to access it is `www.involver.com/applications`. You can display an image on your custom tab or write HTML code to display something more complex.

Involver has also developed several Facebook applications, such as YouTube and Twitter apps, that you can read more about in Book III, Chapter 4.

TIP

Involver allows you to use two of its applications for free; after that, you're charged a monthly fee to use any additional applications. If you're using two of Involver's existing applications, you may want to choose one of the other iFrame applications for your custom tab.

To install the Static HTML for Pages app, log in to Facebook as your personal Profile and then follow these steps:

1. **Go to `www.involver.com/applications`, and scroll down to the Static HTML app.**
2. **Click the Free Install button.**

   A pop-up window appears, listing the Pages you manage. Choose which Page to install the App.
3. **Click the Add to Static HTML for Pages button next to the Page where you want to install this app.**

   You see a place where you get information about the app and select the visibility (who can see the app).

4. **Choose Everyone from the drop-down menu in the bottom-left corner (if it isn't selected already).**
5. **Click Go to App.**

   You see the permissions page.
6. **Click Allow.**

   You're taken to a page where you enter your company name and phone number and accept the terms of service.
7. **Enter your company name and phone number, check the box next to the Terms of Service link, and click Save Changes.**

   You're taken to a page where you can enter your HTML or select an image to display (see Figure 2-13).
8. **Select the radio button next to the type of information you want to display:**
   - *Custom Image:* A browser box appears, and you can browse your computer files to enter the image file.
   - *Custom HTML:* A box appears, allowing you to enter your HTML code.
   - *Custom SML: SML* stands for *Social Markup Language* and requires a license from Involver to use. You can find out more at `www.involver.com/sml`.
9. **Click Save Changes.**

   You see your images uploaded in a preview box.

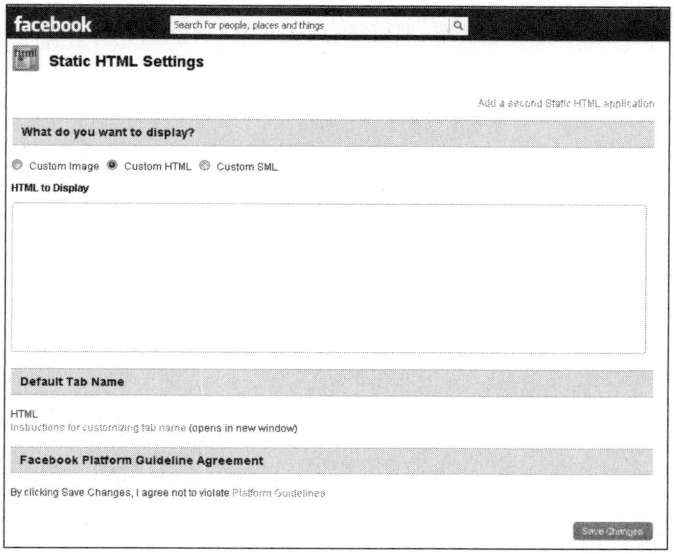

Figure 2-13: Configure Static HTML for Pages.

You're finished and can click Return to Facebook Page in the top-right corner to verify that your custom tab is working properly.

North Social

North Social is a paid platform with 18 Facebook apps. North Social is a good choice if you know that you want a variety of apps, but it has a monthly fee that depends on the number of fans you have. North Social has a lot of great video tutorials, which make using its apps very easy. North Social has fan-gated content available, and you can upload images or use HTML. You can also specify a separate URL for content that you want to bring into the custom tab.

The easiest way to get started is to log in with your Facebook Profile on `www.northsocial.com` and then go to the Pricing page. Select the Fan page and the features you need, pay with your credit card, and start designing. Another great feature of North Social is all the examples of custom tabs that are available for different industries, as shown in Figure 2-14.

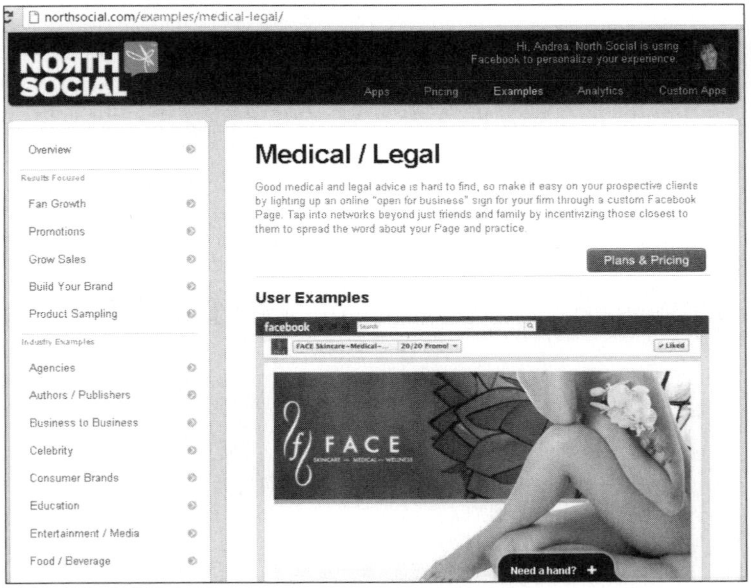

Figure 2-14: Many examples on North Social's site.

ShortStack

ShortStack is a drag-and-drop custom tab editor that offers various widgets that you can add to your tab, as shown in Figure 2-15. With the widgets, you can add photos, text, forms, products, HTML code, and many more features. The widgets stack on top of one another, but templates divide the space into segments that you can edit separately. ShortStack also have a sweepstakes app that you can design yourself.

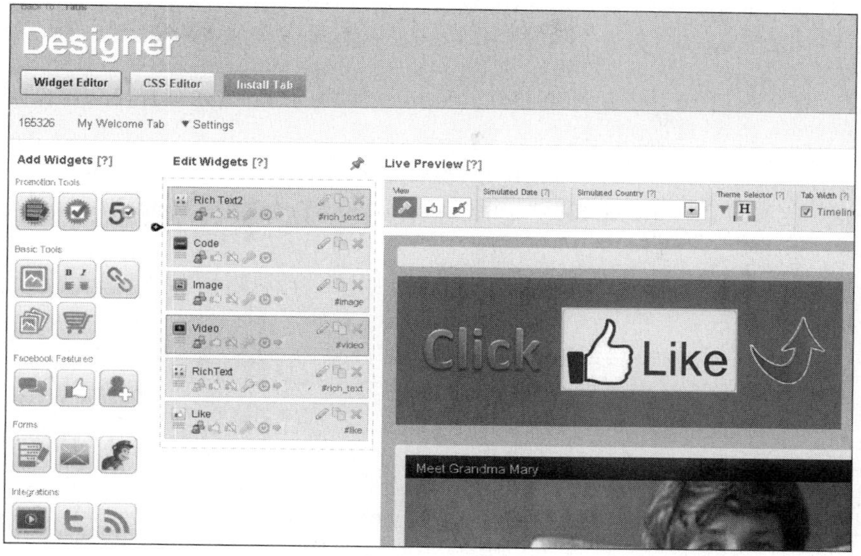

Figure 2-15: ShortStack has widgets that you can add to your custom tab.

ShortStack has a free plan for pages with fewer than 2,000 likes; the prices go up incrementally, depending on how many fans you have. The nice thing about a free option is that you can try your hand at the design tool before committing to purchase it.

To get started, go to `www.shortstackapp.com`, and click the Register Now link, or click the Login with Facebook button to link the app to your Facebook Profile.

Static HTML: iFrame Tabs

With the Static HTML: iFrame Tabs application, you can create fan-only content. This application allows you to upload an image directly (if you have a $7-per-month paid plan), or you can use HTML code to reference an image to display. You can have multiple Static HTML tabs on your page for free if you don't need to have the images hosted.

To use this application, go to `http://apps.facebook.com/static_html_plus`. Alternatively, you can usually find it by searching for the title of the app in the search bar of Facebook; you should see it in the drop-down list of search results. You'll know that you've found the correct app if you see a star icon on the application Page. (With all the similar application names, it helps to know what you're looking for!) You must use HTML coding for this app, but the good news is that the app is free. Also, you can have multiple tabs on your Page with this app for free.

When you're on the Static HTML: iFrame Tabs application Page, follow these steps to install the app on your business Page:

1. **Click the blue Add Static HTML to a Page button.**

   You're taken to a screen with a drop-down menu that allows you to choose the Page where you want to add the app.

2. **Choose the Page from the Add This Application To drop-down menu, as shown in Figure 2-16.**

   The Add Static HTML: iFrame Tabs button appears.

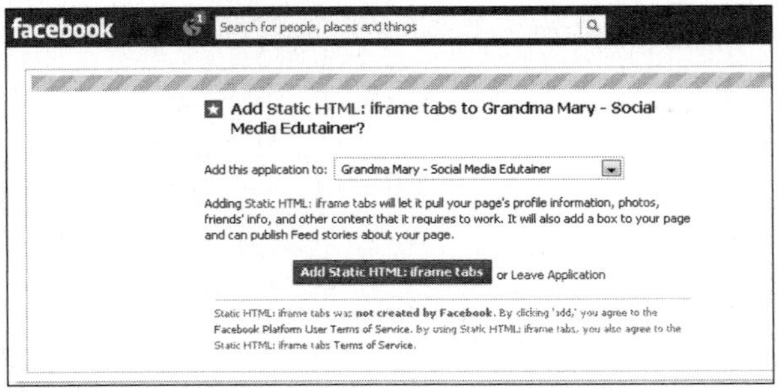
facebook
Search for people, places and things
Add Static HTML: iframe tabs to Grandma Mary - Social Media Edutainer?
Add this application to:
Grandma Mary - Social Media Edutainer
Adding Static HTML: iframe tabs will let it pull your page's profile information, photos, friends' info, and other content that it requires to work. It will also add a box to your page and can publish Feed stories about your page.
Add Static HTML: iframe tabs
or Leave Application
Static HTML: iframe tabs was not created by Facebook. By clicking 'add,' you agree to the Facebook Platform User Terms of Service. By using Static HTML: iframe tabs, you also agree to the Static HTML: iframe tabs Terms of Service.

Figure 2-16: Select the Page where you want to add the app.

3. **Click the Add Static HTML: iFrame Tabs button.**

   You're now taken to your Facebook Page.

4. **Click the Welcome tab with the star icon below your Cover photo.**

   You see the editor page for the app, as shown in Figure 2-17.

5. **Enter your HTML content and the optional fan-only HTML content.**

6. **Click the Preview tab in the top-right corner.**

   You're taken to another window, where you have to view your tab as a fan, view your tab as a nonfan, or go back to the editor.

7. **Click the View Your Tab as a Public and Fans link to make sure that the tab looks right if you are using the Fans-Only content option.**

8. **Click the Edit Tab button to get back into the editor page.**

9. **Click the Save and Publish button in the top-right corner.**

   You've set up your custom tab!

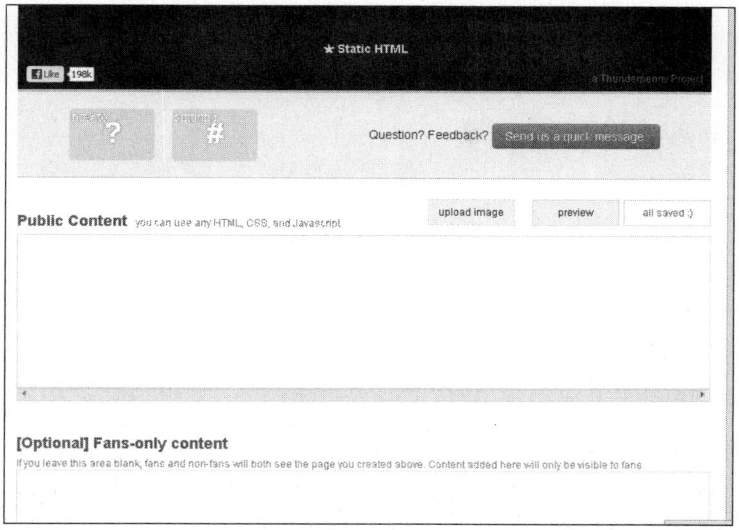

Figure 2-17: Enter your HTML content.

TabSite

TabSite is another iFrame application that you can use to create multiple subpages within one page. TabSite is very versatile, offering a variety of paid plans and a free plan that includes ads (not recommended). When you look at the pricing, note the Bronze plan, which features two tabs and no ads for $5 per month.

TabSite also has several engagement apps available, allowing you to give people deals on your products for sharing the link to your app or pinning the app in Pinterest, or to give a group deal to a certain number of people.

Figure 2-18 shows the design area of TabSite, where you can add widgets or use a template to get started. You can have multiple tabs within the custom tab so that you create a mini website within the page. We don't cover all the steps for installing the app, but you can get started by clicking the Sign Up Free! button at `www.tabsite.com`.

You can find out more about the application at `www.tabsite.com`.

FanPageEngine

FanPageEngine has some great templates that you can customize to give your tab a professional look. It also has photo and video contest apps, as well as a Deals app, as shown in Figure 2-19. Pricing starts at $27 per month for one Facebook Page.

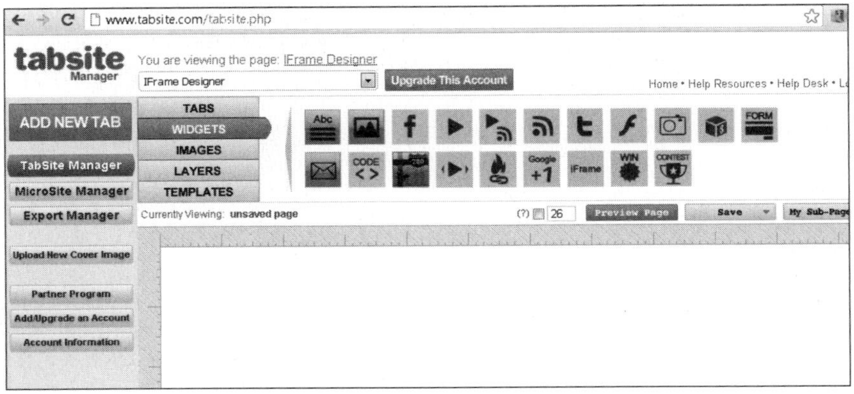

Figure 2-18: The TabSite dashboard.

Figure 2-19: FanPage Engine has video tutorials and contest apps.

FanPageEngine also has great videos that help you see exactly how to set up its apps. To watch some of the setup videos and to get started, go to `www.fanpageengine.com`, and scroll down to click the Choose Your Plan Now button.

Book VI

Making Facebook Come Alive with Events and Contests

The 5th Wave By Rich Tennant

"I know Facebook is great and you want to be a part of it. But you're my mom - you can't be my 'friend.'"

Contents at a Glance

Chapter 1: Creating Facebook Events

In This Chapter

- Creating an event: The basics
- Working around Page event limitations
- Sharing your event with your community

Using the Facebook Events feature can create a lot of buzz around an event, your store, an online event, or even a product or book launch. Facebook Events show up on people's Timelines and within their Events area, and are even searchable by anyone on Facebook. Add to the mix the fact that any time a Friend interacts with your event, that person's Friends all see something in their News Feeds about the event, which gives it a lot of free publicity courtesy of Facebook.

If you've been on Facebook for very long, you've probably received an event invitation yourself, so you may be familiar with Facebook Events. If not, don't worry; in this chapter, you see how to set up an event, the best practices for getting the word out about your event, and tips on using events with your Page.

Getting Started with Facebook Events

Facebook Events can be a powerful way to get your event noticed and shared within the Facebook community. But just as with any marketing activity in Facebook, you need to be mindful of the balance between sharing your event and spamming people with unwanted posts about it.

Because Facebook Events show up in multiple places within Facebook, they are more visible than just Timeline posts. Facebook makes it easy to have Friends invite other Friends to events, and if an event is public, anyone who has a Facebook account can RSVP.

WARNING!

Don't make your event public if your event is at your home. Random strangers have shown up to events that were posted on Facebook publicly and then vandalized the homes.

Facebook Events can be beneficial for many types of events: charity events, book tours, virtual webinars, open houses, big sales at your store, and more.

Figure 1-1 shows a book signing created by Gary Vaynerchuk; note that one of the authors was invited by a Friend on Facebook. News of a Facebook Event can spread through Friends inviting other Friends.

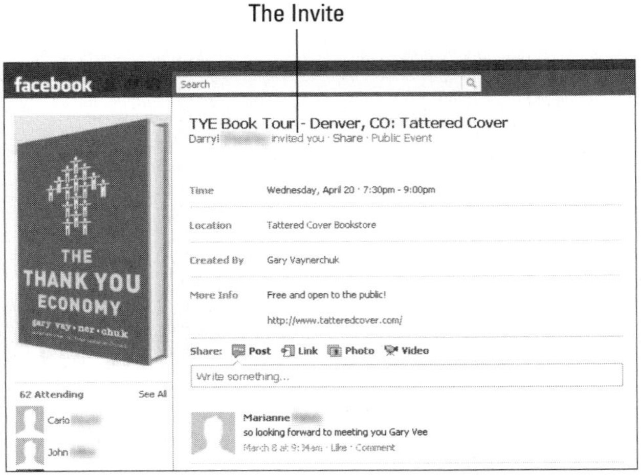

Figure 1-1: A book-signing event.

Social Media Examiner has done a great job of promoting its virtual webinars through Facebook Events. (Figure 1-2 shows an example.) It uses the Event page actively to answer questions about the event and give new information about the event.

Figure 1-2: The Social Media Success Summit was a virtual event.

Facebook Events are potentially seen in five places, which is why you want to create them. You give your connections five ways to find out about your event, as follows:

- ✦ The right sidebar of the home page lists the next upcoming event.
- ✦ The Events link on the left sidebar of the home page shows a link to all the current events you've created or are invited to.
- ✦ When an event is created, it appears in the News Feeds and ticker of all your Friends (if you create the event on your personal Profile) or in the News Feeds and tickers of all your likers. Facebook Events created by a Page are always public. Facebook Events created by personal Profiles can be visible only to invitees or certain personal lists.
- ✦ When people are invited to an event, they get a notification in their notifications area.
- ✦ When people are invited to an event, they may also get an e-mail about the event if they have e-mail notifications enabled.

REMEMBER

When you create a Facebook Event on your Page, you won't be able to invite your fans directly; see the section "Uncovering Limitations of Facebook Events," later in this chapter. However, other people can invite guests if they RSVP to your event.

On the right sidebar of your home page, you see the most current event coming up, as shown in Figure 1-3. You may have to expand the events to see all the ones coming up, as shown.

Figure 1-3: Events appear on the home page.

Having the events listed on the home page of Facebook makes them very visible to potential customers, which is a perfect reason to create events for your business. The events listed are the ones that are either happening now or are coming up next, so this area is good for reminding people of an event coming up shortly but not as effective for events further in the future.

You also find a link to all your events on the left sidebar of your home page. When you click that link, all the events you've been invited to appear on the Events page, as shown in Figure 1-4.

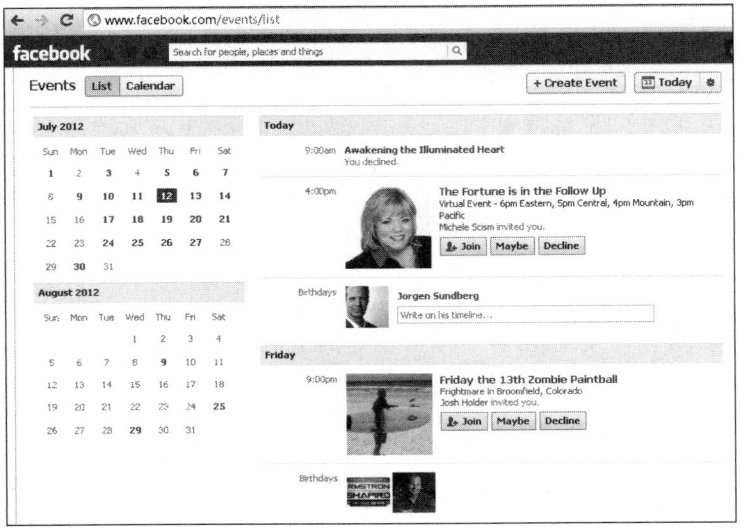

Figure 1-4: All your events on the Events page (in List view).

You get to choose between seeing your events in list form (refer to Figure 1-4) or seeing them in calendar form, as shown in Figure 1-5. To see Calendar view, click the Calendar button in the top-left corner, near the Events heading.

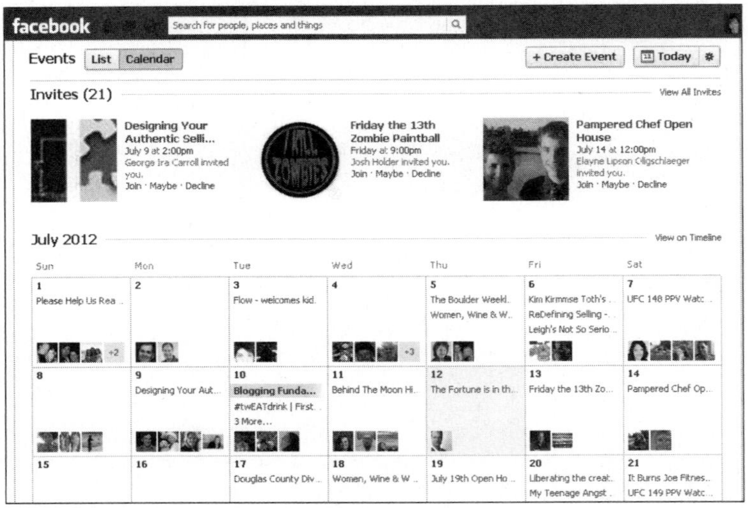

Figure 1-5: Calendar view of your events.

When you get invited to an event, it also shows up in your notifications area (see Figure 1-6). This is another way that your event gets increased visibility. Everyone you invited or who is attending receives notifications when you change something about the event or post about the event. (See SummerToast's post notification in Figure 1-6.) The only people who will not see the notifications are those who weren't invited or have declined the invite. These postings can be great reminders and can give your event increased visibility!

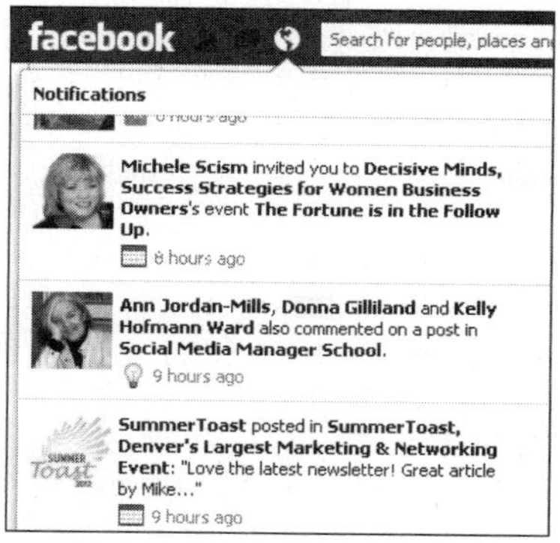

Figure 1-6: You're notified about posts regarding events you're invited to.

You can create Facebook Events through your personal Profile, and you can create them through your business Page (or Page; we use those terms interchangeably). Depending on the type of event you're promoting, we recommend creating an event through your Facebook Page because it's better for your branding and complies with Facebook's terms that disallow you from using your personal Profile for your own commercial gain. There are some limitations involved with creating events on your Page, and we cover the best ways to get around those limitations later in this chapter, in "Uncovering Limitations of Facebook Events."

Adding the Events app to your Page

When you start your Facebook Page, the Events application is available, but it may not be immediately visible in the navigation links on your left sidebar. Events is a Facebook application, meaning that it was created by Facebook (not by a third party).

Your Events tab should (but may not) show up in the Apps area below your Page's Cover photo, as shown in Figure 1-7. Note that you may have to click the arrow on the right side of the Apps area to see the Events App.

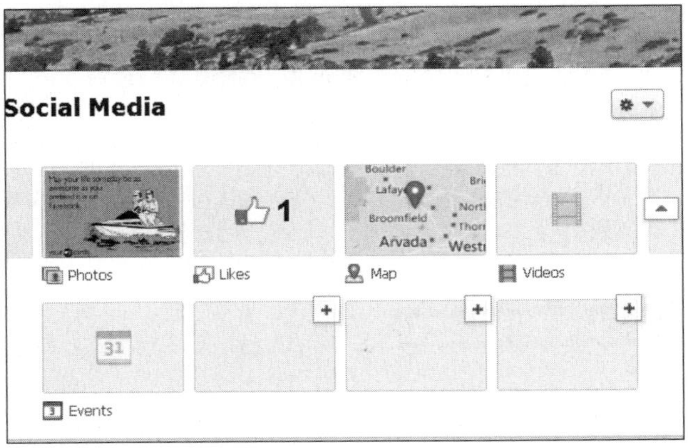

Figure 1-7: Look for the Events tab in the Apps area.

If the Events tab isn't there, follow these steps:

1. **Click the arrow on the right side of the Apps area (below your Page's Cover photo) to show all the Apps.**

   You see all the apps and are able to edit the boxes there. The empty boxes are spaces where Facebook Apps could be installed.

2. **Click the + icon next to one of the empty boxes (refer to Figure 1-7).**

   A drop-down menu appears, displaying all the available apps you can add.

3. **Select the Events app, as shown in Figure 1-8.**

   The Events app is added to your tabs.

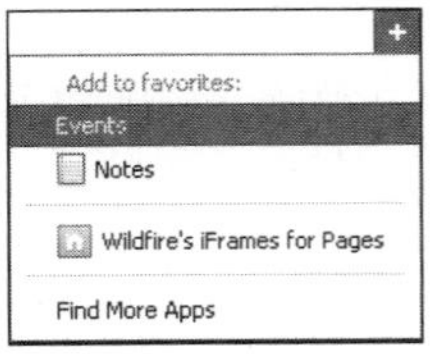

Figure 1-8: Add the Events App to your tabs.

If you have many apps installed, make sure that the Events app is in the first three rows of apps, because only the first three rows are visible to others. To swap the Events app with one of the other apps, mouse over the Events app, click the pencil icon in the upper-right corner of the Events app, and choose one of the apps in the first three rows from the drop-down menu shown in Figure 1-9. (See Book III, Chapter 2 for more information about adding apps to your Page.) The pencil icon will not appear on the app box until you mouse over it.

Figure 1-9: Swap app positions to make sure that the Events app is visible.

To create an event from your Facebook Page, click the Events app and then click the Create Event link, shown in Figure 1-10. ***Note:*** You can also click the Create Event button in the top-right corner (see Figure 1-10) if you have past events that are listed in the screen.

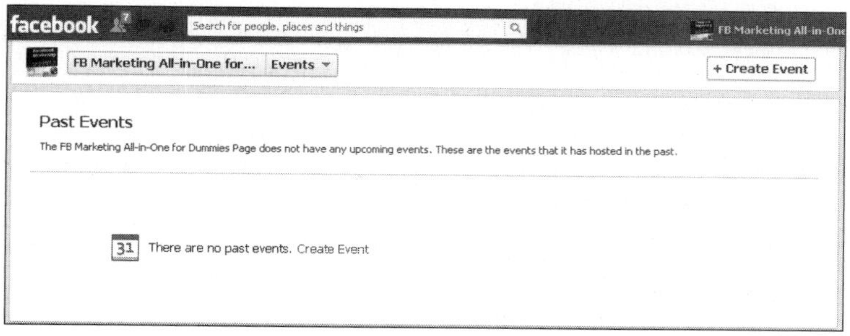

Figure 1-10: Click the Create Event link to start creating your event.

REMEMBER

You can also create an event from the Publisher directly on your Timeline. See Book III, Chapter 1 for more information about using the Publisher to create an event.

Entering the event details

After you click Create event, a window appears (shown in Figure 1-11), where you enter your event's details.

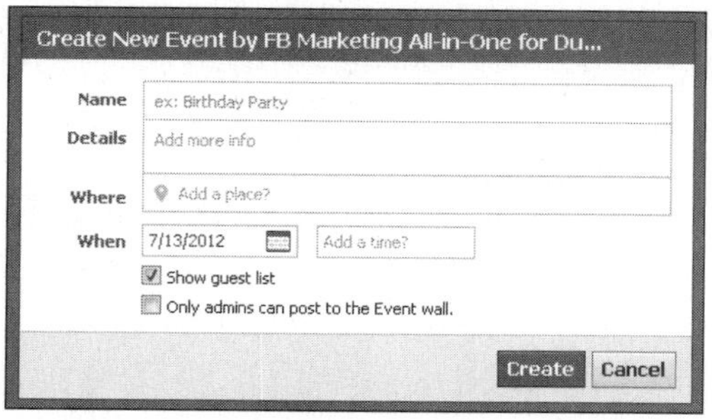

Figure 1-11: Enter the event details here.

You can't start working on an event and save it as a "draft" and then publish it later. So before you start, make sure that you have all the details ready! As soon as you click the Create button, the event will be published. (You can make changes, however, which we discuss in the later section, "Editing your event.")

Enter your event details in the following fields:

✦ **Name:** The event name will show up in people's calendars, in their notifications, and in posts about the event, so make the name compelling and descriptive!

✦ **Details:** Write a description about the event, what you plan to do, why someone should attend, and so on. Put the main information in the first 35 to 50 words (depending on spacing), because that's what people see. After 50 words, users have to click the See More link to see the rest of the description.

  Currently, Facebook doesn't offer a way for attendees to pay to register for events. If your event requires paid registration, you need to send attendees to another site where you can accept payments (such as Eventbrite); put the link to this site in the first part of your description. You can have a very long description in the Details field, and giving people as much information as possible here is a good idea.

✦ **Where:** Fill in this field with a description of where the event is to be held. The information in the Where field also shows up if you post a link to this event or share this event, so make sure that you provide the name of the venue and a description.

  If the event is going to be held at a place that has a Facebook Page, or if the place has been categorized as a Facebook Place, you can start typing the place's name and link to it. That way, people will be able to see more information about the place within your event. If you start typing the address of your event, the Place or Page may come up in the field that's tied to that address, and you can select the Facebook Place or Page.

  If you're holding an online or virtual event, you can add more description to market it, such as "In your pajamas at home" or "An online exclusive event."

✦ **When:** For typical events, you have a beginning time and an end time. If you're promoting an occurrence such as a book launch, you can specify a range of time during which you'll be promoting the event. The benefit of using a range of time is that your event will show up on people's sidebars for the duration of your event.

To enter a range of time, enter the exact time when the event begins, rather than just the date. After you enter the time when the event begins, an End Time? link appears to the right of the time field; click that link to enter the end time for your event.

✦ **Show Guest List:** By default, this box is checked. If you want to keep the attendees list and invitees list private, clear the box. Guests might be concerned about privacy, so keeping the list private is a good idea. Or if you don't want people to know how many (or how few!) people have responded, keep it private. In general, though, it's better to show the guest list.

✦ **Only Admins Can Post to the Event Wall:** By default, this box is deselected. If you don't allow attendees to post on the Event page (also called the Event wall), they can't ask questions, communicate about the event, or connect with other people — all things that you want them to do! Disable this feature by checking the box.

Click the Create button when you've filled out all the fields. Your event will be immediately posted to your Page Timeline, as shown in Figure 1-12. You can hide it immediately if you aren't ready to announce it to the world, but your event shows up on your Events tab.

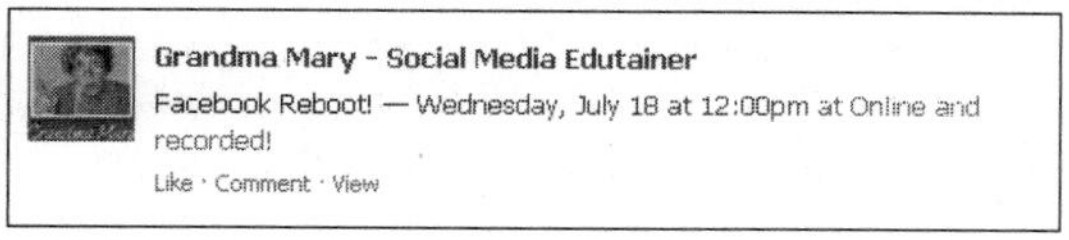

Figure 1-12: Your event is sent immediately to fans' News Feeds.

Right after you create the event, you can add an event picture, as shown in Figure 1-13. (Note that you can't add a picture until after you actually create the event.) Even if you don't have a specific picture to go with the event, find one on the web (making sure that you have the appropriate permissions or that the picture is royalty free), or use your logo. You want a picture to go with your event to make your display eye catching and more visibly interesting than mere text is. Add the photo as soon as possible after you create it so that the event looks more interesting.

Figure 1-13: Click Add Event Photo to add or change your event photo.

If you're hosting a large event, design a picture or image specifically for it. You'll have more branding for your event and get a better response.

Synching events with your personal calendar

After you create an event or RSVP to someone else's event, you can easily export this event to your personal calendar so you don't miss the event. To do so, click the gear in the top-right corner of the Facebook Event page. In the drop-down menu that appears, choose Export Event. A pop-up window appears, as shown in Figure 1-14; this window allows you to choose to save the event to your calendar or send it to your e-mail address. When you select the Save to Calendar option and then click the Export button, the event will be downloaded as a .ics calendar file, which works with Outlook.

You can also turn off notifications for the event from the gear drop-down menu (top-right corner) if needed. The gear symbol appears only after you confirm you are Going or Maybe going to the event.

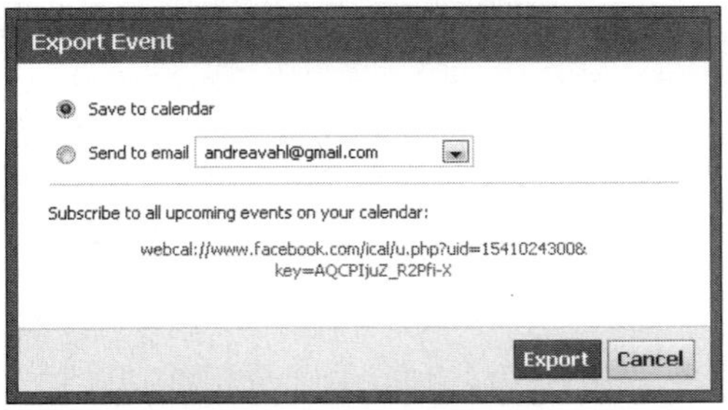

Figure 1-14: The Export Event window lets you choose where to export the Facebook Event.

Editing your event

In case you need to make a change to your event after you create it, editing the event is very simple. From your Facebook Page, follow these steps:

1. **Click the Events tab below your Cover photo.**

   You see your events listed, as shown in Figure 1-15.

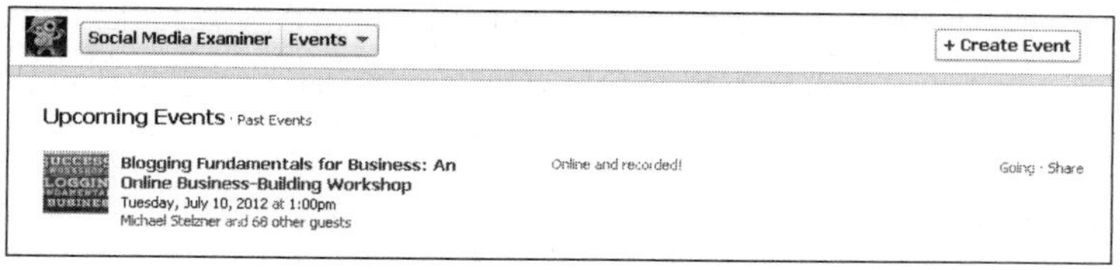

Figure 1-15: Your events are listed when you click the Events navigation link.

2. **Click the title of the event you want to edit.**

   You're taken to the Event details area.

3. **Click the Edit Event button in the top-right corner, as shown in Figure 1-16.**

   Your Edit Event button may be under the drop-down menu you access by clicking on the gear icon if you don't see it as shown in the figure.

4. **Edit any of the event details just as though you were creating the event.**

5. **Click the Save Event button after you've made your changes.**

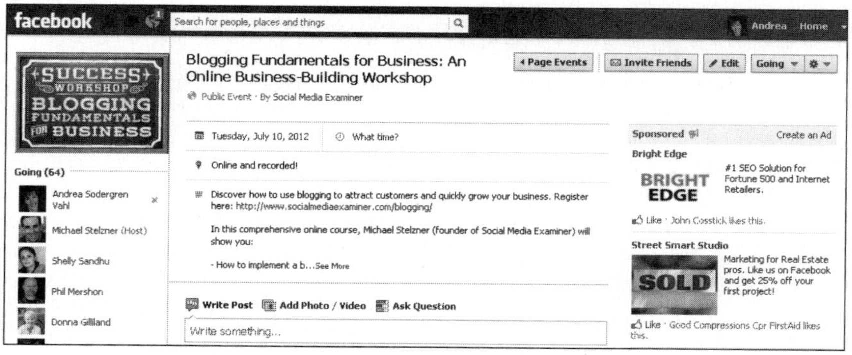

Figure 1-16: Click the Edit Event button in the top-right corner.

Canceling your event

It's easy to cancel a Facebook Event if you need to. Keep in mind that you can edit the Event information if you need to, as discussed in the preceding section. If you accidentally created multiple events or need to cancel an event, however, follow these steps:

1. **Go to your event by clicking the Events tab below your Cover photo.**
2. **Click the title of the event.**

   You're taken to the Event details area.
3. **Click the gear icon in the top-right corner.**
4. **Choose Cancel Event from the drop-down menu that appears (see Figure 1-17).**

Figure 1-17: Choose Cancel Event.

   A warning appears telling you this action can't be undone and asks if you are sure you want to cancel.
5. **Click the blue Yes button.**

   Your event is cancelled. As the warning told you, the cancellation can't be undone, and you'll no longer be able to see the event. Invited guests receive a notification that the event has been canceled.

Uncovering Limitations of Facebook Events

Creating a Facebook Event on your Facebook Page is different from creating the event on your Facebook personal Profile in two main ways:

- **When you create an event via your Page, you can't directly invite your fans to your event.** You can log in as your personal Profile, join the event and then invite your personal friends to it. You may have some friends who overlap as fans of your Page and it can be helpful to invite them. When you create an event on your personal Profile, you can select the guests whom you want to invite from your list of Facebook Friends. These people receive a notification that you've invited them to your event; they also get an e-mail notification if they have that feature enabled. But because Facebook Pages can't invite their fans, you have to get the word out about your event by posting it to your Timeline and encouraging others to invite their Friends from within the event itself.

A business Page can't invite its fans to an event because the guest list could be public information. Facebook does watch out for privacy concerns at times!

- **When you create the Event via your Page, you can't send Facebook e-mails to the people who will be attending the event.** When you create a Facebook Event on your personal Profile, you can send Facebook e-mails to the people you've invited to let them know about any changes or updates for the event. Facebook e-mails are very visible and helpful when you need to let people know about a major change. But any activity within the event will still show up in a user's notifications area (unless they declined), which is also visible.

Even though you have these limitations when you create an event on your Page, we still recommend that you use your Page for any business activities. Facebook Events can still be beneficial ways to promote your event to your community.

Promoting an Event

After you create your Facebook Event, you need to make sure that you promote it. Make your promotion fun and exciting for your community. You may want to post a few teaser announcements about your event to let your community know to be watching your Page. Something like "Big news coming tomorrow about something you won't want to miss" can work well to create some buzz before you post the actual event.

The first step in promoting your event is sharing it directly with your community. You have the initial post when the event is created, but it's important to remind people about your event often, just in case they missed the post in their News Feeds.

There's a line between getting the word out about your event and overpromoting it. To avoid crossing this line, make sure that you still have plenty of value in your other posts. Also, don't just post your event over and over; if you do, people will unlike or hide your Page! A good general rule is to have no more than 10 percent of your posts promotional.

Inviting your community to your event

Because you can't invite your community via a standard Facebook invitation, the main ways to get the word out about your event are posting your event to your Timeline as a link, tagging your event in a Timeline post, and using updates. You may also think about running a Facebook ad campaign that targets your audience or using Facebook Promoted Posts. See Book VIII for more information on advertising. Remember to vary your posts and to keep them fun.

Notifying your Page community of your event

Your event was posted to your Timeline when you created it, but you should repost your event regularly. Some people will have missed the initial post, and others may need to be reminded to RSVP to your event. To continue to get the word out about your event, make sure to share the event as a link on your Page at least once or twice a week.

Each Facebook Event has its own unique URL address just like any other website. You can find the link to the event by clicking on your Event tab on your Facebook Page, and then selecting the event (see Figure 1-18). Include the link in an update as you would any other link: by clicking the Link button in your update and pasting the link. The picture for your event is the one posted next to the event.

The Event URL appears here.

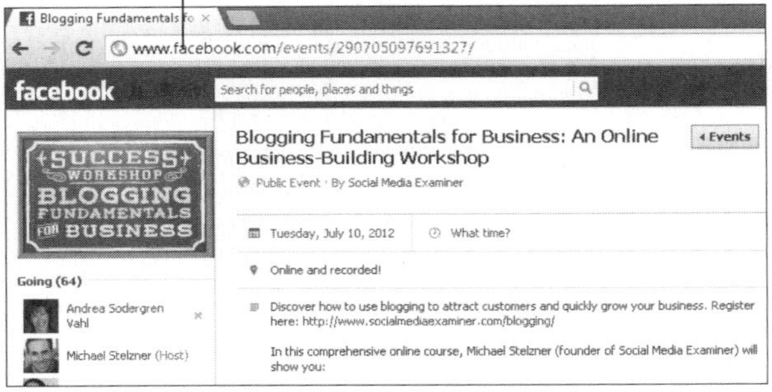

Figure 1-18: Copy the Event's link, and paste it into a post on your Page.

TIP Because you've posted your event as a link, it's easy to share with other people. If the link to your event is in the News Feed, people can click Share to see a pop-up window that lets them fill out their own invitation to the event, as shown in Figure 1-19. In the status part of your post, ask people to click the Share button and spread the word about your event!

Figure 1-19: Encourage people to click Share to post your event to their News Feeds.

TIP

Find ways to vary your posts about your event. Give away a promotional item, feature a particular vendor or sponsor of your event, or add something new to the event to give you a reason to make a new announcement about it.

Tagging events

Another way to keep people informed about your event is to use the status update feature for both your personal Profile and your Page and tag the event so that people can easily click over to it. To tag the event, just type your message in the Publisher on your Timeline, as shown in Figure 1-20. The event name should come up, and you can select it. As shown in Figure 1-20, other events or Pages show up that also have the letters that you are typing. Choose the appropriate thing to tag from the drop-down menu.

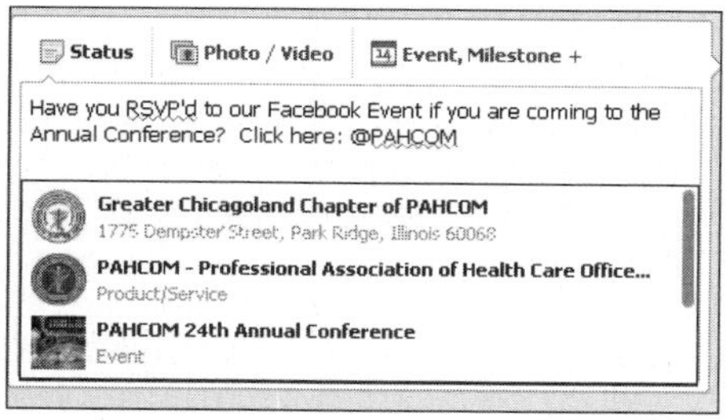

Figure 1-20: Tag your event as a different way to link to it.

Selecting an event's name makes it a clickable link like the one shown in Figure 1-21. Notice that this post added a photo to make it even more eye catching. You can add photos and tag the event in the same post. Tagging is covered in more detail in Book IV, Chapter 2.

The Event name is a clickable link.

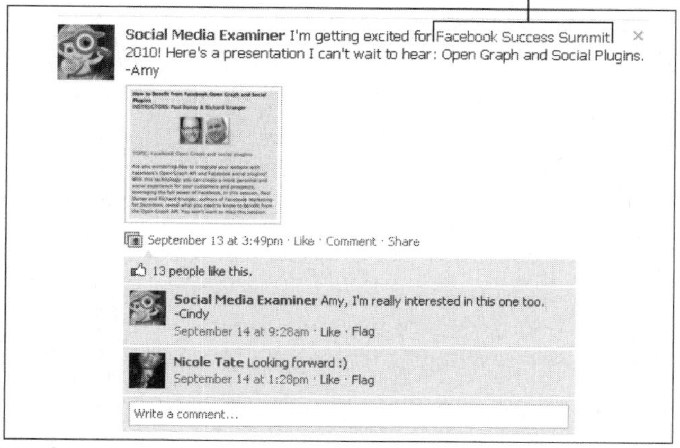

Figure 1-21: An event tagged by Social Media Examiner to promote it and remind people to RSVP.

Make sure to remind people about the event often by reposting the link or tagging the event. Consider posting something about your event two to three times per week at different times of day. You want to post at different times to connect with members of your audience who may be logging in to Facebook at different times. Normally, the best time to connect with most people is morning, so make sure that you make at least one post per week in the morning.

Inviting Friends to the event

After you have created the event, you can invite your Friends. If you don't have any Friends who are also fans of your page or who are interested in your business, this might be a step you don't need to take. But if you have some overlap between your Friends and fans, then take some time to invite your Friends.

You have to be logged in as your personal Profile rather than your Page to invite your Friends. To switch back to your personal Profile, use the down arrow in the upper-right corner and select your personal Profile from the drop-down menu under Use Facebook As. After switching back to your personal Profile, follow these steps:

1. **Navigate to your Facebook Page but remain logged in as your personal Profile.**

   You can do this by typing the URL of your Facebook Page in your browser window or selecting your Facebook Page name from the left sidebar of your personal Profile home Page under the Pages heading.

2. **Click the Events tab underneath your Profile photo.**

   You may have to click the down arrow to the right of the Apps. You see all your upcoming events listed.

3. **Click on the event you will be inviting your Friends to.**

   You see the Event page.

4. **RSVP to the event as your personal Profile by clicking Join (assuming you are going because you did create the event).**

5. **Click the Invite Friends button in the upper-right corner of the Events page.**

   A window appears, with a list of your Friends, as shown in Figure 1-22.

6. **Select the Friends you want to invite and click the blue Save button.**

   You see a message that your Friends have been invited and you are done. Your Friends receive a notification that you invited them and the event will appear in their Events area.

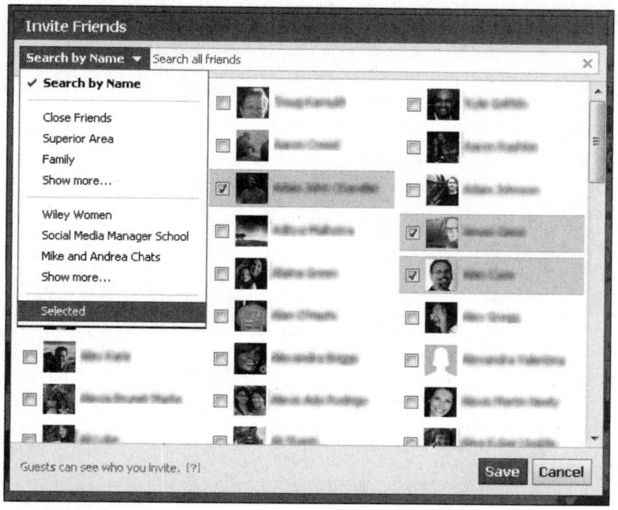

Figure 1-22: Select the Friends you want to invite to your event.

TIP

There is no "select-all" button when inviting your Friends to an event so you will have to select the check boxes next to your Friends' Profile pictures individually. You can also filter your Friends by using the Search by Friends drop-down menu (refer to Figure 1-22). You can then display all the Friends from one of your Facebook Lists to make selecting them easier. This works well if you have created a Facebook List just for your business contacts.

Asking attendees to share the event

The people who are attending the event can be your best advocates for spreading the word, but you may need to educate people about how to share the event and invite their Friends.

Anyone has the ability to share an event, regardless of whether he or she has RSVP'd or has even been formally invited. But you can only invite your Friends to an event that you have RSVP'd for (even if you have declined the invitation you can still invite your Friends to the event). There are four ways to share:

- Click the Share link in the post when the event has been shared as a link as described earlier.
- Go into the event by clicking on your Events tab and then selecting the event; click the Share link on the bottom-left sidebar (see Figure 1-23). A pop-up Share This Event window appears, giving people the opportunity to add their own commentary about the event before clicking the blue Share Event button.

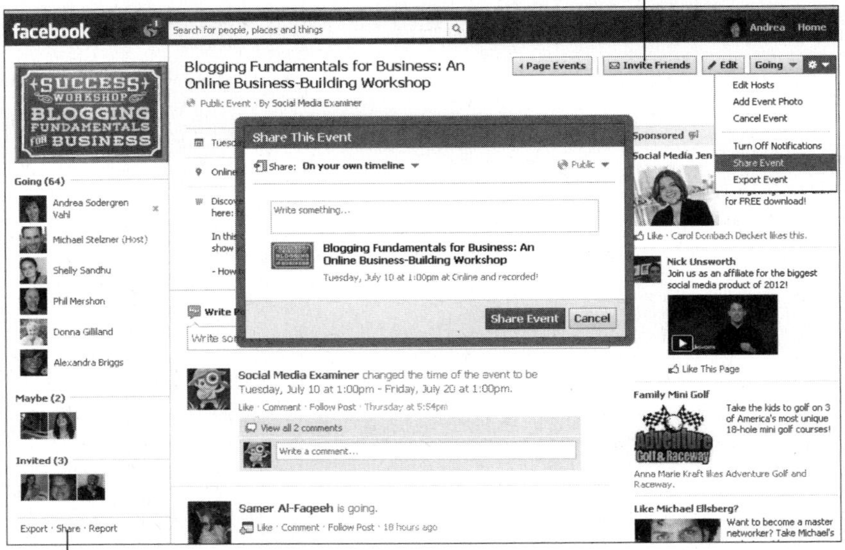

Figure 1-23: Click the Share link in the bottom-left corner to share an event.

- After people have RSVP'd to the event, they have the ability to invite their Friends to the event using the Invite Friends button that appears in the upper-right corner of the Event page (refer to Figure 1-23) in the same way you invited your Friends. The person must have responded to the event by clicking the Join, Maybe, or Decline button on an event before he or she has the ability to invite Friends.

The fewer steps, the better. Telling people to share the post by clicking the Share link is the easiest way; don't make the process too hard!

You may need to educate your connections about how to share this event. When you post your event in a Timeline post, include a call to action such as "Feel free to share this event with your Friends by clicking the Share link below this post." You can also e-mail people, asking them to help promote your event by going to your Facebook Event URL and clicking the Share link in the bottom-left corner. If you want to tell someone how to Invite their Friends to the event, share your event as a Link, tell people to click the event (if they've already RSVP'd) and then click the Invite Friends button to invite their Friends directly.

A word about creating a Facebook Ad for your event

Another way to promote your event is to run a Facebook Ad. Putting together such an ad is fairly easy, and it doesn't have to cost a lot of money. Advertising your event can be an effective tool for reaching your target demographic and connecting to new people on Facebook. When you create a Facebook Ad for an event, people can RSVP easily by clicking the RSVP link in the ad.

We don't cover how to create a Facebook Ad for an event in this chapter, but you can find out how to set up your ad in Book VIII, Chapter 2.

Encouraging interaction within your Facebook Event

Your Facebook Event contains its own page on which people can post messages about the event. They can also post event pictures and videos. If people are posting about the event, make sure that you're responding and connecting. People may have questions about the event, and you want to answer those questions as quickly as possible. Other people likely have the same questions, and the sooner you address any issues that arise, the better for your business.

If your event is a recurring one, post some pictures of past events to show people how much fun or well attended the past events were. You may also want to post pictures of past events on your Page Timeline and then tag the events.

You may also ask some of your close friends who are coming to the event to post on the event's Wall to get buzz going, as well as to provide social proof. *Social proof* means that when you can see your Friends or other people giving good feedback about something, you're more likely to respond favorably to it or to give it a try.

The Event postings aren't sent to the News Feeds of people who are attending the event, but they're visible on the Facebook Event page. People whom you've invited also get a notification when someone posts to the Timeline of the event, which can be a good reminder to RSVP.

Sharing your Facebook Event outside Facebook

Part of your promotion strategy should be to share your event on other sites as well. When you drive traffic to the Facebook Event, you also increase exposure to your Facebook Page. When you send the link to your event, just cut and paste the URL (refer to Figure 1-18). Here are some places to share your event:

✦ **Blog or website:** If you have a blog, post a blog entry when your event is announced. If you have a professional logo, place it on the sidebar of your blog or website, with a clickable link that goes back to the Facebook Event.

- **E-mail subscribers:** Send an update about your event to your subscribers. If they're not on Facebook, they won't be able to RSVP there, but they will be able to view the event. Give them an alternative way to RSVP if they're not on Facebook.
- **Twitter, LinkedIn, and other social media:** If you're on Twitter, tweet the link to your event at least a couple times a week after you announce your event. This can depend on how much you post on Twitter. You want your promotional tweets to stay under 10 percent of your total tweets. Also send a message to your LinkedIn connections and to any other social or professional networks you belong to, if appropriate. If your event is local, for example, make sure that you're inviting only local people from your LinkedIn network, and if certain colleagues have a completely different business focus from the topic of your event, don't invite them.

Chapter 2: Building Excitement with a Contest

In This Chapter

- Choosing a type of contest
- Outlining the details of your contest
- Setting targets for success

According to a recent poll by Econsultancy, the number-one reason why people like a Facebook Page is that the Page notified them about special offers and promotions. With that reason in mind, it's a good idea to run a contest on your Facebook Page.

A contest also gives people a reason to connect with you, makes your Page more fun, and attracts more people to your brand and your site. But what will your contest look like? You have a lot of options to consider when setting up your contest, and in this chapter, we explore how to design your contest, set your targets, and make sure that you're riding on the right side of Facebook law.

Later in the chapter, the terms contests and sweepstakes are clarified. A true *contest* has some type of vote to choose the winner (or you choose the winner through judging) while a *sweepstakes* has the winner chosen at random. Throughout this and the next two chapters, we use the term *contest* more collectively to refer to both contests and sweepstakes. To muddy the waters, Facebook refers to contests and sweepstakes as *promotions*. We are combining all the terms into one and calling them "contests." Whatever the term, your winning strategy lies in the next three chapters.

Thinking about Running a Contest?

The first thing you should consider when running a contest is your goal. Are you looking for more people in your Facebook community, more subscribers to your newsletter, or more brand awareness? If you begin with the goal in mind, the pieces fall into place.

All different types of businesses can benefit from Facebook contests. A contest can draw attention to your business and give you a list of people who want your product or service. You can draw attention to a product or service that you offer as a way to market it. If you're a consultant, for example, you can offer a consulting package that people may not know about. If you're a florist, you could offer a "Fresh Flowers for a Month" package to get your community thinking about treating themselves to flowers every week. If you're a web designer, you could give away free website redesign to prompt others to use your services. When people enter your contest, you have a list of people who are interested in your product or service.

Make sure that you structure your contest to align with your goal. Here are some ways to achieve your goals when running a contest:

✦ **Grow your Facebook community.** If you want more people to join your Facebook community, make liking your Page a requirement for entry.

✦ **Add subscribers to your newsletter.** Be sure to let contest entrants know that they will be added to your e-mail list when they enter (and make sure that they have a way to unsubscribe to comply with spam rules).

✦ **Increase brand awareness.** You can also have entrants check in to your Facebook Place to get extra entries in your contest, which can drive awareness of your business location. Checking in can't be the only way entrants enter your contest, however. (For more about Facebook's contest rules, see the "Understanding Facebook and legal restrictions" section, later in this chapter).

Your prize doesn't have to be expensive or lavish. It just has to be something that your community wants. (A Facebook Page called Chocolate for Breakfast gave away a premium-chocolate prize pack and received more than 700 entries in one week!) You might also receive a glowing recommendation and referrals from the winner of your contest.

REMEMBER

Your contest is part of your marketing budget. A well-run and well-publicized contest can be much more effective than a print ad for increasing awareness and engagement.

Designing Your Contest

How you design your contest can have a big impact on its success. How long will it run? Will you pick a random winner or have a photo contest that is judged? Will you ask people to invite their Friends to enter? Will you have an option to sign up for your newsletter?

One guiding principle for designing your contest is to make it fun. People enjoy the chance of winning something for free. Make it valuable for your audience and beneficial for you.

Also, you need to decide how to administer the contest according to Facebook's contest and promotional rules. The easiest way is to run your contest through a third-party application, which we cover in Chapter 3 of this minibook. The second option for running a contest is to consider designing the contest application yourself. You have more control over how your contest works if you design it yourself but you will have to code your contest on a separate website and then use an iFrame application to bring the website onto a tab on your Facebook Page. (See Book V, Chapter 2 for more information about creating applications.)

You have several issues to consider when designing your contest:

- **Type of contest:** It can be a sweepstakes in which the winner is drawn at random or a contest in which people vote for the winner.
- **Requirements for entry:** Will you have users upload a photo or video, send a short essay about why they should win, like your Page as part of the requirements, or just enter their name and e-mail address? The possibilities are endless. If you make the contest too difficult, you may not get as many entrants. Make sure that you make the contest fun, and you'll have a better chance of having people spread the word about it.

  TIP: If you intend to have people upload content, it can be more entertaining to have the winner picked by a community vote. This method gives people a reason to come back and check on the progress of their picks.
- **Prizes:** Although it helps to have a big budget so you offer something like a seven-night beach getaway (as offered by Sanders Beach Rentals in Figure 2-1), you can still offer something valuable to your community even if you own a small business. Spend some time considering the prize, and maybe even poll your audience members to see what they'd like.

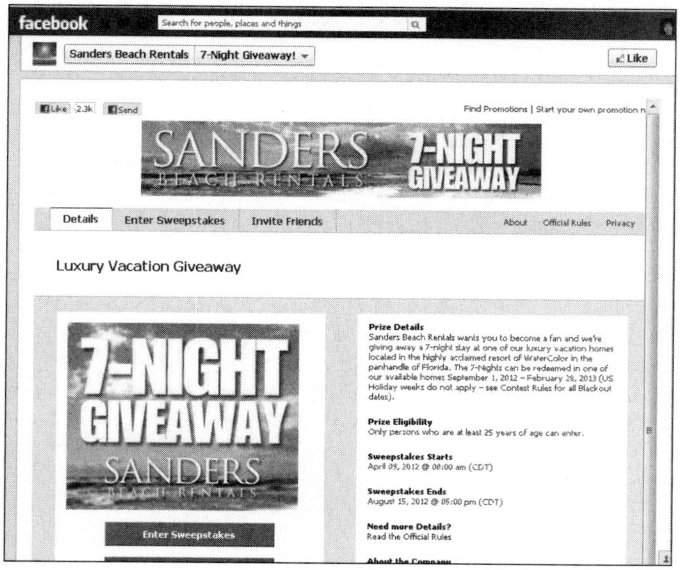

Figure 2-1: Sanders Beach Rentals offers an enticing prize to contest entrants.

- **Length of contest:** How long will your contest run? If it requires voting, how long will the voting period be? Will you have a judging period to narrow the entrants and then allow people to vote on the ones you selected? Many places recommend a one-month contest period to allow time for word of mouth to spread. This period is definitely appropriate if you have photo or video requirements for entry. A sweepstakes can be shorter if necessary. You have to factor in how much time you want to allow for promotion. If you are running the contest for a month, you need to promote it heavily for a month, so factor this requirement into your marketing schedule.

Facebook has strict rules about contests. The biggest rule is that contests and promotions may not be administered through Facebook unless they're administered through an application. You can build the application yourself or use a third-party application designed specifically for contests and sweepstakes (Wildfire, Votigo, and so on). You can't collect entries, conduct a drawing, or notify winners through any Facebook function other than an app. For more information, see the section "Understanding Facebook and legal restrictions," later in this chapter.

Choosing a contest type

You can run two main types of contests: a true contest in which there's some vote to choose the winner (or you choose the winner through judging) or a sweepstakes in which the winner is chosen at random.

You can set up your entry mechanism for your contest in a variety of ways. One way is to have entrants upload pictures for your community to judge. Realtor.com, for example, ran a holiday-lights picture contest that involved having people upload pictures of their houses decorated with holiday lights. The Facebook community voted on the pictures, and the winner won a $100 gift card. In another contest, a coaching professional had people write a short statement about why they wanted to come to her weekend retreat. She judged the entries herself and picked the winner of a free registration to the retreat. Just remember that you have to use the contest application as the place where people will upload their pictures, enter their essays, and actually enter your contest.

Sweepstakes are prevalent on Facebook. The barrier to entry is low, because to access the entry form people typically just have to enter their name and e-mail address, and/or like the Page. Because no judging is involved, the winner is chosen at random. Some third-party applications, such as Wildfire, can assist you in choosing a random winner.

Whether to choose a contest or a sweepstakes depends on your goals. Typically, contests are better for engaging your current community, and sweepstakes are better for growing your community. If you use the Wildfire application to administer your contest or sweepstakes, you can also choose to give away coupons. The following sections offer some considerations for choosing a contest, sweepstakes, or a coupon/giveaway for your product or service.

Contests

A contest increases your community involvement by having users vote and may drive more of the entrants' Friends to your Page. If the entry requirements are too complicated, however, you may not get the turnout you hope for.

Sweepstakes

A sweepstakes is better than a contest for growing your Facebook community or e-mail list. In a typical sweepstakes, entrants provide their names and e-mail addresses, and possibly like the Page, to access the entry form, and these things are very easy for most people to do. Because of the ease of entry, you may get more participation but possibly not as many people sharing word about the contest with their Friends.

TIP

Some people who enter your sweepstakes are interested only in the prize, not in your company. If you can connect the prize with your business, you have a better chance of connecting with the right audience.

Coupons or giveaways

Depending on which contest application you use, you can run a coupon or giveaway promotion. Figure 2-2 shows a coupon promotion created with the Wildfire application. You can also find these promotions in the Promotions application at `http://apps.facebook.com/promotionshq` (which is run by Wildfire). Other applications such as Woobox also support coupons. You add the application to your Page to administer the coupons. Chapter 3 of this minibook covers the various applications that provide both coupons and contests.

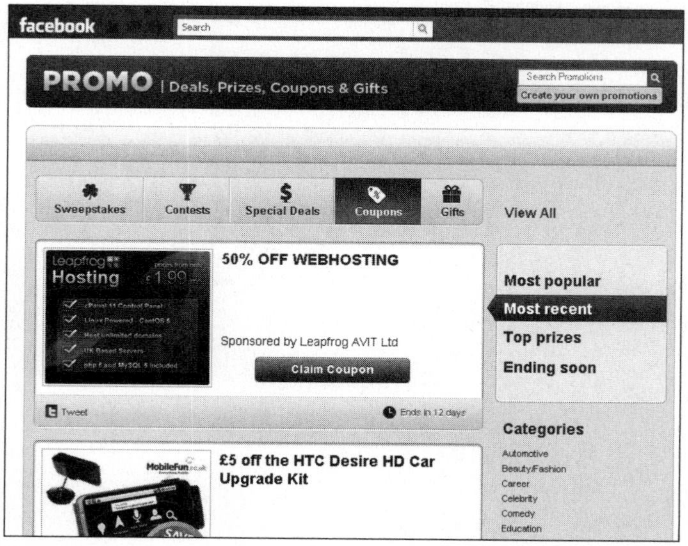

Figure 2-2: All the Wildfire coupons and promotions appear in the Contest/ Sweepstakes area within Facebook.

A coupon or a giveaway is great for attracting attention to your product, building brand awareness, or launching a product. Coupons and giveaways in Facebook are easy to share with Friends, and people love to get special deals.

If you're using an application to run a coupon, make sure you are still promoting that coupon in as many places as you can, just like you would your contest or sweepstakes. CityWide Sewer and Drain, for example, is promoting its coupon for $25 off on its Facebook Page (see Figure 2-3) and on its website (see Figure 2-4).

Figure 2-3: CityWide promotes its coupon that is available on Facebook on its website.

Coupons are nice features, but you may want to consider Facebook check-in deals and Facebook offers as well. Both of these options are free to set up.

See Book VII, Chapter 4 for more information about Facebook Deals and Book VII, Chapter 1 for more information about Facebook Offers.

Figure 2-4: CityWide promotes the coupon on its website and drives traffic to its Facebook Page.

Reaping the benefits of a well-run contest

Before you put your contest out there, make sure that you have everything in place to kick it off with a bang. You may be spending money on the contest application, and you want to make sure that you're getting the maximum benefit. You also want to make sure that the contest is well thought out so that you don't get negative results. The following sections describe some of the good and bad consequences of running a contest.

Benefits

Following are some of the benefits of running a contest:

- **Increased traffic to your Facebook Page:** If you're promoting your contest well and encouraging people to enter via an app on your Page, you'll have increased traffic. Make sure that you set up the marketing schedule so that you promote consistently throughout the contest.
- **Reward for your community:** A contest can reward some of the members of your community and keep them interested in your Page.
- **Increased participation:** By opting in to your contest, your community members are participating more, which encourages more participation in the future, especially if you're having a true contest in which people vote.
- **More likes:** We hope that you're requiring people to like your Page when you run your contest. Just remember that people also have to officially enter within your contest application.

- **More newsletter subscribers:** Not everyone is reading your updates on Facebook all the time (shocking, we know). E-mail is still a great method of communication when you really need to get the word out about something in your business.
- **Buzz:** Well-run contests can generate buzz and get people excited about your product or brand.

Disadvantages

Some of the disadvantages of running a contest are as follows:

- **Investment of time:** Promoting and marketing your contest can take time. Good promotion can take a lot of time, possibly taking time away from your core business. Make sure to plan your contest during a time when you won't be caught trying to do too much at once.
- **Investment of money:** Your contest may cost money to run; the prize also may cost money. Depending on how nice the prize is, you could spend a lot of money. If you don't receive the benefits you were hoping for, such as a large group of new likers, giving out that prize can feel painful. Again, planning and promotion can help you get the benefits you're looking for.
- **Possible community dissatisfaction:** Some people just don't like contests. If judging is involved, people may get angry if they feel that the judging wasn't done properly, and this situation can create some bad buzz around your brand. Others don't like contests that involve voting because it can cause continual updates of people begging for votes.

  One way to combat this potential dissatisfaction may be to think of a special gift for everyone who enters. That gift doesn't have to cost much money. It could be a special e-book or discount given only to contest entrants. Even just a personal note thanking people for entering and for their participation can go a long way to fostering good feelings about your contest.

  TIP

  You can also think about retaining some of the judging rights so that your contest winner isn't based on votes alone. Retaining some of the judging rights also gives you some control over the best candidate when the voting is close.

How will you be able to ensure that your contest is successful? The key is the system you have in place to handle the entries and marketing: the third-party application or the application you design yourself.

The nice thing about third-party applications is that they handle entries, voting, rule posting, and winner selection within Facebook guidelines. The applications make it easy to run a professional, well-designed contest.

TIP

Polling your audience for ideas

Sometimes, you may not be sure what prize you want to offer or what would get the most response from your community. The best way to overcome this obstacle is to ask your users. You can create a poll or survey easily at sites like SurveyMonkey (`www.surveymonkey.com`) and Zoomerang (`www.zoomerang.com`). You can use the Question tool in the Facebook Publisher to create a poll for your Page. You can ask, "What prize would you like to receive if I held a Facebook contest?" and then add prize options that people can vote on. See Book III, Chapter 1 for more about creating a poll for your Page.

You may be deciding among two or three prizes, and involving your audience in the decision builds more about for the prize and also builds more buzz around the contest. If you don't have any ideas, your audience can help suggest things, but you may not get a consensus.

Understanding Facebook and legal restrictions

You should definitely understand Facebook's promotion guidelines before starting your contest. You may indeed see other people violating the terms, but Facebook does state that it can remove materials relating to the promotion or even disable the offender's Page or account, so it pays to follow the rules!

The biggest rule that you should follow is to not administer any promotion through Facebook except through an application. You can use a third-party application designed to administer contests (such as Wildfire or Votigo), or you can program an application yourself to collect entries — a more-complicated process.

What does it mean to not administer a promotion through Facebook except through an application? It means that you can't collect entries, conduct a drawing, or notify winners through Facebook directly; the notifications have to be done though a different tab on your Facebook Page. Also, you can't do any of the following things:

- Put a post on your Timeline that says "Everyone who responds to this post is entered to win a gift card."
- Have people upload a photo to your Timeline to be entered in a contest.
- Announce the winner of your contest with a post on your Timeline.
- Automatically enter in a drawing anyone who likes your Page. (You can have liking a Page be a condition of entry, but it can't be the only way that people can enter the contest.)

You can promote a contest that's being held on your website through Facebook, but the administration of the contest can't take place in the Facebook Timeline.

Here are some legal restrictions that you need to be aware of:

- ✦ The promotion can't be open to anyone under the age of 18. Facebook does have people under the age of 18 on its site, however, and 13 is the minimum age.
- ✦ If you set up a sweepstakes, because of legal restrictions, that contest can't be open to people in Belgium, Norway, Sweden, or India.
- ✦ You can't award as prizes or promote the following items: gambling, tobacco, firearms, prescription drugs, and gasoline.

Again, the nice thing about the third-party applications such as Wildfire and Votigo is that they're set up to follow Facebook's guidelines. For the full set of guidelines, go to `www.facebook.com/promotions_guidelines.php`.

Defining Success

Before you start your contest, make sure that you know what you're aiming for so that later, you'll know whether you were successful. How many entries, new web hits, and/or mentions of your brand are you hoping for? If you fall short of your goals, you can analyze what you could have changed in the promotion or execution of your contest. We cover the analysis in Chapter 4 of this minibook.

Setting targets

How do you set reasonable targets for entries to your contest? Setting targets can be a bit of a challenge if you've never hosted a contest before. You may look at your first contest as a training ground for future contests (and yes, it's a good idea to do multiple contests!).

The number of entries depends on several factors:

- ✦ **Size of your Facebook community:** If you're starting your contest with 25 people who like your Page, a target of 12 entries from your Facebook Page may be reasonable.
- ✦ **Size of your e-mail list:** If you have an e-mail list of 500 addresses and an open rate of 50 percent, you might estimate that of those who open your e-mail, 10 percent will enter, representing 25 entries from your e-mail list.
- ✦ **Other social-media lists (Twitter, LinkedIn, forums, and so on):** You also want to promote your contest on Twitter, LinkedIn, and other places that you frequent online, but the entry rate from these sites may be lower still. You probably can estimate that 1 percent of your Twitter

following and your LinkedIn connections will enter, depending on how engaged you are with these connections.

- **Website hits:** If you have your contest listed prominently on your website, you can estimate that some of your website visitors will enter your contest. Entries may be fairly low — possibly around 0.5 percent of your website traffic.
- **Size of the prize:** You get a higher opt-in for a bigger prize.
- **Length of the contest:** The longer the contest goes, the more time people have to opt in, but don't make the contest run for so long so that people get tired of hearing about it. One month is a good time frame (less for sweepstakes).
- **Other promotional efforts:** These efforts could involve guest posting on another blog to promote your contest, advertising your contest, or distributing flyers about your contest in your local community.

TIP

You may want to set a conservative goal of 5 percent opt-in for your e-mail and Facebook community, and smaller percentages for other places that you participate on the web. Then take a look at that number and see whether it's a worthwhile number for the money and the time you'll be spending.

Goodwill and buzz are hard to measure and hard to put a price on.

Setting your plan

After you set your targets, set your promotion and marketing plan for your contest. Make sure to get the word out on all channels to engage your audience. Here are places to market your contest:

- **Blog or website:** If you have a blog, make sure that you have a blog entry ready to go when your contest kicks off. If you have a website, make sure that you have a link or banner that visitors can click to enter the contest.
- **Facebook Page:** Obviously, you'll be posting about the contest on your Facebook Page because it's easy for your community members to enter on Facebook. Make sure you provide the URL to the contest App tab on your Facebook Page so that people can easily click over to enter. Remember that people are seeing your updates in their News Feeds and without the URL, they won't know where to enter.
- **E-mail subscribers:** To get buzz about your contest going, start with your current customers. Let them know how they can enter, and ask them to spread the word.
- **Twitter and other social media:** If you're on Twitter, make sure that you tweet the link to your contest daily. Send a message to your LinkedIn connections, if appropriate.

✦ **Facebook Ads:** Facebook Ads (see an example in Figure 2-5) are natural places to get people to enter your contest. You can target your demographic in the setup of the ad and send users directly to the link on your Facebook Page that has the entry form to your contest.

Figure 2-5: Ad for winning a shopping spree in Denver.

You also need to have your measurement plan in place. Another nice thing about third-party Facebook applications is that they do extensive analytics of the entries. The analytics the applications provide vary from app to app and Figure 2-6 shows an example of what these analytics can look like.

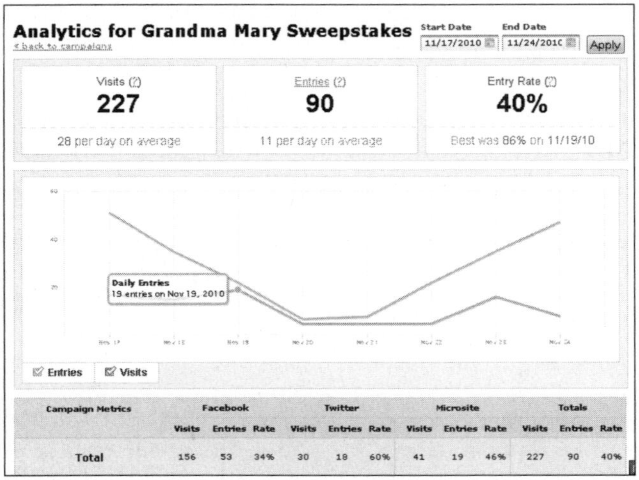

Figure 2-6: A snapshot of the analytics on Wildfire.

We discuss analyzing your contest results in Chapter 4 of this minibook. Make sure that you have Google Analytics on your site so that you're tracking clicks to your contest entry form.

When your plan is in place, you're ready to set up your contest, which we cover in Chapter 3 of this minibook. Remember to keep it fun and exciting so that your community will help spread the word about your contest and make it go viral.

Chapter 3: Using Third-Party Contest Applications

In This Chapter

- **Browsing contest applications**
- **Selecting the right application for you**
- **Setting up the application within your Page**

The easiest way to manage your Facebook contest is to use a third-party contest application. Applications of this type are designed to work within Facebook's contest guidelines, so they make getting started a snap. They give your contest a professional look, and in many cases they include analytics features so that you can analyze your results.

As with other Facebook applications, you have to go through a few steps to add a contest application to your Page, and most of these applications aren't free. Luckily, they're very affordable, and they offer a lot of nice features to help you facilitate a well-run contest.

In this chapter, we look at how to find those often-elusive third-party applications, how to set them up, and how to notify the winners and deliver your prizes.

Finding a Contest Application

Finding contest applications in Facebook can be challenging. The Facebook search function for these apps doesn't always find all the apps that are available, and more contest applications are being added as we write. It can also be challenging to figure out how to add contest applications to your Facebook Page. In most cases, it's best to go directly to the website of the third-party application for directions on adding the app to your Page.

Four of the applications that we cover in this chapter — Wildfire, Woobox, North Social, and Offerpop — are self-service applications, which means that you can set them up from start to finish on your own. We look at the steps for setting them up later in this chapter.

The other self-service contest applications are also fairly straightforward to set up. Some contest applications require you to contact the vendor to get pricing and other information, and typically are better for large campaigns.

Each application has its pluses and minuses, and you should opt for the one that fits your needs. If you're running a large campaign, get quotes, look at the third-party application's past performance, and ask for referrals. Whichever third-party application you use, be ready with all your other promotional efforts, and take some time to analyze your results. We cover both of these aspects of your contest in detail in Chapter 4 of this minibook.

Comparing contest applications on the web

If you'd like to compare your contest-application options, here are some of the current third-party Facebook contest developers:

- **Wildfire:** Wildfire (at `www.wildfireapp.com`) is one of the most popular contest applications. It's an easy-to-use, self-service application that you can set up yourself, and it doesn't cost too much to use.
- **North Social:** North Social (go to `http://northsocial.com`) has a sweepstakes application but not a contest application. North Social bundles all its Facebook apps for one monthly fee. Like Wildfire, it's a self-service application.
- **Woobox:** Woobox (at `www.woobox.com`) is similar to North Social in that it's a self-service application with a sweepstakes option, but it doesn't have a contest option, and all its apps are bundled for one monthly fee.
- **Offerpop:** Offerpop has a suite of 19 different Facebook and Twitter applications to help engage your audience. It's easy to use and customize. Offerpop (at `www.offerpop.com`) is free for Pages with fewer than 100 likes.
- **Votigo:** In the past, Votigo (at `www.votigo.com`) was a full-service application that focused on large brands such as Kohl's and MAC Cosmetics. Now it offers a self-service contest option. If you want to use the custom contest application, you need to go to the Votigo website for prices and details.
- **Fan Appz:** Fan Appz has only a sweepstakes option, and you can't set it up yourself. You have to contact Fan Appz (at `http://fanappz.com`) to get it set up.
- **Strutta:** Strutta (available at `www.strutta.com`) has a very nice photo, video, and text contest application that you can set up yourself. It recently introduced a basic application suite called Mighty Apps that includes coupons, polls, and other tools.
- **ShortStack:** ShortStack has a drag-and-drop sweepstakes form that you can set up yourself for a customized look. ShortStack is free for pages under 2,000 likes and available at `www.shortstack.com`.
- **Easypromos:** Easypromos (at `www.easypromosapp.com`) has a very inexpensive basic version ($15 per promotion) to help you get started with contests or sweepstakes. If you need more features, you can use the premium version ($100 per promotion).

A contest involves some type of voting or judging. A sweepstakes selects the winner at random from all the entries. See Chapter 2 of this minibook for more details on contests and sweepstakes.

Because so many contest apps are available, we can't address all the steps for setting up the apps. Also, if you're using a custom app, the company that offers the app can help you get started. In fact, if you run into trouble with any of the apps, most companies have a very good help department for troubleshooting your problem.

Many of these sites have examples of contests that companies have administered or video tutorials. These tutorials are helpful for showing how the contest applications work and can be good places to start when you're deciding which application to use.

Searching for contest applications within Facebook

Instead of going to a contest application that you already know about directly, you can try to search for a new one. New apps are added to Facebook all the time, and a more recent contest app might work well for you.

The Facebook search feature doesn't always list the proper applications clearly, which can be confusing. When you enter *contest* in the Facebook Search tool, at `www.facebook.com/search`, you may find applications for contests that have been developed for a specific use, as well as applications designed for general use. Filtering your search results by Apps (click the Apps link on the left sidebar after you search for a term) can be helpful, but again, not always accurate as to what apps are for general use.

If you do search for *contest* in Facebook, you'll find the several options, shown in Figure 3-1.

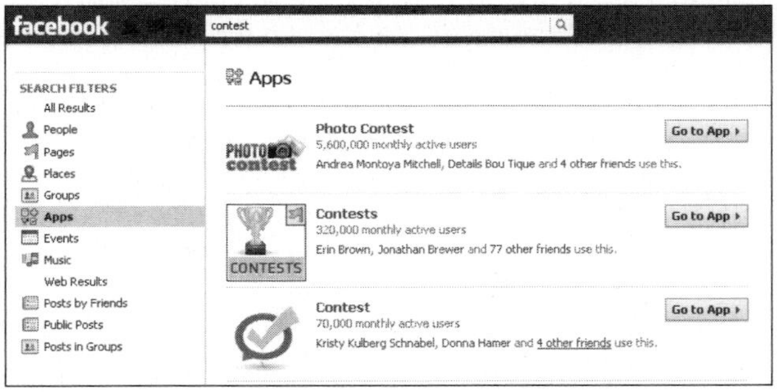

Figure 3-1: Contest applications found in Facebook Search.

Likewise, if you search for *sweepstakes,* you'll find several Sweepstakes applications (shown in Figure 3-2) — but only if you leave the results as All Results, rather than filtering by Apps (to filter a search, click on the Apps field on the left sidebar). As we mention earlier, the Facebook Search feature can be flaky.

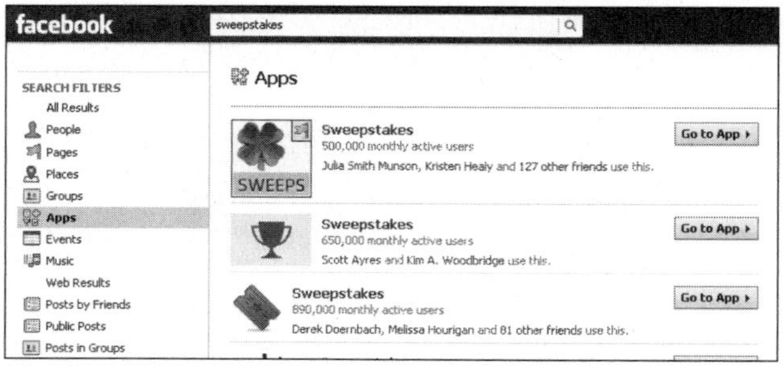

Figure 3-2: Sweepstakes applications found using Facebook Search.

Installing and using the applications can vary from one application to another. You can install some applications, such as Wildfire, from within Facebook. Other applications, such as North Social, direct you to their websites for full installation instructions.

TIP

Appbistro (`http://appbistro.com`) is a third-party Facebook application search tool that can show you different contest applications. This tool may come in handy, as new applications are being added to Facebook every day.

Getting to Know the Contest Applications

In this section, we cover some of the contest applications that you can install and set up yourself: Wildfire, North Social, Woobox, and Offerpop. We don't cover some of the other apps that you can set up yourself because some of them have more variables as you design your contest.

All of these four applications also include the fan-gate feature where you can display an image telling a visitor to like the Page in order to get access to your contest. Once she likes the Page, the contest entry form is revealed. This is a great feature that ensures that only fans of your Page enter your contest. Using the fan-gate feature is optional if you want to allow anyone to be able to enter your contest.

Exploring Wildfire

Wildfire, one of the most widely used contest and sweepstakes applications, is a self-service application that you can easily set up on your own.

Wildfire has the advantage of having an integrated place to enter many contests and sweepstakes from within Facebook. That site is not always easy to find, but it may cause some people who wouldn't have seen your contest otherwise to stumble across it and enter. Figure 3-3 shows the page where people can browse contests run by Wildfire: `http://apps.facebook.com/sweepstakeshq`. As shown in the figure, users can browse by category, popularity, start date, prizes, or end date.

Figure 3-3: Listing of all the contests run by Wildfire.

A Wildfire campaign starts at $5 per campaign, with a $0.99 daily fee for basic campaigns and $250 per campaign with a $4.99 daily fee for premium campaigns.

Looking at North Social

North Social also has a self-service sweepstakes application that's easy to set up. It doesn't have a contest application, but it does have many other Facebook Page applications that you can use for one monthly fee, in addition to the sweepstakes application, as shown in Figure 3-4. The other applications include exclusive coupon offers, a newsletter sign-up offer, an RSS feed, and more.

North Social requires you to use an image file, which you need to create. The image file serves as the graphic for your contest on your Facebook Page. You can easily create graphics with a simple program like Paint (for Windows PCs), but you may want to hire a graphic designer if you want professional-looking graphics and can't create them yourself.

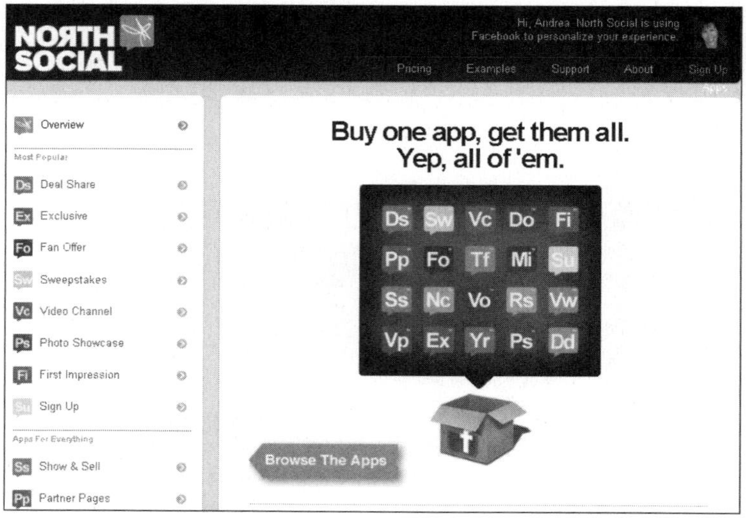

Figure 3-4: North Social and the available apps.

North Social prices by the month and by how many people like your Page. One benefit is that you get access to all the applications, but you may not want to get locked into a monthly subscription cost indefinitely. A campaign for a Page with fewer than 1,000 likers costs only $20 per month (with a two-week trial).

Investigating Woobox

Woobox has a monthly subscription fee that allows you to access all its applications. Currently, it offers four free apps: Pinterest, Twitter, Coupons, and Static HTML Fangate Tab. (The Coupon and Static HTML Fangate Tab apps have additional features if you have a paid subscription.) You can use the Static HTML Fangate Tab application to create custom tabs (which we cover in more depth in Book V, Chapter 2).

Woobox also has apps such as Sweepstakes, Photo Contests, Polls, Rewards, Instant Wins, and Group Deals; you can access these apps through the $29-per-month subscription service. Woobox has some nice features, such as giving people extra entries in the contest if they get a friend to enter.

Understanding Offerpop

Offerpop also has many apps that you can access with a monthly subscription. A nice feature is that you can pay by the campaign or pay a monthly subscription fee if you want ongoing access to all the apps, and if you have fewer than 100 fans, your campaign is free. Offerpop charges according to how many fans you have.

Offerpop has good statistics, such as how many new fans you acquired and how many conversions you had from people who viewed your contest.

Delivering the Prizes

When you're exploring contest apps, you may want to know how the winners are selected and notified. Facebook rules prevent you from notifying the winner on your Page. The Wildfire and North Social apps can help with randomly selecting the winner. With Woobox and Offerpop, you have to download the entries and select one randomly, and we show you the best way to do that in the Woobox section later in this chapter.

If you're using Wildfire to run a contest that incorporates voting, the Wildfire application keeps track of the votes. You can notify the winners in an e-mail that's generated by Wildfire, as shown in Figure 3-5. (This e-mail is generated for both the contest and sweepstakes applications.)

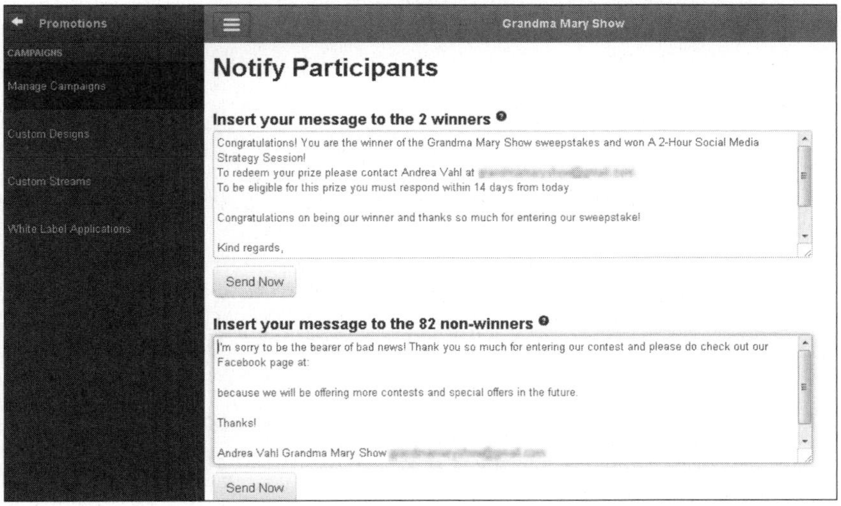

Figure 3-5: Send notifications to the winners and losers of your contest within Wildfire.

TIP

If you have to mail the prize to the winner, make sure that you mention in your rules that you need a proper mailing address. State that if you can't contact the winner to get a deliverable address, a new winner will be selected.

You also may want to give a time frame in which the winner has to respond to the announcement and claim the prize. Give the winner at least three days to respond, with a maximum of one week. That way, the contest won't be too old, and you can still generate some excitement if a new winner must be selected.

Keeping to a Budget

As you set up your parameters, you can see exactly how much the campaign will cost before you start. You can pay for the campaign up front, so there shouldn't be any danger of going over your budget after you commit to the contest.

Wildfire charges you according to the length of the contest or sweepstakes and what features you require. North Social and Woobox operate through a monthly subscription fee. With Offerpop, you pay a one-time fee or a monthly fee, depending on which version you choose.

Your prize will likely be the most expensive part of the contest campaign — and in general, the bigger the prize, the better the response.

Designing Your Contest with the Wildfire Application

You can start designing your contest or sweepstakes with the Wildfire application either within Facebook or on the Wildfire website. As you design your contest, your progress is saved automatically, so you don't have to do the work all at once.

If you're going to have a special tab on your Facebook Page for your contest, you have to add the Wildfire application to your Page before the contest is actually published to your Page. Also note that Wildfire may have some special hints for you along the way, as a first-time user of Wildfire, that don't appear in these figures. You can choose to hide these hints or read more about them in the links that are shown within the hint. In this example, the Sweepstakes option has been chosen. If you choose one of the other options, your screens may have variations.

Adding the Wildfire app to your Page

The easiest way to sign up with Wildfire is to go to `www.wildfireapp.com` and then follow these steps:

1. **Click the Login button in the top-right corner of the home page.**
2. **In the page that appears, click the Sign Up for an Account link.**

   The sign-up form appears.
3. **Enter your first and last name, company name, e-mail address, and password.**
4. **Click Like to like Wildfire on Facebook.**

5. **Select the Agree to Terms check box.**

   You can review the terms first by clicking the terms-of-service link, if you want.

6. **Click the Create Account button.**

   You're taken to the Wildfire dashboard, as shown in Figure 3-6.

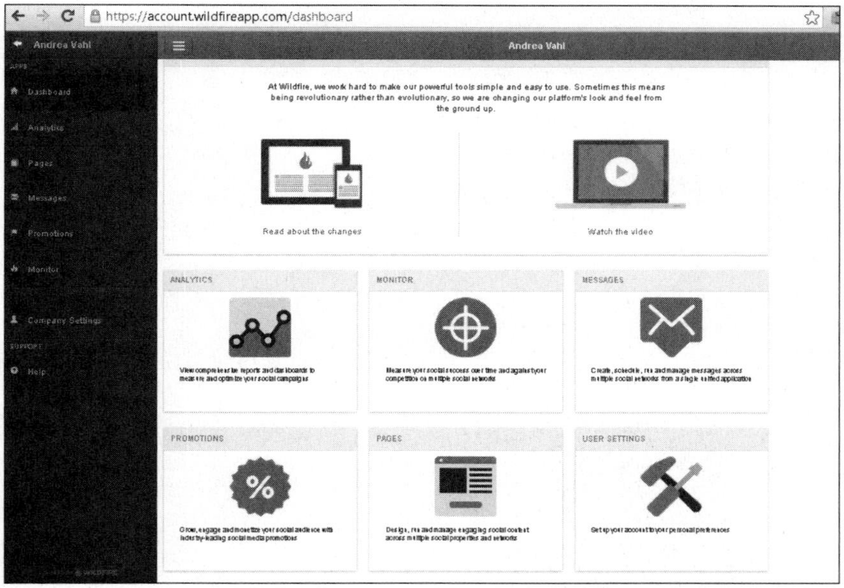

Figure 3-6: After signing up, you see the Wildfire dashboard.

7. **Click the Promotions link on the left sidebar (refer to Figure 3-6), or click the Promotions icon in the lower-left corner.**

   You see a screen that has a list of your promotions if you have created any in the past. Since this is your first campaign, you don't have any listed.

8. **Click the Create a Campaign button.**

   A pop-up window appears, as shown in Figure 3-7.

9. **Select the type of campaign that you want to run.**

   You're taken to the Campaign Details screen, as shown in Figure 3-8. We chose the Sweepstakes option as an example. Wherever you see a question mark in a black circle, you can mouse over the question mark to get more details about what you should enter in that field.

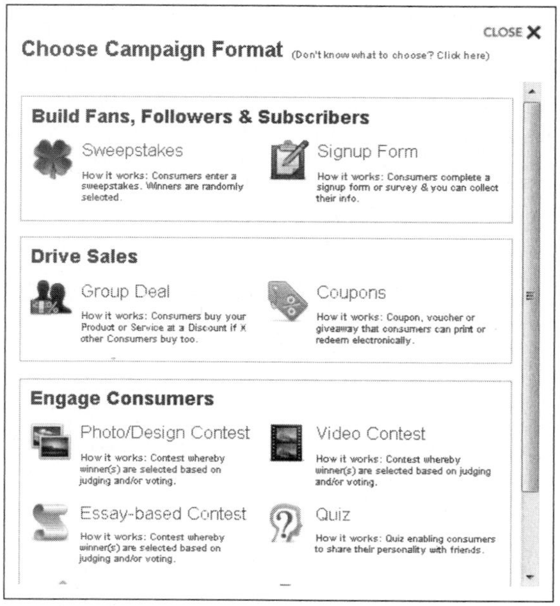

Figure 3-7: Choose which type of campaign to run.

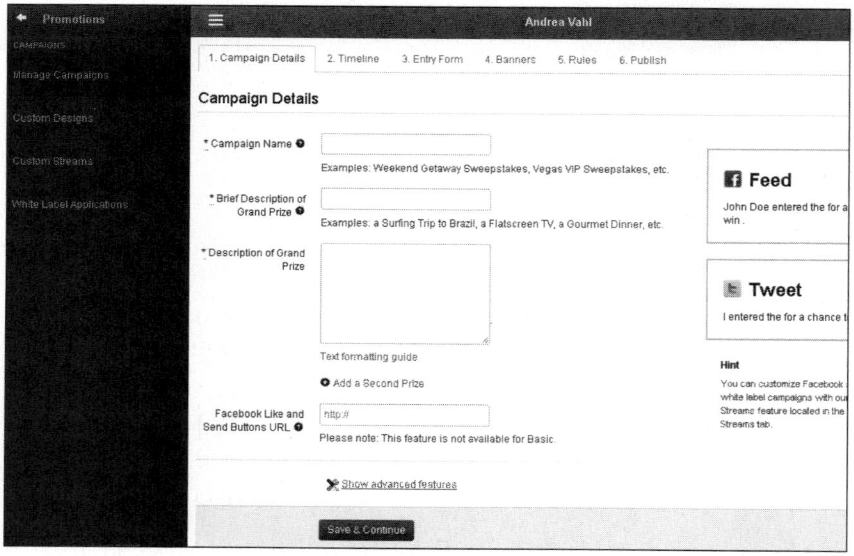

Figure 3-8: Enter the Sweepstakes Campaign Details.

10. **Fill out the details of your campaign, as shown in Figure 3-8, including the campaign name and brief and long descriptions of the grand prize.**

11. (Optional) Click the Text Formatting Guide hyperlink to use boldface text or a big header.

12. (Optional) Add a second prize by clicking the Add a Second Prize link.

13. (Optional) Click the Show Advanced Features link to give your prize a dollar value and place it in a category.

These categories allow people to browse the Wildfire promotions.

14. After you fill out the campaign details, click the Save & Continue button at the bottom of the form.

This step takes you to the Campaign Timeline section (see Figure 3-9).

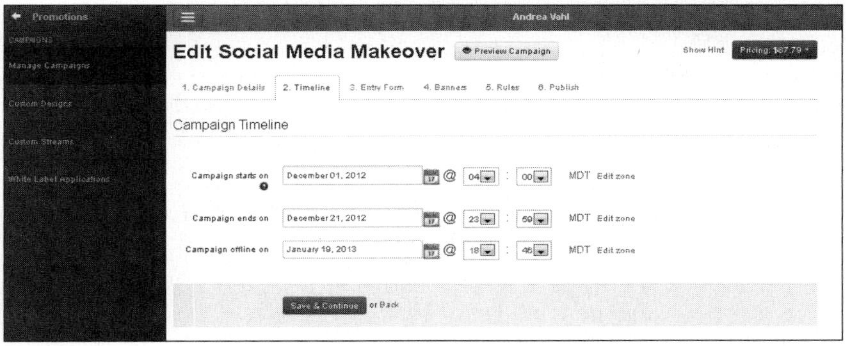

Figure 3-9: Choose your timeline.

15. Choose how long you want the contest to run and then click the Save & Continue button at the bottom of the form.

Chapter 2 of this minibook provides suggestions on how long you should run the various types of contests.

In the Key Features section at the top of this page (refer to Figure 3-9), you can choose what type of campaign you want to run. We recommend choosing the Standard Campaign option because it allows you to export the data from your campaign for analysis.

After clicking Save & Continue, you're taken to the Entry Form tab, shown in Figure 3-10.

16. Choose what information you need from the participants by dragging an item on the left to the blank fields on the right.

You can also choose to have entrants opt in to your e-mail newsletter, an option that's available only for standard-level campaigns and higher. Also notice that you can customize the message that people see after they enter the contest by clicking on the Page 2: Invite Friends button at the top of the form shown in Figure 3-10.

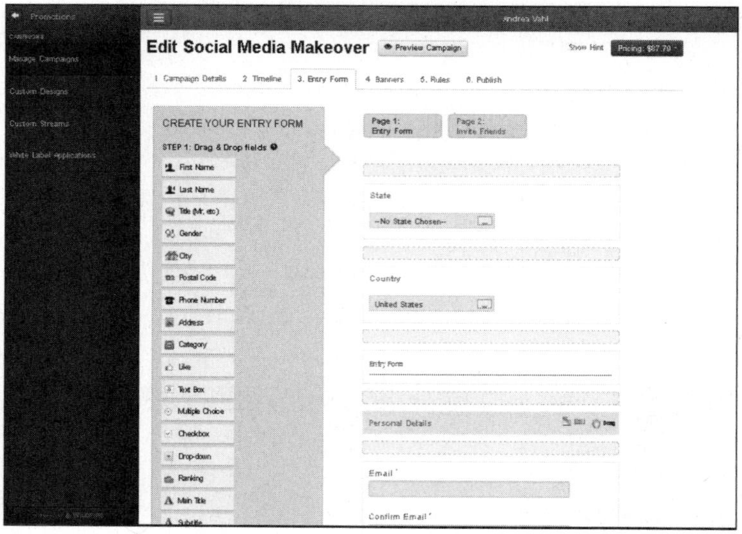

Figure 3-10: Decide what information you need on the entry form.

17. **Select the Age of the eligible participants from the drop-down menu in Step 2 of the Entry Form Page.**

    You may have to scroll down to see Step 2. You can select an age range or a minimum age for entry.

18. **Select the Country of the eligible participants from the drop-down menu in Step 2 of the Entry Form Page.**

    Once you select the country, you can also restrict the location of the eligible entrants by state or province if you would like your campaign to be for local participants only. You can add several states/provinces by clicking the + button that appears after you have selected one state.

    TIP: If you have a white label campaign, you can also select to collect demographic data of your participants in Step 3 on the Entry Form page. This requires permissions from your participants. If you don't have a white label campaign, skip Step 3 on the form.

19. **(Optional) Add a URL address to the URL Redirect field in Step 4 of the Entry Form page.**

    This will send the participant to the URL specified after they have entered. This is optional and you may not want to redirect people unless you have something special to offer them on your site.

20. **Click the Save & Continue button at the bottom of the form.**

    You're taken to the Banners section, where you can upload your banner, as shown in Figure 3-11.

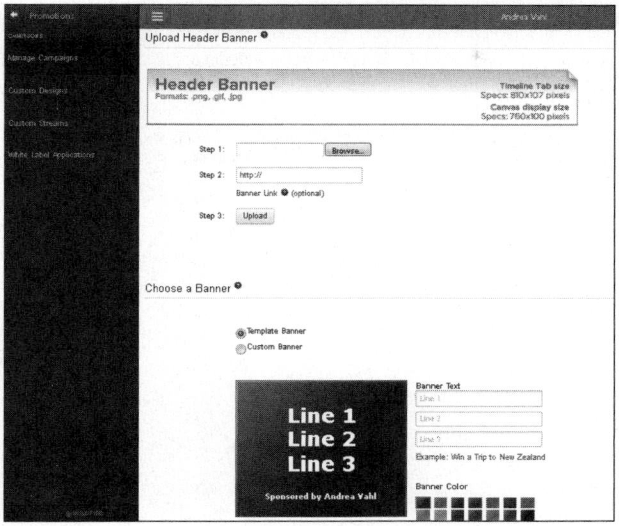

Figure 3-11: Upload your banner or use the template banner.

TIP

If you don't have a custom banner, don't worry; you don't have to have one. A custom banner can help personalize your campaign, however. The banner for the Timeline tab is 810 × 107 pixels. If you can use the banner from your website, it can help with your branding. Or you can use the template banner and add information about your contest. You can also add a 90 × 90–pixel feed banner that shows in the News Feeds of people who enter. Feed banners have been shown to help increase entries.

21. **Click the Save Banner button and then click the Continue button at the bottom of the screen.**

    The Rules tab appears.

22. **Enter the rules for your contest.**

    Make sure that you're following local sweepstakes and contest laws. Also be sure to enter the disclosure statement and privacy policy.

23. **Click Save & Continue at the bottom of the page.**

    A pop-up box appears to collect the payment for your campaign.

24. **Make sure the pricing is correct and click the Pay Now button to fill in your payment information.**
25. **Decide where to publish your contest.**
26. **Click Publish Now (next to the fan Page heading) as shown in Figure 3-12.**

    You're prompted to confirm that this campaign complies with the appropriate local and national laws and with Facebook's Promotions Guidelines.

27. **Check the box next to the confirmation and then click Publish.**

    The next page helps you add the campaign to your fan Page.

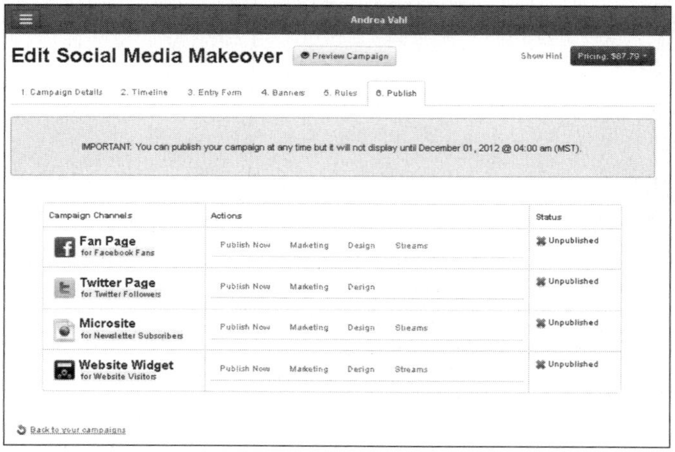

Figure 3-12: Connecting the Wildfire application with your Facebook Page.

28. **Click the Fan Page link to add the campaign to your fan Page.**

    In the screen that appears, a drop-down menu lets you select the fan Page where you want to add the sweepstakes. You can read the tutorial first, if you want. You must be logged in to Facebook as your personal Profile, but you select the Page where you want to add the sweepstakes.

29. **Select the Page to which you want to add the Sweepstakes application.**

30. **Click the blue Add Page Tab button.**

Connecting the contest to your app

You've added the application to your Page, but you're not quite done. You still have to connect the exact sweepstakes to your tab that is now showing on your Page. Luckily, Wildfire has a complete tutorial that appears after you complete the steps in the preceding section. To connect the contest to your app, follow these steps:

1. **In the Admin panel at the top of your Page, click Edit Page.**
2. **Choose Update Info from the drop-down menu.**

   Or you can choose Manage Permissions; either option works.

   You're taken to the Page dashboard.

3. **Select Apps on the right sidebar.**

   You see all the installed apps on your Facebook Page. Scroll down to the Sweepstakes app.

4. **Select Go to App below the description.**

   You see a screen asking for permission for the Sweepstakes app to publish on your Page.

5. **Click Allow.**

   You see a screen that prompts you to log in to your Wildfire account from Facebook, as shown in Figure 3-13.

Figure 3-13: Connecting the application with your Facebook Page.

6. **Enter the name and e-mail address that you use for your Wildfire account, and click Connect.**

   You see a screen with your active promotion listed.

7. **Click the gray Add to Fan Page button.**

Now you have your contest ready to go on your Page, and you need to have your promotional plan in place so that you'll get the maximum buzz! We go over promotional ideas and planning in Chapter 4 of this minibook.

You can set your Wildfire campaign to go live in the future so that you can get all your contest-promotion ideas rolling.

The sweepstakes is now showing in your Apps that appear under your Cover photo of your Page. Depending on how many apps you have there, you may want to change the order of the sweepstakes as soon as it's live so that it appears more prominently in your Timeline.

If possible, you should also change the App thumbnail photo to make it more eye-catching for your sweepstakes.

Using the North Social Application for Your Contest

North Social also has a sweepstakes application that you can set up on your own. You pay a monthly subscription fee based on how many people like your Page. North Social charges by the day and the fee is $0.99/day for a page up to 1000 Fans and goes up to $7.99/day for unlimited Fans at the highest tier. After you subscribe, you have access to all the applications that North Social offers, so if you can use multiple applications, North Social is worthwhile to keep. If you're going to use the sweepstakes application just one time, set up a reminder to cancel your subscription when you're done with your campaign.

To use North Social, you need two mandatory custom images: the Main image, which describes your sweepstakes, and the Thank You image, which is what people see after entering your sweepstakes. These two images must be 810 × 610 pixels.

You can also have a Landing image, which you can use to have fan-only entry to your sweepstakes. This image lets people know that there's a sweepstakes and they have to click Like to enter. The Landing image must be 810 × 610 pixels.

Finally, you can display an optional Thumbnail image next to your sweepstakes description if people share the sweepstakes on their Timeline. This image gives your contest better branding and helps you look more professional. The Thumbnail image must be 64 × 64 pixels.

The necessity for custom image files could be a barrier for some people who might consider using this application. If you don't have the ability to create professional images for your contest within your company, you can consider hiring a designer to create them for you. People who create graphics charge a wide range of prices. You can hire a graphics designer at sites such as `www.odesk.com` and `www.elance.com`.

The benefit of having custom graphics for your sweepstakes is that you have a very professional sweepstakes entry page. Figure 3-14 shows an example North Social sweepstakes on a Facebook Page.

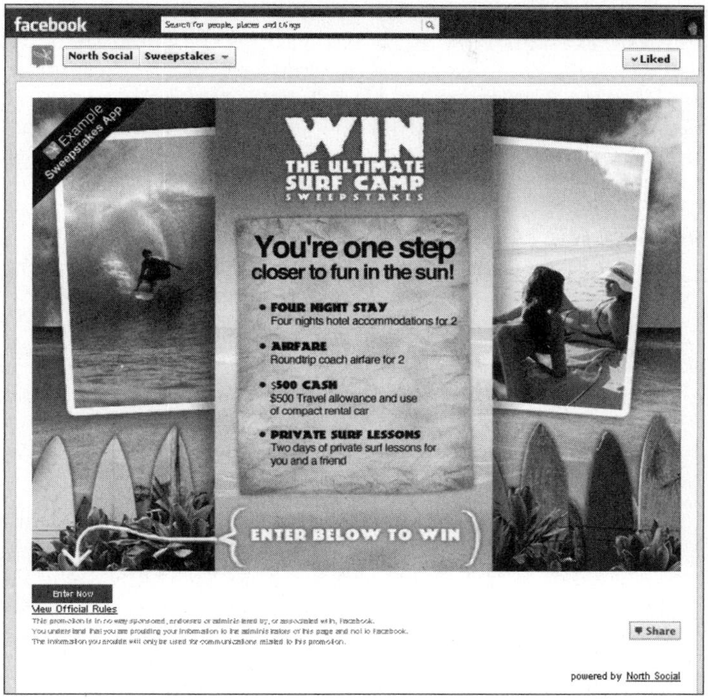

Figure 3-14: A North Social example sweepstakes.

You also need to sign up for an account with North Contact, which is North Social's list-management and form-creation tool. North Contact forms allow you to collect the names and e-mail addresses associated with the entries into your sweepstakes. Before you get started setting up the Sweepstakes application, make sure that you apply for a North Contact account at `www.northcontact.com`. The account is free, but it takes 24–48 hours to get your North Contact login details, so make sure that you allow time for this information to be sent to you.

North Social has a good video tutorial on setting up your campaign and adding the North Contact form to your sweepstakes. You can watch the tutorial here: `http://northsocial.com/apps/sweepstakes`.

Using the Woobox Sweepstakes Application

Woobox has some useful sweepstakes features. The application is easy to set up and has a fan-only graphics page built in, or you can create one yourself to customize your campaign. Woobox is $29/month to use, and you unlock all of the Apps they have available with your subscription.

You can give people extra chances to win if they share your sweepstakes with their Facebook Friends, which can give people an incentive to spread the news about your sweepstakes. One downside of Woobox is that you don't have much space in the Description area to talk about your sweepstakes, but you can use custom images to convey more information about your sweepstakes.

Signing up for Woobox

To get started using the Sweepstakes application, first go to the Woobox website at `www.woobox.com`. Then follow these steps:

1. **Click the red Try It Now button.**

   You're taken to Facebook to connect the app. You may have to switch to your personal Profile. Again, don't worry about authorizing the app from your personal Profile, because you get to choose which Page the app will be connected to.

   You may notice that the app has already selected who can see it, as shown in Figure 3-15. Make sure the App posts are visible to either Everyone or at minimum Friends rather than Only Me in the drop-down box shown.

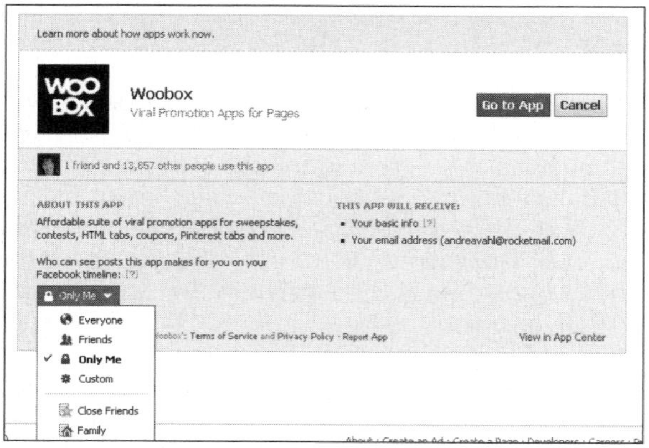

Figure 3-15: Connecting the Woobox application to your profile.

2. **Click the blue Go to App button.**
3. **On the next page, click Allow.**

   You're taken to the Woobox dashboard, where you can manage your free Woobox apps and your paid apps, as shown in Figure 3-16.

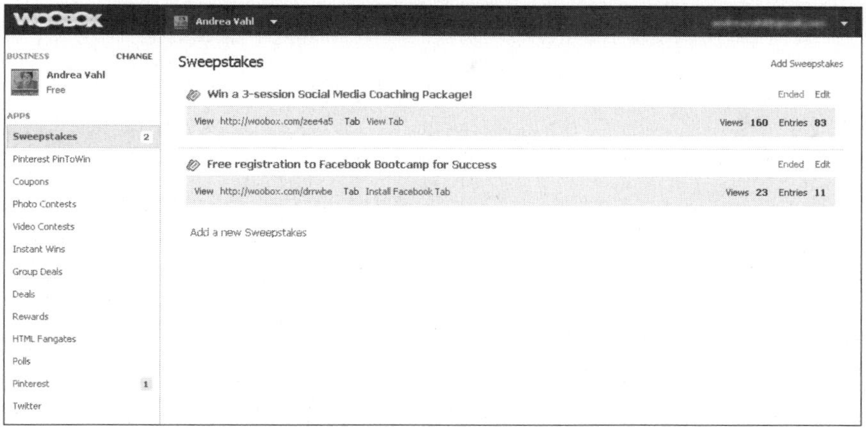

Figure 3-16: The Woobox dashboard.

From this dashboard, you can add sweepstakes, coupons, and other products to any of the Pages you manage.

Adding a sweepstakes

To add a sweepstakes, follow these steps:

1. **Click the Sweepstakes link on the left sidebar of the Woobox dashboard (refer to Figure 3-16).**
2. **Click the Add a Sweepstakes hyperlink.**

   You're taken to the page shown in Figure 3-17.

Figure 3-17: Enter your sweepstakes details.

3. **Add your sweepstakes details (refer to Figure 3-17).**

   The following list details more information about each of the fields on that page (note that not all fields are shown in the figure):

   - *Title:* Enter the title of your sweepstakes. The title can have a maximum 100 characters.
   - *Description:* You have a maximum 255 characters to describe your offer.
   - *Restrictions:* You may want to specify whether the rules call for one entry per person or one entry per person per day.
   - *Start Date and End Date:* Enter the start and end dates of your sweepstakes.
   - *Page Width:* Choose 810px Wide.
   - *Open Graph Sharing:* This option posts a story on the user's Timeline, saying that he or she entered the contest, but the user must authorize the app to do so, which may decrease the entries you receive. This option is off by default.
   - *Fan-Gate:* This option lets you allow people to enter your contest only after they like your Page — a good way to increase your likes. If you have a branded image, you can use it to tell people to click Like to enter. To enable this option, click the radio button next to one of the selections:

     If you select *Image*, you are then prompted to upload an image.

     If you select *HTML,* you are prompted to add your code.

     If you use the *Default* image, no further action is needed.
   - *Entry Page:* Accept the Default setting to show the text details you enter for your contest. If you have a branded image that tells more about your contest, select the Image radio button, and upload your image. If you want to use HTML code to enter information about your contest, select the HTML radio button, and add your code.
   - *One Entry Per User:* You can restrict the contest to one entry per user (verified by e-mail address), one entry per day per user, one entry per Facebook Profile, or one entry per day per Facebook Profile by making a choice from the drop-down menu.
   - *Award Bonus Entries:* You can reward people for sharing your contest by permitting extra entries for sharing. In the text box, enter the number of extra entries people will receive for sharing your contest, and from the drop-down menu, choose how you want to keep track of those entries: by Facebook Friend who enters or by user who clicks the Entrants Shared link. Leave the text box set to 0 if you don't want to give out any extra entries.

You can facilitate more entries if you ask users to share the offer on Facebook.

- *Post-Entry Page:* You can upload a special image that appears after the person has entered your sweepstakes. This image must be a maximum 810 × 1200 pixels tall and no more than 400KB. You can encourage people to share your contest by checking Automatically Show Share Dialog Popup Window check box.
- *Pre-Start Page:* You can upload a special image that appears before your sweepstakes is live.
- *Ended Page:* You can upload a special image that appears when your sweepstakes is over.
- *Official Rules:* If you make your rules available on a website, enter the URL of that website, or just type your rules in the large box.

4. **Click the Save button at the bottom of the page.**

Choosing a payment plan

After you have your sweepstakes saved, you need to pay for a plan to enable the sweepstakes. Follow these steps:

1. **Click the Upgrade hyperlink at the bottom of the Sweepstakes form to choose a plan to pay for your sweepstakes.**

   Some Woobox options are free, but the Sweepstakes plan is paid.

   You're taken to the outline of the plans. Most people need to select the Pro plan, which is the minimum required for a sweepstakes. If you need some of the other features or have more than 100,000 fans, you need the Pro100 or Pro250 plan.

2. **Select your plan.**
3. **Click the Choose Account Level button at the bottom of the screen.**

   The plan is saved.

4. **Click Billing on the left sidebar.**
5. **Enter your credit-card information.**

   You'll be billed automatically for the monthly plan, so if you're running a short contest, remember to stop your monthly plan when you're done.

Note: After you enter your billing information, you need to go back into your sweepstakes (click your name at the top of the page, then click the Sweepstakes title) and clear the Preview Mode check box at the bottom of the Edit Sweepstakes area. Without taking your Sweepstakes out of Preview Mode, the Sweepstakes will not be published.

Adding the sweepstakes to your Page

To add the sweepstakes to your Page, follow these steps from the www.Woobox.com site:

1. **Click your name at the top of the Woobox site.**

   You're taken to the main dashboard.

2. **Click Sweepstakes on the left sidebar.**

   Your sweepstakes are listed.

3. **Click the Install Facebook Tab hyperlink.**

   You see the Facebook Page Tab & App Settings screen, as shown in Figure 3-18. This screen is where you manage your sweepstakes and see the statistics for your sweepstakes.

Figure 3-18: Title the tab, and add a custom tab image.

4. **Enter a name for your sweepstakes.**
5. **Upload an image for your sweepstakes.**
6. **Click Install Tab.**

You selected the Page at the beginning of the process and should see the icon of the Page on which the tab will be installed at the top of the Woobox dashboard. If you need to change, click the Change hyperlink at the top of the Woobox page.

Your sweepstakes is now installed on your Page, and you can change the position of the app, as mentioned in the Wildfire steps previously.

To alert your Facebook community to your sweepstakes, you can share the link to the Sweepstakes tab and let people know to enter there. Or you can copy the Shareable Offer URL that's available in the Sweepstakes dashboard area and post that as a link in your Facebook status update.

In the Sweepstakes dashboard, you can track the entries and views, and see how many people are sharing the sweepstakes with their friends.

Using the Offerpop Application

Offerpop is a very easy application to use. Because it has so many promotional tools, you may want to choose the monthly subscription plan, which is very reasonable, so that you have access to multiple tools. You get one trial campaign for up to 14 days. It's worth trying!

Signing up for Offerpop

To get started, follow these steps:

1. **Go to** `www.offerpop.com`**.**
2. **Click the orange Get Started button in the top-right corner of the home page.**

   A pop-up window asks you whether you want to select Facebook or Twitter as your platform.
3. **Select Facebook.**

   Another pop-up window prompts you to log in to Facebook if you aren't already logged in.

   If you *are* logged in to your Page, you're prompted to switch back to your personal Profile. Don't worry about using this app from your personal Profile; most apps work this way. You select the Page where you want to add your contest a little later.
4. **Click the blue Log In with Facebook button.**

   A pop-up window asks permission for Offerpop to manage your pages. Later, you grant Offerpop access to only one of your Pages.
5. **Click Allow.**

   In the next screen, you enter your company name and information.
6. **Enter the required information (see Figure 3-19).**

   You can choose to select the Page on which you want to run your promotion now, or you can add that information later.
7. **When you're done, click Continue.**

   You're taken to the terms page.

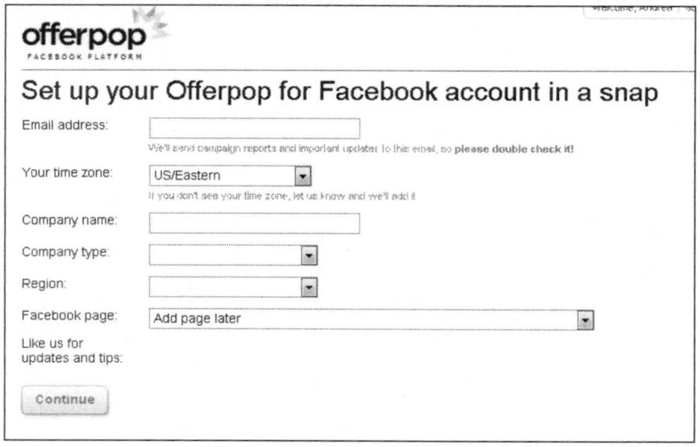

Figure 3-19: Fill out your company information.

8. **Click Accept.**

   You see the main dashboard (shown in Figure 3-20), where you can add Pages, start campaigns, and access the other apps.

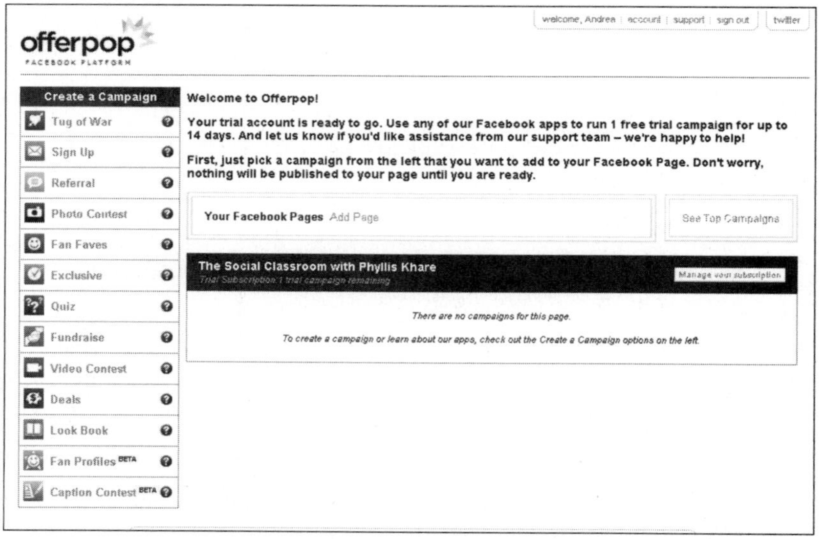

Figure 3-20: Start campaigns from this page.

You can get more information about any of the campaigns by mousing over the question-mark symbol next to the name of the campaign. If you are looking to add a Sweepstakes to your Page, Offerpop titles their Sweepstakes App, "Sign Up".

Publishing a sweepstakes

To publish a sweepstakes, follow these steps:

1. **Click the Sign Up option in the list on the left side of the dashboard (refer to Figure 3-20).**

   You're taken to a Customize page that displays a filled-in example.

2. **Replace the sample information with your campaign information:**

   - *Facebook Page:* From the drop-down list, choose the Page on which you want the campaign to appear (see Figure 3-21). If you don't see the correct page, you need to go back to the dashboard (refer to Figure 3-20) and click Add Page.
   - *Headline:* The headline appears at the top of your Sweepstakes app, as well as in the News Feed when people enter or share the contest. Make it brief, eye-catching, and engaging.
   - *Headline Image:* This image appears at the top of your Sweepstakes app but replaces the Headline. It's best if this image can say something about the contest itself.
   - *Instructions:* Use this area to say more about the contest and how to win. This area supports HTML if you want to use HTML tags to format your instructions.

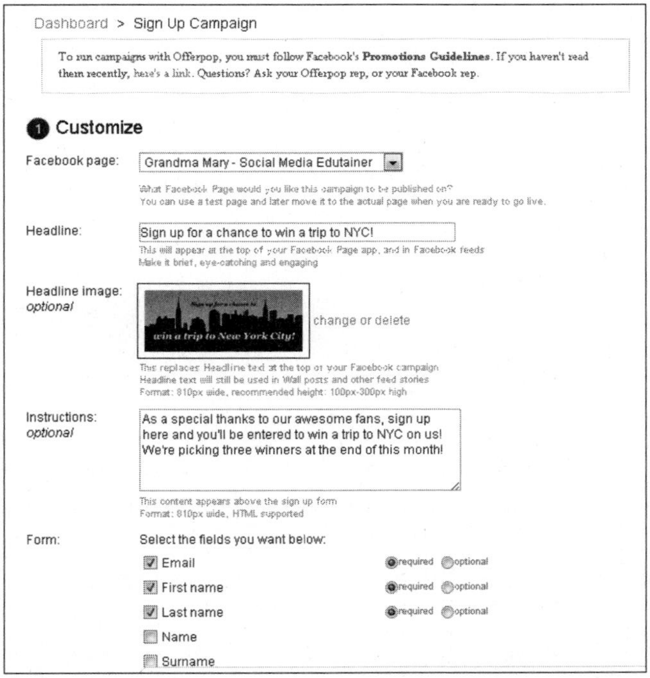
Dashboard > Sign Up Campaign
To run campaigns with Offerpop, you must follow Facebook's Promotions Guidelines. If you haven't read them recently, here's a link. Questions? Ask your Offerpop rep, or your Facebook rep.
1 Customize
Facebook page:
Grandma Mary - Social Media Edutainer
Headline:
Sign up for a chance to win a trip to NYC!
Headline image:
optional
win a trip to New York City!
change or delete
Instructions:
optional
As a special thanks to our awesome fans, sign up here and you'll be entered to win a trip to NYC on us! We're picking three winners at the end of this month!
Form:
Select the fields you want below:
Email
First name
Last name
Name
Surname
required
optional

Figure 3-21: Fill in your contest information.

- *Form:* Specify the fields in which people need to enter information. The less information you require, the easier it is for people to enter your contest, but if you need to mail something to entrants, it's a good idea to require an address. You can also let people check a box to get on your e-mail list. If you're going to add entrants to your newsletter list, you must have them opt in and say that they want to be on your e-mail list.
- *Campaign Ends:* Select the time and date when you'll stop taking entries.
- *Advanced Options:* Select the advanced options that you want to enable. You can fan-gate your content (people have to like your Page before they can enter), customize the page people go to after signing up, and more.

3. **Click Fan View, Non-Fan View, and After Sign Up (see Figure 3-22) in turn to see how your sweepstakes entry looks with those settings.**

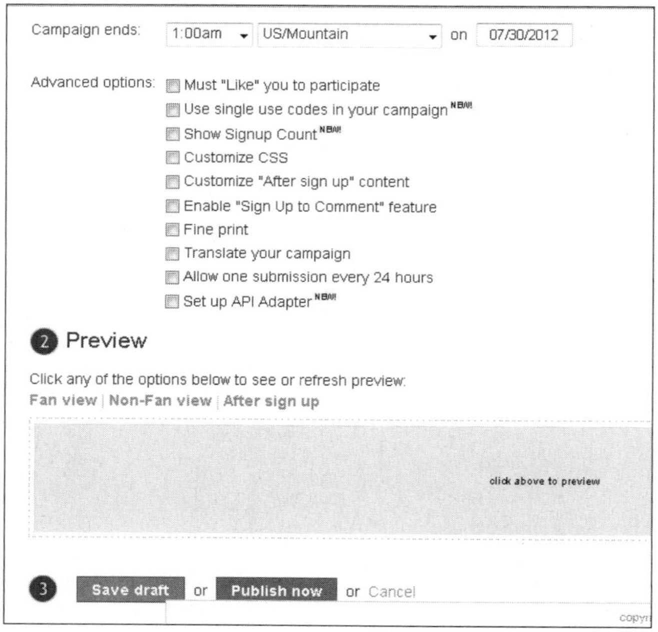

Figure 3-22: Use the Preview section to see how your campaign looks.

4. **(Optional) Make adjustments to your customization choices.**
5. **Click Save Draft or Publish Now, depending on whether you're ready for your sweepstakes to go live.**

   When you click Publish Now, you're taken to a confirmation page, as shown in Figure 3-23.
6. **Confirm your Page, and name your tab appropriately.**

7. **Click the red Publish Now button.**

   You can also click the Do This Later link if you aren't ready to publish it yet. Your campaign is saved and can be accessed from your Offerpop Dashboard.

   You're taken back to the Offerpop dashboard, where you get confirmation that your campaign has been published if you clicked the Publish Now button.

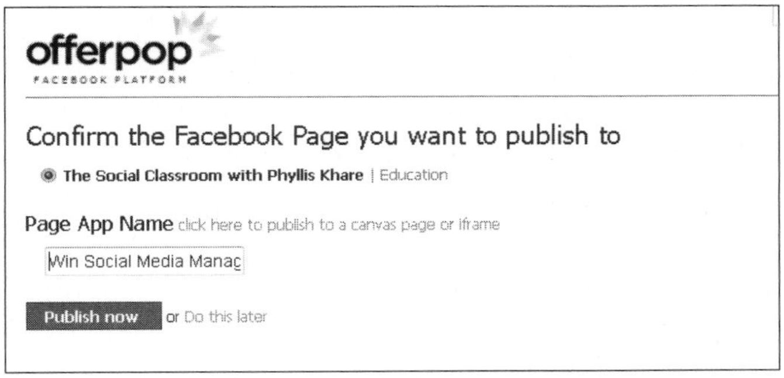

Figure 3-23: Confirm your Page.

Adjusting the App's Photo

The following steps apply to photos for any of the contests we outline in this chapter.

Editing the position of the app

Your Contest app may be installed in a place where the app is not visible to your fans. Only the apps in the first three rows of apps are visible to your fans and if you have a lot of apps on your page, the contest app is installed at the bottom of your apps initially. Ideally, it's best to have the app appear in the top row of your tabs for the duration of your contest for maximum visibility. To edit the position of an app, follow these steps:

1. **Click the pencil icon in the top-right corner of the app (mouse over the app to see the pencil icon), as shown in Figure 3-24.**

   A drop-down menu appears. If you don't have the pencil icon, make sure that all the apps are displayed by clicking the down arrow on the right side of your apps.

2. **From the Swap Position With drop-down menu, choose the app to swap positions with your contest app.**

   Choose one of the apps in the first three rows of apps and preferably one in the top row for maximum exposure.

   The Sweepstakes app swaps positions with the appropriate app.

Figure 3-24: Click the pencil icon in the top-right corner of the app to edit it.

Editing the cover photo of an app

To edit the cover photo for the app if you want it to be more eye-catching, follow these steps:

1. **Click the pencil icon in the top-right corner of the app (refer to Figure 3-24).**

   A drop-down menu appears.

2. **Choose Edit Settings from the drop-down menu.**

   A pop-up window appears.

3. **Click Change next to Custom Tab Image.**

   You're taken to a Page where you can select a new tab image, as shown in Figure 3-25.

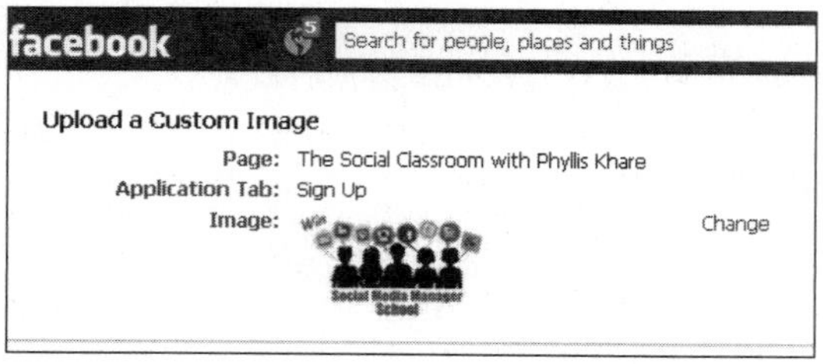

Figure 3-25: Replace the picture with an eye-catching image.

4. **Click Change to select an image from your computer.**

   A pop-up window appears.

5. **Select the file you want to use.**

6. **Click the Open button to add your selected image as the Tab Image.**

   The image is changed.

Chapter 4: Promoting Your Contest and Analyzing the Results

In This Chapter

- Using a blog tour to drive traffic to a contest
- Publicizing a contest on a website or blog
- Allowing entries from anywhere on the web
- Promoting a contest with Twitter, LinkedIn, and YouTube
- Handling external contests
- Watching the numbers
- Making changes based on the numbers
- Strategizing for future contests

Your contest is set up, and the prizes are ready. Now comes the fun part: getting those entries! The success of your contest comes when you can drive more traffic to your entry site. We discuss different things to do to promote your contest in Chapter 2 of this minibook, and we go a little more in-depth in this chapter.

Later in the chapter, we take a look at your contest results, what they mean, and how you can improve them next time.

Setting Up a Blog Tour

A blog tour is a fantastic way to get exposure to a whole new audience, but it does take some planning and legwork. One way to kick off a blog tour is to contact bloggers and ask whether you can write a guest post or whether they can post about your contest.

Some blogs are *single-voice* blogs, meaning that only the original author writes posts, and the blog doesn't have guest posts. Other blogs welcome guest posters, as they give the blogger a short respite from pumping out content. Figuring out which type of blog you're approaching isn't difficult. Just take a look through the posts, and look at the author bylines. If the posts never show a guest poster or an author bio for someone other than the blog owner, you can safely assume that it's a single-voice blog.

When you contact bloggers to ask about promoting your contest, either through a guest post by you or by mentioning it themselves, contact them at least a month in advance so that they have plenty of time to respond.

In the following ways, you can find blogs that are a good fit for your message:

✦ **Research blogs to contact, and have a list of blogs that would be a good fit for your message.**

  You can also start with bloggers you know and have relationships with. Often, these bloggers are very receptive to a guest post. A good guideline is to approach bloggers who have complementary businesses with yours and aren't direct competitors. If you have a graphic-design business and are giving away your services, for example, you may want to look at blogs about business or marketing.

✦ **Perform keyword-based blog searches on the following sites:**

  • `http://technorati.com`
  • `http://blogsearch.google.com`
  • `http://alltop.com`

✦ **Familiarize yourself with the styles of bloggers.**

  Make a short list (or a long one, if you're ambitious) of the bloggers you want to approach about a guest post. Poke around on their blogs, and get to know the styles of the bloggers. You might even comment on some posts before approaching the bloggers.

✦ **Prepare an introductory e-mail about what you'd like to post about, and describe how it can help the bloggers' audiences.**

  It's best if you can offer valuable content that can help the bloggers' readers, in addition to getting those readers to sign up for your contest. Because everyone loves a contest, most bloggers will be receptive to having you encourage contest entries.

✦ **Schedule your blog tour so that it coincides with the time when your contest is live and you can promote your guest posts properly.**

  Then you need to create the content for the blog tour. Get your guest post to the bloggers with ample time for them to review it and suggest any changes.

✦ **When the guest post is live, make sure that you're doing all you can to promote it.**

  You want to help bring traffic to the blog, as well as to promote your content and encourage contest entries. Tweet about the guest post, post it to your Facebook Page, update your status in LinkedIn, and send it to your e-mail list if appropriate.

Promoting Your Contest on Your Blog or Website

You should also have your own blog post about the contest. You may want the post to be simply an announcement, or you can have some valuable content to go with the contest announcement.

If you're running the contest on Facebook, make sure that you link back to the Page where people can enter the contest. You can find that URL by clicking the contest or sweepstakes app link below your Page's Cover photo. It will look something like this:

```
www.facebook.com/GrandmaMaryShow?v=app_28134323652
```


You may also want to post a permanent banner or widget advertising your contest on the sidebar of your website, so that when your blog entry is no longer visible, you're still letting visitors know about your contest. Figure 4-1 shows Ann Taylor's recent contest for a $1,000 gift card. The link at the bottom of each page on the website took users directly to Facebook, where they could enter the contest.

Figure 4-1: Ann Taylor used a banner at the bottom of each page that linked to its Facebook contest.

Golfsmith had a banner ad across the top of its website pages, advertising its Golf Oasis sweepstakes (see Figure 4-2).

Adding your contest information to your blog is not too difficult; all it takes is adding a widget to your sidebar of your blog with an image that links to your contest. If you're using the Wildfire application, for example (see

Chapter 3 of this minibook), Wildfire has a built-in website widget that you can use. If you have a Wildfire account, you log in to your account, go to the Publish area of one of your promotions, and then select Publish on the website widget. You get some code, as shown in Figure 4-3.

Figure 4-2: Golfsmith's banner at the top of its website linked to its Facebook contest.

Figure 4-3: Code to cut and paste into a text box on your blog to create a contest banner.

Wildfire has step-by-step instructions on how to install this code on your blog or website. When you're finished, the banner shows up at the bottom of every page of your site, as shown in Figure 4-4.

Figure 4-4: A contest banner appears on your site.

Using Facebook Open Graph to Allow Entries Anywhere on the Web

You can use the *Open Graph Protocol* (`http://ogp.me/`), a Facebook tool that integrates websites into Facebook, to allow entries directly on your website. By letting people log in with Facebook, you make it easier for them to enter and share your contest with others. Figure 4-5 shows how Blowfish Shoes used Open Graph to let people enter its Shoe A Day giveaway: You can log in with Facebook to enter. Find out more about using Open Graph on the Facebook Developer site at `https://developers.facebook.com/docs/opengraph`.

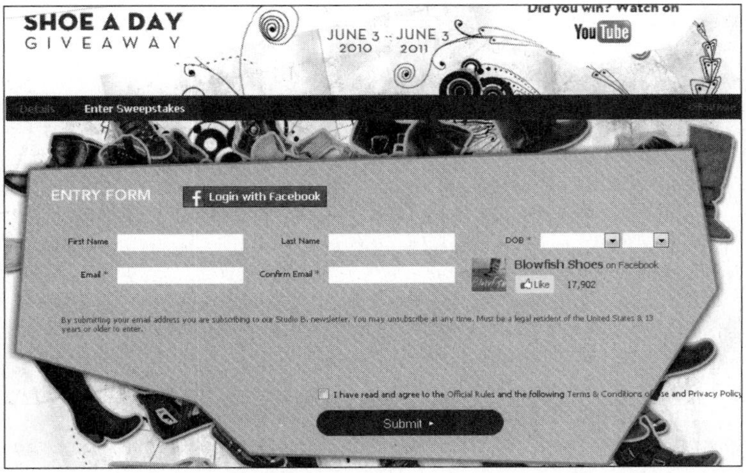

Figure 4-5: The Blowfish Shoes entry form on its website.

Using Social Media to Promote Your Contest

Social media can be critical for getting the word out about your contest. You should post about your event on your Facebook Page, of course, but how much should you emphasize it? You don't want to be obnoxious, but you want to get the word out. Your promotion levels can vary, depending on your comfort zone, but we suggest at least two to three times per week. Vary your posts by saying things like "Have you heard we are having a contest?" or "Thanks to everyone who has entered already. Make sure that you get your entry in!" Make your posts light and fun.

You can also ask other people to promote your contest. Either contact some of your Facebook Friends who would have the right audience, or ask people to share the link with others so that those others can enter.

Make sure that you use an eye-catching graphic as the app cover photo for your contest. (See Chapter 3 of this minibook for more information on changing your app cover photo.) Figure 4-6 shows how Macy's highlighted its VIP Trip to Vegas contest with a custom graphic.

Figure 4-6: Use the cover photo on the app to draw attention to your contest.

Twitter

If you're using Twitter, you should tweet about your contest frequently. Tweet about it at different times of the day. Ask for retweets, and contact some of your Twitter friends directly in case they don't see the tweet.

Twitter also has hashtags that you can use to reach people who are tracking contests to enter. Use hashtags like `#contest`, `#sweepstakes`, `#win`, and `#prize`. Some tweets use lots of those hashtags, as shown in Figure 4-7.

Without getting too deep into Twitter, some people are monitoring certain hashtags to find tweets about that subject. You can search on the hashtag and see all the tweets with that hashtag in it. So you may get people entering your contests who are serial contest enterers and not really interested in your product. Still, you may be able to connect with these people through your posts on your Facebook Page and turn them into customers.

Figure 4-7: MyCoupons.com used several hashtags to promote its Facebook contest.

LinkedIn

LinkedIn can also be a good place to promote a contest. Update your status so that when your connections log in to LinkedIn, they can see it in their LinkedIn Updates area, as shown in Figure 4-8.

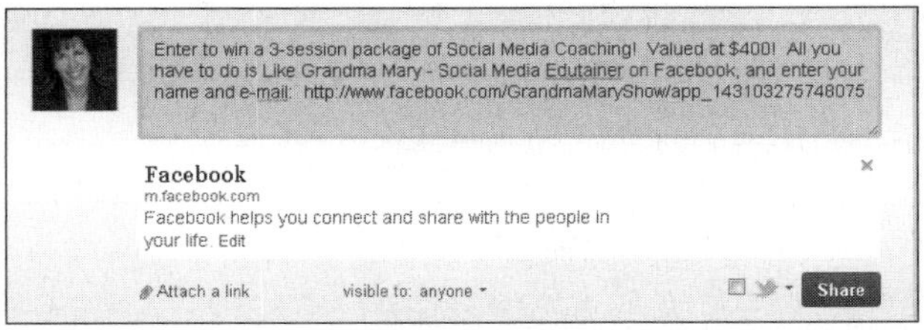

Figure 4-8: Update your status in LinkedIn with your contest.

You can also create a LinkedIn event announcing your contest. Invite your connections to the event, and direct them to your Facebook Page to enter the contest.

Another strategy is to send out an e-mail to your LinkedIn connections, inviting them to enter your contest.

Be careful about some of these strategies, though. Some people don't appreciate getting e-mails of this type and feel that they constitute spam. It's a fine line, and your comfort level should determine how you promote your contest.

YouTube

Another way to promote your contest is to make a YouTube video. You can show off the prize in the video or talk about what you'll be providing. If you're providing some type of coaching, a video can be very beneficial so that people can get to know you a little and see your style.

Blendtec uses YouTube videos to demonstrate its blenders, blending a wide variety of things while posing the question "Will it blend?" It also uses YouTube to promote its contests, as shown in Figure 4-9. In that case, the company was giving away its blender and either an iPad or the remains of a blended iPad.

Figure 4-9: Blendtec promotes its contests with YouTube videos.

TIP

The benefit of having a video on YouTube is that you can then embed it in a Facebook Page or your blog so that people can find it in multiple places. You never know how someone will stumble across your contest, and the more places on the web you can advertise it, the better.

Using Facebook to Promote an External Contest

You can use your Facebook Page to promote a contest hosted on your website. The benefit is that you don't have to contend with all those pesky Facebook promotion rules. But make sure that you still look at the Facebook Promotion Guidelines, contained in Section E of Facebook's Page Guidelines, available at `www.facebook.com/page_guidelines.php`.

Facebook has general guidelines about when you can even mention a contest or sweepstakes on the Facebook platform, and you want to make sure that your contest adheres to those guidelines.

When you're promoting a contest on your website, post the entry link frequently on your Facebook Page. Ask your community members to share the link with their Friends.

You can also incorporate Facebook Connect and Open Graph into your contest site so that people can share and like your contest entry form. That technique ensures that the contest enters the Facebook arena and gets more exposure. See Book VII, Chapter 2 for more information about how to use Facebook Open Graph.

Analyzing Your Contest Results

Tracking your results is critical in any marketing effort, and it'll be very easy to see what you've gained when you have all your contest entries. Analyzing the real effect on your business may not be possible until later, though. You got a lot of entries, but did you eventually get customers and business? Have a plan in place to track later business and see where it came from.

Also, we encourage you to have some type of e-mail subscriber list that your entrants can sign up for in addition to just liking your Page. Contrary to some rumors, e-mail isn't dead, and it can be an effective way to reach your customers with new offers.

Using analytics within third-party contest applications

Third-party sweepstakes and contest applications can make tracking and analyzing the effectiveness of your contest simple. When you use the Wildfire, North Social, Offerpop, and Woobox applications (covered in Chapter 3 of this minibook), you have built-in analytics. Wildfire, for example, provides details about visits to your contest site and entries per day, as well as what websites these entries came from, as shown in Figure 4-10. Offerpop, Woobox, and North Social track slightly different metrics, as you can see in the Offerpop report in Figure 4-11.

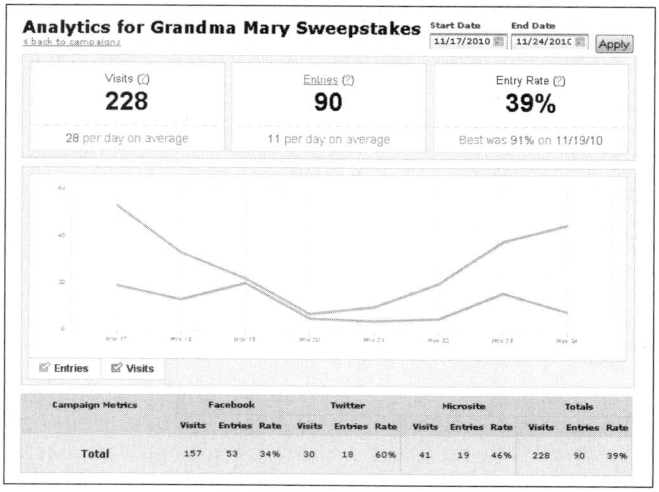

Figure 4-10: Wildfire analytics are comprehensive.

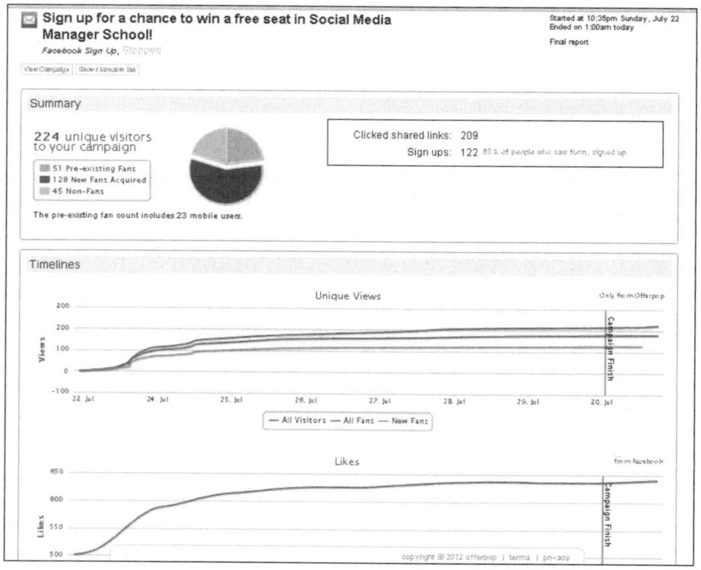

Figure 4-11: Offerpop tracks slightly different metrics.

Monitoring community growth and tracking Facebook Insights

Make sure that you're tracking your new likes on your Page and comparing them with the contest or sweepstakes entries. The newest liker will be at the top of the list. Unfortunately, you have no easy way to download your list of likers, so if someone who liked your Page a long time ago enters your contents, finding that person will be difficult.

Souplantation & Sweet Tomatoes

Souplantation & Sweet Tomatoes has a history of good Facebook contests and promotions. In 2010, the company had a very successful "pucker face" contest in which people submitted photos of themselves after eating a lemon. Sweet Tomatoes ran this promotion to coincide with some of the lemon dishes it was featuring. The winner of the contest won 20 meal passes. Having a photo contest is a fun way to involve your audience, and the prize doesn't have to cost a lot of money. The contest was so successful that the company ran it again in 2011.

Sweet Tomatoes also ran a Refer a Friend contest through the Wildfire app, in which people were entered to win ten free meals when they referred Friends to the contest.

After someone enters the contest, they have the choice of publishing something about it to their Timeline, as well as personally inviting their Friends. These touches in your contest can really help spread the word Then everyone can see some of the positive feedback the winner receives when the winner's name is posted. You can space your contests close together so that your fans are excited to sign up for another round of the contest.

If you're using the North Social, Offerpop, or Woobox sweepstakes application, you have the option of creating the contest as a fan-only application. This means that a visitor to your Facebook Page can't enter the contest unless he or she clicks Like. If you set up your contest this way, you won't have to track whether the person who entered your contest also clicked Like.

Track your Facebook Insights before and after the contest to see how your contest affected the interaction on your Page. We tracked Facebook Insights the prior month and the subsequent month after we ran a contest on a Page, and we saw that the comments and likes to the posts more than doubled, as did the new likes for the Page. See Book IX, Chapter 2 for more information about Facebook Insights.

TIP

Watch the trends of new comments and engagement on your Page. With luck, you'll have an influx of new people who are interested in your brand and decide to connect with you on Facebook.

Adjusting Your Strategy Based on Analytics

Analytics are key in helping you determine where your strategy is working and where to shift your focus. This section takes a look at the analytics for a contest that we ran with Wildfire (refer to Figure 4-10, earlier in this chapter).

At the bottom of Figure 4-10, you can see Facebook had 157 visits and 53 entries (a 34 percent conversion rate), but Twitter had a much better return, with only 30 visits but 18 entries (a 60 percent conversion rate). These statistics tell us that during the next contest, we might be well served by focusing more efforts on Twitter.

You can also see that the entries and views went significantly down over weekend (the dip in the graph), when we didn't promote the contest as heavily as we did during the week. We may want to try changing that situation in the next contest and see whether we can connect with more people who are on the web on the weekend, looking for fun things to do such as entering contests.

You can compare analytics from multiple contests, if you run more than one, to see what improved (or declined) in the other contests. We ran a second contest, and although it didn't get as many entries as the first (mostly because we didn't promote the second contest quite as heavily), it did get a higher entry rate through Facebook, as shown in Figure 4-12. The community members might have seen the testimonials of previous winners and wanted to make sure that they entered the second contest.

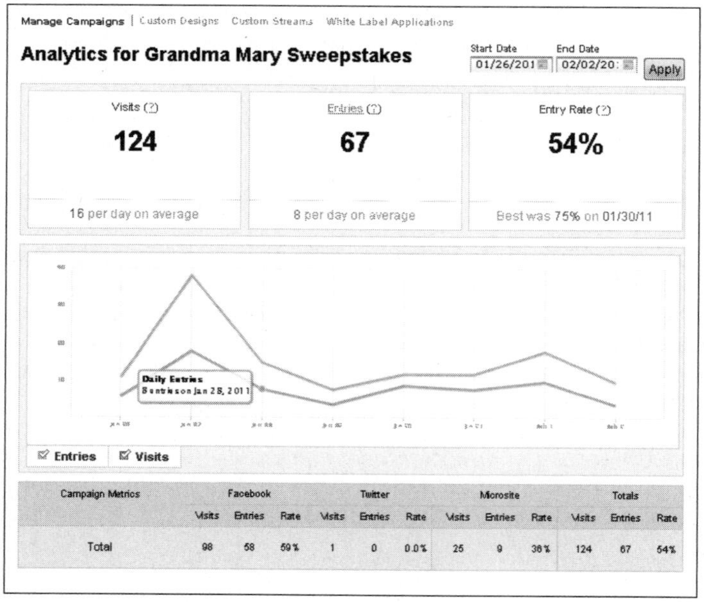

Figure 4-12: Compare the analytics of our second contest.

Planning Future Contests

After you have your first contest under your belt, you can start mapping out your contest schedule. When you've run one contest, you can see the benefits for your Facebook community, such as added members and more interaction.

Maybe you want to run only one more contest, or perhaps three or four per year. Whatever you do, though, running multiple contests is a good idea, for several reasons:

- ✦ You give the people who entered before a second chance to win.
- ✦ You encourage your community to watch your Page because people like contests.
- ✦ It's easy to have others promote your contests because people like to win things.
- ✦ You can showcase some of your services and products as giveaways, which then encourages people to buy them.
- ✦ Contests are fun!

TIP

Plan your contests strategically so that you can promote them adequately. Don't have so many contests so that your community gets contest fatigue, however.

Mapping out your contests for the year

To prevent contest fatigue and to allow room on your calendar for promotion of your contests, make sure to schedule all your contests for the year. How many contests you have and how far apart you space them can depend on the duration of the contests.

If you're running month-long contests, for example, you may want to have a buffer of a couple of months between them so you can focus on other parts of your business. That schedule would allow four contests per year.

Cold Stone Creamery and Papa John's Pizza

Cold Stone Creamery had a Gold Cone Contest, in which people suggested new flavors. The winners traveled to the company's headquarters in Arizona to perfect the winning flavors. Social Media Examiner reported on the contest in this post:

```
www.socialmediaexaminer.com/cold-stone-transforms-the-ice-
    cream-social-with-facebook
```

More than 4,000 people entered the contest, and the Cold Stone Creamery Facebook Page saw about 66,000 new likes over an eight-week period.

Papa John's Pizza saw a similar success when it ran a Specialty Pizza Challenge contest in 2010 and received more 12,000 entries. Papa John's had a live stream to announce the three winners (chosen from the ten semifinalists) and got a lot of buzz from the event.

How many contests you schedule may also depend on the type of contest. Are the contests the same, or are you giving away a different prize each week? Exodus Travels in the United Kingdom gave away a trip a month to each of the seven continents, for example, so its contest lasted for seven months.

Watching for successful contest ideas

If you're planning multiple contests, you should be watching other contests that are running on Facebook so that you can get ideas for your own. It may not be easy to tell how successful a contest is, but you can watch for some clues. If the business is promoting the contest on Twitter, you can search for tweets about it to see whether many people are tweeting about the contest. If the company has a YouTube video of the contest, you can see how many views the video gets. And if you're really paying attention, you can track the new likes on the company's Facebook Page each day because the likes may correlate with contest entries.

You have several ways to search for contests that are running on Facebook:

- Look through the Wildfire site for contests and sweepstakes that are using the Wildfire platform.
- Check Votigo's website for the Case Studies section, which highlights successful contests.
- Look at the Examples page on North Social's website. North Social provides examples from many of its apps but also has a Promotions section that covers examples of its Sweepstakes app.
- Watch the Facebook Ads area to see who is advertising contests.
- Use the Facebook Search feature to see who is posting about contests.
- Use Twitter search to search for tweets about contests.

We discuss each of these methods in depth in the following sections.

Finding popular contests through Wildfire

You can use the Wildfire application to see what contests are being run through Wildfire. When you go to the Promotions area on Facebook (`http://apps.facebook.com/promotionshq/contests`), you can see all of Wildfire's contests listed, as shown in Figure 4-13. (The Wildfire App is not mentioned on this page but all the contests are being run through the Wildfire App.)

Viewing the Votigo Live Showcase of current contests

The Votigo website (`www.votigo.com`) has a Case Studies section of successful contests that have run through its platform, as shown in Figure 4-14. You can access the Case Studies area by choosing Case Studies from the

Clients drop-down menu at the top of the page. Some contests and some sweepstakes are featured. These are not current promotions but previous promotions that have been successful for Votigo's clients.

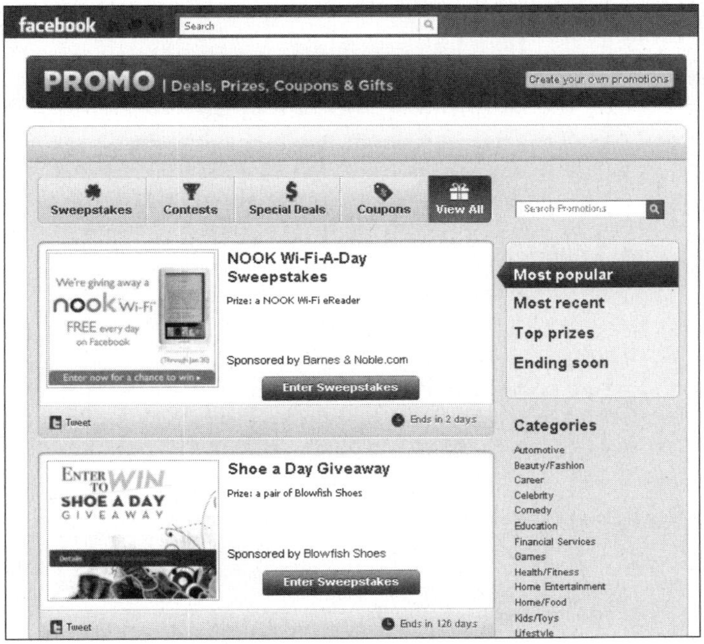

Figure 4-13: Wildfire contests and sweepstakes are listed and searchable in different categories.

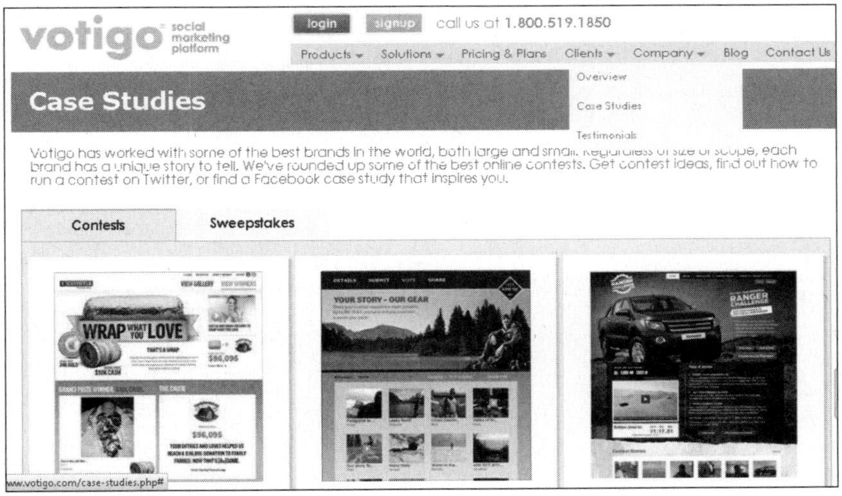

Figure 4-14: Watch for contests and sweepstakes on the Votigo site.

Looking at North Social Examples

North Social also has examples of the promotions using its sweepstakes application. You can see some screen shots of these promotions by going to `http://northsocial.com` and click on the Examples tab at the top of the screen and then selecting the Promotions link on the left sidebar.

Keeping an eye on the Facebook Ad Board

Watch Facebook Ads, because often it's advertising contests. The easiest place to see all the current Ads at one time is the Facebook Ad Board. You can access it at `www.facebook.com/ads/adboard`. When you go to the Ad Board, you see all the Ads that are being served to your Profile demographic at this time, so you need to check back at different times and possibly have people with different demographics checking in.

Using the Facebook Search feature

Use the Facebook Search feature, at `www.facebook.com/search`, to search for any posts within Facebook that mention a contest. When you go to the search area, click Posts by Everyone or Posts by Friends on the left sidebar to filter your search for posts, as shown in Figure 4-15.

Figure 4-15: Use Facebook Search to find posts about contests.

We actually found so many posts containing the word *contest* that we added more keywords to help narrow the posts. We used *enter our contest* in the search field, as shown in Figure 4-15.

Finding contest information on Twitter

You can use Twitter search, at `www.search.twitter.com`, to find people who are tweeting about Facebook contests, as shown in Figure 4-16. You can use keywords like *enter, contest,* and *Facebook* or hashtags like `#contest`, `#win`, and `#facebook` to see who's tweeting about contests.

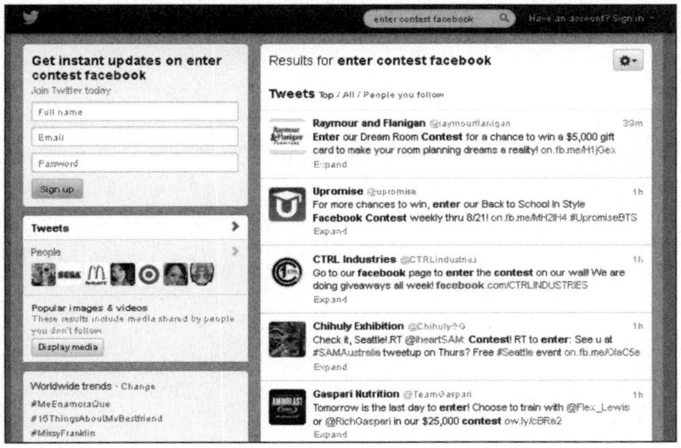

Figure 4-16: Find people who are tweeting about Facebook contests.

Book VII

Advanced Facebook Marketing Tactics

The 5th Wave By Rich Tennant

© RICHTENNANT
Make sure to pick keywords that people will associate with our brand.
How about "sleazy," "tacky," "overpriced" ...
ONLINE ADV

Contents at a Glance

Chapter 1: An Introduction to Advanced Facebook Marketing

In This Chapter

- Refreshing your knowledge of core marketing principles
- Examining advanced marketing techniques
- Putting advanced strategies to work

Clearly, Facebook Pages are quickly becoming essential parts of most businesses' marketing strategies, but how can you find ways to stand out from the competition? You have a lot to consider as you go about developing a successful Facebook Page, and the rewards of brand exposure, loyal fans, and increased revenue are well worth your time and effort. To fast-track your success, consider including some advanced strategies in your Facebook plan.

After you create your Page, optimize it with the essential strategies, such as posting great content regularly, and then build some momentum with your fan base by engaging with your fans. When you have your basic strategies locked in, you can take your Facebook marketing up a notch by exploring some advanced Facebook marketing strategies. Advanced strategies take more time and effort than basic marketing efforts, but on the plus side, they produce much bigger returns.

REMEMBER

You don't have to reinvent the wheel when it comes to Facebook strategies. Instead, take a look at other thriving Facebook Pages, and apply the same success strategies to your own Page. After you give a new strategy enough time to gain momentum, analyze your progress. If what you're doing is working, keep doing it! After a while, if you're not happy enough with the results of your efforts, change direction and try a new tactic. (You won't know if you don't try!)

In this chapter, we give you a quick refresher on the core rules of Facebook marketing; then we take a look at some advanced marketing strategies that can take your Facebook Page from good to great.

Remembering the Nine Core Facebook Marketing Rules

Before you consider experimenting with a few advanced Facebook marketing strategies, make sure that your Facebook marketing foundation is solid. Consider nine core rules when you create your marketing plan. Following these rules will ensure that you stay on track and focus on the most important marketing elements as you increase your Page engagement and number of fans — and ultimately turn your fans into new customers. Although we also mention these rules in Book I, Chapter 2, here's a synopsis:

- **Give your Page a human touch.** Communicate with your fans as though you were talking to your friends, and let your personality come through in each post.
- **Create fresh content.** Always make sure that your content educates, entertains, and empowers your fans to keep them engaged and coming back for more.
- **Cultivate engagement with two-way dialogue.** People love to talk about themselves, so craft your posts and questions around them to get them talking.
- **Create consistent calls to action.** To get your fans to take action, consider offering discounts and specials or asking them to sign up for your newsletter so that you can actively communicate with them on a consistent basis.
- **Make word-of-mouth advocacy easy.** Make it easy for your fans to talk about you by asking them to share your content, getting them to engage in contests, and making the experiences on your Page about them — rather than about you.
- **Encourage fan-to-fan conversations.** Enhance your fans' experience by creating a community that encourages your fans to interact with one another.
- **Focus on smart branding.** Treat your Facebook Page as a mini version of your own website. The key is to create a Page that sparks familiarity with your brand when your existing customers visit your Page.
- **Be deliberate, and manage expectations.** Always stay focused on why you want to have a presence on Facebook. When you understand the "why," your actions are deliberate and have purpose, and your fans clearly understand what your Page has to offer.
- **Monitor, measure, and track.** Make sure that you have surefire methods in place that enable you to consistently track your Facebook marketing progress.

Creating a Facebook Experience

Many businesses just getting started on Facebook worry that they'll be lost in the Facebook abyss. Sure, big brands such as Coca-Cola and Southwest Airlines stand out easily. But what about small to midsize companies? Many of our clients wonder whether they even have a chance.

Here's the great news: There's hope for your Page, no matter how small your company may be! You don't have to be a major brand to gain exposure and build relationships with your clients and customers on Facebook.

One way to stand out from the masses is to create *Facebook experiences* — experiences you execute on your Facebook Page that are unique to your brand and of great value to your fans. No matter how big or small, these experiences can be extremely powerful.

The Social Media Examiner Facebook Page (`www.facebook.com/smexaminer`), for example, created Expert Fridays. Every other Friday, it features a social media expert who answers fans' questions, directly on the Timeline, for one full hour. Anyone can post questions, and the expert answers as many of them as he or she can in that one designated hour, as shown in Figure 1-1. These experiences have proved to be a huge hit!

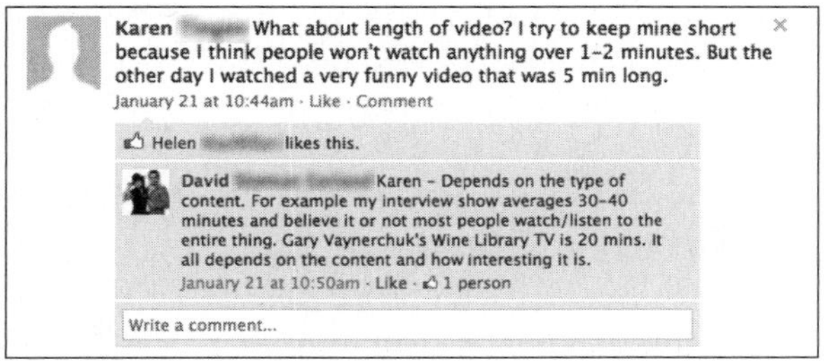

Figure 1-1: An Expert Fridays session on the Social Media Examiner Facebook Page.

Planning the experience

If you like the concept of an experience and want to create something unique to your brand and your mission, here are four steps to get you started in the right direction:

1. Decide on the overall vibe you want to create with your experience.

   Do you want to add value? Perhaps you're looking to entertain. Is your desired outcome to educate, create excitement among your fans, or all the above? Determine the kind of experience that will resonate with your fans.

2. Get clear on what your company does best.

   What's your company known for? What does it do best? What do your clients tell you when they're singing your praises? Use this insight to fuel your ideas about unique experiences.

   When you're brainstorming, think of experiences you can duplicate (do multiple times). An experience that you can execute consistently is key to building momentum with your Facebook community. After you create your list of ideas, choose the experience that your audience will embrace most fully (and one that your team will enjoy delivering!).

3. Map out your execution plan.

   You want to document the process of your experience. Before Social Media Examiner began Expert Fridays, it followed this step. The team talked about ways to find the ideal experts, the best day to announce the weekly experts, how to post the questions and answers, and all the other specifics involved. After the team talked all this out, they created a Microsoft Word document that explained the process for doing Expert Fridays sessions. At any time, the team could refer to the document for guidance. If they discovered better ways to deliver the Expert Fridays sessions, they updated the document to reflect the changes. It's a work in progress.

4. Commit to your plan.

   For some people, this is the toughest step! When you decide on your signature experience, it's crucial that you deliver. If you say that you intend to do something once a week, do it. If you don't follow through, you could lose trust with your fans, and that's something you don't want to mess with!

Optimizing the experience

After you create your experience, begin to think about how you might repurpose the content or information that comes from it. If audio is involved, perhaps you can create a podcast. Or if your experience involves video, think about using that video in an opt-in strategy for anyone who might have missed it that week. This could be a great way to build up your list.

You can also take the content from your experience and post it in new ways weeks later for those who may have missed it. Doing so allows you to continually post great content. Repurposing the content or elements of your experience creates multiple touch points throughout your marketing strategy.

Signature experiences and other "out of the box" ideas are vital to keeping your Facebook community engaged and enthusiastic about your brand. The key is to find something that you can duplicate and build on over time.

Building Social Proof with Sponsored Stories

Before most people make a buying decision, they want to know that their choice is a smart one. To get reassurance, we look to our friends to give us their advice and recommendations. With the rise of social networks, word-of-mouth recommendations are essential for businesses in their efforts to gain popularity and expand the ranks of their clientele. Studies show that when it comes to buying recommendations, people trust friends' recommendations more than they do the actual brand. Facebook has capitalized on this behavior by creating Sponsored stories.

Sponsored stories take word-of-mouth recommendations from Friends and promote them in Facebook Profiles as Facebook Ads. This means that when you go to Starbucks, for example, and use Facebook Places to check in, that story is posted on your Timeline and sent out into the News Feeds of your Friends. Now, with Sponsored Stories, that post is also displayed next to the Starbucks ad (see Figure 1-2). Starbucks has something even better than an ad; it has social proof.

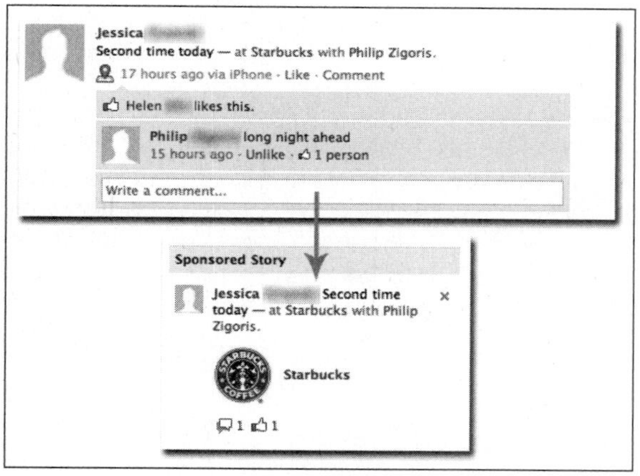

Figure 1-2: Example of a fan's Starbucks Facebook check-in next to a Starbucks ad.

The term *social proof* refers to the psychological phenomenon of people being motivated to do things that they see other people doing. Interactions on social media sites, such as Facebook, have increased the influence and reach of social proof because now it's much easier to instantly see what your friends are doing at any time.

The posts from Sponsored stories make it seem as though your Friends are saying "I bought this!" or "I just ordered the best burger ever at Rocket Burgers!" These posts are viral, instant recommendations and may be more powerful than traditional Facebook Ads. As Facebook put it, you have the "ability to promote your content with a user experience focus." Research on these unique ads has shown increased brand awareness, including ad recall and likeliness to recommend to a Friend.

As you explore your opportunities with Facebook Ads, we encourage you to test Sponsored stories. The word-of-mouth feature is a powerful tool to entice new users to check out your Facebook Page and your business. If you think this strategy might work for your company or product, see Book VIII, Chapter 1, where we go into more detail about setting up your own Sponsored stories.

Experimenting with Custom Apps

In Book III, Chapter 2, we explore custom apps. Custom apps (also known as custom pages or tabs) in many ways are the most important piece to your Facebook marketing strategy. You can create multiple pages inside your Facebook Page. One powerful advanced strategy is to create a custom page to promote special products or events. Custom pages can give your product or event extra promotion and give it the push it needs to get even greater exposure.

If you have a physical event coming up, you might consider creating a custom page with a video from past events to showcase the experience. Then you can include the Facebook comments feature from the social plug-in options to encourage people to talk about the event. This strategy showcases your event via your video, and the comments section on the tab gets people talking.

When we worked with Tony Robbins, we created a special tab for his live event (see Figure 1-3). We included a video as well as features to highlight the event benefits and the pricing structure. In many ways, the tab was like a mini website.

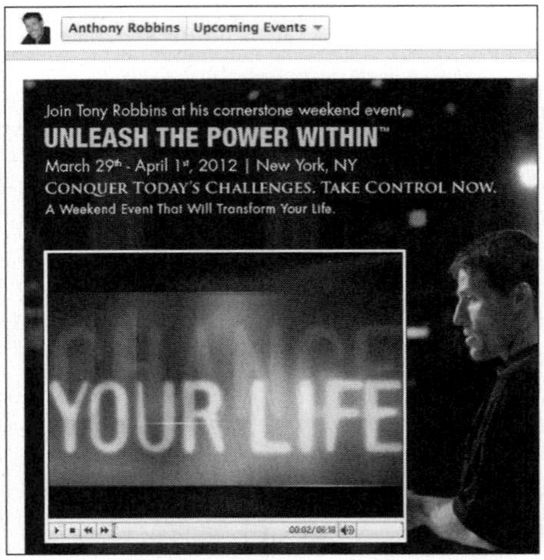

Figure 1-3: Promoting a live event with a custom app.

Targeting Your Audience with Custom Lists

As we discuss in Book II, Chapter 4, when appropriate you can use your Profile for business networking. Keeping up with all your Facebook Friends on your Profile can get a bit tricky. If you're anything like us, you have a mix of family members, friends, acquaintances, potential clients, current clients, and even a few complete strangers as Facebook Friends on your Profile. At times, that volume makes it difficult to decide what you want to share with everyone on your Facebook Timeline.

The good news is that Facebook created a way to segment your Facebook Friends into special lists: smart and custom. The benefit of both types of lists is that they allow you to share your posts with smaller groups of people.

Smart lists — which Facebook creates for you — stay up to date based on Profile info your Friends have in common with you, such as family, the city where you live, workplaces, or schools. Although Facebook creates these lists automatically, you can edit them at any time. To access your smart lists, look on the left sidebar of your Facebook Profile home page for the Lists section. Depending on the info in your Profile, you might see smart lists of your relatives, Facebook Friends in your town, and Facebook Friends you went to school with.

Custom lists are what you create as a way to selectively group certain people whom you've added as Friends. Click More next to Friends (see Figure 1-4) to see your custom lists. The name of your custom list and its members are visible only to you. If you send a post to a custom list, those on the list can see who else that post was sent to, but they won't see the name of your list. If you name a list Prospects I Plan to Land as Big-Money Clients, for example, the people on that list won't see what you called it — so get as creative as you like!

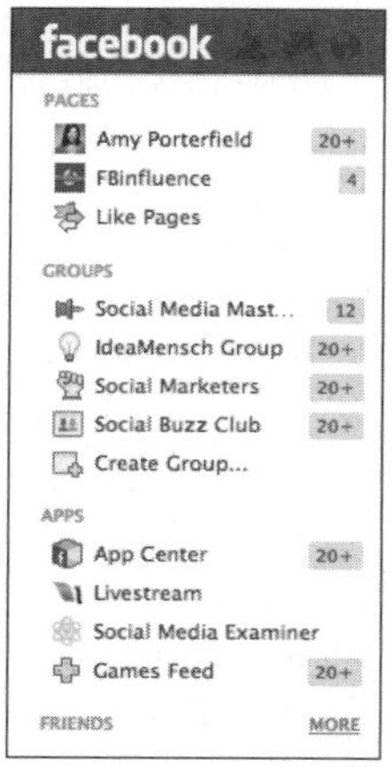

Figure 1-4: To access your Custom lists, click More next to Friends in your left sidebar.

A benefit of using both smart lists and custom lists is that they allow you to share your posts with smaller groups of people. If you just had a family reunion and took a bunch of photos, for example, you may choose to share those photos only with those in your Family smart list. Overall, these lists allow you to intelligently choose whom you talk to and what you want to share with them.

Whenever you want to share something with a specific list, you can use the drop-down audience selector in the status update box and pick one of your lists. (For more info on the audience selector, see Book I, Chapter 1.)

So how does all this relate to your Facebook marketing strategy? We allude to it a bit when we jokingly mention the list Prospects I Plan to Land as Big-Money Clients earlier in this section. Because it's very likely that you have potential clients and customers mixed in with your Facebook Friends via your Profile, custom lists are a great way to segment your personal friends from current and potential customers. You can communicate with them on a regular basis from your Profile.You can create multiple lists — depending on how you want to communicate with different groups — and then post information, photos, videos, and promotions that you know each group will find valuable. When you laser-focus your communication with custom lists, your marketing messages will pack a bigger punch — and get you even better results.

Creating your custom lists

Here's how you set up a custom list:

1. **Point your browser to** `www.facebook.com`**, and log in to your account.**

   By default, you land on your home page.

2. **In the left column, hover your mouse over the word *Friends*.**
3. **When the word *More* appears, click it.**
4. **Click Create List (top-right corner of your screen).**

   A pop-up window appears, prompting you to name your list.

5. **Type a name for your list.**

   The name of your list will be visible only to you — not anyone else on Facebook, including those you add to the list.

6. **In the Members box, below the List Name box, type in the names of the people you want to add to your new list.**

   Each time you begin to type a new name, a drop-down list appears with potential Friends to add, as shown in Figure 1-5. You will want to know the name of the Friends you want to add in advance so you can type them in at this time.

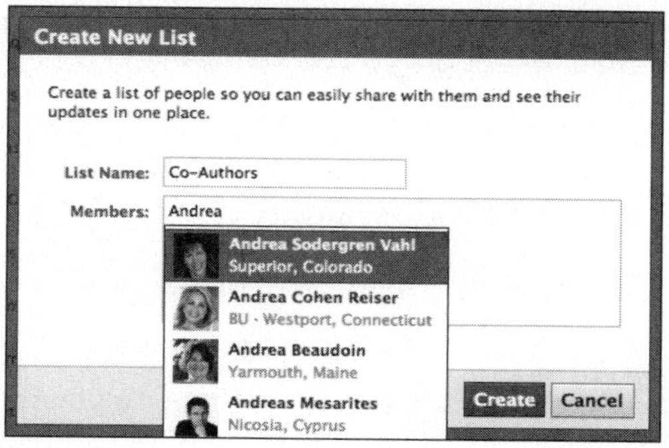

Figure 1-5: Type the name of the Friends you want to add to your list.

Adding custom lists to your Favorites

Custom lists come in handy when you're posting, but you can also use them to filter which posts you see in your News Feed stream. To see only the updates from people in a specific list, you just click that list; Facebook filters your posts on your News Feed page to show you only status updates from the people in the specific list.

To make things even easier for you, you can add custom lists to your Favorites. The Favorites section appears in the top-left column on your home page as a way to quickly access the links you use most. To add a list to your Favorites, follow these steps:

1. **Point your browser to** `www.facebook.com`**, and log in to your account.**

   By default, you land on your home page.

2. **In the left column, hover your mouse over your custom list.**

   A little blue pencil (the icon Facebook uses to indicate an edit opportunity) appears to the left of the list name.

3. **Click the blue pencil.**

   A drop-down menu appears, with the option to add this list to Favorites.

4. **Click Favorites.**

Creating Interest Lists to Focus on the People who Matter Most to Your Business

Because of the sheer number of people on Facebook (more than 1 billion!), it's easy to get overwhelmed by all the information users are posting. One smart strategy for staying focused is to customize your News Feed to ensure that you're seeing only the Facebook posts that matter most to you and the success of your business. One way to make this happen is to create Interest Lists.

Interest Lists are different from the custom lists mentioned earlier in this chapter because you can add people you're subscribed to, people you're Friends with, and Pages you like to Interest Lists, making them even more useful and interesting.

Advantages of creating Interest Lists include

- ✦ Not missing out on important updates by your favorite people and Pages
- ✦ The ability to share your Interest Lists with the world
- ✦ The convenience of adding yourself or your Page to your own Interest List so that when others subscribe to it, they subscribe to your updates as well

To see what Interest Lists look like, go to `www.facebook.com/addlist` and check out the Add Interests section.

Alternatively, you can go to your Facebook home page; on the left side, you see Interests below your Favorites, Groups, Friends, Pages, and Apps (see Figure 1-6). You may have to click the More link to find it.

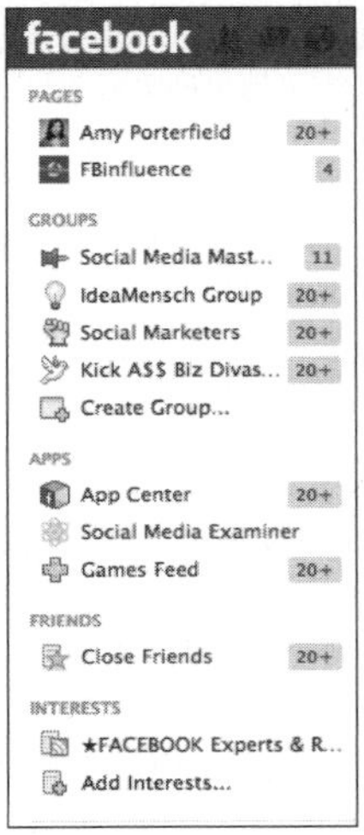

Figure 1-6: Facebook Interest Lists in the left sidebar.

If you want to start creating your own Interest List or subscribe to popular ones created by other Facebook users, click Add Interests. As you can see from the first few suggested Interest Lists shown in Figure 1-7, the popularity of Interest Lists can be great. Some have more than 75,000 subscribers!

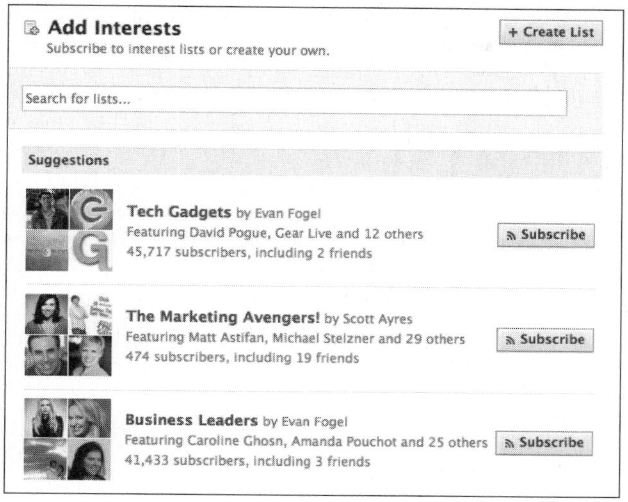

Figure 1-7: Facebook offers suggestions for your Interest Lists.

To set up an Interest List, follow these steps:

1. **Point your browser to** `www.facebook.com/addlist`**, and log in to your account if necessary.**
2. **Click the +Create List button.**

   The window that pops up allows you to search Pages you like, people you subscribe to, and Friends. You can also browse people and Pages by category.
3. **Click to select the Pages, Subscriptions, or Friends you want to add to your list.**
4. **Click Next when you finish adding people and Pages.**
5. **Type a name for your list.**
6. **Choose whether you want your list to be seen publicly, by Friends, or only by you.**
7. **Click Done when you're finished.**

After you create your list, you're taken to that list immediately, and you see the latest updates by the people and Pages you added.

To edit your new Interest List, click the Manage List drop-down menu near the top-right corner of the page. There, you see the options to rename your list, edit your list (including the option to add or remove people and Pages), choose update types, set notification settings, or delete the list.

To access your list, find the Interests section in your left sidebar. Your newly created or subscribed-to lists are displayed here, but you may have to click More to find them. If you'd like to get easier access to your list, hover over the list name, click the pencil icon when it appears, and select Add to Favorites. Now your Interest List will be below your Favorites near the top of your left sidebar.

TIP

You can add a Profile or Page to your Interest Lists (or create new lists) when viewing a person's Profile or Page by clicking the settings icon (gear) under the Profile's or Page's Timeline cover photo. In the drop-down menu, you see Add to Interest Lists, as shown in Figure 1-8.

Figure 1-8: From a Profile or from a Page, you can add people to an Interest List.

Creating a Facebook Offer for Your Local or Online Business

A Facebook Offer is like a coupon that people claim and then either bring in to your place of business to redeem or redeem online at your website. When you create and promote your offer, it goes out into News Feeds, and your fans can click it to claim it. Facebook Offers are created through the Publisher on your Facebook Page. When they claim it, they add their e-mail addresses to the form, and the Offer is sent to them. The great thing about offers is that they can be very viral. When someone claims your offer, your offer posts to that person's News Feed for all of his or her Friends to see.

Creating a Facebook Offer

Facebook Offers are a fantastic way to expose your Facebook fans and their Friends to your special offers.The great news is that offers are extremely easy to use and take just minutes to get going. Essentially, you create special offers on Facebook and then market them to your fans and Friends of fans with a Promoted post. We break this strategy into two parts to help you understand the process. In the first part, you create the Facebook Offer; the second part involves promoting the offer.

You can use Facebook Offers to create a deal of the day, a promotional coupon, or another incentive to encourage fans to shop your online store or a store at their location, as shown in Figure 1-9.

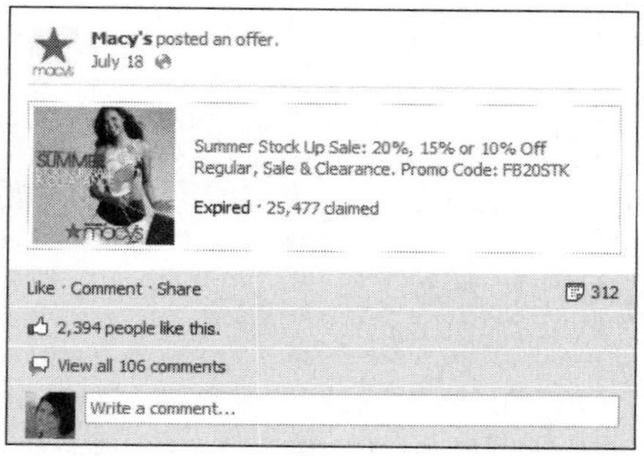

Figure 1-9: Example of a Facebook Offer from Macy's.

REMEMBER

You must have at least 400 fans to access the Facebook Offers Feature. Pages with fewer than 400 fans cannot run offers at this time. You will see the Offer option inside your Publisher on your Facebook Page, as shown in Figure 1-10.

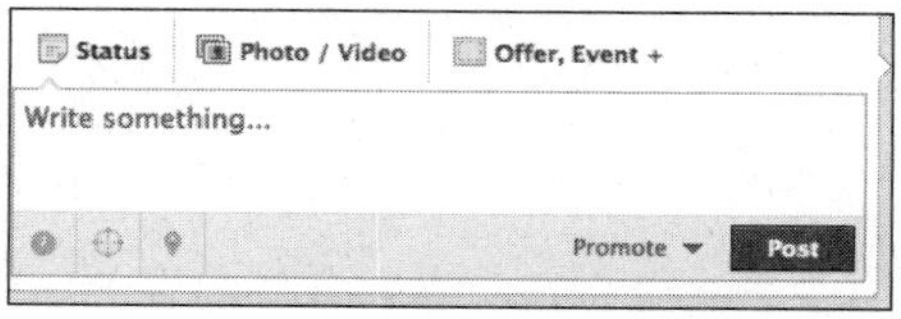

Figure 1-10: The Facebook Offer option inside the Publisher on a Page.

TIP

You have three options when creating a Facebook Offer. You can create offers for in store only, in store and online, and online only. As mentioned, when users claim an offer, they receive an e-mail with details to redeem your offer. You cannot customize the e-mail message that's sent to the person who claimed your offer; it tells them to bring this offer into your business to claim it or go to your website to redeem.

Promoting your offer

Once you create your offer, the next step is to promote it via Promoted posts or Facebook Ads. Promoted posts are status updates that you pay for to get even greater exposure in the News Feeds, which is why this strategy is great for promoting your new Facebook Offer.

Running a Facebook Promoted post is relatively straightforward. There's no bidding process; you pay a flat fee to push your post to a certain number of your fans. The post organically reaches a certain number, and then you're paying for Facebook to show your post to Fans and Friends of fans who may not ordinarily have seen your post in their News Feeds. (For step-by-step instructions on how to create Promoted posts, see Book VIII.)

The overall strategy of creating a Facebook Offer and using a Promoted post to market that offer is a great way to introduce your Facebook fans to your special promotions, discounts, coupons, and the like. If you have a local business and are looking to gain even more foot traffic for your business, you definitely want to test this strategy!

Putting your offer together

Facebook Offers are very easy to set up. To get your Facebook Offer started, follow these steps:

1. **Click the Offers, Events + icon in the Publisher.**

   A drop-down menu appears.

2. **Click Offers.**

   A box appears where you can enter the details of your offer, as shown in Figure 1-11.

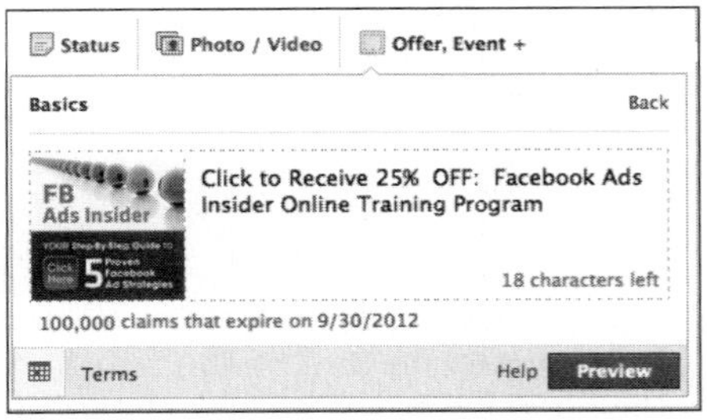

Figure 1-11: Fill out the details of your offer and add an image.

3. **Add a thumbnail photo by clicking the Upload Thumbnail link.**

   A list of files from your computer appears, allowing you to select your photo. A product photo is best. The photo will size to 90 × 90 pixels, so try to pick a square photo. Select the appropriate picture.

4. **Write a headline for your offer in the large box.**

   You have only 90 characters, so you need to make the headline compelling and succinct.

5. **Click the Unlimited hyperlink below the photo area to limit the number of offers available, if applicable.**

   A drop-down menu appears, allowing you to select a preset number of offers or create a custom number of offers.

6. **Click the date hyperlink below the headline area, and in the drop-down menu calendar that appears, select the date to limit the length of time your offer can be claimed.**

7. **Select the Terms field to add any terms and conditions to your offer.**

   A box appears where you can type any terms and conditions.

8. **Click the Preview button.**

   You see the offer as it will appear on your Timeline, and you receive an e-mail notification about the offer information that Facebook will send out when someone claims the offer. If you need to edit further, you can click the Edit link.

9. **Click the Set Budget button.**

   You see two options. You can either promote your offer inside the Facebook Ads dashboard or you can choose to run a Promoted post where you choose a dollar increment at the time you create your offer, as shown in Figure 1-12.

Figure 1-12: Choose a dollar amount to promote your new offer.

10. **To create a Promoted post, choose a dollar increment directly from the Offer Set Budget page.**

    Your offer will run immediately.

11. **To run an ad via the Facebook Ads dashboard:**

    a. *Click Promote Later Using Another Facebook Ad Tool, as shown in Figure 1-13.*

Figure 1-13: Choosing to set up your offer ad via the Facebook Ads dashboard.

b. *Go into the Ads dashboard, click the Create an Ad button, and choose your offer in the Specific Post drop-down menu, as shown in Figure 1-14.*

If you choose to create an ad for your offer inside the ads dashboard, your ad will not run until you do this step.

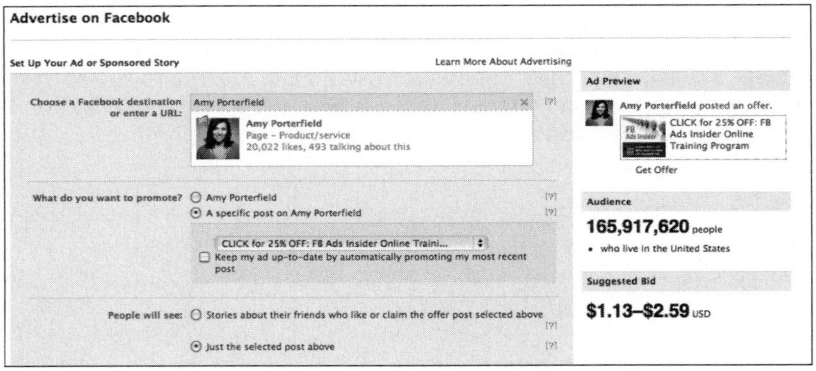

Figure 1-14: Creating an ad for your offer in the ads dashboard.

When your offer has been published, you can see how many people have claimed your offer but not who claimed it.

After you set up your offer, you're ready to move on to the second part of this strategy: creating a Promoted post to market the new offer.

Expanding Your Page's Exposure

The way to get seen on Facebook is to create multiple reasons for people to engage with your Page. Try these tips to increase the chances that your Page will be seen often:

- Set up your vanity URL for your Facebook Page. See Book II, Chapter 3.
- Create a Timeline cover image that's the maximum size available to give your Page a professional, well-branded look and feel. See Book II, Chapter 2.
- Create a custom fans-only page through which you offer an incentive for those who click your Like button. This strategy increases nonfan curiosity and incites action in the form of nonfans clicking the Like button. See Book III, Chapter 2.
- Add a Facebook app to your Page. Consider one that will increase activity and encourage more users to visit your page. See Book V, Chapter 1.
- Run a Facebook Ad campaign for 30 days. (For extra credit, test the Sponsored stories feature, described earlier in this chapter.) See Book VIII, Chapter 1.
- Create a special promotion and test out Facebook Offers by creating a coupon and post about it on your Page.
- Embed a social plug-in on your website to drive up the number of likes on your Page. See Book VII, Chapter 2.

Engaging with Fans

Communicating with your fans helps keep them engaged — and coming back. Here are a few ways to keep the lines of communication wide open:

- Create a Facebook experience to execute on your Business Page. Think of what your fans want most from you, and deliver it as a Facebook experience. See "Creating a Facebook Experience," earlier in this chapter.
- Ask more questions. The more you make things about your fans and less about you, the more your fan base will flourish. Mix up your questions so you have some related to your business and industry, some that get people thinking in new ways, and some that entertain and keep things light. See Book IV, Chapter 2.
- Set up notifications to get continuous alerts when your fans post on your Page. See Book II, Chapter 3.
- If you're having an event online or offline, consider setting up a special custom app to promote the event. (For extra credit, embed a video and a comments plug-in.) See Book III, Chapter 2.
- Turn your Facebook Page into a lead generator by adding a name and e-mail box to your Facebook Page. This box will help you capture the e-mail addresses of your Facebook fans. See Book II, Chapter 2.

Getting Viral Exposure

Going viral isn't so great in the offline world, but it's the best of all possible worlds online. Here are a few ways to position your Page to get lots of viral exposure:

- ✦ Connect your other social media accounts, such as Twitter and LinkedIn, to your Facebook Page to ensure that your posts are getting even better reach and exposure. See Book III, Chapter 4.
- ✦ Stream a live video on your Facebook Page by using the Livestream application (`www.livestream.com`). Live activity will create a buzz! See Book VII, Chapter 3.
- ✦ Create an event by using the Events feature on your Facebook Page. See Book VI, Chapter 1.
- ✦ Pull your blog into your Facebook Page by using the Networked Blogs app. When you publish a blog, it automatically gets pulled onto your Facebook Timeline and into the News Feeds of your fans. See Book III, Chapter 3.
- ✦ Run a contest on your Page, and offer an enticing giveaway to help spread the buzz. Try the Wildfire app or Offerpop for contest support. See Book VI, Chapter 2.

Chapter 2: Marketing with Facebook Social Plug-ins

In This Chapter

- Exploring social plug-ins
- Integrating Facebook with your website
- Finding the right plug-ins to fit your business goals
- Using social plug-ins as part of a marketing program

At one time, users searched the web independently of their peers. Today, users look at what their networks of friends are doing, and they take their friends' activities and recommendations very seriously. Social plug-ins allow you to take advantage of this new way of surveying information.

In this chapter, we cover the basics of social plug-ins: what they are, why they're important, and how you can use them to expand your online presence. When it comes to social plug-ins, you have numerous options. Therefore, we dedicate a separate section to each Facebook social plug-in, as well as offer suggestions for open-source Facebook-friendly plug-ins. Open-source plug-ins are developed outside the Facebook platform, but they integrate seamlessly with Facebook and your website. (We get more into open source later in the chapter.) Overall, this chapter can help you decide which social plug-ins are the right fit for your business goals and how you can integrate them with your overall marketing program.

Understanding Social Plug-ins

Social plug-in tools connect your website with Facebook users and enable social activity among users directly on your site. With Facebook social plug-ins, you create an identical experience of your Facebook Page while maintaining control of your content and brand. Considering the high number of people on Facebook today, social plug-ins can be extremely powerful tools. Plug-ins have many benefits, perhaps one of the most important being their capability to encourage your website visitors to spend more time on your site.

The plug-ins appear as buttons and boxes on websites, and the content populating them comes directly from Facebook activity. If you have a plug-in on your website, when your visitors are logged in to Facebook, they can interact with their Facebook Friends directly from your website. Specifically, they see their Friends' Facebook activity (such as what their Friends have liked, shared, recommended, and posted) via the plug-in on your website.

Here's an example of how social plug-ins work. Suppose that you click a link that you received in an e-mail and land on a website that includes a Like button. If any of your Facebook Friends clicked that button, you see some of their names or Profile images (depending on how the site owner configured the button). Seeing that your Friends have interacted with the site makes you more likely to explore the site's content — and possibly share it with your own social networks. The Like button plug-in lets this activity take place directly on your website rather than going through Facebook — which is exactly what marketers want. Read on to find out why.

Integrating your website with Facebook via plug-ins

So why do you want to integrate your website with Facebook by using social plug-ins? Easy answer: You gain viral visibility. You increase your exposure when you create more opportunities for users to consume your content on your website or blog. Also, by showing how multiple users are interacting with your content every day (ideally), the plug-ins create social proof and increase the credibility of your content.

REMEMBER

The term *social proof* refers to the psychological phenomenon of people being motivated to do things that they see other people doing. Although marketers have used social proof as a fundamental principle for many years, the popularity and growth of social media has strengthened its influence and reach.

Social plug-ins enhance the social proof strategy because they highlight the friends and acquaintances of the people you're directly trying to influence. In many ways, social proof acts as a "foot in the door" strategy because it takes viewers' initial interest and quickly turns that interest into acceptance. The acceptance happens when they see their peers' interactions with the information they are currently consuming. The familiarity builds trust.

Social proof is crucial in creating a successful Facebook marketing plan. The goal is to show your visitors what their peers are talking about, liking, and posting — and in turn, your new visitors will naturally match those behaviors.

The key is to create multiple opportunities for your users to see their Friends interacting with your website. This activity increases traffic to your site and encourages site engagement overall. Social plug-ins aid in this marketing endeavor.

One example of a website that uses social plug-ins successfully is Stay N' Alive (`www.staynalive.com`). Site owner Jesse Stay has implemented two social plug-ins: an Activity Feed (see Figure 2-1) and a Recommendations bar. (We discuss both in detail in this chapter.) Both plug-ins are optimally placed in the right column of the home page for high-traffic viewing. The plug-ins are not only prominently placed, but also extremely active, meaning that Stay posts content to his Facebook Page and website consistently, keeping the social plug-ins updated continually.

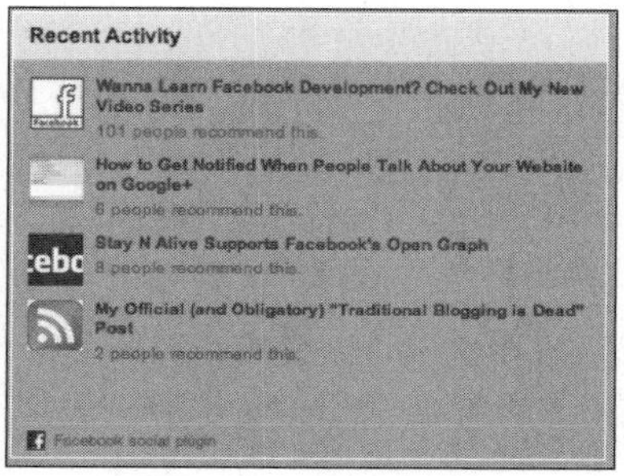

Figure 2-1: The social plug-in Recent Activity used on a website.

Choosing the right plug-ins for your business

You have many options when it comes to social plug-ins for your website. To make things easy, we've separated your options into these two categories: Facebook's own social plug-ins and *open-source plug-ins,* which incorporate Facebook activity but are created by third-party developers.

Facebook offers 11 social plug-ins, and each one has a specific function with unique benefits and multiple features:

- Like button
- Send button
- Like box
- Login button
- Recommendations box
- Recommendations bar
- Activity Feed
- Comments
- Facepile
- Registration
- Subscribe button

Installing these Facebook plug-ins isn't exactly simple, however. In most cases, if you're not familiar with programming code, installing these plug-ins will create some frustration for you rather quickly. If you're not familiar with code, we suggest that you turn this task over to your webmaster. All the details needed to install the plug-ins are available here:

```
http://developers.facebook.com/docs/plugins
```

The open-source, Facebook-friendly plug-ins are developed especially for your website and are much easier to install. (Later in this chapter, we cover how to install these plug-ins on your WordPress site.) Before we get to the installation details, however, we cover in detail what each social plug-in can do to expand your online marketing presence by dedicating a separate section to each plug-in in this chapter.

TIP

You can use just one social plug-in on your website, or you can combine multiple plug-ins based on your overall marketing goals. Understanding the function of each plug-in can help you decide what will work best for your site.

Finding Leads through the Like Button

The Like button plug-in allows anyone who's signed in to Facebook to like the content on your web page, such as a blog post, video, or product. When a user clicks a Like button on your website or blog, a short summary of the content — a *story* — with a link back to the content on your site, is posted to the Facebook Timeline of that user's Profile and also sent out into the News Feeds of all the user's Friends. This feature results in great viral visibility for you, which is why using the Like button in multiple places on your site, such as on each blog post, is a good idea.

Figure 2-2 shows a story (the first few lines from the article and a link back to your website or blog post) posted to a Facebook Timeline after a user clicked a Like button on a website.

Figure 2-2: A story posted to a Facebook Wall by a Like button plug-in.

You may be wondering about the difference between a Like button and a Like box (covered later in this chapter). You can place the Like button next to specific content on your site, such as a blog post, or even next to specific items on your site, such as a product or program you offer. A Like box, though, is associated directly with your Facebook Page and is placed on your website as a way to attract more fans to your Facebook Page.

When setting up a Like button, you have the option to add a comments feature with the button: Users can leave a comment after they click the button. Allowing users to leave comments when they click Like can be an extremely powerful marketing strategy, because Facebook weighs the comment with the link to the blog post more heavily than it would just the link. In Book IV, Chapter 2, we talk about EdgeRank and the algorithm that Facebook uses to decide which posts get the most exposure in the News Feeds. When a user clicks the Like button and also leaves a comment with it, that post gets more weight than if the user didn't leave a comment when clicking the Like button. The extra weight can increase the chances of your content getting seen by more people on Facebook. Figure 2-3 shows an example of the option to leave a comment after clicking the Like button.

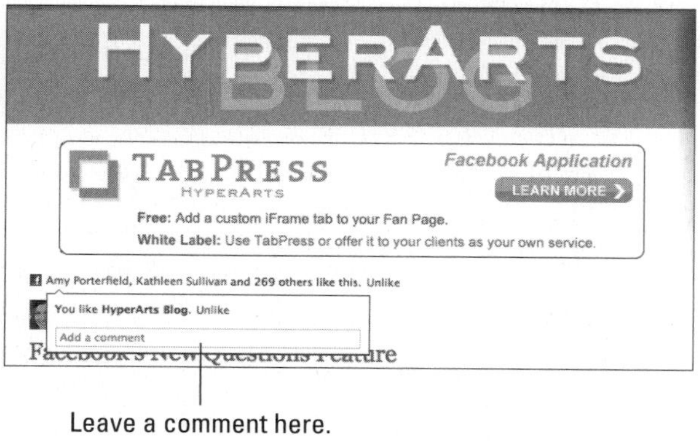

Figure 2-3: Give people the option to leave a comment after clicking the Like button.

Like-button best practices

According to Facebook, websites that used the following best practices experienced three to five times greater click-through rates (CTR) with the Like button:

- Use the version of the Like button that includes thumbnails of users' Friends.
- Enable users to add comments.
- Add the Send button alongside the Like button to increase exposure.
- Place the Like button at the top and bottom of articles and near visually appealing content, such as videos and graphics.

When you set up a Like button, you have a few options that determine how it displays. You can choose a Like button that also displays the number of Likes next to it, or you can choose just the button with no Like count showing. If you opt for the layout with the Like count next to it, the Like count is the sum of the number of likes, shares, comments, and inbox messages containing a URL that can be generated from both the Like button and the Send button. In the next section, we discuss the Send button and how to link it to the Like button to increase your like count and overall exposure.

Optimizing your Like button with Open Graph

With the Open Graph protocol, Facebook enables your website to establish a connection with your visitors and the Facebook platform. Facebook uses a (jargon alert) Open Graph protocol to interact with other websites. You can use the Open Graph on any website or blog. When you use it, the Open Graph provides Facebook the technical tool to link information from outside Facebook with the information on the Facebook platform. By linking the information, your website becomes equivalent to a Facebook Page.

Why does this matter? There's tremendous value in Open Graph when you use it in conjunction with the Facebook Like button. Open Graph allows you to integrate your web pages into what Facebook calls the Social Graph. The Open Graph protocol can be used without Facebook, but because we're talking about Facebook marketing, we focus primarily on how it's used with Facebook.

In this chapter, we discuss the simple, one-step social plug-in process. When a user likes a web page by clicking the Like button, for example, the social plug-in automates an update in the user's News Feed. It's as simple as that, and it stops there. When you add the full Open Graph application programming interface (API) code to your website, however, here's what happens when a user clicks a Like button on your site:

- An update is automatically published on that user's News Feed inside Facebook.
- The updates you publish on your Facebook Page now also appear in that user's News Feed (thus giving you greater exposure).
- Your Page shows up in Facebook search results.
- You can create ads that target people who have liked your content.

How does this work? It all starts with setting the right tags to define the content being liked. Open Graph tags are tags that you add to your website to describe your page's entity — what your page represents, such as a band, restaurant, or blog.

First, there are tags to make the connection with Facebook. With Open Graph, you set tags for your web pages to define them for Facebook. Using the Open Graph tags on your web page makes your page seem as though it's on Facebook. When a reader clicks the Like button on your web page, a connection is established between your web page and the reader. Your page will appear on the reader's Facebook Profile just as though that reader had liked a Facebook Page.

There are also tags to provide context for what is being liked. With the tags, you define this information. Using the Open Graph, Facebook can collect a large amount of information about your fans, prospects, and clients — the people you most want to connect with. You can easily imagine cross-referencing some of this information to find people who are an exact match to a very specific Profile you define — specifically, a Profile that would likely be interested in your products and services.

The Open Graph protocol is pretty technical. If you're not familiar with code, we suggest that you save yourself a lot of unnecessary stress and call your webmaster for assistance. To learn more about Open Graph, visit the Facebook Developer site: `http://developers.facebook.com/docs/opengraph`.

TIP

Encourage your site visitors to like your blog posts and other content on your pages — and also ask them to leave a comment. The gentle reminder will encourage more users to take action.

Sharing Selectively with the Send Button

The Send button is very similar to the Like button and usually appears next to it on websites and blogs. It differs from the Like button, however, in that the Send button is used for selective sharing, whereas the Like button has public sharing capabilities. When a user clicks a Send button next to an article or on a website page, a pop-up window appears, displaying a link to the URL of the page the user is viewing along with a title, an image, and a short description of the link. The user has the option to send the link to specific Facebook Friends, a Facebook group, or a specific e-mail address. The user also has the option to add a personal message, as shown in Figure 2-4.

In many ways, the Send button is designed to be Like's companion, meaning that you often see the two buttons side by side. Some users like to customize their messages and selectively choose whom they're sending to, whereas others like to share more openly. We recommend adding both buttons to give your users sharing options. As mentioned earlier in this chapter, the Like button count is the sum of the number of likes, shares, comments, and inbox messages containing a URL that can be generated from both the Like button and the Send button, so the two truly work hand in hand to increase your overall exposure through social sharing from those who visit your site.

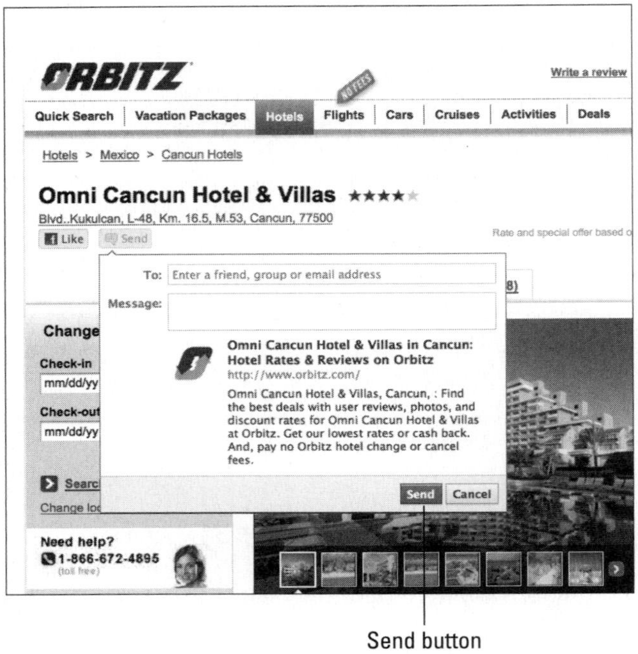

Figure 2-4: The pop-up window that appears when you click the Send button.

Using a Like Box to Grow Your Fan Base

A Like Box plug-in brings attention to your Facebook Page while visitors are on your website and also allows your users to interact with your Page. As we mention in the previous section, a Like button is used to promote individual content on your site, whereas a Like box is associated directly with your Facebook Page and is placed on your website as a way to attract more fans to your Page. Specifically, a Like box allows visitors to like your Facebook Page without ever leaving your website or blog, which is something that marketers see as highly advantageous.

In addition to allowing people to like your Page with just one click, a Like box gives you the option to add the posts from your Facebook Page, encouraging even greater social interaction on your website. We suggest that you use this option because it gives your visitors the opportunity to be exposed to even more of your content.

The best place for a Like box usually is your home page, but you can place it on multiple pages throughout your site. You can also include thumbnails of your user's Friends to instantly indicate to your site's visitors which of their

Friends have already liked your Page. We recommend this option and suggest that you display at least ten Profile images, because the more users you show, the greater the social-proof appeal is.

You can adjust the dimensions and number of fans who show up in your Like box. This feature allows you to choose the size that suits your website design. You also have the option to include your Facebook Timeline feed as well as a "Find us on Facebook" header.

Finding Out More about Your Visitors with the Login Button

The Login Button plug-in allows your users to sign in to your website via their Facebook accounts. Take a look at Figure 2-5 to see how Mashable uses this plug-in on its website. When you install this button, you can access data such as a user's name, e-mail address, Profile picture, and list of Friends. This information is valuable to use as you communicate and market to your Facebook audience.

When a visitor clicks the Login button on your site, he first sees a Request for Permission window (see Figure 2-6), where he's prompted to click Allow to move forward with the login.

When users who have already clicked your Login button return to your website, if they're logged into Facebook, they're automatically logged in to your site when they click the Login button and won't have to click the Allow button again. If they try to log in to your site and aren't logged into Facebook, though, they're prompted to log in to Facebook first.

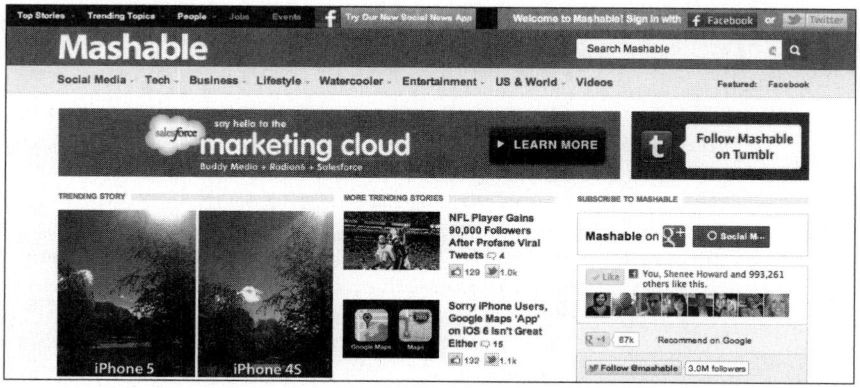

Figure 2-5: The Login button on the Mashable website.

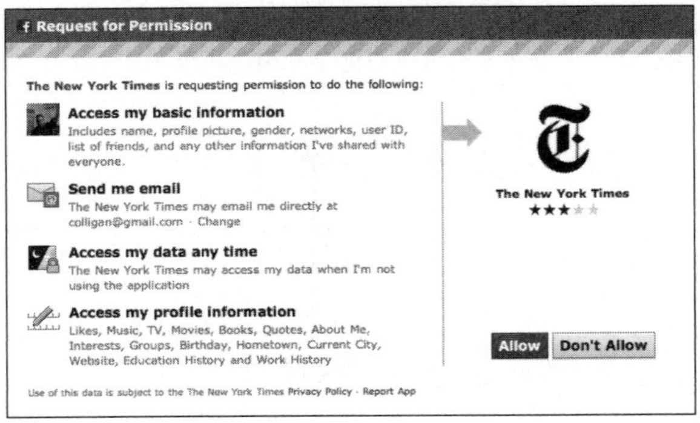

Figure 2-6: The Request for Permission window.

In addition to using the login feature, you have the option to add the Profile images of the users who click the Login button. When the Login button with Faces is placed on your website, visitors initially see only the Login button. After visitors click Allow (meaning that they're giving their consent to be logged in to your site via Facebook), their Facebook Profile images appear inside the Login button box on your website, along with all their Friends who also signed in to your website via the Login button.

TIP

You have the option to not include the Profile images with the Login button, but you'll increase your social-proof appeal if you include the images of your users. These images will entice Friends of the users who visit your site to log in with the Login button.

Now you have access to all the public Facebook information on that user, including a user's name, Profile picture, interests, list of Friends, and more. As we mention earlier, this information could be valuable as you collect data on the demographics, likes, and interests of the users who visit your site.

Using Recommendations for Social Proof

The Recommendations box plug-in shows the most popular content on your website or blog, as well as the number of times that content has been shared. Specific content is listed in the Recommendations box based on the number of times your viewers like or share content from your site on their Facebook Profiles and Pages. This means that if someone clicks the Like button attached to an article on your site, that article is considered to be one recommendation. The blog posts, articles, videos, or other forms of content that are socially shared the most are highlighted in the Recommendations box. You can see this box in action in Figure 2-7.

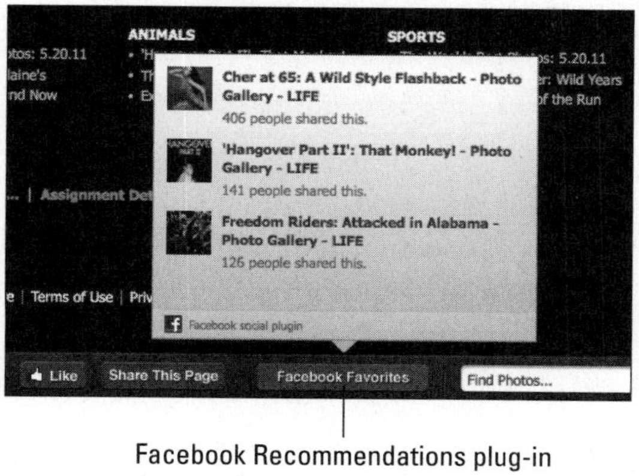

Figure 2-7: A Recommendations social plug-in on a non-Facebook website.

Visitors to your site will see the recommended content regardless of whether they're logged into Facebook. If they're logged into Facebook, they see the content that their Friends have shared at the top of the Recommendations box.

The benefit of this plug-in is its capability to spotlight your most popular content for visitors new to your site. When the Recommendations box pulls in your content that your users interact with most, there's an increased chance that new visitors will interact with your content and in turn learn more about your business.

Offering Smart Suggestions with the Recommendations Bar

The Recommendations bar helps your website visitors find articles based on what their Friends like and share from your site. The Recommendations bar functions similarly to the Like button. When a website visitor likes an article on your website by using your Recommendations bar, a story is published to that person's News Feed and also to her Friends' News Feeds, giving your site and articles maximum exposure.

The Recommendations bar is docked to the bottom-right or bottom-left corner of the screen. When a user goes to your website, the Recommendations bar is automatically collapsed, and the user has the option to like your Page. As the user scrolls down your page, the social plug-in actually expands. The expanded view shows the user a few social recommendations of the next articles to read on your site, based on her Facebook Friends' activities on your site (see Figure 2-8).

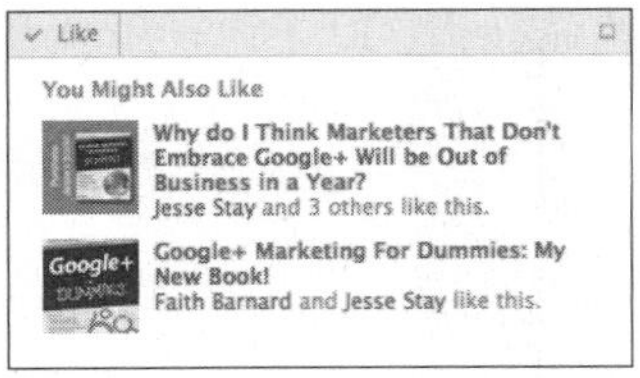

Figure 2-8: A Recommendations bar on a website.

Spotlighting Your Latest Content with the Activity Feed

An Activity Feed plug-in allows users on your site to see what their Friends are interacting with, such as liking or recommending the content on your site. It's very similar to the Recommendations box plug-in, but it highlights the person and the action that the person took, such as "Amy Porterfield liked 8 Ways to Improve Your Blog." Visitors can also see the number of times certain content on your website has been recommended.

A visitor to your site can see the recent activity on your site regardless of whether he's logged in to Facebook, but if he's logged in to Facebook, he sees only the activity of his Friends. The plug-in gives you the option to include recommendations, meaning that the top half of the Activity Feed box is activity by the user's Friends, and the bottom half is recommendations (likes and shares) from everyone on your site. We suggest that you show the recommendations on your Activity Feed. Figure 2-9 shows an Activity Feed social plug-in at work.

Figure 2-9: The contents of the Activity Feed plug-in.

The Activity Feed plug-in is a great way to guide your visitors to the content that their Friends and peers have already shown interest in. Because people in the same networks tend to enjoy similar content, your new visitors will likely also be interested in the content that their Friends recommended.

Optimizing the Comments Feature

The Facebook Comments plug-in allows you to add an interactive posting and discussion feature to specific pages on your website. The most popular way that this plug-in is used is to allow users to add their comments to your blog site.

Encouraging your website or blog readers to leave comments on your site is important, because it allows users to share their thoughts and be heard, and also gives them an opportunity to connect with other users of your site. Further, comments act as social proof for your site, because the perceived value of your content increases as the number of comments increases.

When you use the Facebook Comments plug-in, your visitors who leave a comment have a few options: They can leave a comment as their Facebook Profile or as any Page they administer, or they can also choose to have their comment posted to their Facebook Timeline (on their Profile or Page, depending whether they posted as their Profile or their Page). When they leave the Post to Facebook check box selected, a story publishes to the News Feeds of their Friends or fans. This option increases the visibility of content on your site, because the story links back to your blog post or website.

What makes Facebook Comments different from other blog-commenting systems is that the comments are posted on your blog site as well as on Facebook. This allows Friends and fans to respond to the discussion by liking or replying to the comment directly in their News Feeds on Facebook or in the comments area of your blog site. Also, *threads* (strings of conversations in the comments area) from inside Facebook and from the comments area of your website stay synchronized, meaning that no matter where the comment is made for the original blog post, it always shows up in your comments box and on Facebook. The conversations are indented, making it easy to identify separate conversations, as you see in Figure 2-10. Also, all the likes on the comments are synced in both places. The viral exposure from this plug-in is extremely powerful. Figure 2-10 shows the Facebook Comments plug-in at work on the TechCrunch website.

The Facebook Comments box also uses social relevance to order the blog comments. That means that each user logged in to Facebook sees what Facebook calls "relevant and interesting comments" — comments made by the user's Friends and Friends of Friends, as well as the most liked and active discussions — at the top of the Comments box. The comments that Susie would see at the top of a Facebook Comments box would be different from the comments that Sally would see because Susie and Sally have different Friends and connections on Facebook. The experience is personalized for everyone.

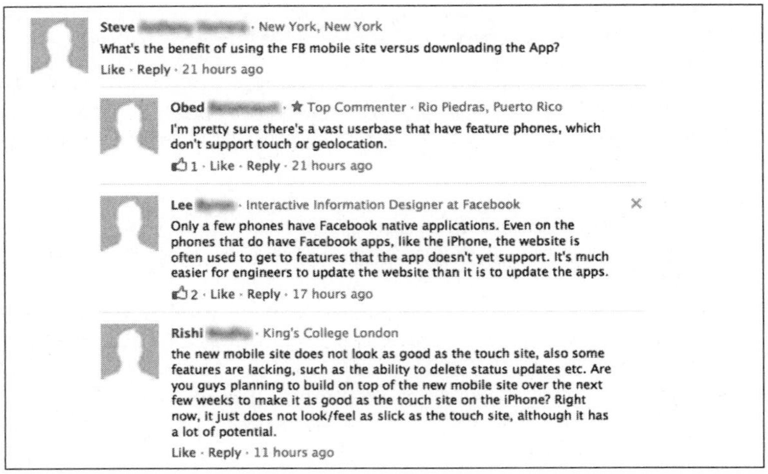

Figure 2-10: The Facebook Comments plug-in at work.

You have multiple ways to optimize the comments system on your site:

- Enable the Comments plug-in in multiple areas on your website, including specific web pages, articles, photos, and videos. This allows your users to interact with your site in more ways than one.
- Respond to your users' comments often and in real time when possible. This allows you to create one-on-one relationships with the visitors to your site. Refer to Figure 2-10 for an example of a Comments box on a website.
- Encourage users to post comments by asking for their feedback about your article, video, photo, and so on or by asking a question at the end of your post.

If your site doesn't already offer comment functionality, or if you're using a comment system that's getting minimal interaction, consider installing a Comments plug-in. You have great potential for your online exposure to increase as users share their comments on your site.

Optimizing Your Connections with Facepile

The Facepile feature shows users the Profile images of their Friends who have signed in to your website or have liked your Page (see Figure 2-11). One benefit of this feature is that it doesn't display if the user doesn't have Friends who have signed in to your site. Therefore, the social plug-in displays only when appropriate.

Figure 2-11: The Facepile social plug-in on a non-Facebook website.

Don't worry if you don't have a lot of fans for your site. The Facepile plug-in resizes its height dynamically, so it won't look awkward if only a few Friends are featured in the box.

You have two options for configuring the Facepile plug-in:

- **Include a Login button.** When you include this button (refer to the preceding section), your users can sign in via the button; then the faces of their Friends who have already signed in to your site appear in the Facepile box.
- **Omit a Login button.** If your website has a separate sign-in process that's not connected to a Facebook Login button, you can install the Facepile box without the Facebook Login button; then the Facepile box displays the faces of those who sign in to your site via your separate sign-in process.

Following the social proof-appeal strategy, when you have the opportunity to display Friends' faces on your site, do it! People are more likely to look to their friends for recommendations and suggestions than they are to search independently on the web. The Facepile plug-in creates social proof by showing users which of their Facebook Friends have already signed in to a website or liked your page. Depending on your preferences, you can customize your Facepile box to show just a few Profile images or multiple rows of user images.

Seeing a familiar face on a website can create an instant connection between the visitor, her Friends, and your site. Also, it's easier for your visitors to "know, like, and trust you" when they see that their Friends have already embraced your site.

The more users your site attracts, the greater the chances are that your new visitors will see their Friends' Profile images in your Facepile box. If your site is brand new, you may want to wait a little while to build some momentum before you install this plug-in. The plug-in will have greater impact if your users see many of their Friends inside the Facepile box.

Capturing Audience Data with the Registration Plug-in

The Registration social plug-in allows your users to sign in to your website with their Facebook accounts. Non-Facebook users can also use this plug-in to register for your website.

To use the plug-in, all you need to do is add a single line of code to create a registration form on your website. When users log in to Facebook and click the Registration button on your website, the form prepopulates with information from their Profiles, as shown in Figure 2-12.

If users aren't logged in to Facebook when they come to your website, the Register button automatically reads *Login* instead and prompts the user to log in to his Facebook account. After the user logs in to Facebook, he sees the prepopulated form to register for your site. *Prepopulated* means that a user's name, e-mail address, birthday, gender, and current city can appear in the form automatically, depending on how you set up the Registration plug-in. This prepopulation feature in the Registration plug-in reduces drop-off during registration, because users (obviously) find filling out the remainder of the form much easier. This ease of use in turn increases the number of users who complete registration on your website.

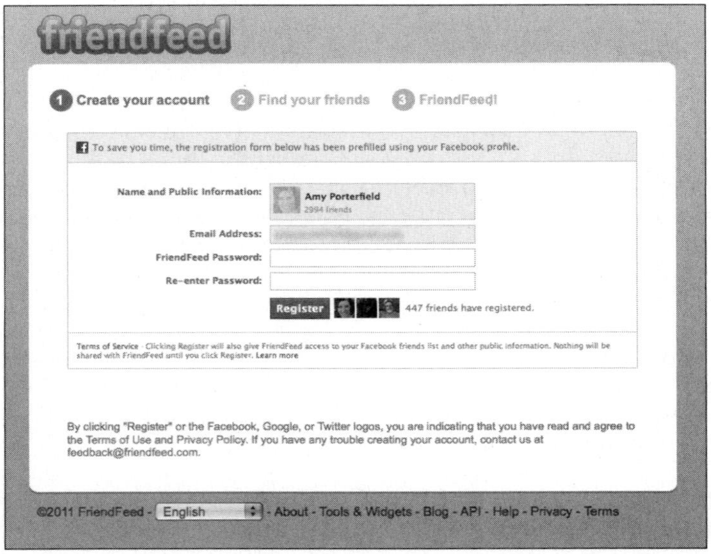

Figure 2-12: A registration sign-in form on a website.

You may be wondering how this plug-in is different from the Login plug-in. Think of the Registration plug-in as being an advanced Login button with additional features and benefits. Both buttons allow you to collect data about your users upon login/registration, but the Registration button also allows your users to create a username and password to log in to your site. They can use that username and password each time they return to your site.

In addition, the form that the plug-in creates allows you to add fields to ask for additional data not supplied by Facebook. When a user logs in for the first time, you can prompt her to answer questions you create. You may want to ask users questions related to your niche. If you own a wine shop, you might ask users to tell you their favorite wine. If you're a Realtor, you might ask users to add the zip code of the location in which they're looking to buy a home.

To read more about the flow of the Registration button and to get ideas about to use it, go to `http://developers.facebook.com/docs/user_registration/flows`.

Attracting a Larger Audience with the Subscribe Button

The Subscribe button social plug-in allows your website audience to subscribe to your public Facebook updates that you post on your Profile. When you're a subscriber to someone's Profile on Facebook, you don't have to be Facebook Friends with that person to see her public posts.

There's a very clear marketing strategy behind activating your Subscribe button on a personal account. If you're branding yourself, consider activating the Subscribe button on your personal Profile. We cover this strategy in more detail in Book II.

REMEMBER

To be clear, there's a Subscribe button that you add *to your Profile* (discussed in Book II), and there's a Subscribe button social plug-in that you add *to your website* (as shown in Figure 2-13) to encourage visitors to subscribe to your Facebook Profile. Both elements do the same thing. One is located on your Facebook Profile, and the other is located on your website.

Figure 2-13: Facebook users can subscribe to your public Profile posts via a button on your website.

Finding and Installing Open-Source Facebook Plug-Ins

Open-source Facebook-friendly plug-ins incorporate Facebook activity but are created by third-party developers outside the Facebook platform. These plug-ins are very similar — some being almost identical to the Facebook social plug-ins — but are much easier to install (no coding!). Open-source plug-ins include access to Facebook activity, and some of them also include access to multiple social networks, which can expand your overall online reach. We explore some plug-ins that include multiple social networks in the section "Using Share buttons for multiple social networks," later in this chapter.

Considering the most popular open-source social plug-ins

If you're considering adding a few open-source social plug-ins to your website or blog, and you're looking for some help in choosing the best ones, we suggest starting with the following:

- Like Button
- Like Box
- Comments

As a refresher, we suggest that you add the Like button to the top or bottom of each of your blog posts. This gives your content greater viral visibility and attracts new visitors to your site when it gets posted in the News Feeds of your visitors' Friends.

We suggest using a Like box as a great way for a visitor to become an instant fan of your Facebook Page without ever leaving your website. Because the goal is to keep visitors on your site as long as possible, the Like box is an extremely useful marketing tool. We also suggest that you choose the option in this box to show your Facebook Page activity as well. This gives your Facebook content even greater exposure on your website.

Finally, the Comments box is crucial for your blog. Without active commenting on your blog site, you can't gauge your audience's interest in your content. Also, blog comments are great social proof. Although the Facebook Comments box has many useful features, we especially like the commenting system Disqus. Although this commenting tool doesn't post comments directly to Facebook, it does allow easy commenting and includes the threading feature we mention earlier in this chapter; you can comment directly below another user's comment, which keeps specific conversations synced. Also, many blog readers have Disqus accounts and are familiar with the system, making it more likely that they'll leave a comment on your blog post.

You can access the Disqus WordPress plug-in by going to `http://wordpress.org/extend/plugins/disqus-comment-system`.

Using Share buttons for multiple social networks

Social media Share buttons are great options if you want to combine multiple opportunities for visitors to share your content. These buttons offer your visitors choices about how to share your content with their social networks without ever leaving your site.

You have several open-source Share button plug-ins to choose among. Here are two of our favorites:

✦ **Shareaholic:** This company offers a variety of plug-ins that connect your website and blog posts to different social bookmarks and social networks, such as Facebook, Twitter, and LinkedIn. We like the Sexy Bookmarks tool best. With the Sexy Bookmarks tool, your reader can place his cursor on any of the icons to see it pop up on his screen. Then he can click the icon and share your content directly with that social network or bookmarking site, as you see in Figure 2-14. To access the WordPress option for this plug-in, go to `http://wordpress.org/extend/plugins/sexybookmarks`.

Figure 2-14: The Sexy Bookmarks plug-in on a blog site.

- **Digg Digg:** This plug-in provides multiple ways for your visitors to share your content on their social networks. They have two versions of this plug-in: a static version and one that floats to stay in view as your reader scrolls down the length of the post. You can see this plug-in as it floats in the middle of a blog post in Figure 2-15. To access the WordPress option for this plug-in, go to `http://wordpress.org/extend/plugins/digg-digg`.

Digg Digg social sharing tool

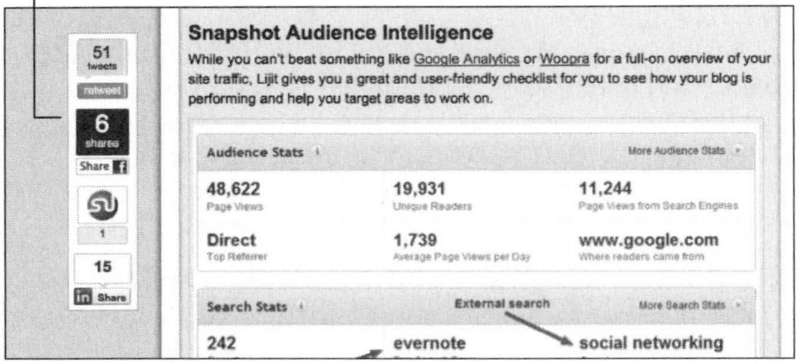

Figure 2-15: The Digg Digg plug-in on a blog site.

Installing a WordPress plug-in (The easy way!)

WordPress, the most widely used blogging platform, offers hundreds of social plug-in options. Here are the universal steps for installing a plug-in on a WordPress platform:

1. **Log in to your WordPress dashboard.**

   In the left column of your dashboard, you see multiple categories, with links below each category.

2. **Click the Plugins link.**

   You can find this link in the left column on your dashboard. After you click the Plugins link, you see a list of plug-ins that are already installed on your WordPress site.

3. **Click the Add New button (near the top of the page).**

   Now you see a search field.

4. **Type** Facebook Like Button **in the search box, and click Search Plugins.**

   Multiple plug-ins appear in a list format. Each plug-in has a short summary explaining its features. You can take the time to research which plug-in meets your needs, or you can do a little research in advance and search for the one you already know you want.

TIP

If you want a suggestion, our favorite WordPress Like button plug-in is Facebook Like Button Plugin for WordPress, by Dean Peters. This plug-in is likely to appear when you search for *"Facebook Like Button"* in the plug-ins search field.

5. **When you find the plug-in you want to install, click Install Now below the specific plug-in's name.**

   You may see a page that asks you to enter your FTP username and password. This information is required to host the plug-in on your web server. If your FTP username has already been added, you may not be prompted for this information.

6. **Enter your FTP username and password, and click Proceed.**

   Note: If you don't remember your credentials, you can contact the company that hosts your website to get this information.

   You see an Installing Plugin page. The installation starts automatically. Wait a few seconds, and you see a `Successfully installed plugin` message and an Activate Plugin link.

7. **Click Activate Plugin.**

   You're ready to set up your plug-in.

8. **Click the Settings link to the newly activated plug-in.**

   You can find the Settings link of your plug-in by locating the Settings category in the left column of your WordPress dashboard. After you click your new plug-in, you see a page with options to change the settings of the plug-in. Each Settings page differs, depending on the plug-in.

   If you have questions, you see a link back to the official page of the plug-in that you just installed. You can click that link to find out more information about your plug-in and get answers to any questions you may have.

Chapter 3: Discovering Live Video Streaming on Facebook

In This Chapter

- Exploring how streaming live video can enhance your business
- Choosing a video-streaming application that's best for you
- Setting up your live-streaming application
- Marketing your streaming event

Live streaming is used to stream live video of different types of events, from college football games to company announcements. It can be used for brand events and business events, wherever they are. It's also a great way for musicians and all kinds of other artists to connect with their fans. Live streaming gives you an additional communication platform for your event, and simultaneous live-streaming chat boxes can make these video events even more interesting for everyone.

In this chapter, we first look at what live streaming can mean to you. Then we discuss some of the most popular live-streaming applications available to you today and show you how to set them up. Finally, we tell you how to use these tools to get more out of your live events.

Understanding the Benefits of Streaming Video

Streaming adds a whole new social dimension to any event. Here are the reasons why:

- **Audience reactions:** You can see who is participating in the event and gain insight into how well your event is going over with your audience.
- **Increased traffic:** The live social stream drives more traffic to your event. Viewers post updates to their social networks and bring in more of their friends to watch the event. With a relatively small number of well-connected viewers sharing your content, you don't need to have a huge budget to create a popular event.
- **More social engagement:** The most important social addition is the increased engagement you can create for an event because viewers can participate. This is why you want to share your event in the first place, right?

For a glimpse of the social video experience, have a look at Facebook's official live streaming Page at `www.facebook.com/facebooklive`.

Attracting viewers with chat

Live social streams work best when they're used in conjunction with a live event broadcast through streaming video, because the stream of comments from other viewers naturally pulls others in to share their own thoughts and comments.

Combining a stream of comments with your video broadcast is a way to grow your audience organically during the broadcast itself. Facebook makes it easy to build a larger and more interactive community around your event.

Live-streaming your event with a real-time Facebook chat box increases your exposure to your fans and their Facebook Friends. These real-time chat boxes (also called live social streams) allow you to have millions of viewers interacting at the same time. Chat boxes are powerful communication tools when they're used on the Page next to your live-streaming video content. The chat box invites viewers to participate by reading other viewers' comments and sharing their own. Chat boxes also include embedded Share buttons (see Figure 3-1).

Figure 3-1: Live-streaming video with a chat box and Share buttons.

Getting closer to customers

Facebook is a social platform; it's where people come to chat with friends. In this social environment, live streaming is a tool that helps businesses get closer to their audience. With a little planning for both social media and offline promotion, it's easy for businesses to cultivate interaction, create buzz (see the last section of this chapter), and expand their audience, thanks to social media.

Supplementing traditional advertising

Given the size of Facebook and the viral nature of social media, live streaming through Facebook can give you as much visibility as any form of traditional media advertising. A live chat box helps you engage a large audience for your live-streaming video.

Keep in mind, however, that you won't be able to control all aspects of your live-streamed marketing communication. Streaming gives your viewers a platform to share their opinions, exchange ideas with friends, and read all the comments posted by other viewers.

Choosing Your Streaming Application

Currently, you have a few options for streaming live video on Facebook. In this chapter, we examine two popular applications:

- **Linqto:** The Linqto application is a live online platform that's easy to use and doesn't require you to download anything to get started. It's available as a Facebook application (at `www.linqto.com`); a standard URL provides an additional entry point to the live site. Linqto is inexpensive ($8 per month). It takes just a short time to get it up and running. If you are brand new to Facebook and/or live video streaming, Linqto is a great platform to experiment with. It's important to understand that this application doesn't live on your Facebook Page; instead it creates your own application inside Facebook (see Figure 3-2). Your live sessions, as well as the recordings of the sessions, will be accessible via your unique application.
- **Livestream for Facebook:** The Livestream for Facebook application (at `http://apps.facebook.com/livestream`) supports both do-it-yourself video broadcasting and live stream chat boxes on your Facebook Page (see Figure 3-3). If you need a tool to broadcast your live videos inside Facebook, the easy-to-use Livestream application is for you. There is no cost to use the basic version of Livestream to stream and record video on Facebook. The basic version should be all you need to get started.

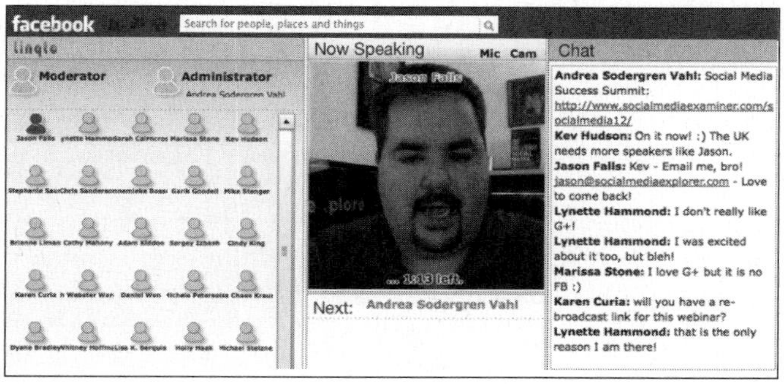

Figure 3-2: The Linqto platform on a Facebook application.

Figure 3-3: The Livestream application on a Facebook Page.

Linqto and Livestream are third-party applications. To better understand third-party applications, go to Book V.

How do you know which application to choose? Your choice depends on what you need to do:

- If your business needs to stream live video to your Facebook community, no more than 300 people will be participating in your live chat, and you don't require the live stream to be embedded in your Facebook Page, Linqto may be a good option for you. It's easier to use than the Livestream application (not as many bells and whistles).
- If your business needs a robust, professional broadcasting tool and wants to take full advantage of your Facebook community, with no audience-size limitations, you'll want to look at the Livestream application for publishing your videos directly on your Facebook Page.

Things change rapidly in this field, and other solutions may exist at the time you read this chapter. Other companies that you should check out for live video streaming on Facebook are Ustream (`www.ustream.tv`), Justin.tv (`www.justin.tv`), and Vpype (`http://vpype.com`). Also, Google has been talking about a live-streaming application for YouTube, so don't forget to watch developments there as well.

In the next two sections, we show you how to create a live stream with both Linqto and Livestream.

Streaming Your Live Broadcast with the Linqto Application

Here's how to get started with the Linqto application:

1. **Go to** `www.linqto.com`**, and click the Try It Free button.**

   Here you will see details about the 30-day free trial offer.

2. **To receive the 30-day trial offer, click the Log in button.**

   You're taken to a login page that asks for permission to log in to your Facebook account. On this page you need to choose who can see the posts that this app makes for you on your Timeline. You can choose to make the posts public, only visible to your Facebook Friends, or you can choose to make them visible only to you.

3. **Click Log In with Facebook to access Linqto via your Facebook account.**

   You're prompted to create a site name and URL for your visitors to use to access your site, as shown in Figure 3-4.

Site Name and URL Address
×
The first step in creating your own Linqto site is to give it a name, and to specify the application URL address which will be used by your visitors to access your site. This URL address must be 7 to 18 characters long, all lower case, and only letters from the alphabet. You must create a Site Name and URL Address in order to create your site, but you can also change them until you activate your free trial.
Site Name: Amy Porterfield's Live Facebook Marketing Videos
URL Address: amylive
Suggest
Visitors can find your site on Facebook or directly on the web at these URLs:
On Facebook: http://apps.facebook.com/amylive
On the Web: http://www.linqto.com/rooms/amylive
Save

Figure 3-4: Choose your site name and URL for your application.

4. **Type a site name and URL that best represent your business and the type of videos you'll be streaming and then click Save.**

   After you set up your site name and URL, you're taken to your personal Linqto application. This page is what your users will see before they enter a live-video viewing room. You can add details about your upcoming videos and links to other websites, as shown in Figure 3-5.

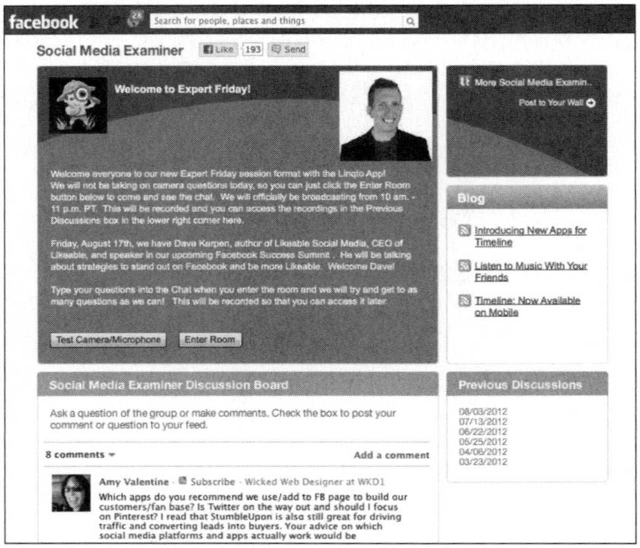

Figure 3-5: The Social Media Examiner Linqto application.

5. **Click Activate.**
6. **Enter your credit-card information in the next page and click Activate Subscription.**

   You'll be billed $8 per month as long as your account is active.

   After you activate your account, your Linqto URL address is live.

Streaming from Your Facebook Page with the Livestream Application

Are you ready to try your hand at broadcasting an event directly through your Facebook Page? You can create your own real-time broadcast and have a real-time chat box at the same time, directly from your Facebook Page, thanks to the Livestream application!

There's no fee to set up your Livestream application, but you have to go through a simple verification process before you can have more than 50 viewers at the same time. Livestream uses this process to limit piracy. After you go through this initial process, you have access to live streaming to an unlimited number of viewers.

REMEMBER

The Livestream application doesn't work on your personal Facebook Profile. You need a Facebook Page to use this application. Your broadcast will be set up on a tab on your Page. Facebook is known to change things, however, so check back to see whether it becomes available on Facebook Profiles, too.

Creating a Livestream account

If you want to use the Livestream application to create and broadcast your own video through your Facebook Page, you need a Livestream account. (If you want to broadcast from an existing Livestream account, whether that account is your own or someone else's, you can skip this process.)

To set up a Livestream account, follow these steps:

1. **Go to** `https://secure.livestream.com/myaccount/selectwizard`**.**

   You see a screen that asks, "What would you like to do?"

2. **Click Broadcast.**

   You go to the Livestream Account Center page.

3. **Enter a name for your channel.**

   As you type your channel name, Livestream populates the Short Name and Channel Page fields, and instantly lets you know whether the name is available. (If not, you need to choose a new name.) See Figure 3-6.

Figure 3-6: The Account Center page.

4. **On the same page, click Launch Free Channel or Launch Premium Channel, as shown in Figure 3-7.**

   The premium channel lets you stream with no advertisements; however, that channel costs $350 per month. If you're okay with ads, choose the free channel.

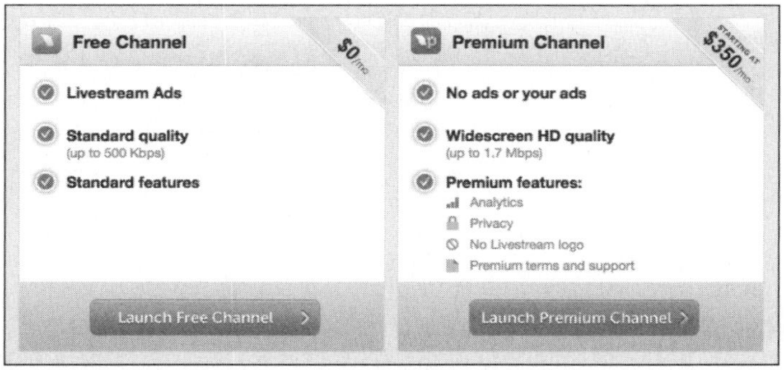

Figure 3-7: The two channel launch options.

5. **Enter your sign-up information.**
6. **Click Sign Up in the bottom-right corner.**

   A Congratulations! screen confirms your sign-up.

Installing the Livestream application on your Facebook Page

After you establish a Livestream account, you're ready to install the Livestream application and add it to a Facebook tab on your Page, as follows:

1. **Go to** www.facebook.com**, and log in to your account.**
2. **Go to** http://apps.facebook.com/livestream**.**
3. **Locate the Page where you intend to use the Livestream application.**

   If you already have several Facebook Pages, you see all of them listed below Pages without Livestream, as shown in Figure 3-8. If you've created only one Page, you see only that Page listed.
4. **Click the Add Page Tab button for the Page where you intend to use Livestream.**

   You're taken to a permission request page.
5. **Click Add Livestream to accept the permission request (see Figure 3-9).**

   Livestream requires permission to access your basic information, including name, Profile picture, gender, networks, user ID, list of Friends, and any other information you've shared with everyone.

Figure 3-8: The Livestream for Facebook application setup page.

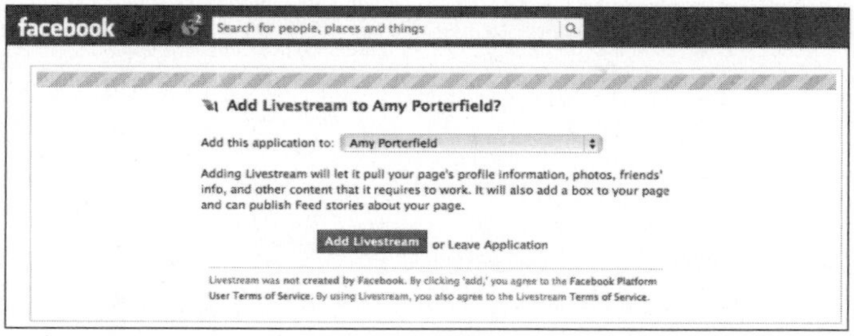

Figure 3-9: Permission request for the Livestream application.

After you accept the permission request, you're taken to your Page. Your new Livestream tab is viewable, along with your other existing Page tabs, as shown in Figure 3-10.

Figure 3-10: Locate your Livestream Page tab on your Facebook Page.

Adding Livestream to a tab on your Page

Here's how you get started with your new Livestream application:

1. **Click your new Livestream Page tab from your Facebook Page.**

   You see an option to Start New Channel or Use Existing Channel, as shown in Figure 3-11.

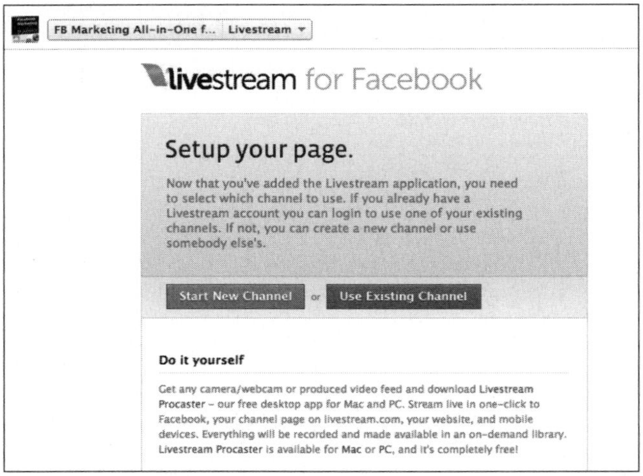

Figure 3-11: Setup page for your new Livestream application.

If you are new to Livestream, you will choose Start New Channel. You are then prompted to log in to your Livestream account, as shown in Figure 3-12.

2. **Log in.**

   Now you see Channel Name and a drop-down menu. Choose the Start New Channel option in the drop-down.

3. **You are prompted to choose a name for your new channel. Type in a channel name and click Launch Channel.**

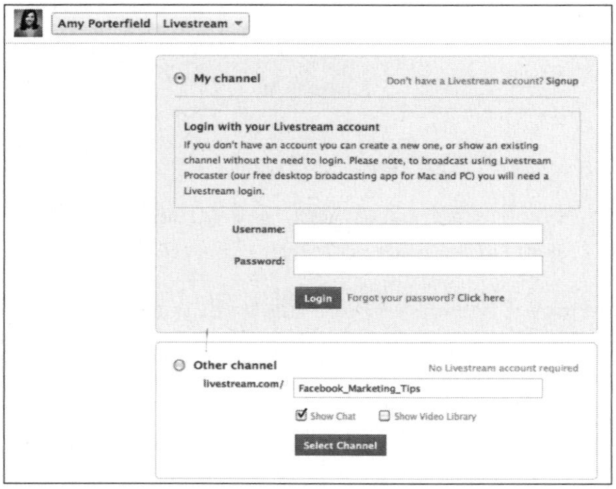

Figure 3-12: The login page.

You see more options to set up your channel, including the channel description. A channel is just like a TV channel that you select from Livestream. You get to choose what you intend to broadcast. It can be your own channel or a channel that already exists on Livestream.

After you select your channel option, you see the Channel Settings page.

4. **Select the channel you want to show from the drop-down menu list.**
5. **Add the channel description.**

   Your audience will see this description, so make it good!

6. **(Optional) Upload a banner by clicking Browse and choosing a banner image from your computer.**
7. **Click Save Changes.**

   Your Livestream Page tab is created.

Congratulations! You're done installing the application, so all you need to do now is follow the steps to broadcast your video.

TIP

To broadcast your live video on your Facebook Page, try the Livestream Procaster. You can download the Procaster by clicking the Options button on your Livestream Facebook Page tab and then choosing Broadcast Now. You can broadcast video directly from a camera or from a webcam. You can also broadcast what you're showing on your computer screen, such as a Microsoft PowerPoint presentation. For more details on broadcasting with the Livestream Procaster, visit `www.livestream.com/platform/procaster`.

Creating Buzz about Your Live Stream

After you have your live stream up and ready to run, you want to get people interested in your live-streaming event — and this is where your Facebook marketing skills come into play.

Posting to your Facebook Page

Before your live-streaming event, remember to post an update on your Facebook Page to let your audience know what's coming:

- Tell them about your live-streaming event.
- Tell them why they'll find it interesting.
- Tell them how they'll be able to participate.
- Ask them to tell their friends.

Keeping Facebook users interested in the stream

As with creating other experiences on Facebook, you'll benefit from a communication plan to promote your live-streaming event. Here are a few key tips to help you maximize your live-streaming experience:

- Let people know about your live-streaming event before, during, and after the event.
- Reach out to people in different ways and on different communication platforms.
- Share the link to your live-streaming event on Facebook, Twitter, and LinkedIn, as well as on your website and blog. Also, e-mail your prospects and clients, and invite them to your live broadcast.
- Use a positive, conversational tone in your updates.

During your live-streaming event, be sure to let your audience on your Facebook Page know what's happening live, and give them the link.

You can also create a Facebook Event and promote your upcoming event there. To read more about Facebook Events, go to Book VI, Chapter 1.

Posting to your personal Profile

Before your event, you can share the updates on your Page and your Facebook Event page. Doing so gets those updates in your personal Profile and published in your News Feed.

During the live-streaming event, your viewers can post comments in the live-stream chat box with their Friends on Facebook. Their updates are automatically published on their personal Profile pages. This means that their updates are also visible in their News Feeds for their Friends to see. These updates have links back to your live stream, which potentially gives you exposure to a new audience.

Additionally, the comments from your viewers give your event extra coverage, and more people are likely to come to see the event while it's going on.

Sharing viewer comments with other social media

It's easy for viewers to share their comments on Twitter as well as to their Facebook Profiles. There's also a Tweet button on the live-stream chat box.

You want to encourage your audience members to use these social buttons often to get the viral exposure necessary to draw a crowd to your video. Calls to action are extremely important during a live-streaming event. Remember, the link generated when people use these social buttons sends people back to the live-stream chat box, bringing in more viewers and facilitating even more interaction around your event.

Partnering with other events and organizers

One cool thing about live streaming is that you don't actually need to have your own live-streaming video to chat about it. You can create a live-stream chat to talk about someone else's video content, if you want. You just need to be able to access the video feed.

Look for interesting upcoming live-streaming videos on the Livestream new event listings at `http://new.livestream.com/home`. Check out these events to find content that your audience would love to see.

If you create your own videos, find people who have audiences that are interested in your content, and partner with those people. Your video broadcasts will reach wider audiences, and you'll build an interactive community experience around your event.

As you look for opportunities to bring content publishers and communities together, remember the opportunities that mobile devices offer. It's easy to access Facebook on all mobile devices, and it's also easy to record videos on many of those devices. With so many possibilities, we're sure to see more live-streaming events.

Chapter 4: Stepping Out with Facebook Places and Facebook Deals

In This Chapter

- **Understanding Facebook Places**
- **Getting your Facebook Place up and running**
- **Creating incentives with Facebook check-in deals**
- **Promoting Facebook check-in deals**

Facebook Places and Facebook check-in deals present exciting opportunities for businesses that have physical locations — the bricks-and-mortar businesses across the country. The two applications combined can create a highly valuable tool for gaining new exposure and promoting your business online.

As we mention in Book II, Chapter 1, Places is an effort by Facebook to create a community experience with your Friends while you're out and about. Facebook check-in deals allows you to create specialized discounts, offers, and rewards for new and returning customers.

For business owners, combining Facebook Places and Facebook check-in deals creates word-of-mouth marketing at its best and can dramatically increase your exposure and reach.

In this chapter, we tell you how Facebook Places work, how to access Places from a mobile device, and how to claim your Place if you have a physical location. From there, we move on to Facebook check-in deals, telling you what they are, how to create them, and what you can do to promote your deals to gain even greater exposure and attract a larger audience.

Exploring Facebook Places

Facebook Places allows users to share their location with Friends, find out where their Friends are, and discover new places in their area. When Facebook users find a favorite hot spot — say, a new coffeehouse, nightclub, yoga studio, or hair salon — with one click of a button, they can tell all their Friends about it by checking in to the location.

Places for consumers

Before you dive into the specifics of how your business can benefit from Facebook Places, it's important to understand how consumers — your potential customers — will interface with this location-based feature.

When you check in to a location, your check-ins create a story. By default, this story appears in your Profile (see Figure 4-1), in News Feeds (see Figure 4-2), in the ticker, and in the activity stream for that Page (see Figure 4-3).

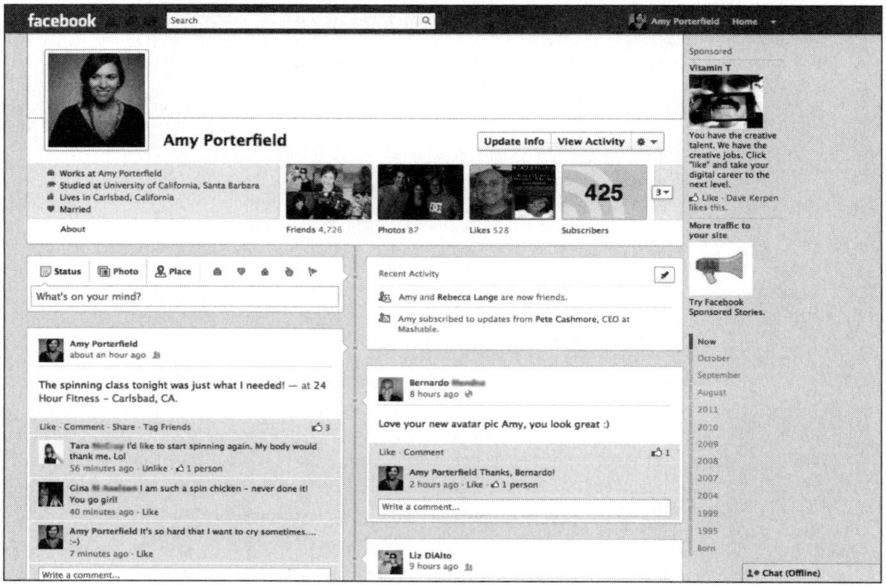

Figure 4-1: A check-in story in a personal Profile.

Figure 4-2: A check-in story in a News Feed.

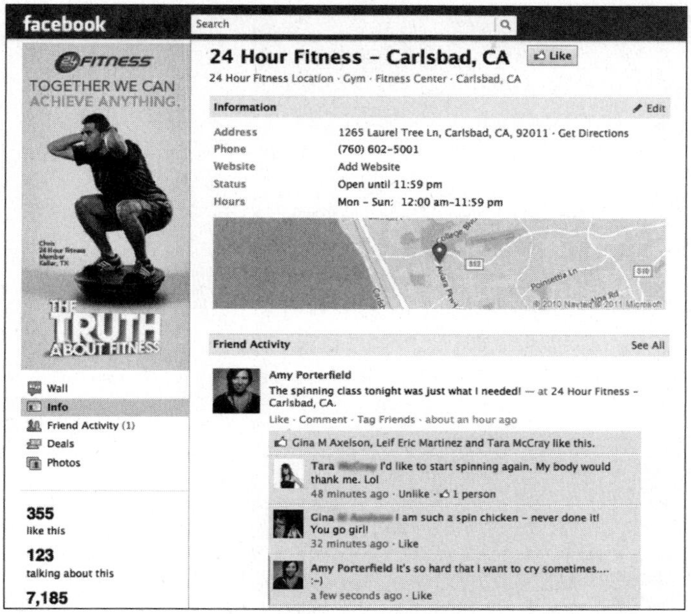

Figure 4-3: A check-in story in the Places activity stream.

Checking in to a Place on Facebook

You can check in to a Place via your mobile device, such as a smartphone or tablet. The Facebook Places platform uses GPS to enable the Location Finder feature in a GPS-equipped mobile device. You don't have to download the Facebook app to access Places and check in to a location. You can access check-ins directly from your browser on your smartphone or by going to `http://touch.facebook.com` or `http://m.facebook.com`.

In this section, we walk through a check-in via a browser on your smartphone.

Here are the steps you follow to check in to your location via your smartphone:

1. **Using your smartphone (or any GPS-equipped mobile device, such as an iPad or other tablet computer), point your browser to** `www.facebook.com`**, and log in to your account.**
2. **Tap the Check In icon in the top-right corner of your screen (see Figure 4-4).**

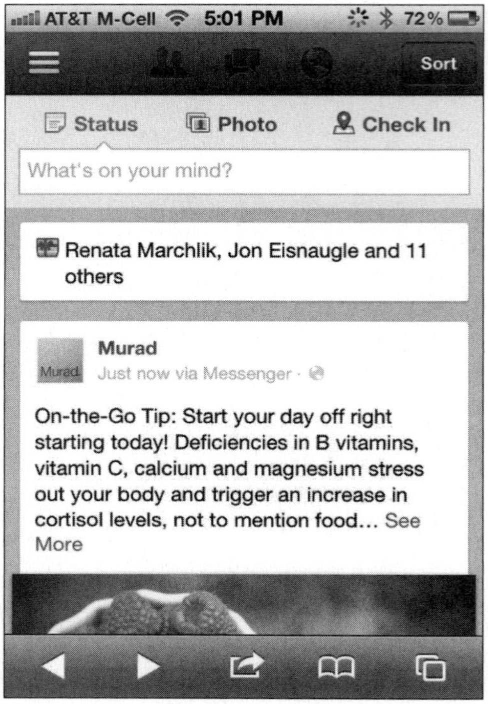

Figure 4-4: Check In icon in a mobile browser.

Facebook asks to use your current location.

3. **Tap OK.**

   You see a list of places around your current location, as shown in Figure 4-5.

4. **Tap the location where you're going to check in.**

   The name of the location populates as a hyperlink in your status update.

5. **Type a personal note.**

   To personalize your check-in, you can type a note to let your Friends know a little more about where you are and what you're up to.

6. **Tap Post.**

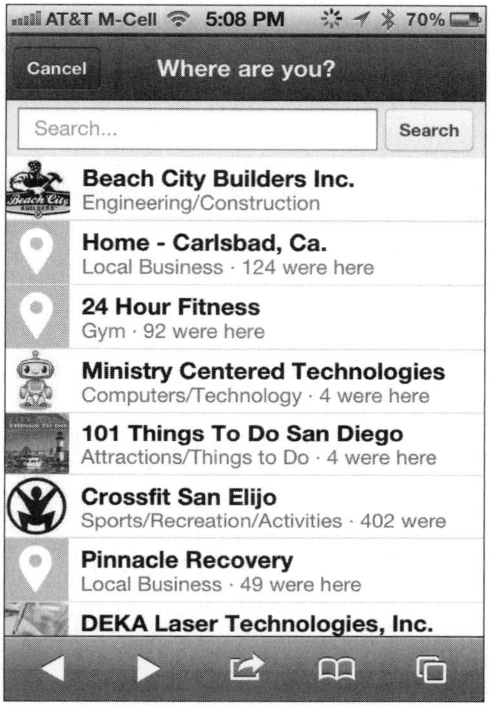

Figure 4-5: A list of physical locations in an area.

Before you check in by tapping Post, or if you return to your check-in later, you can tag the people you're currently with. *Tagging* (as we discuss in Book IV, Chapter 2) allows you to identify and reference people in your status updates, photos, and videos. Just as you can tag a Friend in a photo on Facebook, now you can now tag the people who are with you at your location. ***Note:*** If your Friends have set their privacy settings so as not to allow Place tagging, you won't be able to do this. For more info on privacy, see "Exploring privacy options," later in this chapter.

REMEMBER

Speaking of tagging, now is a good time to point out an important distinction between *location-tagging* a physical location and actually checking in to a physical location. These are two different activities.

In a way similar to checking in to a Place via Facebook, you can use the location-tagging icon in your status updates to tell people where you've been and where you're going. Location tagging doesn't mean that you've actually checked in to that establishment.

To location-tag a location, click the location icon (shown in Figure 4-6) in the status update box in either your Page or Profile, and choose your location. The great thing about location tagging is that it's based on the city you type as your location, so unlike with mobile-device check-ins, you don't have to be in a specific physical location to tag a nearby Place. This means that you can go back to your old posts and location-tag your photos and older status updates, bringing even more depth and info to your existing posts.

Figure 4-6: The location-tagging icon in your status update box.

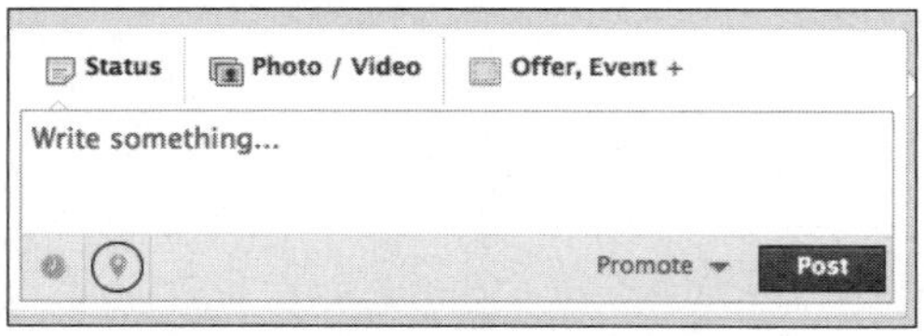

Checking in via a Facebook app on a mobile device

To check in to Facebook Places on a mobile device using a Facebook app, follow these steps:

1. **Download the latest Facebook application to your mobile device, if you haven't already.**

   If your mobile device can download apps, locate the apps section on your device and search for Facebook.

   After the app is downloaded and you log in, you see your News Feed with three buttons at the top: Status, Photo, and Check In (see Figure 4-7).

2. **Tap the Check In icon.**

   You see a list of places near you.

3. **If you're asked whether Facebook is allowed to know your location, tap Allow.**

   You enter the Check In interface and see a drop-down menu with a list of locations nearby.

4. **Choose your location.**

   Tap your location in the drop-down menu. If you don't see your location in the list, search for it by entering the business name in the top bar, titled Search near *(Your Location).* If the location doesn't yet have a Facebook Place, you can tap Add to create it.

   The name of the location populates as a hyperlink in your status update.

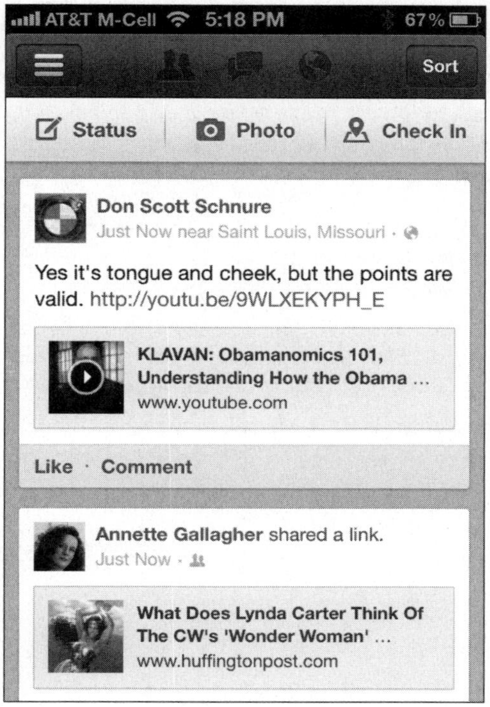

Figure 4-7: The Facebook application home screen on an iPhone.

5. **Type a personal note.**

   To personalize your check-in, you can type a note to let your Friends know a little more about where you are and what you're up to.

6. **Tap Post.**

   Your post lands on your Profile Timeline and goes into the News Feeds and tickers of your Friends.

Connecting with others at your location

Another great feature of Facebook Places allows you to find out who else is currently at your location. After you check in, if some of your Friends are also checked in to the same location, you see their picture on the Places check-in page (if their privacy settings allow).

Exploring privacy options

Mark Zuckerberg, the founder of Facebook, said that Facebook Places is about finding places and sharing them with Friends, not about sharing your location with the world. You get to decide who sees your location and how much information about your location gets shared with others. You're in control of your location on Facebook.

Third-party apps for Places

Facebook Places now allows developers to access areas of Places. This means that developers can create applications to pull in information about people, locations, and groups. Facebook Places has already begun to integrate third-party apps. Specifically, you can benefit from the third-party apps that you can use to track check-ins.

Leader boards, also called *dashboards,* can help you monitor your customer check-ins. A *leader board* shows you the people who have checked in to your location most often. You can make a game of encouraging your visitors to compete for the top spot. You can offer deals or specials to the top check-in customer, for example. This type of game can be extremely powerful for boosting sales.

To find options for leader-board apps, we suggest doing a search for *"leader board"* or *"places"* inside Facebook.

Facebook never shares or exposes your location automatically. To be clear, only Friends can tag you and check you in to a place if you set your privacy settings to allow it. Non-Facebook friends can't check you in.

In addition, you don't have to add your location to your Facebook posts. You can turn off the location-tagging feature at any time.

Another area of control for Places is the Privacy Settings page for your Facebook account. (Privacy settings are covered in detail in Book I, Chapter 1.) When you're on the Privacy Settings page, you can change your options to meet your needs. Your default privacy settings and your Timeline and tagging privacy settings (both on the Privacy Settings page) will help you control how your location posts appear in Facebook.

Places for businesses

When you understand how a consumer interacts with Facebook Places, you can see the benefits of this location-based feature to a bricks-and-mortar business. Your customers can tell all their Friends that they're at your location and can add comments and/or pictures about their experience.

This type of information exchange serves as valuable social proof. As mentioned earlier, people trust their friends' recommendations more than they trust brands and businesses, and the Places check-in functionality can serve as a powerful recommendation from your customers.

Launching a Facebook Place

Getting your Facebook Place up and running involves two steps:

✦ Your Facebook Place must be created, either by you or a customer.

✦ You must claim your Facebook Place to gain control of it.

The following sections describe both steps.

If you create a Facebook Page and select the category Local Business or Place, Facebook automatically makes it a Facebook Place, meaning that you don't have to create a Place separate from your Page.

Locating your Place

Your Facebook Place is created when someone is physically at your location and attempts to check in. (Or, as we mention in the preceding section, if you have a Page that's categorized as Local Business or Place, your Page automatically becomes a Place.)

If this check-in is the first one that's been attempted at your location, the person who's checking in can search for your location and tap Add on his or her mobile device; then your Place is created automatically. After your Place has been created, you can claim it as your business (see the next section).

Multiple Places may have been created for your Page, so you may need to claim multiple Places. Once you claim your multiple places, you can delete the irrelevant ones and keep the Pages you want to focus on.

If your business name doesn't have a listing on Places yet, no one has tried to check in to it. The easiest way to create a Place is to use the mobile interface to add your business, check in there, and then go back to the computer and claim your Places Page. Alternatively, categorize your Page as Local Business or Place, and you're ready to go.

If you use your smartphone to create your Place, you need to be physically present at your business location. This program is a geolocation program, so your phone's location is what Facebook puts on your Places page.

To locate your Place, follow these steps:

1. **From a GPS-enabled mobile device, go to** `www.facebook.com`**, and search for your business name.**

   The Search bar appears at the top of every Facebook screen.

2. **If you don't see your Places Page, create it.**

   If your business name doesn't have a listing on Places, no one has tried to check in to it.

3. **Use your Facebook mobile app to add your Place.**

   a. *Tap Check In, and type in the name of your Place.*

If the Place hasn't yet been created, you're prompted to add it by tapping the name you just typed.

b. When you see a screen with a map of your location and an Add button in the right corner, tap the Add button.

You've now created your Place.

Claiming your Place

If you have a bricks-and-mortar store, you need to claim your Places Page as it shows up in mobile Facebook. Then you have the opportunity to merge your Places information with your official business Page on Facebook. A good process would be to create your Official Business Page first and then go and claim your Places Page.

To claim your Place, follow these steps:

1. **Go to** `www.facebook.com`**, and search for your business name.**

   You don't need to be on a smartphone to do this step. Also, you can use the Search bar at the top of every Facebook screen.

2. **If your business's Place already exists on Facebook, click or tap it to visit its page.**

   If it's a Facebook Places Page, it's listed below the Places heading, as shown in Figure 4-8.

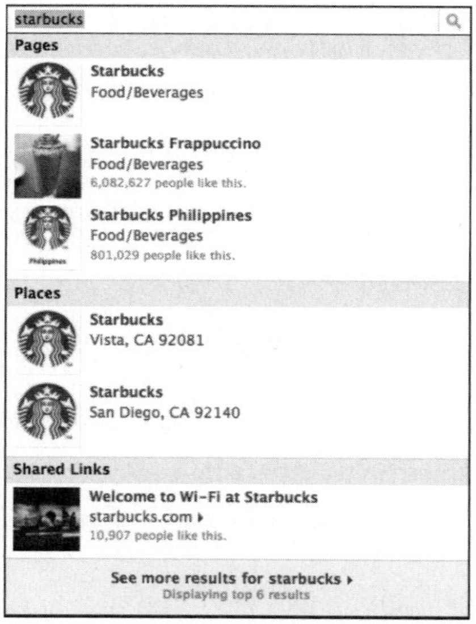

Figure 4-8: A Places Page listed in the Facebook Search menu.

3. **Click or tap the link titled Know the Owner? in the left column. You also have the option to click the gear icon under the Timeline Cover photo and choose Is This Your Business?**

   A pop-up window asks you to verify that you're an official representative of the physical location.

4. **Click or tap the verification check box and then click or tap the Proceed with Verification button.**

   You see a claiming-process page.

5. **Enter your business information, and click or tap Continue.**

   To claim your business, Facebook asks you to provide the following information:

   - Official name of business
   - Business address
   - Business phone number
   - Business website
   - Third-party listing (such as a Yelp! or Better Business Bureau listing)
   - Your relationship with the location (such as Owner)

6. **Verify your business by providing additional information.**

   You're asked to verify that you're the owner of the business through an e-mail or a document-verification process.

   TIP: Your e-mail address must be a business address (one that has your business name in the domain name). If you choose document verification, you have to provide scanned images of a phone or utility bill that includes the business's name and address.

7. **Click or tap Submit.**

After your claim is confirmed, you own your Place on Facebook. Even though you already have all the information that a Places Page contains on your regular business Page Info tab, by claiming your Place, you can manage your Place's address, contact information, business hours, Profile picture, Admins, and other settings that people see in their Facebook mobile application.

Now you can go back to your computer, search for your Places Page, and edit the settings or provide more information.

REMEMBER: Facebook may ask you whether you want to merge your Places Page with your official business Page.

Merging a business Page and a Places Page retains everything from your business Page (photos, posts, events, video, ads) and adds a map, check-ins, and a place on the Page Timeline for recommendations.

A merged Page not viewed on a mobile device looks like Figure 4-9. Note that the number of check-ins (shown as `were here`) appears in the data beneath the business's name. A number here tells you that the Pages have been merged.

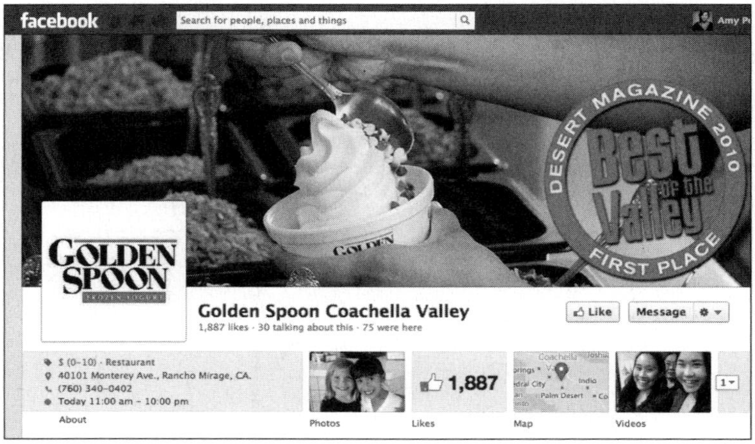

Figure 4-9: A merged Places and business Page.

A merged Page viewed on a mobile device looks like Figure 4-10. Notice the addition of the Check In button.

TIP

When you create a Place or merge a Place and a Page, you have the option to add a Recommend This Place button that appears on the right sidebar of the Page for users who live near that business. This feature is a great opportunity for your business, because users can write a recommendation of the business, which goes out into the News Feed and is shown to those users' Friends when they visit the Page. It's fantastic exposure!

If you don't see the Recommend This Place button, follow these steps.

1. **From your Pages/Places Page, click Admin Panel.**
2. **Click Edit Page.**
3. **Click Update Info.**
4. **Select the "Show this map on the Page" check box.**

Facebook allows Recommendations only for Pages that have not only provided a physical location but chose to display a map within their applications. If you deselect the check box to display the map, the Recommendations box disappears.

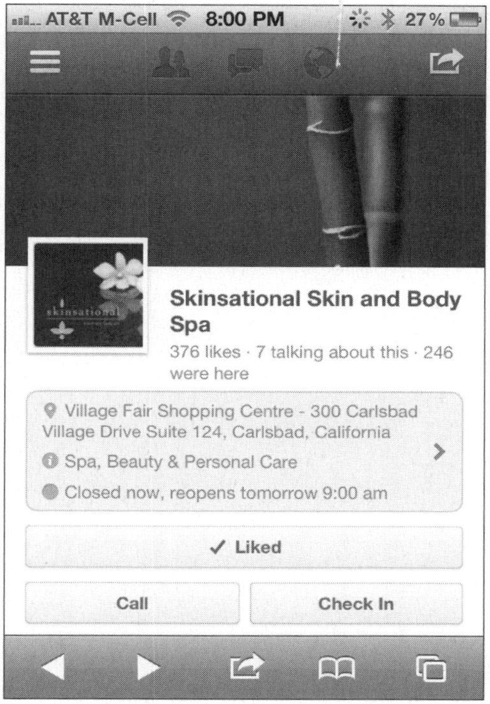

Figure 4-10: A merged Places and business Page viewed on a mobile device.

Introducing Facebook Check-in Deals to Your Community

Check-in deals (`www.facebook.com/deals/checkin`) is a location-based rewards service that offers special discounts and giveaways to visitors of physical locations who check in using Facebook Places. To view a Check-in deal on a smartphone, see Figure 4-11.

Using check-in deals is a terrific way to drive traffic to your bricks-and-mortar locations and bring in more customers. The opportunity to create these unique deals gives you a vested interest in claiming your Place on Facebook. When users are looking through a list of possible Places to check in to or when they check in to your location, they see a yellow or green ticket next to your location to let them know you're offering a deal. Deals entice customers with discounts and other special offers to help you build raving, loyal customers and attract new business.

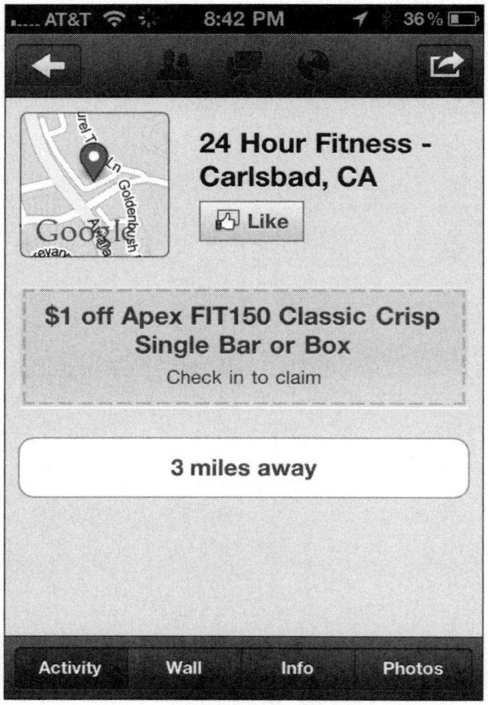

Figure 4-11: A check-in deal on a smartphone.

You have several compelling reasons to experiment with Facebook check-in deals, including these:

- **Build customer loyalty.** Deals allows you to build valuable relationships with an interested audience. For the customers who are already at your store, you can create incentives for them to keep coming back by offering great deals they can't refuse.
- **Spread the word.** Typically, Facebook users have Friends. When someone checks into your business and finds that you're offering a deal, that person's 230 (or more) Friends potentially can be exposed to your offer. This word-of-mouth marketing is priceless!
- **Attract new customers.** More than 543 million people use Facebook on their mobile devices. By offering a deal when people are searching their location, you give them a great reason to stop by your business.

Choosing a deal

You can offer four types of Facebook deals:

- **Individual:** To create incentives that encourage people to visit your business, you want to create a high-value individual check-in deal.

✦ **Friend:** Friend deals allow you to create a deal for multiple people who come to your store together. When they check in together, they're rewarded with a special group deal. You can offer deals to up to eight people when they check in as a group. Because several people have to come in together to claim your discount, you can increase overall exposure to your business.

  Often, some people in the group are new to your business, so this deal attracts both loyal customers and new ones. Encourage existing customers to bring along their friends.

✦ **Loyalty:** In the past, businesses had to get punch cards or rewards cards printed in advance to promote a loyalty program to their customers. Now you can see this same model in a digital format and set up your loyalty program in minutes.

  You can set up a loyalty program that tracks people who check in to your business numerous times. Loyalty deals keep customers coming back often. A great feature of a loyalty deal is that the number of check-ins can vary. You can have your customers check in no fewer than 2 times and no more than 20 times.

✦ **Charity:** This deal allows you to make a donation to the charity of your choice each time someone claims your deal. You have to manage the donation process on your own. A charity deal allows you to combine giving back with growing your business — a win–win situation for everyone involved.

REMEMBER

You can run only one type of deal at a time.

Defining your offer, and setting deal duration and quality

In addition to choosing the deal, you need to write a short summary of your offer, as well as define how customers can claim it. To make your offer easy to claim, we suggest that you ask your customers to view the offer on their mobile phones' screens. That way, they don't have to remember to print the offer before they visit your store.

You also need to decide on the deal's duration and quantity. The duration is the length of time you want your deal to run. After you set the date and time, Facebook manages the rest.

As for the deal quantity, you can limit the number of specific deals you're giving out. This setting is important, because if you're giving a steep discount or a physical giveaway, you want to monitor your quantities closely. You can do this by selecting the number of people who can redeem your deal. If you don't mind how many people redeem your offer, you can choose Unlimited.

Last, you can limit the number of times a customer can redeem your offer. Currently, you have two options: once per user and no more than once every 24 hours.

Promoting a deal

The social distribution factor of Facebook deals is a highly attractive reason to experiment with this app. When a Facebook user claims a deal, that information is shared in the News Feeds of his or her Friends, allowing all their Friends to reap the same deal if they choose.

When you create a new deal, you want to make sure that you consistently promote it to your Facebook followers on your Facebook Page and Place. You can also share your offer on Twitter, LinkedIn, and your blog. The more places your customers and potential customers see your offer, the more likely they are to take you up on it!

You can also place a Facebook Places decal on your window to tell all your customers how to find you on Facebook. This decal is one of the best ways to advertise that you're on Facebook. You can order the Facebook decals from a number of different vendors on Amazon.com.

You can promote your deals by purchasing Facebook Ads. You can be laser-focused with these ads, targeting specific demographics and locations to attract your ideal customer. (You can read more about Facebook Ads in Book VIII.) In addition to promoting your offer on social networks and experimenting with Facebook Ads, Facebook helps you by promoting your deal when users are near your location.

Here's how it works. Suppose that you have the Facebook app loaded on your iPhone, and you've opted to receive notifications from Facebook. (Notifications are similar to text messages and appear on your phone as pop-up windows.) Facebook sends a store's offer to your phone as a notification when you're near that location. If you aren't already aware of the store, the notification of a special offer may pique your interest enough for you to visit it. If you check in to the location, the deal appears on your Places check-in page.

Setting up a deal in Places

There's no cost to set up a Facebook check-in deal. Here are the simple steps to create an active offer:

1. **Go to your business's claimed Facebook Place or if you have combined your Page and Place, go to your combined account.**

   Deals can be created only on claimed Places, so make sure to claim your Place right away. (We discuss the process in "Claiming your Place," earlier in this chapter.)

2. **Click Edit Page in the top dash of the Page.**

   You see a drop-down menu. Click Manage Permissions in the list of options. You see a page with multiple options in the left column.

3. **Click Deals in the left column.**

   You're taken to the Check-in Deals dashboard.

4. **Click Create a Check-In Deal for This Page.**

   You see the four types of Deals: Individual, Friend, Loyalty, and Charity. (Refer to "Choosing a Deal," earlier in this chapter.)

5. **Click the deal you want to create.**

   You see two sections where you need to fill in offer details.

6. **In the Deal Summary section, enter your offer.**

   You might enter something like **25% off when you spend $50 or more.** You have a 50-character limit for your summary, so choose your words wisely.

7. **In the How To Claim section, enter instructions for claiming the deal.**

   You have just 100 characters, so be brief. You might enter something like **Show this offer on your mobile device at check-out to redeem your deal.**

8. **Specify how many check-ins are required before the customer can claim the deal.**

   The number of check-ins applies only if you're creating a loyalty deal.

9. **Specify the duration of your deal by choosing a start and end date and time.**

10. **Choose the deal quantity.**

   Make sure to choose a quantity that you'll be able to fulfill. If you don't deliver on your offer, you could have many angry customers expressing their frustration on Facebook and other social networking sites. This exposure isn't the kind of exposure you want!

11. **Decide how many times a customer can claim this deal.**

   You can choose Claimable Once Per User or Claimable Once Every 24 Hours Per User.

12. **Click Save to submit your deal for review.**

   All deals are subject to review within 48 hours. And deals that Facebook considers low-quality deals can be rejected or pulled from Facebook at any time. Be sure your offer shows an obvious value to your customer and is relevant and appropriate to your audience.

After submitting your deal, you receive a message that confirms your deal's start and end dates, as well as information on best practices to help you prepare your business to run the deal, such as ideas for promoting your deal and making sure that you have enough supplies on hand if you're doing a giveaway.

When your deal is approved, you can begin promoting it by posting a status update on your Facebook Page or Place.

Train your employees on all the specifics of tracking and honoring your deals. You want to make sure that all employees have all the details of the offer, including what the offer is, how many items you intend to give out, and your specific terms and conditions. If your employees are well trained, your Facebook deal strategy can be executed flawlessly.

Book VIII

Facebook Advertising

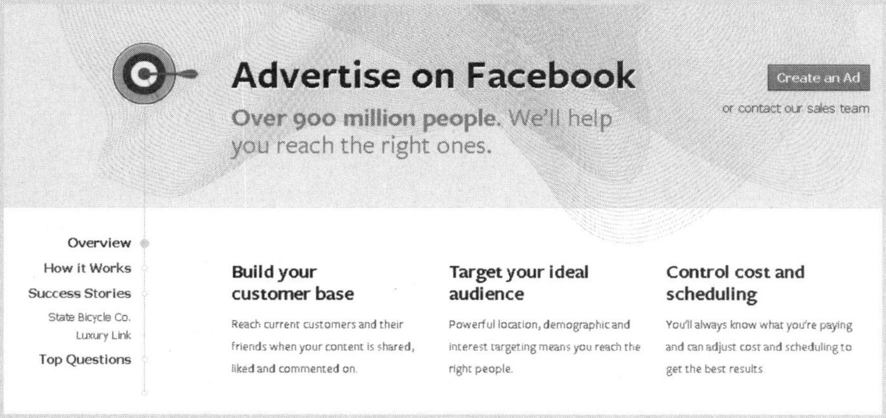

Advertise on Facebook
Over 900 million people. We'll help you reach the right ones.
Create an Ad
or contact our sales team
Overview
How it Works
Success Stories
State Bicycle Co.
Luxury Link
Top Questions
Build your customer base
Reach current customers and their friends when your content is shared, liked and commented on.
Target your ideal audience
Powerful location, demographic and interest targeting means you reach the right people.
Control cost and scheduling
You'll always know what you're paying and can adjust cost and scheduling to get the best results.

Contents at a Glance

Chapter 1: Advertising in Facebook

In This Chapter

- **Attracting new clients with Facebook advertising**
- **Designing your campaigns to meet your goals**
- **Setting your budget and timeline**

According to eMarketer (`www.emarketer.com`), Facebook ads will bring in more than $5 billion in revenue for Facebook in 2012 and are projected to bring in close to $7 billion in 2013. That's a lot of money, so it shouldn't surprise anyone that Facebook makes an effort to keep that revenue stream a-flowin'. Clearly, Facebook has a vested interest in making the ads an easy and pleasant experience for both the marketer and the Facebook community.

In this chapter, you dive into the basics of Facebook advertising and find out how to start making the right decisions that will get you the results you want. You discover how to set your goals, allocate a budget, and set your timeline.

In Chapter 2 of this minibook, you get to set up your first campaign, target your ad, and start running it. By the time Chapter 3 of this minibook comes around, you'll be ready to hone your advertising skills by doing some ad testing, measuring your test results, and modifying your campaign if needed. Hang on — it's going to be fun!

Introducing Facebook Advertising

Placing ads on Facebook provides one of the most targeted advertising opportunities on the Internet today. You decide the exact demographic to see your ad; your choices include age, gender, education, location, and even keywords in your targets' Profiles. You can even choose to advertise only to people who have a birthday that day. When you can narrow the audience who sees your ad to that granular level, you can be pretty sure that whoever clicks your ad is your target customer.

Within Facebook ads, you can advertise an external URL (directing people out of Facebook to your website), or you can advertise something internal to Facebook, such as your Page or Place, an Event, or an application. There are two different bidding processes for advertising: One process is for advertising something internal to Facebook, and the other is for advertising something external. Before we dive deeper into Facebook ads, we want to make sure that we introduce you to all the terminology.

When you're advertising an *external URL*, Facebook structures its advertising bidding similarly to Google Ads. You opt for one of the following:

- **Cost per click (CPC):** *Cost per click* is a model in which you pay your host only when your ads are clicked.
- **Impressions (CPM):** You pay based on how many thousands of people see your ad — a measurement known as *impressions,* or CPM. (*CPM* stands for *cost per thousand.* Okay, really, it stands for *cost per mille; mille* means *one thousand* in French.)

Facebook uses an auction-based system, in which you bid on how much you're willing to pay for each action. (By *action* here, we mean each time someone clicks your ad or each time Facebook places your ad in front of 1,000 people.)

When you're advertising something internal to Facebook, the bidding process is said to be *simplified.* When you're advertising a Page, Event, or application and want to place an ad, you can choose an *objective* for that ad so that the ad is shown to particular people, such as those who are most likely to like your Page, join your Event, or install your app. Or you can choose the objective of showing your ad to people who are most likely to click your ad or Sponsored story. When you select the latter objective, the bidding uses the CPC model. When you opt for any of the other three objectives, Facebook uses the CPM model, but there is no bidding. Facebook optimizes these campaigns for you. When Facebook optimizes them, you don't have any control over your actual bid; Facebook chooses it for you based on who else is bidding. Based on experience, the bidding is fair and you can always shut down your campaign if you feel that the click price is higher than you want it to be.

You can easily set things up so that your ad shuts off when you reach a daily limit, and you can target the times of the day when you advertise, along with many other variables. Find more coverage in Chapter 2 of this minibook.

Facebook's Promoted posts are structured a bit differently, as you pay a flat fee to have Facebook to push the post directly into the News Feeds of your fans (rather than on the right sidebar, where the other ads appear). We discuss Promoted posts in more detail later in this chapter.

TIP

You may want to test both objectives to see which one gives you better results. Your ad testing will show you the better bidding strategy.

Facebook advertising differs from Google Ads in one important respect, though: With Facebook, you choose your audience by demographics, whereas Google Ads (also known as Google AdWords) target advertising based on keywords in searches. Because you can show your ad to a specific demographic, knowing your target demographic is critical. You may have some general thoughts about who you're trying to reach in terms of your marketing efforts, but we recommend going through your customer list (or a small sample, if your list is large) and charting the following attributes:

- Age
- Gender
- Location (if you have a business that isn't local)

From your Facebook Page, take a look at the Insights area — Facebook's statistics area, which shows your community demographics including gender, age, and location — to find out more about what demographic you're currently connecting with on Facebook. Here are the steps to get to that demographics info via Insights when you're logged into Facebook as your Page:

1. **Click the See All link (shown in Figure 1-1) in the Insights box of the Admin panel.**

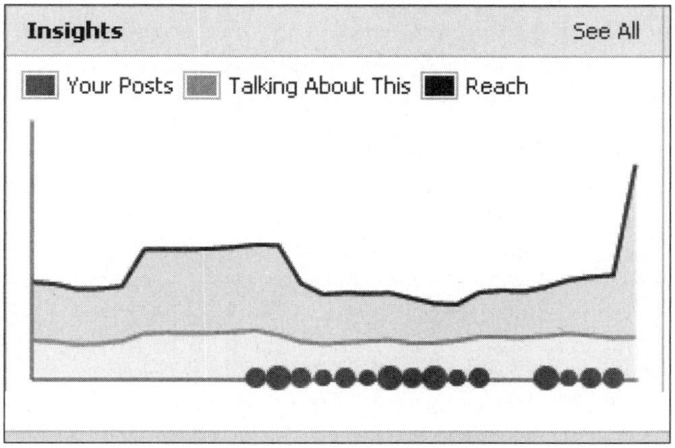

Figure 1-1: Click the See All link to see your Page statistics.

   You also see the main Insights area for your Page. The first graph shows the weekly total reach of your posts. Insights are covered in more detail in Book IX, Chapter 2.

   The Overview is the main set of statistics you see when you first navigate into the Insights. Click the links at the top of the graph — Likes, Reach, and Talking About This — to see additional pages of statistics.

2. **Click the Likes link at the top of the page.**

   You see detailed information about the demographics of your fans. Fans are broken down by age and gender, as shown in Figure 1-2. These demographics on your Page will help you decide which demographics to target in your ad campaign.

Figure 1-2: View Page demographics here.

REMEMBER

You need to decide not only the target demographic for your ad, but also what to advertise. You can create a Facebook ad for your Page, for a Facebook Event, for a Facebook application, for an external website, and more.

So why would you want to pay to advertise your Page? The new Facebook advertising options enable you to reach out to new people who might not have another means of discovering you and your expertise, product, or service. You may want to

- Reach a wider range of people who may be interested in your Event or application.
- Use Sponsored post stories to reconnect with your existing audience.
- Target the Friends of your community to show *social proof* (that is, your Friend likes me, so you should, too) with a Sponsored like story. You learn more about the different types of Sponsored stories in Chapter 2 of this minibook.
- Push an important sales message or update into the News Feeds of your community for people who may not see your updates with a Facebook Promoted post.

In essence, you're paying for people to like you — highly targeted people who'll see your updates every day (assuming, of course, that you're in fact posting every day and they're watching their News Feeds). These new members of your community will value your expertise in your field, get to know you, and at some point (ideally) buy something from you.

If you're advertising a paid event, you can probably see right off the bat the value of paying for advertising. But what if you're advertising a free event? How can that end up making money for you? Simple — by giving you a new connection. After you meet someone in person, you've made a connection with the person and have the potential to deepen your relationship to get that person to know, like, and trust you. Then, when he or she needs your goods or services, you end up being the first person who comes to mind.

Understanding How Facebook Advertising Works

We're sure that you've seen Facebook ads in the right column of a Facebook Page below the Sponsored heading. (If you haven't, though, check out Figure 1-3.) If you've ever wondered how these ads know that you live in a certain city or are interested in this or that, precise targeting is the answer.

In the Facebook model, ads appear in the right column. As many as seven ads are displayed in the column at one time, depending on where you are within Facebook. One ad is displayed on your home page and is reserved for clients with an ad budget of $30,000 or more per month.

Look here for Facebook ads.

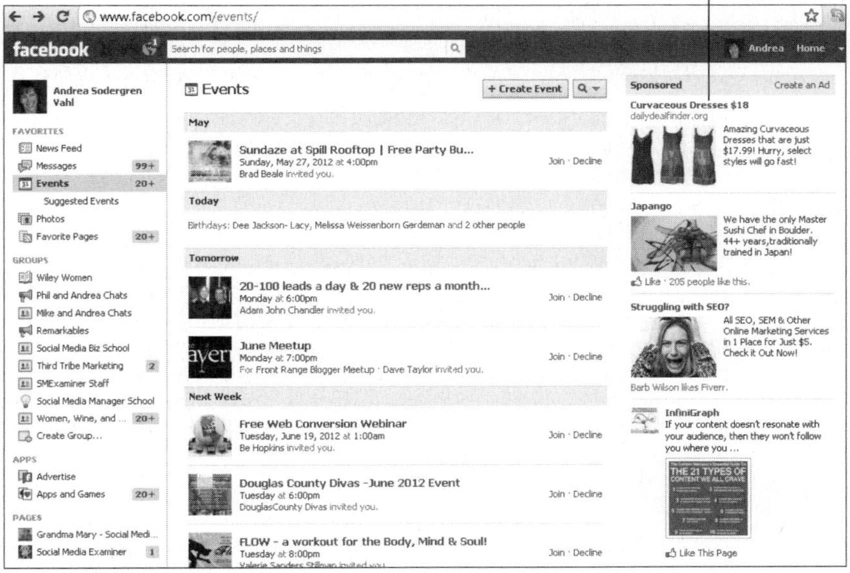

Figure 1-3: Ads are located in the right column.

As mentioned earlier, Facebook's newest ad offering, the Promoted post, now appears directly in the Facebook News Feed and shows a Sponsored message just below the post, as shown in Figure 1-4.

Figure 1-4: A Promoted post in the News Feed indicates that it's sponsored.

Up to seven ads are typically displayed on your Timeline or on fan, Event, or group Pages. You can't choose whether your ad will receive the top, middle, or bottom position, but the bid you place for the ad and how many clicks your ad is receiving affect the placement. (You find more on bidding strategies in Chapter 2 of this minibook.)

Before we walk you through the mechanics of setting up an ad, we want to give you a bit of background on how Facebook advertising works so that you can have a successful advertising campaign. (Think of it as our gift to you.)

Advertising on Facebook versus other platforms

Facebook ads work a little differently from Google or Yahoo! ads or even banner ads. (If you aren't familiar with banner ads, don't worry; we go into a little more detail on that topic in a bit.)

Similar to Google and Yahoo! ads, Facebook ads work on an *auction system*. You place a bid for ad space, essentially letting Facebook know how much you're willing to pay per click or per 1,000 impressions (refer to "Introducing Facebook Advertising," earlier in this chapter). Depending on how many other people are bidding, you may pay less for your ad, and if you bid too low, your ad may not be shown at all. Again, if you're advertising something internal to Facebook, and you optimize your ad to show it to people who are most likely to click Like (or to join your Event or install your app), Facebook does the bidding for you.

As a point of reference, for ads placed within the search-engine platforms — the Google or Yahoo! approach, as it were — you select certain keywords entered in the searches and bid on those keywords. If your business is car insurance, for example, you could opt for *"car insurance," "car insurance quotes,"* or *"auto insurance"* as your keywords. CPC prices can range from 10 cents to a few dollars, depending on how competitive the market for those keywords is. But Facebook is different from this model because people are not actually searching for something as they do in Google and Yahoo!.

Banner ads are ads placed on targeted websites or blogs that you believe your customers will visit. These ads typically appear at the top, bottom, or sides of the page. You typically pay a flat rate per month to display a banner ad. A sample banner ad is shown in Figure 1-5.

When people click your banner ad, they're taken to your site. More highly trafficked sites charge a higher monthly rate to host your banner ad. Banner ads are typically placed on a website when you purchase space directly from the owner of the site or are placed on several websites when you purchase an advertising package from a broker who works with multiple websites. The *click-through rate* (CTR) — the percentage of visitors to the site who click your ad — typically is fairly low for banner ads.

Facebook takes a different approach. Within Facebook, you're selecting the demographic viewing your ad, and people within that demographic (after all) may or may not be searching for car insurance. Suppose that you determined that your ideal customer is a 35-year-old male college graduate who lives within 25 miles of your city. You can easily enter those target demographics in your ad so that only people who meet those criteria see the ad.

Figure 1-5: Banner ads appear on web pages or blogs.

You can also enter keywords in the Likes and Interests area of the Targeting section of the ad-placement page, using keywords that your audience members are likely to have entered in their Profiles. Perhaps their keywords say that they like volleyball or yoga, or that they liked The Beatles's Facebook Page. Figure 1-6 shows some of the interests in one of the author's Profiles that will translate into keywords. If a vineyard ran an ad with *wine* as a keyword, that ad would potentially be shown to her on her sidebar in Facebook.

When you create a Facebook ad, as we show you how to do in Chapter 2 of this minibook, you can enter the demographics and the Likes and Interests in the Targeting section. Figure 1-7 shows the Choose Your Audience section of Facebook ads. You can see how specific you can be with your demographics.

WARNING!

Be careful when using keywords in Facebook advertising, because people might or might not have chosen to add those interests or keywords to their Profile. You might be excluding potential customers, which is always a risk when you narrow your target audience.

The biggest difference between Facebook ads and search-engine ads is that within Facebook, the CTR may be lower than within the search-engine advertising you'd use with Google or Yahoo! because people may not be actively searching for what you're advertising. (That's bad.) But if people do click your advertisement, you know that they're your target demographic. (That's good.)

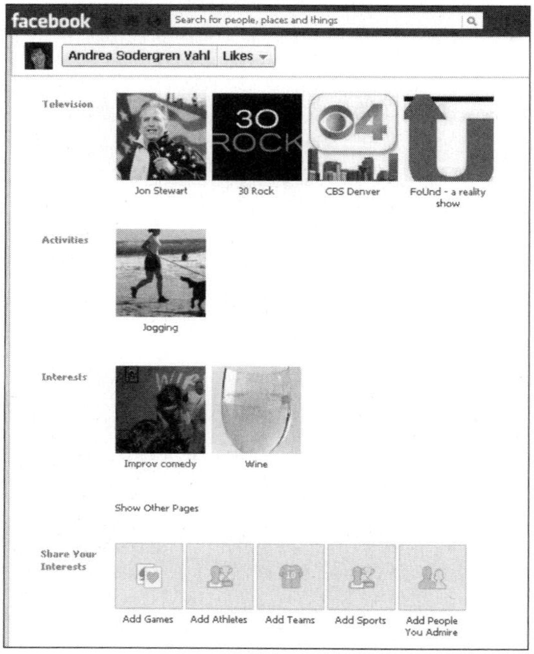

Figure 1-6: The Info area of your Profile shows your keywords.

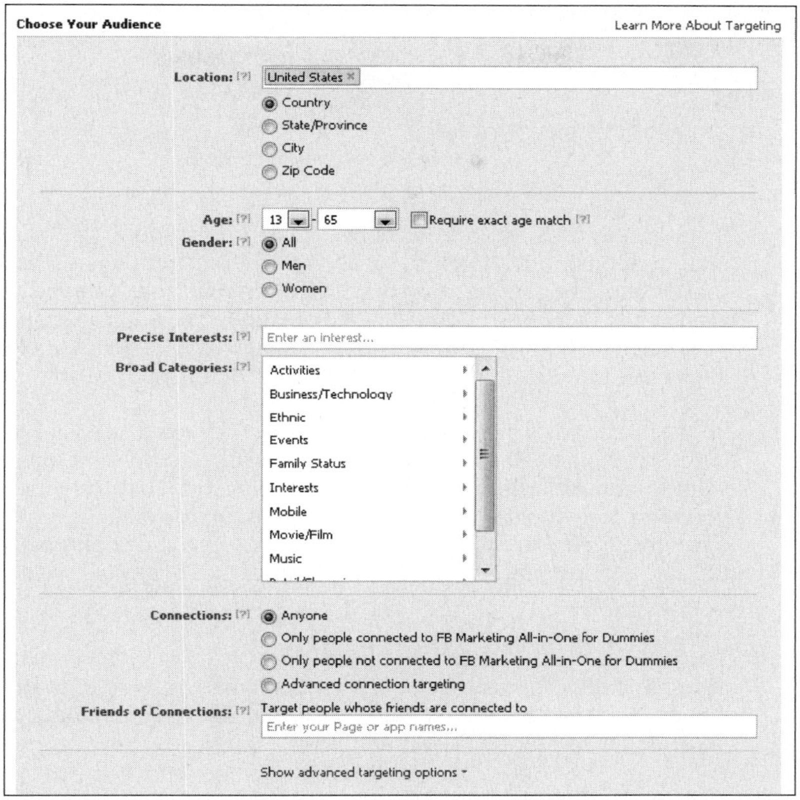

Figure 1-7: Target your Facebook ads by choosing demographic details.

Defining ad types

Facebook allows you to create many types of ads. You can advertise

- Pages
- Events
- External websites
- Applications
- Sponsored stories
- Individual posts in the News Feed

When you advertise something internal to Facebook — such as your Page, group, Event, or application — you're creating an Engagement ad. An *Engagement ad* allows people to respond to your ad without actually leaving the Page by clicking Like or clicking to RSVP to your event. Figure 1-8 shows some sample Engagement ads.

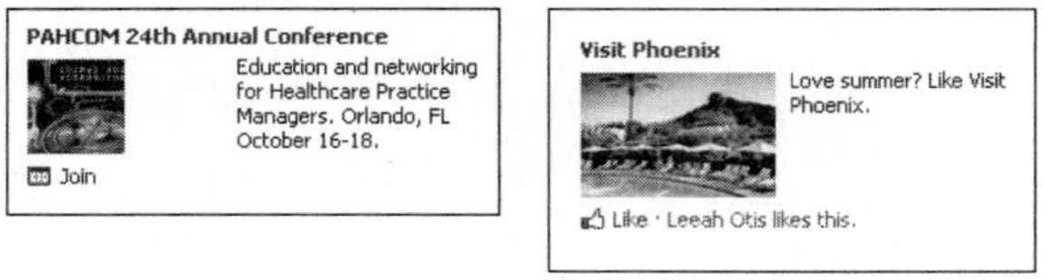

Figure 1-8: Sample Engagement ads.

If you're advertising your Facebook Page, for example, the Like button is included in the ad, allowing the person to like your Page without ever going there. Also, people can join your group or RSVP to your event in the same way. When someone clicks the Like button in the ad, he automatically likes your Page and starts getting your status updates in his News Feed. If he clicks the Join link in the ad, he can RSVP right from the ad.

Engagement ads are good things because they make it easier for people to like your Page or RSVP. If you have powerful ad copy that makes people want to connect with you, you lessen the chance that they'll forget to like you after they look at your Page. Engagement ads make it easier to get the outcome you're looking for — someone liking you or responding to your RSVP. This outcome is extremely powerful and emphasizes the need for good ad copy.

You don't need to do anything special to create an Engagement ad. Facebook automatically creates this layout for you when you indicate that you're advertising your Facebook Page, group, or Event. Read about how to create your ad in Chapter 2 of this minibook.

If someone does click the Like button or RSVPs to your event, you'll be charged for a click. Facebook tracks the people who click the Like button as Actions in the Stats area of your Page, as shown by the Actions number in Figure 1-9. Then you'll know how many likes you got right from the ad versus how many people clicked the ad to go to your Page. (In-depth statistical analysis of your ad performance — including info about how to work effectively with the Stats area of your Page — is covered in Chapter 3 of this minibook.)

Facebook also has a type of ad called Sponsored stories. You can advertise activities that happen in the News Feeds, such as individual posts, likes of your Page, or check-ins with Facebook Places. Then the Sponsored story is shown to a Facebook user's Friends. Sponsored stories also appear in the right sidebar of a Facebook Page.

Sponsored story ads don't have text in the ad body. If the Sponsored story is promoting a specific post, the body of the ad consists of that post. If the Sponsored story is about people liking your Page, the body lets people know that one of their Friends liked your Page. Read more about creating Sponsored stories in Chapter 2 of this minibook.

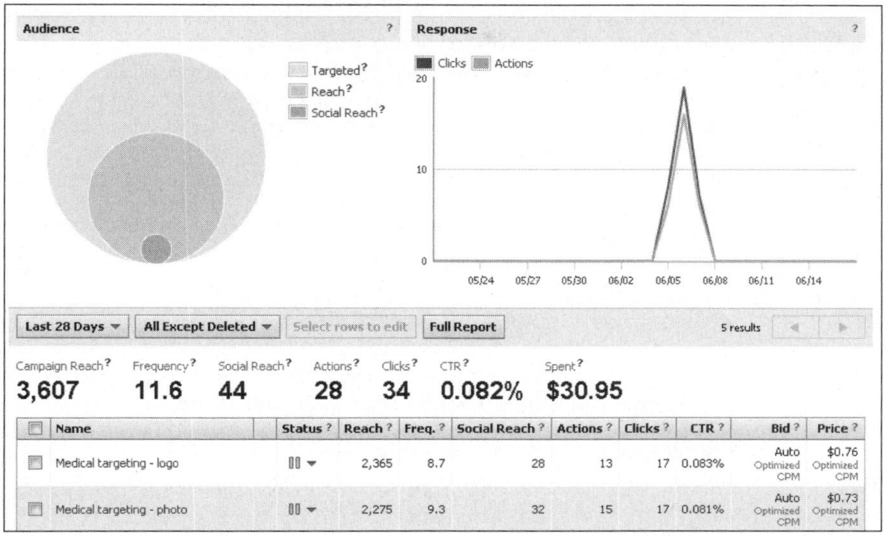

Figure 1-9: Facebook ad statistics tally Actions and Clicks.

Figure 1-10 shows an example of a Sponsored story from Starbucks in which the company is advertising check-ins. In this case, Jessica checked into Starbucks' Facebook Place, and Jessica's Friends will see this ad in their right sidebar. The Sponsored story can increase trust in the Starbucks brand.

Figure 1-10: A Sponsored story ad.

You can also advertise individual posts to encourage new connections. When someone likes or comments on a post on a Facebook Page, the Sponsored story is shown to that person's Friends. The ad could encourage comments on the post and likes to the Page. We cover Sponsored stories in depth in Chapter 2 of this minibook.

Facebook has recently introduced Sponsored results. This new advertising tool allows advertisers to appear in the Facebook search results when a user types in a keyword. As of this writing, the ads are available only through the Ads API in the Power Editor, a feature that is beyond the scope of this book. You can read more about this type of ad at https://developers.facebook.com/docs/reference/ads-api/sponsored-results/.

Looking at Promoted posts

Promoted posts are Facebook's newest type of ads, created right from your Facebook Timeline on your Page. This type of ad involves no targeting or bidding. You're choosing only to push the post into more of your fans' News Feeds.

Facebook has made it clear that not all posts by a Page are seen by the people who like the Page. At the Facebook Marketing Conference in February 2012, Facebook stated that on average, each post is seen by 16 percent of a Page's fans. Over the span of a week or a month, you reach a percentage higher than 16 percent of your fans with all your posts collectively, but they aren't going to see *every* post.

The reason why the reach is so low is that people are connected to a lot of Friends and can like many Pages, so it isn't possible to show all the updates in their News Feeds. Facebook uses the EdgeRank algorithm to determine whether or not a person is shown a post. (See Book IV, Chapter 2 for more information on EdgeRank.) So if you haven't had your fans interact with your posts, they may stop seeing the posts in their News Feeds. Oh, no!

Engaging content is the best way to solve this problem for free. Make sure that your fans are watching for your posts, and make sure that you're posting fun things to keep the likes and comments rolling in for each post. From time to time, though, you may need to give your Page a boost with a Promoted post.

You also may want to consider which posts are best to promote. Certainly, Facebook Offers (discussed in Book III, Chapter 1) are leading candidates for this advertising solution. Other good options are fun posts that get a lot of interaction; occasional sales messages that you don't want people to miss; and intriguing photos that interest your audience and boost interaction. Or you may want to watch the interaction a previous post receives and then decide to promote it after the fact to reach more fans with a post that is already a winner.

Designing campaigns with ads

In the Facebook Ads Manager, you arrange your ads into campaigns. A *campaign* is a group of similar ads that have the same purpose but slight variations. You can run multiple ads to test which ad title, picture, or copy converts best, for example. By *convert,* we mean attaining the outcome you desire. If you're advertising your Facebook Page, your goal is to get people to like your Page. So if you run an ad and get 30 clicks, but only 15 people like your Page from those clicks, your conversion rate is 50 percent. If you change the copy of your ad, and 30 people click your ad and 20 people like your Page, your conversion rate is 66 percent. The second ad is converting better and gets you more for your money.

TIP

The Ads Manager is the place where you can see all your campaigns in one place and access your reports and settings. We discuss the Ads Manager in Chapter 2 of this minibook.

You can also run campaigns around geographic locations, demographic targets, or likes and interests. Figure 1-11 demonstrates the hierarchy of campaigns and the ads within them.

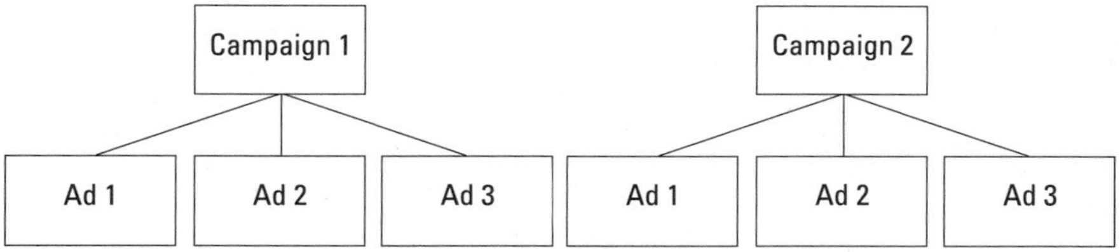

Figure 1-11: Hierarchy of an ad campaign.

For every product, service, or goal you have, you'll want to create a new campaign. You can set daily budgets for your whole campaign and for each individual ad. You can run a single ad, but it will be placed under a campaign heading that you choose. Create a new campaign when you're advertising

- A particular product
- A particular product in a region or country
- An event
- Your fan Page

Within those campaigns, you have different ads to test the performance of your copy, your call to action, and different targeting or bidding strategies. Check out the details of two campaigns in Figure 1-12, which are based on different variables.

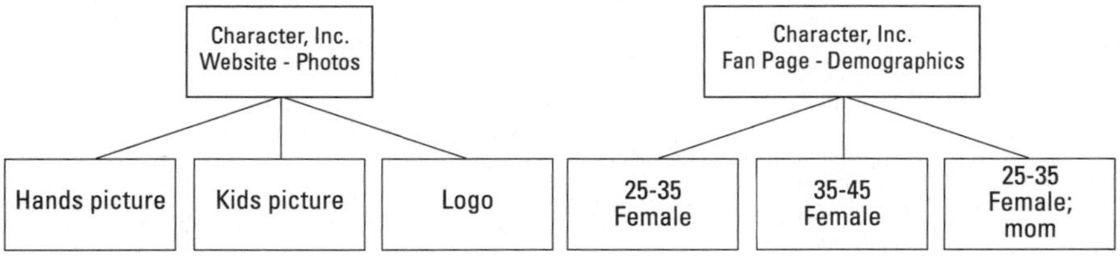

Figure 1-12: Two campaigns with different ads based on different variables.

You may want to run two identical ads — one using the CPC model and one using CPM — to see which gives you a better return on investment (ROI).

Typically, you want to run some test campaigns with small budgets first to find out which ad performs best. Lest you think that this testing will break your bank, you can set a daily budget so that the ad stops running automatically when it reaches your limit. Then, when you know which ads are performing best, you can run them for longer periods with bigger budgets.

Knowing what you can't advertise

Facebook has guidelines about what you can and can't advertise. It reviews each ad for appropriate language, content, and formatting. If your ad doesn't comply with the guidelines, Facebook *will* reject it. Some of the items that you can't advertise include

- Work-at-home sites that promise easy money for little or no investment
- Multilevel-marketing opportunities, such as Mary Kay and Avon
- Sites that have *domain forwarding,* in which the listed URL forwards to another website

  Even if your site is innocently forwarding the domain, many places that do have domain forwarding can be doing so for shady reasons, and Facebook has drawn that line in the sand.
- Landing pages that have a pop-up window

  Having a pop-up window may be an innocent way to get subscribers to your e-mail list, but many people don't like pop-up windows, and sometimes, they can't even close them. Facebook decided to control this item for its users.
- The obvious stuff
  - Tobacco
  - Gambling
  - Pornography

Some advertisements heavily restrict the language you can use in the ad and the demographic you're targeting. See the Facebook Advertising Guidelines at `www.facebook.com/ad_guidelines.php` if you're advertising any of the following:

- Dating sites
- Alcoholic beverages
- Health products
- Diet supplements or weight-loss products
- Subscription services (such as ringtones)

Identifying Your Goals

Before you start spending money, have a goal in mind. What does a successful ad campaign look like? Attracting 50 more fans? Selling 25 more widgets? Having ten people sign up for your newsletter? Getting ten comments on a post? Whatever goal you decide on, write it down, and come up with a way to track your progress.

TIP: Make sure that you know where your baseline rests. How many fans do you get per week through your current efforts? How many website hits from Facebook do you currently receive? With that info in hand, you can assess whether it's cost-effective to pay for your campaign.

Gaining connections

Advertising your fan Page is one of the best things you can do with Facebook ads. You know that the people who click your ad are in your target market and enjoy Facebook. Connecting with new people on your fan Page allows them to get to know you and your company.

Before you begin your ad, collect some baseline data on how your Facebook Page is performing currently. The Insights feature on your Page makes it easy. Some measurements to note are

- How many new likes to your Page do you get per week, on average?
- To what extent are your current fans making the extra effort to interact with you — likes, comments, and so forth? This statistic is indicated by the People Talking About This number.
- What is your current demographic?

We talk more about Insights in Book IX, Chapter 2, but the following steps list shows you how you can access the numbers for your baseline data. Log in to Facebook as your Page, and follow these steps:

1. **Click the See All link in the Insights box of the Admin panel.**

   Doing so takes you to the Insights Overview area, which has some nice graphs, as shown in Figure 1-13. You can download your data to do weekly or monthly totals.

2. **To download your data, click the Export Data button in the top-right corner of the page.**

   A window pops up, asking what date range and what file format you prefer: a Microsoft Excel spreadsheet or a comma-separated values (`.csv`) file. See Figure 1-14.

3. **Select Page Level Data, the format you prefer, and the date range; then click the Download button.**

With these settings, you can get the data to graph how many likes you're getting per week, how many likes and comments you receive on your posts, and your demographics.

Write down all these baseline measurements or save them in a file so that you can compare them with your Insights after you run the campaign to make sure you're reaching people on Facebook who will interact with and be part of your community.

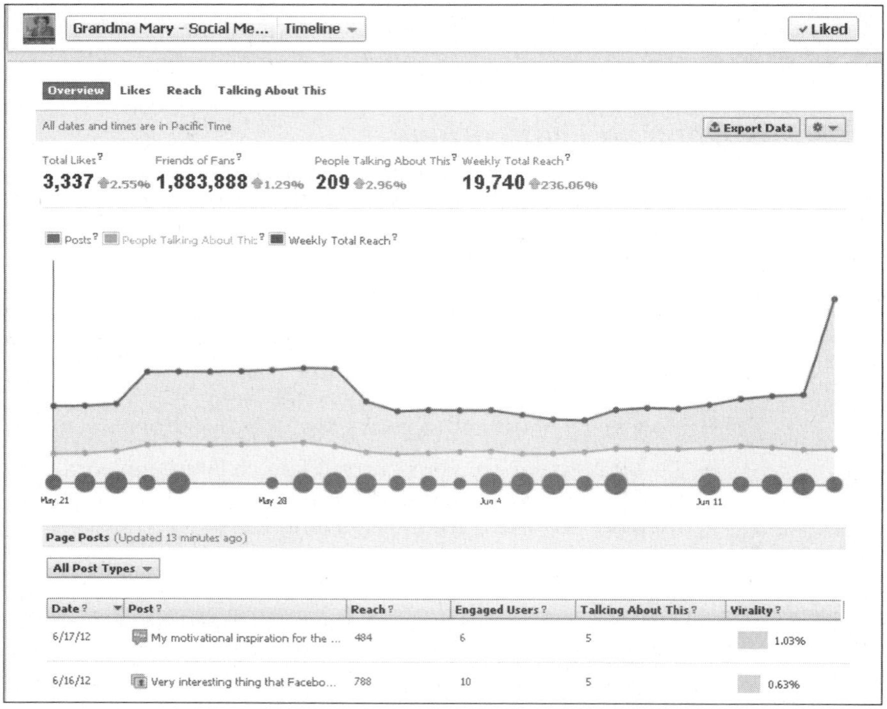

Figure 1-13: The Insights area shows your reach, and the trend of how many people are liking and commenting on your posts.

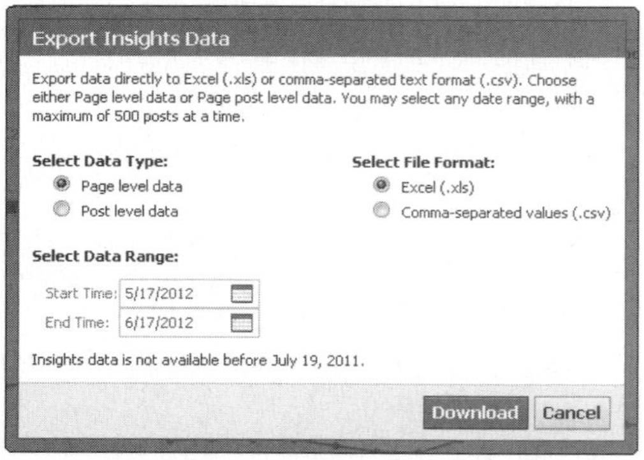

Figure 1-14: Select the date range and the file format.

If your current Facebook community isn't too large, see whether you can determine how many of your fans are actual customers and how much money they've spent with you over time. With that information in hand, you'll have a more accurate picture of the effect that your Facebook community has on your bottom line. That's not to say that having a community isn't of value in itself, but you're running a business, after all, and your advertising dollars need to be well spent.

REMEMBER

Facebook's Engagement ads make it easy for people to like your Page right in the ad and potentially give you greater return on your ad. But if people are going to click over to your Page to see what you're about first, consider sending them to a special Welcome tab rather than to your Timeline. You can use Facebook Ads to send people to any tab on your Facebook Page. (See Book VI to learn more about adding tabs to your Page.)

A special tab should tell more about your business and give users a compelling reason to join your community. Figure 1-15 shows the REI Trail Mix tab, which tells visitors to click the Like button, shows the store locator, and offers some special blog posts with expert advice and information about the company.

Figure 1-15: REI has a call to action to like its Page and gives you information about the company.

Acquiring leads

Acquiring leads for your business with Facebook ads could be your goal. Maybe you'd like your potential leads to sign up for your newsletter, a free half-hour consultation, or a free quote. In this case, you've probably set up your ad so that clicking it sends users to a website outside Facebook. When you do this, make sure that the site that you send users to — a site often referred to as a *landing page* — correlates directly with the Facebook ad.

You may want to have a special landing page that clearly sets out your call to action. If you send visitors to your general website, they may not see the small box where they need to request your newsletter, or they may be distracted by all the other nice things on your website and forget to request a quote. It's okay if the landing page is part of your website, but just make sure that the call to action is very clear.

Figure 1-16 shows an example of a good landing page. The only thing users can do on this page is click the Try It For Free! button (people always like free) or give the company a call. There's no menu to start clicking, and there are no distracting ads on the side.

If your goal is simply to drive awareness of your brand rather than acquire leads, you may want to have your phone number or store address in the ad so that someone doesn't necessarily have to click to contact you. If you're having a grand opening or open house, put as many details as you can fit in the 90 characters you have available in the body of the ad. See Chapter 2 of this minibook for more information on creating your ad.

Figure 1-16: This landing page doesn't distract from the call to action.

Reconnecting with your community

By using some of the Facebook ad features such as Sponsored stories and Promoted posts, you can reconnect with your current community and get interaction from dormant fans. As we mention earlier in the chapter, and as you can see at the bottom of each of your Page posts, only a portion of your community is seeing each of your posts. When you drop out of the News Feed of one of your fans, it's very difficult to get back into that News Feed organically, and you may have to use some advertising to reconnect with that person.

You can use Sponsored stories and target only the people who have connected to your Page (that is, your fans) in the Connections area of the Choose Your Audience section. Then this Sponsored story ad will appear in the right sidebar of Facebook pages. Or you can use the Promoted post option to push the post directly into the News Feeds of fans who otherwise may not see it.

Making Your Initial Decisions

Map out your strategy before you start. You need to decide how long to run your ad, how much to spend, and how often to change things.

Allocating a budget

Allocate a budget and time for the initial testing, as well as the longer-term Facebook ad. You don't want to be spending money week after week on an ad that isn't converting as well as it could be.

Your initial testing budget should be, at most, one-tenth of your entire ad budget. Run each variation of your ad for a short time. Even after just 20 clicks, you can start to see whether one is outperforming another significantly.

In allocating a budget, knowing what your clicks are worth to your bottom line is critical. How your product is priced and how many conversions you need to be profitable are factors to consider when you set your budget. Think of it this way: If you need 100 people to visit your site before you get a sale, and each sale of your product earns you a net profit of $20, it doesn't make sense to spend more than 20 cents per click.

Rotating your ad

Plan on rotating your ad every couple of days to keep things fresh, especially if you're advertising to a small demographic. Again, this strategy isn't a "set it and forget it" campaign. Ideally, after you finish your testing, you'll have zeroed in on a couple of ads that perform well. Facebook makes it easy to run one ad for a couple of days, turn it off automatically, and have the next ad start running for a couple of days. (For more on rotating your ads, check out Chapter 2 in this minibook.)

Figure 1-17 shows a series of ads that performed well for a client. These ads have eye-catching pictures and engaging headlines. The ad campaign targeted moms who responded well to the ads by clicking them.

Figure 1-17: A series of ads that convert.

You can always go back to an earlier ad, but plan to rotate ads regularly.

TIP: If you aren't getting as many clicks as you'd like, try adjusting your demographics to a slightly wider range by adding more keywords, a larger age range, more cities, or cities included within 50 miles if you previously chose 25, for example.

Setting a timeline

How long should you run your ads? This question is intimately tied to your budget and how effectively your ad is converting. Make sure to allocate time to do your testing. Testing may take a few weeks, depending on how many campaigns you're testing and how many ad variations you have.

REMEMBER: Allow time for your ads to be approved. Ads are reviewed manually at Facebook, and approval can take anywhere from a couple of hours to a full day. After the ad is approved, it starts running automatically. The ad-approval process is covered in Chapter 2 of this minibook.

Chapter 2: Creating a Facebook Ad

In This Chapter

- **Writing your ad copy**
- **Finding your demographic**
- **Placing your bid**

You'll find many places to start an ad, because Facebook wants to make spending money with Facebook easy. In this chapter, we show you one of the many places to start a Facebook ad. Keep in mind, though, that you may see links in other areas of Facebook, such as in your sidebar of your personal Profile or on your business Page, that lead you to the area where you can create your Facebook ad. All the links essentially end up at the same place — that is, to the area where you can start your Facebook advertising campaign.

One point to understand in the Facebook ads process is that you create all ads from your personal Profile. This may feel counterintuitive when you are creating an ad for your Facebook Page but it is the way that Facebook ads work. So don't get nervous if you are redirected back to your personal Profile when starting an ad. That is where you are supposed to be.

In Chapter 1 of this minibook, we cover the basics of Facebook advertising: how to identify your goals and set your budget. This chapter will be Facebook's favorite because it covers how to give Facebook some of your money by creating an advertising campaign.

Designing a Click-Worthy Ad

What makes an ad click-worthy? Is it a good headline? An eye-catching picture? Or some really enticing copy within the ad? The answer is most likely a combination of all three. This section gives you some of the keys to creating an engaging and click-worthy ad.

The following sections cover advertising an *external* website, as well as advertising something *internal* to Facebook, such as a business Page, app, or event. The main difference between these two types of ads is that Facebook fills in some of the information for you if you're advertising something internal to Facebook.

As mentioned in Chapter 1 of this minibook, when you create an ad for something internal to Facebook, you create what's called an *engagement ad,* which lets users like your Page or RSVP to your event right from the ad itself. You should keep this feature in mind as you consider what types of ads you want to create.

Advertising an external web page

Advertising an external website differs slightly from advertising something internal to Facebook, in that you choose your own title — *and* you need to upload a picture.

To get started, log into Facebook as your personal Profile, and take the following steps:

1. **Go to** `www.facebook.com/advertising`**.**

   You can just type this URL into the browser after you've logged in, or you can open a new window and go to this website. You're taken to the Facebook Ads Overview area, shown in Figure 2-1.

2. **Click the green Create an Ad button in the top-right corner of the Facebook Ads Overview page.**

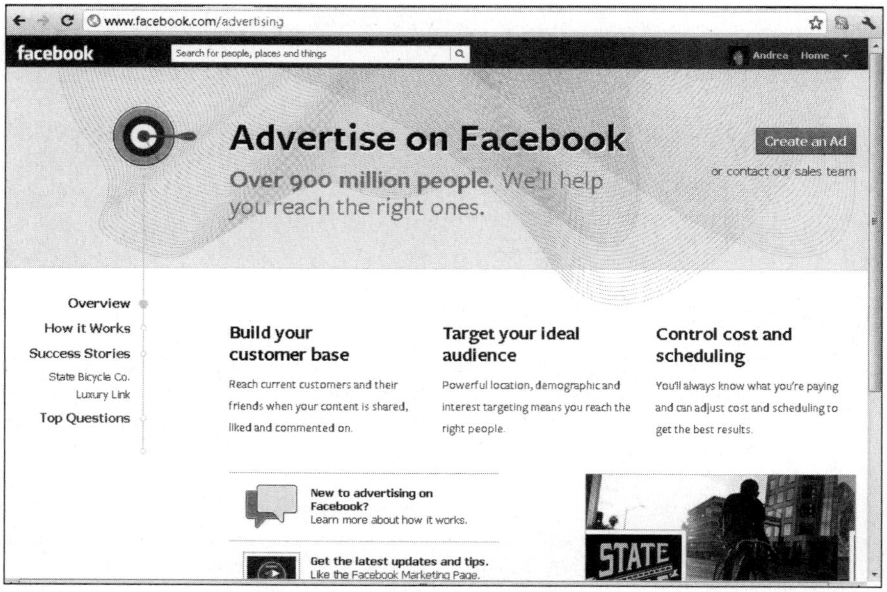
www.facebook.com/advertising
facebook
Search for people, places and things
Andrea
Home
Advertise on Facebook
Create an Ad
or contact our sales team
Over 900 million people. We'll help you reach the right ones.
Overview
How it Works
Success Stories
State Bicycle Co.
Luxury Link
Top Questions
Build your customer base
Reach current customers and their friends when your content is shared, liked and commented on.
Target your ideal audience
Powerful location, demographic and interest targeting means you reach the right people.
Control cost and scheduling
You'll always know what you're paying and can adjust cost and scheduling to get the best results.
New to advertising on Facebook?
Learn more about how it works.
Get the latest updates and tips.
Like the Facebook Marketing Page.
STATE

Figure 2-1: Use the Facebook Ads Overview section to help you with your ad campaign.

The area where you design your ad appears, as shown in Figure 2-2. All your Pages, Events, and Apps are shown as possible choices; you also have the option to choose an external URL.

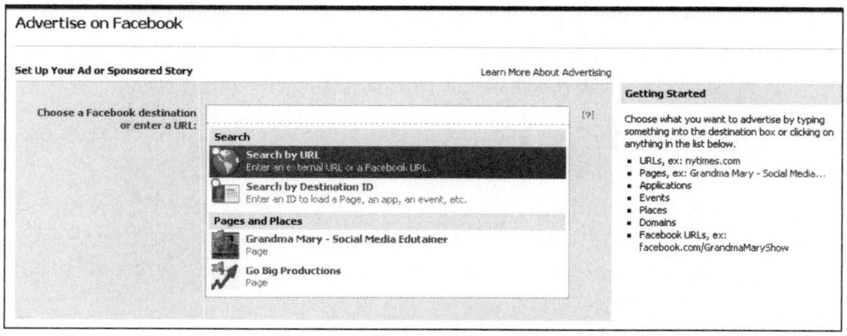

Figure 2-2: Designing your ad begins with this screen.

3. **In the Choose a Facebook Destination or Enter a URL section, enter the destination URL.**

   The destination URL is the full name of the website where you'd like to send your advertising traffic, such as `www.socialmediaexaminer.com`. Once you add the URL, you see the main ad setup screen where you can enter the headline, text, and image for your ad, as shown in Figure 2-3.

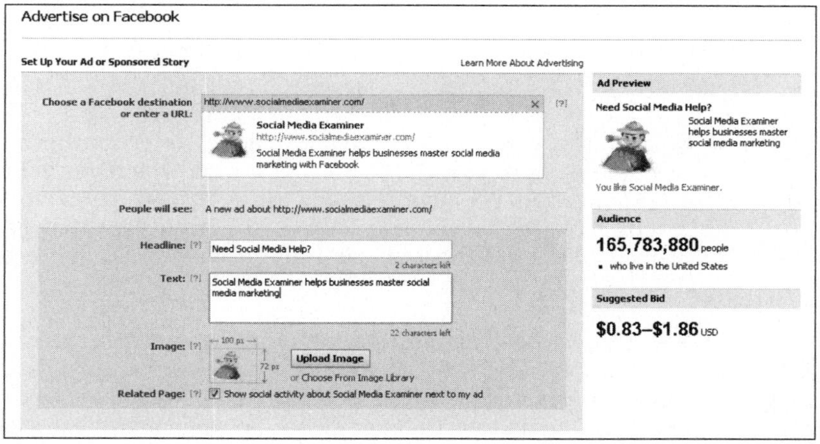

Figure 2-3: Add the details of your ad copy.

If you have a question about any field, click the question-mark symbol to its right for more explanation of what to enter.

After you enter the destination URL, you see a Suggest an Ad link, and you can click it. . . . but wait! You probably don't want to use the ad that Facebook suggests for you, for the following reasons:

- ✦ The suggested ad copy is pulled from the information in your website description, which may be too general.
- ✦ The picture placed in the suggested ad could be from anywhere on your website and may not be relevant.

Your ad will be more effective if you craft your own message — with your own title and text, and an appropriate picture. You can use the suggested ad tool to pull in a logo quickly; then you can modify the ad as necessary.

Writing a title

The title appears above the picture and should be interesting! You have to make it interesting *and* concise, though, because you get to use only 25 characters.

Check out the following fewer-than-25-characters examples to see why they're effective:

Do Your Teeth Have Stains?	(Poses a question)
Try Our Free Samples	(Offers something for free)
No More Aching Back	(Solves a problem)
Attend Our One-Day Sale	(Sends out a call to action)

In your ad title, you're allowed to have capital letters at the beginning of each word, in contrast with the body of the ad, which doesn't allow excessive capitalization. We have seen ads with entire words capitalized, but Facebook typically doesn't let you do that. See the "Meeting Facebook's terms and conditions" section, later in this chapter, for more grammar and capitalization rules.

To see many more examples of what other people are currently advertising and perhaps garner ideas for titles, take a look at Facebook's Ad Board. The Ad Board consists of all the current ads that could be shown to a Profile based on the ad's target demographics. So when advertisers set up their ad to be shown only to women ages 45–55, if you're a woman in that age range, you can see that ad in the Ad Board area. Go to `www.facebook.com/ads/adboard` to see them. You may have even seen some of them already in the sidebar of your personal Profile, but by using the Ad Board, you can see the ads all in one place.

Crafting your message

You have 90 characters to work with in the text of your ad as shown in Figure 2-3, so you want to make them count! Start by considering the keywords you want to have in the ad that attract attention.

TIP: Make sure that you emphasize the benefit that your offer provides to your ad's readers. What problem do you solve for the customer? Starting your text with a question or two can work well to engage the reader and give him or her something to relate to. Then follow the question by identifying the benefit that will solve the problem. Here are some examples:

> Are you always short on time? Have someone else do your house cleaning!
>
> Would you like to earn your degree? You can in just six months with our online program.

Take a look at the sample ads in Figure 2-4 for examples of good ad copy.

Figure 2-4: Examples of compelling ads.

Make sure to include a strong call to action at the end of the body text. Tell your audience what you want them to do. "Click here to find the best shoes," "Click to access the free report," and "Click to get your free quote" are all good calls to action.

REMEMBER: As we mention in Chapter 1 of this minibook, make sure that your web page or landing page matches the call to action in the ad. If you're asking your ad audience to sign up for your newsletter, direct them to a place on your website where they can easily enter their information to get it. (If you make the process the least bit inconvenient or confusing, you'll lose ad responders in a flash.)

Choosing an image

Images make your ad more eye catching, and Facebook now requires them anyway. An image can be a logo, photo, or icon and should relate to the title and body text of the ad.

The photo should be clear and not too "busy;" it'll be only 100 pixels wide and 72 pixels tall. Once you have selected your destination URL and crafted your message, as mentioned in the previous section, you are ready to add your image. To upload your image, follow these steps:

1. **Click the Upload Image button next to the Image field.**

   A pop-up window appears, displaying the files on your computer.

2. **Navigate to your image by finding the folder that the image is in, and click the image you want to use in your ad.**

   The filename of the image appears in the File Name field in the bottom of the pop-up window.

3. **Click the Open button next to the File Name field.**

   The pop-up window closes, and you see the image in the preview window of the ad, as shown in Figure 2-5. Uploads must be smaller than 5MB.

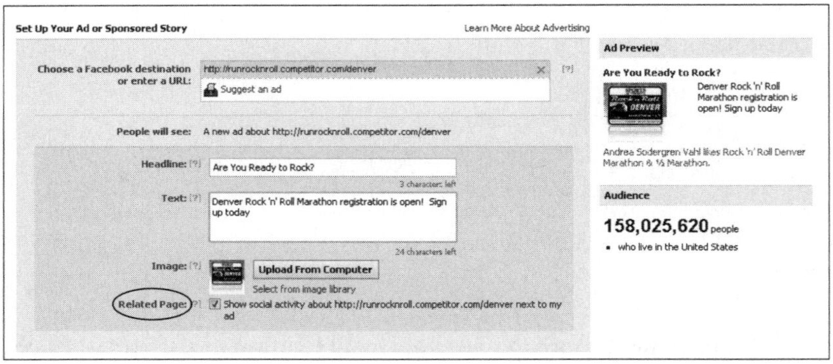

Figure 2-5: Your ad is shown in the preview window while you write it.

TIP

You see in Figure 2-5 that Facebook found the Page related to this external URL. People who view the ad will potentially see mentions of their Friends who have liked the Page, and they can click the link to get to the Facebook Page rather than the URL you're advertising. This option isn't a bad one if they then like the Page and you can connect with that person on Facebook. Just be aware that you'll be charged for a click. This option is off by default; to turn it on, you have to click the box next to the Related Page option. If you don't want the related Page to show up in the ad, leave the box deselected.

Your next step is choosing your audience with the targeting options that Facebook allows. You can skip ahead to the "Using Laser Targeting" section to complete your ad or read the next section to find out more about other types of Facebook ads.

Facebook Creative Library

You can save the design for any ad in the Facebook Creative Library (`www.facebook.com/ads/manage/creative_library.php`). This is a feature that Facebook might be phasing out, but it is a good tool to save your ads to edit later and then publish when you are ready. You must begin the process from the Creative Library link. Then you can use the ad you created in a campaign by clicking the Select Existing Creative link at the top of the Creative Library page when you're ready to start running the ad.

Advertising a Facebook Page, App, or Event with Engagement ads

As we mention at the beginning of the chapter, there are a few differences between creating an Engagement ad — something you have on Facebook, such as a Page, an app, or an event — and creating an ad for an external website. The process that you use for an ad for an external website begins with the same steps that you use for an Engagement ad, but when you create the Engagement ad, the title and image are automatically filled in for you. Facebook uses the title and picture from your fan Page, app, or event. Cool, huh?

An advantage of an Engagement ad is that people can join, like, or RSVP right from the ad itself, without even going to your Page. In addition, Engagement ads show the Friends who have already liked your fan Page (see Figure 2-6), are attending your event, or are using your app, depending on what you're advertising. When people see that their Friends like something, they're much more likely to become fans themselves. *Social proof* — the idea that if your Friends like it, you might like it, too — is a powerful tool.

Figure 2-6: Social proof in Engagement ads allows you to see which Friends are already fans of the Page.

Another nice thing about Engagement ads is that they give users the ability to like your Page (the desired outcome, of course) with one click, and the more convenient you make things for the user, the better. You don't want users to have to click your ad and have to be transported to the Facebook Page; they might forget to like it! That would mean that you'd get charged for a click without getting the fan.

TIP

When users click the title, image, or body of the ad, they're taken to the Facebook Page. When users click Like, they like the Page and aren't taken to the Page. You're charged for a click in both instances. See Chapter 1 of this minibook for more information on cost-per-click advertising.

To begin creating an Engagement ad, log in to Facebook as your personal Profile, and follow these steps:

1. **Click the down arrow in the upper-right corner.**
2. **From the drop-down menu, select Create an Ad.**
3. **Select from the list what you want to advertise.**

   TIP

   If you don't see the internal Facebook site that you want to advertise, enter the URL of the Page, Event, or App in the URL field. Facebook connects the ad to the right place.
4. **In the next section, select the radio button for your objective.**

   If you're advertising your Page, for example, you have the options of Get More Page Likes, Promote Page Posts, or See Advanced Options (which allow for advance pricing options), as shown in Figure 2-7.

   If you're advertising an App, you have the options of Get New Users, Increase App Engagement, or See Advanced Options.

   If you're advertising an Event, you have the options of Increase Attendance or See Advanced Options.

   For this example, select Get More Page Likes.

   Promote Page Posts is for creating a Sponsored Page Post story (covered in the later section in this chapter , "Using Sponsored Stories").

   TIP

   You can easily start an ad for your Page from your business Page by choosing Create an Ad from the Build Audience drop-down menu in your Admin panel, as shown in Figure 2-8. If you select Create an Ad from your Business Page and you are logged into Facebook as your Page, you're reminded that you're using Facebook as your Page and you need to switch to your personal Profile. If you're logged in as your personal Profile, you're taken straight to the Ads area.

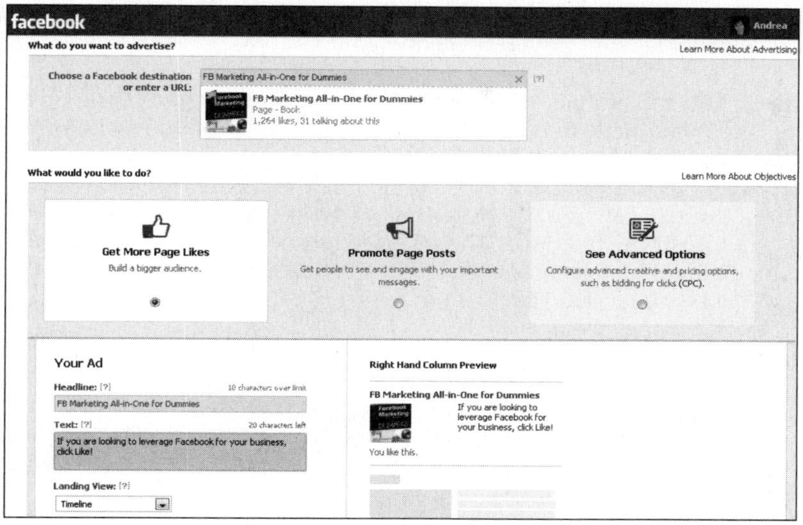

Figure 2-7: Select the Page name to create a new ad about the Page.

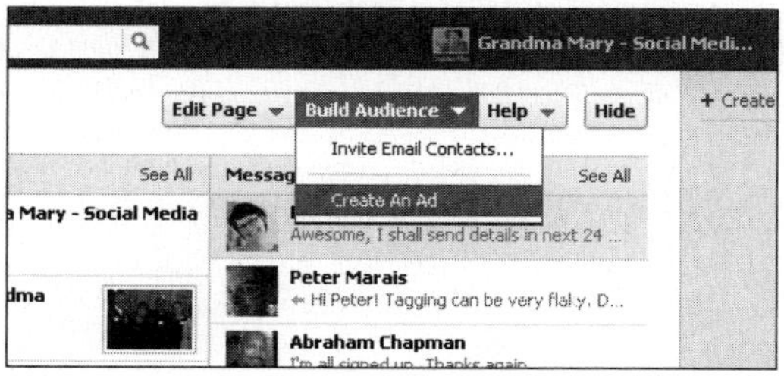

Figure 2-8: Create your ad right from your Facebook Page.

We cover the remaining fields that are visible in Figure 2-7 — Headline, Text, Image, and Landing View — in the following sections.

Seeing why the title matters

When you advertise something internal to Facebook, the headline of the ad is automatically filled in with the title of your fan Page, app, or event — and you can't change the title, so we hope that you like it! Take a look at the preview on the right side of your screen to see how your title appears.

If you have a long title for your event, fan Page, or app, Facebook will cut the title short because of the space it fits into. Unfortunately, you can't do anything about that, either, but you can compose the body text in such a way as to make your advertisement clear.

You can actually change the title of your ad to your Page by typing the URL to your Page in the Choose a Facebook Destination or Enter a URL field. For example, Figure 2-7 shows "Grandma Mary – Social Media..." as the title of the ad because it is too long. But if you enter the URL — such as `www.facebook.com/grandmamaryshow` — in the destination field, you're able to edit the headline. The ad no longer allows people to like your Page right from the ad as it does in a true Engagement ad, but it may be worth having a headline that isn't cut off.

Using the body text to encourage engagement

Your ad allows for only 90 characters of body text, so you have to make your body text very compelling. Be sure to compose it with your desired outcome in mind, whether that outcome is to get your readers to like your Page, RSVP to your event, or use your app.

If you're advertising your Page, mention in the ad what the reward is for liking your Page. Give people a reason to click the Like button right away rather than have to look at your fan Page first. What do you offer on your fan Page? Tips, tricks, discounts, or free things? Work the benefits of becoming a fan into your body text.

If you're advertising an event, what is the benefit of attending your event? Community, knowledge, networking? Always work to answer the question that's on the mind of the customer: "What's in it for me?"

Make sure that you provide a very clear call to action in your body text. If you're advertising your Page, for example, say, "Click the Like button." If you're advertising an event, say, "RSVP now."

Choosing an image

Although the ad you're creating will automatically be populated with the image from your event, Page, or app if you have an image loaded (and you should!), you can change the image file. For the purpose of promoting your brand, it's better to keep the image consistent in all your ads and Pages, but if you have a compelling reason to change it, just follow these steps to place a new one (continuing from the ad setup area in Figure 2-7):

1. **Click the Upload Image button next to the Image field.**

   A pop-up window appears, listing the files on your computer.

2. **Navigate to your image by finding the folder that the image is in; then click the image you want to use in your ad.**

   The filename of the image appears in the File Name field at the bottom of the pop-up window.

3. **Click the Open button next to the File Name field.**

   The pop-up window closes, and you see the image in the preview section of the ad. Uploads must be smaller than 5MB.

TIP

You may have the image you need in your image library, which you can access from the link right below the Upload from Computer button. Look for the Select from Image Library link. Your image gallery includes images that you previously uploaded to ad campaigns.

Setting a landing view

By default, the landing view is set to the Timeline, but you can select your ad to go to any tab installed on your Page. Sending your traffic to a different tab on your Page can be a great idea if you have a special video or a way to capture e-mails from your ad traffic right on your custom tab. You can accomplish this task with many of the apps (which then become your tabs) that we outline in Book V, Chapter 2.

To change the landing view, from the Landing View drop-down menu, shown in Figure 2-9, choose the tab where you'd like the ad traffic to go. The ad traffic will still be able to navigate to the Timeline of your Page from your custom tab.

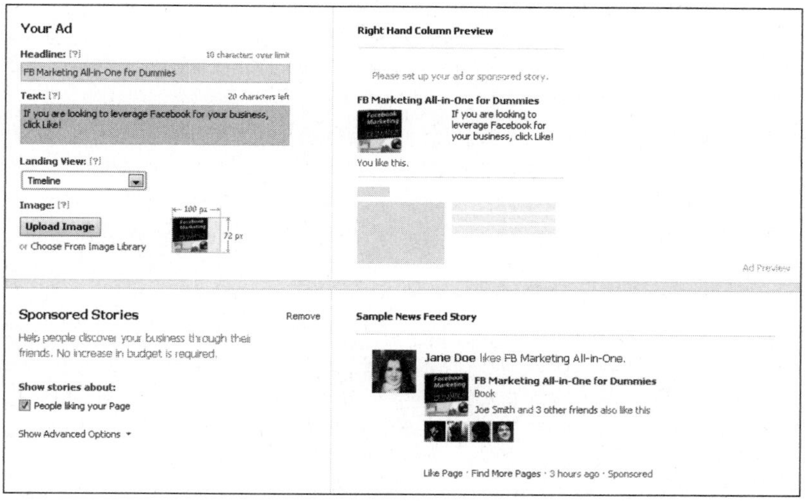

Figure 2-9: Select the Page name to create a new ad about the Page.

Also notice in Figure 2-9 that Facebook automatically creates Sponsored stories when you choose the Get More Page Likes. The Sponsored Story will be a News Feed story that is advertised to the Friends of your Fans about people who Like your Page.

Facebook is currently enabling this advertising option for no additional budget. If you do not want this option, you can either click Remove or uncheck the box next to People Liking Your Page. But if your goal is to get more likes, Sponsored stories placed directly in the News Feed can help. For no additional budget, why not? (Advanced options allows for URL tags, a subject that is beyond the scope of this book.)

Your next step is choosing your audience with the targeting options that Facebook allows. You can skip ahead to the "Using Laser Targeting" section to complete your ad or read "Using Sponsored stories," later in this chapter, to find out more about creating a Sponsored story.

Meeting Facebook's terms and conditions

As you craft your ad, be aware of Facebook's terms and conditions (listed at `www.facebook.com/ad_guidelines.php`) so that your ad isn't rejected, thereby resulting in the waste of your precious time. In Chapter 1 of this minibook, we cover some of the sites and products that you're not allowed to advertise. Facebook also prefers that you adhere to some basic grammar, punctuation, and capitalization suggestions within ads. Facebook used to be a bit more strict about what ads it would approve based on these "rules" but it has since relaxed a bit. If you want your ad approved the first time, we suggest you follow these guidelines:

- **Grammar:** The ad body must be grammatically correct, with complete sentences and correct spelling. The ad can't contain excessive repetition, such as "Buy, buy, buy." (You don't want to sound like a used-car salesperson anyway!)
- **Capitalization:** Ads must use proper, grammatically correct capitalization. You may not capitalize the first letter of every word or an entire word, such as "BUY NOW." Acronyms can be capitalized, however.
- **Punctuation:** Use logical, grammatically correct punctuation. Don't use unnecessary punctuation, such as multiple exclamation points, as in "Buy now!!!" Also, you can't use exclamation points in the title of the ad.
- **Symbols:** Symbols must be used according to their true meaning and can't be repeated unnecessarily. Also, you can't substitute a symbol for a word, such as an ampersand (&) for *and,* a dollar sign ($) for *dollars,* or the at sign (@) for *at.* You may use the $ symbol, however, if it's paired with a dollar amount, as in $100.

TIP

Facebook ads are reviewed by a group of people who sometimes have different standards as to what meets the Facebook guidelines. You may find that some ads that are approved violate the suggestions. To better your chances of getting your ad approved quickly, use the previous suggestions. It's Facebook's sandbox.

Using Sponsored stories

Facebook's newest ads are called Sponsored stories. You can advertise specific Facebook activities such as individual posts (a Sponsored post story), likes of your Page (Sponsored like story), or check-ins with Facebook Places (Sponsored check-in story). The Sponsored story is then shown to a Facebook user's Friends. Sponsored stories currently aren't widely used, and some debate exists about their effectiveness.

Facebook recently changed the Sponsored Story Ad creation so that Sponsored like stories and Sponsored checkin stories are automatically enabled when you advertise your Page or your Place. Now the only separate Sponsored Story you can advertise is a Sponsored post story.

You can use Sponsored stories for Facebook Pages and apps, and to advertise when someone checks in to your Place. The idea behind the ads is that they show when someone is liking your Page, using your app, or checking into your Place, thereby giving you the social proof that we mention earlier in this chapter (and throughout the book). But people are questioning whether social proof is enough to move someone to act without the call to action in the copy. The ads look different from a traditional Facebook Ad because there is no text in the body of the ad for a Sponsored like story. In a Sponsored post story, the text of the ad is determined by the Page post, as shown in Figure 2-10. Also note that for Sponsored post story ads, you get added information about the post in the ad, such as the likes, shares, and number of comments.

Sponsored like story

Sponsored post story

Figure 2-10: Sponsored story ads.

Creating a Sponsored post story

To use the Sponsored stories feature for a Page post story, follow these steps:

1. **Log in to Facebook as your personal Profile.**
2. **Go to** `www.facebook.com/ads/create` **to get to the ad-creation screen.**

   You can type this URL in the browser after you've logged in, or you can open a new window and go to this website. You see the Set Up Your Ad or Sponsored Story page.

3. **From the list, select the Page or app that you want to advertise.**

   If your page doesn't appear in the list, enter the URL of your Page in the URL field.

4. **In the What Would You Like to Do? section, select the Promote Page Post radio button.**

   The ad is set to promote the most recent post, but you can change that setting. You can also select the optional Keep My Ad Up-to-date by Automatically Promoting My Most Recent Post box.

5. **Select the post you would like to promote from the drop-down menu.**

   You see the preview of the ad on the right side of the page, as shown in Figure 2-11. Facebook also automatically creates a Sponsored News Feed Story about people liking, commenting on, or sharing this post. Uncheck these options if desired but more people may see your ad in the News Feed rather than in the areas where Ads normally appear.

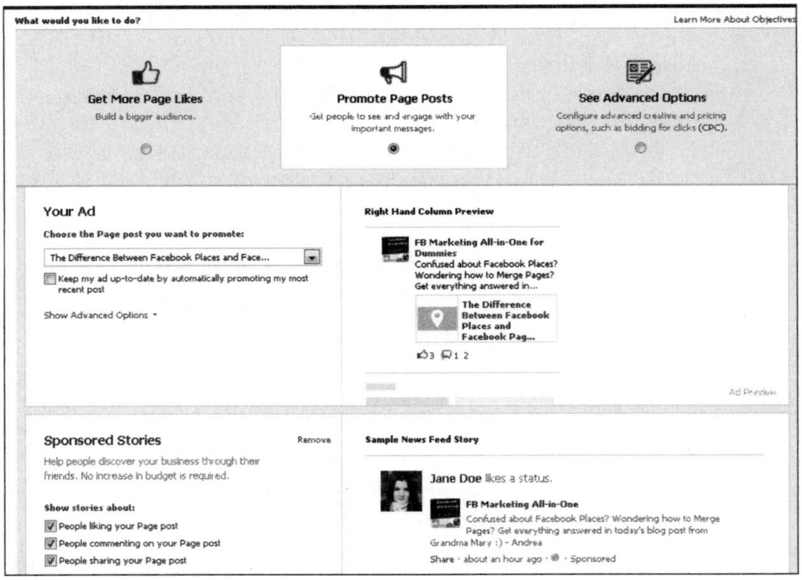

Figure 2-11: Select the post you want to promote.

TIP: Create your Page post with the ad in mind before you create it. Also note that you can create a Sponsored post story from a Facebook Question (thus creating a mini poll within the ad), or you can create an ad from a post of a YouTube video, which can be very engaging. See Figure 2-12 for examples.

Figure 2-12: Examples of unique Sponsored post stories.

A carefully crafted Facebook Page sponsored post story sometimes gets better results than a Facebook Ad. Because you can do unique things with a Facebook Page sponsored post story, such as show a Facebook Question or a YouTube video, you may want to experiment with ways to make Sponsored stories work for you.

Your next step is choosing your audience with the targeting options that Facebook allows. You can skip ahead to the "Using Laser Targeting" section to complete your ad or read the next section to find out more about creating a Sponsored story.

Creating other Sponsored stories

If you're creating an ad for an App or an Event, Facebook automatically creates a Sponsored story for your App or Event about people using the App or joining the Event. You can opt out of these ads if you like but as of this writing, Facebook is not charging extra to create these ads. You can select more targeting for your ad if you choose, which we cover in the next section. By default, your Sponsored story is being shown to Friends of people who like your Page or, if it's your app, Friends of people who use your aptp.

Seeing Advanced Options

If you select the See Advanced Options radio button, the advanced options include bidding options (covered in the "Setting Your Bidding and Pricing Goals" section later in this Chapter.)

Using Laser Targeting

Now the fun part of designing your ad begins: targeting your audience! When you add different demographics, you can see exactly how many people your ad is potentially reaching. We think that this is the most interesting part of the ad process, because as you tweak and change your targeting fields, you see how many people may be in your market. The targeting fields include location, age, gender, education, likes, and interests. The better you know your customers, the easier this section is to work with.

Here's a review of the steps to get to the Advertise on Facebook page, where you design your ad:

1. **Log in to Facebook as your personal Profile.**
2. **Go directly to the ad-creation screen by going to** `www.facebook.com/ads/create`.

   You can type this URL in the browser after you've logged in, or you can open a new window and go to this website. You see the Design Your Ad page.
3. **If you haven't done so already, follow the steps in the preceding sections of this chapter to complete the Set Up Your Ad or Sponsored Story section.**

   The choice is based on what you're advertising: an external URL or something within Facebook.

When you finish filling in the Set Up Your Ad or Sponsored Story section, scroll down to the second section, titled Choose Your Audience, shown in Figure 2-13.

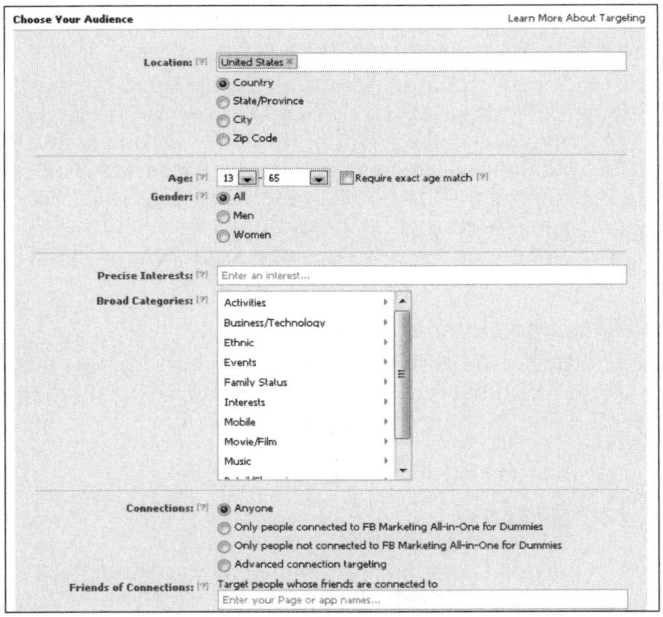

Figure 2-13: The Choose Your Audience section of the Advertise on Facebook page.

Location

The first way to narrow your audience is by the location of your business. If the product you're selling is useful to a strictly local audience, entering a location in the Choose Your Audience section (refer to Figure 2-13) is especially beneficial to you. If, for example, you have a dry-cleaning store in Des Moines, you have no reason to show that ad to people in San Francisco.

To enter a location, follow these steps:

1. **In the Location section (refer to Figure 2-13), enter the country your business is in.**

   The default country is the one you live in (as set in your personal Profile). You must enter at least one country. If your business is global, you can add up to 25 countries per advertisement. To add another country, start typing the country in the text box and a drop-down menu appears, listing the countries you can select. If you add more than one country, you lose the option to select the state/province, city, and zip.

2. **Select one of the following radio buttons: Country, State/Province; City; or Zip Code.**

   If you select By State/Province, you can enter multiple states in the box that appears.

   If you select By City, you can also choose multiple cities and cities within a range of miles — 10, 25, or 50 — of the specified city. If you select By Zip Code, you can choose multiple zip codes. (***Note:*** The latter option is available only in the United States.)

TIP

As you narrow the target audience, you notice that the Audience counter, on the right side of the page, changes (see Figure 2-14). The *Audience* is the number of people who could be shown your ad based on the information in their Profiles.

Demographics

Targeting by demographics is a great way to reach your ideal client. If you know, for example, that your most responsive audience consists of females between the ages of 35 and 50, you can enter that in the Age and Gender sections (refer to Figure 2-13).

Facebook gives you the option to require an exact match within an age range if you select the Require Exact Age Match check box. This means that if a user turned 51 yesterday, that user won't be shown the ad for which you selected the age range 25 to 50. It's better not to require an exact match, however, because Facebook will give you a discounted bid for people slightly outside the range who click your ad. (Facebook doesn't provide an exact idea of *slightly,* however, and it doesn't specify its definition of *discounted bid.*)

Interests

A great way to reach your perfect customer is by using the Precise Interests field — a powerful targeting tool that you can use to focus on likely customers. When you aim to grab the attention of a specific niche, your ad is more powerful. If your personal Profile states that you like yoga, for example, you're likely to click an ad for a new yoga studio in your area.

You can target interests with keywords that match users' interests based on what those users entered in their Profiles and what Facebook Pages they've liked. If you're selling running shoes, for example, some good keywords to enter are *running* and *jogging,* as shown in Figure 2-14.

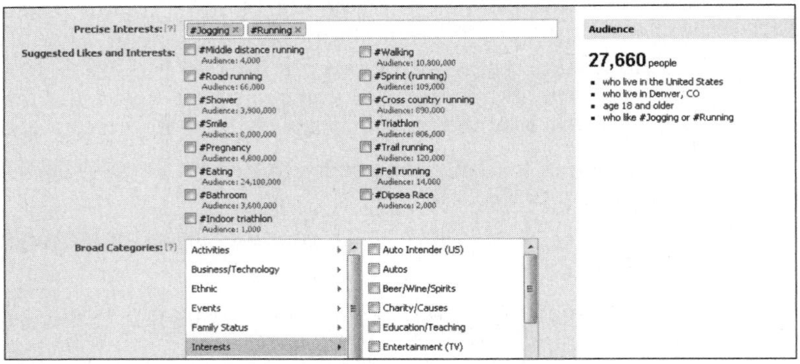

Figure 2-14: Entering interests.

As you start typing a word in this field, a drop-down menu appears, listing possible matches for your word. These matches can be helpful for finding likes and interests keywords that you hadn't thought of. Your selected keywords appear in separate gray boxes as shown in Figure 2-14.

Topics indicated with the # symbol, as shown in Figure 2-14, include overlapping Precise Interests. Many Pages or interests may use the term *jogging,* and by selecting the #Jogging option, you include all of them so that you don't have to select them individually.

TIP

You can also use the Broad Categories section to select a broader range of general terms, such as Small Business Owners.

If an interests keyword that you enter doesn't appear in the Precise Interests field, Facebook didn't find a match for that keyword. In the example shown in Figure 2-15, *accountant* is a match, but *accountant department* is not.

Figure 2-15: Make sure that your keyword is in the small gray box.

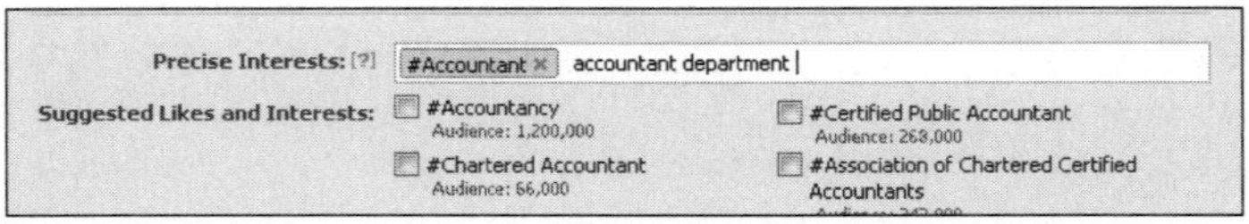

Depending on the keywords you enter, Facebook may (or may not) offer some Suggested Likes and Interests (refer to Figure 2-14). If you decide that the suggested keywords are also a good fit, select the boxes to have those keywords appear in your ad.

TIP

All the keywords you enter use Boolean operators including AND, NOT, and OR. This means that every keyword you enter should give your ad wider reach by targeting people who have those keywords in their Profiles. If you enter the keywords "cats," "dogs," for example, your ad is shown to everyone who has *cats, dogs,* or both terms in his or her Profile, rather than shown to only those people who have both terms in their Profiles or fan Pages.

One of the most effective ways to use the Suggested Likes and Interests area is to target fans of a particular Page — specifically, fans of your competitors. If your business is a large chain of fast-food restaurants, for example, you can target the fans of another large chain. Powerful stuff! And it's all kosher within the Facebook advertising terms. Just type the name of the competing Page in the Suggested Likes and Interests section (making sure that it appears in the gray box, which signifies a match).

You may even decide to mention the competition in your ad. Be careful of trademark infringement, of course, and definitely don't use the other company's logo.

Here's another, similarly powerful angle: Suppose that you're in a musical group that's trying to make a name for itself. Pick a famous band whose music is similar to yours, and create an ad that targets the fans of that band. The body text of your ad might say something like this: "Hey, [Famous Band] fans, if you like [Famous Band], you'll love us." An ad like that receives many more clicks because it lures people who already have a strong interest in a particular style of music.

REMEMBER

The more clicks you receive, the lower your cost per click.

Connections on Facebook

The next area in the Choose Your Audience section is Connections. This area offers five types of connections:

- **Anyone:** Default selection — no connection restriction.
- **Only People Connected to [*Page Name*]:** You can limit your ad to show to only people who like your own Page as a way to engage your own audience by advertising to them.

- **Only People Not Connected to [*Page Name*]:** Use this option to make sure that you don't spend money advertising to your own fans.
- **Advanced Connection Targeting:** If you select this radio button, you see two additional fields:
  - *Target People Who Are Connected to:* Enter a Page, app, or event on Facebook that you control as a way to cross-promote to a different audience.
  - *Target People Who Are Not Connected to:* Enter a Page, app, or event on Facebook that you are an Admin of as a way to exclude the members of that audience. We do not see a practical use of this option.

Advanced targeting options

You use the Advanced Targeting Options section of the Advertise on Facebook ad-creation page to target people in very specific ways. To access this area, click the Show Advanced Targeting Options link below Friends of Connections. These options may come in handy in unique situations.

Other possibilities for advanced targeting are single people, married people, people who speak a particular language, and people who work at a certain company. You can use the Education & Work area to target college graduates, people who attended a specific college or majored in a specific subject, or people who work at a specific company. Many Facebook users don't enter this information in their Profiles, though, so we suggest that you leave this area blank unless you have a very good reason to target these niche audiences.

REMEMBER

Narrowing your reach too much may result in fewer clicks. It's a balancing act between finding your perfect target and making sure you get enough clicks. If you aren't getting as many clicks as you want, you may have to widen your restrictions and use a broader target audience. You don't have to use all the targeting options that are available.

Setting Your Bidding and Pricing Goals

You have your ad designed and your niche targeted. Now it's time to pay the piper. How much are you willing to spend for your ad? After you've completed the Targeting section (covered in the preceding section of this chapter), scroll down to the Objective section to select the goal for your campaign:

- You can show your ad to people who are most likely to Click on Your Ad or Sponsored Story (see Figure 2-16), which allows you to bid on the CPC model discussed earlier.

- ✦ If you select to show your ad to people who are most likely to Like My Page, Facebook automatically changes your campaign to the CPM model and optimizes your bidding for you, as discussed earlier in the chapter.

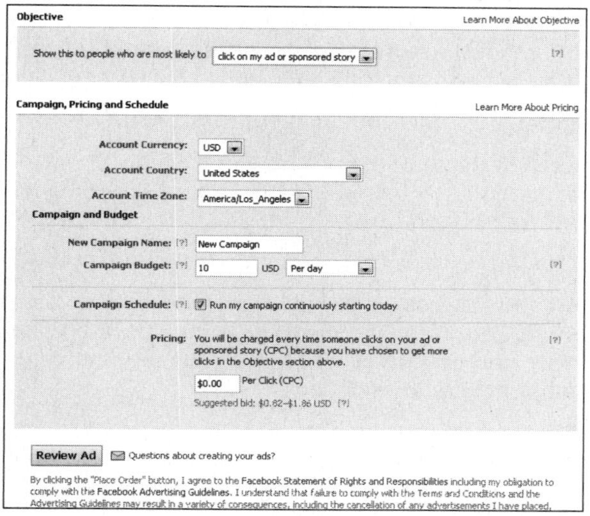

Figure 2-16: The Campaign, Pricing and Scheduling section as it appears for new users.

Now you move down to Campaign, Pricing and Scheduling. This is the last section you have to complete before placing the order for your ad.

If you've never created an ad or campaign before, you see the screen shown in Figure 2-16. If you've created an ad before, you see a Use an Existing Campaign link in the upper-right corner. Click this link to select a previous ad campaign in order to group the ad with that campaign. This makes sense when you're running similar ads and split testing them as outlined in Chapter 3 of this minibook. If you have run an ad campaign before, you won't have to set the Account Currency and Account Time Zone options (as shown in Figure 2-16) because you entered that information for your previous campaign.

To complete the Campaign, Pricing and Scheduling section, follow these steps:

1. **From the Account Currency drop-down menu, choose the currency you'll use to pay for the ad.**
2. **From the Account Country drop-down menu, choose the country you are in.**
3. **From the Account Time Zone drop-down menu, choose a time zone so that Facebook knows when to run the ad if you select specific times.**
4. **In the New Campaign Name field, enter your campaign name.**

The default name is New Campaign, but you should enter something more descriptive. In Chapter 1 of this minibook, we describe designing your campaign; refer to that chapter for ideas about how to structure your campaign names to reflect the types of ads within that campaign. You can always edit the campaign name later if you decide to make it more descriptive. See Chapter 3 of this minibook for details on changing the name. If you want to put this ad within an existing campaign, click the Use Existing Campaign link and select which campaign to use.

5. **In the Campaign Budget field, set your daily budget.**

   When you reach the limit of your budget, Facebook shuts off your ad automatically. You don't need to worry about spending more than you thought or forgetting to turn off your ads at the end of the campaign.

   TIP: If you're running test ads first, keep this daily budget low.

6. **If you want your campaign to run during specific dates, clear the Run My Campaign Continuously Starting Today check box and then enter the start date and end dates by clicking the respective calendars in the Campaign Schedule section.**

   These settings are handy if you want to run your ad for only five days, for example, and then automatically turn it off. If you leave the check box selected, you have to remember to turn off your campaign.

7. **If you chose See Advanced Options in the What Would You Like to Do section, you can Optimize for Clicks (the CPC model) and choose your own bid or Optimize for Impressions (the CPM model) and choose your own bid. If you chose Get More Page Likes or Promote Page Posts, you have the default CPM Facebook-optimized bid.**

   Facebook gives you a suggested bid range for the CPC or CPM model. We recommend using a mid-range price in the suggested bid range or possibly going a bit higher initially so that your ad appears prominently, and you can see whether it's converting. If you bid too low, your ad may not be shown and won't perform well from the start.

   REMEMBER: If you're advertising something within Facebook, and you're optimizing your ad to get likes or joins for your Event, Facebook will be optimizing your bidding for you by using the CPM method.

8. **Click the Review Ad button at the bottom of the section.**

   You're taken to a page that shows you how your ad looks and reviews your targeting information.

9. **If you want to edit the ad, click Edit Ad.**

10. **When your ad looks good, click the Place Order button.**

At the start of your campaign, it's hard to tell whether you should pay for clicks or pay for impressions, so determining which method is better requires some experimentation.

When you select the objective of Get More Page Likes, you're using the CPM model. In this case, you pay for a certain number of people to be shown your ad (which doesn't mean that all of them will actually see your ad). If you pay 60 cents for 1,000 people to be shown your ad, and only 100 people actually click it, you still pay 60 cents.

When you select See Advanced Options, you can use the CPC model. In this case, you pay for each click. If you bid 60 cents per click, and if 500,000 people are shown your ad and 100 people click it, you pay $60. In this example, it's better to go with the CPM option; both methods produced only 100 clicks, but the CPM option cost only 60 cents.

The general school of thought is that CPM is better for raising general awareness because you're paying for the people who are shown the ad. CPC is more effective when you want a specific click or response. But at the end of the day, you're trying to make money — not spend more. Test to see which method is cheaper for you. We cover this topic in more detail in Chapter 3 of this minibook.

After you place your order for the ad, the Facebook Ads team reviews your ad to make sure that it complies with Facebook terms. Depending on the time of day and the level of activity with Facebook Ads, this review can take anywhere from a few minutes to a few hours. Your ad status is Pending Review while your ad is being reviewed. You receive an e-mail when the ad has been reviewed; the e-mail states whether your ad was approved and is running or whether your ad was rejected. If your ad was rejected, Facebook doesn't tell you exactly why. The e-mail sends you the link to Facebook's terms and conditions, and lets you figure out the reason on your own.

Running a Facebook Promoted Post

Running a Facebook Promoted post ad is relatively straightforward. No bidding process is involved; instead, you pay a flat fee to push your post into a certain number of your fans' News Feeds. The post organically reaches a certain number; then you're paying for Facebook to show your post to people who may not have ordinarily seen your post in their News Feeds.

Promoted posts are good options for reengaging members of your current audience, as mentioned in Chapter 1 of this minibook. To start a Promoted post, simply go to your Page and find the post you want to promote. Then follow these steps:

1. **Click the Promote link below the post you want to promote.**

   A drop-down menu of budget options appears.

   If the Promote link isn't available, that means that you've never run a Facebook Ad before. You have to run an ad before you can enable this feature. At this writing, there's no way to set up your billing without going through the process of running an ad.

2. **Select your Audience by either clicking the radio button next to show the Promoted post to just People Who Like Your Page or People Who Like Your Page and Their Friends, as shown in Figure 2-17.**

   The People who like your page and their friends will cost more because you are showing your ad to more people.

Figure 2-17: Starting a Promoted post ad.

   The Budget drop-down menu shows you how many people you can reach and the cost of reaching that audience. At this writing, it costs less than a penny per person to push your post out. If you have a large Page, it can be expensive to reach the thousands of people you may not be reaching currently.

3. **Select your budget (and subsequently how many people you will reach) from the drop-down menu.**

4. **(Optional) If necessary, change your payment method by clicking the gear icon in the bottom-left corner and choosing Change Payment Method from the drop-down menu.**

5. **Click the blue Save button.**

   Your campaign has started. You can see data from the post itself while your campaign is running, as well as after the campaign, by going to the post and clicking the blue Promoted For button, as shown in Figure 2-18.

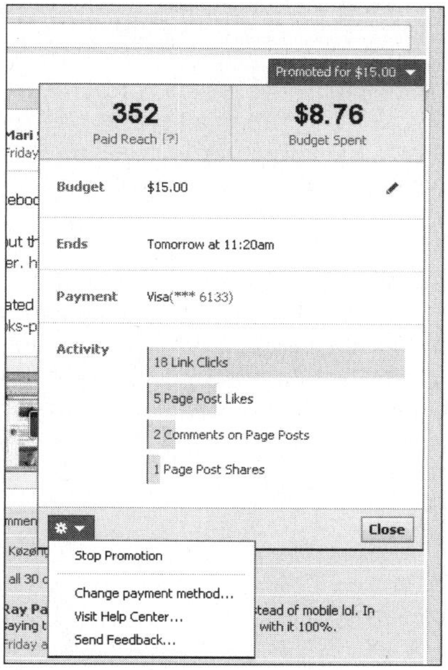

Figure 2-18: Watch the data as you run your Promoted post.

TIP

If you need to stop your Promoted post before the budget has been reached, you can click the gear icon in the bottom-left corner (refer to Figure 2-18) and choose Stop Promotion from the drop-down menu. Otherwise, your promo- … ue to run for three days or until the budget has been reached.

… ber of people who saw your post because of your campaign, … mber of organic and viral views, click the People Reached … n-left corner of the post, as shown in Figure 2-19.

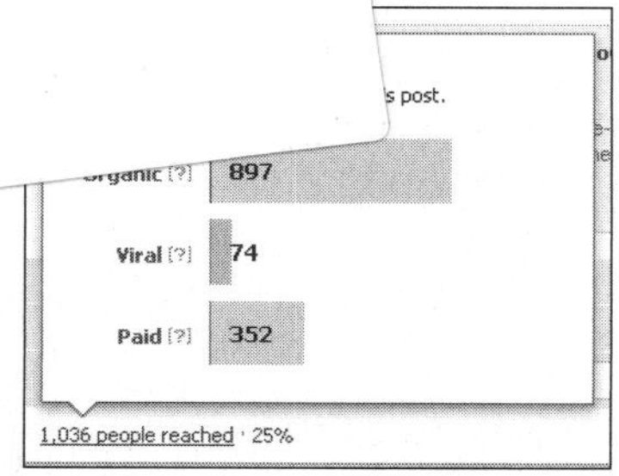

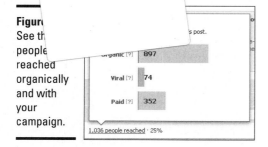

Figur… See th… people reached organically and with your campaign.

The Reports section of the Ads Manager has additional data about your campaigns, and you can find out more about it in Chapter 3 of this minibook.

Getting Help from the Facebook Ads Team

The Facebook Ads Help section is one of the most complete areas within Facebook Help. You can find step-by-step instructions for setting up your ad, case studies, and a glossary. Also, whenever you see a question mark (?) next to a term or box, you can click it to get an explanation in a pop-up window.

Facebook has a very comprehensive guide to advertising at `www.facebook.com/business/ads`. The left sidebar of that page has links to many frequently asked questions about the various aspects of Facebook Ads, including targeting, budgeting, and analyzing. Facebook likes to help you have a good experience while you give it money!

Chapter 3: Testing, Measuring, and Modifying Your Ad

In This Chapter

- **Becoming familiar with the Ads Manager**
- **Exploring split testing**
- **Making sense of the reports**
- **Optimizing your campaign**

Testing, measuring, and modifying your ad are among the most important things you can do to ensure that you're getting the most for your dollar. Unfortunately, testing is one of the most overlooked aspects of the Facebook advertising experience because it can be overwhelming.

Because of the many variables to test and tweak, you may feel daunted at first, but if you approach your Facebook ad campaign systematically, you can come away with an ad that has a high click-through rate at a low cost.

In this chapter, you begin by familiarizing yourself with the Ads Manager, where all your ad campaigns are displayed. Then you discover how to begin your split testing, view the Facebook ad reports, and optimize your campaign.

Now it's time to ratchet up your Facebook advertising expertise!

Understanding the Ads Manager

The Ads Manager is your Facebook Ads dashboard. Here, you see an overall picture of each campaign, the campaign status, and how much you're spending. From the Ads Manager, you can drill-down into each campaign and get the campaign statistics.

After you create your first ad, as discussed in Chapter 2 of this minibook, you're taken to the Ads Manager whenever you click the Ads Manager link on the left sidebar of the Facebook home page or your personal Profile.

The Ads Manager shows you all your ad campaigns in one place, as shown in Figure 3-1.

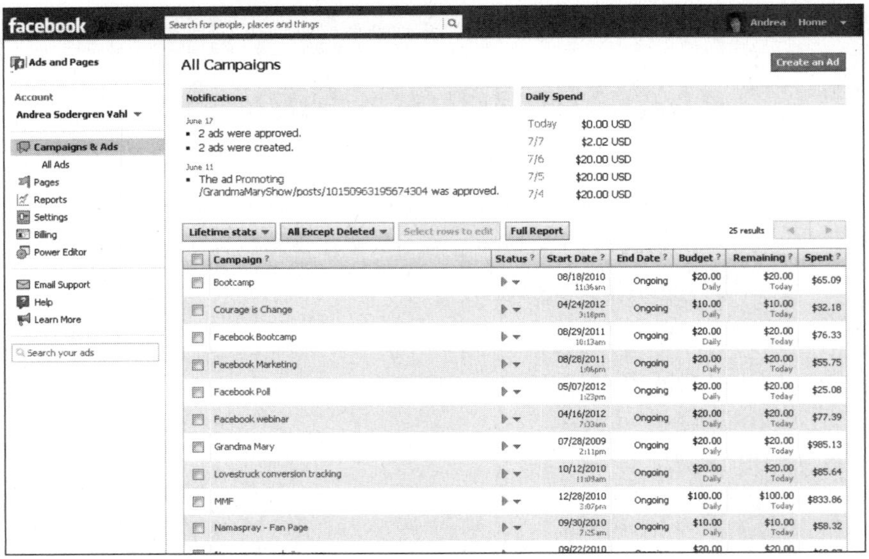

Figure 3-1: The Ads Manager page shows you an overview of all your Facebook ad campaigns.

You can also get to the Ads Manager directly at `www.facebook.com/ads/manage/campaigns`.

At the top of the screen, you see your Notifications and Daily Spend. Notifications include updates such as whether your ad was approved or declined or your credit card was charged. Daily Spend is a running total of how much you've spent each day across all campaigns.

Below the Notifications and Daily Spend areas are four boxes (refer to Figure 3-1):

✦ **Lifetime Stats:** When you click this box, you see a drop-down menu, as shown in Figure 3-2. You can adjust the range of dates for the Ads Manager to Today, Yesterday, Last Week, or Custom. If you choose Custom, you see a date range that you can input manually. Choosing any of the other options filters the Ads Manager table to display only those selected dates.

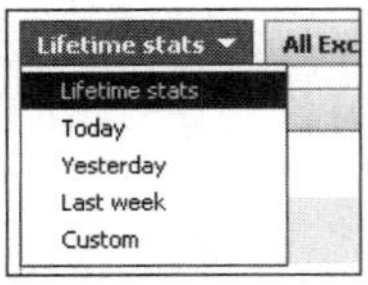

Figure 3-2: Adjust your range of dates.

- **All Except Deleted:** This drop-down menu allows you to select which campaigns are displayed in the Ads Manager. You can choose to view All Except Deleted (the default), Active, Scheduled, Paused and Completed, or Deleted. When you choose any of the selections, the Ads Manager changes to reflect your selection.
- **Select Rows to Edit:** This button is dimmed until you select the check box next to one or more campaigns, as shown in Figure 3-3. When you select a campaign's check box, the Select Rows to Edit button changes to Edit Row. Click this button to edit the titles or budgets of individual campaigns. In the case of Figure 3-3, the button text switched to Edit 2 Rows because we selected two campaigns. We don't find this feature to be particularly useful unless you have a large number of campaigns for which you need to change the budgets.

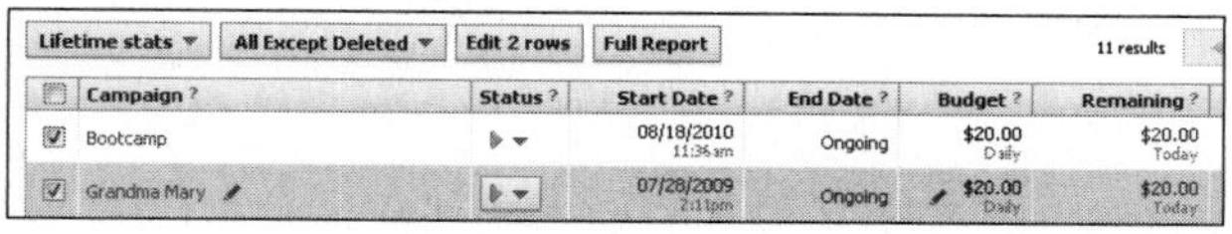

Figure 3-3: Select rows to edit.

- **Full Report:** Click this button to get your overall Advertising Report. This report shows in-depth statistics from all your campaigns in one place. We cover this report later in this chapter.

Just below the buttons, you see a table with several columns, as follows:

- **Campaign:** This column lists the names of the campaigns. A campaign may have several ads within it.
- **Status:** Each campaign is running, paused, completed, or deleted. The status is indicated by different symbols:

  - *Running:* Green arrow.

  - *Paused:* Pause symbol (two vertical lines, similar to the pause symbol on a CD player).

  - *Completed:* Check mark. An ad campaign is completed if you run an ad for a set amount of time.

  - *Deleted:* Red *X*.
- **Start Date:** This column lists the start date of the campaign.
- **End Date:** This column lists the end date of the campaign. You may choose to run a campaign for a specific length of time or stop the campaign manually.

- **Budget:** This column lists the maximum amount you're willing to spend on a campaign per day or during the life of the campaign. Each ad can have its own budget, and the campaign can have an overall budget.
- **Remaining:** This column lists the amount still available in the campaign's daily or lifetime budget.
- **Spent:** This column lists the total amount you've spent on the campaign.

TIP

Your Promoted posts ad statistics are also displayed in your Ads Manager. The campaign name defaults to a long name with a link to the Promoted post. It's a good idea to rename the title of the Promoted post campaign to something more meaningful by clicking the pencil icon next to the title.

The left sidebar of the Ads Manager contains several links that let you navigate to different areas, as shown in Figure 3-4.

Figure 3-4: Access different areas of your Ads Manager via links on the left sidebar.

Most of these links are directly related to Facebook Ads, but you can also access your Pages and Facebook Page Insights from the sidebar. Here's the scoop on each of the sidebar items:

- **Campaigns & Ads:** Clicking this link displays all your campaigns on the right side of the screen.
- **All Ads:** Clicking this link displays all your ads from every campaign on the right side of the screen. You see more stats and information. The effect is similar to clicking the Full Report button in the Ads Manager.
- **Pages:** Clicking this link takes you to a list of all the Facebook Pages you administer.
- **Reports:** This link takes you to the Reports area of Facebook Ads, which we cover later in this chapter.

✦ **Settings:** From here, you can change your Facebook Ads account information, add permissions so that other users can access your Facebook Ads account or reports, and change the notifications you receive. We cover this area shortly.

✦ **Billing:** Click this link to change your billing method and track how much you spend each day.

✦ **Power Editor:** This link takes you to a Facebook tool that allows you to create, upload, and manage your ads in bulk, even across different ad accounts. We have found the tool to have a few bugs and to be useful only if you're a true Facebook Ads power user. For more about the Power Editor and how to enable it, see the later section "Enabling the Facebook Ads Power Editor."

✦ **Email Support:** Clicking this link takes you to an area where you can specify what questions you have about your Facebook Ads. You can select questions in several categories: Costs and Payment, Understanding or Improving Performance, Reporting, and Other. If you don't have a Facebook ad currently running, you won't see this link.

✦ **Help:** Clicking this link takes you to the Facebook ads help section.

✦ **Learn More:** Clicking this link takes you to an area where you can view success stories, go through some tutorials in the Facebook Marketing Classroom, and find out more about how to use Facebook for business.

✦ **Search Your Ads box:** Use this search box to search your ads or campaigns. The search finds an ad or campaign with keywords you enter in this box. The search includes ad titles or campaign names but doesn't include the text of the ad.

Adding an Admin to Your Facebook Ads Account

You can add an Admin to your Facebook Ads account so that someone else can have access to the ad campaigns (General User) or access to the Ad Reports alone (Reports Only). This setting can be helpful if you want someone else to be able to change your ads, manage your campaign, or just view the reports. To add an Admin, follow these steps:

1. **Log in to your Facebook account as your personal Profile.**

   You see the home page of your personal Profile.

2. **Click the Ads Manager link on the left sidebar.**

   You're taken to the Ads Manager.

   TIP: You can also access your Ads Manager by clicking the down arrow in the upper-right corner of the page and select Manage Ads from the drop-down menu.

3. **Click the Settings link on the left sidebar (refer to Figure 3-4).**

   You may have to reenter your Facebook password. Then you see the Settings area for Facebook Ads.

4. **Scroll down to the Permissions section, which is shown in Figure 3-5, and click the Add a User button on the right side.**

   A pop-up window appears. In this window, you can add a user and select the access the user has to your Facebook Ads.

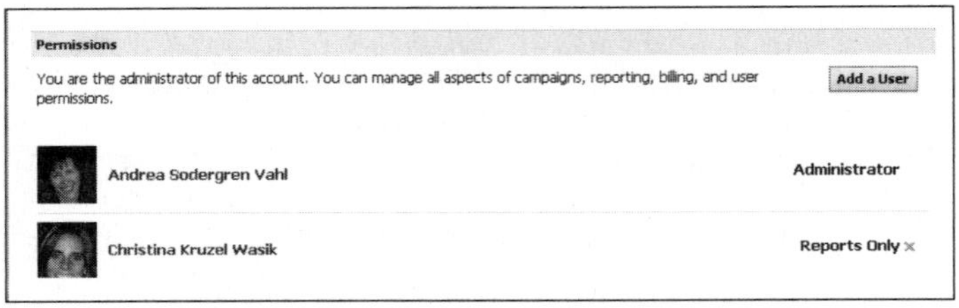

Figure 3-5: Add an Admin to your Facebook Ads account in the Permissions section.

5. **When you start typing the name of the user you want to add, a list of your Facebook Friends appears; select the name of person you want to add from the drop-down list.**

6. **Choose General User or Reports Only from the drop-down menu shown in Figure 3-6.**

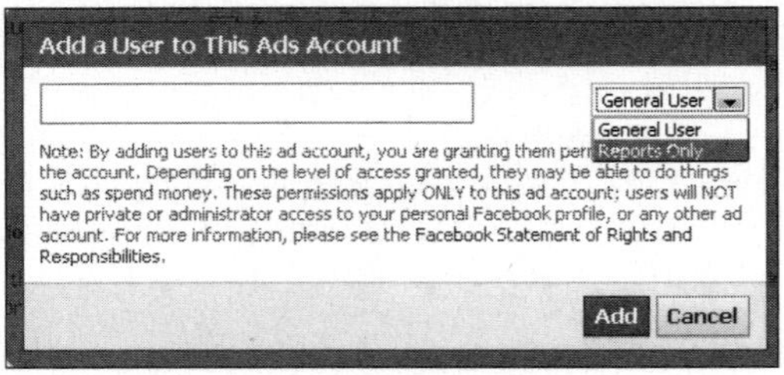

Figure 3-6: Select General User or Reports Only.

7. **Click Add.**

   The person you're adding appears in the Permissions section.

Now that you understand how to navigate the Facebook Ads Manager, you're ready to drill-down into the Facebook campaigns and test your ads. (See Chapter 1 of this minibook to see how to set up campaigns.)

Testing Your Ad

With any type of Facebook ad that you create, you want to test several variations to find out which one performs best. Ads that are performing well have a higher number of clicks and are rewarded by Facebook with lower cost. See Chapter 2 of this minibook for more information on how bidding and cost per click (CPC) works.

REMEMBER

Your bid price isn't the same as what you actually pay, but what you're *willing* to pay. Facebook adjusts the actual CPC based on what other advertisers are bidding.

To create these variations, Facebook makes it easy to copy an existing ad that you've created and then change the copy, image, targeting, website, or bidding. For any major change, though, we suggest creating a new ad instead of just changing the existing ad. That way, you'll have a record of ad performance to compare.

REMEMBER

For each campaign that you run, rest assured that you don't have to change each and every variable. That would be exhausting and time-consuming. Instead, map out two or three changes to test. Maybe select two different titles but keep the copy, image, and targeting the same, or keep the body text the same but change the title and the image. You get the idea.

This approach is called *multivariate testing, A/B testing,* or *split testing.* As we mention earlier in this section, you typically want to change only one or two things at a time and keep the other variables the same. Changing one thing at a time is best if you have the budget and the patience, because then you know that any difference between the two ads is attributable solely to the one thing that you changed. Choose what variables you want to test for each campaign, and map out your plan so that it's systematic. Maybe you run an ad one day with one call to action, run a different ad the next day with a different call to action, and then compare the two.

TIP

Make sure that you have enough data to make a valid conclusion. We recommend having at least 20 clicks and running the ad for at least two days so you can make a sound comparison. You don't need to have the same number of clicks to compare two ads because many of the variables can be different, such as the bid price and market. You can use a more relative number to compare the ads, such as click-through rate (CTR) or click per thousand (CPM), because these rates are percentages, not absolute numbers.

Your main goal is to get a high *CTR,* which is the number of clicks your ad receives divided by the number of times your ad is shown on Facebook *(impressions).* After all, Facebook judges your ad on how many people click it, and Facebook rewards ads with a higher CTR by showing them more often and giving them a lower CPC.

If you're running a campaign for your Facebook Page and selected the Show This to People Who Are Most Likely to Like *your page* option, as mentioned in Chapter 2 of this minibook, your bidding method defaults to the CPM method, and Facebook controls the bidding and ad price. Facebook optimizes your price and gives you a better price if your ad is performing well.

You run through a cycle similar to these steps:

1. Create a new ad.
2. Run the ad for a certain period to gather statistics.
3. Analyze the results of the ad (CTR, demographics, and action taken).
4. Decide which variables to split-test.
5. Repeat.

Split-testing your three ad variables: Copy, image, and targeting

The easiest way to do split-testing is to copy all the information from a previous ad to a new ad. That way, you can tweak the one thing you want to change and keep everything else the same. To create a new ad from an existing ad that you've created (as shown in Chapter 2 of this minibook), follow these steps:

1. **Log in to Facebook as your personal Profile.**

   You're on your personal home page.

2. **Click the Ads Manager link on the left column.**

   You're taken to the Ads Manager page.

3. **Click the name of the campaign that your ad is in.**

   You see a screen with the ads within that campaign and the various statistics they have. Assuming that you're just starting, you see just the one ad that you've created.

4. **Click the ad's name.**

   The ad area expands to show you the stats and an ad preview.

5. **Click the Create a Similar Ad link below the preview, as shown in Figure 3-7.**

   You're taken to the design section of Facebook ads. All the information from the earlier ad is automatically filled in, and you can change the copy, the image, the title, and the demographics for your split-test.

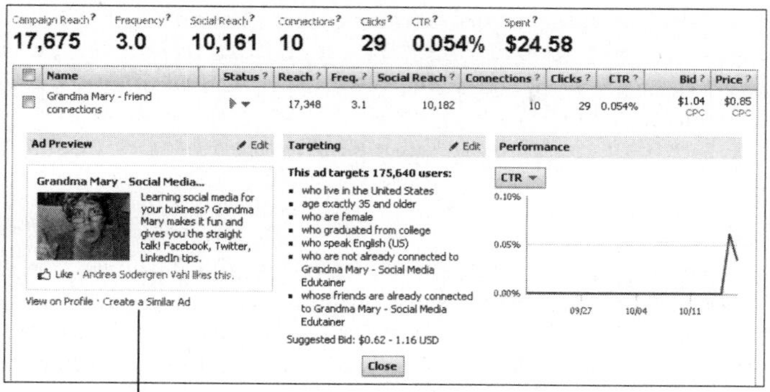

Click to see the ad design section.

Figure 3-7: Start here to do ad split-testing.

You can save a draft of the ad in the Creative Library, but you won't be able to save the targeting. You can set the campaign to run at a certain time in the future if you want to save all the information for later.

Copy

Your *copy* includes the ad title and body. If you're advertising something within Facebook — such as your business Page, a group, or an event — you won't be able to change the title of the ad. If you have a longish name for your Page, group, or event, it will get truncated to fit the 25-character title. Unfortunately, you can't do anything about that.

If you're advertising a website outside Facebook, you can change the title, though. Try two different titles to see which encourages more clicks. Figure 3-8 shows two titles that were split-tested. The one on the right performed better. Sometimes, you won't know exactly why a certain title or copy performs better, and this is why you split-test. In this case, the idea of creating leadership resonated better with people than the idea of boosting confidence did.

Also make sure to test the text in the body of the ad. Test different language and calls to action.

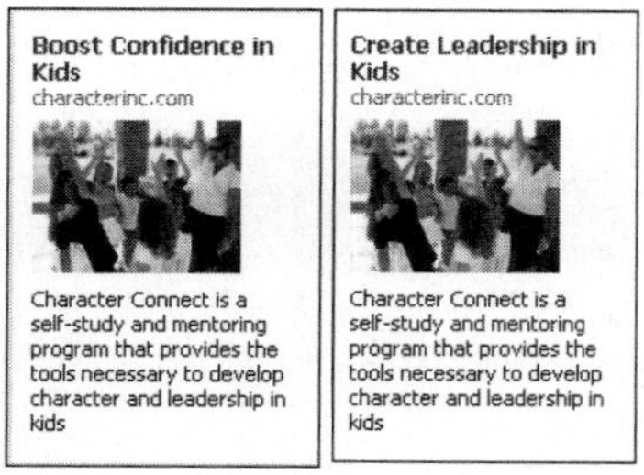

Figure 3-8: Split-testing ad titles.

To get ideas for different copy, take a look at the Facebook Ad Board at `www.facebook.com/ads/adboard`. You may have to enter your password to see this page. These are ads that are currently running on Facebook that are using demographics matching your Profile. They may or may not be successful ads, but they can give you an idea of what ads are running now.

Image

Your ad image can be very important for catching people's eyes. Try split-testing your ad between your logo and a picture of your product, for example. If you're advertising something within Facebook, we recommend keeping the image the same so that when someone goes to the event, fan Page, or group, the image is consistent.

The maximum image file size is 5MB, but the image displays at only 100 × 72 pixels in the ad. Make sure that the picture is clear and not too intricate.

Targeting

After you run an ad, you can take a look at the clicks and break them down by demographics. That data is listed in the Responder Demographics report, which we discuss later in this chapter.

To change the targeting, scroll down to the Choose Your Audience section, and adjust the location, age range, Precise Interests, Broad Categories, and others settings that you may want to change. To delete Precise Interests that you previously entered, for example, click the *X* next to Precise Interests. You may want to try split-testing two ads, using certain Precise Interests in one and using selections from Broad Categories in the other, as shown in Figure 3-9.

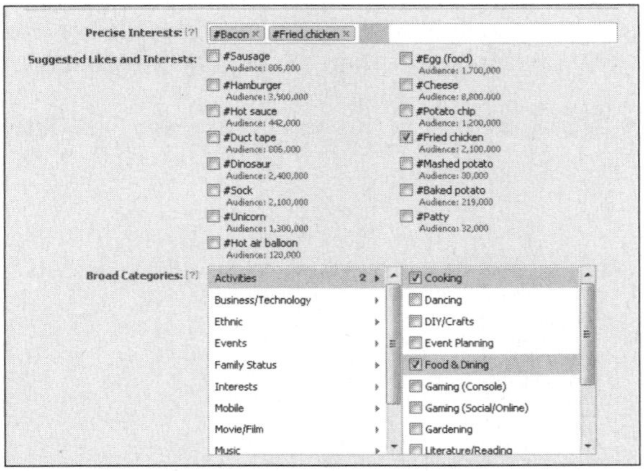

Figure 3-9: Adjust your targeting.

After you make one or two changes to your ad, click Place Order at the bottom of the section to send the ad to the Facebook Ads team for approval. You've created a new ad, and it must go through the approval process even if you've made only a slight change to the ad. The approval process can take up to 24 hours.

Testing your landing page

If you're advertising a website outside Facebook, you want to make sure that your website is optimized for what you're advertising. If you'd like someone to sign up for your newsletter, send that viewer to a web page that shows the benefits of the newsletter, a box for her to enter her name and e-mail, and not much else. If you're advertising a sale, send those viewers to the web page where you talk about the sale. Don't make the user hunt through your website to find the relevant content.

That said, you can also split-test your landing pages. Design two similar pages, and see which one gets better results when you send traffic to it. In this case, you want to keep the actual ad copy the same within Facebook so that you can really measure the difference.

Split-testing landing pages doesn't have to be too hard. If you created a page about your product along the lines of www.*yourwebsite.com/productname*, create another page on your site such as www.*yourwebsite.com/productname2*. The two pages should be identical except for the different copy, layout, or images you want to test. Send traffic to each of these pages with your Facebook Ad to see whether one page is better at converting visitors to buyers. Make sure that you have an analytics program installed on your website to measure the traffic, and watch when people are purchasing your product from one landing page or the other landing page. Google Analytics (`www.google.com/analytics`) is a perfect tool to help measure the traffic on your website.

Viewing Facebook Reports

Facebook Reports is a gold mine of data. Sometimes, sifting through that gold mine can be a bit tedious and confusing, but you can always find some good nuggets. Facebook Reports is the area in the Ads Manager where all your data on your ads is available, such as impressions, clicks, actions, actual cost per click, and more. The two most helpful reports are Advertising Performance and Responder Demographics.

You can access the reports in a few ways. The easiest way to drill-down into data for a specific ad is to follow these steps:

1. **Click the Ads link on the left side of your home page in Facebook.**

   You're taken to the Ads Manager page.

2. **Click the Reports link on the left side, as shown in Figure 3-10.**

   You're taken to the Ad Reports area, where you can drill into each campaign's reports and each ad's individual reports.

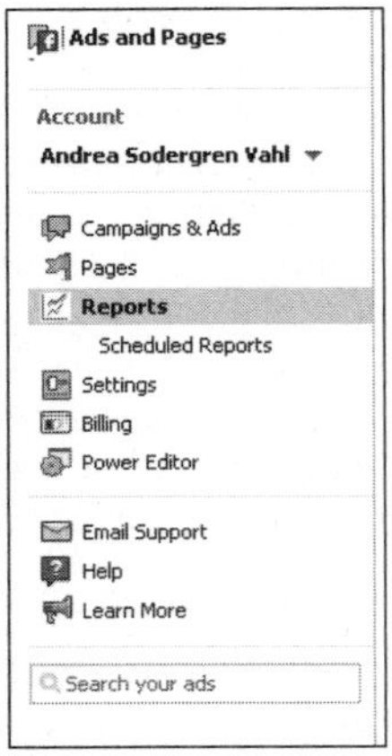

Figure 3-10: The Reports link takes you to the Ad Reports area.

The Ad Reports area has a drop-down menu from which you can choose the type of report you want, and you can filter the report summaries by campaign or ad. If you have multiple Facebook Ad accounts, you also have the option to filter your reports by account. You have multiple accounts if you've been added to other ad accounts as an Admin, as mentioned earlier in this chapter. Figure 3-11 shows the Ads Reports area.

Figure 3-11: Select what type of report you want.

Running and reading the Advertising Performance report

The first report in the drop-down menu is Advertising Performance. This report includes statistics such as Clicks, Impressions, Click Through Rate, and Spend. Similar information is available in the Ads Manager, which you can find on the left sidebar of your personal Profile home page, but the Advertising Performance report goes a step further and tells you conversions and cost per conversions if you're advertising a fan page.

To get your Advertising Performance report, follow these steps:

1. **Choose Advertising Performance from the Report Type drop-down menu (selected by default).**
2. **Choose Ad from the Summarize By drop-down menu.**
3. **Choose Campaign from the Filter By drop-down menu.**

   Now all your campaigns are available. You can select one or multiple campaigns to have in the report.
4. **Make a choice from the Time Summary drop-down menu.**

   You can choose Daily, Weekly, or Monthly. The report in Figure 3-12 shows Weekly.
5. **Select the appropriate date range in the Date Range fields.**
6. **From the Format drop-down menu, choose the format you want your report to be presented in.**

   You can choose Webpage (.html), which displays the report on a web page; Excel .csv; or Multilanguage Excel .csv. We say more about downloading your report into Microsoft Excel shortly.
7. **(Optional) Check the Include Deleted Ads/Campaigns box if you also want this information in your report.**
8. **Click the blue Generate Report button.**

   Figure 3-12 shows a sample Advertising Performance report for one campaign.

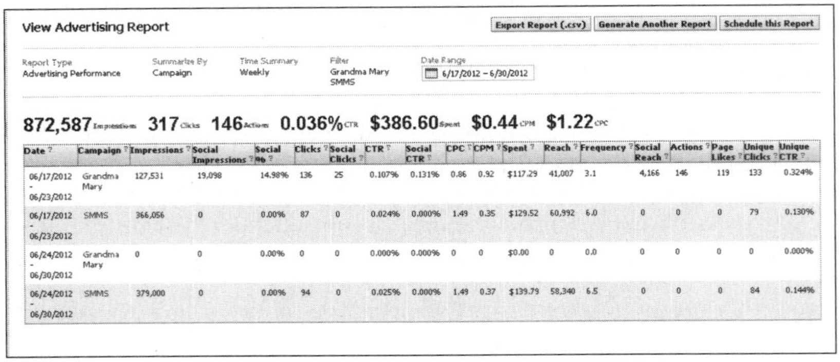

Date	Campaign	Impressions	Social Impressions	Social %	Clicks	Social Clicks	CTR	Social CTR	CPC	CPM	Spent	Reach	Frequency	Social Reach	Actions	Page Likes	Unique Clicks	Unique CTR
06/17/2012 - 06/23/2012	Grandma Mary	127,531	19,098	14.98%	136	25	0.107%	0.131%	0.86	0.92	$117.29	41,007	3.1	4,166	146	119	133	0.324%
06/17/2012 - 06/23/2012	SMMS	366,056	0	0.00%	87	0	0.024%	0.000%	1.49	0.35	$129.52	60,992	6.0	0	0	0	79	0.130%
06/24/2012 - 06/30/2012	Grandma Mary	0	0	0.00%	0	0	0.000%	0.000%	0	0	$0.00	0	0.0	0	0	0	0	0.000%
06/24/2012 - 06/30/2012	SMMS	379,000	0	0.00%	94	0	0.025%	0.000%	1.49	0.37	$139.79	58,340	6.5	0	0	0	84	0.144%

Figure 3-12: Compare all the ads from your campaigns in an Advertising Performance report.

If you haven't run ads before on Google or other web platforms, some of the terms in the Advertising Performance report can look like Greek. Here are the definitions of the terms in the Advertising Performance report shown in Figure 3-12:

- **Impressions:** How many times the ad has been shown to a Facebook user. Ads can be shown multiple times to users if they're logging in several times during your campaign, or, if they're browsing through different areas of Facebook, they are shown your ad in multiple places. Each time a user is shown your ad, it counts as an impression.
- **Social Impressions:** How many times the ad was shown to a Facebook user and one of his or her personal Friends liked the Page or attended the event. This report is valid only for advertising things within Facebook, such as fan Pages, events, or groups.
- **Social %:** What percentage of the total Impressions were Social Impressions.
- **Clicks:** The actual number of clicks of the ad. This report can include a click if someone liked your fan Page right from the ad itself. A single user could click on your ad multiple times, and you are charged for each click. Theoretically, someone could drive the cost of your ad campaign up in this way, but that isn't typical.
- **Social Clicks:** How many clicks you received from an ad showing that a current fan's Friend liked your fan Page or responded to an event RSVP. Again, this report is valid only when you advertise fan Pages, groups, or events.
- **CTR (click through rate):** How many times your ad was clicked, divided by the number of times your ad was shown (impressions). This is a straight ratio of the Clicks divided by Impressions.
- **Social CTR:** Social Clicks divided by Social Impressions. Theoretically, this number should be higher than the CTR, because the ad included a personal Friend who liked the Page and thus provided social proof.

✦ **CPC (cost per click):** How much each click your ad received actually cost you. This number is calculated even if you didn't bid on the CPC model, which is helpful for comparison. It takes how many clicks your ad received (even if you're paying by impression) and calculates how much each click cost you.

✦ **CPM (cost per thousand impressions):** How much each 1,000 impressions cost. Even if you didn't bid with the CPM model when you placed your ad, Facebook Reports will calculate it for your reference. This report is helpful if you decide to switch to the CPM bidding model because you can compare how your ads with different bidding models are performing.

✦ **Spent:** The amount you spent for the time summary you chose for the report: Daily, Weekly, or Monthly.

✦ **Reach:** The number of people who saw your ads. The reach is different from the Impressions because it only counts the unique people who have seen your ad. So if someone saw your ad five times, the reach only counts that person once rather than the five impressions.

✦ **Frequency:** The average number of times each person saw your ad. This is the Impressions divided by the Reach.

✦ **Social Reach:** The people who saw your Sponsored ad or Sponsored story, with social info about the people and Pages they're connected to on Facebook, such as whether they saw that one of their Friends already liked your Page. This report doesn't apply if you're advertising something external to Facebook.

✦ **Actions:** The number of actions taken by people within 24 hours of viewing an ad. You see data here only if you're promoting something internal to Facebook.

✦ **Page Likes:** The number of people who like your Page within 24 hours of viewing your ad or Sponsored story, or within 28 days of viewing the Page. This number can be beneficial because you can see when you have generated awareness that led to a like within a month.

✦ **Unique Clicks:** How many different clicks you received. This data is helpful for knowing whether the same person happened to be shown your ad twice and clicked it both times, because the second click wouldn't be a unique click.

✦ **Unique CTR:** Unique Clicks divided by Unique Impressions. Again, in relation to Unique Clicks and Unique Impressions, you want to know whether new people are clicking through to your ad or whether one person is clicking your ad over and over. It's best to have your Unique CTR come close to your CTR, but there's nothing you can do to control who is clicking your ad.

TIP

When you're comparing campaigns, make sure to compare the numbers like the CTR and CPC to get fairer comparisons. If you're going to compare two ads, try to run them with similar bids and at similar times of the day to get a true picture of which ad performed better. You can set the ads to run at certain times of the day when you create the ads.

Reading the Responder Demographics report

Another report that you can run is the Responder Demographics report. This report gives you great information about the types of Facebook users who are viewing or clicking your ads. To run this report, follow these steps:

1. **Start from the Ads Manager page, as described earlier in this chapter.**

   You can also go there directly at `www.facebook.com/ads/manage/campaigns`.

2. **Click Reports in the left column.**
3. **From the Report Type drop-down menu, choose Responder Demographics.**
4. **Choose Ad from the Summarize By drop-down menu.**
5. **Choose Campaign from the Filter By drop-down menu to see a list of your campaigns.**
6. **Check the box next to the desired campaign.**
7. **Select the Time Summary and Date Range you want to see.**
8. **From the Format drop-down menu, choose the format you want your report to be presented in.**

   You can choose Webpage (.html), which displays the report on a web page; Excel .csv; or Multilanguage Excel .csv. We say more about downloading your report into Microsoft Excel shortly.

9. **(Optional) Check the Include Deleted Ads/Campaigns box if you also want this information in your report.**
10. **Click the blue Generate Report button.**

This report shows people in certain age ranges who actually clicked your ad; Figure 3-13 shows an example. You may think that your target demographic is the 45–54 age range, for example, but a larger percentage of people in the 55–64 age range may have clicked the ad. With this information in hand, you may want to adjust your ad to target only that age range to get more clicks and more traffic.

The Responder Demographics report also shows you the percentage of users in various regions who saw your ad. The columns of this report may be blank if an insufficient number of impressions occurred or no users in the selected demographic group clicked your ad, but that doesn't necessarily mean that the number is zero.

Date ?	Campaign ?	Ad Name	Demographic	Bucket 1	Bucket 2	% of Impressions	% of Clickers	CTR
Dec 2010	Grandma Mary	Grandma Mary - Social Media Edutainer 2	country	US		100.000%	100.000%	0.072%
Dec 2010	Grandma Mary	Grandma Mary - Social Media Edutainer 2	gender_age	F	25-34	0.206%	0.000%	0.000%
Dec 2010	Grandma Mary	Grandma Mary - Social Media Edutainer 2	gender_age	F	35-44	33.511%	20.642%	0.044%
Dec 2010	Grandma Mary	Grandma Mary - Social Media Edutainer 2	gender_age	F	45-54	36.653%	31.193%	0.061%
Dec 2010	Grandma Mary	Grandma Mary - Social Media Edutainer 2	gender_age	F	55-64	21.800%	38.532%	0.127%
Dec 2010	Grandma Mary	Grandma Mary - Social Media Edutainer 2	gender_age	F	65-100	6.158%	7.339%	0.086%
Dec 2010	Grandma Mary	Grandma Mary - Social Media Edutainer 2	gender_age	F	Unknown	1.672%	2.294%	0.099%
Dec 2010	Grandma Mary	Grandma Mary - Social Media Edutainer 2	region	Unknown		0.935%	0.000%	0.000%
Dec 2010	Grandma Mary	Grandma Mary - Social Media Edutainer 2	region	us	Alabama	1.734%	0.000%	0.000%
Dec 2010	Grandma Mary	Grandma Mary - Social Media Edutainer 2	region	us	Arizona	1.738%	0.000%	0.000%

Figure 3-13: This report breaks down who saw your ad and who clicked your ad by age range.

If you click on any of the columns shown in Figure 3-13, you can sort the data by that column from highest to lowest or lowest to highest. Using that feature makes it easier to see the highest percentage of impressions if you use that column to sort. Then you can easily see which demographics are seeing your ad.

The Responder Demographics report doesn't always show the % of Clickers and CTR columns, so be aware that these numbers may not be available.

Exploring Actions by Impression Time

Another report type is Actions by Impression Time. This report shows the number of actions organized by the impression time of the Facebook Ad or Sponsored story. An action is tracked by the length of time between a user's view or click of the ad or Sponsored story and the action, such as a like or joining an Event (0–24 hours, 1–7 days, 8–28 days, and so on).

This report is somewhat interesting in that it tracks lag time. We don't see too much strategy adjustment that can occur based on the results of this report, but the data is available if you're interested in how long it takes someone to view your ad or Sponsored story before clicking the Like button. To view the report, choose Actions by Impression Time from the Report Type drop-down menu, and follow the steps for viewing the other report types.

Understanding Inline Impressions

The Inline Impressions report can give you information about how people are interacting with your ad. This report is valuable if you're using some of the features described in Chapter 2 of this minibook, where we discuss using a Sponsored post story to advertise a video. You can see how many people interacted with your content right from the ad itself, as shown in Figure 3-14. Choose the Inline Impressions report type, and then select the necessary date ranges and ad types, as outlined in the preceding steps.

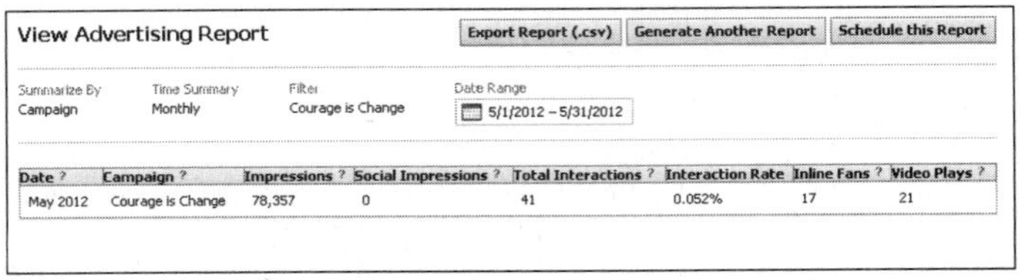

Figure 3-14: Inline Impressions gives you more information about interaction in your ad.

Exporting to a CSV file

To analyze the data in your ad reports more fully, consider exporting your reports to a CSV file, which you can use in Excel or a similar program. You may want to export the data to give yourself a visual graph of the numbers or to compare the numbers of two campaigns side by side. You can export your data from a few areas:

- **Ads Manager:** See all the campaigns you've ever run and then export the statistics.
- **Campaign:** Within each campaign, you can export the overall statistics.
- **Reports:** Within the Reports area, you can get more-refined data.

To export the data within the Ads Manager, first click the Full Report button. You see the data for all your campaigns, as shown in Figure 3-15. Then click the Export Report (.csv) button at the top of the screen.

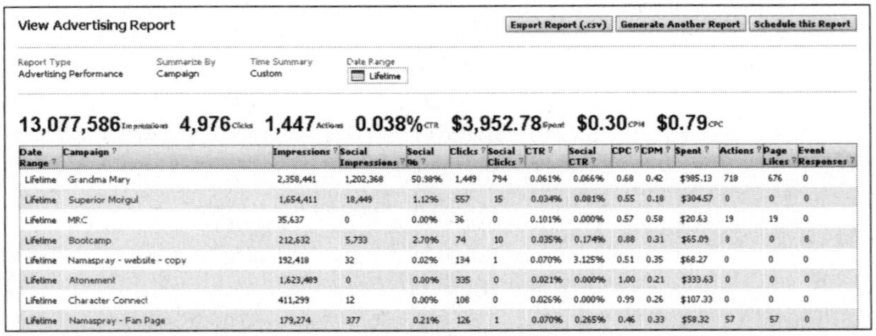

Figure 3-15: Export your data from the Ads Manager to a CSV file.

To export the statistics from a report that you run, follow the steps for whichever report you are creating as outlined in this Viewing Reports section, but select Excel .csv rather from the Format drop-down menu.

Enabling the Facebook Ads Power Editor

If you're becoming a Facebook Ads *power user* (that is, you create a lot of Facebook ads), you may want to enable the Power Editor so that you can have more control of your campaigns from one access point. The Power Editor makes it easy to create, edit, and manage ads and campaigns in bulk, even across a large number of different ad accounts. The Power Editor is also a way to access the Facebook Ads API to create ads such as Sponsored search discussed earlier in this chapter.

REMEMBER

The Power Editor can be a bit buggy and occasionally gets hung up when you are trying to create ads but you may find it useful if you're running a lot of Facebook ads.

To enable the Power Editor, follow these steps:

1. **Go to your Ads Manager at** `www.facebook.com/ads/manage`**.**
2. **Click the Power Editor selection on the left sidebar.**

   You see some information about getting started with the Power Editor.
3. **If you need to install Google Chrome, click the link shown in Step 1 of the onscreen directions, or go to** `www.google.com/chrome` **and click Download Chrome.**
4. **If you already have Google Chrome, or after you install it, move to Step 2 of the onscreen directions, and install the Power Editor by clicking the Here hyperlink.**
5. **If you see a pop-up window warning about extensions and apps that may harm your computer (this one is safe!), click the Continue button.**

   A Confirm New App window opens.
6. **Click Add to add the Power Editor app.**

   You're taken to a browser window where the Power Editor is enabled.
7. **Click the Power Editor icon.**

   You're taken back to Facebook, where you're prompted to select which of your ads and campaigns you want to show in the Power Editor.
8. **Select the accounts you want to add to the Power Editor.**
9. **Click Download.**

   Depending on how many ads you've run in the past, downloading may take a little while.

When the download completes, you're ready to use the Power Editor.

Adapting your campaign

After you have the data, what do you do with it? For starters, always make sure that you're digging into the reports deeply enough and watching the right stats; the data can be tricky! Suppose that you have two ads that ran with exactly the same copy; only the picture changed. From the data in Figure 3-16, you see that the ad with pic 2 performed better in terms of CTR and CPC. But notice that the actual Page likes are better for the ad with pic 1. The conversions to fans are better for the pic 1 ad, which is what you ultimately want!

179,274 Impressions **126** Clicks **57** Actions **0.070%** CTR **$58.32** Spent **$0.33** CPM **$0.46** CPC

Date Range ?	Campaign ?	Ad Name	Impressions ?	Social Impressions ?	Social % ?	Clicks ?	Social Clicks ?	CTR ?	Social CTR ?	CPC ?	CPM ?	Spent ?	Actions ?	Page Likes ?
09/26/2010-10/23/2010	Namaspray - Fan Page	Namaspray™ Yoga Mat Disinfectant-pic 1	93,601	246	0.26%	59	1	0.063%	0.407%	0.48	0.30	$28.32	32	32
09/26/2010-10/23/2010	Namaspray - Fan Page	Namaspray™ Yoga Mat Disinfectant-pic 2	85,673	131	0.15%	67	0	0.078%	0.000%	0.45	0.35	$30.00	25	25

Figure 3-16: Comparing initial data for two ads.

TIP

You can access the Advertising Performance report, which is shown in Figure 3-16, within a campaign by clicking the Full Report button in the Ads Manager.

Also take a look at the demographics responding to your ad (refer to Figure 3-13, earlier in this chapter). If you're getting a higher response from a certain age range, consider removing the underperforming age ranges from your ad targeting and focusing on the responsive age ranges for a better CTR.

REMEMBER

Rotate your ads every few days to keep them fresh. If you're targeting a narrower range of people, those people will potentially see the ad multiple times, and the ad won't be as effective.

Testing and tracking your Facebook ad may take some practice. There are lots of things that you can vary to see what gives you the best CTR or the highest conversion rate. Don't get discouraged if creating a good Facebook ad seems hard at first. After a while, you'll see a real difference in the performance of your ads, and you'll get a lot more for your hard-earned advertising dollars.

Book IX

Measuring, Monitoring, and Analyzing

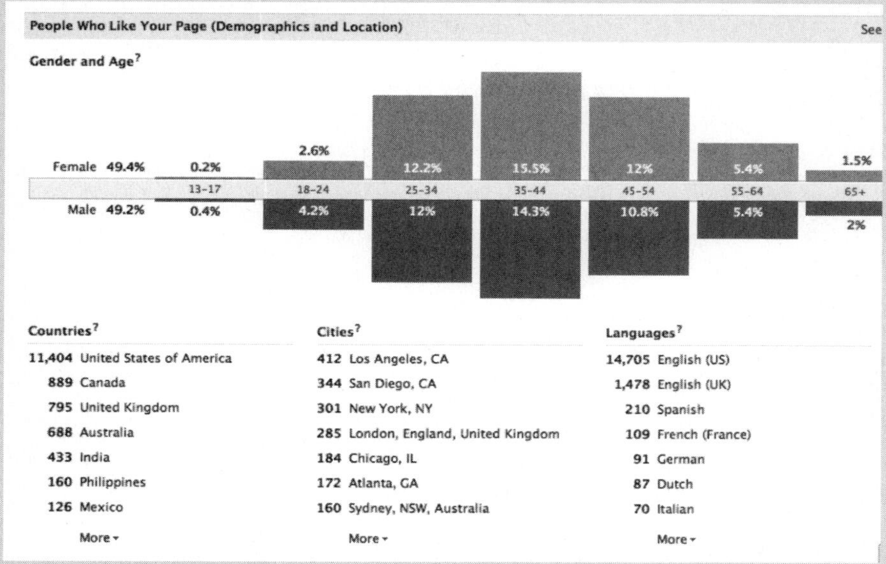

Contents at a Glance

Chapter 1: Setting Realistic Targets to Identify Success

In This Chapter

- **Understanding the difference between social monitoring and social measuring**
- **Knowing the benefits of real-time engagement**
- **Determining the best social metrics for your business**
- **Understanding the importance of social media measuring**

Gone are the days when businesses could operate behind closed doors. The popularity (or should we say massive explosion?) of social networking has busted open those doors, and there's no turning back.

Your customers are now *social customers.* They love to share, chat, post, like, and comment — and when they have something important to say (good, bad, or worse), they're quick to share it on their social networks. Their comments run the gamut from the best raves to the worst rants.

This chapter first examines the importance of social monitoring and describes ways that you can take advantage of the social conversations related to your niche and your business. From there, we explore strategies related to social measuring, discussing how you can best measure your prospects' and customers' social activities, and then use this information in your marketing messages to get your fans to take action.

Your customers and prospects are going to be social with or without you, so it behooves you to pay attention, take notes, and get into the conversations at just the right times. This chapter helps you do just that!

Exploring Social Monitoring and Measuring

If you're just dipping your toe into the ever-changing Facebook waters, the idea of taking on social data tracking may be a bit daunting. You may be wondering, "Where do I start?" When you do collect the data, you might ask, "What the heck do I do with it?" We address both of those questions and many more throughout this section.

The purpose of tracking online activity is to identify the overall impact of your efforts. The data that you collect can help you support your customers, promote your brand, and grow your business. Although we've been exploring Facebook marketing throughout this book, it's important to note that you should take a holistic approach to monitoring and measuring social media activity. By *holistic approach,* we mean including all social activity that is important to you, no matter whether it's coming from Facebook, Twitter, YouTube, or a different social network. All sites that matter to your clients should matter to you.

In addition to listening to your fans, you should do a reality check to find out whether all your social media marketing efforts are worth your time and effort. Is what you're doing really working? When you're exploring monitoring and measuring strategies, you first want to set your key performance indicators. Ask yourself these questions:

- What do I want to achieve?
- What does success look like?
- What are the indicators of my success?
- By what date will I complete this goal?

Although you'll find some overlap in the data, monitoring and measuring are two different processes. When it comes to taking action, you analyze and use that data differently. This chapter closely examines both processes so you can better understand what overall tracking can do for your business.

The Importance of Social Media Monitoring

Monitoring is a bit like eavesdropping while pressing your big digital ear against the computer screen. You get to listen to all the chatter about you and your company, as well as hear what's being said about your competitors and industry. In this section, we explore what it means to monitor social media activity and what you can do with the data you collect to improve your overall marketing initiatives.

Monitoring involves identifying a set of keywords relevant to your business and brand. Knowing what words your prospects and customers are using online to research your niche or business is paramount to overall marketing success.

After you identify your keywords, you plug the keywords and information about your social media accounts into a monitoring tool. (We review your options for monitoring tools in depth in Chapter 3 of this minibook.) The monitoring tool tracks the communications that are most important to your niche and business, and organizes the data for you in a way that's easy to digest, such as comprehensive charts, tables, and lists. Overall, monitoring allows you to know who's talking about a topic (by means of specific keywords that you've identified) and what they're saying about it.

To put a successful social monitoring plan in place, you must understand why monitoring is important to your business and look closely at what you can do with the information you collect.

Seeing why monitoring online conversations is important

Monitoring is all about listening to online conversations with the intent to learn, engage, and support. The benefit of social media monitoring is the opportunity to join the conversations that matter most to your business and its relationships with its fans.

When it's working in your favor, Facebook can function as a word-of-mouth machine, broadcasting every customer rave that hits its airwaves. When you're engaged with your fans and firing on all cylinders, Facebook can be your best friend.

At some point, however, all best friends have spats. Sooner or later, someone will use Facebook to tell the world that your product is lacking, that your delivery department is slow, or that your call-center response time is horrendous. It's bound to happen.

In both cases — that is, in the "singing your praises" scenario and the "lackluster results" scenario — your goal is to be prepared to engage. You want to respond to both types of posts as quickly as possible. That's why monitoring is a crucial component of your overall social media marketing strategy.

In the case of the raving, happy fans, catching them in the moment only elevates their appreciation for you and their admiration of you. They feel heard and appreciated. See Figure 1-1 for an example of a positive exchange on Facebook.

In the case of the ranting, frustrated customers, keep in mind the two main reasons why responding quickly is crucial:

- **You want to take care of your customers.** If someone's upset, you want to genuinely meet his or her needs and put the fire out quickly.
- **You want the rest of your online audience to see that you take care of your customers.** What you say and do for one client or customer directly affects all viewers' perceptions of you, so this situation is your chance to make lemonade out of lemons and shine a good light on yourself.

Figure 1-1: Admins from the Facebook Page Social Media Examiner are quick to respond to fans' appreciation.

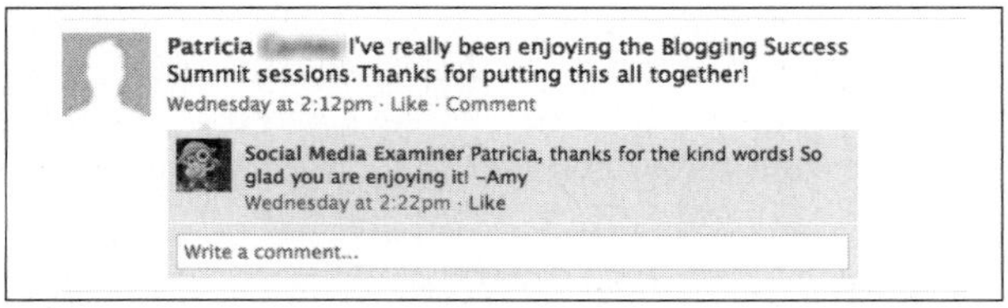

Situations like these give you the opportunity to protect your brand. One goal of an effective monitoring strategy is to guard your brand's reputation and keep it polished at all times. Also, you can increase your brand's social proof by engaging in these important, in-the-moment, two-way dialogues, which increase fan trust and admiration.

Understanding the importance of real-time engagement

Monitoring online conversations is important if you want to stay in the loop about conversations related to your niche and your business. That said, the optimal outcome of social media monitoring is to take full advantage of the opportunity for real-time response. The goal is to get in on the conversations that matter most at just the right time. In this section, we give you a few examples to illustrate just how important real-time response is for your business.

Suppose that you're the owner of an online store that sells wine, and your goal is to increase overall sales. Monitoring for phrases such as *"wine pairing," "the best wine that goes with,"* and *"wine recommendations"* can help you help others. Knowing when people are talking about your area of specialty gives you an online icebreaker; it allows you to join the conversation at the right time and even do a little consultative selling, where you offer suggestions and advice focused on the products and services you sell. Best of all, because you're monitoring in real time, you're joining the conversation at a time when people are open to suggestions and in need of help. In essence, they're raising a digital hand and saying, "Hey, I need your expertise over here!"

Real-time monitoring is crucial when you want to make an impact online. To help you grasp the magnitude of real-time monitoring, we want to tell you about a post that was shared on Twitter and Facebook. Tim Ferriss, the best-selling author of *The 4-Hour Workweek* and *The 4-Hour Body* (Crown Archetype), was trying to give a $100,000 donation to St. Jude's Hospital. Not too shabby, right? Although he tried to contact the hospital multiple times, his calls were never returned, so out of frustration, Tim took to the social media airwaves, as shown in Figure 1-2.

Figure 1-2: Tim Ferriss posted these status updates on Facebook and Twitter.

Imagine that you were St. Jude's Hospital and saw Tim's post online, in real time. You'd be sure to reach out immediately, right? If a fan posts something negative about you or perhaps asks advice of you, and you delay your response, someone outside your company will likely step in to defuse the situation or offer a better solution. That "someone" just might be your biggest competitor coming to the rescue.

Almost 200 people responded to Tim's post, making suggestions for his donation. (***Note:*** St. Jude's did reach out to Tim quickly, and he posted that he was talking with the hospital about his possible donation, as shown in Figure 1-2.) Now do you see why real-time response is so crucial?

Monitoring the right way

Social media monitoring is not just about identifying and responding to your online detractors. To develop a clear picture of what's being discussed online, you should monitor more than just your customers' and prospects' conversations about you. In this section, we take a look at additional ways to use these monitoring strategies to take your marketing initiatives to the next level.

An additional way to use monitoring strategies is to follow the conversations of industry thought leaders, your top competitors, and your partners. The goal is to cover all the bases. Also, consider monitoring keywords that are associated with products or services that may be complementary to your own. The conversations may give you insights and ideas about possible partnership opportunities or brand extensions.

Monitoring is keyword based, so choosing the right keywords is crucial. Here are some suggested keywords that you can monitor:

- The names of key people in your company
- Your company name
- All brand names associated with your company
- Product names
- Names of your services
- Your top three competitors' names
- Names of industry thought leaders
- Names of businesses that you partner with
- Competitive product names and services
- Industry or niche keywords

TIP

Clearly, when it comes to monitoring, you have a lot of information to pull. You can monitor all the public conversations that are taking place online at any given time. To start off right, you should monitor the communication that's posted on Facebook as status updates; posts where your name or business have been mentioned in a post (also called @tagging) or comments; Twitter updates; and comments on blogs.

Identifying your monitoring outcomes

Here are some outcomes of monitoring social activity:

- **Spy on your competitors.** What are they doing online? What do their customers say about them?

- **Understand your ideal client.** Find out what she wants and needs, what makes her tick, and what words she uses when talking about your brands and services.
- **Participate in conversations.** You want to join the real-time conversations that matter most to your business. When people online are talking about your industry (niche, topics, and so on), you want to get in on those conversations to generate exposure for your company. You can offer advice or just share your thoughts and insights.
- **Gather market intelligence.** You want to listen to what people are saying in your industry so that you can create better products and services.
- **Manage your reputation.** You want to know what your customers are saying about you. You want to see both good and bad comments in real time so that you can address them quickly.
- **Set up a listening portal.** You want to set up a support team to monitor your clients' needs and concerns and to address issues quickly. (We talk in detail about setting up a successful social media team in Book I, Chapter 2.)

REMEMBER

Setting up a listening station is the most important piece of social monitoring. While listening, observe with the intent to genuinely understand group dynamics and behaviors. Look out for the influencers and leaders, because these people are the ones who can spread the word about your business. Notice how people interact, and pay close attention to the community norms. Make sure that you understand the rules of engagement before you begin to interact and add value.

To review, here are some of the most important benefits of social monitoring:

- You're more responsive to your fans' needs when you can help them in their time of frustration or confusion.
- By jumping into online conversations at the right time, you stay relevant and at the top of your fans' minds.
- By monitoring regularly, you begin to fully understand your customers.
- Monitoring online communication allows you to hear others sing your praises. When your fans post compliments, rave reviews, and praise, these communications are great social proof. Take screen shots of these posts to use in your marketing materials. (The term *social proof* refers to the psychological phenomenon of people being motivated to do things that they see other people doing.)
- Monitoring allows you to spot trends, keeping you on the edge of your industry.

- When you understand what your fans are talking about when it comes to your brand, you can better deliver the features and benefits that your audience is asking for.

The Importance of Social Media Measuring

Measuring is more statistical than monitoring and occurs over a period of time versus in real time. In the following sections, we explore how measuring your social activity allows you to evaluate the success of your social media efforts, as well as to better understand the behaviors and habits of your customers and prospects. We also examine what data is best for you to measure, depending on your marketing outcomes. With all the data on the web today, the last thing you want to do is to get bogged down in too much information! When you know what to measure, you can streamline your efforts, saving yourself a lot of time and stress.

Seeing why measuring online activity is important

The benefit of measuring activity that relates to your brand, company, and industry on Facebook and other social networks is to spot trends, behaviors, and reactions early. The goal is to analyze the data quickly and act on it to get your biggest bang for your time and efforts. Constant benchmarking is crucial to ascertaining whether things are working in your favor.

Measuring online activity as it relates to your social networking sites is important because the data allows you to see fairly quickly what's working and what isn't. This valuable data will help you stay on track and continue to move toward your desired results. For example, let's say you are a wine seller. When measuring your data, you find that over the past few months your fans engaged with your content (clicked on links, commented, and shared your posts) more often when you posted about wine pairing versus when you posted about the types of grapes used in specific wines. This data will help you determine what content your audience wants to see more of, therefore eventually increasing your overall engagement and reach.

To begin measuring, first identify the keywords that reflect your business and brand. Useful tools for researching and identifying the best keywords for your niche or market include Google Keyword Tool (`http://googlekeywordtool.com`), Scribe SEO (`http://scribeseo.com`), and Google Alerts (`www.google.com/alerts`).

Keyword tools make it easy to find out what people are searching for online. With Google Keyword Tool, you can enter a word or phrase, and the tool returns other popular keywords or phrases that are searched for online, as shown in Figure 1-3. Then you can do some research to find out what words are searched for most and determine the words that best fit your brand.

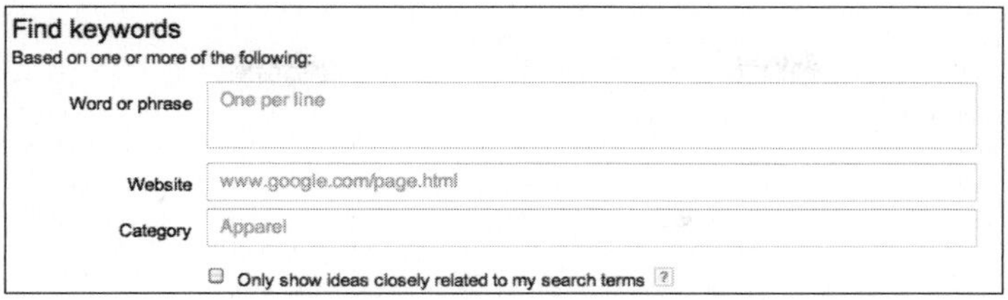

Figure 1-3: Keyword suggestions from Google Keyword Tool.

Next, plug your keywords into a monitoring tool. (Again, we review monitoring tools in depth in Chapter 3 of this minibook.) The monitoring tool scans the Internet; grabs all blog posts, online articles, videos, and so on that contain those keywords; and disseminates the information in different data combinations, building patterns that tell a story about the social activity collected. The tool might tell you the specific keywords that were mentioned on specific social media channels and how many times they were mentioned. This type of data is useful for finding out what people are talking about online and where they're talking.

After the tool grabs the information, the measuring starts. Monitoring and measuring tools allow you to analyze the data, to slice it and dice it in different ways to gain full understanding of its meaning.

REMEMBER

One of the major benefits of measuring the data is that measurement keeps you accountable. When you see what's working and what's not, you can take action to do more of what's working and tweak what's falling short.

Determining what you should measure for your return on investment (ROI)

When monitoring and measuring, it's important to pay attention to your return on investment, meaning you want to make sure that your time, efforts, and dollars are delivering real results toward your specific goals and outcomes. When it comes to tracking and measuring online data, you have numerous options. Therefore, it's important to identify the metric indicators that are most important to you. If you post content with links to your blog, for example, it's important to track which links get the most clicks from your fans by using a link-tracking tool such as bit.ly (`https://bit.ly`).

A free tool, bit.ly allows users to shorten, share, and track links (URLs). You copy and paste a long URL into bit.ly's portal, and the tool automatically generates a shorter link that you can use on social networks or anywhere else on the web. These shorter links are trackable, meaning that bit.ly will tell you how many times that link has been clicked and on what social sites it has been shared, as shown in Figure 1-4. Over time, this data helps you see which content your fans interact with most.

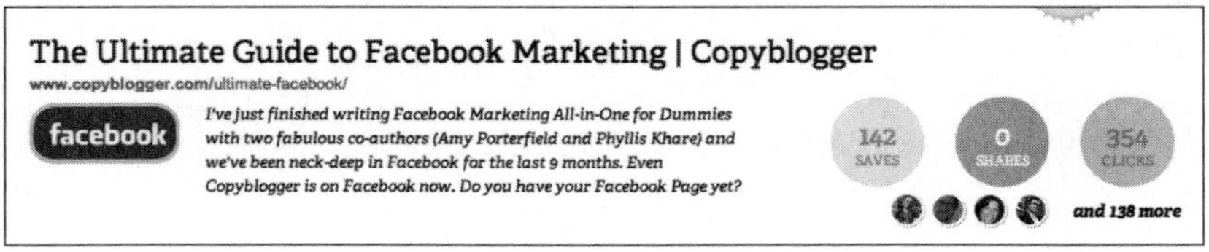

Figure 1-4: Click metrics from a bit.ly dashboard.

If you're looking to increase the comments on your Facebook Page, you may want to use Facebook Insights to track which posts are getting the most comments. *Insights* is Facebook's built-in analytics dashboard. You can use it to look at trends in the activity on your Page, including how many comments you're getting from your posts. We talk in detail about Facebook Insights in Chapter 2 of this minibook. This tool can paint a picture of what types of posts your fans respond to best — most favorably and most frequently.

One of the ultimate benefits (and goals) of monitoring and measuring, after all, is uncovering information that allows you to increase the impact of your social media posts. Tracking the time of day you generate the most activity on your Page, such as clicks and comments, can help you decide the best time of day to post a call to action.

Suppose that you own a store for runners, and you're currently having a special on running shoes for men. By analyzing your data, focusing especially on how many men are engaging with your content, the time of day they're most active on your Page, and what content they're engaging in, you can find out the best time of day to post your promotion and how to craft your post around this data.

By measuring these behaviors at this depth, you can reach more of your targeted audience with each post and turn your fans into loyal, paying customers.

Read on for specific ideas about what to measure, based on your business outcomes and goals.

Turning social activity into key metric indicators

When it comes to social media activity, you can track and measure numerous indicators. Here are the most important areas to consider:

- Engagement
- Brand awareness
- Influence
- Sentiment

- New likes/unsubscribes
- Click activity
- Financial return
- Volume
- Demographics

To help you understand how these indicators can support your marketing efforts, we dive a little deeper in the following sections, exploring the benefits of each indicator. To decide which indicators are a good fit for your business, keep your marketing goals in mind as you read the options.

Engagement

Engagement refers to the relevance of the Facebook Page to users and the actions they take when they visit the Page. You can measure engagement by taking a look at the types of activities users engage in, such as becoming a fan, writing on your Timeline, liking or commenting on an update, uploading a photo or video, or mentioning your Page in status updates. You can monitor this information weekly and monthly with Facebook Insights (see Book IX, Chapter 2 for details) and by spending time on your Page on a daily basis.

You can also monitor and measure all the words and phrases that your fans and prospects use when they talk about your brand. Are these words and phrases what you expected? Are they the same words that you're using to explain your programs and services? These words and phrases are key to understanding how people are talking about your business! In addition, when you know the words your fans use online, you can build rapport more quickly because using the same words creates a connection.

Brand awareness

Brand awareness refers to how much your company is talked about on the social web and, even more important, why people are talking about you. It also refers to how recognizable and known your brand is to your ideal audience. Is it in relation to a product announcement, a press release, or some company news you've played a role in? Or did someone write a review or mention your company in a blog post? Regardless of where the awareness comes from, you don't want to be the last one to hear about it.

You may want to add a reference point to your social mention tracking to see how many times your company and products are mentioned along with your competitors' during a 30-day period. This type of monitoring is often called *share of voice*, meaning you are sharing this social space with your competitors and monitoring and measuring how often your brand is mentioned compared to theirs. You can access the information you need to monitor share of voice through third-party monitoring tools. You add up all the mentions of your business and the mentions of your competitors, and then divide your mentions by the total to arrive at your share of voice.

Influence

Influence refers to how much your company is referenced and respected on Facebook. If a company whose Facebook Page has 10,000 engaged fans posts a link to your new video on YouTube, and your video goes viral overnight as a result, you'd be able to attribute your success to being discovered on that company's Facebook Page. Then you'd be able to monitor the increase in comments, likes, and shares on one of the social listening tools, such as Netvibes (www.netvibes.com), as shown in Figure 1-5. You'd also want to send a shout-out to the company for helping make your video a success. In the future, when you launch a new video, you'll probably want to add that company to a list of companies to alert.

Figure 1-5: A Netvibes listening station.

Sentiment

Sentiment comprises both positive and negative reactions to your brand on Facebook. Perhaps someone ordered a product from you and was dissatisfied with the color or the overall quality. Perhaps that person went to your Facebook Page and wrote that he'll never order another product from you. But what if your customer service reps were monitoring the page in real time, and one of them offered to take the product back, refund the customer's money, and send him a new model? You could nip the situation in the bud, not only undoing the negative sentiment, but also turning it around significantly.

New likers/unsubscribers

It's important to measure how many new likers can be attributed to individual updates and your collective activity on Facebook. If people respond favorably by liking your Page, and especially if they respond to a specific update, you can gain a good sense of how your users feel about that type of content. If videos get more attention than other links do, for example, you want to post more videos for your fans.

On the other hand, if users unsubscribe in reaction to a particular update, that situation gives you invaluable information, too. Perhaps users don't want to see that type of content from you, or maybe you've overloaded your users with too many updates. Although ascertaining why you lose one fan here or there may be hard, a major exodus would be very revealing. You can monitor the number of new likers and unsubscribes on Facebook Insights.

Click activity

Click activity refers to the times when a person clicks your Facebook Ad and is taken to your website or a tab on your Facebook Page. It's important to measure click activity so you'll know how effective your ad campaign is and whether you want to run it again or tweak it the next time around. You can monitor this type of data by using Facebook Ad reports. (See Book VIII, Chapter 3 for more about these reports.) Clicks are also tracked for Page likes and event RSVPs. You'll want to know whether your event is drawing people in on Facebook; if not, you may need to change the description or the date. Will you have enough interest to run it? You can see information about likes and RSVPs in the Facebook Insights reports. (For more on Facebook Insights, see Chapter 2 of this minibook.)

Financial return

Financial return is the same as return on investment (ROI) and looks at the efficiency of your efforts in terms of time, resources, and dollars; it compares those efforts to your end results. When examining your financial returns, you want to make sure your efforts are paying off, meaning they are moving you toward your overall goals.

Asking yourself specific questions related to your goals and marketing outcomes will help you determine if you are moving toward a financial return. For example, what are you getting in return for the time you spend on your Facebook marketing efforts? Have you increased your number of fans? Sold an online or in-person event via Facebook promotions? Brought more people to your web page and in turn sold them your programs or services? Had people download a white paper or report that, in addition to adding value, promoted a product or service? Brought more people to a special offer through a Facebook-specific promo code?

To see a real financial return on your social media activity, think in terms of conversion. The goal is to convert an interested potential customer to an actual, paying customer. Social media allows you to add value and to create engagement, trust, and affinity with your fans. After you capture your fans' trust, it's time to sell them your programs and services.

Tracking tools can show you how much traffic is generated, what content is of interest to your fans, and how often fans engage with you. To see a financial return on your social media activity, use these metrics to generate activity and to create and sell products, programs, and services for your ideal audience.

Volume

Volume is how frequently people search for your company in search engines. Facebook Pages come up in search-engine results for your company name, so someone who's looking for your website might also decide to check out your Facebook Page. Google Analytics shows which Facebook custom apps on your Page sent traffic to your website, which is all the more reason why you want to make sure to display your URL prominently in the About box of your Facebook Timeline and on the Info tab.

Demographics

Commonly used *demographics* include age, race, gender, language, location, and household income. Tracking tools such as HootSuite (`www.hootsuite.com`) can show you a breakdown of likes by region (as shown in Figure 1-6), and Facebook Insights can show a breakdown by gender, countries, cities, and languages, as shown in Figure 1-7. You may already know the demographics that are most associated with your products and services, but if you suddenly discover, through monitoring your Facebook Insights reports, that a significantly different group is coming to your Facebook Page, that discovery could not only potentially affect your social media marketing efforts, but also demonstrate that your company is connecting to a different demographic than you realized! You may want to adjust your products and services accordingly.

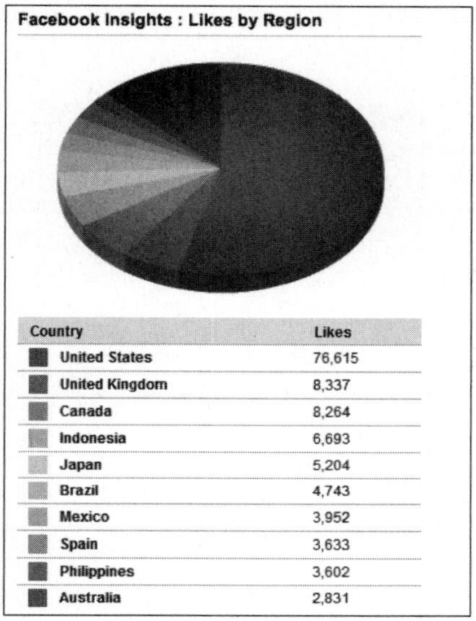
Facebook Insights : Likes by Region
Country
Likes
United States
76,615
United Kingdom
8,337
Canada
8,264
Indonesia
6,693
Japan
5,204
Brazil
4,743
Mexico
3,952
Spain
3,633
Philippines
3,602
Australia
2,831

Figure 1-6: Regional Facebook data generated by HootSuite.

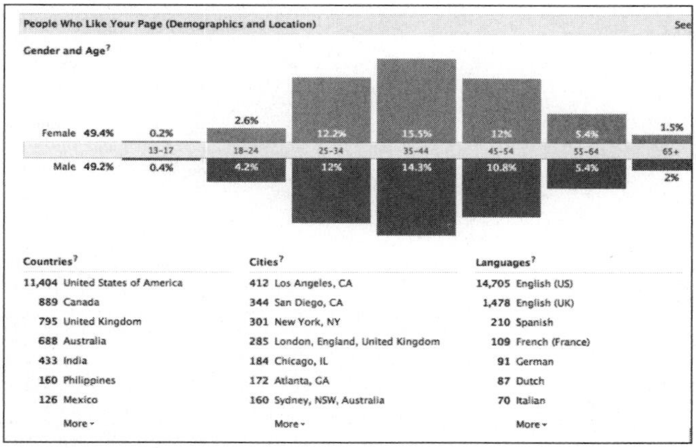

Figure 1-7: Demographic metrics generated by Facebook Insights.

Chapter 2: Exploring Facebook Insights

In This Chapter

- **Using Insights, Facebook's built-in monitoring tool**
- **Interpreting Insights's tracking details**
- **Deciding which data to track**
- **Using the data to create a thriving Facebook Page**

Insights is Facebook's built-in analytics dashboard, which you use to look at trends revealed by the activity on your Page. Insights helps you get a feel for who is using your Page and how those users are interacting with it. In this chapter, we dive into the data and explore ways to better understand your Facebook users' behaviors in relation to the content you share. The key is to find out which of your marketing strategies are working and to replicate those efforts — and, conversely, to understand what isn't working so that you can create more productive and meaningful interactions. Now who doesn't like to do more of the good stuff and less of the bad stuff, right? Don't worry: We've set up this chapter so that exploring the analytical data of your Facebook Page won't be painful, we promise!

In this chapter, we look at how to interpret the myriad graphs and charts that Facebook Insights offers, as well as how to use the data to generate a positive effect on your social media strategy.

Making Sense of Insights Information

Think of Insights as your personal road map to Facebook success. That may sound a bit cheesy, but Insights truly can help you navigate your way to a thriving Facebook Page. To understand the true value of your Facebook efforts, you need to know how many users have been exposed to your posts, how much of your audience is actively responding or interacting with your posts, and which posts are the most popular with your ideal audience.

By diving into your Insights, you get a better understanding of how to interpret your unique Page information, and you can make informed decisions about the direction in which to take your content and how to bring more users to your Page.

Understanding analytics is a crucial component of creating, implementing, and maintaining an effective strategy. By moving beyond clicks, likes, and posts, you can begin to understand what your audience expects to gain from its interactions with you as a brand, and you're in a position to fulfill your audience's expectations.

Understandably, marketers want to ensure that their Facebook marketing efforts produce a return on investment, but without taking the time to review Facebook Insights information, figuring out how best to use Facebook for your business is like shooting in the dark. Fortunately, no matter what goals you have for your campaign, you can use the metrics to guide your next steps.

REMEMBER

At least 30 people must like your Page before the Insights dashboard becomes available for viewing.

Exploring Insights data

In this section, we examine the data that Insights collects. We also explore in detail the three subcategories of Insights: Likes, Reach, and People Talking About This. By diving into each category, you better understand your fans' demographics and behaviors, who's talking about you, and what those people like most about your Page.

To access Insights for your Page, simply go to your Facebook Page. Above your Timeline Cover photo is your Admin panel, where you can quickly see your page's Notifications, Messages (if you added Messages; see Book II), New Likes, Insights, and Page Tips, as shown in Figure 2-1. Just click the Show button, and the entire Admin panel will open above your Timeline Cover photo.

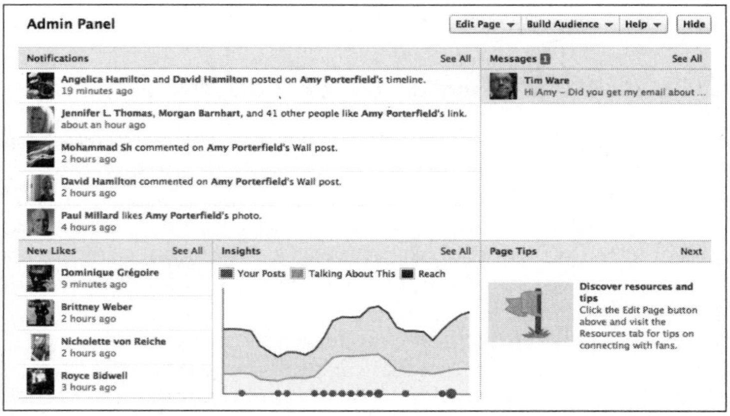

Figure 2-1: The Admin panel dashboard.

Insights

When you click the Insights graph on your Admin panel, you see four metrics at the top of your Insights tab: Total Likes, Friends of Fans, People Talking About This, and Weekly Total Reach, as shown in Figure 2-2. These metrics allow you to understand the size and engagement of your audience.

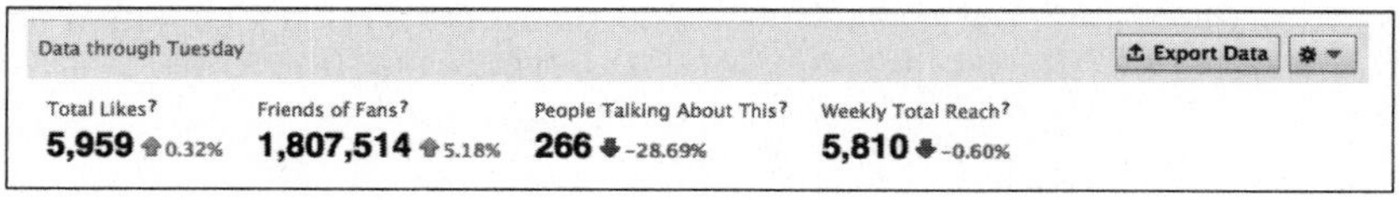

Figure 2-2: The four key Insights metrics.

Here's a brief explanation of each metric:

- **Total Likes:** This metric is the number of unique people who have liked your Page.
- **Friends of Fans:** This number can be a bit confusing. It's the number of unique people who are Friends with your fans, but it also includes your current fans. What's interesting about this metric is that it represents the total number of people you could reach if all your fans were talking about your business to their Friends. That's why the number is much higher than any other number you see on the Insights dashboard.
- **People Talking About This:** This metric is the number of people who have mentioned your Page (also known as those who have created a story about your Page) in the past seven days. Fans can create a story by doing several things inside Facebook, including liking your page, commenting on or sharing your post, answering a question you posted on your Page, responding to your invitation to an event, mentioning your Page in one of their posts, tagging you in a photo, or checking in to or recommending your Page.
- **Weekly Total Reach:** This metric is the number of unique people who have seen any content associated with your Page in the past seven days. (This number also includes any Facebook ads and Sponsored stories pointing to your Page.)

TIP

To see the time frame of each metric, hover your mouse over the question mark next to the metric. A pop-up window appears, showing the date range.

The row of the four key metrics have little green and red arrows and percentages next to each set of numbers (refer to Figure 2-2), to show you the difference from the previous week.

The only two metrics that are visible to anyone who visits your Page are Total Likes and People Talking About This. Both metrics are meant to show Facebook users how popular, active, and engaging your Page is. That's why it's extremely important to track these numbers and to continue to focus on increasing your fan base and overall engagement.

On this same dashboard tab, directly below the four key metrics, is a graph that helps you understand how your posts directly affect your overall engagement and reach. The graph shows metrics for Posts, People Talking About This, and Weekly Total Reach (see Figure 2-3).

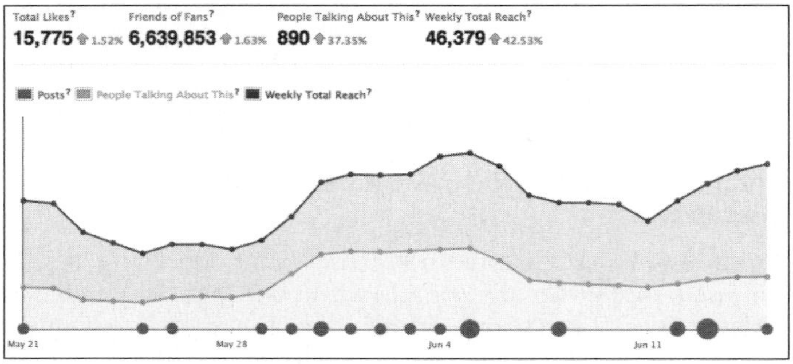

Figure 2-3: Insights graph for Posts, People Talking About This, and Weekly Total Reach.

Here's what each metric means:

- **Posts:** The number of times you posted. The sizes of the bubbles in the graph represent the number of times you posted on your Page that day.
- **People Talking About This:** The number of unique people who have created a story about you in the past seven days. The more people you get to talk about your Page, the more people you reach.
- **Weekly Total Reach:** The number of unique people who have seen any content associated with your Page in the past seven days.

When these three metrics appear in one graph, they tell the story of your overall Facebook efforts. Think of them as a sequence of events that touch one another. You post on your Page, people talk about it or engage with it to some degree, and that level of activity with your post increases or decreases the total reach of your message.

The last data group you see on the main dashboard consists of Page Posts. Each time you post something new on your Page, you can see how it performs. Here's the data that displays with each post:

✦ **Date:** The date when the content was posted.

✦ **Post:** An abbreviated name of the post. Click the post to see the full story, as shown in Figure 2-4.

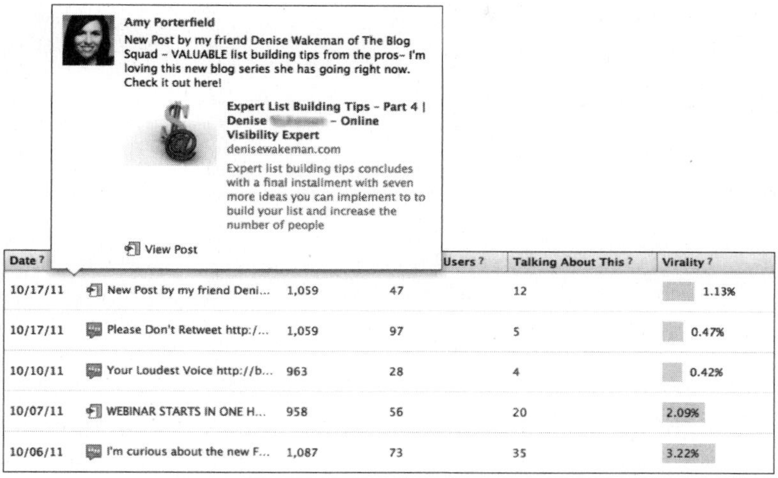

Figure 2-4: A pop-up window showing the Page Posts metrics.

✦ **Reach:** The number of unique people who have seen your post within the first 28 days after its publication. Click this number to see a pop-up graphic with more details about that post's reach, as shown in Figure 2-5.

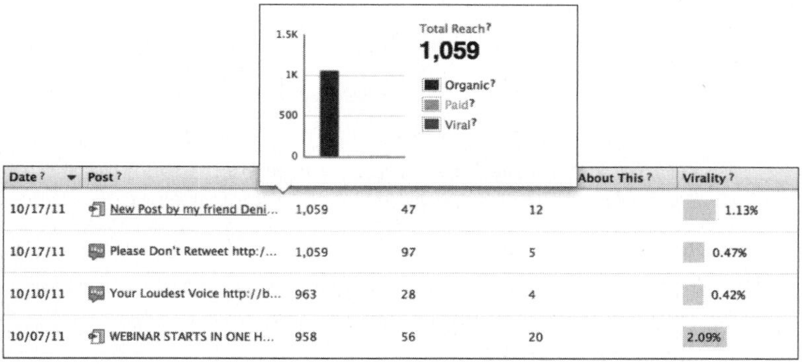

Figure 2-5: The Total Reach pop-up graphic for Page Posts metrics.

✦ **Engaged Users:** The number of unique users who have engaged with your posts within the first 28 days after its publication. This number includes any click in the post. Click this number to see a pop-up chart with more details about this metric, as shown in Figure 2-6.

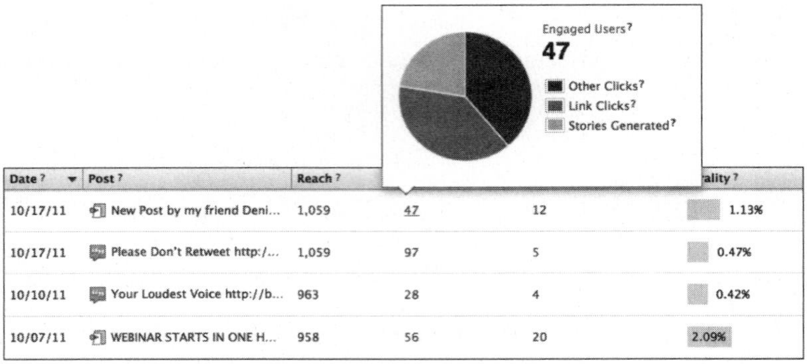
Engaged Users?
47
Other Clicks?
Link Clicks?
Stories Generated?
Date ?
Post ?
Reach ?
rality ?
10/17/11 New Post by my friend Deni... 1,059 47 12 1.13%
10/17/11 Please Don't Retweet http:/... 1,059 97 5 0.47%
10/10/11 Your Loudest Voice http://b... 963 28 4 0.42%
10/07/11 WEBINAR STARTS IN ONE H... 958 56 20 2.09%

Figure 2-6: The Engaged Users pop-up graphic for Page Posts metrics.

- **Talking About This:** The number of unique people who have created a story from your post within the first 28 days after its publication. Click this number to see a pop-up chart with more details about these stories, as shown in Figure 2-7.

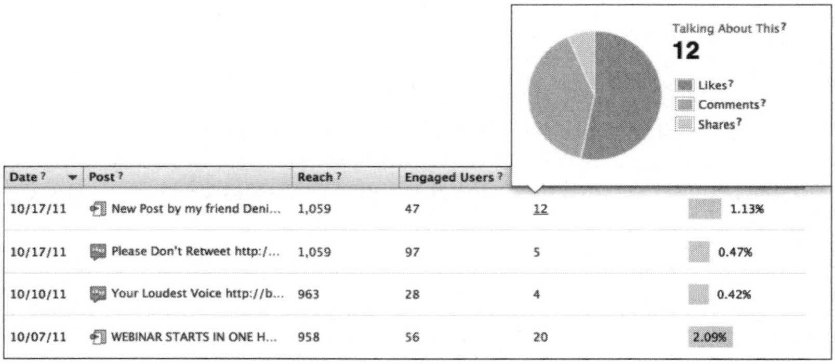
Talking About This?
12
Likes?
Comments?
Shares?
Date ?
Post ?
Reach ?
Engaged Users ?
10/17/11 New Post by my friend Deni... 1,059 47 12 1.13%
10/17/11 Please Don't Retweet http:/... 1,059 97 5 0.47%
10/10/11 Your Loudest Voice http://b... 963 28 4 0.42%
10/07/11 WEBINAR STARTS IN ONE H... 958 56 20 2.09%

Figure 2-7: The Talking About This pop-up graphic for Page Posts metrics.

- **Virality:** The number of unique people who have created a story from your Page post as a percentage of the number of unique people who have seen it.

Using these metrics, you can identify which types of posts are most popular with your audience and tweak your content strategy to post more of what's working best.

You can also see Insights at a glance on your Page's Timeline itself. Below each of your posts, you see the number of people reached. When you hover over the number of people reached, you see the number of unique people who saw the post, split among Organic, Viral, and Paid, as shown in Figure 2-8. ***Note:*** You will only see Paid in the chart if you used Facebook Ads to promote your post.

Figure 2-8: Insights posts data showing the number of unique people who saw the post.

Later in this chapter, we discuss how to determine the most important data to track, as well as how you can use the Insights data to reach your ideal audience. Before we jump into examining the data, however, it's important to drill even further into the Insights data to see what information you can access. Here, we explore the three subcategories of Insights: Likes, Reach, and Talking About This.

REMEMBER

For all three subcategories of Insights (Likes, Reach, and Talking About This), you can select the date range of your choice. At the top of each of the subcategory pages is the date range. Click the drop-down arrow next to the date range and then select the range you want to analyze.

Likes

The Likes tab gives you a good understanding of who your fans are and how they found your Page.

The first set of metrics you see is a graph of your fans' demographics. *Demographics* refers to the aggregated demographic data about the people who like your Page based on the information they provided in their user Profiles regarding age (13–17, 18–24, 25–34, 35–44, 45–54, 55–64, and 65+); gender, country, and city where they live; and the default language setting selected when they accessed Facebook.

The second set of metrics on this tab is Where Your Likes Came From; it tells you where your new fans are coming from on the web. Are people finding your Page in their News Feed or ticker, or perhaps in a social plug-in on your website? This data is valuable because you can use it to research new ways to drive traffic to your Facebook Page.

TIP

You can also see the number of new likes and new unlikes for the date range you specified. Keep your eye on your new unlikes. If you find that people are unliking your Page at an alarmingly high rate, you need to look at what you're sending and make sure that it matches what people thought they were liking in the first place.

Reach

The Reach tab gives you a good understanding of who is actually seeing your content. The first set of metrics you see is Reach demographics. Just like the demographic data on the Likes tab, this section shows information about age, gender, location, and language.

In addition, this tab shows you how you reached people. Facebook tracks how you reach people in several ways:

- **Organic:** The number of unique people who saw content from your Page in their News Feed, on their ticker, or on your Page. The more engagement you create on your Page, the more likely you are to get out into the News Feeds and tickers.
- **Paid:** The number of unique people who saw a Facebook Ad or Sponsored story that pointed to your Page. (For more information on Facebook Ads, see Book VIII.)
- **Viral:** The number of unique people who saw a story about this Page published by a Friend. This metric includes liking your Page; posting to your Timeline; and liking, commenting on, or sharing one of your posts. As you attract more fans and get them to interact with your Page, you start to see more and more viral opportunities.
- **Total:** Includes all three metrics, Organic, Paid, and Viral. The Total metric shows the number of unique people who saw any content associated with your Page (including any Ads or Sponsored stories pointing to your Page).

In this same section is a graph called Unique Users by Frequency. Here, you can see how many people saw any content about your Page, broken down into how many times each person viewed this content. Figure 2-9 shows the graphs for Reach and Unique Users by Frequency.

For both Reach and Frequency data, you can segment the type of info shown in the graphs. From the drop-down menu directly above the two graphs, you can choose options that let you see the data in the following ways: All Page Content, Your Posts, and Stories by Others (see Figure 2-10).

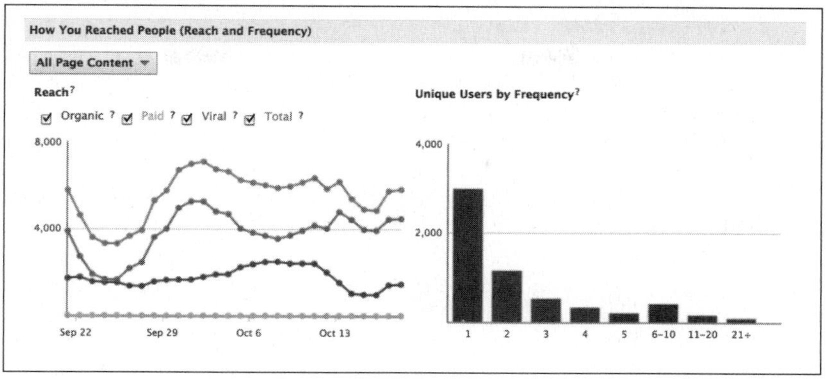

Figure 2-9: Graphs for Reach and Unique Users by Frequency.

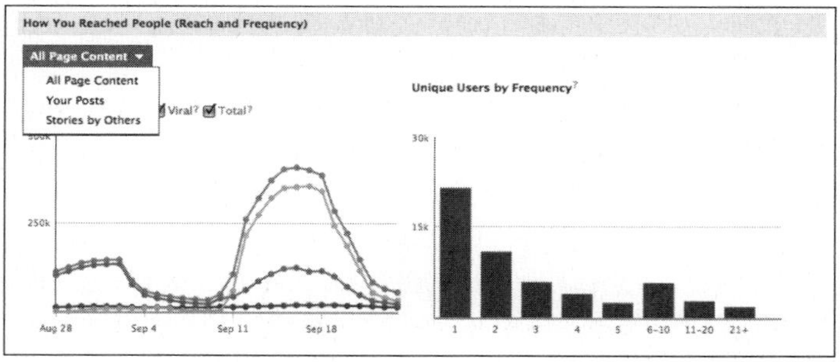

Figure 2-10: Drop-down menu for Reach and Unique Users by Frequency graphs.

The last set of metrics on the Reach dashboard is Visits to Your Page. In this area, you find

- **Page Views:** The number of times your Page was viewed on each day during your selected date range
- **Unique Visitors:** The number of unique people who visited your Page on each day during your selected date range
- **Total Tab Views:** The number of times each of your Page tabs was viewed during your selected date range
- **External Referrers:** The number of times people arrived on your Page from a URL that isn't part of Facebook.com during your selected date range

Tracking which external sites are sending traffic to your Facebook Page is important because it can give you clues about your audience. Pay attention to the content on the external sites that are referring traffic to your Page. This content is likely the content that attracts your ideal audience. We discuss referrer sites in more detail later in this chapter, when we look at tracking activity outside Facebook.

Talking About This

The Talking About This tab gives you a good understanding of who's interacting with your Page and who's talking about you on Facebook.

Just like on the Fans and Reach tabs, the first set of metrics you see on this tab is the graph representing demographics. This data shows you the ages, genders, countries, and languages of the people who have been talking about you during your selected date range.

The next section, How People Are Talking About Your Page, includes two graphs: Talking About This and Viral Reach. This section gives you great insight into your audience's Facebook behaviors. Here's what each metric tells you:

- **Talking About This:** The number of unique people who have created a story about your Page in the past seven days, for each day during your selected date range
- **Viral Reach:** The number of unique people who saw a story published by a Friend about your Page in the past seven days, for each day during your selected date range

At the top of the two graphs is a drop-down menu with options that change the info in the graphs. You can choose to see activity from all stories, Page likes, stories from your posts, mentions and photo tags, and posts by others (see Figure 2-11).

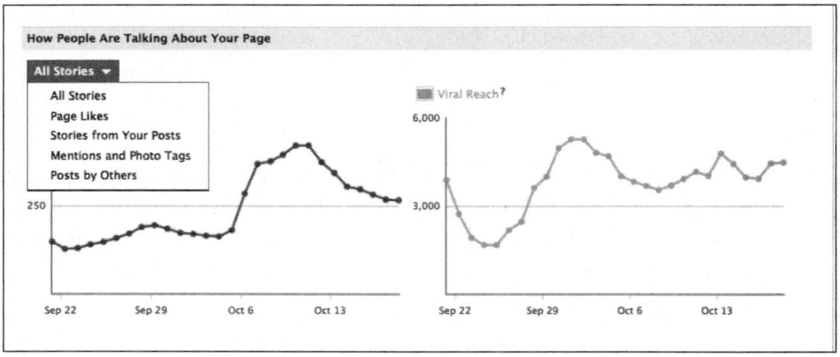

Figure 2-11: Drop-down menu for How People Are Talking About Your Page graphics.

This data can provide valuable information about the ways users are interacting with your Page and no doubt can help you strategize the next steps for enhancing the content you share on Facebook. We explore these topics later in this chapter, when we discuss evaluating the impact of your content.

Exporting the data

At any time, you can export the data on any of the Insights tabs. Here's how you export data from any of the Insights dashboards:

1. **Click the Export button in the top-right corner of the dashboard.**

   The Export Insights Data dialog box appears.

2. **Select Data Type: Page-Level Data or Post-Level Data.**

   Page-level data is aggregated data about your Page, and *post-level data* shows you data on each of your Page posts.

3. **Select a file format (Excel or CSV).**
4. **Select a date range.**
5. **Click the Download button.**

   This data file goes to your Downloads file or to where downloads are configured to go on your computer.

After you download your data file, you have a very rich file to analyze — meaning that you have a boatload of information to check out! Don't worry, though, because you don't need to analyze all of it.

All the data available in the report may or may not be of use to you, depending on your overall marketing goals. You likely will find the key metrics to be most useful, because they tell you a great deal about the activity on your Page. If you have a bricks-and-mortar business, however, the city data will be of great interest to you as well. The data you will find most valuable depends on your type of business and your goals for your Page.

Determining the Most Important Data to Track

In this section, we explore your Facebook tracking options. We determine what activities are most important to track, based on your overall Facebook goals and business strategies. Specifically, we look at your like activity, the effect of your content, Facebook comments, and unlikes. Also, we explore ways to reach your ideal audience, and we take a look at your Facebook Page activity that occurs outside the Facebook platform. So put on your analytical hat, and dive in!

Tracking your like activity

Users can tell you specifically what they think about your Facebook Page every step of the way, from the initial like to every item they share, post, or comment on. From this data, you start to see a clear pattern that explains what your fans think about the content you post.

Content is king! If you produce content that your fans enjoy and find valuable, they keep coming back for more. That's why evaluating what content gets your users' attention most often is so important.

Perhaps every day for three days, you posted a link with a message about a new post published on your blog. One of those posts receives 21 likes, another receives 11 likes, and the third receives 5 likes. What types of things should you be looking at? Well, you might be curious to see the day and time of day when the posts were made. Maybe the post that received 21 likes occurred on a Tuesday at 3 p.m., the post that received 11 likes was made on a Monday at 4 p.m., and the 5-likes post was made on a Friday at 9 a.m.

Over a period of time, you can see whether a pattern emerges. Are more people engaging with your Page on Tuesdays than on Fridays, for example? Or are your users inclined to be on your Page late in the day rather than early?

You also want to take a look at the topics of the posts. Was the post that received 21 likes about a topic that your users are most interested in? Was there something special about the way you posted your message? In the 21-like post, perhaps you started your message with a catchy question or added some humor. You want to evaluate all these variables to see whether you can detect a trend to take advantage of.

Also, not every post you make on your Facebook Page is related to a blog post. Suppose that you simply post a question to try to get your users engaged in a conversation. One question you post is about weekend plans, and it receives 2 likes; another question asks who will be attending the South by Southwest (SXSW) Music and Media conference this spring, and it receives 18 likes. What can you tell about the differences in the questions? Perhaps your users really don't care about what others on your Page are doing on the weekend, but they really connect to the SXSW conference. You can't make sweeping statements based on only a couple of reactions, of course, but if you make a point of reviewing which questions and conversations generate the most likes, you'll start to see what is most important and relevant to your users. You may even discover that a huge potential customer base will be going to SXSW, so maybe you should be going too!

Evaluating the impact of your content

What is the impact of your content, and who are you currently reaching? Evaluating the impact of your content can help you decide whether you're on the right track or whether you need to make adjustments to your content strategy. In the following sections, we explore ways to evaluate your content strategy as it relates to the data you collect from Insights.

Setting goals for your content

To begin with, your Facebook content will have very limited impact if no one is seeing it. One of the first numbers you should look at and keep in your mind's eye is how many Total Likes your Page has. Perhaps your Page has a total of 500 people who have liked the Page. You might set goals for increasing the numbers each month. For that, you need to be thinking in more detail about the activities you're doing outside Facebook to bring people to your Page. We get into the ins and outs about your activity outside Facebook a little later in this chapter, but for now, keep that topic in the back of your mind.

At this point, you want to pay attention to whether increasing the number of posts you make each week will create more likers, and the only way to find out is to experiment. For a few months, you may want to shift how you've previously been doing things. You can do this by adding more posts, varying the days and times of your posts, paying attention to the messages of your posts (begin by asking a question, for example), using keyword-rich language, adding humor, or making posts shorter.

When you look at your Insights graphs, you want to see whether you have an increase in Total Likes and what your monthly and weekly numbers look like after you alter your posts.

Suppose that you've posted similarly for the first quarter of the year, and your People Talking About This number is significantly lower for February and March. What can you surmise about the dip in numbers?

You may want to look at several other variables, such as what topics predominated in January's posts versus those of February and March. Perhaps you did a series of posts about predictions for the new year, and those didn't resonate with your users as much as your posts about how-tos for Facebook and LinkedIn did.

Alternatively, maybe your users weren't spending as much time on Facebook in January after getting back to work following the holiday season, or maybe the decrease had nothing to do with your content but more about your users' schedules.

TIP

You can affect some things when it comes to the content you post, but you can't influence everything. A good rule of thumb is to replicate to the best of your ability what's working and to omit the actions that aren't generating good results.

Delivering content that people like

Although the rules of content aren't etched in stone and certainly don't produce the same types of results on every Facebook Page, Facebook users are known to favor three types of content: video, audio, and photos. As you embark on the process of evaluating your content, take a look at past months to see how media has been received on your Page. If media hasn't been a regular part of your content strategy, now may be a good time to explore using it.

Large brands can teach you a few things about Facebook. Coca-Cola, which has the most fans of any worldwide brand (more than 44 million at this writing), has made it a point to post videos and photos on its Page regularly. Fans have followed suit by adding their own videos and photos to the Page. Although your business isn't Coca-Cola, who can argue with the strategy of a brand that has more than 44 million fans?

Likes, comments, and unsubscribes — Oh, my!

Insights data are good storytellers, and the stories come from facts, not imagination. The graphs can tell you the days on which your posts received likes, comments, and — heaven forbid — unlikes. No one wants to see unsubscribes on his Page, but in the event that you do, you definitely want to take note. What happened that day on your Page? Were comments posted that may have been off-putting to users? Had you increased your number of posts, and users were getting tired of seeing your updates in their News Feeds? You won't have any sure way to tell.

The best you can do is to ask yourself a few questions to see whether you can find any explanations on your side. People are always coming and going on Facebook Pages, and you can't take that fact personally; but while you're taking a look at the effect of your content, it's worth thinking about. If you see a mass exodus, however, that's another thing!

You also want to see which days generated the most likes and comments so you can find out whether you're reaching your users with content that they can relate to.

Perhaps one of the most interesting stories the Insights data can tell you is about Page posts: the messages you posted; the dates when they were posted; and their overall Reach, interactions with Engaged Users, and number of people Talking About This for that post.

What posts received the largest reach? How many Engaged Users did it attract? How can you explain why some posts are viewed more times than others? Is it the topic? Is it the wording of your post? After tracking the data consistently, you begin to see patterns that answer these questions. In these cases, tracking the data and a little experimentation can pay off.

You built it, but did they come?

Assessing the effect of your content in relation to the number of Engaged Users and the People Talking About This graph can be compared with the notion that a picture is worth a thousand words. If your Page is receiving a high number of mentions, and people are writing on your Timeline, adding new discussions, and uploading videos, suffice it to say that your content is inviting. You have the kind of Page that people want to hang out on and be affiliated with.

It's not a given that a Page with even the best intentions will generate that type of activity. The difference between success and failure may be whether the Page fosters community or is filled only with its own updates. "Why do some Pages and brands attract more users than others?" may be the million-dollar Facebook question, but our hunch is that engaging, informative, and unique content plays a big role.

Reaching Your Ideal Audience

You have to love demographics; they can be so revealing at times! By taking a look at the demographics graph for all three subcategories — Likes, Reach, and Talking About This — you can tell a lot about your Page and who it's attracting and keeping. In the following sections, we examine the most important analytics to track so that you can determine the best way to attract and communicate with your ideal audience.

Seeing who's been viewing your Facebook Page

By knowing who's visiting your Page and interacting with your posts, you can take your Page to an entirely new level of success. Knowing more about your fans and viewers allows you to deliver exactly what they want and encourages them to continue to build trust in you.

Insights data will tell you the gender and age of your fans, along with the cities they live in and languages they speak. This data can guide you as you create content and offers for your existing fan base.

Suppose that you're introducing a new product line for men between the ages of 35 and 44. Sixty percent of your overall users are women, and 30 percent of them are between the ages of 35 and 44. In addition, right now more women than men are talking about your Page, according to your Talking About This metrics. As part of your social media marketing strategy, you may want to attract your target audience to your Facebook Page. Think about the content you're posting so that it has a greater likelihood of appealing to men 35 to 44 years old. Consider, too, that your product will more likely be used by men in a warm climate; it's January, and the majority of your users are in the Northeast region of the United States. You may need to adapt the types of posts that would reach users in other regions.

Evaluating activity outside Facebook

When it comes to evaluating activity outside Facebook, you want to be sure to monitor one graph on a regular basis: the Visits to Your Page graph on the Reach tab of the Insights dashboard. This graph contains two important words: *External Referrers.* Like all activity on the web, the number of external referrers can make or break a website. You may have experienced the good fortune of having someone write about your Facebook Page, without any involvement on your part, in a hugely popular blog and suddenly see a surge in activity on your Page. That outcome would be good fortune (or perhaps a little more like magical thinking). That said, chances are good that the external domains that refer traffic to your Facebook Page have something to do with actions you've taken outside of Facebook.

What kind of actions are we talking about? We mean things like the following:

- Putting social icons on your website and blog
- Adding your Facebook URL to your LinkedIn profile
- Integrating your Twitter and Facebook updates
- Promoting your Facebook Page URL on other sites where you comment
- Adding your Facebook Page URL when you write a guest blog post
- Adding the URL to your e-mail newsletter signature

In other words, promote, promote, promote!

You want to know which sites generate the most referrals to your Page so that you can think strategically about when and how to promote your Page.

Chapter 3: Using Third-Party Monitoring Tools and Analyzing Results

In This Chapter

- **Finding the best tool for your business**
- **Reviewing popular third-party monitoring tools**
- **Turning results into your next steps**

Now that you understand the power of monitoring and measuring your social activity, it's time to talk about third-party monitoring and measuring tools. After all, you shouldn't take this on alone. The torrent of data at your fingertips just might make your head spin!

The great news is that numerous third-party monitoring tools have been designed to streamline the monitoring process. These tools scan, grab, and organize your data for easy digestion. And here's the great news: Many of these tools are free or inexpensive.

In this chapter, we look at the key factors you should consider when choosing a monitoring tool for your business. In addition, we examine the core features of multiple different third-party monitoring tools to help you make a well-informed decision for your monitoring and measuring needs.

Choosing the Tool That's Best for Your Business

When you begin to monitor your social media activity, keep it simple and streamlined. Just because a tool might have 20 features doesn't mean that you should try them all from the get-go. To save yourself some frustration and stress, first get comfortable with the tool's basic features, and move forward to the more-advanced features only after you've mastered the basics.

When choosing a monitoring tool, you need to be clear about what's important to you and your team. The price of a tool may be your number-one deciding factor, for example, whereas another company may be more concerned with a tool's reporting features. Your tool preference depends on your business goals and needs. The following sections describe some key factors to consider when researching third-party monitoring tools.

User flexibility

Although you may start by having just one person in your company monitoring your social media activity, you may later decide to add multiple people to your tracking strategy. You want to make sure that you're satisfied with the way the tool allows multiple users to interact at any given time. Not all tools are user-friendly in this area.

Ease of setup

If you select a good tool that meets your needs, the most time-consuming task will be setup. After you take care of this step, the rest will be easy — and, in many cases, automatic. Before you get to the automation, however, you must enter all the data you want to measure.

When selecting a tool to fit your needs, make sure that you've compiled all the login details for your social sites, as well as a list of your needs, including the types of filters (demographics, regions, languages, and so on) and all the keywords you want to track. This data, when compiled before you start to search for a tool, can help you determine which tool has the features that best fit your needs.

Ease of use

You must feel comfortable using the user interface, or you'll quickly abandon the tool. User-friendly dashboards are essential. In many ways, deciding on the specifics of the dashboard layout is a personal preference, and you'll benefit from taking a little time to test a few tools before you make a final decision.

TIP

Many tools have guided tours that you can explore before signing up. A tour is a great way to get a sense of how you navigate the tool. We discuss tours in "Training and support," later in this chapter.

Ease of reporting

Each tool has a different depth-of-analysis capability; therefore, you want to determine just how much reporting you need. If you want to keep reporting simple, you might decide to track just a few metrics, including weekly click rates, the number of comments on a post, and the number of likes on your Facebook Page. If that's the case, you won't need a tool that promises depth of analysis and extensive reporting templates. Be careful not to pay for what you don't need.

Cost

If you're just starting and aren't confident that your tracking outcomes are on target with your business goals, taking baby steps may be wise. We encourage you to choose a tool that offers a free version and then upgrade to a paid version when you're certain that the tool will work for you. Also, when looking at cost, consider how important your monitoring needs are and how much time you can dedicate to monitoring.

Training and support

Many tools, both free and premium, offer great guided tours to review before you make your decision. Take advantage of these tours.

In addition, before you choose a tool, find out whether the tool comes with training videos to help you get started quickly. Tutorials and training videos that walk you through the features and benefits of the tool are extremely useful, allowing you to get up and running quickly. They also give you a good sense of where to start and what you may want to build up to when you feel more comfortable.

Choosing Monitoring Tools: Your Third-Party Options

After you're clear about the features of a monitoring tool that are most important to you, it's time to get down to business and choose a tool. In this section, we look at just a few of the many third-party tools that are on the market today.

Each of the following tools differs in its approach, metrics, depth of analysis, channels measured, reporting ability, and user interface. If your goal is to keep costs down, you may find that a combination of free tools works best for you. If you're willing to pay a premium, just one tool may be all you need to cover everything you want to do. The key is to identify your tracking needs first and then research which tool, or combination of tools, best meets your needs.

TIP

Many of the tools discussed in this section offer multiple levels of membership. When you find a tool that fits your needs, make sure to research it closely to find the level of membership (if applicable) that best fits what you're looking for in features and functionality.

bit.ly

`https://bitly.com`

bit.ly is a free tool that allows users to shorten, share, and track links (URLs). You copy and paste a long URL into its portal, and bit.ly automatically generates a shorter link that can be used on social networks or anywhere on the web. You don't need to set up an account to shorten a link, but we encourage you to set one up so that you can view all your links easily in one interface. bit.ly makes shortening your link easy by allowing you to copy and paste your URL into its tool right from its home page, as shown in Figure 3-1.

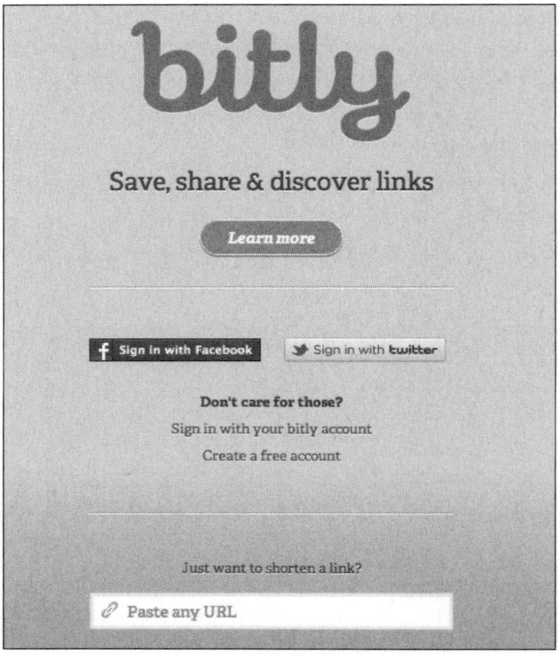

Figure 3-1: The bit.ly home page allows you to shorten a link without having an account.

Another perk of creating an account with bit.ly is you can view real-time traffic and referrer data, as well as location and metadata related to your click activity for all your links. This tool is useful for tracking metadata such as the locations where your link is getting the most activity, along with the dates and times when people are clicking your link most frequently. Figure 3-2 shows the bit.ly user interface.

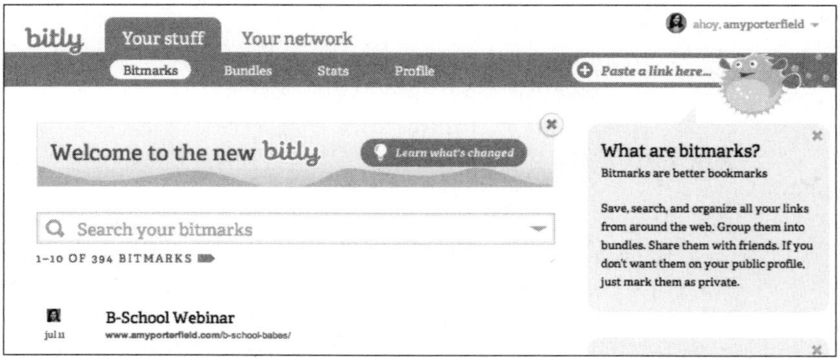

Figure 3-2: The bit.ly user interface.

Google Alerts

www.google.com/alerts

Google Alerts is a free service that includes e-mail updates of Google results that users set up based on the choice of query or topic. You can specify what you want to receive by update types, frequency, and volume. To take full advantage of this free tool, we recommend that you set up multiple alerts, including keywords and phrases related to your niche. Provide your name and your company name, as well as the names of your competitors and their products and services. Also, if you're involved in an event, track the event name before and after the event to find out what people are saying about it. Figure 3-3 shows the Google Alerts user interface.

Figure 3-3: The Google Alerts user interface.

Google Analytics

www.google.com/analytics

Google Analytics is a free tool that provides insights into website traffic and marketing effectiveness, allowing users to see and analyze traffic data. To set up Google Analytics, copy and paste a few lines of code into your website to get the tool you need to start tracking activity on your site. One of the many great features of this tool is its capability to uncover trends in your visitor activity — meaning that it gives you a visual representation of how your users are interacting with your site over specific periods. This data can help you identify what your visitors are responding to most on your site. A Social section is devoted to your visitors from social networks, including Facebook. Figure 3-4 shows a Google Analytics Social Value report.

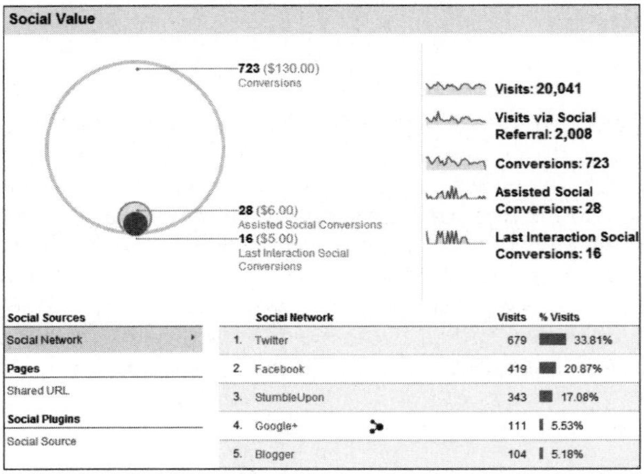

Figure 3-4: A Google Analytics Social Value report.

HootSuite

`http://hootsuite.com`

HootSuite's social media dashboard helps organizations identify and grow social media audiences by tracking campaign results and industry trends in real time. HootSuite has a web-based dashboard, so you don't have to download any software to use it, and you can access your data online from anywhere. One of the best features of HootSuite is a tool called Hootlet. Hootlet is a button that you place on your browser's toolbar. When you come across an article or blog post that you want to share with your social networks, you can schedule a post to multiple social networks simultaneously with a click of a button. Hootlet makes it easy to share great content with your fans and customers.

In addition, the multiple-panel user interface makes managing multiple channels easy. Figure 3-5 shows the HootSuite user interface. Notice that the different tabs make it easy to manage multiple social sites from one dashboard.

Multiple accounts can be listed on the same screen.

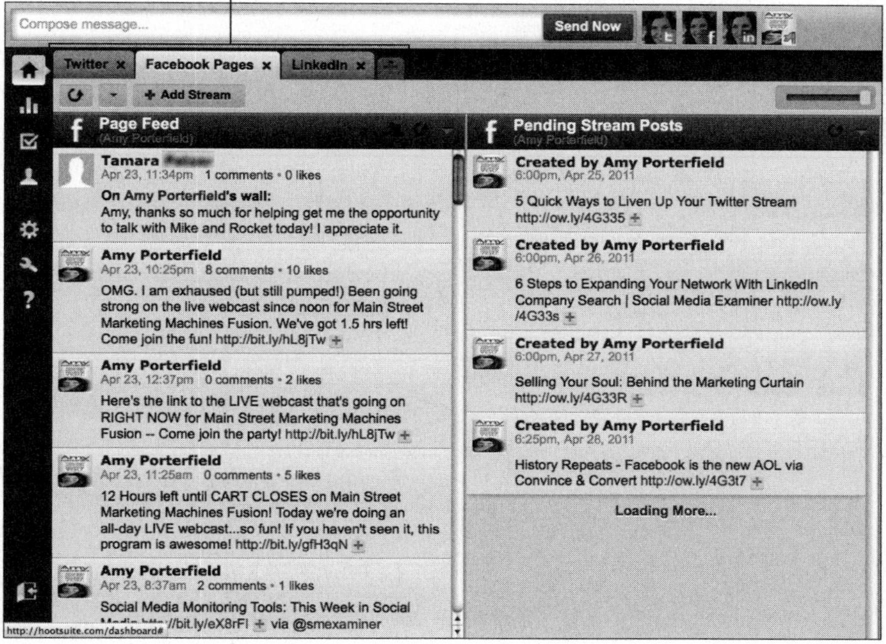

Figure 3-5: The HootSuite user interface.

Social Mention

`www.socialmention.com`

Social Mention is a free service that's very similar to Google Alerts, except that it specifically tracks data from more than 80 social media networks. Its real-time social media, search-and-analysis platform allows you to track and measure what people are saying about your company and products on Facebook and other social media properties. The service can send you daily e-mail alerts on the keywords you want to track. One unique feature of this tool is its analysis service, which reports on the likelihood that your brand is being discussed online, the ratio of positive to negative mentions, the likelihood that people who are talking about your brand will do so repeatedly, and the number of unique mentions of your brand online. This data is extremely valuable for identifying how people feel about your programs and services. Figure 3-6 shows the Social Mention user interface.

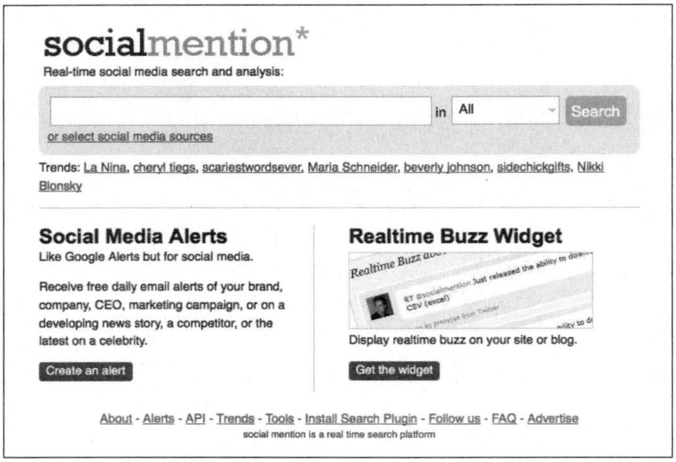

Figure 3-6: The Social Mention user interface.

Crowdbooster

`http://crowdbooster.com`

Crowdbooster shows analytics based on your business and social media strategies to help you achieve an effective presence on Twitter and Facebook. This tool measures your follower and fan growth, impressions, total reach, engagement, and other meaningful statistics; then it gives you specific ways to improve each one of these areas. It also gives you insights into your audience and allows you to manage multiple Twitter accounts and Facebook Pages in one location.

You can sign up for a free plan with one Twitter account and one Facebook Page that gives you all the social media metrics and tailored recommendations, plus weekly account summaries sent via e-mail. To manage more accounts, you can upgrade to the Professional or Business premium plan.

Figure 3-7 shows the Crowdbooster user interface.

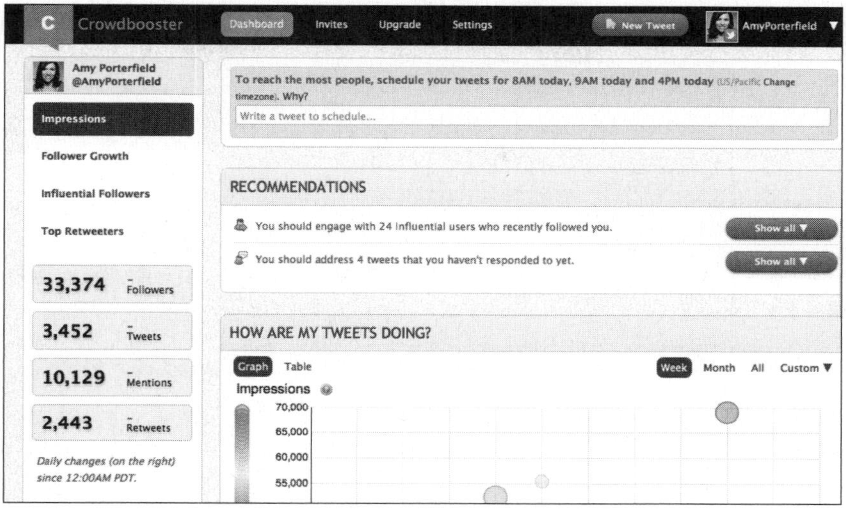

Figure 3-7: The Crowdbooster user interface.

AgoraPulse

`http://agorapulse.com`

AgoraPulse is an all-in-one Facebook marketing and customer relationship management (CRM) solution that helps small businesses and large brands measure their Facebook return on investment (ROI). Features include a community manager toolkit for managing your Facebook Page, including scheduled publishing, content tagging, and e-mail alerts. It helps you find out more about your fan base and how much your Facebook fans are worth based on specific information you collect from them. The beauty of AgoraPulse is it supplies you with easy-to-use tools to collect the data from your fans without being too intrusive or pushy. For example, you can create a contest that offers a giveaway in exchange for some key data you want to collect from your fans, making the contest strategy a win-win for both you and your fans.

You also get access to premium Facebook apps that allow you to add quizzes, sweepstakes, contests, and other functionality to your Facebook Page. Plans start at $9 per month.

Figure 3-8 shows the AgoraPulse user interface.

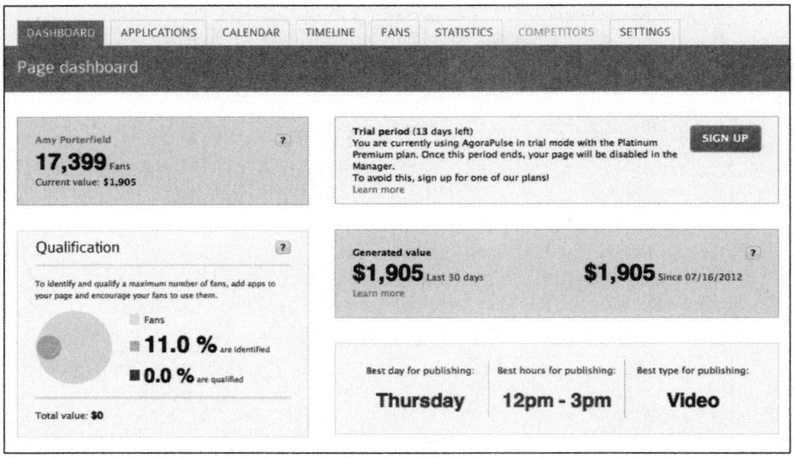

Figure 3-8: The AgoraPulse user interface.

Hyperalerts

www.hyperalerts.no

Hyperalerts is a free tool that allows you to sign up for e-mail alerts whenever someone posts and comments on your Facebook Page. You don't have to be an administrator of a Facebook Page to receive alerts, which makes it a great tool to encourage your fans or employees to use to keep up to date with your latest Facebook activity. It's also a handy tool to monitor your competition. Figure 3-9 shows the Hyperalerts user interface.

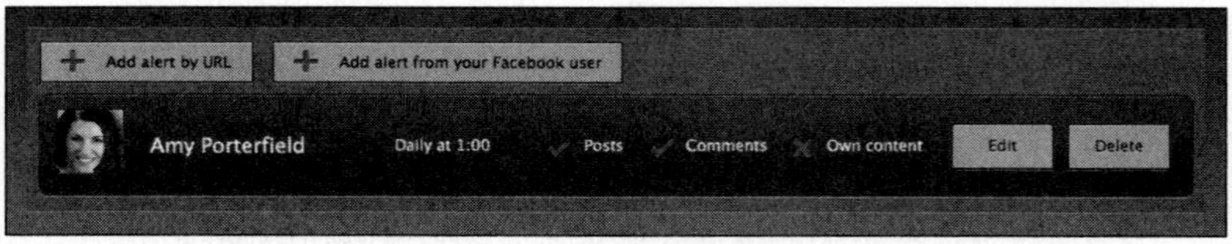

Figure 3-9: The Hyperalerts user interface.

Sprout Social

http://sproutsocial.com

Sprout Social monitors key metrics, discussions, and connections with users, and helps businesses increase brand awareness across demographic groups. Two great features of this tool are the engagement and influence scores. These scores are determined by your engagement activity, as well as by your fan growth and interest level over time. The tool aggregates average influence and engagement scores of Facebook users; shows you how your scores compare to the average scores on Facebook; and gives you advice to help you increase your overall scores. Plans start at $9 per month. Figure 3-10 shows the Sprout Social user interface.

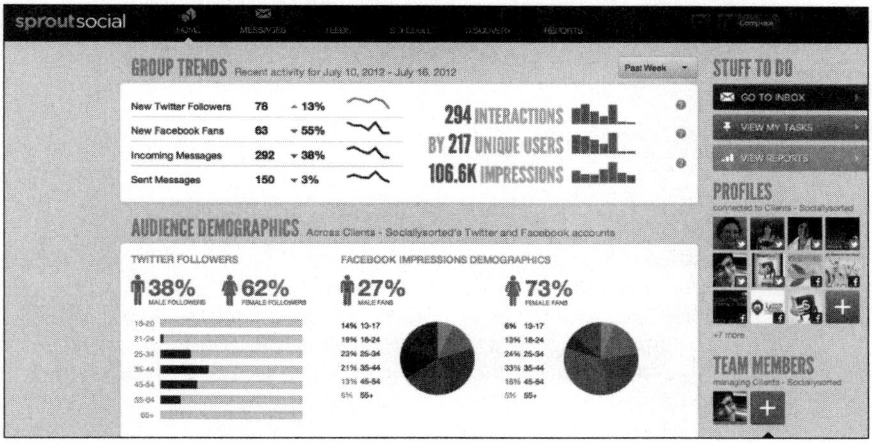

Figure 3-10: The Sprout Social user interface.

Topsy

http://topsy.com

Topsy is a free, real-time search engine that indexes and ranks search results based on trending conversations that people are having about specific terms, topics, pages, or domains queried. What makes this search engine different from traditional search tools is that it tracks what people are actually talking about, meaning that you see what people think and feel about the topics being discussed. Understanding the sentiment and the human side of these online conversations gives you better insight to your potential audience.

Figure 3-11 shows the Topsy user interface.

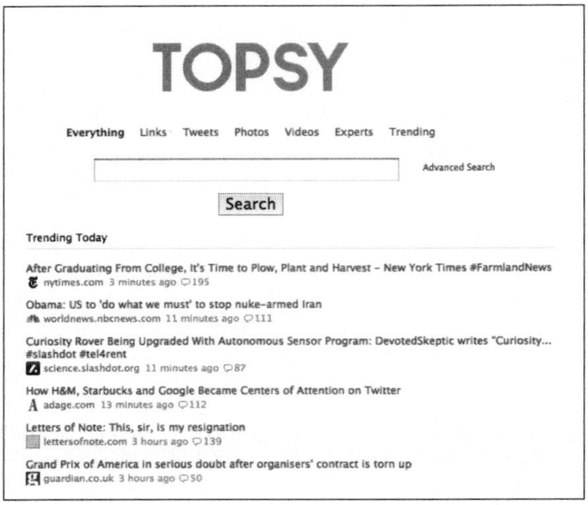

Figure 3-11: The Topsy user interface.

Klout

`http://klout.com`

Klout is a free influence-tracking tool. It gauges the influence level of any social media user by combining several data points (followers, comments, clicks of links, retweets, and so on). You can use it to identify your most influential customers with the intention of communicating with them, to see who's most influential in your industry, and to find out where you fall into the influence mix. After you know your own influence score, you can monitor it to see whether it increases or decreases based on your social activity. This tool is a great indicator of what's working for you.

Figure 3-12 shows the Klout user interface.

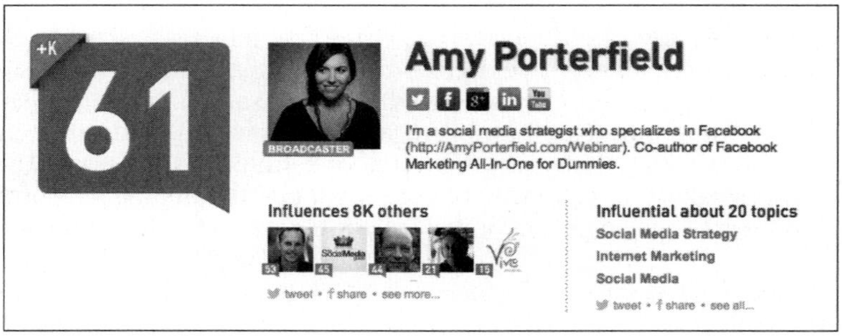

Figure 3-12: The Klout user interface.

Finding the Biggest Payoff with Your Monitoring Efforts

After you're clear about the data you want to collect, you may decide that you need to grab data from Facebook Insights, Google Alerts, and HootSuite. Managing multiple tools takes some organization, no doubt, but if combining tools meets your needs, you should do that.

Specifically, Facebook limits what information third-party developers can access and monitor. That limit is why it's important to use the data from Insights if you can't get the data you need from other tools. As you know, however, Facebook Insights monitors only activity related to Facebook. Therefore, you need to research third-party tools to expand your monitoring beyond Facebook.

Your decision on which monitoring tools you use comes down to your tracking goals, resources, time, and money. Only you can determine what's best for your business.

TIP

The more actions you can link to the results you obtain from your tracking data, the bigger the payoff. If the data you collect helps you streamline your support team, correct a flaw in your product, ignite a new idea for a partnership, and/or solidify new relationships with potential clients, your tracking strategy can become a vehicle for growing your sales. You can increase the ROI on your time, money, and efforts when you use the data to see real results in your business.

Analyzing Results and Taking Action

One of the ultimate goals of Facebook marketing is to move your fans to action. To do this, you must try different strategies to discover what works best for your team, which is why monitoring and measuring are key to your success. By analyzing this data, you can strategically decide what your next steps should be.

In this section, we explore how to create a plan to take the data that's most crucial to your business and put it into action. In addition, we touch on the importance of eliminating time-wasters and being as flexible as possible so you can change your strategies when challenges arise. In social media marketing, your ability to course-correct quickly is critical to your success!

Building a tracking guide

In Book IX, Chapter 1, we discuss the importance of monitoring and measuring and explain why they're crucial to the success of your social media plan. Here, we show you how to create an overall tracking plan. The key to streamlining your monitoring and measuring process is creating a quick guide for easy reference. The payoff for this extra step is big and worth the time! After you put a plan of action in place (in the form of a tracking guide), the data becomes manageable, and you can more easily understand how to use it to your advantage. The result: Having a growing number of fans and increasing engagement won't feel like work, but will be an enjoyable experience. What a concept!

Creating a monitoring schedule

Inside your company, identify your front-line listening and response teams — specifically, who will monitor the data and who will be assigned to respond to the conversations in real time. These people will be the faces of your company, so choose them wisely! In addition, decide who will analyze the data behind the scenes.

When you're putting your monitoring schedule together, remember that quick response is the goal. Therefore, make sure to cover all bases. What is your plan for nights and weekends, for example? If your company isn't a 24/7 company, one option is an alerting system. Some third-party tools send you a text message when a post has been made. Although you don't want to get messages all the time if you have active accounts, this solution might be a smart one to use when you can't be around a computer. When you're choosing your monitoring tools, be sure to look at alerting features.

In addition, depending on how often you and your team members will evaluate the data, decide how often you should run reports. We suggest starting with just one report per week to track your progress. As you expand your social media activity and start seeing more engagement, you may want to track biweekly. Also, decide which reports to run so that that running them becomes an automatic weekly task.

Mapping out a communication plan

When it comes to your communication plan, you have two paths to explore with your team: internal communications and external communications.

First, create an *internal path* within your company. For your internal path, look at your data and ask, "Who needs to know?" Many small to midsize companies have different departments that follow different metrics. We suggest that you meet with your team to clarify what information needs to be sent to specific teams. You should consider the following teams when you create your internal communication plan:

- ✦ Sales
- ✦ Marketing
- ✦ Customer service
- ✦ Human resources

- Research and development
- Management and executives

In addition to looking at your internal team, you should consider how you will be communicating with your customers and fans — your *external path* of communication. As you monitor online conversations, different situations will arise, and you want to be ready for them. Here are some specific questions to answer:

- **How quickly will you respond to customer questions, concerns, complaints, and issues?** It's ideal to respond in real time, meaning at the time your fan has posted her questions. However, it's not always realistic to instantly reply to posts on your Facebook Page. You want to determine your response time during work hours and also nonworking hours to ensure the entire team knows what is expected. As a rule of thumb, because Facebook is "always on," it would be smart to work out a plan to respond to all inquiries on your Facebook Page within a few hours of the time the inquiry was posted.
- **How will you respond to people who post questions about your products or services?** Also decide how you'll respond when someone asks about something related to your area of expertise. Will you offer your support (and, in the process, take advantage of consultative selling, which means you can offer advice and insight while subtly suggesting your own products and services)? Plan this strategy so that you're prepared!
- **What will you do when a crisis arises?** You need to document this plan, identifying who on your team should be responding and what responses should be used in specific situations. If you sell products on your website, for example, and your site goes down, many frustrated customers may post on social networks that your site isn't working. A crisis plan for this situation may be to designate one person on your team to communicate on your social networks when your company is having challenges with its website. By informing your fans and customers right away, you eliminate the potential of negative chatter before it starts.
- **How will you respond to negative and positive posts?** Make it a goal to respond to all comments about you, good or bad. How will you respond to an angry blogger who posts negative feedback about your number-one product, for example? You want to have your plan in place and your team trained.
- **How will you respond to posts on your Timeline that aren't aligned with the goals that you've set out for your Facebook community?** It's common, for example, for some fans to post promotional details about their own products and services on your Timeline. These posts tend to clutter the Page and detract from the conversations your fans are having. Define which posts aren't acceptable on your Page and how to address them so that your team will be ready to handle any situation that arises.

Allocating manpower and resources from analysis

After you've been collecting your data consistently, you begin to see patterns and areas you could tweak for improvement. When you get a clear picture of what you need to do, you also need to decide whether additional staff or other resources are needed. As always, focus on the growth of your business, and when you're making a decision about taking on more work or changing what you've been doing, weigh the financial, time, and manpower implications against the overall business goal.

Identifying the time-wasters

When considering whether to pursue a particular goal or strategy, ask yourself: Are you doing it because you truly believe that you should or just because everyone else is doing it? With the popularity of social media, taking on a new shiny "social media strategy" just because everyone else is doing it is a common mistake. We hear all the hype about a tool or a strategy and jump on it, thinking that we'll be left behind if we don't use it. The real question you need to ask is, "Does this make sense for my business?" Stay focused on expanding your business, and take on only the projects that you expect to produce valuable results.

Making adjustments on the fly

Whether you're a new user of social media marketing or have been using it for a while, you're likely to stumble at times. Don't get bogged down by these events: The goal is to fail fast and move on. With a tracking system in place, you can identify issues quickly and rectify them before too much damage is done.

Social media moves fast. The good news is that when you do have challenges, if you respond to them quickly, they're more easily forgotten. Media are always changing, especially Facebook! If you stay in the know and are aware of trends and behaviors early on, you have a huge competitive advantage.

Building on your success

As you continue to build momentum with your social media strategy, pay close attention to your own best practices. Which strategies are working for you on Facebook? Has a pattern emerged regarding the strategies that are working? Your fans are likely to respond well to certain things, while other engagement attempts of yours fall flat. As long as you monitor your success and continue to make adjustments on the fly, some clear best practices will surface over time. (Remember what we said earlier: If it ain't broke, don't fix it.)

When you find a strategy that's producing good results, continue with it and build on it. Add more of what's working, and abort the strategies that aren't showing you the results you're after.

Index

A

C

E

F

G

H

I

J

K

L

M

N

O

P

Q

R

S

T

U

V

W

X

Y

Z